THE ROSE OF PARACELSUS

THE ROSE OF PARACELSUS

On Secrets & Sacraments

William Leonard Pickard

May this forever be
a secret between
yourself and me…

- Lewis Carroll

Insolent vaunt of Paracelsus,
that he could restore the original rose or violet
out of the ashes settling from its combustion…

- Thomas De Quincey (1785-1859), *Writings*, XIII, 345
"The Palimpsest of the Human Brain,"
Suspiria de Profundis

So that we are far away the most ancient of all things blest,
And that we are of love's generation
There are manifest, manifold signs
We have wings…

- Aristophanes

ISBN: 9780692509005 (paperback)
ISBN: 9781957869001 (ebook)

Cover design by Matthew Morse
Cover Art from Alchimia (Alchemy) by
Giorgio Perich, Trieste, Italy
Layout by Richard J. Ryan III

Printed in the United States of America

Synergetic Press
Santa Fe, NM 87508
London, WCIN 3AL, England

www.synergeticpress.com
www.theroseofparacelsus.com

For the One Who Wept

Author's Note

Gather about, all ye blessed of Allah. Listen, all ye true believers,
and I shall unfold to you the wondrous story of many-petaled Love.

- Arab street story teller

These writings are a literary experiment. It is an extrapolation of the government's fictions at a federal trial, hypothesizing the existence of an international psychedelic conspiracy, and evolved as well from the poetry and stories of Jorge Luis Borges.

The experiment is to discover whether a classical form, in the mannered language of Borges, can be applied to a theoretical drug trafficking organization, and to psychological phenomena often inaccessible through prose. The cities and characters at times may seem unreal, as is the narrator, and these very words, the atoms of thought.

In the form of a memoir describing a researcher's observations on a seductive group with special gifts, the tale is an effort to emulate certain works of Borges, and thereby to embrace the medieval, the erotic, the infinite.

It is the author's hope that the reader will find something memorable in these pages, even though the commonplace yields to the transcendent, at a moment's reflection.

- WLP

An Invitation

Reading is an activity subsequent to writing, more resigned, more civil, more intellectual.

- JLB

When you're reading late at night,
and the words don't seem quite right,
but they are,
we just wrote it like that.

- (apol) Lennon, Northern Song

The careful and accurate reader now enters this labyrinth of science, myth, and sensuality, cognition and compassion, surveillance and deception, and the trying of the human spirit. One might approach the material as it was written: slowly.

Such a reader is invited to contact the author, with comments, suggestions, and corrections. This is a living work, a roman à clef, subject to revision and expansion. Those whose efforts are incorporated into subsequent editions will be cited or acknowledged, at their thoughtful discretion, and with enduring gratitude.

- WLP

I

A Simple Monk

…the dreamers of the day are dangerous men,
for they act their dream with open eyes,
to make it possible.

- T.E. Lawrence, *Seven Pillars of Wisdom*

Report to the Human Subjects Committee

Harvard University

Faculty of Arts and Sciences

With the assistance of a grant through Harvard Medical School, a series of interviews has been conducted among the principals of various drug trafficking organizations (DTOs) in an effort to quantify the economics, public health burdens, and prevalence of certain drugs; and

a. in the instance of non-lethal drugs, both novel and synthetic (LSD, ayahuasca, etc.), to explore the lifestyles, personalities, characters, and motives of manufacturers; and

b. in the instance of lethal, addictive drugs (heroin, fentanyl, cocaine, methamphetamine), to observe the drug's progress from the farm gate or clandestine laboratory to the street user, and the toxic outcomes from uncontrolled use.

The enclosed report consists of a personal field journal over four years, including relevant scenes in Cambridge and in foreign settings, focusing initially on the study of psychedelic manufacturers.

As the Committee will observe, there are inherent difficulties in preparing rigorous ethnographies on the psychedelic group; the challenges are similar to those experienced by ethnopharmacologists living for extended periods among remote Amazonian tribes during their practice of syncretic religions. Richard Evans Schultes of the Harvard Botanical Museum, and his graduate students, have applied these methods to indigenous groups in the Orinoco basin and the Pantanal.

Due to the unusual phenomena encountered, numerous historical recollections are provided in the report. They may be helpful in distinguishing the observer from the observed.

As a caveat, the Committee will note that – while illegal activity is not condoned herein – the descriptions of altered and visionary states often parallel existing records in the medical, forensic, and psychiatric literature, to which these special histories may be supplemented.

Respectfully submitted,

WLP

Cambridge, Massachusetts

Chapter 1.

Highlander

But where was one to find them, if they wander the earth lost
and anonymous and are not recognized when they are met with
and not even they themselves know the high mission they perform?

- JLB, *The Man on the Threshold*

I think that any group of people who have a system of belief
that encompasses practically everything, and who act upon it,
are bound to be interesting to any scholar.

- Edmund S. Morgan, Sterling Professor of History, Yale

You had to live -- did live, from habit that became instinct --
in the assumption that every sound you made was overheard and,
except in darkness, every moment scrutinized.

- Orwell, *1984*

The stars began to crumble and a cloud of fine stardust fell through space.

- Joyce, *A Portrait of the Artist as a Young Man*

HER EYES WERE EMERALD and hermetic, her weathered face lit as if by benign witchcraft. An agile, elderly woman of dignity and bearing, with waist-length white hair in loose braids, she was an *éminence rose* bundled artfully in woolens of purple and red. An unexpected apparition, she descended to sit beside me. The dying sun in silver streams yielded to the moonrise.

"They are coming for you," she said.

We watched as before us a solitary piper began playing to the full moon, standing with his fur sporran among the heath and harebells on our isolated hilltop. His double jacket bonnet ribbons fluttered in the sea wind. The plain mantle over his left shoulder was held by a broach, his kilt the Hunting Stewart tartan. His black brogues shined beneath white spats.

He was etched against fogbanks cascading to the darkening ocean, as tall dry stalks of broom leaned in the cool dusk. Amid the salt air and spiky gorse, he fingered a haunting melody on his chanter. The five pipes and low octave drones seemed but a dirge, until the skirling grew high and free, resounding "Scotland the Brave."

It was the Hunter's Moon celebration on this crisp October eve, when once each year only local villagers of Point Reyes, California knew where to gather on Inverness Ridge to attend the piper. In crocheted pullovers or clustered within blankets we listened, while below the lonely moors stretched like grey counterpanes to the edge of nothingness.

"They are coming for you," she said again, more intently. "Now."

"How shall I recognize them?" I asked. She could not hear the quickness of my heart.

"They are like stumbling through a mirror, traveling across the sky."

She whispered a few directions in the cultivated voice of a ballet *grand dame*, rich with Central European dialects, perhaps Hungarian or Czech. Her words were like a roomful of moonlight to one's imprisoned blood. She had a spectral air, the holiness conferred by secrecy. Though formidable, she spoke almost inaudibly, as if presenting to the Inquisition.

She referred to six people in the world who had the capacity to synthesize kilograms of LSD. She said they moved about the shadowy earth with salutary motives, as the most devoted of societies. Others described them as an invisible cartel of theologians and mystagogues, without weapons or violence, reputed by some within the underground to possess the preternatural equanimity of the battleground.

I was visiting from Cambridge, and graduate studies at Harvard's Kennedy School of Government. A simultaneous appointment at Harvard Medical School, as a drug policy fellow and research associate in neurobiology, supported an interest in novel drugs and organizations.

Through a baffling, labyrinthine series of seemingly accidental encounters, I became aware of them, and they of me. Yet they remained eternally elusive, unlocatable, unknowable. At an uncertain time, an unknown person had disclosed vaguely, one of the Six might approach; after each encounter and vetting, perhaps another might appear, but ultimately only five of the Six.

It was a trackless mystery of no identities. Their names were to be replaced by shades ascending from scarlet, as were painted Homer's ships: Crimson, Indigo, Vermilion, Magenta, Cobalt.

At the appointed hour, I walked northward in the violet evening far along Limantour Beach. There were no signs of human existence, only a monotony of ocean and wind-carved dunes. The surrounding fog was phantasmal with loneliness, as if one had left earth's embrace. High seas were running, with immense clouds of spray.

Shivering, I kindled a small fire from driftwood, and by its warmth began listening to a recording of Wagner's *Der Ring des Nibelungen*. The white noise, as the booming waves folded in upon themselves, became double basses and bassoons, sustaining for an unearthly one hundred and thirty- six bars the E-flat chords of *Das Rheingold* in the Ring Cycle, announcing the creation of the World.

◯

AT THE 108th MEASURE, Crimson materialized silently beside me. There was no fright at the presence of this international quarry, but an odd sense of greater safety. Upon leaving his small sailboat moored in a distant inlet on Tomales Bay, he had walked ten miles through the National Seashore hiking trails. He was casual, admiring the Pacific, mentioning sailing off Cape Cod and the South China Sea, and the coastlines of Goa and Ibiza.

His eyes were deeply set like a Navaho Roadman, the visage of having seen the dancing flames and prayer fans and movement of spirit until the dawn woman brought water. His face of many years was smooth, as though reborn. Tall, with grey hair close to a crew-cut, a beatific countenance at moments, he had the quick acuity of a heavily scheduled surgeon. His language mingled with scholarly asides.

He wore a heavy, dark red cable knit over jeans and running shoes. Rangy and well-exercised, he could have been a Princeton crew alumnus, a rower carrying sculls from the boathouse to the Lake. In his late fifties, his voice was at times retreating and academic, reflecting years of isolation in deserts and mountains, surrounded by literature and ranges of light. His eyes were hazel, like leaves in late autumn.

⬡

HE OFFERED A SIP of mango juice from an antique silver flagon, as if it were holy water. Within minutes the sea floor itself, perhaps the entire continent, seemed to move ever so slightly, like some microscopic, profound, and irrevocable tectonic shift.

The fire's heat against the cold sea air became the allegory for the worlds balanced by practitioners of these clandestine arts. I could only listen to his fantastic web of recollections and foretelling, as he spoke softly, confiding mythic tales of remote laboratory sites.

"Sacred glass furnaces disgorge illumined fragments of mind in blinding rivers. Alone and on their knees at these fountains of consciousness, singular beings pray for an end to suffering. Eternal evenings become crystal daybreaks, pierced by the morning star."

At first thinking him messianic, pontificating, perhaps a proponent of some arcane religious heresy or ghastly folly, I felt mixed elation and alarm. There was a moral unease at his description of what only could be mere simulacra. But the changes were beginning.

With his words, the beach became luminous as noon, as though the sky had knocked open. There was the crackle of stars, then blood-red shelves of Magellanic clouds. The ocean was billowing, cold and black, percussive between the screaming silences. The dunes were a moonscape of rubble.

"There is fission then fusion of thought and feeling, as forgiveness for all blasts heavenward. Dissolute chaos renders to absolute certainty; wrenching ignominy and confusion transmute to clarity and peace. The tranquil vales of Elysium are welcoming us."

He fell silent. The sound of the sea began to evolve out of night, the hum of existence whispering secrets like some fantastic drug, but not so cruelly, for mind that evening was so vast no mere substance dare mimic its majesty. It was the power of Grace that compelled us.

The seas cradled and released, as in play; they flowed in bright streams, reflecting the plumed branches of heaven above. Unrolling firmaments were full of incoherent raptures.

I sat speechless in a hypnogogic state while he seemed to transform, in the shifting firelight and white noise and the reflections of ten thousand fingers of fractal silver waves, into a spectrum of beings. He reaggregated as the alchemist Paracelsus, as the Gnostic wizard Hermes Trismegistus, as an ecclesiastical conspirator in 16th Century Basel, as an itinerant tinker on a Scottish beach. He displayed the Dionysiac intoxication recalled by Euripides in *The Bacchae*, yet the solemnity of a Delphic priest as clouds of myrrh trailed from his oracular pronouncements. He became robot flesh from synthetic DNA and future avatars penetrating the present for just this one encounter, then a Miocene hominid speaking unknown tongues before the advent of fire. He became the angel that St. John saw in the sun, then all the healers and medicines of the world: the heretical anatomy of Galen and Vesalius, the antisepsis of Lister, the anesthesia of Crawford Long.

Finally, the dreamlike light show slowed, the changes merging into a single, still, perfectly clear prospect. There appeared at last only Crimson himself, simply poking the embers around and placing driftwood, as though nothing at all had occurred except two friends warming themselves beneath the universal canopy. After the psychic conflagrations, I took quite some moments to recover.

"Something more you wished to know?" he said, with gravitas.

THE NIGHT was a Damascene conversion into a privileged heterodoxy, like a bewitchment conferred by priests of concealed knowledge. In the end, one was grateful to discover, all was perfectly lucid. It first had seemed a trial by self-immolation, where the duplicitous would go mad, but in the purity of my inquiry I survived this first encounter, perhaps the last stage of their background check.

I had been permitted a carefully limited glance at the edges of a worldwide system, the existence of which had never been proven. My writings henceforth were but a fitful remembrance, not only of these most uncommon of interviews, but of complex ephemera barely recordable yet absolute. They were so utterly unforgettable that, in order for the observer to function, they must be forgotten.

Rendered mute by all that had been said and seen, none of which was suitable for Harvard peer review, I managed to remember a question, finding a barely articulate voice.

"The mind…the mindset…what is required for your work?"

"Other than the syntheses conducted by each of the Six, I specialize in basic security; the foci of the other five are different. My perspective cycles among only a few realities, then repeats. Moving from window to window, I may in one view predatory opposing forces with weapons; in another, daisies strewn in a field like laughter. In another the nightingale's cry on a Southern night, or an unmarked car at the wrong time of day, or sublime ranges of forests and mountains and no walls. It is the schizophrenic life of a sentient herbivore, at any moment devoured pitilessly, but living the long peace, grazing in serenity beneath untroubled skies."

"How do you live…each day?"

"Upon waking, I meditate on boundless tranquility and freedom, then through every hour keep submerged the cold sweat, the awareness of pervasive surveillance technologies, ubiquitous cameras, facial recognition, dossiers, and databanks. I constantly recognize fearfully armed governments, the control of radical thinking and non-obeisance, the data mining for single actors and organizations beyond the state's understanding. As I walk through cities I am cognizant of aerial, automotive, and pedestrian surveillance, the small armies of police disguised as laborers, bankers, cabbies, barflies, cocaine traffickers, and earnest fellow travelers."

At this overwhelming disclosure, which at first seemed a highly functional paranoia, I noticed that Crimson was an island of contrasts. His hands were toughened from splitting cords and fire making, at the same time without tremor, possessing a connectedness between earth and sky. Yet his carefully manicured fingers seemed capable of calligraphic flourishes, the precise rotation of stopcocks, and the fine analytical measurement of exotic reagents. He emanated an electrical excitement, suggestive of some great and wonderful secret. He unnervingly anticipated my every thought, withdrawing gently when I grew fearful of his presence. Near this remarkable being, one of the Six, it seemed no time for careless trivia.

"How do you avoid detection?"

"I dress, act, and speak quite conservatively, striving to be forgettable, to leave no memory. One must be a gray man, perhaps a mild accountant of little means, to hide without a trace personal responsibility for the ecstasies, the orgasmic religiosities in millions of minds."

At this frank admission, he looked to the sea. I was saddened by this painful description of his dichotomy, the chilling and necessary mechanisms for covert actions coexisting with his heightened aesthetic. His poetic stream of observations and acts rendered every moment deeply felt. It seemed the greatest irony that one who espoused divine unity and harmony would suffer in such cause a lifetime of being a virtual outcast. I seized upon his assertion of mimicking common habits, mores, and clothing to appear normal, even as he controlled some vast, chimerical, and stealthy machine.

"You practice a form of social invisibility?"

"We dress for the environment, like chameleons. So there are no sartorial affectations or signals as we move unnoticed among the mainstream, no capes or long hair or shaved skulls or tattoos or any distinguishing features; one becomes boring visually to peers, the ultimate conformist, hopeless to underground art and fashion. Yet the women have been known to affect fascinators among the pomp of English receptions, or torn Levis for a dismal bus ride to Corpus Christi."

The sands were white meadows beneath the moon, drawing the brilliance of open sea. Crimson seemed a persecuted ecclesiastic, fleeing gothic halls and cloisters, his intrigues majestic as the night horned with stars. Rather than sensing criminality, one felt the presence of great virtue.

"And your behavior is normal?"

"We are considered wild men among a few, but our manner is entirely conventional, even drab or self-effacing. Forsaking all recognition for the improbability of detection, we practice blending in seamlessly. Upon contact with the public, we have easy courtesies and friendly eyes, exchanging simple words, as though one has nothing to hide, but also to not frighten anyone, or provoke suspicion or even remembrance."

White caps were racing, colliding into light showers of spray. The winds were a chanting sort of litany, conjured up by fairies.

"But how do you remain balanced?"

"As with Daniel among the lions, one's heart cannot be conflicted, even momentarily. Such enduring duplicity must be conducted with fearless grace. The life is difficult; only by devotion to cognitive evolution can harboring constant deceits be made honorable. I speak here not of small syntheses, a hundred grams or a million doses on occasion, but the requisite practices over decades for planetary scale batches."

⬡

CRIMSON WAS NOT BEING SENTENTIOUS, but perceived correctly he was the prey, constantly hunted by unseen international law enforcement and intelligence agencies. I listened to this lonely warrior behind enemy lines, who spoke of a small but widespread underground that provided him with a modicum of respect, tolerance, and safety. He had committed a felony that would be penalized by life in prison, not once, but for a lifetime. It was disconcerting that in beholding his face, one saw not some cabalistic darkness, but a luminous compassion.

Crimson, as one of the Six, was a dedicated psychedelic manufacturer since his first exposure to a classical hallucinogen. In rare instances my inquiry was permitted into other techniques by which he somehow had evaded arrest for decades. I learned of the rogue chemist's methods, of the tradeoff of an unthreatened life for an inspired alienation which must not be shared, even with those he loved.

He ceased his introspections for a while, then remarked, "As you say in Zen, 'a hairbreadth's deviation and you are out of tune.'"

I had never once referred to my years before Harvard as a monk at Hoshin-ji monastery. The Six had investigated me. Somewhat undone, I suggested taking some air.

We walked in an unhurried way, arms crossed, even as the chill of the rolling grey ocean began to reach through us. We passed masses of kelp and Sequoia driftwood, watching the sandpipers at the edge of riplets and gulls sailing over the crests, while the sighting of kestrels, eagles, and egrets redeemed our intrusion into this sacred shore. Stopping at last, we saw in the mists flowing over our distant embers the sleeping eye of some great beast. Returning, we hastened our fire with eucalyptus. Warming ourselves, we faced the sea, and talked of magical things, then of desperate moments.

"The covert lifestyle," Crimson mused, "the practice necessary to support clandestine psychedelic manufacture, may be applied to any severely outlawed activity. The hidden other life, terrible in its stress, requires the most delicate decisions. Metaphorically, perhaps the only way it can be described, the path is fine as a silver web, treacherous as an icy couloir. Yet success, the completion of a synthesis, is like the dawn, the end of dreams."

Trails of smoke from our fire dwindled away among the stars. Ribbons of darkness turned throughout the enigmatic diamond sky. Light sea winds invigorated the blue-black littoral of the coast.

Eager to learn more, and not wanting to divert him from his poetic allusions, I offered him jasmine tea from a flask. My questioning became very gentle, like a novitiate who knew nothing.

"And what decisions might those be?"

"It is as if we were early Christians," he ventured, "clinging together among hostile Romans, or pagan Visigoths before legions worshipping Saturn. One decides early on whether one's elixir is sacramental or poisonous, whether the outcome is benevolent or criminal, a hallowed duty or a tragic caprice. The moral issues are resolved through repeated personal sufferings and illuminations, agonies and ecstasies, no less than any acolyte. We were among the first exposed to the substance."

"And you concluded that distribution of psychedelics was, in the aggregate, benign?"

"Among a narrow subset of the population who wish it. Not for everyone. LSD is only the first synthetic non-lethal compound in an accelerating psychopharmacological revolution of evolutionary magnitude, the dimensions and social impact of which we hardly can anticipate."

"Evolutionary magnitude?"

"Consider the primordial fire makers of *Homo erectus*, the cave artists at Lascaux or Grotte Chauvet-Pont d'Arc. Think of the coming of the prophets, the transition from papyrus to electrons for communication. For those who first knew of the light, special knowledge and practices were closely held, for the future unraveled in manifold directions, both that of plague and salvation. Societies divided on the issues; moral introspection was paramount. What does one do with the sacred? With utterly transforming technology? Withhold it, or release it? None were decisions for governments, but for the makers."

I waited for his elevated, almost scholarly discourse to resolve into actual precepts that could be recorded. Although he possessed several distinct voices, his language at this time was antiquated, Dickensian. It seemed stilted to the modern ear, as though he had spent years alone removed in hidden settings, comforted only by Victorian literature, or the writings of Virgil, St. Augustine, or Plotinus.

"How do you protect yourself, and those who protect you?" I asked, conceding both his moral imperative and his fiercely armed opposition. He looked somberly at me.

"Would a brief tutorial be helpful? A day in the life of a hypothetical chemist or distributor of some future drug?"

I assured him it would, stirring the fire gently to not distract him.

"Let's assume a compound that induces profound religiosity. Its adherents are persecuted, no longer by Caesar, but by governments preferring sole control over advances in neurochemistry. The same security rules would apply to clandestine chemists confronting another inevitability: the first substances significantly enhancing cognition, memory, and learning. Imagine the social outcomes, not only of these, but of erotogenics that heighten libido."

Crimson, clearly safe at our obscure campfire up this secluded coastline, began expounding with vignettes on furtive arts seldom practiced in our civilized interdependency. I remained quiet throughout the night as he described, in staccato bursts or long reveries, how not to attract attention while constructing a type of psychological nuclear bomb. Affecting millions, it was carried easily in one's pocket in the form of a drug potent in micrograms. Although too specialized to be included in any rigorous research monograph at Harvard, his portrayals were tantalizing, and interruptions unthinkable.

The iron of night became fleetingly veined with trails of light, manifold spectra recalling the dialectical dreams of the first imagery. The fire behind Crimson was radiant unto a halo around him.

"Together here we are considering the mystical intersection of mind and brain, in service of humanity," he observed, "even while some regard distribution as foolhardy and criminal. Others honor it."

He alluded to the Kabbalah's description of the thirty-six keepers of the mystery, men and women spread across the earth in trivial occupations – cobblers, camel herders, beggars – but upon whom the world unknowingly may depend. He deliberated thus *ex cathedra* for some time, his words punctuated by the sharp crying of a gull, the pounding of the winter storm surf on the beachhead. Upon the fire we placed redwood, washed down from the cloud-bound Humboldt coast. As it steamed and snapped in the blazes, he looked intently at me. He stopped theorizing.

"It is better that we all teach you in small ways. There are six chemists. Of four others I shall speak," Crimson confided. "We may be thought of as occupying the surface of a modern Eucharist, a crystal. While within the jewel, we all prepare the sacrament individually in remote sites, but each thereafter in returning to the world is responsible for different facets. We then focus separately on practical aspects that ensure continued viability of the system."

"What are these practical aspects, beyond the synthesis?"

"I develop fundamental security, the habits to make arrest or seizure improbable. The others, whom we will designate by the cryptonyms Indigo, Vermilion, Magenta, and Cobalt, have different roles. We constantly share what we learn."

"Tell me of the others."

"Indigo contemplates ritual preparation of the Eucharist, the sanctity and precision of labs, and their surreptitious transfer from site to site. Vermilion monitors distribution; he conducts downstream counterintelligence with gifted women operatives who employ forms of tantric unions, esoteric erotic practices.

At this he hesitated, processing some emotional memory. He went on.

"Magenta is concerned with research, the future, anticipating neuroscience, the next touchstone of evolution. Cobalt considers high-level threats, infiltrates governments, and watches intelligence and enforcement agencies. Spy versus spy. Together, we survive."

"And the sixth man, or woman?"

"That discovery we must leave to you, and your readers."

I STACKED rough pine driftwood until our ceremonial flames grew hotter and more luxuriant against the translucent purple night. With the gunshot crackling of resins, live sparks swirled upwards like fire flies, the sea air cool and delicious. The sky freshened, the smashing breakers and hissing foam finally all that could be heard.

Barely visible waves, now exposed by the dissolution of mists, reflected in broad paths of light to the far edge of the waters the fullness of the October moon. Suspended in high, horizontal dark clouds that curled and pointed as though in a Tibetan painting, its lunar whiteness was of sublime and eternal beauty.

Before me, a second shift in perception occurred, for the veil was removed this night. The orb seemed to possess a powerful, mute aesthetic, one increasingly disturbing in its perfection. It became an apocalyptic profundity, rendering a sudden comprehension of the divine, then the irrefutable art of God. I had to turn away so that I could function and not, before its unutterable presence, wildly dance and shout, or kneel.

As he observed my staggering glimpse, his voice arose in a grounding way, in the sepulchral tones of a vast auditorium.

"You wish to learn the mechanics of it all, you say?"

"Whatever…is comfortable for you," I returned, with the greatest effort.

He said nothing. Avoiding only with difficulty the ineffable transcendence so starkly plain before us, I managed only a few words.

"Your special arts might live forever."

He hesitated at my awkward overture, then viewed internally some realm of future and past. Regaining my footing somewhat, I cautiously tried again, appealing to his historical perspective.

"Read one day by someone in need: a revolutionary in time of oppression. A soul on your path. Why not pass the knowledge on?"

"Would that not be the apex of Narcissistic illusion? But so it is with all true callings, from neurology to theology to, dare I say it, the prosecutor's imperative."

He became pensive, then solemn. The firelight began flickering like sheet lightning, plunging us into anonymity. A small premonitory unease manifested, a tingle of disaster that labored then fled like slow wing beats through the spokes of darkness. A stream of ants, escaping the smoking castaway pine branches, fell one by one into the fire. Crimson, down from his reveries, considered the subject.

"The occult life, in modern times, in America and Europe, Russia and Southeast Asia – the domains of my experience excluding South America and its obscene cocaine trade – is an exercise in cultivating two or more parallel worlds, and moving easily among them."

A pale rinsed dawn was breaking. We were sticky with dampness and salt. My wavering, skeptical mind had foundered against his most exalted dedication. One felt a foreboding of terrible perils, for this sage spirit was encircled by genuine enemies. I pressed him with care.

"What are the rules of conduct?"

"One could write a treatise on them. They must be observed as religiously as the three hundred vows of Vipassana monks in the Thai forests. At the slightest misjudgment, one is swept away from the purity of graceful practice into the cesspool of captivity. Let's call them 'Washington Rules,' as in D.C., followed so one's demise is met with dignity, rather than walking abused in forlorn circles around a prison track."

The undertow drew its hissing breath at the terrible cruelty of his fate; above a froth-chained sea, the gulls screamed and herons rasped. The useless horror of penal servitude forever shadowed the Six. Immured behind some wall, one could be driven half-mad by the squalor of confinement. Beyond our fire, piles of rotted, lichen-encrusted redwood logs were trapped in moon bright sand. I thought of the last caribou crawling in heavy snows, their shaky, frightened calves, the frolicking wolves.

"Washington Rules, then," I agreed, quite eager to learn.

It was nearing first light; he abruptly turned to go. Confused, and apprehensive at perhaps overstepping my charter with invasive questions, I mumbled some apologies, then absurdly asked for his phone number. As the night had taught, he had thought far ahead of me.

"Experience is more indelible than rhetoric, friend. Visit San Francisco Saturday, anywhere downtown, at sunrise. I'll find you."

Quickened, I rushed to reply lightheartedly, recalling his penchant for many costumes.

"How should I dress?"

"Bring your gym clothes," he said simply.

A little smile. He then slowly raised his hand and walked away, his fire-lit body receding like a phantom into pale obscurity, by the singing sea.

With the weariness of this immensely long vigil, I trembled quietly at his sudden disappearance. I remained crouched on the beach for hours as the fire withdrew to embers then to ash, the moon not unusual, fading now into the ocean. The incoming tide like the slow pulse of the earth erased in great rhythmic sweeps his footprints, until at last there was no trace whatsoever to be found.

〇

THE DANK MOIST-GREEN SAN FRANCISCO WHARVES were like a shattered fragment of an abandoned temple. A cold dawn exhaled rising damps and flotsam under the optic of the sky. As the edge of day filtered from the Berkeley horizon, the Bay bloomed with iridescence; mirages flickered across the water. My position had been chosen randomly; I looked for any movement. It seemed an unlikely place to be pinpointed, even by a crack surveillance team.

The massive 19th Century clock on the Ferry Building ticked to 4:30 AM. Glowing in the twilight, its circumference breathed with the last effects of Crimson's fireside revelations. Even in the devout stillness of the morning, the leaves of tall imported palms still fluttered almost imperceptibly in the breeze of mind.

It seemed I stood at the crossroads of past and future, seeing in all directions, for nearby the monks and nuns at Hoshin-ji monastery moved with hands folded in prayer to the zendo for morning meditation, as the great temple bell sounded sonorously, while in Cambridge students hurried to the Memorial Church bells, tracking a new frost in Harvard Yard and giddily discussing Heidegger. In Moscow a mathematician's daughter kissed her father farewell as he grappled with the Poincaré conjecture, and in Mazar-i-Sharif heroin cooks in dirty loincloths squatted before kerosene-soaked pits filled with morphine paste, and conjured devils that fled to the West.

It was a cloudless morning, the Bay with small skirmishing wavelets, the seafront windless. I leaned against heavy pylons in the cold salt air, infused with these memories and premonitions of worlds to come. All finally resolved to a single scholar at no place in particular, awaiting those with no name, and who would dare release to entire populations their antidote for addiction, even at the cost of their own lives.

As I nursed hot tea from a Thermos, Crimson in his unnerving manner came from nowhere, bid good morning in soft Russian and German, and smoothly collected me. We walked together as the City ceased its fitful dreaming, until we breakfasted in a run-down coffee shop that catered to drunks and the homeless. Old men wearing dirty knitted gloves with no fingers rattled on nonsensically, while a slatternly, tired waitress poured coffee beneath a hand-written sign:

"No refills."

She kindly allowed the destitute their sinecure of a warm corner. Greasy menus were duct taped to wooden tables; resigned eyes looked vacantly through smeared windows at forbidden skyscrapers. Crimson sat across from me, wearing sweat-stained coveralls from the Salvation Army free box, and had a two-day-old stubble.

Eager to hear of covert methodology, even over chipped bowls of instant gruel, I asked about Washington Rules. Crimson deftly held the conversation to the prospects of his finding food stamps, menial labor, or public assistance. He left a twenty-dollar tip under the plate for a two-dollar meal, because of the waitress's soft eyes for the lost.

"We speak in public only that appropriate to the listeners, even complete fictions," he said.

Loitering near a bus stop, he was indistinguishable from an indigent person. After some minutes, I realized he had no car, and awaited no one. We boarded the Folsom bus, standing at rush hour, riding wordlessly into humanity's ocean of personal agendas: tourists both determined and directionless, workers asleep or awakened, those worried or frivolous, the pursuers and the pursued.

A tall, slender girl in ripped Danskins and denim jacket, carrying a book bag with the pale logo of the university at Maastricht, stood gripping the top of a seat. She appeared a severely dressed-down model with no makeup, an ivory face, spectacles with fine gold rims and her bright blond hair in Eastern European braids. Above her endless black leggings flashed a slice of Black Watch tartan microskirt.

She edged slowly through the compressed crowd like a gymnast, leaving in her wake a little frisson of heat and disquiet. Eyes down and excusing herself in almost unheard Dutch but with an evident Glaswegian overtone, she stepped out with head held high and a practiced pirouette of her narrow hips over the gutter, as if in another age she were delicately disembarking a phaeton assisted by a liveried footman. Looking neither to the left nor right, she disappeared as an anomaly in America, past sullen Negro boys and confused street hustlers rendered mute at her passage.

Crimson with a rural Alabama accent engaged a toothless, grizzled veteran about the Highlands of Vietnam, his long red dirt vowels gravely recalling the killing at Quảng Tri, the A Shau Valley, Khe Sanh, and Dien Bien Phu. We finally descended into the dissolute drug and sex bazaars of the Tenderloin. The street lay ravaged in the abhorrent morning from the tawdry night of the craven and the crazed, the small-time rip-off artists and purveyors of abused flesh.

We arrived at some flophouse, in part a shooting gallery for addicts, but also catering to the dispossessed who had begged enough handouts to afford a room with thick brass locks and chains and no questions. The halls had the penetrating smell of urine.

Crimson's small space had a sprung bed, torn lace curtains revealing desiccated shades, a banging iron radiator thickly painted and peeling, and a small writing desk embossed by cigarette burns and crescents of stains from cheap wine. From the window, down two floors, one saw a small enclosure from adjacent buildings that was filled with prophylactic wrappers, shattered bottles, broken glass pipes, and scorched tinfoil. The hollow echoes of lust and addiction, death and poverty, all faded now, washed clean for a moment in the purifying daylight. The curtains moved lightly in the morning air.

"Welcome," he said, "to an example of one type of temporary safehouse, easily acquired and discarded. Another may be an architectural study on a promontory above the sea, or a sheppard's cottage in an alpine valley. This kind doubles as a reminder of human frailty, and of the demons we oppose through our practice, so that we don't ever forget."

I said nothing, stunned not only by the fluidity of his movement among divergent worlds, by his changing appearances, dialects, mannerisms, and identities, but also by his comprehension of the darkness.

⬡

HE DISMANTLED A PORTION of a closet ceiling and removed a folded set of clothes and a briefcase, then rifled through the contents to produce a Belgian passport and an electric razor from a duty-free shop in Hamburg. Shaving and donning a cutting-edge black suit, then seizing a gym bag, he showed me along the street for blocks, arriving at the desk of an executive gym on the 10th floor of a *luxe* high-rise hotel.

We were passed into the lockers by the thin receptionist. She was Celtic in post-punk swept-back black hair and mauve singlet over her small, high breasts. Her lipstick was a fashionable Laurent Rouge Pur Couture. She had eyes of lustrous heights, as if they had seen everything, as if they had been taken by the sky.

We proceeded into a lengthy, serious workout, I with a prison calisthenic routine made for cramped cages, Crimson into heavy aerobic strides on a precipitously inclined treadmill, both ending with floor sets, slow yoga, and a steam. Barely visible in the clouds, Crimson outlined the Washington Rules.

"You are in the setting of my choice, not yours, so there is minimal fear of surveillance; no devices, no recorder taped to skin or agents behind these walls. Your young revolutionary today must adapt to each decade's technology; the basic rules are old spy craft applied to modern threats, evolved from the code of the Peloponnesians, the writings of Machiavelli, from the Staatspolizei, the Cheka. From the NKVD. MI-6."

"Tell me."

"A mnemonic is 'ABC' or 'Automation, Behavior, Containment.' Too briefly summarized – first we consider Automation: cameras are everywhere, cars and digital devices are locatable, all electronic footprints are retrievable. Second is Behavior: be forgettable, act normally, move between identities easily, change lifestyles only operationally. The last is Containment: almost everyone talks, pillows are not for secrets, only ignorance is invincible to inquisitors."

"And of personal habits?"

"Work closely only with those known for more than ten years. Exercise daily. No drug use other than the rare sacrament, for all is too serious for indulgence. We avoid even caffeine rather than whipping our senses daily. Embrace deep yoga, meditate with every movement, every step, like breathing."

"And of your security routines?"

"Each morning, religiously, ask 'What if they came now?' Then carefully examine all notes, computer files. Discard numbers, receipts, anything that leads to sensitive individuals or locations or those that know them. Once each week, do 'Security Day' – sever or create a relationship, drop negative habits, switch locations, review the Rules. Constantly assume the opposition on the periphery. Study investigative probes at the edges of things: people arrested, surveillance, odd statements by desk clerks. Anything suggestive of hostile forces, so our loving matrix doesn't unravel into the unforgiving world where people die in small steel enclosures."

We sat in silence, then showered, toweled, and dressed. We passed the girl at the desk, who only nodded. She was strikingly lean in her tight leather pants and heels, dreaming of her nights dancing among blasted Goth tribes in the artists' SoMa district. In the noon crowds, Crimson revealed her background.

"We watch her, as we do selected persons, for we might approach her one day, asking for some small and harmless but critical service."

Crimson described the girl as first appearing one sunrise on the empty streets, careening about joyously with her boyfriend, obviously survivors of a psychedelic night.

"Confronting me suddenly, before walking away, she said 'We're not high on *drugs* or anything.'"

The girl dismissed Crimson as some conservative businessman, ignorant of her revelations, disapproving of her gleaming morning. A pavement artist, one skilled in tracking by foot, located her crash pad and found her a safer job, anonymously.

"She doesn't remember our encounter and will never be reminded."

"How many people do you provide for, or develop?"

"There are hundreds, perhaps thousands, monitored indirectly by the Six. Within a hierarchical cartel of devotional equality, each may be called upon for some small event, but unknowing of the reasons. Although shared consciousness is an ancient tribe in spirit, the small operational side beyond the Six is structured in cells, no one aware of the others. They are all ages, all walks of life. Except for Vermilion's *bonbonnière* of erotic models, which are forever young."

"You mentioned the tantric practices of Vermilion, and his counter-surveillance. Would he include this girl?"

"Perhaps, if she possessed a certain irresistible animal magnetism, and the refined intelligence of a chessmaster. But our sexuality is varied: two are practitioners of high monogamy throughout their lives, faithful only to one person, as am I. Another is nonsexual, anhedonic, Apollonian. One conducts serial monogamy. Vermilion is both tantric and Dionysian."

"But how would each employ her?"

"If she were a skilled hacker, Cobalt might request that she breach security for a database. If she could trail a coat in spy craft terms, she may be asked to walk naked by the fires at Burning Man and engage someone we wish to study. If she were a graduate student in pharmacology or policy, Indigo or Magenta could involve her through multiple cut outs. For now, she sees all staff and guests at this hotel, quite close to City Hall and the Federal Building."

I did not pursue the subject. Crimson led the way as we walked along the boutique district, its restaurants and bars filled with young professionals confident they had it made. He pointed out the clusters of cocaine users, those monologuing hyperkinetically between bouts of craving and begging more lines.

"I think of the Berlin epidemic of 1930," he said, "where men and women sold garments from their backs for just moments of unbridled lust. Now, as then, they make a Faustian bargain of exorbitant payment for what is, as the final joke, free for everyone, and heavily available among those conducting the erotic rites. Vermilion will speak of such worship."

"Do psychedelics displace addictive drug use?"

"From the earliest days, our hopes included prevention of the great infections. By these means we try to inoculate against the poisons of cocaine, heroin, methamphetamine, and alcohol, providing users and addicts with insight into their psychic vampires, if you will, that drain their life force. Sadly, they substitute a ridiculous powder for all rewards. They forget the power of normal orgasms, indeed all human pleasures: the laughter of children, racing clouds at the edges of storms, the ennobling dignity of kind acts, the triumphant bliss of natural mind."

We took a cab to Golden Gate Park for the afternoon, watching young families and cyclists about the meadows. Beyond the Half Moon Bridge, by a formal Zen garden and pond of white carp, we sipped herbal teas at the Japanese Tea House.

"How is money regarded?" I inquired, a salient economic detail in any study involving Harvard, one that would exclude the divinities of our fireside, the unwritable subtleties of mind.

"Money is a by-product of the synthesis. It cannot be avoided, and to it we are neither attracted nor repelled. It is merely paper, a convenience for food, shelter, movement, the intricacies of identities and security apparati. Drug traffickers singularly focus on profit, growing mad with greed. But psychedelic synthesis, with its chronic exposure to the substance, quickly eliminates those who hope to sate such hunger. One stands beside a furnace of consciousness, as if it were an Ark of the Covenant, where silver and gold are vaporized instantly, and there is neither surplus nor lack."

I thought of the Rhine maidens, where stolen river gold was made into the Ring, and desire to possess it led to Götterdämmerung, the end of the world.

"A gold louis betrayed Louis XVI fleeing near Varennes," Crimson remarked, ever the sensitive, always reading me.

To these pronouncements I hardly could reply. Crimson continued in his ruminations, finally speaking in an aside.

"Others of the Six may comment on the paper. Profit is a misconception of the inexperienced, but to us a distraction from duty. We prefer not to trade our soul for the whole world, but rather admire the words of Epictetus, in his contempt for gold. We live briefly in mansions and hovels, which have the same flies. It is only love itself that is sought, which cannot be bought or sold. In its presence, a tin-roofed shack becomes a palace; in its absence, the glory of kings is but a beggar's tatters."

We walked along the trails in the Park to the ocean. Dusk loomed, then swallowed the sunset, the City curving away from the frail golden light on the Pacific. The sea was brilliant, curling and flexing, then moody, awaiting in wonder the first constellations.

⬡

IN THE EARLY EVENING we hailed a taxi and arrived in the Mission near 16th Street, where we chanced upon a cluster of illegal immigrants on a street corner. Crimson approached with fluent and familiar salutations in Spanish, quickly retrieving several vials of crack and giving them a thick packet of phone cards. We removed together down an alley, where he smashed the vials underfoot.

"The cards will be used to call narcotics vendors from Mexico to Colombia, confusing any software aggregating names and numbers, and generating schools of red herrings for hostile analysts."

His was a basic sanity, full of practical wisdom. He had a perfect aplomb, his every confidence delivered with the prudence of a seminarian. But when he crushed the vials, I thought he muttered violent epithets. They seemed to be Latin phrases, as in some rite. I recognized only the name of Lucifer.

We straggled during our long walk to the Warehouse district, finally arriving at the cheapest of Laotian restaurants, haphazard with Montagnard weavings. We were restored with a simple meal of vegetables and rice. Crimson exchanged a *wai*, a bow to the owner, and made his small daughter giggle incessantly with comments in H'mong. I noticed she had a blue ribbon in her hair, and that Crimson placed his chopsticks reverently, as though it were some subtle practice.

⬡

THE EVENING FELL upon us like the neon cool of subterranean blues. We entered the pounding Folsom venues, their entries plastered with club posters under black light, where mobs of mohawked, pierced youth and funereally black Goths danced in broken-loined rhythms. Sonic walls of electronic dance music were visceral with techno, drum and bass, trance, jungle, emo, and math rock.

Couples lay devastated across lush pink cushions, chilling in tranquil ambient lounges, while below massed dancers linked arms like the telepathic future celebrants in Clarke's *Childhood's End*, who moved in serpentine swarms of religious ecstasies across the planet.

We mingled with separate groups and danced until exhaustion, clothes clinging and the last shreds of inhibition blown away. Powerful electromagnetic pulses, from massive dynamos electrifying the City, were transmuted by musicians' fingertips and holy concentration into the primal rhythms of epochs before speech and fire.

In the ambient rooms, Crimson slowly moved among the subdued and transformed, a ministering spirit conferring blessings, speaking softly in his gentle way like a physician among the newly born. Those who could speak returned earnest words of innate trust, their faces open to him, their eyes like pools of night reflecting fields of stars.

⬡

AT 4:30 AM, as if synchronous with the previous dawn, we departed the clubs and walked for blocks, finally sitting on an isolated sidewalk, with Crimson resting peacefully against the cement wall of an undistinguished building. I knelt beside him, drained and mute after the *comédie humaine* of intersecting tribes and electric youth, their revelry like the frantic joy of immortals.

On the edge of vision the Folsom bus groaned and slid diagonally down an anonymous alley, its fluorescent glare exposing elderly Mexican and Filipina women in shawls, punks swinging crazily from chrome poles, and unconscious drunks crashed across plastic seats. Like security at the price of loneliness, a fog horn sounded its wet lips. A faint Pacific breeze began to move eastward across our hot faces. Crimson awakened me from a reverie, tapping the wall behind him thrice, slowly and sharply, then spoke.

"One last warning, a counterpoint to our night's vulnerable ecstasies. This 6-story building with no marking is 611 Folsom. On the 5th floor is the Northern Telecom switch for much of the internet and phone traffic from the Western Hemisphere. Zettabytes of information from undersea cables converge here, all monitored by an optical splitter reflecting content to NSA. There are many such sensitive, compartmentalized facilities."

He had seen an adversary, that of liberty constrained. Crimson was a study in religious devotion; his words were hushed as before a great battle, imagining a world in fetters. A chromatic scale, like membranes of light, lit up the edge of sky.

"All information, every keystroke, movement, conversation, is analyzed for terroristic intent. The scrutiny will evolve to ever lessening crimes, minor infractions. Pre-Crime analysis. Ultimately behavioral and thought control technologies will influence every individual. Magenta and Cobalt will address these issues, and the end of revolution. We feel one must act quickly."

At that cold prescience he stood. Taking my hand warmly in both of his, he wished me at length safety and peace.

"Until another space and time," he concluded happily.

"And where do you go now?" I ventured with bravado, holding for precious seconds.

"I must make breakfast for my children," he said, "and see them off to school."

I thought then it was some cryptic parting. As a magician behind the silk robe of the lessening night, he was gone.

FOLSOM STREET WAS EMPTY but for grinding sanitation trucks. Weary, I slid down the wall, legs askew, as light crept down the tips of old warehouses under a dusty flash of blue sky. My flight to Cambridge, and the rigors of Harvard, was due in only two hours. Half awake, I recalled how I had begun this study of six chemists and their international trafficking organization, and how I had arrived at Harvard. I nodded for a while, dreaming of other walls, some of metal smeared with blood, some fragrant with jasmine and roses, caressed by soft bells.

Chapter 2.

Beginner's Mind

On the one-ton temple bell
A moon moth, folded in sleep
Sits still.

- Tanuguchi, *Busoan*

A special transmission outside the scriptures
Not depending on words or letters
Directly pointing to the mind
Seeing into one's true nature.

- Bodhidharma

I'm looking for the face I had
before the world was made.

- Yeats, *The Winding Stair*

Le couvent n'est pas comme le monde, monsieur.

(The convent is not the world, sir.)

- James, *The Portrait of a Lady*

Who vanished into nowhere Zen...

- Ginsberg, *Howl*

THERE IS THE SCENT OF LILACS. I am facing a wall, seated on a cushion in a monk's formal sitting robe, legs crossed and back straight. Across the darkened hall an incense offering burns. I notice my breath, as it flows in and out, and focus upon it.

Distractions appear in the form of thoughts and feelings, sound and light, in physical sensations from the disciplined posture. These go away for a while, then reappear. I think of plans and people, feel anxiety and desire, hear the faint muffled traffic, and see upon the wall a shaft of sunlight.

Within this eternal circle of perceptions, I have fleeting moments of pure consciousness. The Dalai Lama has described this essence of mind as clear and all-knowing.

We are practicing at Hoshin-ji, Beginner's Mind Temple in San Francisco, the oldest and largest training monastery in America in the Soto Zen tradition. We practice arts from the lineage of Japanese Zen master Dogen, from 1250 A.D. It is a place of ancient courtesies and unworldly kindnesses, each morning opening into the rose window of the East.

As heirs to the final teachings of Hoshin-ji founder Shunryu Suzuki Roshi, we are in residence for months, years, or a lifetime. We learn about simple but difficult mental practices, about graceful conduct, aesthetics, the perfections of manner and, within all of these, the iron rail of discipline. After *zazen*, or meditation, we engage in calligraphy, *hibana*, or flower arranging, *chano-yu*, or tea ceremony, gardening, and service to the dying. As a path to enlightenment, or "Big Mind," some Soto monasteries also may practice the martial art of Aikido, the non-injurious rendering of physical aggressors by their momentum to the floor. The soft, elegant litanies of Hoshin-ji are merciless as diamond.

Indistinguishable from one another, fifty Zen priests, monks, nuns, and students sit side-by-side facing the wall in the *zendo*, or meditation hall, a rectangular room in the 16th Century style with a hand-polished wooden floor and elevated areas for sitting meditation.

Sometimes our restless normal consciousness, affectionately labeled "monkey mind," ceases playing, subsides, and becomes quiescent. We occasionally gain glimpses of "no mind," the space between thoughts. It is completely silent, and just before dawn.

⬡

OUTSIDE, through the zendo walls of rebar and brick, we hear two young lesbian lovers frantically clutch and rip at each other's clothing, pressing against doorways, sobbing, their footsteps shuffling back and forth in attraction and repulsion. They are coming down hot, in jangles, crashing from their long, sleepless night. They yearn at loss and gain, the fear of surrender, the tantalizing promise of new couplings. Their tender, fruitless urgencies cry to unify the spirit through flesh. Their voices are without bodies.

"Don't go!"

"I hate you! I can't be with you anymore."

"Please don't go. I love you. I gave you all my coke!"

Convulsive with tears, they run up and down the alley behind Hoshin-ji, past the monks sitting in silence. Passion and calm are separated by an aged, implacable wall, embossed with wet lichens and lapped by the City's mists. We hear the cycle of unsatiated cravings, the pleading, the chasing and embraces, the tearing away and returning, the long, low moaning. For them, it is an ugly and poignant hour, when Samsara – the illusion of the world – becomes delicious imaginings, unchecked passion, and the cruel severing of their hearts.

Their anguish fades in the barely perceptible sounds of distant motors, opening doors, salsa music, the ignition of engines, children's voices ready for school, drunks shouting execrations. Two junkies from nearby projects prowl trashcans and mutter like aimless lunatics, already jonesing for the next fix.

The background becomes subdued as we attend to the breath. It is quiet once again. There remain only the whistles of swifts as if from abbey walls, and the smell of rain-shining streets. No one moves; not a word is uttered.

We sit in silence, awaiting the next manifestation of thought and feeling, sound and light, bodily sensations. Before it is lost on the out-breath, a haiku by Zen poet Basho arises.

> "Below, the autumn tempest rages,
> While above, the sky is motionless."

A bell is struck softly. The sitting period is ended. We turn on our cushions, gather our flowing robes, and stand simultaneously with eyes lowered, hands folded one upon the other. As the bell rings again, we turn left together. From the zendo in a single file, we slowly walk away.

⬡

I HAVE ENTERED this world by begging admission the same day as released from prison. Captive for a misunderstanding about laboratory equipment, one had been consigned to a hellhole of lethargic suffering. By this different confinement of monastic practice, I seek healing and purification, a cloistering from endless brutality.

For a thousand years, supplicants meditated by temple gates for weeks, until their earnestness was recognized by passing monks. My years of isolated meditation, in the midst of knives and blood, may be apparent. Possessing only the second-hand clothes I wear, remnants from a cardboard box that day, I ask for refuge, and am given shelter.

The howling violence, the ferocity of oppression, is gone now. My body is lean and tight from relentless exercise beneath rows of razor wire in nameless, lonely yards. Monasteries, some say, are places for desperate people.

⬡

I BEGIN TO WALK these halls, past perfectly placed lilies, minimalist arts, sculptures and paintings, where each of us bows in passing with hands pressed near the heart in prayer, or *gasshō*. Contemplative mindfulness reigns. Such frequent bowing, traditional among Japanese and highly cultivated in Zen practice, is explained to Westerners as "lowering the mast of the ego" so that others can be seen more clearly. The slightest loudness, anger, or vulgarity is seized upon and extinguished through examination and insight. With each step I thank the Good Lord that Buddhists do not recognize, or the spirit that is the mystery, or the essence of mind, for this blessing, this teaching. Late at night I sometimes wander alone in the empty, silent halls, freedom's shadows emptying and splashing, and see through the tall windows under a clear sky the high riding moon.

Yet the monastery is proving far more demanding than gun towers. I slowly am making progress in not being an unruly creature, unconscious of these graceful, steely arts. As we practice before first light, always returning to the pool of silence, a tall, gaunt priest one day announces in a deep, true voice a haiku, to help us cultivate body, speech, and mind.

"Rhinoceros!
Crashing through the underbrush
Becomes white deer
In the moonlight."

I HAVE STUMBLED directly into Rohatsu Sesshin, the winter seven-day silent period that even for monks with thirty years of practice is a rigorous, even grueling, continuous meditation. It is broken only by highly formal meals, or *oryoki*, and walking meditation, or *kinhin*. This stringent, scrupulously detailed practice involves such absolute attention that I become as a prisoner again, not of the gross, but of the subtle.

A few of the new students physically shake during meditation, as random, powerful images manifest. Others, relaxing deeply for the first time, de-repress old memories in silent tears. Some may flee rather than continue to look inside. The monks consider these first phenomena as distractions by an ego less than eager to observe itself. Occurring not infrequently among beginners, they are called *makkyo*.

A single small window, high upon the wall, opens to the edge of a pale and bloodless late moon. Behind us, as we face the wall in the long hours of zazen, we hear the almost imperceptible passing of bare feet, the rustle of a robe as a priest slowly circumambulates the zendo.

A phantom, he carries a long, wooden awakening stick, the *kyosaku*. He stops to administer it upon the shoulders or backs of students whose posture is flagging. My form is perfect, but not perfect enough. Courteous unto death, he bows. Then he strikes me.

At the startling impact my spine elongates, the thrill of alertness heightening awareness until the flames of bodily sensation are recognized. They pass away like the many worlds that come and go. After a moment, there is neither pain, nor pleasure.

○

AT THE END of morning zazen, before an identical afternoon and evening, a priest rings a bell for the ritual service of *oryoki*. We do not ramble to the dining room, but bow to the wall, turn together on our cushions, then produce our oryoki set. Facing each other now, with eyes lowered, hands in prayer, we all bow again in a single hush of robes.

Within a square white cloth, tied twice at the diagonals, are a white ceramic bowl, a wooden spoon, a pair of chopsticks, and three nested lacquered bowls. All are arranged with a certain perfection. Still in zazen posture, legs crossed, we open the cloth and place each item upon it in the prescribed order. Chopsticks in the wrong direction or not parallel is a flaw in the oryoki practice, as is the small lacquered bowl placed to the left rather than to the right, or the cloth not tied properly. We are training, not to be obsessive, but to be mindful of small things.

We each lay out the oryoki set as silently as possible, then wait until the last of the fifty persons is done. We all bow as one. The *Ino*, head of zendo practice, claps two blocks of wood together to signal several servers in robes, queued by the zendo doorway. Each server, carrying a single large bowl of rice, vegetables, tofu, or sliced fruits, appears in a silent row. The food is the most pure, and adequate; there is no feeling of a renunciative philosophy, of being lost in the desert, purging guilt on a diet of locusts and wild honey.

The serving monks and nuns walk in single file, not to the nearest person, but circumambulate the entire zendo, passing everyone. They arrive to stand before the first recipient, who is holding her hands in prayer. Both bow to each other.

She offers her large lacquered bowl, one of three, by first raising it to her forehead, as a bow with her hands full. The server with the rice then bows, steps forward, ladles out a portion of rice, steps back, and bows. The second server then bows, the process continuing until all of the first recipient's bowls are filled. All bow again. The next person then is served, with this formal procedure continuing through all fifty people. The Abbess is served last, even after the beginning students.

I realize that the unearthly din of confined men no longer is heard; it is replaced by the nuns' murmurs of devotions, their soft countenances, in this antipode of Hades past.

A formal oryoki service may require a half-hour or more. Not a word is spoken. No one moves other than to bow. The Ino, seeing everyone served, strikes a bell for the meal prayer, or *gatha*. We chant in part in honor of those who grow and bring food.

"We should know how it comes to us…Desiring the natural order of mind, we should be free from greed, hate, and delusion…"

The bell rings, and we begin to eat our rice thoughtfully, drink our miso soup, and consume slowly the mixed fruits in the small lacquered bowl. We taste each flavor, feel each texture.

I reflect on the almost two thousand days in the madness of prison chow halls: the surly, angry lines shuffling to receive through a porthole in a cement wall plastic trays filled with industrial byproducts, the lowest-quality processed food for penal institutions, and carelessly heated in vats. A *Shigella* outbreak hospitalizes eighty inmates because a worker placed feces into the food. Meals are consumed hastily as guards shout threats. Kitchen workers steal as much as possible. Tightly crowded tables are filled with murderers, addicts, the dysfunctional and crazed, the clearly evil. Dark countenances drain the smile from any face.

But all that is gone now, and I dare lift my eyes slightly, for the briefest of moments, to see these many people practicing this ancient art. I now am surrounded by children of light.

Remembering to return to the breath, and at this moment to the oryoki service, I pick up the last grain of rice with chopsticks, for these portions are "just enough" to sustain practice. Each person wipes their bowl with a sliver of *daikon*, pickled radish, then eats the daikon. The Ino, seeing everyone has finished, claps the blocks and the servers reappear with pitchers of hot water, repeating the bowing procedure one by one, with each person swirling the hot water in their bowls, drinking the water, then drying the bowl with the oryoki cloth.

Through the high small window, the buttery dawn of light is now a pastoral blue. A whipping rain has ceased; the thin rays of the sun touch the ceiling. The first of three daily oryoki meals is finished.

The bowls are nested, the cloths tied in the formal manner. We as one place the oryoki sets next to the wall and to the right of our *zafus*, or sitting cushions. The times of cages, of beggared friendships and destroyed love, are no more. A bell sounds to begin the all-day meditation in the first of seven silent days. We bow.

This refined and gracious service, these simplest of meals, and all other ancient forms at Hoshin-ji are conducted with the same perfection and reverence. About this practice, performed as if each of us were a sacrament, one can never forget.

Suddenly, I see tattooed faces in prison yards, hear the screaming, feel the cruelty of feedlots, the black hole of a human abattoir. I awake to see only the nuns' luminous faces. My internal voice comforts me.

This is the right place.

○

ON THE SEVENTH and last day of Rohatsu Sesshin, in the pre-dawn quietude, the esteemed Abbess of Hoshin-ji glides in her robe behind those meditating and without a word touches a monk or student on the shoulder. This is the summoning to *dohatsu*, a private interview with the Abbess, to discuss difficulties we may be having with the practice. At the touch of the Abbess, I arise and follow her to the dohatsu room, eyes lowered. I can see only the swaying hem of her robe.

For thirty years, she has taught the 13th Century art of sewing traditional monks' robes: the *rakasu*, or little robe, and the *okesa*, the fine priest's robe. Each requires thousands of hand sewn stitches, in a manner defined for seven hundred years. With each stitch, the words "Namu Kie Butsu," the name of Buddha, the first teacher of this way, are softly intoned.

Walking three stories up the narrow hallways to the dohatsu room, she enters and closes the door. I wait outside, as is the custom. On either side of the door, we settle for a while, I with knees folded and sitting on my heels in *seiza*, the alternative pose to the legs-crossed posture of zazen. After some moments, she strikes a bell lightly. I rise, enter, bow, and sit before her in seiza. I bow to her three times. She returns the bows.

She is in the gold, grey, and brown robes of a *Rōshi*, a direct descendant in the lineage of the first teachers, and one to whom *Inka*, the seal of illumination, has been transmitted. Her hair is white, shaved almost to her scalp. She sits erect, balanced, intelligent, compassionate. One feels as though one is being diagnosed by a master physician, for the malady with no name.

We sit in the silence of mutual regard. I try not to waver, for there is no place to hide. We talk for a while, before the essential questions.

"How long will you remain?" she inquires.

"Until I am married or accepted to graduate school," I propose, balanced on the gate to a new world.

"Our practice is very rigorous, some say. Very difficult. Will you be able to manage it?"

My cumbersome efforts in the zendo are clear to her. New students are obvious, restless, distracted. Confusion and irreverence are like a rock thrown into a pool of moonlight.

"I have come from a world of men, where for five years every hour of the day was highly structured. Awakening, meals, working, sleeping. Not unlike here, but less peaceful."

I do not describe the white scar of memory, the iron parallelogram in which part of me remains forever. She does not inquire further. From her discretion, I feel she knows.

"Your occupation?"

"My research interests are in medicinal chemistry," I respond, avoiding memory's spiritual precipice.

"I, too, was a chemist at the University of California at Berkeley, before studying Zen."

She explains that she is from Alabama as a girl and has four children. Her husband is with her in the practice. I also am from the Deep South as a youth. She will encourage the *Tenzo*, the head cook, to include biscuits now and then in the mornings. We smile.

"Why don't we try it for a while?" she says.

She gently rings the summoning bell. I bow, she returns the bow, and I leave, bowing a final time at the door. I close it in the way monks enter and leave rooms, by turning the handle and seating the door soundlessly.

Assigned to a lay monk's bare cell, I must move from my comfortable visitor's accommodations. From this moment, I truly enter the monastery for the first time, not as an observer, but as a member of this exquisitely rare community where every small action – sitting, standing, walking, sleeping, speaking – must be conducted with mindfulness.

○

BEFORE DESCENDING to my monk's cell, I go to the roof of Hoshin-ji, where there is a small garden and an expansive view of San Francisco. The brilliant, open western sky is blue and hard. The spire of the carillon at the Berkeley campus pierces a low fog across the Bay; its own temple bells are calling the academic faithful to their devotions, to another form of enlightenment. It is a tolling to which I too ultimately must yield, as is my heritage. But reborn in this cleansing practice at Hoshin-ji, I vow to remain until these precepts can be applied to scholarly effort, to the promise of a new life.

To the south is Stanford and Silicon Valley, their bandwidth electrifying our planet. I bow in that direction in honor of the beings we all are becoming. Yet as a cloud passes before the sun, I notice to the northeast the Federal Building. There, technology is being turned inward upon us through fearsome surveillance methods and databases with millions of files, instantly retrievable for monitoring subjects of interest.

Against the shadow's coldness I pull my sitting robe closely, anticipating that such careful scrutiny of the population is leading to Indra's Net, the Sufi concept of a universe of eyes looking at each other, but this time in judgment. Perhaps they still consider me as a target, one who inexplicably has gone to ground in a religious retreat.

I remember the CIA Director of Intelligence in the Cold War, Yale poet James Jesus Angleton, who was fond of the phrase "wilderness of mirrors." Angleton used it to describe the illusion of a straight line, in truth always twists and turns in any games involving mutual deceptions.

Certainly my own file still exists, among the many more worthy of attention. Established the same year as DEA was formed, it must be long inactive and paltry with its lack of weapons or violence. My robe is flowing in a light wind. The sophisticated machines nearby might fail against the skills of Hoshin-ji's practice, far too subtle to be comprehended by different breeds.

Turning into the monastery, I remember to let such distracting thoughts go now. With gratitude, I begin rigorous training, erasing the pain that came before. This clockwork of sustained meticulous effort measures every hour for the next seven hundred days. Perhaps forgotten now by the watchers, I have become only a simple monk.

○

AT THE END of the first year, I still have the same dream. Running wildly, escaping from the suffocation of tortuous cages. I am pursued relentlessly across bleak and mythic landscapes, under a cold moon, saved by the kiss of a woman never seen. Within this nocturnal sea is heard the awakening bell, and the practice day at Hoshin-ji begins.

The sound of the awakening bell is not the clear resonance of a small singing bowl on a silk pillow in the zendo. An alarming, brisk clanging down the hallways, seeming to hover near every door, it grows and recedes in magnitude from horizon to horizon like a slow steam locomotive. It is accompanied by the sound of running, for a robed monk or nun is swinging a large bell on a wooden handle in broad vertical sweeps, moving through every hallway, up and down the staircases, before vanishing as abruptly as they appeared.

I enter the physical realm, tensing hands and legs and stretching, then sit up slowly in the prescribed manner. I am again in my temporary suit of bone and hair and tissue. My body becomes an automaton, working through exercises learned in prison cells so cramped one hardly can turn. The blood begins to rush.

The confined use these routines to survive weeks or months of lockdowns from gang violence, to sharpen one's spirit against insurmountable odds. My heart is leaping, lungs gasping. With slow yoga, I recover, becoming as a child again, then bow in gratitude.

Out the window of this cloistered bare room is only the chill deadness of a winter's night. No surveillance teams lurk on the pavement anymore, no unmarked vans with UHF antennae are down the street. There is only a star-cancelled sky. It is 4:30 AM, precisely.

Slipping on a grey kimono, and wearing sandals of tatami mat, I enter a procession of monks, splash cold water on my face to elicit the alerting reflex, then return to don a long black sitting robe with full wide sleeves. The tendrils of night visions become frail. We walk mindfully in single file down flights of stairs, worn at the center through decades of practice, towards the darkened zendo.

The awakening bell is replaced by a sharp, methodical, singularly resounding rap. It is the repeated concussion of a wooden mallet, administered every two minutes by a robed monk with his back to us, upon a suspended flat hardwood "han." Defeating any thought of sleep, and acting as a timer before we all must be seated in the zendo, the startling sound of the han echoes insistently throughout the building, quickly soothed by the silence of night.

As black swans upon an obsidian lake, we flow in our swirling robes, hands folded, only sandal heels and edges of robes seen by our lowered eyes. We are silent apparitions. There are no whispered salutations or any words or interactions, just the movement of our robes, a silent peace train.

The monk facing the han stands immobile, awaiting the exact moment for the next strike. I lift my eyes to the inscription carved into the han, a wide, thick hardwood flat suspended from the ceiling by ropes. Its words are the first we see each day.

Awake! Awake!
Great is the matter of birth and death.
All things are passing.
Don't waste this life.

◯

WE EACH ENTER the darkened zendo on the left foot and bow. The Ino, head of practice, bows and instructs us where to sit. A single votive burns. Not gazing about, we stand by our *tan*, the elevated sitting area, all facing each other. Upon a bell sounding, we bow simultaneously, turn to the left, then sit in zazen posture on our zafu cushion to face the wall.

The han is struck faster, once each minute for five minutes, then every fifteen seconds, then every second, then as rapid a staccato as the monk can manage before stopping. After a pause of five seconds, a final, very loud rap penetrates every crevice of Hoshin-ji. We all begin meditation. It is 5:00 AM.

The monk by the han strikes a heavy wooden mallet on the massive, three hundred pound iron *densho* bell, its surface covered with Japanese sutras. Each stroke produces inescapable, deep sonorous vibrations felt at the cellular level. The monk strikes the bell three times, letting each ring completely subside, a pause before the next strike. The sound is of utter gravity.

It is rung once for the Buddha, the Indian prince Siddhartha Gautama, who first developed this mental practice. The second is for the Dharma, the teachings arising from that realization. The third is for the Sangha, the community of those who practice the Way.

The swirling swans have become black crows, side by side on a power line to the infinite, to Big Mind. With heightened wakefulness, they step back from the restless cortex and examine psychic contents with great attention.

Past the wall, much of the City still slumbers. Our thoughts are like incense, rising, curling, and vanishing. Our limited human awareness awaits the miraculous impossibility of the day. Through the high and narrow window, and just below the edge of the world, dawn begins to illuminate the eastern sky.

◯

EXTERNALLY, meditation is quiescent, motionless. Within, transcendent rivers of mind merge and flow in the darkness. I am not so skilled and on an in-breath, clusters of vivid images erupt.

Memories of volunteering in emergency rooms. The Trauma Unit of San Francisco General Hospital. Four dying 19-year-olds, double dates, now screaming on gurneys, a vehicular mass casualty from the driver's cocaine overdose and cardiac arrest. Only twenty minutes earlier they were speeding over the Bay Bridge, music blasting, laughing, drinking, snorting lines, rushing, horny, clutching the girls' silky thighs. Unconscious of the Beast, about to pluck them all.

Two survive, shrieking to their voiceless friends now quiet as death. Blood everywhere. The driver's ribcage sliced open without anesthetic, pried apart with a steel rib spreader for hands-on direct massage. The most extreme remedy, life's last chance. Every resident is there, crowded together with victims, nurses, attendings, paramedics. A resident calls the deaths at 5:13 AM, just as it is now. All walk stunned from the trauma room to their private confrontations with God, before the next patient in a line that never ends.

Left alone, I say a prayer for the young man, holding his lukewarm hand while no one is looking. His eyes are open, glassy like a doll. I close them, remove the rib spreader, and glance at the exposed heart, hanging and still. I slip a body bag over him. The janitor, a very elderly black man, mops a floor slick with carnage, squeezes out the mop, says nothing. A resident approaches; we seal the bag, the victim's face disappearing. We push the gurney to the morgue. We talk a while to come down from seeing fresh spirits so suddenly devoured. We hover between the two worlds, colors seem unreal, faces look away. We change subjects, for Armageddon's cold visage has passed us by, this time.

There is no greater privilege than the witnessing of life and death. I apply to medical school, work at the Trauma Unit, death's main stage on Saturday night. I see everything. Dying junkies with scars like ropes. Latinos deranged on PCP with lacerated skulls from baseball bats, their wrists broken from struggling while handcuffed to gurneys. Countless young mothers in wheelchairs delivering in elevators as life giveth and taketh away. The wealthy and prominent rendered mute and helpless by stroke, now quickly discarded.

My own world dies, for I am arrested over some disputed laboratory equipment from a recycler. My acceptance to medical school arrives in jail the same week. I kiss the letter, and pray for guidance. Five years follow, smothered in steel enclosures, born again now. Sadness, failing, falling, useless…

With only a beginner's mind, not yet quick to notice long-submerged feelings arising, I finally recognize the florid cognitive display of this makkyo de-repressed from the subconscious. I awaken to return to the breath. The makkyo resolves itself in a vow to act compassionately. It seems so simple. I become as a tranquil, clear stream.

○

A SOFT BELL SOUNDS and the spell is broken. Each morning, for seven hundred days, I gather my robe, stand, turn, and walk in silent single file with all monks and nuns to the Buddha Hall. It is empty except for elaborate figures of Buddha, Bodhisattvas, and Kannon, goddess of compassion, all above an altar with votive candles, incense, and flowers. On a shelf there are small wooden boxes containing the ashes of past residents at Hoshin-ji.

Fifty tatami mats and black zafu cushions are in order on the floor to seat us into two groups, each with rows of monks and nuns facing each other. Priests in okesas walk between us to the altar, lay prayer cloths, then kneel and touch their brows to the floor. We all together kneel three times as well, then collect our robes and sit in zazen. We bow as one, as a drum and a large wooden fish, the *mokugyo*, are struck in time for chanting in Japanese or English. A steady slow beat commences.

With our deepest voices, we chant the Heart Sutra, for seven hundred years recited each morning in Soto Zen monasteries throughout the world. The monks chant in Japanese, their many voices in a basso profundo described as a deep abiding, or being settled in the heart of being alive, or like walking on the bottom of the ocean. The strong, slow rhythmic chant, on the transience of all phenomena, begins "Makka Hanya Haramita Shin Gyo," an English fragment being:

Form is emptiness, emptiness form

Not born, not destroyed

Not defiled, not immaculate

Not increasing, not decreasing

In emptiness no form, no feeling, no thought

No volition, no consciousness

No eyes, no ears, no nose, no tongue, no body, no mind

No sound, no taste, no touch, no object of mind

No vision, no ignorance and no extinction of ignorance

No old age and death and no extinction of old age and death

No suffering, no origination, no stopping, no path

No cognition, no attainment and no non-attainment

No hindrance, no fear…

At the ceremony's end, still heady with chanting, we turn and file into the hallway, to queue before the Ino. She is standing in her robe and kimono, her hands in prayer. Each person approaches and leans close to her, where the Ino dispenses the work orders for *Soji*, the temple cleaning period. She bows and whispers.

"Third floor hallways…garden…street…toilets."

We lift the fine black sleeves of our sitting robes, tie them with two strands of cloth sewn into the robe, and roll up the kimono sleeves. The prize assignments are the toilets. The monks vie for this lesson in humility, already known to me from the prison years of scrubbing cells on hands and knees. I sweep the sidewalk around Hoshin-ji in robe and sandals at 6 AM, clearing away leaves, candy wrappers, cigarette butts, and from the hedges the crack vials, wine bottles, and prophylactics from the nearby projects.

Busy commuters stalled in traffic hardly glance at us, this being San Francisco, perhaps mistaking us for Catholic novitiates in a seminary. Summer and winter, in light rain or mist, only the mindful sweeping and the commuters' hurried frustration occupy the dawn streets.

The paranoia from incarceration fades into a certain peace. I no longer sense or imagine government teams in dented parked cars down the streets, for their ghosts have fled with the light. There remains for any observers only the dreary spectacle of a monk, sweeping with head down, day after day, reciting softly spoken prayers. I have become nothing special.

One morning, in the pearly dawn from a receding fog, a young beginning Zen student, who has traded in chronic cannabis, alcohol, and caffeine use for clarity of mind through the practice, inches close by as we sweep with our brooms. After weeks of wrestling with Zen's difficult merger of delicate forms with absolute discipline, he divulges quietly a certain truth.

"Now I know why this place is considered the Marines for seekers."

I smile, but continue sweeping.

○

ON THE SECOND FLOOR of Hoshin-ji one encounters a small alcove with tatami mats, flower offerings, and candles, all before a black lacquered statue of a figure in robes, carved from Bolinas burl. It depicts Shinryu Suzuki Roshi, the founder of Hoshin-ji and the sister monasteries at Green Gulch and Tassajara and, arguably, Zen in America. Although Suzuki Roshi passed away many years ago, once each week since then after morning ceremonies our lines of monks congregate on the stairs below the effigy to chant in honor of his teachings.

Once in place and everyone silent, a diminutive, elderly Japanese woman appears, grey hair pinned back, walking with tiny steps from an adjacent hallway to cross before us. She and the priests bow to the effigy, light incense, recite Japanese prayers, and bow again. Our low honoring chant fills the hallways, passing into silence.

At the end, this single, small Japanese woman, affectionately known as Oku-san, or temple mother, slowly and very reverently bows alone, three times to Suzuki Roshi's statue, hands in prayer. She turns and bows to the priests, then to us, the monks and nuns cascading down the stairway. She folds her hands and, with great dignity, walks away into the recesses of Hoshin-ji, not to be seen again until the following week. The ceremony is conducted over the decades since Suzuki Roshi's death, never failing, never changing. For a year, I assume Oku-san is simply an aged nun. Finally, I whisper on the stairway.

"Why does Oku-san come each week?"

A nun, Chang-san, hands in prayer, whispers back.

"Why, that is the widow of Suzuki-Roshi. She appears each ceremony in devotion to her husband. For thirty years…"

Whenever Oku-san bows now, my secret self only can bow to her, in veneration.

◯

NEVER FORGETTING HER HUSBAND, Oku-san evokes memories of some unnamed loss, or prescience of a future life. Sensitized to the irreplaceable heart by Oku-san's quiet honor, I feel emotions like islands in a sea of emptiness.

A performance becomes stirring when, accompanied by the atonal sounds of a samisen, a Geisha in jet-black perfect hair, silk kimono, obi sash, and holding a parasol, performs a five-hundred-year-old dance so slowly as to be motionless. With no change of expression on her oval painted white face and small heart-shaped red lips, but only with limited movements of her feet and hands and parasol, she expresses falling in love. She symbolically cuts her hair, before a ritual suicide at her plight, because for a Geisha love can never be.

The feeling arises again from an old image in the Hoshin-ji library. A mother in a ragged kimono, stunned and lost, is carrying her newborn child. Her eyes are unspeakable. She stumbles through a crematorium, the aftermath of the firebombing of Tokyo.

Sitting in zazen, there are memories of fathers forced from their families in prison visiting rooms, of mothers denied the nursing of their crying babies, of a distraught child being carried out prison doors, of their small hands waving goodbye forever, of all their hopeless eyes. Images manifest of

Oku-san's reverent bows, the Geisha's desperate heart, the lost mother in Tokyo. I see a future where the sad eyes of my own wife and child turn away one day, and all seems connected to that wailing darkness where love departs, and we are left so very alone.

◯

I FIRST NOTICE HELEN, a very elderly nun with snowy hair, when she bows so deeply in Oku-san's presence. I often escort her about the monastery, but never ask of this homage. As she gradually becomes infirm, then an invalid, I find a blue silk kimono for her, one with streams and lilacs and branches of laurel.

On the night of Helen's death, she shows me photographs of her youth, when she was a sophisticated, attractive, artistic woman, a San Francisco bohemian with green eyes and red hair in a high French cut. One photograph catches my eye, though, of an aged, blind Japanese woman with one arm.

"Her name is Ishizaki. She taught me Zen meditation," Helen explains, "as a very young girl. Perhaps we were six or seven."

"Tell me of those days."

"I was the daughter of missionaries in Japan. The war years. The time of starving families, the devastated, haunted cities. We were among the last residents at a foreign consulate. Ishizaki and I played by the river, under the Sakai bridge."

"How did she lose her arm?"

"A sunrise that never ended, a star on earth. A multi-headed dragon that spread across the horizon, and ate the very sky. The images of the slaughtered were written on its face. Hiroshima…"

I can say nothing, but only listen.

"The poisoned sunlight was shining with the dead faces of sleeping infants. They were carved into a fanatical rictus, like white leprosy."

I am hearing her final words; I think she must be dreaming.

"Evil spirits hung about like great bats, then roamed the earth like reptiles among the dying, like beasts of the Apocalypse…"

Perhaps she is delirious. I open her Japanese fan and try cooling her face. We are behind a small *shoji* screen for privacy, in her simple, spare room. Incense lifts in whorls in the air. I try to bring her back.

"Where were you both?"

"I was in blue satin and patent leather pumps that day. We were pretending a tea party in the garden of the walled estate, singing children's songs. She was laughing and pointing up at the kites, when the light blinded her. We staggered outside. The silhouettes of schoolchildren were etched into the consulate walls. Mothers with prams, the pink kites, our little friends, the rose gardens, all gone…"

I keep her windows open this last night, flaring at the moon. Somewhere, someone is playing a *shakuhachi* flute.

"The shockwave came next, the howling of a trillion banshees, the instant flattening of buildings, bridges."

"And the survivors? What were they like?"

"We saw grisly humanoid figures as they collapsed into dust. Japanese families were naked in the river, their clothes burned off. They looked like great blisters. Some had no faces. Others moved with their arms out, flesh hanging in shreds, as though they were reaching for a lost world. It was so eerie. There was no sound, but for the weeping."

"Where was your friend?"

"I found her beneath the rubble, and drew her out. Her leg was broken, her face burned. Her left arm was in the river with the heads and bodies, the stump cauterized by the blast. Yet my friend gave me a plum she had kept in her right hand. We shared it and stayed together until the consulate survivors found us. They said we were embracing each other, and singing hymns.

"What were you singing?"

"A song I taught her, for her meditation lessons. We sang it over and over, until they came."

And she begins to sing, in her frail, high voice.

"We shall gather at the river,

the beautiful, beautiful river.

Yes, we'll gather at the river,

that flows by our home up above."

Deathwatch beetles sometimes tick in the timbers of Hoshin-ji, until the cool silence engulfs us yet again. Some monks die in zazen posture, for meditation is like one's death at morning. After Helen's passing, I find an envelope addressed to me in her handwriting. It contains the photograph of her beloved Ishizaki, as though it were a message no one else could read.

At the very end of her formal funeral ceremony, with fifty monks chanting to bells and drums, a priest calls out her name to the skies, as if she were listening.

"Helen!"

We file from the Buddha Hall. Her ashes are on the shelf in a cedar box, inscribed in Japanese.

I often visit the Hoshin-ji roof now, with its flowering of roses, the new aspiring violets, the garden scent of limes. There is a plum tree Helen always cared for. I meditate here sometimes, overlooking the City, the last rays of the sun playing like august lions. The sunset blows fresh and keen; autumn's coloring is moist. I remain for hours, as ruffled feathers of moonlight embrace the City in cobwebs of light and mist.

Swallows are gathering below this hermit *in extremis*; midnight ravens crow sleepily. I can see all the way up the fretted coast; the ocean and mountains are like a Chinese water print. The world becomes encrusted with lights; an enigmatic fan of planets stretches across the cosmos. Hours pass. There is a high moonlight, full of monochrome beauty; the sea drains of its colors.

I begin to sing for Helen, fragments of "The Old Rugged Cross," chants in Japanese, lines from a mourner Kaddish. I sing the Islamic *azan*, the call to prayer, then remember the hymn at the earth's end. Until the light of dawn, I sing softly for her.

"We shall gather at the river,

the beautiful, beautiful river…"

I hear the rustling of black robes behind me, smell incense of green laurel, but no one is ever there.

⬡

I AWAKEN NOW at 3:30 AM, before zazen, then run through the barren San Francisco streets until speechless with fatigue. Sometimes the sky folds back like great wings hovering in the sky. There is a strange confusion of scents from nowhere: jasmine, rose, laurel, blood, sulfur, the head of a newborn. The pavement is cracked and faded, but I still dance a little now and then, for out of darkness one is moon splashed, with an audience of stars.

With the passing of Helen and her memories, my conscientious scruples are ignited. I think of the madness of the world, the suffering she described. In the evenings, beginning with only small scribblings on bits of paper, I decide to change reality.

○

FOR THE SECOND TIME, I apply to med school and, as a gesture to some impossible contact with decision-makers, to the Kennedy School of Government at Harvard. The application has less than stellar transcripts from seven schools spread over decades, an admission of the prison years, and standardized test scores obtained between controlled movements from one locked area to another. There is a desperate mention of being among the forty Science Talent Search finalists, once Westinghouse and now Intel, as if secondary school remained pertinent. No explanation is given for the curious white spaces in the curriculum vitae.

To med schools I propose expanding American medical curricula online for the Third World. To Harvard, I propose policy research from the perspective of certain special experiences. The applications are truly anomalous, radioactive. I feel foolish, presumptuous, but as a monk can act only in the service of others.

○

THE SECOND ROUND of med school requests for recommendations slowly trickles in, together with outright rejections. Hopelessness flourishes. Resigned to continual defeat from years of trampled spirit, I sit in meditation facing the wall in my barren room, praying a path will open.

A letter appears under the door, the soft padding of a nun's sandals retreats down the hall. The Cambridge return address is unsurprising; no doubt it is my rejection by Harvard. Zen practice teaches us not to be too reactive to sorrow or joy, so I bow out, sigh, place the letter on a shelf, and go to the dining room to arrange tableware mindfully for fifty people at the evening meal.

I work in the kitchen these weeks under the Tenzo, the head cook, for each of us circulates through all duties at Hoshin-ji. I chop vegetables grown in ocean fields at Green Gulch monastery, slicing with methods taught at Tassajara, preparing monks' food for monks. The thin letter remains unopened; it merely confirms again one's failure in life.

I wash dishes for fifty people, silently. I think of the first blast of white light, and how a policy analyst could have influenced decision-makers, achieving surrender by detonating the devices ten miles out in Tokyo Bay.

Neglecting the letter for weeks, I sit on the stairs before Hoshin-ji in the afternoons, or sometimes watch children playing in a local park. They are laughing, singing. One day there is a little girl, flying her pink kite before the setting sun.

At this small omen, I drag myself to the room and see again the dusty envelope. I open it with resignation, for it is like all the rest. It begins in an elegant script.

"We are pleased to inform you…"

As I stand in my monk's cell, the universe turns in the pale dusk. I hear the soft rustling of a robe nearby, and open my door, but the hall is empty.

⬡

IN THIS INSTANT, the path becomes not minimization of thoughts, but of bathing in them. Of entering for years hence an almost wholly foreign environment of unfamiliar books, lectures, deadlines, memorization and finals, all among the most skilled competitors, all in the study of bureaucracies, federal agencies, the military, financial systems, warfare, and non-governmental organizations. I have never thought in these terms before.

Sitting on the steps of Hoshin-ji, I watch the ambulances, the rush of commuters, the derelicts with watery eyes, the first stars now. With the quiet rhythm of the blood, I think of pink kites, and the harmony of all things.

I know many entering students are from Oxford or Princeton, the mid-career people from CIA or State or the Pentagon. The syllabi are on topics completely unread in my exclusively scientific undergraduate courses. A new language must be learned. It all seems too much.

Yet it is a path from which one must not wander, like being at gunpoint in prison, or wintering the difficult forms of Hoshin-ji. Derided as a convict, inexplicable to many as a Zen student, but now conferred with the credibility of Harvard, I remain – under the changing perceptions of others – only this simple monk.

○

DOWN THE HALLWAY, already torn about leaving this perfect community for the trappings of conventional success, I see a hanging scroll in charcoal brushstrokes. It is a poem from the *Blue Cliff Record*, a centuries-old Zen text where the monk Oshin describes two rivers in China, the Sho and Tan, encompassing the area when Zen was first practiced. It reads:

> "South of Sho and north of Tan
> The land is filled with gold.
> Under the shadowless tree, a ferry boat.
> No one notices,
> In the emerald palace."

Turning from the calligraphy, I see nearby a kind Chinese nun down on her knees, scrubbing the floor. She smiles, places her hands in prayer, and bows. Returning this simple gesture for the ten thousandth time, I pass through the silent simplicity of the hall, with the flowers placed so very carefully in the spiritual practice of hibana. I am leaving this refuge, this palace of mind, with a sad yearning, a sense of irrevocable loss.

As the final months pass, at every ceremony and with each practice, I drink in the sights that remain forever with me: the black hems of the robes trailing above the floor, the endless bows, the faint smiles beneath lowered eyes. I see the gold of autumn, the noiseless rain, the venues of falling leaves. The *Shuso*, the head monk, makes a pronouncement to us during zazen, but I feel it is meant for me.

"When you step outside the gate,

the multi-colored dragon will eat you up.

But remember.

This is your home,

you can always return."

In the last week, there is a formal ceremony in the zendo for one leaving the community. The Ino speaks of my assiduous practice with a smile of tolerance, recollecting the ox only dreaming it was a deer. Around me flows a stream of realizations, and refined, humble beauty. I am leaving the womb. The final separation is announced by the sharp, loud, reverberating stamp of a long, wooden staff on the floor. I file from the zendo for the last time.

The morning ceremony is now without my cushion, but I hear down the halls the monks and nuns in sonorous rhythms reciting the *Sandokai*, the "Song of the Precious Mirror." We chant it in Japanese and English on frequent mornings.

"Now you have it; preserve it well.

A silver bowl filled with snow; a heron hidden in the moon.

Move and you are trapped; miss and you fall into doubt and vacillation.

Turning away and touching are both wrong, for it is like

a massive fire.

To portray it in literary form is to stain it with defilement.

In the darkest night it is perfectly clear;

in the light of dawn it is perfectly hidden.

Like facing a precious mirror, form and reflection behold each other.

In the end, it says nothing, for the words are not yet right…"

I stand and listen. Light is coming in overhead, as if there were clerestory windows high up in the vaults. The walled gardens are still rosy, but only with the last blossoms, like the precious mirror of our lives. The monks and nuns are chanting in warm waves.

"Penetrate the source and travel the pathways.

You would do well to respect this; do not neglect it.

With cause and conditions, time and season, it is serene and illuminating.

So minute it enters where there is no gap;

so vast it transcends dimensions.

A hairsbreadth's deviation and you are out of tune.

Whether teachings and approaches are mastered or not,

reality constantly flows.

An archer with skill can hit a mark at a hundred paces,

but when arrows meet head-on, how can it be a matter of skill?

With practice hidden, function secretly, like a fool, like an idiot.

To do this continuously is called

the Host within the Host."

I fold my robe and kimono in the ritual manner for the trip east; a few clothes, futon, and computer my only other possessions. This gracious community of devoted monks and nuns in which I have lived for years is to be replaced quite suddenly. I vow to carry the teachings with me always.

I know that the next monastery is one of competitive students and learned faculty, all striving to solve social problems: world hunger, cyberwarfare, overpopulation, biowarfare. Rather than votives and incense and disciplined holy tranquility, the world soon is becoming strange briefing books on CIA assessment of threats from rogue state and non-state actors, or optimal fleet sizes for nuclear carrier destroyer escorts.

There are no reverent bows on this path, no aesthetic arranging of flowers, no space between soon relentless thoughts. The next world is a whiplash of conflicting moralities, one as stringent as the transition from the violent chaos of filthy cells, to the Way.

Summoned by the Abbess, I appear in the dokusan room for the last interview. After the respectful bowing, she speaks.

"And what have you learned here?"

I describe my limited grasp of the teachings, but feelings of loss soon overcome theological discourse.

"I will miss you," I cry, coming undone before her for some moments.

"I will miss you also," she replies gently, bowing a last time.

As I bow again at the door, the Abbess leaves me with a final teaching.

"Remember not to let your head get too far from your heart."

Gathering my things, I bow deeply in reverence to my monk's room. The stairs and halls already are empty, lonely, without soft smiles. On the 700th day of formal practice, I open the gate of Hoshin-ji. My old ghost is there, restless, unfocused, frightened, asking for refuge. The eastern sky is light. With only a hairsbreadth's deviation, distracted by thoughts of the journey ahead, I step directly into the dragon's mouth.

Chapter 3.

What the Doorknob Said

Enter to grow in wisdom.
Depart to better serve thy country and thy kind.

- Inscription over Dexter Gate
entry to Harvard Yard

There was talk of the world, and daring thought, and intellectual insurgency;
heresy has always been a Harvard and New England tradition…
No matter who you were or what you did,
at Harvard you could always find your kind.

- Radical journalist John Reed, '10, author of
Ten Days that Shook the World on the Bolshevik
Revolution, and buried outside Kremlin walls.

Snow is bruised lilac, in half-light.

- Sonmi-451, in David Mitchell's *Cloud Atlas*

THE HEAVYWEIGHT EIGHT CREW, pulling the long blades of their rowing sculls in tandem, raced down the Charles River toward Longfellow Bridge. It was a halcyon August at fair Harvard: the brilliant plumages of students, umbrellas adorning the wide mossy banks of the Charles's tawny waterway, the summer curving in from some mystic latitude.

Sails of small boats filled and tossed; there were obscure movements of oars and arms above the glittering water. Students crowded the Coop for texts or strolled Harvard Square; many paced along the Charles beneath the cupolas and bell towers of Eliot, Lowell, and Dunster Houses – the elegant, Neo-Georgian revivalist piles for upperclassmen and women. Some students were electrified by their prospects, some fearful; others soberly entered the Houses as the faithful to mosques, but all were preparing for the intense labor of thought and ritual to come.

A long-legged undergraduate girl, slender as an Easter lily and almost naked but for shorts, lay unsheathed reading a volume on the decryption of Linear B by Mycenaean scholars. The gold and blue domes of Lowell and Eliot Houses were nippled minarets, caressed by white doves upwards. The distant singing and music of those gathered here to learn evoked ancient, robed muezzins at dawn reciting the Ebed.

"I praise the perfection of God, the Forever existing…"

We were assembling on the Charles embankment in these first days, retreating from the loutish reality of the world, thrilled and anxious scholars hearing legends of Cambridge and its jasmine-petaled nights. We walked down the remembered streets, at moments even dancing among their novel innocences. In these treasured handfuls of the last blue days of summer, with soft cloud formations high above, white puffs of blossoms scattered in Harvard Yard. We all became encompassed by the university's sky-floating mirages of our futures, and its granite monuments to the dead.

Many were from the far corners of nations, but all had arrived in this capital of memory to rework our personal, and the world's, realities. Among the burnished arbors of leaf-green ivy, a new sense of self-possession was kindling. At first, like travelers relating only to sullen cashiers, we were isolated by loneliness, yet from the balm of frequent receptions soon arose a new village of lightning friendships. Although garden party hats and gloves were seen no longer in the mauve dusks, the exclusions and rigors of expected excellence still prevailed.

The towers of Winthrop and Adams Houses looked upon us: the newly anointed, the fleet, and those uncertain of their gifts. All too soon a blood-red moon sometimes would wander, as term progressed, above the white steeples of Memorial Church in the Yard, waiting for our fear of the ungraspable lecture or assignment and our dismal, irrevocable, public failure.

○

BUT ON THIS SPECIAL NIGHT the moon was high and white, turning over Harvard Square; it was the evening before orientations for the undergraduate classes in the Yard, and at the Kennedy School of Government, now Harvard Kennedy School (HKS). The moon seemed of other faiths, the Square full of its light upon a sprawling subcontinent of castes and creeds, as students from a hundred cultures gathered to worship the gods of thought.

Ranks of mathematicians and cyberneticists locked in royal chess by the patisseries, while young tattooed and pierced townies sat in small groups before the MTA entrance with exaggerated purposelessness. Low mists trammeled the outline of the Charles, as ghostly sails like wings went down moonbeams in the water.

It was a *tableau vivant* of song and intrigues, cooperation and competition. Student *a cappella* groups serenaded: the undergraduate Krokodiloes in tuxedos and green shoes singing "Istanbul Not Constantinople," the Radcliffe Choral Society with madrigals in counterpoint with the Collegium Musicum, while Elizabethan minstrels preformed among skirling bagpipes.

Lackluster pigeons began to flap beneath the excited crowds. A shiver of tambourines announced the haunting gentleness of Peruvian flutes, while buskers played the Beatles and sang, "you say it's your birthday." Students and faculty, laughing or in somber homage, considered the graduate schools of Law and Medicine, Arts and Sciences, or Mallinckrodt laboratories where insulin, lysergic acid, chlorophyll, quinine, and napalm first were synthesized.

Dog-eared jazz flowed from street saxophones, idlers squatted or walked apathetically offstage, and fellow Kennedy School matriculants with name tags began practicing the elaborate kindnesses of diplomats. By the Charles, alone, I sang to myself.

"We shall gather at the river,
the beautiful, beautiful river…"

I STRUCK UP a conversation with Chris, an entering HKS student. We sat on the steps of Holden Chapel (1744) in the northwest side of the Old Yard, beneath Mrs. Holden's coat of arms. Young men and women, required to live in the Yard in their first year, were struggling with sofas into Pennypacker and Wigglesworth halls. A few had the look of inheritors, some seemed the children of tradesmen or merchants, others from straightened circumstances, but all with the gifts upon which no value could be placed.

"The Yard seems too small for everyone," I opened, tentatively.

"After freshman year, they go to the Houses: Cabot, Leverett, Quincy, others by the Charles or near Radcliffe Quad."

"But look at this diversity. How does Admissions choose?"

"Harvard could fill its freshman class with perfect SAT scores, but seeks the ineffable 'potential for greatness.' Not to worry, we're merely *grad* students."

"A lesser breed?" Many of us were in our thirties or later, and struggling even now.

"Already proven failures at being titans," he said, smiling broadly.

He seemed admirably balanced in perspective.

"Can you distinguish who's who yet? Among the freshmen?"

"Some are poor Indians with the mind of Ramanujan, whose equations could change the world. Another might be the future Aga Khan with a string of chateaux, or the daughter of a seamstress."

"So it's a matter of mind, not circumstance?"

"That's it. Even the president of the university, an English Literature scholar and noted expert on the verse of Sir Philip Sidney, is the son of a guard at Danbury Prison and a lifelong waitress. Harvard is the ultimate meritocracy."

He had me for a moment. I said nothing. Thankfully, he went on.

"The Houses all have formal dining rooms, music rooms, lesser works of Old Masters. They smell of potpourri and antiquarian books, wax polish, candles and camellias. And brow sweat and sex, although less often the latter."

We considered a trio of Radcliffeans, now Harvard women, very much arm-in-arm and trouncing onward, singing "Ode to Joy" in German.

"The Cliffies are so fast, academically at least, that if we were horses," he reflected airily, "they would be in the paddock at Longchamp." He spoke with the wistfulness of the inexperienced.

We lost each other in the mad ramblings of Harvard Square, but I wandered late, agape at the angel-haunted spaces of the Aiken Computer Lab, the site of the first computers and Internet node. At the Law School, I fell asleep on couches beneath paintings in the Treasure Room. Its windows looked in upon a sealed space – designed to protect atomic secrets during World War Two – that opened to secret underground tunnels to the physics labs. Penetrating closer to the decision-makers, I dreamed of a star on earth, and a dragon that ate the sky.

⬡

A SURREAL JOLT, early orientation at the Kennedy School was a torrent of unfamiliar words and concepts, a wonder-working cure for our huddled anonymity. On a break, some students seemed agoramaniacs like inbred politicans, others had a heightened social awareness, while a few at first were completely at sea. By noon, it was a raucous gaggle of the blessed, mixing in the trumpeting sunlight.

Ever surrounded by the university's unconscious pageantry of feudalism, in these first weeks before midterms, there were to our delight the vertiginous pleasures of imagined competences and equality. We toasted each other, suspending our prior mental sloth, private wildernesses, and obscure missions. We smiled affectionately, and had undisguised fervor for our future professions as analysts. Our need for reserve and solitude though, as we began scrambling to survive the progressive cognitive challenges, too soon made us recluses. No less than Hoshin-ji, we were scholar monks mediating on information, as streams of data merged and flowed in our darkness.

Multi-national in origins, ethnically diverse, HKS students inevitably possessed a certain high-strung quality. Fully grounded competitors born to excel, they frequently were magnetically engaging, while some – more rarely – were withdrawn in such an academic way that one erred in thinking them timid, then later confronting a ferocious intellect. While a few retained a sense of entitlement as heirs to the university's imprimatur, all students soon were tempered by a pervasive feeling of constantly drowning together, overwhelmed both by the rings of the world's sorrows, and its unimaginable promise.

CHRIS REAPPEARED, forever *au courant* with university lore and politics. I spotted him being ejected from a closed and gloomy subterranean library, relying on his default of good manners. Vaguely amiable and bespectacled, with shiny black Oxford brogues, and the physical size and mental agility of T.E. Lawrence, he usually had an air of grave preoccupation. Ever so courteous and cautious with Harvard women, he tried social endearments and avuncular tricks of speech, occasionally managing a date.

In battles of wit, he fell back upon Schopenhauer, Hume, or Spengler, but his personal kindnesses were disarming. His fine brows and future were unclouded. He never mentioned or inquired as to others' backgrounds, attracting me with this gentlemanly quality.

Lighthearted at moments, he soon felt it his duty to demolish my monk's liturgical air. To that end, he delighted in mimicking esteemed Cambridge notables, but took particular pleasure in the drawl of Strom Thurmond, then Chair of the Senate Intelligence Committee, with his wicked quotidian platitudes.

"Ahm askin' yew 'bout *intel-li-gence*, suuuuh," (Chris's hand affects to cover a microphone) "we deal in *intel-li-gence* fo this heah intel-li-gence committee, even if yew *cain't* pass no lit-tu-ruh-cy test. Now, where's ma *briefin'* book?"

I termed him privately the "Hulk," for his diminutive size was offset by the playful muscularity of his thought. Between our exhilarated but timid arrival, and our staggering but glorious departure years later, there was – beside the information and faculty – only the wonder of such bright souls.

OUR FIRST CLASSES were pervaded with a sense of self-satisfaction at having arrived, but also with fright at the thought of not remaining so. Papers shuffled, lights trembled from eyes contracted with adrenaline, welcoming or exultant gazes were replaced with expressions of malaise at irremediable gaffes. While several students were surviving dual-degree programs at the medical or law school, I was burdened by a simultaneous appointment at Harvard Medical School. As a new officer of the university, I soon became aware of the six international psychedelic chemists, and – among proliferating research topics – sought to study them.

In lectures, young assistant professors evoked nervous laughter by their hope that in a few weeks we might be "up to speed." Distinguished older faculty peered in upon us with labored, almost hieratic movements. I noticed a faint blue love bite, a rarity never to be seen again among Harvard's fairest, fading upon the long, lovely neck of a daughter of a leading Buenos Aires family. It was the last kiss of an Argentine night.

I scribbled in the margins of a dream, while others addressed themselves to sheaves of notes, stunned but affecting to think. The air became charged with the savagery of competition. Mind and spirit grew restless; the first deadlines for insoluble problem sets were in sight. I began studying the love bite as it disappeared, her quiet profile bending over inscrutable passages. In the mental saturnalia to come, we would all play the role of a *machine à plaisir*.

◯

A SEA OF ACADEMIC STARS confronted by ceaseless, insurmountable waves of data purposely generated by faculty to be almost unmanageable, all somehow persisted through their sense of duty to public service, and in part from their origins. Half the students were international, the gifted youth of small villages in India and Russia, chosen for this privilege, brought to America, exposed to the democratic ideal and – through such harvesting of talent – trained to lead, influence decision-makers as analysts, or become high-level officials. Harvard continually reseeded nations with future policy makers – and connections – yielding a porosity of intelligence information among peers worldwide that no covert action ever could accomplish.

◯

LA FEMME MURPHY, the students' name for her, bounded into view. To me she was "Murph the Surf." A Boston Irish redhead with a disputed overseas history and uncertain friends in Malibu, she was rumored to be a Wellesley survivor. Displaying perfect graces and the *de rigueur* tailored navy blue suit, cut slightly too high, she was beautiful in an etiolated way, with legs as long as an Ibis and almost trembling with life force. Surf was windblown when she arrived, spring dew without a flaw. Her skin flushed lightly. She sometimes had a low, melodious voice among her many dramatic poses, like a woman ruefully aware she was marooned on some inaccessible moonscape.

Surf still had a little cream on her lip from a *café viennoise*; a blue velvet ribbon surrounded her throat. She had noticed my guileless admiration in class. Just out of our lecture on childhood poverty in the Bangladeshi slums, she was dismal, tearful, moving awkwardly. In a sweet high register, her blue eyes changing to smoke, she made a broken pronouncement, quoting her beloved Yeats.

> "She comes, the human child
> To the waters and the wild
> With a fairy hard in hand
> For the world's more full of weeping
> Than she can understand."

Her looks that day were unguarded and shy as a small, ancient, trusting girl. We had no idea of her personal experiences. Although Surf at times had an unconscious coquetry, she was unmated among the diverse heredities at HKS, for her subtle wildness was fearsome to conservative academics. At lecture she had a powerful grasp of policy matters, and prevailed unshrinkingly, like a medieval scholar splitting theological hairs. She could be stern, with those splendid eyes.

⬡

LESS ABOUT KNOWLEDGE than acquiring personal confidence to engage in serious dialogue from boardroom to national laboratory to defense establishments to palace halls, HKS first taught us intellectual fearlessness, then evolution from competitive Harvard *arrivistes* to eager cooperation in groups. We trained to submerge lifetimes of one-upmanship for the broader public good. One student circulated through HKS mind fields to become the youngest Minister of Serbia, another mid-career CIA officer returned to the duplicities of spy craft to ferret out the next traitor in the ranks, yet another to dusty encampments in Tibet to lay water lines and treat endemic high-altitude glaucoma.

Many others went to the White House or State or Congress as staffers or policy analysts, some to the financial sector and leisurely lunches in Brussels and the Hague, another to the World Bank to make loans for milk for a hundred million children on the flood plains of India. A few were destined to Wall Street's golden handshakes and trading in arbitrage, even as a cluster went to the Peace Corp for food and a tent while teaching disaster management to thin, bedraggled refugees digging latrines in Eritrea's famine belt.

⬡

CLASSES BEGAN PROMPTLY on Harvard time, seven minutes after the hour, a habit some alums continued all their lives. In these first months, as dreaded midterms approached, we became filled with forests of heartbeats, for our thoughts were those of startled hares. Some of the lectures had evolved into such fusillades of words that we became as poor worshippers in a cathedral of sighs. While statistics professors eagerly loaded whiteboards with indecipherable nests of flow charts, Surf took to making suicide gestures across her delicate throat with her long perfect fingers.

Against this deluge of demands, an intellectual rigor mortis soon developed; only flickering electric signs of the imagination occasionally flashed down from the firmament. Even Hulk, after being summoned to stand and deliver a summary of the week's salient points, surreptitiously placed his head in his hands.

Under such stress, the elms and oaks in the Yard began to seem like crude Dadaists' paintings; Wigglesworth was a bristling fortification. On good days, we mistook the Yard's failing light in the Fall for some hopeful vernal landscape. Hulk, stricken with the pace, began appearing with a cold, marmoreal cast to this skin. Surf, though, whom one might think the fruit of perfect breeding, pretended a studied naturalness, claiming with careless hair tosses an impatience with partial information, and a mania for exactitude. But Surf, and all of us by that time, were merely waxworks, lost in a house of economists' mirrors.

⬡

NOT ALL WAS GLORY. One hapless visiting researcher in a small seminar intoned axioms in a listless voice, espousing the dogma of a sect, but with an expression as though he were bequeathing knowledge in a shower of silver arrows.

"(unintelligible)…and the prevailing egalitarian sympathies of Keynesian theory," he fluted.

At the very edge of hysteria, we all listened gravely, pens motionless over paper. The excellence of HKS professors had made us hypersensitive to cant, imperiousness, or illogical thinking. We rebelled at this seminar, at the portentous circumlocutions of his meddlesome pedantries. With the fervor of amateurs in a new medium, prone to unhesitating argument, we were a difficult audience.

Distracted from the drone, I suddenly noticed through the window an unearthly light, one I forever kept to myself. The last of the camellias, their foamy white blossoms loose with petals, were infused with music and radiance. I had just returned to Cambridge from interviews with Crimson on the beach by the fireside, the night of illumined moon and sea. My notes on that ungraspable event, some written in an alley in San Francisco, were in disarray.

It still was an uncertainty that analysis of an international psychedelic trafficking organization would be achievable at Harvard Medical School, with its primary concerns about addictive drugs. In haste, over masses of economic graphs, I wrote "Crimson" in large block letters on my note pad. Hulk, obliquely overseeing this reminder, thought I referred to the Harvard student newspaper or the athletic teams. Pretending to listen to the lecture, I failed to dissuade him. A petal floated through symphonies and choirs, and worlds upon worlds, to the earth.

The visiting researcher, a contented dogmatist, was assailed by wry comments. His fifty minutes no more, he grew specious, then seemed more attentive to the oriental allurements of our Filipinas, sisters from a notable banking family in Manila. Decidedly unimpressed with his occidental piety, they abruptly did a *volte-face*, long hair flinging, glasses perched on noses. A roaring northern rain began, the last of the fall. The camellia petals were swept downstream. A telephone shrilled as a thousand scholars marched to the next ganglion in our HKS nervous system. We, thankfully, were among them.

⬡

I RECOGNIZED a lean, solitary figure besieging a young HKS woman, who began yielding her perceptible coolness with a grudging but obvious pleasure. David K, who became the most gracious of friends, was "Hammersmith" or "Hammer" to me, named for his absolute, incisive mind and concise arguments, always directly *en pointe*.

Hammer was a Kentucky boy with a Judaic gloom and a Levantine shadow of a beard despite attempts at being clean shaven. He had surrendered his private life to HKS and Harvard Law School as a dual-degree student. A provincial at heart, with a formal politeness and bright, tired eyes, he was a king of complex absorption.

While HKS students were learning deportment, diplomacy, speech and oratory, networking, analysis and briefing-book writing, Hammer conceived and promulgated secretive barbed poetry. In a seminar with a Pentagon official, he passed a hand-written note, resorting to Blake.

"…and the hapless soldier's sigh, runs in blood down palace walls."

I first noticed Hammer in a national security lecture, lifting his eyebrows to me, like someone signaling from an unknown universe. In class confrontations he often had the last word; his logical summations dropped like falling stars, and expired in the astonished silences.

Hammer had dark, appraising eyes. He admired the HKS woman's surly magnificence, her own satin eyes, like a thundercloud brooding over fertile fields. Hammer the lad was clever, not pressing. He waved to me, then sauntered with an umbrella and his new acquaintance past the line of black limousines and duty cars of visiting dignitaries, through the HKS gates. He had exemplary dispatch, and a profile of crisply cut features. I heard him entertaining her with Cambridge quotes, in his clearly enunciated way.

"Francis Crick would seduce undergraduates by saying, 'Dear, do come up and see my *Nobel*.'"

She tittered and smiled. They cut in front of the Defense Minister of Lebanon, Hammer unsettling me with a look while describing his lost weekend and paraphrasing Arthur Koestler.

"I had the secret of the universe last night, but this morning, I forgot what it was."

◯

WITH SUCH LAYERING of personalities, introductions, histories, futures, and hidden reasons for being at Harvard, a moment's encounter resulted for many in a project anywhere in the world, under any government, researching weapons systems or children's diseases, fragile oceans or toxic atmospheres, diplomatic intrigues in Namibia or Malaysian finanical systems. HKS case studies were directed at leaderships or controlling parties, while training increased one's ease with high officials. But most of all, for the public good, instruction concerned how organizations could be made more humane, or more lethal.

Mid-career students who were night fighter pilots were at first unaware of others nearby who were prospective or actual intelligence analysts. They both separately considered from their prospect of the trigger or the pen – as they walked and conversed in excited groups in HKS courtyards – how war craft might be refined against those who would violently oppose the interests of the United States.

⬡

I FIRST OBSERVED a splendid, young 6-foot Princeton woman, now an HKS student in clinging gossamer-grey cashmere, when she giggled during lecture at the elitist tone of an Indian Oxford alum's comment on "populist manners." She reappeared at the HKS gate, breathless and bouncing in a skin-tight black tracksuit, her slender eyebrows narrowed, her blond hair in a runner's pony-tail, provoking me with a question as she continued to jog up and down.

"Given the demands of our *evenings*…do you think a Polish *immersion* course is insur…*mountable*? I mean…as an elective? Could one…*squeeze it in*?"

Through the Old Yard, then dancing lightly in her long black coat up the steps of Widener Library past the massive granite lions *couchant*, she trailed a wake like comet's hair fanning. Her smoldering blue eyes, unconscious of their effect and focused on the data at hand, induced in others a starry ache. She was long-waisted, slinky from a perspective, strikingly European. Once past this formidable exterior, one found a secret warmth, an endearing candor. I could only give her the sobriquet "Hagendas," so much was she fancied by Harvard men, like ice cream by the Charles on a summer's afternoon. She tasted like strawberries, rumors held.

But within her physical vessel lay oracular thoughts; she was an unimpeded academic since her childhood at the Lycee Francaise in New York City and Le Rosey in Switzerland. The daughter of an accomplished couple, surrounded as a girl by artists and writers and scientists who frequented her home and dinner table, Hagendas was always a step ahead.

Her failings included the touch of envy in others, but she preserved her graces. When in the night she passed the inviting doors of Wigglesworth or Pennypacker, she became a legitimate idolatry for undergraduate men, and even a few women who in their scholarly tensions still retained a certain ardor for school mistresses.

Handsome and reserved, she had a cool, clear, honeyed voice, perhaps in F major, except when in opposition or annoyed. Her secret followers imagined her divine splendor in bed; but if she had lovers, they remained forever conjectural. In lecture, she caught my eye, her arm held behind her head, stretching, pushing back the fair hair, a little mild stargazing. I got her wavelength.

Hagendas, golden blond, writing in Widener in her exquisite hand with long silken fingers, often seemed like a Victorian gentlewoman painting watercolors. My experiences prior to Harvard though, and more so during Harvard when later exposed to the majestic erotic practices of the Six, led me to a tolerant admiration of her, rather than some disturbing, inconvenient, unquenchable desire.

⬡

THEY ALL CORNERED me one day: Hulk, Surf, Hammer, Hagendas, a tall white Afrikaner woman, and an eternally serious Albanian girl from Tirana.

"How does data swamping turn us into leaders?" said Hagendas, born to direct.

"We're becoming data rats, burrowers," said Hulk, overlooking the moles.

"Statistics notes, anyone?" said Hammer, ever cautious at sneak attacks by observant faculty with pop quizzes.

"Penny loafers!" cried Surf to my horror, pointing gleefully at my new conservative footwear.

I had arrived from Hoshin-ji with only a few clothes in underground, ascetic black, the fashion of the day. Later adopting Crimson's practice of not being noticed, but blending in seamlessly, I had acquired dull grey slacks and sports jacket, and was indistinguishable from overstressed junior faculty.

The white Afrikaner had the last word. Thinking I had succumbed to Harvard's dubious sartorial flair, she dryly commented, to nods all around:

"I don't let this place get to me."

⬡

THERE WERE COUNTLESS receptions on the top floor of HKS, with its mandarin calm, cinnamon walls, green baize tables, roped-off sitting rooms, New England paintings, and overview along the Charles from Harvard to MIT. Here we learned the easy aridities of social practice, and our hearts were bright.

Several exceptionally promising young doctoral candidates were visiting. We arrived at one of the myriad gatherings for students to engage with faculty, governors, Nobelists, and a rainbow of former White House officials. The latter commonly were defrocked high-level bureaucrats waiting out the current administration with HKS teaching appointments.

Mingling with this eclectic assortment of potential encounters, each a railway to traditional worlds, we passed a gallery of Presidential portraits from Washington to Eisenhower. Through the vocal scholars, beyond the well-tended lawns, sunshine was rippling on the Charles. We soon spied a tidy, poised gentleman in his early seventies, standing somewhat apart.

With tailored suit, tight military haircut, pale blue eyes and bow tie, he was reminiscent of a headmaster at St. Paul's or Choate. After light pleasantries, we entered into commerce with Ken Knaus, a senior officer late of the CIA Operations Directorate, now the National Clandestine Service. He chatted as amiably as any Gloucestershire vicar, rather than one protective of unspeakable secrets. He was a master of war.

Knaus was a prime example of the legendary CIA spies always in residence, hobbyists all as talent spotters who harvested analysts from HKS classes. He was writing a manuscript on his early days as the young case officer who smuggled an adolescent Dalai Lama out of the Potala Palace in Lhasa, through regiments of Chinese seeking His Holiness for other than religious purposes. On a train of mules accompanied by monks with prayer flags and bells, porters with bricks of tea and yak-butter tsampa, together with a small coterie of armed CIA personnel with encrypted radios, Knaus and the Dalai Lama carefully treaded across the ice abysses and couloirs in the high passes of the Himalayas, from Tibet down into the lush lowlands of Daramsala, India.

Knaus deflected our tentative inquires into CIA tradecraft by easy and inoffensive verbal parries, the skills of a lifetime. He did acknowledge knowing Ken Olson, the biochemist under CIA psychiatrist Sidney Gottlieb, who died suddenly by defenestration, plunging twenty stories – either pushed or suicidal – after being overdosed by CIA employees ("Yes, I'm aware of Olson").

CIA Technical Services Staff purposely administered Olson LSD as an unwitting experimental subject in Operation MK-ULTRA during CIA's effort to weaponize LSD as an interrogation agent in the Cold War. Knaus said little about Olson. Our benign generalities otherwise were not too pressing for him, so that we parted in an urbane way. I remained gratified by the gentlemanly manner of the secret services, if not their artful circumspection of actual intelligence information, for they were deft in creating a black hole from which no light emitted, save the smile of a Cheshire cat.

⬡

SURF AND HULK AND I sought refuge on a Saturday night, as fall term began to coil toward winter. We came from Memorial Hall in the Yard into the Square, where before the MTA entrance was a scattering of club kids with smudged eyeliner, and one likely predator with an uncouthness of mien.

On the far, dark bank of the Charles, as though it were the last of summer evenings, a lavish girl with cascades of black hair, wearing only a Mount Holyoke tee-shirt and quite snug pink short shorts, sat barefoot with her long legs tightly embracing a thin Boston Conservatory student. His violin case was opened wide, exposing folds of soft, red velvet. In slow movements, a kind of *andante glissando*, he in perfect time caressed her burgeoning cleft. As she approached the beatitudes, eclipses of the moon began spreading across her face.

In the fecund silence, the sky in those long moments seemed molten stars. In an *accelerando*, her muffled cries were inaudible but to us. We withdrew past the Anderson Bridge, to give them peace; Hulk grew quiet with sympathetic adoration at the simple beauty of shamelessness.

"Clearly a summer student," Surf remarked with irreverence, the spell evaporating.

In a huff, she paced restlessly, turning here and there with pangs of envy, but still transfixed on the distant passion.

"There have been no orgasms at Harvard," she said, "since the Business School shorted Wall Street in 1929."

Surf referred to the apparent lack of sex among grad students. Although many walked purposely, intent on world conquest, one rarely saw anyone even holding hands. One's calendar of desire was penciled in lightly, and mostly erased, among impossibly scheduled hours, weeks in advance. Our relentless, hyperactive undergraduates, with those prepossessing frontal lobes and the obligations of genetic drift, were quite another matter.

○

WE CONTINUED up the Charles in the evening, where Memorial Drive traffic had been blocked off all the way to MIT. Beneath grand tents, almost-nude Taiko drummers in sweaty loincloths struck great drums in racy, overheated rhythms. Flocks of skaters swayed like seagrasses as they flowed down open lanes, semi-professional student mourners wore skeletal masks in a burial procession for the Chemical Weapons Treaty, Danish women engineers picked suggestively at the tassels of soft cushions beside owlish, frozen MIT students, while strobes and lasers shot from high suites in Lowell and Eliot Houses.

The light show precipitated thoughts of Crimson, and how Harvard students were not unlike the Six. Both groups had a global theater of operations; they were exiles of circumstance from many worlds, yet there was a fantastic poetry to them.

Floating to the Square, we saw Harvard women, fresh from encounters down the cobbled streets, teetering in heels in the Walk of Shame for puritans or the Stride of Pride for libertines. Parisian students sat with languid, fruitless airs, having lost their half-dozen pliant French mistresses, and now confronted by thinking women with advanced cognitive skills. They claimed no taste for a girl that night.

Posses of diverse women students were practicing the samba down Mass Ave. Reeling Hasty Pudding dramaturges, flouncing in diaphanous lace and chiffon spikes, affected messy chic party hair and faux whorish latex pencil skirts. Clusters of cosmological physics students from Lowell Observatory wore fitted tops, corset belts, killer heels with vanity straps, or houndstooth and snakeskin pumps. Others, the last of the Egyptologists, danced with Professor Gropius's Bauhaus School designers.

We had stumbled upon some celebratory *haute couture* catwalk of academic orgyists, where excluded and less well-feathered males grouped in local bars, resorting to dropping the "H-bomb," their matriculation in Cambridge, in hope of a date. College girls from west of the Charles to the Pacific were visiting. UCLA undergrad women on leave wore Mouse Ears, Dunster House men wore Moose Ears, Leverett House men wore Rabbit Ears. Mass Ave was rather like a galactic watering hole.

I thought of the Harvard Botanical Museum nearby, where the inestimable Amazon explorer and ethnopharmacologist Richard Evans Schultes often had startlingly elegant, formidably serious grad students. Arrived from hot tribal nights in primitive villages in the Orinoco Basin, they insisted on keyboarding about hallucinogenic snuffs administered through blowpipes, while in the muggy Cambridge summers the women writing their PhD theses were simply adorned with a macaw feather on a leather string, and were otherwise naked to the waist.

○

WITHIN THESE VISIONS, with their assumption of permanent excellence and privilege, the corrective sense of midterms came softly toward us. They were clouds filling our horizon, condensing in the mind like dew. The autumn lucidity became smoky; a strident curt reality began to set in. Leaves rained down in drifts to motley patchworks, as did our progressive sense of desolation.

All wired together now to survive, HKS students bewailed their misfortunes about Machiavellian problem sets. The libraries at HKS and Widener became machine-like with robot intensity. Hammer began clutching his notes, his face ashen and furtive, as if economic analysis were a crime. Ad hoc study groups proliferated fearfully, our mingled voices like prayers for knowledge to be contagious. In her round, violet sunglasses, Hagendas pretended a cool exterior, but we all trudged on in dogged misery.

A few HKS students tried late transfers to the Woodrow Wilson School at Princeton ("more scholarships") or the Safety School (Yale). The images of eight U.S. presidents and forty-eight Nobelists from Harvard seemed guardian angels ascending into the blue, expanding like some mystical rose, until the harsh truth of our frantic incompetence dispersed these Hosts with blistering candor. In our half-dreary stupefaction, some tried to catechize the silences with sacraments of caffeine and chocolate, but by that time thought had perished. There was mental shrieking; the air was rank with fatigue and wet overcoats.

In the last dusk before midterms I walked on a break, through the variable airs of the Charles, to a far jetty. Thinking of the night with Crimson, I saw overhead an unforgettable grandeur: the lightest of silver rains from the north, the last of the dying sun opposing a young rising moon, the cobwebs of changing light as if the sky had gone mad.

Returning to HKS for the final push, I remembered that the faculty had been exemplary; they were rhetoricians of peace – then of war – even as their speech in the first months had the cadence of immortal poetry. But as we lost control of the information, and our fear broke loose, lectures sometimes seemed orotund, then doggerel, the poetics of distraction. Withdrawing into anxiety, we only half-heard what had become wretched words. I saw that the faint blue love bite had yellowed; the days of golden anticipation were no more.

Even rushing to Widener would waste precious minutes. In the HKS library was Hagendas, her flawless head bent down to take long drafts of impenetrable arcana. Our Mediterranean women, puzzling over great tomes, had Byzantine faces, their profiles like frescoes. Hulk crouched over a statistics problem, totally anesthetized. Surf had a not altogether mock resignation. Hammer, his reserves depleted, approached the next page with reticence, almost shame. An iron band was around all our heads, putting us out of humor; we began to read widely, fretfully, with a sulky emphasis. Mawkish and callow undergrads, fleeing from Widener, looked on us with pity. We tried clearing our minds of the debris of fumbling calculations, one eye on our inadequacies and the other on janitorial careers. At closing bell, we all detached ourselves from our study carrels, clumsy and taciturn.

Those pulling all-nighters walked in somnambulant shrouds by the darkling Charles, I among them, lost in a maze of breathing, amorphous data. Someone was sailing under the moon, heeling on a freshet, waters lapping the prow, then tacking with one running light down the channel as though it were the Venetian Grand Canal. Clouds of silver pigeons climbed in wisps and puffs, diving upwards to moon-white clouds. Still sensitive from my encounter with Crimson, I briefly banished midterms from my mind with the scent of their enigma.

I remembered the transformations by the fire with Crimson, where all the ages of history passed like a storybook. It seemed some mythical calculus of hermetical lore, but others would think it mumbo-jumbo, a kind of parlor mysticism. It was then I firmly decided to investigate such visionary states through the appointment at Harvard Medical School, secondary to a study of the economics and methods of the Six. From these recollections, my mind fired; I sat reviewing notes by the Charles until dawn overtook the sky.

We entered the lecture hall in a dream: blank, lightly crazed, our confidence a poor joke. Hours passed in white light. Torn Blue Books, hastily inscribed with best guesses and parroted fragments of misinformation, circulated limply back to the proctor. The only smiles were those of relief. Suddenly midterms were over, where the first now became the last; then we were free, like bandaged patients climbing from gurneys, into the delicious morning air.

THE WEATHER WAS CHANGING. Great winter storms lurked off Kennebunkport up the rugged Maine coast; wet leaves lay in mounds in the Yard. Students were bound up tightly by the alien integers of their mid-term grades; there were histrionic silences, and a pervading melancholy under cold rains. Intermittent stabbings of reality assured us of our imminent demise.

The Charles was choppy with white crests from magisterial north winds; even in calms a heavy damp came off the river, with dense, blurred ground mists. A last sailboat wallowed and yawed for a while, then suddenly heeled before the wind. laying in sheets, shaking down the jib, coming about and tacking to shore to make fast. It finally turned on the stern anchor, helpless before the incoming weather.

The high-spirited little warrior tribes of Harvard Square dwindled into gossip of the lazy and envious. Unconscious moral judgments flashed about; one unfortunate girl, common and fast-looking, kept swinging her leg, so close to the needles and sores.

After the hushing of the rains, as rare sunlight dried its damp facades, Massachusetts Hall became an old faded daguerreotype. We moved through cold currents, the air full of static electricity; our colored fantasies soon drained in the insistent river wind. The nights became frozen, the stars brilliant. I often walked by the crisp beauty of Eliot, Quincy and Lowell Houses, alight by the lonely waters of the Charles, thinking that this marathon intellectual orgy was but a spiraling labyrinth of concealed motives.

The survivors thus far only whispered bruised affections, for our piercing happiness was suspended until finals. The grad students looked for traction; the undergrads yielded their infectious high spirits, their Champagne tipsiness, their spent kisses, for new constellations of profound effort.

Odd gleams of sunshine riddled the Yard, torrents of brass brown leaves swirled until the first heavy frosts peeled the sky clear. Lean, long-haired, well-featured senior women undergrads stalked the steps of Widener, their chilled cheeks blushing, wearing long mufflers, fine gloves or mittens, legwarmers, and ankle-length coats nipped at the waist. Lovely in their focus, they sought warm silent alcoves to ponder Goethe or Swedenborg, with furtive glances at Exeter or Andover alums, or at each other.

⬡

I SPIED HULK, a victim of the historical virus, explaining with a cordial futility to ice-bound tourists the Three Lies of John Harvard's statue, as if the tale were dismembered fragments of a novel. I surreptitiously joined the group.

The statue of John Harvard in the Old Yard was throughout the year, but particularly during Commencement, an academic Mecca. A bronze figure of a seated youth in the 1600s, it was akin in religious terms to the massive shrouded cube of the Ka'bah, about which Islamic devotees on the pilgrimage of Hajji circumambulate counterclockwise in reverent masses. The statue attracted much devotion among international groups of visitors, no less than the rumored white meteorite within the Meccan shroud, now turned black from absorbing the sins of the world.

In the Yard, tourists congregated hourly before the statue, which had become a type of djini representing the limits of human consciousness. Hulk encouraged tourists to rub the bronze buckled boots of this hursuit founder with his fine countenance and frockcoat, like actual students who appeared at the statue to coax scholarly excellence to emerge before Reading Period.

Harvard's sanctuary was allotted often to the truly accomplished, and more rarely to wandering monks of questionable backgrounds. Visitors sometimes mistook these privileges for the tawdry commonality of prestige, a word derived from prestidigitation, or the making of illusions. However it was regarded by passersby, or what sins it harbored so mutely, it was regarded with affection as the "Statue of the Three Lies."

Hulk was pontificating marvelously, and winked at me.

"Cast by Daniel Chester French before he sculpted the Lincoln Memorial," he said, "the inscription reads 'John Harvard, Founder, 1638,' but none of this is true. The statue is of Sherman Hoar, class of 1882, descendant of a prior president."

I whispered, "Don't forget his pluck." Hulk threw me a foul look.

"…sixteen years after Pilgrims landed at Plymouth Rock, Massachusetts Bay Colony purchased the acre of land that became the Yard and founded the College in 1636. John Harvard, minister at Charlestown, donated in his will 400 volumes and 779 pounds, now an endowment of 35 billion…"

I began to flap my arms behind the transfixed tourists.

"…17th Century Harvard accepted tuition as wheat, Indian corn, apples, honey, firewood, sheep and…ah, chickens."

As the visitors moved on, Hulk and I remained at the statue, observing there were not three lies, but five. The seal on the left side of the statue read "Veritas," but the original motto was Veritas Christo et Ecclesiae ("Truth for Christ and the Church"), and in all other images the seal was of a shield with three open books, but the statue had the middle book facing downward, a puritan reminder that not all knowledge is written.

From these unsteady bases, the moral imperative of "Veritas" unseated the prestidigitation of those early board members whose nimble wits first conjured the statue's lies. Passing this icon frequently, we were reminded to look beneath accepted reality, even that written in stone and bronze for centuries, to question even the underpinning of the university itself. We discerned with amusement our first and final lesson – that the true can be false – so that when we were at last set upon the world, standing in caps and gowns before John Harvard's statue at Commencement, it was as if we were favored politicians at a landslide, recorded forever before a background of lies.

○

THE HARVARD SQUARE DENIZENS, a polyglot congregation of medieval historians, chess masters, Hasty Pudding fashion models of the year, fry cooks, CIA analysts, panhandlers, nervous parents, faculty with clutches of admirers, pretenders to Bavarian thrones, pot dealers, ethnographers, medicinal chemists, and Lampoon staff burgling the Sacred Cod of Massachusetts, all buckled down for what might be considered by New Englanders as "cooler weather."

The unsuccessful French students occupying the boulangerie Au Bon Pain, panicky and wrapped in long black coats against a serious change in climate, assumed a forlorn but waspish attitude of no moral responsibility. They kept checking Harvard's "Let's Go!" office for cheap Air France tickets for weekends in Paris, fleeing presumed sapless puritan women in their urgency to, as one delicately proposed, *ramoner une poule.*

A great livid winter cloud, scratching the sky, heralded an ice storm. Imminent snow burials were announced, students became frantic for comforting dates in the long winter; unpaired undergrads roved in wan packs. Condensing breaths were rising; anxious student meteorologists began rushing about with skyward faces. Overnight, it befell us.

The Yard became the ruins of a snowbound Norman castle. Fingers of thick ice marched across shadowy oaks; fearsome spikes of frosted grass lascerated Cliffies' knee-length boots. Nor'easters began whipping us mercilessly as students ran down Mass Ave shivering uncontrollably, actually howling into the freezing pelagic spray. Leaning into the eye of a ceaseless blizzard, I negotiated snow drifts in High Sierra expedition gear to the steps of Widener; the monumental brace of granite lions, now with snowy manes and muzzles of icicles, looked upon disordered thickets of cross-country skis and snowshoes.

⬡

SURF WAS WITHIN, BANGING snow from her boots and gloves. Hulk brushed the stars from her hair with a stealthy, manly glance at her milky-white skin, his eyes then softening in their austerity. We hovered on a broad staircase with carved balustrades in this paragon of Harvard's 70 libraries, with Widener's 17 million volumes on 8 levels, 4 underground, the world's largest academic library, second only to the Library of Congress.

Two massive John Singer Sargent murals occupied facing walls, the diptych flanking the entryway to memorial rooms with a Gutenberg Bible. Hulk kept quoting graduation dates ("Sargent, '16"). We found leather chairs and green lamps beneath the rococo ceilings.

"Quite a setting," I opined, ripping off stiff ski gloves.

Hulk, the HKS class curator of Harvard lore since his senior days with the Crimson Key Society, seized the moment.

"The *Titanic* built this place."

His hypnotic, hushed delivery captivated me.

"Imagine, the White Star Line flagship Titanic, on her maiden voyage out of Southampton: crystal tinkling, chamber music, leading families, then the tear in the hull, the screaming, the black icy death."

Slender women from Radcliffe Quad and Lowell House stood with their elegant hands poised over medieval texts. Bootless, with thin black stockings and twilled wool scarves, they had the luminous quiescence of bewitched Madonnas. Pre-med refugees from the basement of the Cabot Science Center, eyeing the beatific feminine, argued with sophomore computer scientists on the maternal inheritance of mitochondria. Hulk persisted.

"There was 27-year-old Harry Elkins Widener, class of 1907—for whom our surroundings are named—with his father in the madness of death and bravery, helping his mother Eleanor, her maid, and John Jacob Astor's wife into Lifeboat 4. Harry's brother, Vincent, was a freshman. Too busy for the trip".

"Did they make it?"

"Well, Harry was a devoted collector of rare first editions, an antiquarian; his will conferred the collection to Harvard."

"But…"

"Harry remembered that he left a precious volume in their stateroom, and rushed back. His father waited. The stacks were exploding, the Titanic at a frightful angle, people singing hymns, praying, fighting, scenes of courage and cowardice."

A girl was sniffing a grand bouquet of white lilies; her long hair spilled in slow waves before an early 20th Century photograph in silver frame of a very proper young man.

"Harry and his father, George D., perished. Eleanor provided these memorial rooms for her son, and the Library itself, and insisted on fresh flowers daily, forever in perpetuity. The photograph is of Harry."

I thought to plumb Hulk's depths.

"What was the book?"

"A 1598 edition of Francis Bacon's *Essays*. There's probably one at Houghton Library, through a secret tunnel underneath Widener."

"And the women?"

"Eleanor and her maid survived, with Mrs. Astor. Eleanor demanded architect Horace Trumbauer, who designed the campus at Duke, do the drawings. Everything we see is the expression of a mother's love."

Surf was contemplating the distant John Singer Sargent murals, apparently lost in some dream of shellfire and poison gas, but listening to Hulk's tale of the flaming, frozen night.

"That affidavit you signed swearing you knew how to swim?"

I vaguely recalled some university requirement.

"Eleanor demanded every freshman have swimming lessons. After the Titanic, it spread throughout the Ivy League."

By then we were in the central suite with its massive chandeliers, where Harry's collection was housed, with its deep thirty-foot high embrasures and rotunda of ten circular windows. Hulk lectured, elated in a way, rolling with Harvardiana.

"At the 1915 dedication, Eleanor gave President Lowell the key. A graduating senior gave a class oration on 'The New Art.'"

"e.e. cummings!" Surf piped, in minor key, then in major key related a woman's right.

"Harvard refused to give Eleanor an honorary degree," she said, "simply because she was a *woman*."

Hulk, newly appointed feminist, did the apologia.

"Then again, the Yard dorms were only fitted with bathrooms, showers and electric lighting in 1914."

Surf again, trumping Hulk, a mistress of detail.

"One honorary was the dashing Alexander Hamilton Rice (Hulk, injecting, "'98, M.D. '04"), physician and explorer of South America. Mrs. Widener soon was Mrs. Rice."

She wheeled about, striding away, long red muffler flowing, kitten hips, wizard of politics, tough and tender.

"Come on, you two, people are dying."

⬡

STRICKEN, WE HURRIED to Surf. Always the poetess, she took us by the hands to the Sargent murals on the main staircase of Widener.

Hulk, somber. "President Lowell's commission to honor the 373 Harvard dead in World War I; 43 were undergraduates, and 11,400 served."

I looked up at the "Coming of Americans to Europe," a phalanx of doughboys with identical faces ("Everyman," Hulk noted). All were reaching for the hands of anthropomorphized Britain with Grecian helmet, Belgium with broken sword, France a young heroine and nursing mother. She was blond with sallow, dark, circled eyes, red chapeau, and a suckling babe in arms.

Surf: "Think of them, the chlorine gas attacks at Ypres."

The second mural, "Death and Victory," took me away. A dying soldier, lying beneath a faceless phantom grappling with a triumphant angel of victory, her face and arms heavenward, her lavish breasts, her back arching.

The unearthly light of the camellias, before the rain washed the last petals away, manifested for some seconds. After Crimson, archives of the unconscious sometimes emerged. Shells burst overhead, heads blown off, entrails eviscerated. Harvardians in the Royal Scot Fusiliers, Royal Canadian Highlanders, and even foreign students in the German army, all slaying and slain. Radcliffe women, volunteer ambulance drivers at the front, at night no headlights, shell-pitted roads, the rapes, the poison gas, the killings…

Hulk's voice over bodies in trenches: "First to show the American flag in France was Norman Prince, '08, '11. Founded Lafayette Escadrille, trained under the Wright brothers."

Surf, to me: "Are you not *feeling* well?"

I quietly collected myself. "Oh…yes. I just have an appreciation of…desperate moments."

⬡

THE YARD SUGGESTED a forgotten winter palace, its serenity belying the periodic colossal mental breakdowns in the undergrad Houses. We passed the archway at Sever Hall, with its conduit of distant whispers. We could hear breathing, murmurs, no…light moans of one, a straining virginal undergrad with the accent of the Dordogne, urging her companion before Reading Period to *depucéler* her.

Harvard Square had dug out. Old people teetered carefully about, snowball sabotage rampant. Folk singers emerged. A well-bundled three-year-old with masses of curls bounced with snowflake happiness in her pram, then cried with fervent tears "Mickey, Mickey!" as her mouse balloon floated upwards from her grip, loss and impermanence soon assuaged by copious hot chocolate.

A hive of faculty manses streamed beneath crisp winter skies, the street again a honeycomb of faces and mental gymnastics. I thought of Cambridge as a filter from which technocrats and meritocracies arose, a kind of dragnet of the seed.

Surf now, with a *café crème*, and her fetching little movements, settled on an icy iron bench among durable chess players, teasing Hulk with harmless sallies and elaborate rhetorical devices. Nearby was a downcast physics major of eighteen, engrossed in a text on quantum mechanics. Surf swore she sensed that his failed calculated charm at mixers, his subsequent renouncing of worldly pleasures, had terminated in *Ejaculato Praecox*. He was expressionless, assaying incalculable matters of naked Providence.

The thin sun shone upon us, the stunning cold making ghosts with our breath. The Charles was a lusterless sheet of lead, overhung with mists like low-lying clouds, the sun dying into amethyst. Frosts crystallized on chess pieces. As Surf was musing on the physics major, Hulk launched his wit.

To Surf: "Do I intuit a disenchanting sense of professional inadequacy?"

Always the one-upswoman, she lobbed it back.

"No, that was my pre-final expression of neuralgic vacancy."

Laughter at each peal of church bells, as they argued about which was more wicked, more wayward, the flesh or the mind. Hulk concluded it would depend, like Harvard students' prowess and the university itself, on "the monomania on which it is built."

Mass Ave was broken with flagrant street hustlers, one confiding with a grin that he made hundreds each day, more than many in the public sector with Harvard degrees.

"Excuse me, excuse me, sir, sir, ma'am, ma'am…"

We defected to the embrace of the Kennedy School, where we became face down on the texts, flat against the wall of information, our progressive insanities as yet unchecked.

⬡

FROM THE YEARS as a lay monk at Hoshin-ji, I had developed the habit of handling objects quietly, from dishwashing to sweeping to placement of silverware or pens or paper, rather than the clattering of unconscious movements. In restaurants I still noticed if plates were placed with care, or in haste. Of the hundreds of faculty and students rushing past the heavy glass entryways into HKS departments each day, I may have been the only one who didn't let the doors slam. Even within the frenetic activity, I turned the knob slowly, opening the door in half-time and seating it soundlessly. It was a monk's sleight of hand, for other methods of passing doorways seemed discordant.

No one noticed this private exercise, while I found it comforting; except for the cloistered hallways within the Divinity School, it was one of the reverent, ancient disciplines outside the expertise of Harvard. As I silently slipped past the entry adjacent to the office of the crime scholar Francis X., who normally tolerated the door crashing loudly throughout the day, he called me into his office.

"You know, you're the only person who doesn't slam the door, which I appreciate. How did you learn that?"

Frank was Boston born and bred, early sixties, wiry with an ascetic air. Taken aback at being detected, I could only mumble uncertainly.

"Before Harvard, I was for some years a lay monk in a Zen monastery, if that doesn't sound too odd."

"Not at all, I thought it might be the case," he said with a confiding smile, "I was trained in such practices as well, as a Jesuit priest."

Although excited by this senior instructor's awareness of such subtleties, but too shy then with faculty to accept his offer of lunch and the inevitable scrutiny such intimacy entailed, I finally submitted to a curious offer he made.

"Why don't we walk over to a place next door? Something I'd like to show you."

I assented. We strolled through the Kennedy School walkways, under arbors of bare dogwood trees facing the Charles, finally encountering a Gothic entry with massive wooden doors and a broad, elaborate iron frontispiece. We had arrived at a monastery.

"I come here most every day," he said, opening the interior door to the Nave, "and sometimes when things get too confusing or rough, or just to lift the spirit."

We sat in the stark hewn oak pews, beneath stained glass and by tall beeswax votaries, surrounded by a few elderly Cantabrigians and the profound mysteries of Christendom. Within moments, from the vestries beyond the heavy stone walls, appeared two rows of white-robed full-bearded monks. All walked slowly, their hands clasped under swaying robes, singing the processional of Verilla Regis of Venanitus Tortunatus.

"Impleta suni quoe conciniti,

David fidelil carmine,

Dicendo nationibus,

Regnavit a ligno Deus…"

The twenty men collected in two groups on both sides of choral pews perpendicular to us and facing each other. Motionless, we all were suspended in time, in perfect silence.

One voice in Latin song lifted upon the stillness like a single flower petal buoyed upon a soft breeze. The monks responded with a thousand-year-old liturgical chant in plainsong. Back and forth the voices rose, turning, majestic, humble, devoted, spiraling inward upon themselves and ceasing unto peace.

We were only steps away from the Kennedy School's intrigues: its defense intelligence reports of kill radii and Raptor missile lethality, the criminal justice analysis of cocaine overdoses and violent prison gangs, the manipulation of Third-world governments by covert operatives, in general the business of minimizing or maximizing deaths per policy alternative.

When the plainsong ended, we gave a little bow in the monastic tradition, then wandered back into the complexities of Harvard. In the weeks that followed, we again visited the brothers to hear their chants from the Dark Ages, when only the rare monk scribe was literate, and cunning and malice reigned. We received these graceful teachings, for we both had heard, long ago, what the doorknob said.

⬡

A STRANGE PALLOR OCCUPIED the days, finally clearing into everlasting winter; the windowsills were frosted, the snow weighing down black branches of oaks, and smoothing the graves in Cambridge churchyards. Promising an invigorating tour and a jog, Hammer and Hagendas intercepted me in the Harvard Coop as I contemplated an eight-seat rowing scull and oars mounted high on the wall. We withdrew to Mass Ave.

Hagendas, clutching an orange juice, her skin flushed, her breath of clouds. On this fine ringing morning, always a gallant creature, she smelled like apple blossoms.

Hammer had his customary morose hangdog expression of a Sunday, but a thrilled, gravelly voice. His powerful introspection was sharpened by a weekend of incessant review, stretched out on bare mattresses in cheap housing, of rigorous texts and nubile tutors.

They were like finely bred animals; Hagendas, with a lilac afterglow, gave me one of her conspiratorial looks. As we warmed up with a walk in the Yard, the sky had a glassy freshness; my first semester unawareness of locale soon was enlightened.

"Massachusetts Hall," Hammer pointed with his cup, "second oldest building in the country, after Christopher Wren's admin building at William and Mary."

"And if the doorknobs could speak?" Hagendas grinned. She had observed my modest habit, now apparently common knowledge.

"Washington's troops were stationed in the Yard during the Revolution," Hammer explained, "Continental Army soldiers melted down Mass Hall's doorknobs and metal rooftops for ammo."

"But there they are," I retorted gamely.

"The University was the first corporation in the Western Hemisphere, existing long before the United States. First institution to sue against the new government, demanding payment for the doorknobs, and won."

Moving quickly now, gaining heat, we soon passed Lowell House. Within were white naperies on long tables, candles, slender stems of glass. Snow laced the tall filigreed ironwork gates. Leafless topiaries in baroque planters. Old ballrooms with replicas of Queen Anne and Chippendale chairs. Tarnished Edwardian mirrors.

"Their motto is *occasionem cognosce*, recognize opportunity," Hagendas observed. "There is Thursday tea in the Master's residence, on May Day they do Champagne toasts on Weeks Footbridge."

Lowell House bells were ringing in a mournful joy, like the end of the War of the Roses.

"The seventeen bells are from St. Danilov's Monastery in Russia," Hammer noted, "Stalin was melting church bells for cannon, but a Harvard alum, philanthropist Charles Crane, slipped them out of the country. Our Klappermeisters ring them every Sunday afternoon."

"*Svyato* Danilov Monastery," Hagendas insisted, "They are going back soon, with our blessings. The Vera Foundry in Voronezh is making seventeen new bells for Lowell House." I noticed her Russian accent was flawless, like Crimson's, but said nothing.

◯

CROSSING OVER THE CHARLES, we loosened up by the aged grey stadium, with its thick mats of ivy roots in the winter deadness. Like plants, students had a sessile lifestyle, and combated their immobile scrutiny of data with serious athleticism. Hammer, doing deep knee bends, provided background.

"This is the world's first massive reinforced concrete construction. 1903. Like Greco-Roman coliseums." Lunges, stretches, our eyes on Hagendas's whipping ponytail. "National historic landmark, like the Rose and Yale Bowls."

Hagendas on tiptoes, stretching to the sky and our devotion, then with legs spread wide and strong, folding forward, grasping ankles, ponytail swinging, face inverted, we attentive.

"1906," she breathed, upside down, "the Classics Department did *Agamemnon*. Chariot racing, troops of horses, and Grecian temple…last theatrical was (head touching ground now)…Euripides in 1992."

Hammer, in a triangle pose. "This stadium created football's forward pass."

"Pass?" I was monosyllabic with effort, remembering only my semester goal.

"1906. President and alum Theodore Roosevelt, to reduce violence at football games, had to decide whether to widen fields by forty feet. Because Harvard stadium could not be widened, the forward pass was introduced…greatest innovation in football."

Our straining threesome now gasped together in a composition lane, Hagendas between us and leading, Hammer close behind her, and I last, fueled by the lonely hours of prior incarnations, running hard under the blinding white sky.

◯

READING PERIOD EMBRACED US the silent two weeks before finals. The winter's cold cut to the very bone of thought; we wound along against obstinate winds in painful dusks. The campus was virtually deserted; the archways loomed with thinking students who moved ponderously, with the gravity of churchwardens.

I resided in Radcliffe dorms this term; during frequent storms the small window by my desk ticked with flecks of tossing snowflakes. At Brain Break, the hiatus at 9 PM when everyone stopped tearing hair and smiting breasts, the wandering halls were a maze of students; they suddenly appeared and disappeared as in a house of mysteries. I came upon a nearby door, opened so very slightly upon a room rosy with candlelight and the urgent night-odor of flowers. A single curtain moved softly like a sail in the air. Within were the sounds of some resurrected Aphrodite astride an unseen lover, a glimpse of a satin duvet bunched at her waist, the plunging of her hips yielding shrill incoherent cries. A tartan shawl with a white broach lay loose over a Harvard chair. Absolute humanity replaced my logic with entangled emotions; I listened like some anxious voluptuary until one could bear it no longer, then retreated to blank pages.

⬡

THE LAST LECTURES and reviews had passed. We reeled with images of bioterror outbreaks, statistics of Swine Flu, decision trees on air cover at the Bay of Pigs, all of us obsessively meticulous over fine points as if we were senior microbes. Snow fell steadily past tall windows in the numb drowsiness of winter. Coughing and whispering, brooding and worrying, we looked absolutely pious.

Battles of resignations were won or lost those long nights. Even Surf, with her faintly apprehensive solicitude, began showing elements of despair. I fled one night to trek up and down Mass Ave. In a ghostly derived light, from street lamps on decaying snow banks, Hulk staggered up with his thick binders of notes. With a light fatalistic glance, he summed up our predicament.

"One financial analyst, on her way to the World Bank, just told me that she can mechanically *do* the stat problems, but is hopelessly confused. She said it's like mumbling some debased liturgy well, without realization."

Hulk had it. By only a hairsbreadth's deviation, we lacked ultimate comprehension of the data. At Harvard, we all had beginner's mind, floating like strange, solitary jewels, hovering late and early over the river of information while mankind slumbered. In these weeks, Hagendas temporarily foundered;

Hammer obviously suffered. Everyone had the nursery troubles of teething competence. With rueful attitudes, we closed our books, then wished we could die upon the snows, under a high moon.

We tried painting fine landscapes of correct solutions with brushstrokes of thoughts, but always slipped on our overbred finesse. As we walked to our rooms, we shivered in the chill air as sirens pierced the night all the way from Boston Harbor. Glory or disgrace, our futures hung on the Reading Period.

Sheltered from the powdery snowfalls, we found some relief in huddling under Sever arch with cups of hot cider, listening to undergraduates' secret kisses. Benign snatches of moonlight crossed frost-laced paths. "Lamonsters," bleary students emerging from all-nighters at Lamont Library, weaved bloodshot on caffeine overdoses underneath dying elms.

The university's hollow-eyed, gaping towers and spires, like a tinted cyclorama, considered this fourth century of classes implacably. For relief, Hagendas, Hammer and I began to run at night, crunching on the frozen track in the then undomed bowl as the brindled moon striped the endless, fatiguing lanes. Returning to HKS or Widener, for a moment aerated and alive, we too soon became again like Tokyo's *otaku*, the reclusive computer people, in the requisite *taedium vitae* of our isolation.

On Brain Break at Widener the night before finals, as students retreated into panic, the Harvard Band entered and, as a form of redemption, launched into "Yellow Submarine." Surf rose and sang brightly in her soprano, coaxing morose undergrads from their desperate labors. We whirled outside to drink in the freezing air on Widener's steps, our puritan consciences swept away by the shrieking of naked students sprinting in the Yard. It was the Primal Scream, the ritual nude laps of streakers before finals, as hundreds of delighted onlookers danced and howled. If we didn't command the information by then, all was lost anyway.

⬡

I COULDN'T SLEEP. I took the shuttle to Countway Library at Harvard Medical School; the bus had only a few slumped, speechless students staring at bleak snowfields. Under the deep night with rising moon, the Charles curling, inky water was swollen with blocks of black ice.

At Countway, beneath paintings of physicians in frockcoats conducting the first surgical procedures with ether, I thought of Brigham and Women's Hospital close by, with its soft blooms of pediatric cancers, the children on uncomfortable steel beds concealed down long, green anonymous corridors. I wondered if they had flown pink kites. Fatigue, with its ghostly anesthesia, had clipped the angels' wings.

Concentration was futile. It had been only months since I sat in a San Francisco alley, after the events with Crimson. Reflecting on the Six, spread about the earth with their potential medicine for the cancers of hatred, I felt they had an elementary moral beauty, one alien to the lesser manufacturers of addictive drugs, one worthy of study as a policy fellow. The night was spent reading 19th Century medical literature on visionary manifestations and altered states: the work of Alexandre Brierre de Boismont, the records of Charles Bonnet on phenomena among the blind.

I was due in Vienna after finals to interview researchers at the United Nations Drug Control Program on proliferation of heroin and cocaine, a topic more fundamental to Harvard's concerns with the public health aspects of lethal narcotics. My itineraries through varying countries often were impromptu; the next of the Six were unlikely to find me overseas.

Others studying all night at Countway were staring at graphs, grasping at elusive facts, far too late for understanding. Snow raced past in razor winds until a grayness, a faint light, touched the east. The dawn came beating up white, with a thin snowstorm and gusts of light. The shuttle to the Yard was noisy, careening, like the harsh metal of doom, grinding past the Charles. Slow flights of long-necked geese were bracketing the low winter sunrise.

Students, pale with apprehension, sat possessed before proctors; most, assailed by dreams, had sullen, immobile features. Having long surrendered to the power of each word, always clutching at the grains of thought, we had the nerves of lovers, and trembled slightly.

Hulk was fascinated by the ceiling, as if waiting for some signal from outer space. Surf danced down the rows, blowing frightened kisses. Hagendas was drawn, internalized, shadows under her eyes. Hammer had a chewed pen dropping from his mouth, like a cigarette before a firing squad. With dignity, he saluted.

It passed like a fitful dream among sleepwalkers; we wrote what we knew or supposed, filling voids with hopeful conjectures puerile to the accomplished. Marginal costs blended with statistical deviations, nuclear weaponry with cholera, presidential advisors with street people, humanity with extrajudicial killings.

The clock hands swept the last hour; my ignorance was revealed, replaced with a sober humility. I saw the trees bordering the Kennedy School lawns, all adorned with soft snow, blown white in the wind. It was a December morning of crystal, where the very sounds transmitted with clarity. The riverside was dark with evergreens, cold and snowy like white flowers, the frost hoary and blue in the pure, sweet air.

AT BOSTON'S LOGAN AIRPORT on Christmas Eve, I weaved noticeably. Ragged, with a dirty-blue pallor, I stumbled into an aisle seat on Lufthansa's evening departure to Frankfurt and Vienna. The Charles soon became scattered pieces of silver on the impassive earth. A tide of darkness overcame the clouds, while above appeared a swarm of stars, an immense stillness.

The flight was a purgatory between worlds. I still wondered when and where others of the Six might appear: Indigo, Vermilion, Magenta, Cobalt. Crimson had seemed uncanny, strangely familiar, while I – daily mingling with the Kennedy School's many covert personnel – had become a fabulist of superimposed identities, of doubles.

I wore a cheap blue jacket, and a Harvard tie to strike conversations with researchers during journeys. Like the leather wristbands or piercings among the little warrior tribes of the Square, the tie denoted another tribe: faster, more ruthless, with the outrageous freedoms of academic privilege. Penurious, on a small stipend and full scholarship, I occupied the last row in tourist. One had grown far from the camp fires of the Sierras, the magical nights, the dancing and celebration of the forests, the transcendent Pacific. And even farther from the tranquil simplicity of Hoshin-ji.

Over the cold Atlantic, to clawing fatigue and relentless beating of my heart, I remembered being a small boy, marching to Communion, toward *Veritas Christo et Ecclesiae*. Through the window, with the solemnity of perfect solitude and its infinite nameless colors, was the evening star. Music was playing, a poignant, rare recording from post-war Berlin of Marlene Dietrich; it alternated with the same song by the Simeone Chorale. Our crossing was to music from Austria's High Holy Days.

Hört ihr Leute, parampampampam

Kommt alle her geschwind, parampampampam

Zum neuen Königskind, parampampampam

Bringt ihm das Beste all, parampampampam

Lauf auch Du zum Stall, parampampampam

Kleiner Trommelmann

Come they told me, parampampampam

A new born King to see, parampampampam

Our finest gifts we bring, parampampampam

To lay before the King, parampampampam

So to honor Him, parampampampam

When we come

Lieber König, parampampampam

In kalter Winternacht, parampampampam

Hab' Euch nichts mitgebracht, parampampampam

Nicht Gold und Edelstein, parampampampam

Nur mein Lied allein, parampampampam

Hört mich doch an

Baby Jesus, parampampampam

I am a poor boy too, parampampampam

I have no gift to bring, parampampampam

A gift to give our King, parampampampam

Shall I play for you, parampampampam

On my drum?

II

Into the Mystic

I come now to the ineffable center of my tale;
it is here a writer's hopelessness begins.

- JLB, *The Aleph*

She said it was like a fog coming over her face
And light was everywhere and a soft voice saying
'You can stop crying now.'

- Kenneth Patchen, "Do the Dead Know What Time it Is?"
in *Collected Poems*

We were born before the wind
Ah, so much warmer than the sun
And we shall sail as One
Into the Mystic.

- (apol) Van Morrison, "Into the Mystic"

Chapter 4.

Edelweiss

The Company, with godlike modesty, shuns all publicity.
Its agents, of course, are secret.
Yet another declares that the Company affects only small things…
the crying of a bird, the half-dreams that come at morning.
And others, whispered…
The Company has never existed, and never will.

- JLB, *Lottery in Babylon*

His eyelids trembled as if they felt
the vast cyclic movement of the earth and her watchers,
trembled as if they felt
the strange light of some new world.

- Joyce, *A Portrait of the Artist as a Young Man*

Above my head various sopranos
floating in spasms of miraculous sunlight.
There are fires on the sea
and wandering tongues in the meadow
The telephones…whisper together.

- George Hitchcock, *Messages*

We have removed thy veil, and thy sight is piercing.

- Qur'an

SALZBURG'S BAROQUE CHURCHES and towers flowed past the Mercedes on this few days exploration after interviews in Vienna at the United Nations Drug Control Program. My driver and I slowed at the Mirabellplatz, passing a few ruddy, fair and beaming Austrians in Lederhosen and Tyrolean caps. Already out in the early morning, their knee-length stockings had sheaths with hunting knives.

Departing my room at the Goldener Hirsch, I walked over the Staatsbrücke on the river Salzach, the sunrise now lighting homes on the great hill of the Feste Hohensalzburg and far beyond, the snows on the looming Mönchberg, the Monks' mountain. Wandering before inexpensive cafés crowded with Salzburgers consuming schnitzel with coffee and Steinhäger at 30 schillings, I noticed near the bridge a striking young woman in bright blond braids. She was not unlike the lissome student from Maastricht on the Folsom bus with Crimson. Glancing my way, the girl darted down the Linzergasse and back over the bridge. I assessed improbabilities and dismissed the coincidental.

I rested at a café where locals were eating cakes and drinking *Doppel Expressos* or glasses of pink Himbeersaft. An elongated, bespectacled man with a professorial air appeared outside, then approached a string quartet that had settled near the café window. In his late fifties but emanating the wiry strength of a marathon runner, he made a silent request to a woman with a viola. Entering, he looked about absently, then as commonly done in Europe asked if he might share my table. I nodded.

He possessed a fine bearing. Wearing a perfectly cut but frayed herringbone jacket, he was meticulous in unfolding a freshly ironed copy of the morning newspaper *Salzburger Nachrichten*. He had the benign academic air of a preoccupied Oxford don, perchance visiting faculty down from the *Universität* or his lodgings at a thrifty pension. Sitting erect, he applied a certain focused thought to his reading. His watch was forgettable, some cheap plastic Timex. By contrast, his barely perceptible scent was that of an expensive French cologne with a base of ambergris and roses, perhaps from a recent and heated assignation.

In flawless Österreich dialect, he ordered only peppermint tea, no sugar. Folding the *Nachrichten*, he withdrew from his pocket a well-thumbed and annotated copy of Herodotus, *The Histories*. He began to read, occasionally murmuring Greek phrases, and once audibly mentioning Lycurgus, the lawgiver of Sparta, in his training of young warriors. I listened to Donizetti's *L'Elisir d'Amore* being played by the itinerant quartet.

After some time at our ease, and my second cup of tea, he reached into his other pocket and – in an almost surreptitious move – laid upon the scarred wooden table a well-used, studio-size crinkled metal tube of Windsor and Newton oil color, a finely ground pigment in linseed oil. At this inexplicable gesture, he kept reading. As the music and the moment coalesced in wild comprehension, I thrilled to realize the Donizetti was *The Elixir of Love* and the oil paint was Indigo. Fearing an overture to one of the Six might be a foolish mistake, I said nothing.

He placed his teacup upon the saucer and turned a page of the Herodotus. Fixating on the Windsor and Newton, I then looked hopefully at him, my senses alive with the conundrum of a casual encounter in Europe being a carefully wrought surveillance coup. As amicably as an old and dear friend on a summer's afternoon, he paid both our bills and made a quiet invitation.

"Shall we?"

○

I COULD ONLY STUMBLE beside him into the Salzburg light. Only hours before, Indigo and the others of the Six were nameless numbered files lost in the massive databases of the UN Precursor Control Program, an intelligence clearinghouse for heavily armed worldwide police agencies that enforce entombment or death for the actors of violent drug cartels. Yet this tranquil scholar seemed vulnerable and alone, leading me carefully through narrow 17th Century alleys crowded with Salzburgers, past the pushcarts of fruits and vegetables on the Sigmundplatz, then at leisure down the Getreidestrasse to stand in homage before the house of Mozart's birth.

He finally arrived at the Gstättentor, one of the old gates of the city, where we were confined to a single lane. To my delight, he proved to be an eager walker, so that we began following the river, ranging beyond the rural villas and farms to a considerable altitude above the Mönchberg. We rested against an outcrop of stones inscribed with lichens, a derelict wall from the reign of the learned Holy Roman Emperor Frederick II.

Before us, a very young farm girl in her dirndl skirt appeared. With a long, thin stick, she gently guided her flock of waddling Imperial geese and goslings slowly across our path, all in a single row.

"*Ach, Österreich*," Indigo whispered.

Hailing in Austrian the smiling girl, he fell in behind the geese. I followed as well, for the day had unraveled into illimitable possibilities, and at this lovely encounter the razorwire of the UN fortress was forgotten.

He motioned for me to sit at a rude, hand-hewn picnic table under a spreading black oak, then disappeared into a nearby farmhouse, returning with a pitcher of homemade Kir and bowls of blueberries. We sat for a while, I dumbfounded and unprotected by my notes or questions, in the unheralded, informal presence of one of the most hunted people in the hemispheres – a primary Interpol target and one of the Six.

In this quite pleasant setting we nibbled on our blueberries, teetering between opposing and highly trained teams of operatives: those elusive acolytes of his singular colleagues and the world's law enforcement agencies. All the while we exchanged thoughts on the pleasures of opera, and the staging in Salzburg of the Queen of the Night in Mozart's *Die Zauberflöte*. In this no-man's land of a beautiful afternoon, we were protected it seemed only by the light and grace of a little girl with her harmless armada of pet geese.

○

POSSIBLY I WAS VERY FATIGUED at this altitude, or disarmed by the bucolic scene, but the moment magnified intensely, as when tongues of silver waves broke into permutations under Crimson's hypnotic fireside voice. Partaking of the Kir, I gazed past Indigo at the verdant hills cascading down into Salzburg as they infused with radiant beams, with shifting rainbows over softly grazing sheep and pastoral huts and crystalline streams, as if one were in a vision of the Impressionists.

Gliding flights of doves passed dreamlike over the valley beneath, as a cone of silence descended. Yet I could hear simultaneously a brook flowing kilometers away, and a pinecone dropping through tiers of branches in the descending forests, and Indigo's many and distant voices, and the sound of a far cowbell ringing like a vicar's summons. The wind in a great susurrus moved over terraced lands and patches of thistles and Queens Anne's lace as if all were the comforting wish of a restful deity.

The brilliant azure sky was ablaze with heaven's light. A transparent canopy of portentous colors, it was not ominous, but inescapable and absolute, like a state of Grace. Breathing deeply, I at last could only submit to the glory.

Through a tunnel of my introspection, Indigo's murmur separated from the streams and birds and thunderous quiet of alpine valleys. He had a companionable and easy mirth, as though resting on a hike with friends, but his words were of a different order entirely and not for the common ear. I leaned into his delivery physically, to manage somehow the startling rate of information, but also to not panic. I comprehended his words only in midsentence.

"…and we are one organism, this small community of makers, as you know, so I am aware that Crimson discerned your mind can now, after the initial disclosures, increasingly receive transmission of data at the light speed of cognition. I am crossing dimensions within and subconsciously beyond the limits of human speech. You remember that, other than syntheses common to us all, I consider ritual preparation of Eucharists and secure transfers of lab sites, but can speak to the concerns of Crimson, Vermilion, Magenta and Cobalt."

I remained mute as he continued at the outskirts of my understanding. His voices ranged from an indefinable Eastern European accent to that of the Nebraskan plains to the flat vowels of the Georgian Piedmont to a spectrum of British class dialects: Cockney to Oxbridgian to a Dorset burr to vernaculars from sooty mining villages in the iron and coal fields of Derbyshire. It was either a *tour de force* of mimicry or from immersion in widely divergent linguistic habitats, like a traveler who was never in repose sufficiently for a single identity to form. Sensing my discomfort, he settled upon the precise pronunciation of British public schools: Old Harrovrian with a periodic twang of educated 19th Century Midlands English.

He mused so very quickly, in a soliloquy of images, casting visions and experiences in a kaleidoscopic manner. His spinning globe of discrete realities unwound with such rapidity it seemed as though I were a child only beginning to read, or think, or grasp words from a distant future civilization toward which one inexorably was being swept.

⬡

INDIGO'S DELIVERY at first seemed a dialectical frenzy, then a harmonious, subliminal transfer of data and dreams and effectively unknown esoterica involving the discovery of LSD's subjective effects on April 16, 1943 by Dr. Albert Hofmann at Sandoz Laboratories in Basel, through the second human exposure of Dr. Walter Stoll, then its secret proliferation among the pharmaceutical heads at Sandoz and thereafter spreading from person to person like a sea of radiance.

I glanced about. There were dream trees breathing, and the drifting of dark owls. The ground rotated with intersecting mandalas. Above us was translucent divine machinery; there were great wheels in the sky. I listened again to him.

He described their sacrament being given reverently, a magical gift, throughout the community of Jungian analysts from Berlin to Zürich, then its adoption by CIA in Operation MK-ULTRA and the human subjects exposed to the substance at 80 universities. He reflected on the first clandestine labs and the great public distributions of the Brotherhood of Eternal Love, of Augustus Owsley Stanley and Nick Sand and Tim Scully. He finally alluded to the rise of the Six, he among them, and how their identities and movements remained mythopoeic and – as yet – undisturbed.

I could only receive his words. Everything he said seemed finely crafted as diamond sutras, then structured in alexandrines, his perfect poetic forms almost Homeric in their profundity.

I felt like the barbarian Droctulft, when he first witnessed the temples, statues, arches and marble amphorae of Ravenna, and who deserted his ravaging and primitive hordes to defend the pristine city. I felt as Borges described the rude warrior, stunned before the magnificence of stonework and fountains and art, the very devices of advanced thought.

"As we would be struck today by a complex machine whose purpose we know not but in whose design we sense an immortal intelligence at work."

He ceased speaking. There remained only the water music of invisible brooks. The last silken threads of insight receded from my understanding; mere fragments and tendrils of mind could be recalled from the light storm of data that had passed through me. From such blessed forgetting one might hope to regain a certain normalcy, but throughout our encounter this day and night the phenomena reoccurred in the form of waves with some magic frequency: quiescent, then raging, then archaic silence, then the roar of creation, then an unutterable and calm abiding.

As I raised my eyes a host of cheerful finches blossomed overhead, while in the distant valleys sunlight glistened matchlessly. Shifting masses of air moved like the breath of slumbering transparent dragons. Perfumed Arabian oases gathered in the painted pastoral landscapes, appearing and disappearing in the fecund ground of being.

For an instant it suddenly all passed, becoming simply a still, sublime afternoon of gratitude and relief. Above us a bluebird was singing, attending its young.

⬡

THERE WAS A TUG at my shirtsleeves. The young shepardess, now angelic in a sky blue shift, curtsied brightly and placed a plate of cheese and fresh black bread on the oaken table. "*Dankeschön, mein Fräulein, bitte*," I managed, but Indigo offered her a present in return. A simple and delicate being, she stood transfixed as he lifted his voice and softly sang "Edelweiss" to her.

"…small and white,
clean and bright,
you look happy to meet me.
Blossom of snow,
may you bloom and grow,
bloom and grow forever…"

It was surprising to hear the Austrian lass ask in Dutch if he would sing it once more. Remarkably, he did. This transnational cypher, this wanted man, became for the little girl a fluent Holländer, a gentle kindergarten teacher from Utrecht.

"Teer en fijn,

breekbaar klein,

Schijn in duistere tijden

Bloesem van sneeuw

die de storm doorstaat,

Laat de wind maar loeien…"

As he sang she danced, twirling her pretty skirt in great circles, arms out and barefoot with her white golden ringlets loosening, eyes closed and face lifted to the sun. At the end, she hovered motionless before us, until there was only the sound of the alpine breeze. In an endearing, childlike gesture of delight, she smiled and clapped her hands and curtsied again, then skipped gaily to the thatch-roofed farmhouse through a garden of herbs with its rows of rosemary, sage and hyssop.

At this benign vision, Indigo suggested that our peak experience hardly could be surpassed, so that after sharing the bread and cheese we might wander downward along the many trails through copses of pine and birch to Salzburg to listen to Vesper bells. He withdrew from his jacket a small German edition of *The Secret Garden*, carefully inscribing it on the flyleaf, and leaving it as a present for our child sheppardess. As though he knew her, he dedicated it with the affectionate *Blüemi*, Swiss-German for "Little Flower."

◯

I STOOD, collecting our things as the sky and earth turned in blissful motion. Yoked again only lightly to our bodies, we descended under the firmament's still-billowing spectacle. Alpine cows with hooves of ivory lowed on far ridges, resonating like Tibetan prayer horns guiding pilgrims to the transcendent. Our very core was perfused with countless thoughts and rivers of light.

The food was modestly restorative, and the lower altitude settling, so that my charter to question Indigo again seemed urgent, yet now impertinent.

"How does it feel to make millions of doses?"

"Hundreds of millions," he returned. "For each of us the average batch is now over 800 grams, twice the lifetime output of Owsley, some 16 million doses every month or so."

"But how do you bear it?"

"After the changes, all that is left is humility," he said simply and finally, deflecting further inquiry.

We pressed on through the failing light toward the still, small town of Salzburg, our bodies loose and flowing, conversing on the way. The beckoning night became oddly roseate, our steps soft, as if the very grass were warm fleece. On a long trail through groves of beeches, he grew ever more genial, and our hearts were light. We glimpsed hares and foxes and ptarmigans, and saw to the far high valleys of the Vorarlberg in the Alps. A million leaves moved in the windless twilight.

Encountering a rocky fall of talus, we began picking our way carefully around the massive granite boulders. To Indigo, the obstruction appeared as some omen. Without explanation, he began alluding to my prior interlocutor at the mythic fireside. In this sensitive state, his unexpected disclosures were abrupt, jolting, like the buffeting of a cold, sharp wind.

"And you are aware of Crimson's most valiant security measure?"

"I know only of the Washington Rules."

At this, Indigo disclosed a highly sophisticated operation of the Six, the reality of which I at the time did not fully grasp.

"For the first deployments to large populations of a technologically advanced psychoactive such as LSD, ruthlessly creative techniques were required."

"Can you tell me of them?"

The next wave came upon us. Forests of holy trees began crystallizing from the jeweled earth, rising like great repositories of molecular information.

"Listen carefully," he said. "Crimson conceived of the psychedelic project Ivy Mike."

"Does the name have meaning?"

"It's a cryptonym, appropriated from physicists at Los Alamos."

"For what, exactly?

"The first hydrogen bomb detonation over Eniwetok Atoll. Our project had opposite karma."

"And the project's goal?"

"To sustain distribution against the inroads of law enforcement agencies."

"By what means?" I inquired, trying to find my way across a heavily inclined scree fall of sharp stones, but shaken at the import of his revelation. A lone hawk wheeled in silence above the dense forest below, looking for the slightest movement.

"By the specialized protocols of Ivy Mike – the first counterintelligence operation against the newly formed DEA."

I almost slipped at his aside, with its unanticipated brutality, but regained my footing. Indigo though seemed unperturbed. As we walked beyond the scree fall at a good pace, I dared not interfere with his continuity of thought, for this day one was only a neophyte confronting an old priesthood.

Stopping by a stream, we drank from it, sharing handfuls of sweet watercress. As prisms of light spilled among the still slowly turning foliage, we rested under a copse of birch trees. Indigo in a crystalline moment disclosed the dark side.

"Small clusters of devoted youth from the Sixties counterculture were recruited and instructed on infiltrating federal agencies," he continued, "with the sole directive to identify personnel and methods. Their hair was shorn, their dress and manners returned to the conventional. They became known to agencies as 'walk-ins,' those without pending criminal charges who supposedly appeared voluntarily to assist law enforcement as informants. But their true agendas were as double agents to study those who threatened us."

"How did Crimson arrive at this technique?"

"DEA employees regularly penetrated homes and celebrations camouflaged as turned-on youth, but failed to consider the sophistication – the dedication – of their adversaries. We adopted and greatly refined their own methods. We didn't oppose them on violent heroin and cocaine organizations, but were wholly devoted to protecting the psychedelic community. From Ivy Mike, which ran for decades, we characterized DEA protocols and agents throughout the world, even as they – unwitting of Ivy Mike – watched us."

"How did the Six monitor the agencies?"

Around us, the world now was a labyrinth of defiles and grottos, with mountain mists curling upwards as if from burning censers, and Indigo a venerable priest unrolling the secret canticles of new religions.

"We photographed them, monitored their task forces at clubs and venues, followed their vehicles. Sometimes our Ivy Mike infiltrators made controlled calls from the San Francisco DEA office to psychedelic targets DEA selected, then later those evenings joined us to share laughter and prayers with the same targets as we debriefed the Ivy Mike double agents."

"Does it continue?"

"Our people still attend every acid trial, photographing agents and informants for our databases using covert digital devices that elude courtroom security measures. Even our brave artists do surreptitious sketching. But now Ivy Mike is highly modified, for most low-level agents and prosecutors have been characterized."

"A modified form?"

"Cobalt studies only the leaderships – headquarters officials and analysts primarily."

"Of course no one could ever know the Ivies' identities?" I opined.

"Quite so, or even of the project. The Ivies, who were among the most honorable, could never divulge to agencies or most friends such magnificent duplicities. On the occasions they were arrested in later years, some made bail by claiming to be DEA informants for decades, then fled forever with the Diaspora to Goa, Nepal, Southeast Asia, Amsterdam. Sadly, some were reviled by portions of the psychedelic community not privileged to their feats."

In my heightened state I felt the inconceivable bravado of matadors with their deceptive capes of crimson, felt too close the hot breath of bulls enraged and red-eyed, their scarlet horn tips slashing.

"How could one distinguish an Ivy from an actual informant?"

"A simple task. Actual informants send psychedelic people to prison, a matter of public record. Ivies by contrast claim complex relationships with DEA for their defenses at hearings and trials, and DEA thereafter issues denials and confuses juries on the issue. Because of the Ivies' action, the community is much safer."

The trees had become steel bars imprisoning dying, forgotten men. From the darkening sky, great black poppies were dropping softly in silence, like private tears.

"A most delicate gambit," I said, quite nervous.

"But inspired. A hallmark of great courage. It made the agencies transparent, as was the vision."

"How do you remember who's who?"

"Double, even triple, psychedelic agents are the loneliest of numbers. Their accomplishments are sealed in the recollections of a handful of elders. Consider that CIA awards medals incognito and retrieves them with the other hand to be hidden in agency safes. Our safes are but a small circle of hearts and minds, among those with very long memories."

"And it runs today, a more advanced form of Ivy?"

At this, his speech became measured. Rocks were sliding with the sounds of cuffs and chains, the air smelled of buried decay. Boulders were the stone walls of dungeons, their crevices stuffed with dead flowers and shreds of old love notes. Evil trees had hanged men like warning gibbets. Even as he continued, I grew very afraid.

"Ivy Mike was the first of Crimson's devotional exercises in high security. As the intrusions were detected by agencies, we evolved to more sophisticated measures, at higher levels of government. To these Cobalt alone may speak."

Sharp spikes and tussocks of tall, harsh grasses now roughly enclosed us with their edges of barbed wire. Storms rushed up the valleys, mad as beasts. He saw I was shivering, and quickly let the matter drop.

Indigo stood, then in a shamanic ritual slowly raised his arms and open hands to the sky. Before the unceasing movement of the world, he in his deep voice offered a Navaho blessing to the four winds.

"Peace above us."

Tumultous clouds were now a flock of white manes.

"Peace below us."

The ground of cold swords was warm eiderdown, strewn with living opals.

"Peace behind us."

The chargers of heaven followed, our protectors always.

"Peace before us."

With his prayer the way again became sweet and soft, for a sea of bluebells flooded from forest to field, opening into the evening light like the simple trust of a young child's heart.

◯

HE REMAINED INTERNALIZED as we tramped steadily down toward the village of Salzburg. Violets came out by the streams, and bright anemones appeared in the verdure. Thatched-roof cottages burgeoned before us, their bulging windows and eaves alive with crocuses and wallflowers, their doors unlatching to the possible, to secret bedrooms and immaculate kisses.

Down from the heights but not yet reintegrated, we passed among the tiny, glowing Konditorei shops, each packed with lighted faces. All had decks and views over the obsidian river Salzach as it prowled into nothingness, its surface forming and reforming with shining black facets. The patterns reticulated like Escher's tessellations of devils and angels as the water's edges dissolved into arcane geometries.

Salzburg overwhelmed us, emanating pungent scents of cabbages and wursts, of ripe and hidden bagnios, of fresh potpourri of hyacinths and daffodils, of elderly ladies and schoolgirls trailing the indefinable fragrance of innocence. Sounds of subdued traffic evoked hooves and carriages and whips, while sporadic techno beats and sitar ragas and measures of *Die Meistersinger* evolved from the quietude. Sonorous cathedral bells marked with solemnity our reluctant pace to and from the infinite. Giddy at the synesthesia of sight and sound and touch and smell and the moving specters of ancient edifices, I stopped for some moments to recover, seizing a wooden railing until the field of being settled and became motionless.

Down the old Residenzplatz, we wandered with caution into the phantasmagoric dusk of eventide, agape at the density of objects and people and the translucency of twilight lanterns. Women's faces glowed like benevolent wraiths. Seeking unfrequented places where a few might be alone drinking cold, young Heuriger or consuming bowls of savory Gulaschsuppe, we passed along before empty and forlorn shops down the Schwarzstrasse. Indigo brought me with a kind of tenderness to a booth in the Café Tomaselli. Bereft of customers in these early hours, the café's warmth provided refuge from our dazzling trek.

I was blown away. My every cell was alight. I clung to my impossible ethnography for Harvard, now rendered utterly trivial. Although nothing could be said, I hoped to confirm Crimson's portrayal of the Six, and began to grasp at linear thinking.

⬡

"AFTER A SYNTHESIS, when each of you reenters society, what then?"

"Ahh, conventional mind regathers itself," he said, with an unexpected air of merriment.

I was uncertain of his meaning. Everything still turned. Perhaps he had divined my metaphysical anguish.

"Look about you," he said. "When we return from a clandestine site, every place at first seems a projection, a *mise-en-scène* of our calling, our expertise and duties."

The café was empty, the walls rippling with every thought, every feeling.

"A priest," he tried to explain, "sees good and evil and the intervention of grace. A prosecutor sees victims everywhere. A physician sees maladies."

"What do the Six see?"

"The exaltation of thought. Cortical evolution. Surveillance and secrets. Sensuality."

Through the café window two alluring women *modèles artistes* pressed against a Peugeot, coupling rather intimately in the fading light. By the kitchen a retarded workingman in a hand-me-down shooting jacket slowly swept the premises, his slack face lowered to his broom, vacant and bemused. A foreign counsular car moved with tentative stops down the cobbled street, the sturdy, crewcut passenger in his mid-fifties glancing at the women.

"But of our respective roles," he said. "I consider the rituals – the liturgies during fine synthesis. And the covert transfer of a metric ton of custom laboratory glassware, exotic reagents and analytical instruments."

The models by the Peugeot were long and thin, striking at two meters each, with matching blond and black coifs cut in a high French curl. Dressed in tight, black leotards, they were head to head, *couer à couer*, it seemed. As one intently stroked the other's elegant neck with her fingertips, I noticed the fabric of their scarves was the McGilreath tartan. Lifting his shaded eyes to them, Indigo described the other chemists, murmuring a tantalizing prospect.

"Vermilion's summoning of Eros is harnessed for countersurveillance."

"And his women," I hastened to ask, "what are they like?"

"Our wild white swans, our priestesses. They have fair breasts and throats; their very touch is a soundless explosion. At first you may think them unbridled with paganism, or slaves of lust. They will find you soon. With their inevitable eyes."

A sensuous musk filled the café. The lapping of warm waves ran up my blood. The walls floated with amber lotus flowers and orchids, the floor swam with luminous traces of sacred bronze and silver carp. The shadows of inviting doors unfolded like Japanese fans and paper parasols, spread open like cherry lips beneath lowered eyes, and the secret parting of silk kimonos.

Lost and uncomfortable with this impossible synchronicity of people and actions, I tried to stop the movement by focusing on the café's simple night janitor, with his muscular arms and silver ring, his rhythmic broom, his vacuous countenance.

"And of Magenta?"

"Magenta monitors a biotech revolution in memory and learning drugs, and erotogenics. Our sweeper could have the mind of an archangel. And the loins of a satyr."

The embassy car returned, crawling with stealth, looking for an address, or for someone.

"Cobalt penetrates high-level government offices," he continued.

Paranoia. I felt surrounded by some organization, as if everyone everywhere were a coconspirator. At the connectedness of all things, my defenses became porous. Memories of the police scrutiny at the UN interview in Vienna now agitated me, bleeding into this grand conspiracy of those administering enlightenment.

Unseen hands replaced the café's Schumann piece with *L'Elisir d'Amore*, the measures where the alchemist flees. In a cataclysmic apprehension, I thought the entire setting from café to street was staged, from the janitor to the ravishing models to the silver Mercedes. All were some coordinated underground intelligence team, a bestiary of surveillance. Sensing fear, Indigo took my hand with earnest words of comfort.

"Forgive us. It is not meant to frighten. Know that we would never harm you."

He lit a taper. The candlestick was an empty bottle of Lacrimae Christi. He folded his hands and bowed to the solitary, peaceful flame, then to me. With his simple kindness, the anxiety subsided, tranforming into echos of a benediction. There remained only an afterglow, a sublime rapproachment. We floated downstream in silence, but for the soft Donizetti. Yet it had all been too wild, too chaotic. In a moment of clarity, I dared ask the obvious.

"Did you…did you *dose* me?"

○

"NEVER," he responded, without guile. "The phenomena you experience sometimes occur in our proximity, as if you remember our ancient language. It happens where 'two or more are gathered together', it has been said. A contact high from shared subconscious archetypes; the opening of neurological regions among the experienced."

Certainly he had misjudged my background, overestimated my paltry abilities. Before the next wave, I pressed him, trying to find firm ground.

"The visual displays are not a drug effect?"

"The phenomena are not the teachings, but seem to reflect constellations of neurons that are learning. A quickening. As when our fetal neural cells began aggregating toward consciousness."

"When did it appear among the Six?"

"After our initial profound doses – the classical psychedelic experiences – we each independently observed a fortuitous and persistent cognitive enhancement."

"But the neuroscience of it?"

"Perhaps from the neuroplasticity of random dendritic spines sprouting or pruning in the hippocampus and the cortical association areas."

"By chance? Unrepeatable?"

"Not altogether. We attribute the enhancement in part to a global neurogenesis arising from microdoses, the daily subthreshold exposure in clandestine labs. The neurogenesis occured during – and was guided by – our rigorous physical and spiritual practices over years. Magenta's experimental compounds also may have contributed. We first noticed a superfunctionality, then a hypersensitivity to all things, but even more so – to each other."

"So the acute, single psychedelic rendered awareness of the possible, then by practices and low-level doses you retained special traits, and developed them?"

"You may prefer to think the paranormal phenomena are only drug-induced, an artifact of intoxication. But you now know that brain regions can be unlocked by sequences of phrases, by these very words, like notes in the *adagio* of the *Pathétique* may access the heart of those who have never heard music."

"Only words?"

"We also have observed almost extrasensory, emotional fields below conscious awareness. Consider the herd reflex at a predator's approach. Or old lovers' awareness of each other at a distance."

"You are proposing a new human sense."

"It would be naive to conclude there are no unknown extradimensional fields. Writing his equations by a whale oil lamp, Maxwell characterized electromagnetism. Newton's gravity was discarded by Leibnitz as occult."

"And you understand this? You assert it is reproducible?"

"Neither. We – the Six – fail to comprehend even this vanishing glimpse we have had, but only know it triggers a most uncommon form of learning."

"But always dependent on a substance?"

"No. Remember new human forms always are evolving. Some then become a heritable species. Universities have been breeding intelligence genotypes since the the Age of Enlightenment and the Reformation."

"Does it happen often?"

"So very rarely. And it differs with each of us. It seems to manifest only as a compassionate act, in safety – in the absence of the inexperienced. Those who cannot understand."

We no longer were talking about a drug. I was chasing him to get at the truth.

"Can it happen now?"

To this Indigo only smiled patiently, so that I thought he would never speak. He placed his hands together in supplication, then brought his forehead to mine.

"*Listen*," he said.

20.2 kilometers above the Serengeti, floating as though a geospatial satellite, low clouds and land mass rotating beneath. From the edge of Ngongoro Crater, the high desert wind. Over Congo at Mai-Ndombe Lac, ten thousand snowy egrets rising as one. Over Laos, a bamboo flute played by a naked child, and the clapping of an old man in loincloth. The children of all the earth jublilant, shrieking – Laplanders, Yakut, Arctic Inuits. Viennese crowds sobbing, trying to touch Beethoven's casket. Howling dark wreckage of a dying planet. The silence of this precious island earth, moving through unfeeling space, so very alone. A single soprano singing *Missa solemnis*.

"*Look*," he said.

15.1 kilometers above Vinson Massif, Antartica. Last calvings of the Larsen Ice Shelf. Sunrise over jungles of the Pantanal. Moongate light upon Gobi dunes. Sunrise over the last hunter-gatherers: the Malaysian Bajau, the Tanzanian Hadza, the Tsimane of Bolivian Amazon. Sunrise over Yemen, the slums of Madinat ash Sha'b. Moonrise over orphanages of Battambang. Through rough camel skins of Bedouin tents, the divine brillance of the Pleiades. Sunrise over Krygyz boy milking yak in the Afghan Pamir Mountains. Volcanic furnaces of Iceland. Aurorae dancing, reflected in eyes of a newborn Aleut girl. Stars gathering for the Hosts. The far dawns of once and future centuries.

"*Think*," he said.

All thought a sphere of 10^{-24} centimeters, expanding to the diameter of an atom, to the Schwartzchild radius, beyond the edge of universe. Every instant of comprehension, everlasting. The moment we all learned to tie our shoe strings. An unborn girl, in the womb of a destitute mother in a filthy favela on a Rio hillside, dreaming of the day her equations will revise the Standard Model. The ultimate intelligence of humble prayer. The fields of mind: all knowledge, all cognition, all senses, all understanding, everything all at once. And, dear God, the Light.

"*Feel*," he said.

Sorrow, desire, joy, anger, hatred. Eight-year-old lepers without faces in Bombay alleys. The endless tears of Christ. The irresistable hot river of a billion climaxes. The birth of angels. Two-year-old girl in El Paso being beaten to death for soiling her diaper.

I have not the capacity to record further here this unspoken exchange, at once so familiar and fantastic. Almost as an act of mercy, he lifted his head.

Our separation was like a mother's warm kiss on one's sleeping eyes, the last sound her unknown language, the last thought her perfect love, the last look her face filling the sky, and I helpless in her arms, naked, crying, reaching for her. The last feeling was sadness, such unspeakable sadness, at leaving our species behind.

Nearby in the crepuscular majesty of old Salzburg, the four stately bells of Vespers sounded, then from 14th Century towers were ringing the medieval monks' awakening bells, the *horologica excitoria*. At this simultaneous event, our thoughts externalized for the last time, like the fields of bluebells that softened the path before us. We remembered only unlimited grace.

"It is finished, for now," he said.

His words were gentle, barely heard, like a night whisper. They were the caress of innocent clouds, like a blessing from a benevolent sorcerer, a bearer of light. New recognitions arose with each of my heartbeats. I felt like a child hearing their first poem, as if it were the springtime of our mind.

⬡

A WAITRESS PASSED, trailing scents of roses. Moist syncopated hips, complicit smile, infinite eyes. Indigo said nothing, but soon a hearty vegetable broth appeared, with thick slices of pumpernickel, fresh butter, and cups of hot cider. Ravenous, we ate with wordless pleasure, placing to rest all vestiges of other worlds. Reveling in the solidity of our bodies, we seemed down from our resplendent journey.

With the food, normal consciousness returned with its ponderous, irreverent viscosity. I recalled that hard data was required, not the unrecordable preternatural intelligence of the day. My interviews were of six underground chemists, not an investigation of a cult proposing conscious control of evolution. As a writer fears madness, but seeks the edge of things, an ethnographer fears the seduction of belief systems, and seeks testable hypotheses through controlled, random, double-blind clinical studies. Stronger now, I ventured a question, hoping his answer would be suitable for Cambridge, at least among adepts at the Divinity School.

"And within a clandestine laboratory, what occurs that so few have witnessed?"

"We say our prayers during every synthesis, each chemist then a lay monk or priest in his own tradition: Christianity, Judaism, agnosticism, Hedonism, Vedanta, Buddhism."

"But of the extremes, the phenomena during synthesis?"

"The night has been long, friend. Perhaps a discussion tomorrow? In Vienna, before your flight? I'll find you."

My rational mind seized control. My itinerary had been known only to the UN. Standing too quickly I staggered, but Indigo collected me with a kind and forgiving solicitude. The night was over for us. From the café of synchronicity, we strolled toward the Goldener Hirsch, I unsteadily at first, then with more confidence over the Staatsbrücke. The river Salzach again was only a river, its powerful fluidity glasslike with indefinable colors and unseen faces and the last of evening lights scattered like forgotten dreams.

PARTING FROM INDIGO with a warm grasp, I watched as he blended into the night, walking in his threadbare herringbone jacket to his modest pension in a depressed neighborhood of Salzburg. I fought a desire to rejoin him, then followed instead from a distance. In perhaps a foolish effort to observe one so accomplished at surveillance, and at some risk to my study, I discovered the secret character of this most isolated of beings.

In the empty hours, Indigo wandered among the lost and dispossessed: those huddled in doorways, the destitute, the harlots, the aged drunks. To each he gave a few schillings, to the men a handshake and encouraging word, to the women a *Handkuss*, a bow to the hand as if they were elegant ladies of a bygone age. He continued until his pockets were empty.

Spying an impecunious young Turk student laboring over a tattered book at a falafel stand, he gave away the Herodotus. Admitted by a grudging, rumpled night porter to a coarse rooming house for indigent transients, he went up the stairs and never looked back. Down the street at the edge of vision was the embassy Mercedes, facing my way.

My room. Hot bath. Long naked yoga. Candlelight meditation. Worlds upon worlds falling in upon themselves, realization upon revelation. Eons of night becoming sunlit stillness, sky swirling doves. An hour's rest before morning croissant and fruit. The phone call like heaven's clock with the first human voice after my last rebirth. My driver's muted voice.

"Guten morgen, mein Herr."

○

VIENNA APPEARED like a mirage of the baroque, its centuries of Hapsburg rule overlain by the frosts of Cold War deceits. At the noon hour the Ringstrasse was crowded with prosperous, bourgeois Viennese; my driver suggested tarrying at the Hotel Sacher to enjoy its renowned *Torte*. Staff in morning coats and grey striped pants acquired my valise, then conducted me into a small, barely-lit cave lush with dark rose draperies and green silk chairs and gilt ormolu. Encased clocks with engraved pendula ticked under azure ceilings graced by cherubs. The very air, scented with dowagers' perfumes, suggested even more discrete pleasures.

Alone at the banquette, before a long-stemmed Champagne flute of pomegranate juice, sat an extraordinary young woman. Clearly just awakened, she wore an evanescent cheongsam and a high collar beaded with seed pearls, its bodice silken and slit to the waist and illustrated with streams and finches and lilacs. Her complexion was identical to the child sheppardess. Her eyes were atmospheric blue.

I never knew how the Six found me. Transformed into bespoke Armani, Indigo soon arrived. Upon his entry the girl arose, her cheongsam clinging tightly to her lean movements and small, pert breasts. She glided through the chamber with refined deportment, moving from the dark lair as a pantheress escaping the night. In the atrium, she glanced back over her bare shoulder at Indigo, then stepped onto the Ringstrasse in the direction of the Staatsoper. Ravishing and spectral, she dissipated in the sunlight. At the passing of this apparition, we sat together in the emptiness. Very quietly.

"Vermilion will see you next," Indigo casually remarked, never again mentioning our illuminated night. As an afterthought, he considered the girl.

"Spies and diplomats have entertained here since the Great War."

For the first time, I felt the delicacy of his life, its true complexity, but I felt even more his exceptional vulnerability. The formidable adversary of the UN drug program was nearby, implacably tracking the pulse of the Six, they in turn with sophisticated gentleness both vetting me and monitoring agencies. Watching the interplay of both opposing realms, I likely was identified in the soundless crossfire.

Indigo with his finely mannered confidences tried to put me at ease, ordering to my amusement a small lunch of blueberries and Kir and Austrian waters and cakes. I struggled to set aside the soft music playing, *Die Zauberflöte*, as merely a coincidence of Vienna's heritage, rather than a reminder of our afternoon with the little girl and her pet geese.

"Wolfgang Amadeus took long evening walks down these streets," he said, "clutching ink-blotted parchments of this libretto." Forever reading me, he requested instead the Jupiter Symphony, to which we listened over Kir.

"Mozart did the contrapuntal invention of the finale upside down and in canon," Indigo said, "all five themes played at once. Showing off in rapture, just because he could. Imagine his singular neocortex, his inspired joy. Imagine his loneliness."

⬡

THE ROOM WAS BARREN except for a somewhat removed but attentive waitress and an elderly man in a white jacket who was bussing tables. His frail, blue-veined forearm bore a faded tattoo of crude, hastily scrawled numbers. I detached my gaze only with some difficulty, which Indigo noted. I tried collecting my thoughts, for the night was still with me. There were no phenomena this day.

Perhaps this was my last opportunity with Indigo. Having survived thus far our spectacular encounter – and their microscope – I returned to my simple study of how it began, how it was distributed. I braved a request for everything.

"Can you describe the approach to a clandestine laboratory? The first days?"

"I can say, for now, that for security one detaches from the world, as a monk to a hermitage, painfully forsaking all society and family. The social fabric which comforts us is torn. With elaborate countersurveillance techniques we go alone through alpine forests or deserts to the remote site, to the place of many voices and visions. Returning from a synthesis, we are open like children but so very shy, and only gradually engage others. It is tentative at first, this finding of our way back to normalcy and relief, and long before the smiles return."

"And when one arrives at the secret site – the house?"

"As the horizon's distant lights fade with the fear, we come at night in reverence, beneath starlight, to remember the holy. We stand outside and scan for hours the Magellanic clouds, and watch for the meteor's trace, and listen to droplets of melting snow and the trickle of streams, or to the winds down the mountainsides, or to the far coyote's bark. There are no sounds of civilization. This tranquility is a membrane, sensitive to the slightest threat."

"And beyond the threshold?"

"Before entry and commencement, we place a hand upon the door, and offer a prayer for peace, for survival, and for the medicine to be benign. Within, we light a votive as a type of protector. I prefer a votive with an image of Mary, mother of Christ, standing in her purple robe of stars upon Satan's horns. Our Mother of Guadalupe I believe, common among Mexican Catholics. Some also burn smudge sticks of sage and open the windows, as the Navaho do, to let the dark things leave. Beyond varied, extreme spiritual practices there remains overall the rigors of pure science, the absolute molecular domain, the chemistry of which must be flawless."

"What occurs next?"

"By the votive's pale light we check the countersurveillance devices: concealed motion detectors and recorders and a web of failsafe chits and threads. Past a wooden door, actually a veneer over metal plate with steel door frames and magnetic locks, we behold sheer walls of glass apparati, custom twenty-two liter reaction kettles and massive teardrop-shaped separatory funnels and vacuum ovens and thickets of fine labware, all perfectly arranged to produce the polar opposite of a nuclear weapon."

"And after that?"

"In blackness, we scan the room with ultraviolet light, so that the LSD fluoresces brightly and can be visualized like ephemeral blue spirits. We then activate a range of the deep red overhead lamps –

the only illumination under which syntheses are conducted – to prevent damage to fragile molecules. Bathed in scarlet light, we don a protective moon suit with faceplate and breathing device. The scene is extraterrestrial, as if one were an interstellar astronaut on a planet of advanced technology, a world turning under the red giant Betelgeuse. In those moments, I play Gregorian chant, and pray."

"And then?"

"And then it hits."

"What does?"

"The first wave of a psychic tide, the herald of an ocean of mind, ever transmuting. Even with protective garments, the first exposure to the substance can be ten or a hundred or a thousand doses. This profound neuronal cascade, the initial detonation, consumes the earth. I can speak of it only allegorically."

"The first night, if you will."

"The *droit du seigneur*, to God that night we are wed. Cognition flashing across the galaxy, changing every subatomic particle. Shiva the destroyer rampant leaving all minutiae intact and without blemish. The fabric of dark matter reweaving, strong and weak nuclear forces interchanging. The unified field and divine mystery permeated by Grace."

He often was reminiscent of Crimson with his cosmic allusions, as if they were religious devotees returning from repeated ordinations. I tried a difficult question.

"How does exposure to the actual substance in the laboratory differ from the phenomena we shared in Salzburg?"

"One is a sacrament; the other is received knowledge."

"First one, then the other?"

"With the sacrament we lay gasping, naked before eternal love. With the other we hear for the first time the cry of a heron at dawn, the wind's laughter, the singing in children's hearts."

"But with either we must return to the mundane world?"

"Always. To not be lost. To rest for all of our life in the great gift."

"And what is that?"

"Our natural mind."

◯

"MEIN HERR, BITTE," the waitress said, approaching too quickly. With disturbing haste, she whispered, "A phone call for you at the desk."

With his hand on the rose damask linen, Indigo nodded to her, looked at me, then glanced at his watch for a long beat. His cheap plastic timepiece was gone, replaced by a museum quality Breguet Grande Complication or convincing replica. Sapphire crystal in platinum bezel. Its face had astronomical events, displaying equinoxes and eclipses, and tracked the motions of the Sun, Moon and Planets.

It was symbolic of this careful, meticulous organization. Wheels turned within wheels as in Revelations or Blake's light. The Breguet's flying tourbillion escapements and spiral cone fusees, balances and mainsprings all eluded gravity as it mimicked the planetary cosmology of Copernicus's *De Revolutionibus*.

Like Crimson, Indigo changed his look and manner with each setting, so that his elegant chronometer and bespoke black suit blended perfectly, like a rare chameleon indeed against the antiquarian clockworks and tapestries of this velvet hideaway. To elude capture, the practice of his peers was not to be different, not to be noticed.

I saw it was the full moon, and Jupiter was aligned with Mars. A portent from the night rekindled, and the Breguet became an omen. The sweep of the seconds seemed to traverse our lives, its discrete movements irrevocable and harshly indifferent, pointing to some instant when without warning time and the world of the Six would end. I sensed Indigo was nearing an invisible precipice into which he – or we together – might fall. Therein lay an infinitude, not of ecstasies, but of abysmal miseries.

He stood with reluctance. The augury vanished. I had so many questions, now unrequited. With an abrupt formalism, he concluded our interview.

"Do forgive me. With the greatest regret I must now depart, but wish you Godspeed. If it pleases you, then again one day."

With the ancient courtesy of an Afghan tribesman, he placed his hand over his heart, held it there, and bowed. Turning, he crossed the salon with the waitress while engaging in some intent, unheard exchange. He hesitated only before the aged busman with the tattoo of scrawled numbers. Unclasping the Breguet, he provided it to him with a kind word, as if it were a mere gratuity. His image merged into the Ringstrasse in the direction of the illustrated woman in her silks of finches and lilacs and waterfalls. I saw him no more. He never used the phone.

After some protracted moments, quite alone with my notes and fond memories of Indigo, I spoke to his absence in the blessed stillness of the room.

"Thank you. Thank you for…everything."

Chapter 5.

The Rhythm Section

We travel not for trafficking alone,
By hotter winds our fiery hearts are fanned.

- James Leroy Thacker, *Golden Journey to Samarkand*

A core of secretarial ladies kept records of the Emperor's cohabitation
with their pens dipped in imperial vermilion.

- Daniel Boorstin, The Missionary Clock, in *The Discoverers*

She was absolutely gone, in her own incantations. She was absolutely gone,
like a priestess utterly involved in her own terrible rites.
And he was part of the ritual only, God and victim in one.
God and victim.

- D.H. Lawrence, *Aaron's Rod*

"She seems possessed by three different beings."

"No, there is only one."

- (apol) Peter Blatty, *The Exorcist*

Let the flesh instruct the mind.

- A. Rice, *Interview with a Vampire*

I PASSED IN BERLIN beneath the chariots and spears, the muscular equine necks, flared nostrils and lavish manes of warhorses in the Quadriga of Victory atop the Brandenburger Tor. From behind my driver, as the evening approached, I could see the shadowed and debauched provocations of the verdant Tiergarten begin to manifest along its hidden walkways. The chauffeur with his fine leather gloves soon neared a small manor several kilometers off the Kurfüstendamm; I had been summoned by phone by an unknown woman while in the international transit lounge at Tempelhof. She had a cultivated delivery, evocative of scholarly Prague salons, but underlain with the low husk of one still unsated after weeks of unrestrained ardor.

The manor and its ten-hectare park were, as my driver disclosed with a subtle yearning, long of German nobility. It was rumored to host on the equinoxes pagan celebrations or *clubs échangistes* by European hedonists with lineages in the *Almanach de Gotha*. At the assigned moment, I stood with uncertainty in the estate's entryway until staff guided me within and then retreated. Designed by Lagerfeld, the marble foyer was a harlequin chessboard, its rococo armoires beneath cool blue bas-relief, all offsetting sitting rooms redolent with mysteries and candlelight and myrrh. Within its stately silence, I was startled to hear from behind the thick doors of a distant suite overhead a woman's muted but long and almost religious ululations, her frenzied spasms consummating some unimaginable pleasure. My consciousness quickened. From these aspects of possible felicities, I assumed Vermilion was near.

⬡

I WALKED HESITANTLY to French bay windows opening upon a broad stone veranda; in the far uncultivated gardens of a too early spring were gladioli and blood-red daffodils, and a German wedding. The bride and groom had faces flushed with joy, while a soprano sang from Bach's Wedding Cantata the aria "Wenn die Frühlingslüfte." Rose petals were strewn in front of the holy sacrament by six little girls twirling about in flowers and lace, arrayed as angels, each with feathered wings and a halo. One small girl was summoned by her mother, a classic Teuton with blond plaits curled upon her head in the Germanic manner. The matron was a fulsome Amazon in white bias cut satin that cleaved her hips, clinging from ankles to her high neckline, her figure proud as if she were the manor's *châtelaine*. She kissed the girl's upturned face, and pointed to the foyer.

Within minutes, this chosen of the seraphim, less than a meter in height and with a winsome innocence, entered the hallway with hesitation, proceeding in wide delicate arcs, and arriving tentatively before me. She presented a lilac-scented *billet-doux*, remarking with a little curtsey, "*Pour vous, Monsieur*," then rushed away in a blaze of small petticoats and flying pumps. Her tiny anklets were pink diamonds over blue argyle, like the last descendant of the clan of Campbell.

I sighed at being surrounded again, submitting to their exquisite surveillance. The unsigned note, in calligraphic vermilion ink from an antique fountain pen, instructed me to leave my valise and proceed to the Wilhelm Suite. I did so, guided by a distinguished, elderly major domo in white tie and tails, who ushered me in to an antechamber, then bowed and left. Beneath a shaded lamp and in a heavy gilt frame was a fine reproduction of two women reclining *au naturel*: Gustav Courbet's *Le Sommeil*. On the opposing wall was a *trompe l'œil* replica of Veronese's beatific St. Catherine, dreaming by a window. I had entered some realm of the sacred and profane.

◯

THE SUITE beyond was expansive, with clusters of Louis Seize chairs and commodes, and one wall of French windows open to the gardens beneath. There was a large tapestry of enchanted and horned bull antelopes, reminiscent of the woven *La Dame à la Licorne* at the Musée de Cluny.

An elegant figure of a man entered, beckoning me to sit. He spoke English with a Schweizerdeutsch overtone, but claimed to be American through his teens. He had tight curls going to grey, and lithe leanness to his form. Although he displayed perfect manners, one sensed an undercurrent of absolute seriousness tempered only by a pronounced attention to the sensual.

He offered pomegranate juice in an angular Steuben Martini glass, then sat and exchanged trifling cordialities as the wedding culminated to Lohengrin. Below us, after all of the girls like winged fairies ran joyously to the bride's embraces, the Berliner's bourgeois sensibilities soon dispersed the party happily to their beds. The velvet fingertips of late dusk began caressing the darkening topiary, so that we were left alone in emptiness and solitude.

Vermilion was dressed entirely in black, from his Italian slippers to his custom shirt from Turnbull & Asser. His voice was low and relaxed, his conversation indirect. He was abysmally sophisticated, almost teasing but respectful and gracious. On his nearby escritoire I saw editions of Pliny's *Naturalis Historia* Volume VI, de Quincey's *Writings*, and excerpts from Seneca. Yet he seemed not effete but quickly capable, in the service of enlightenment or his sybarites, of the staggeringly primitive.

"I understand your hike into Salzburg was challenging," he said, "and that you enjoy Mozart."

Without waiting for a reply, he offered a recording of "The Abduction from the Seraglio." The erotic scent of early orange blossoms wafted through the open windows. In the lessening light it became as if we awaited our reward of houris in paradise, the flowers' ripe promises like Islamic perfumes.

Indigo had cautioned me of the contact high from the Six, with each chemist's teachings that of his first knowledge after walking on the surface of the sun. Crimson was obsessed with security, Indigo with ritual preparation of eucharists, but Vermilion with his electrical presence, his knowing and unhurried silences, presented a moral atmosphere of some inevitable abandonment into which I was being procured. There was a sensation of the long dormant kundalini at the base of my spine uncoiling with fire and life, from my tongue to my genitals. At its writhing like Eden's serpent, I knew this interview would be like no other. I attempted to recover, but my voice had become hollow, giving me away.

"You do countersurveillance of downstream distribution?" I persisted, recalling Crimson's and Indigo's description of him, but transparently avoiding mention of his voluptuous methods.

"Our operatives, only those first illumined, are trained from late adolescence in the arts. We can access the secrets of most men and women, from the aristocracies to rough underground trade, from stoned music tours to insular government offices, from esoteric military laboratories to refined diplomatic circles. We often employ elaborate variants of KGB honeytraps, although more professional from being sacrosanct."

"How did you choose this specialty?"

"Upon my first survival from weeks of synthesizing 10 million doses, all alone and far from human closeness, I was nursed in the arms of several sisters of the Sapphic arts, a coven of models, who searched and found me wandering lost one night in Amsterdam near the Oudezijds Voorburgwal. Many years ago. We now use protective measures."

I could not help but ask, "Did you…do you have sex with them?"

"For long periods, nothing. Then constantly every day and night as a lifestyle, at the slightest whim of any party, I in their service, they in mine if they wish, all free and without shame. Master and servant interchangeably, body worshippers, devotional yogis and yoginis. The special dynamics of Queen and King *ménages à trois, à quatre*. The sisters are of course far more active than men dream, men frequently being so trivial. We live for months consuming little but each other, traveling about the hemispheres, occupying hovels and castles for a few nights, seeking the extremes of human experience, our only comfort one another."

This stunning admission was offered unaffectedly, in the hushed tones of a devoted choirboy, his face clear before the Mother of God. I wanted every detail.

"You were disoriented until such friends found you?"

"Yes. Planetary quantities consume the soul, the intellect. They are not the single doses used for introspection and aesthetic enhancement. Only a handful of people have been in the presence of such amounts. Indigo lived through the greatest human exposure in history."

"I wasn't aware."

"Ask him of that lucid night, when the ellipse of his orbit next intersects your path," Vermilion suggested, bemused at his humorous aside.

"So it's not lethal at any dose?"

"None of which we are aware. We know of police and addicts insufflating lines of LSD, thinking it was cocaine they had stolen. A fifty milligram line could be a thousand doses, Indigo was exposed to millions of doses within seconds."

"Perhaps under the red light of an operating lab?" I suggested, recalling Indigo's descriptions. "Like working on a planet near Betelgeuse?"

"I rather think of it as the scarlet light of Antares, but with two white consorts," Vermilion replied, granting a rare smile.

◯

THE SOUND OF A WOMAN in primal ecstasies split the dusk, her lengthy and repeated contractions just behind the suite's walls. It was far too feral, even guttural, to be the licit nuptials of some shy young couple on their marriage night. As it continued I gripped the arms of my chair and looked wildly about, starting to rise until Vermilion with his imperturbable self-control held me steadily. An almost Arabic wail slowly transformed into sobbing invocations of "*O Dio mio*," then into low, vulnerable moans, finally extinguished by the whispering comforts of others. Vermilion's eyes were gleaming yet tranquil. A period of silence. The running of a tap. A girl's voice singing a sweet lullaby in Ukrainian. Laughter and adorations followed, until at last I heard a brief benediction in Latin, chanted seriously. Vermilion continued to watch my face. I had no resources for these events, and was speechless.

An impeccable matron of Mediterranean descent appeared from the bedroom with a sultry air, tugging the hem of her tailored suit below her knees. Her *derrière* was round and firm as an apple. I glimpsed through the door sumptuous matrimonial sheets. Stealing a glance at me, she blushed to her crown, closed the door, pulled down the net of her black cloche hat, and with a slight awkwardness adjusted the straps of her Gucci pumps. With her flawless oval face and jet black hair, she could have been the wife of the Italian counsel in Berlin, defying prudence for her obvious preferences. She wore Bulgari rings and had a black snakeskin clutch in one hand. A wedding band scintillated.

"*Grazie, Professore,*" she managed, hurriedly leaving the suite without another look.

"*Signora,*" Vermilion replied, standing as was his chivalric nature.

He seemed to host an international *beau monde* in his intrigues with sensuality and surveillance. I was beguiled by the splendid openness and seductive air of his ways; his framing of natural drives with devotional practices, but at a loss to explain such flagrant indiscretions to Harvard.

The bedroom door opened and closed silently, as if by the passing of a monastic nun detaching herself from meditation and prayer. An electrifying *haute couture* model emerged, somewhat disheveled. She was bare but for scraps of diaphanous attire stretched across her narrow hips; her abdomen was hard and sculptured, her high, small breasts carelessly displayed nipples of *couleur de rose*. Bewitching, impossibly tall and with marvelous skin, she with a queenly air strode across the suite. With close-cropped pale blond hair as though from eternal days at the Arctic Circle, she had blue, intelligent eyes that seemed to reflect unspeakable tragedies and glories, and insensate lust.

Vermilion and I stood in a form of veneration, while I was introduced. I was flustered by her effective nakedness and direct, inviting gaze. Rather than an embarrassed volubility, I grew uneasy. He turned to me.

"This is Polyhymnia, our muse of sacred song," Vermilion remarked, "we may think of her as V-1."

She held my hand in hers, a strong, vibrant grip beyond the perfunctory. Her fingers were hot, and scented with musk, although her body's fragrance was that of an ethereal Eau de Givenchy. I bowed reflexively, trying to contain myself, my face uncontrollable and uncertain of its expression. With reserved courtesy, I resorted to banal etiquette.

"I am so pleased to meet you."

Her attitude was not salacious or frivolous, but that of a distinguished woman neurologist examining a patient, so that I could not flee from her unnerving presence either by sophisms or idle banter.

"*Merci infiniment*," she replied, in the tone of one's most earnest lover, dropping the slightest curtsey I dared not admire, "*et toi, aussi.*"

I was transported, and thought of Schiller, "*Her movements are so mysterious and her figure so elegant; who can she be?*"

The intimacies had begun. Excusing herself with no attempt at modesty, she assumed the bench of a harpsichord before the flowing draperies of opened windows, her head turned into the air, feeling for the movement of the night. She carefully sorted a vase of buttercups, peonies and dahlias as a Zen priestess in the flower-arranging practice of hibana. At the aesthetic perfection, she approached the sheet music, and began to pick her way through a Bach chaconne, then a saraband, settling more confidently upon transposing a Chopin nocturne from memory.

A scarcely decent demi-goddess, her erect back revealed the delicately inscribed muscles of a gymnast. Her hips had low dimples in alabaster skin, her waist narrow and curved like a precious violoncello. She was lean with some unsated hunger. Had she lived a century ago, she could have been an English ballerina in Monte Carlo, before which transfixed rajahs hopelessly tossed Buddha's eyes. During the nocturne, Vermilion disclosed some of her background.

"Her physical attractions may be deceptive. She qualified in medicine in St. Petersburg, neuroscience doctorate at Leipzig, research in Gdansk. For periodic amusement she danced at the Crazy Horse, refined her desires, did fashion from Copenhagen to Helsinki. Her cluster of bisexual models prefers the rare psychedelic."

"And for the Six?"

"She studies sex and the energy around it. Accomplished at the recruitment of female operatives in governments, as Cobalt may request. On occasion, she does exorcisms of the infected."

"I'm sorry, did you say…*exorcisms*?"

"Removal of the vampire's teeth. Women cocaine addicts, preferably. She remembers the enslavement and degradation of many innocent souls."

Although Crimson had alluded to the devastating epidemics of cocaine and methamphetamine, I was confused at first by Vermilion's reference to absolute evil, and so asked of a different threat. As we contemplated the perilously attractive sylph V-1, my efforts to maintain a neutral artist's *oeuvre* had become futile. I felt the sheer insolence of desire, and envy, but also the tragic fragility of his beautiful arrangement. The ticking of Indigo's chronometer had awakened a continuing paranoia, for myself in their proximity, but most of all for them. They were hurtling toward martyrdom.

"Are you not afraid," I proposed, "that it all might end?"

"We follow Crimson's Washington Rules, and meditate and pray. We rely on essential goodness. And I have six eyes."

His statement was perplexing, until from the same bedroom as V-1 and her dear Italian *mignonne* came forth yet another vision. The almost identical twin of V-1 manifested, a glorious nymph of Athena, varying only by slightly darker hair in a short Eton crop and a tigerish look. She wore Christian Louboutin six-inch heels in red, and a wide choker of pearls, but otherwise floated in the merest wisp of *crêpe de chine* and essentially was unadorned.

⬡

WITH IMMACULATE POLITENESS she nodded, passing by me so closely her fragrance of honeysuckle blended with a magnetic warmth. She strutted boldly to V-1, who hesitated in the Chopin to raise her lips and receive a long adoring kiss. Pressing their heads together, they turned their open faces to us, and then lifted their veiled eyes, revealing themselves to be lost in the secret apostasies of their hearts and minds and loins. At this intimate disclosure, they sat and slowly resumed the nocturne, playing together.

"*Madame* is our muse of memory," Vermilion finally said. "She is Mnemosyne or, if you will, V-2."

"Remarkable similarities," I oafishly observed, already trapped in their gifted allure, privately imagining the heated perfections of their late evenings' *soixante-neufs*.

"V-2 has an eidetic memory," Vermilion continued, quite aware of their effect on me, "she is a favorite of Magenta, who insists the cortical revolution will be driven by substances enhancing learning and memory, and libido. She helps penetrate laboratory groups inaccessible to the public, and monitors the emergence of new structures."

"Training?" I managed tersely, focused on the swan-like backs of the Graces.

"Dual citizenship at birth, Canadian through Choate Rosemary, then Ukrainian, educated in Kiev and Warsaw as an intel analyst, trained in a subset of espionage by inactive elders of the GRU, the *Glavnoye Razvedyvatelnoye Upravleniye*. She also is of great value to Cobalt. She plays speed chess, Fisher random chess, 3-D chess, Kriegspiel. Like V-1, she is an *agente provocateuse*." His Russian indicated complete familiarity with the idiom.

"What sort of espionage?"

"A rare form. Spying at the edge of science and mathematics. She entertained graduate students close to iconoclast Grigori Perelman subsequent to his resolution of the Poincaré conjecture, the same with colleagues of Andrew Wiles at Princeton after the proof of Fermat's Last Theorem. She enjoys Asian women students, those near Shinki Mochizuki at Kyoto, to anticipate the impact of his ABC conjecture. She entertains the odd Silicon Valley billionaire, preferably their wives. We suggested to her even more important cortical concerns."

"An extraordinary array of beauty and mind. They are almost too perfect."

We watched as V-1 played the G-cleft upper scale melody with her right hand, as V-2 played the C-cleft lower scale accompaniment with her left, their free hands moving across each other's thighs and pulling them closer. They were as a single being. Abandoning my reserve, I could only imagine one caught within their private symphony of desire.

"We are bound by their intellect," Vermilion observed astutely, "their bravura, and their devotion. Beauty, we have found, is so common."

I was at the center of some sensual cyclone, a vortex of carnality, exhilarated by those immodestly adorned, and being invited, it seemed, to obscure pleasures and secret nudities. The Chopin piece ended. V-1 and V-2 walked holding hands to Vermilion, each kissing him with unalloyed desire. The shadowy outlines of their silver bodies showed, a prelude to more sensuous visions. They sat beside him, V-2 in the midst, and all three turned to look directly at me. They said nothing for long, uncomfortable moments. Transfixed within their torch lights of attention, I could not move or entertain some nervous utterance, glancing guiltily at the women's fine breasts.

V-1, without breaking her gaze, her eyes now imperial purple, reached with tantalizing slowness and parted slightly one of V-2's legs, their ivory leanness promising even headier delights. Vermilion with the lightest touch seemed to open delicately V-2's other leg. V-2, her eyes ultramarine, tensed as V-1 began to stroke the inside of her thigh. Finally submitting, her eyes clouding as she looked at me, she responded with slowly increasing urgency. The contact high from the threesome was of celestial import. A glorious nimbus of light radiated outward from the edge of their faces, and embraced them. I heard both women speak distinctly, although their lips did not move.

"Would you like more juice?"

◯

ABOVE THEM THE CEILING of cerulean blue broke into displays of dryads and naiads, tree and fountain nymphs, and sons of Poseidon with Triton shells. V-1 and V-2, sitting with their legs wide and overlapping, pleasured each other before me, their eyes now aquamarine, now with diamond radiance. They became expert witches perusing abstruse treatises on potions, their arms multifold like Hindu deities. Spectra of erotica displayed, reflected in infinite mirrors, as V-1 and V-2 became the newly born, schoolgirls, mothers, toothless wrinkled crones, then offal and stench and dust. Their beauty became the face of God, then starlight so holy I was prostrate. Their perfumes and voices were of the harlot goddesses at the crest of fabled Mount Meru, made of blue sapphires and rubies, then transformed into the prayers of revered nuns in demure robes kneeling before Christ incarnate. Their frantically copulating hips were orgiastic with the cries of birth and death, their climaxes like the crash of majestic breakers on pristine shores, the silent expansion of supernovae, the picosecond of universal creation and the casting of worlds.

As their hands moved between their legs in driving concupiscence, their faces became vulnerable and unblemished in adoration of the Godhead. Fields of lush breasts and hardened milky teats roiled to the edge of reality, and thick forests of painted fingernails protruded from the wet-lipped earth. I felt as though the sky were my lover and I, rampant with ardor and immortality, rent the moist fields with bolts of lightning as the winds scattered life and the cries of those to be born echoed through eons undreamed.

Before me, the women's beauteous minds and bodies seemed the apex of evolution, their DNA entwined irrevocably through stone age fires and billions of childbirths, until I felt at last the yearning of all lost loves, and saw its manifestation as a pure young girl in a long dress with broad hat and ribbons, wandering far from her thatched-roof cottage, all alone among the hedgerows on a grey and desolate moor, fair and sorrowful, remembering her missing lover with all her secret heart.

⬡

I DON'T KNOW how long I was gone. In the end, there were suddenly no naiads on the ceiling, no dryads, no Triton's horns, just the sound of the late evening breeze across the gardens and the connubial scent of flowers in efflorescence. Sipping tea primly from translucent china cups, V-1 and V-2 comforted me as if I were an unruly schoolboy lost from his studies. They acted as though the Second Coming had not occurred before us, while I perspired lightly and could not find a voice. They wore antique buttoned leather shoes and long blue calico dresses with embroidered cotton to their necklines, without makeup, dressed down and plain like Mennonite schoolteachers. Yet they had the same eyes, the color of sapphires. They both carried the Mennonite Bible. Still not moving their lips, they posed a difficult question.

"How often can you come?"

Before I could respond inappropriately to such virtuous discourse, Vermilion interceded at last, inviting me to a window to take the air and settling me gently. The women in their long skirts began to walk slowly to the bedroom, holding my eyes. Worried at this juncture, I addressed Vermilion in a voice now muted and hoarse.

"Where…are they going?"

"To save a soul," they replied.

To my distress they left the bedroom door slightly ajar. Vermilion held me by the far window, lest I in my disinhibitions stumble to join them. He ruminated on arcane aspects of Eros in his scholarly asides.

"There were of course the Histrioni, or Abysmali, who refused Christian dogma, and believed that one has a double in heaven who did good deeds and was sanctified if one on earth engaged in insatiable wantonness."

"Must one deny Christianity in such service?" I mumbled in bewilderment, still unsteady at the revelatory displays.

"Never. The early Christian Adamites, to initiate their sacred orgies, prayed together, and before extinguishing the candle recited the Good Lord's instruction 'Go forth and multiply.'"

The yellow acacia blossoms below were bursting in full flower, the haze of pollen like fine clouds. I stood and wavered, lacking any indication of my role in the night, thinking only of the tempting bedroom. Vermilion distracted me.

"Rhodopsis the courtesan, celebrated throughout Greece, was a fellow slave of Æsop the fable writer. She was rumored to have built a pyramid from her encounters. She cast irons to roast whole oxen for the offerings at Delphi. She was redeemed for a vast sum by Charaxus, brother of Sappho, the poetess of Lesbos, and who traded in Lesbian wine."

At this cryptic aside, my imagination smoldered, and I detached myself toward the bedchamber, hesitating only to seize the Mennonite Bible left upon the desk. It was not an illusion. Vermilion walked closely nearby, still the historian.

"There were the Devadasi, or ritual female prostitutes in Hindu temples, in honor of the Babylonian goddess Mylitta."

I long had ceased to ask academic questions, becoming more mute and dark, but Vermilion intercepted and managed me easily. He had seen these reactions in others. The black leather Bible was bookmarked with a blue ribbon. I opened the gilt-edged leaves and found a note, upon which was scribbled a list.

"1. alcohol, 2. morphine, 3. cocaine, 4. methamphetamine, 5, 6, 7."

Vermilion watched as I studied the note in the guise of a drug policy analyst. Returning the paper, I saw beneath the blue ribbon a portion of Revelation.

"And there came upon me one of the seven angels which had the seven vials full of the seven last plagues."

I closed the book, finally comprehending that Vermilion and his companion stars did not trifle in pleasures, but practiced an esoteric art of medicine, arguably the most fundamental healing. Their exquisite, erotic devotions were not indulgences, but religious conduct. I collected myself from unbridled dreams, humbled and respectful.

⬡

V-1 AND V-2 REAPPEARED, this time in ankle-length black robes with caftans. We silently partook of sliced fruits and yoghurts and nuts, and became grounded in our bodies, subdued from the events of the early evening. I could only await their direction. With little discussion we removed to two vehicles, identical black Mercedes in the manor courtyard. The women led in one car. As a habit from a previous life, I could not help but notice their license plates. Oddly, they were CH, Confederatio Helvetia, Swiss.

"Our target tonight is a young woman cocaine addict," he remarked, "a clerk at the former Stasi headquarters, now part of the *Bundeskriminalamt*, the German federal police."

We tailed V-1 and V-2 as they filtered toward the bombed-out bunkers and warehouses of East Berlin near the former Checkpoint Charlie, where those who ran for freedom were executed like wild beasts. We rode in the late Berlin blackness down forbidding streets derelict with the horrors of the Reich, arriving at an intimidating, destroyed pile, an underground venue with no name.

It was packed with garishly tattooed skinhead thugs with broad, sinewy arms and vests of rawhide. Platinum-coifed and rail-thin but bosomy dominatrixes, ghostly pale in severe leather coats with pointed collars like vampires, moved through the tawdry scrum. Groups of surly Moroccan dealers with evil looks trailed their victims, while excited German, Dutch and English girls slummed dangerously to salve their addictions.

The pounding metal rock and growling low, German dialects of Rammstein were deafening. Small bars dealt iridescent liquids and paper bindles with dragon stamps. Emaciated women with smudged eye makeup and the torn silk of heroin chic, bound with ropes or handcuffs, swayed languorously in elevated cages.

As we entered the unworldly crush, every woman's eye followed V-1 and V-2. Towering over the Moroccans, both disrobed simultaneously. They revealed matching scarlet and ebony leather corsets pinching their already vanishing waists. Only their florid hips and tumescent nipples barely escaped the grip of tight leather against ivory skin; their legs were satin down to fearfully sharp and lofty heels. An impromptu and mesmerized entourage desperately followed their progress, too stunned even to speak with them.

V-1 and V-2 produced short whips and passed easily though the crowd, standing for tantalizing moments to graze lightly with their whips the swollen breasts of a woman bound inescapably with ropes. She was inclined back against a huge Coptic cross, her arms and legs extended and forced apart with iron spreaders gaffled to cuffs on her delicate wrists and ankles. A hooded, gnarled figure dripped hot beeswax from a thick white liturgical candle upon her reddening breasts as she twisted under the slow stinging drops.

Deeper into the caverns among groups of men and girls in lurid pursuits, the huntresses searched for their patient. They moved relentlessly as the ribald shrieks of lost sirens sounded in the heat, the press of bodies like the pawing of restless stables. Within one isolated cave, dimly lit by guttering black candles, V-1 found her. She was seated tearfully before several Moroccan coke dealers, the powder and craving evident, as they stood before her trading lines for sexual favors, manhandling her youthful flesh and resigned lubricity. We were in some infernal Baal.

One fixed his sordid eyes on V-2, who responded by spewing loud and vile invectives in Arabic. The mood thickened with danger, like the smell of fresh blood. They all turned with menace, scowling, and one rushed at V-1. Shouting obscene commands from the brothels of Marrakesh, she flogged him mercilessly with painful strikes of her whip, demanding he kneel before her. He halted, staggered and confused, thinking it was dominance play by a brace of stellar lesbians who ravished the caves for white slaves.

V-2 placed one endless leg onto the seat by the girl, stretching her finely toned white thigh and her filmy black G-string close to her face, as V-1 took the girl forcefully by the hair and pulled her head back, blocking access to the men. The Moroccans, dazzled by these salacious gestures, retreated awkwardly. They considered the extended stiletto points of their fierce heels, their ankle straps encrusted with diamonds, beneath the flawless musculature of improbably long legs.

Whispering in High German, V-2 very gently brought up the girl's dazed eyes and kissed her bruised lips. Seizing the girl as their captive, V-1 and V-2 stormed from the cave. One Moroccan tried to follow, dissuaded by Vermilion and a burly doorman with bad teeth and a full facial tattoo of a grinning death's head.

THEY KEPT HER BOUND as we burst through the exit door into the waiting Mercedes, the girl now with one shoe, craving more drug and expecting to be for the night an odalisque in some cocaine harem. Vermilion and I followed them to the manor, the captive seated tightly between V-1 and V-2. They covered her with a robe, their prize still bound and now barefoot, the trio flowing past the astonished but obeisant footman. Vermilion pulled carefully onto the gravel sweep of the manor, and doused the lights.

After observing the darkened suite become oddly roseate with some pale fire, Vermilion invited me, surprisingly, for a stroll in the garden. We passed at a funereal pace among the verdant foliage, only the suite's French windows subtly lit above us, as stone gargoyles between the 17th Century cornices protected the manor, grimacing with thickened lips and lavish fangs and tongues.

"They'll need a little time," he explained.

"Tell me of the procedure."

"They may bring her off the cocaine craving with small doses of MDMA, which we regard as glorified speed with useful empathogenic properties for rare interventions. Once pretreated and displacing the devilish sexuality of cocaine with the superior sensuality of MDMA – itself limited by its toxicity – we'll invite her introspection and awakening, if she wishes, with a non-lethal classical psychedelic. They'll bathe her very slowly first, as a purification ceremony. With V-1 and V-2 as guides, her mind and body will become radiant. After the transfigurations."

"What transfigurations?"

We moved in slow circuits toward the manor, ever vigilant. He finally spoke.

"We may hear them but not see them."

THERE WAS LITTLE EVIDENCE of their presence in the suite, save a crystal decanter filled with frappe of blueberries and three fragile Champagne flutes, while the small steady flames of three equidistant votives in dark purple glass illuminated the center. All the lamps had been draped with red silk, their harshness dimmed; the suite appeared as a baronial rouge bordello, or a sanctum for the Epicurean erotic mysteries. Three sticks of sandalwood incense burned, curling into horizontal drifting vapors, while "Song to the Moon," an aria from Dvořák's *Rusalka*, played with poignant air. Within this occult scene, there was a sense of some primordial teaching being handed down. A shower was running, and other sounds were muffled. I could not determine if mingled with the water were tears of joy or sorrow.

Now in lucent shining robes, they appeared across the suite. Laughing gently, they were dancing like fairies in a courtly allemande. V-1 began playfully stroking the girl's erect breasts. At this overture, she became quite serious, pouting and complaisant, even as she grew more taut and excited. She stood very still, then shivered, stretching her legs firmly to receive more fully their incessant adorations.

Now an eager captive, her growing cupidity and the jaunty upward tilt of her rosy tips flagrant before us, she was pushed and pulled in opposing directions by V-1 and V-2 until her prudence at being witnessed was overcome. She began quivering, responding to every touch with ever more heated indiscretions. V-2 danced before her as an alluring moonlit will o' the wisp, her opalline robes oscillating hypnotically. Panting heavily, the girl reached for her. At this frank admission of the girl's true erotic nature, they pressed her between their unattainable bodies and against a Louis XIV table, so that she either had to bolt, or to submit.

Tantalized by magical sylvan nymphs on this night of nights, their mesmerizing hands coaxing her dampening crevice, she with a lavish swoon yielded completely, shaking and loosening her thighs like Leda before a brace of white swans. Her hands gripped their backs. She began to plead. With heated kisses they moved in dreamlike haste to the bedchamber.

Vermilion and I remained, as the aria from *Rusalka* transformed into ecclesiastical chants from the cloistered nun Hildegard von Bingen. We managed to sip flutes of the frappe, finding some relief in the hypnotic liturgical glorias. Vermilion's countenance was grim, for the girl's willing seduction was to be far more serious than an evening's sex.

◯

FROM THE BEDCHAMBER, lilting gasps of pleasure rose from the girl, until she began groaning with utter abandonment.

"Ja...ja...Leibling...ja..."

Her intermittent cries became unintelligible, culminating in long, slow, heaving contractions. But to our concern the frenzy mounted further, her lust becoming insatiable. She began to mutter then shout indiscriminant invocations, hysterical and begging in a rough voice not her own for even more wicked pleasures. She became lost in a frighteningly wanton delirium, and invited the urgent thrusts of hooved satyrs. It was as though some dark and winged creature of desire in the girl had been recognized and provoked and battled to be released.

The rhythm of her initiation quickened over the hours; V-1 and V-2 began singing in plainsong exchanges a 16th Century Latin rite of exorcism from the *Rituale Romanum*. As the girl convulsed endlessly under the devoted ministrations of their hands and mouths and hips, they each sang a Litany of the Saints, and lines from the *Pater noster*. At the peak of her unquenched desire they briefly conjured the princes of Hell from her by the names Acheront, Astaroth, Magoth, Asmodeus, and Beelzebub, then precipitated each wild climax by adjuring and driving them out with the sacred invocations of Emmanuel, Jehovah, Adonai and, it seemed, the wordless Tetragrammaton, the Hebrew name that cannot be spoken.

They ceased only to repudiate with her in soft exchanges the horror of addiction, then again fell into each other's clenching ecstasies. Their multitude of orgasms became seizures, thunderous waterfalls of light not of this world, the intensity of their spiritual intercourse far beyond mere physical movements. Hours passed, but the sensual fascination of their entwined bodies and moaning prayers did not.

◯

IN THE EXHAUSTING EARLY HOURS Vermilion, trusting me now, elected to return to the garden for meditation with a volume of elegiac poetry, leaving me alone to listen to this sensational conversion. I respected their path to the healing of an unfortunate, but could not remain seated. The bedchamber door remained slightly open. I walked silently, reverently, just to glimpse for a moment the transfiguration of a soul being freed with the blessing of Eros.

The *tableau* was illuminated with lunar whiteness from the rising moon, with one votive across the room. V-1 and V-2 clasped the girl acolyte between them, moving as alabaster forms of living statuary, as though they were animated Elgin marbles. Their naked and licentious figures were outlines in ivory like a forbidden intaglio, their skin pale as white honey.

The girl, slim and yearning, was being transubstantiated as a holy *virgo intacta* beneath two angelic succubae. Her come face was beatific, turned deeply into a lush down pillow as she convulsively grasped silk and flesh. She was urged into erotic seizures by their long graceful fingers, whose slightest gesture had the eloquence of blessings.

Now supine, constantly caressed into voluptuous paroxysms, her back repeatedly arched at each fervent exhortation. She was twisting restlessly to offer her tumescent breasts. Her exquisite ankles, porcelain in the moonlight, moved shamelessly in the perfumed, musky air, rising and falling slowly like courtesans' fans, then circling in wide, slow arabesques, then flexing and trembling violently. At last, she began uttering one long syllable of worship, a roulade to a forgiving deity, its florid embellishments broken only by her drowning gasps and almost screamed German phrases of elevated religiosity.

In the deepest night, the beast at last had fled. Their happy voices became those of children, of virtuous schoolgirls. Knowing they finally were safe, and being deeply fatigued, I managed to fall asleep on a couch. Just before dawn I half-dreamed the trio stood before the open French windows, arm-in-arm, rapturously singing to the horned moon with its white aura. There was in the end, for all of us it seemed, a feeling of boundless peace, of infinite solace.

⬡

I AWAKENED IN MID-MORNING, to fresh blue hydrangeas and yellow roses in a pair of antique celadon mint green vases by each end of my couch. Vermilion, V-1 and V-2 and the girl were not to be found. Alarmed, I hastened to the bedchamber. The sheets were stripped. There remained only a great emptiness, the bleak absence of angels that perhaps never were. A Navaho smudge stick of sage had been burned, and the windows were all open. A recording of the sainted courtesan von Bingen still played quietly. The Champagne flutes had been polished, as was every surface in the bathrooms. There were no fingerprints to identify them; no record they ever existed. I rang the major domo and asked for the register of guests. The suite was in the name of Dr. Leopold von Sacher-Masoch of Gstaad, obviously a literate ruse. Even the harpsichord keys had been wiped.

Badly stung by their abrupt departure but admiring their professional acuity, I grimly adjusted the dual combination locks of my valise and opened it to prepare for my own urgent flight. Therein was a folded note, which I quickly put in my pocket. Below, upon my shirts, had been placed a little girl's feathered angel wings and a furry white halo.

Behind my silent driver, en route to Tempelhof and down the Unter den Linden, I saw the Reichstag pass, then the burned skeletons of the Wilhelm Memorial and Nikolai Churches, destroyed by Allied bombing. They rose against the troubled sky like shriveled fingers from unkempt graves. The horses' manes and chariot of the Brandenburger Tor receded above me, their frozen grey images recalling the Prophylaea in Greece, victorious forever. But from Berlin ever after I remembered not war, not the howling Reich, nor the enslavement of innocents, but only their antidote, the Athenian ideal, the Graces, the goddesses of mind.

Only the note in my pocket remained. Upon opening it, the scent of Eau de Givenchy arose. Unsigned, in broad strokes of vermilion ink, was a fragment from Puccini's *Madama Butterfly*, an aria of Cio-Cio San. It seemed for our interview a riddle of benediction, or commencement, in this insoluble maze of desire and loss.

"I will return to the roses, in the season of joy."

Chapter 6.

The Fire Hose

Dulce est periculum.

(Danger is sweet)

- motto of The Advocate,
Harvard's literary magazine, oldest in U.S.

I stood beneath the mystic moon
An opiate vapour, dewy dim
Exhaled from out her golden rim.

- Poe, *The Sleeper*

Ten year old girl on a street corner
Sticks the needles in her arms
She died in the dirt of an alleyway
Mother said she had no chance, no chance
Heartbreaker, pain maker
I want to tear your world apart.

- Jagger, *Heartbreaker*

HARVARD'S SNOW-LIT ENTRANCES – its twenty-six ironwork gates – were still clad in heavy, transparent ice, for New England had no false spring. The Yard's wedding-cake trees and jubilant snowscape seemed no less an engrossing delusion than events in Salzburg or Berlin though, for in Cambridge – as among the Six – one mingled with dream projections, and seemed entrained in great events.

Both Harvard students and the Six, through their dedication, practiced the hallowed and unhallowed arts; at times the presence of either group was like living in some enchanted medieval castle, one that exploded prismatically at the very touch of thought. Both arguably had airs of omniscience, both induced mixes of elation, terror, doubt, and slowly maturing astonishment. While Harvard had been a phantasm of cognition for centuries, and our own mad alchemists had invented napalm, I had to force myself to not reflect on the Six, and the unforgettable transformations witnessed with Crimson, Indigo and Vermilion. There were no interpreters of visions here, so far.

We all had scrambled back from the edge of the earth, glowing with tentative affability from our mysterious interludes, and frequently arriving with mock contrition at the last moment. On this first night, Harvard snowbound was alight with a blue kinetic beauty; our still-refocusing thoughts swam above the books, like mirrors of ink in the nether darkness.

Around us were gardens of whiteness, above us perfect blackness and cold stars. Within Widener were silent glades of intense scholars, all spinning in the sky of mind. I wondered how much Salzburg and Berlin had affected me, now having passed through a warp in the fabric of reality, and returned to our normal world of weaponry, overpopulation, and bioterror.

Cambridge itself seemed a whole bright mirage of well-rehearsed acolytes and tender disciplines. The foreground was crowded with the first evening receptions as clusters of dignitaries filtered into the Kennedy School, the hard-won territory of our desires. I tended to speak in terse phrases, too somber at first. Hulk brought me down gently.

"Man, we're *all* freaking out. You know what Dean Light at the Business School said about the first year at Harvard?"

"Enlighten me."

"It's like trying to drink from a *fire hose*."

Ah, there was Hagendas, always a grounding moment. But no, her golden whorls shined even brighter; she had a new self-possession, inducing murmurs of delight in passersby. She nodded gravely, sympathetically, aware of the bitter fruits of last term's finals, and the fears to come. With expressionless calm, she smoothly played her opening moves.

Heavy snow fell in bursts, as razor winds gusted. Even the frost hurt. Translucent daggers of icicles thrust downward in macabre pantomime of Damoclean threats. The Charles was iron-black, and rolled into episodes; windy grabbles of talk emanated from fearful, joyful returnees. Hammer slid by with a certain determined elegance and thrilling suavity, lifting his round sunglasses in circumspection at the diplomatic impedimenta blocking Kennedy School doorways.

Weak moonlight was advancing over the Charles as the marine-blue twilight subdued into early evening. Surf came forward with her manic concentration, but lissome as a ballerina, waving her long, scrupulous fingers. An apparition appearing from nowhere, she was gifted with insights on the long semester break. Without salutations, she began unexpectedly, abruptly, with a poignant, private truth.

"We are nourished by our senior loneliness."

She meant that we congregated now, finally together from childhoods spent as outcasts, when perhaps we were too introspective, too scholarly, or too outreaching not to wonder where the others of our kind were. Gathered here from our isolations, so excited by finding each other at last, we nonetheless affected a devout nonchalance.

At Harvard, among the hubris and overweening, we all yearned for new thinking, and were vulnerable in that aspect. Our guides through the clouds of unknowing, HKS professors painted thoughts with magnificent subtlety; they guarded us from the sorceries of false politics and imperfect information. But our hearty blood was turning slowly to quicksilver, for it began to conduct the electricity of fierce logic. While we girded ourselves for whiteboards of formulae, I sometimes in lectures recalled from Salzburg the very failure of words, and from Berlin the hot moon.

○

THE CRIMINAL JUSTICE POLICY AND MANAGEMENT section at HKS attracted high-level law enforcement officials from across the globe. On my left sat Rahul, the future drug tsar of India, who extended an invitation for dinner. He and his young family lived at their Spartan cement apartment in Harvard's bleak grad student towers by the ice-bound Charles; it was a formidable contrast to his palm-etched, sun-beaten lair in Mumbai.

He regaled visitors with tales of seizing cargo containers of Quaaludes, synthesized in the Transvaal by unreconstructed witchdoctors whose crude scales also apportioned animal feedstocks, and whose technicians were illiterate children and legless men in wheelbarrows. These bush seers' powders then were pressed into tablets and transshipped from the African veldt to the miserable addicts of the subcontinent, a few trickling to the silken nymphs spread invitingly among the mirrored whirlpools of Paris.

Rahul entertained, while his six-year-old daughter and toddler son, both with large, dark, solemn eyes, watched the strange, oversized and pale dinner guests who tried to amuse them; we succeeded only with our dismal, boxy Western clothing in lieu of saris, and our unintelligible American accents.

"We do have some charming rogues," Rahul went on, proudly displaying a photograph.

A string of battered, dark-skinned faces looked back: diminutive, guilty Thugees in tatters, all handcuffed together like a string of dead mackerel.

"Here we have lined up the smugglers, after beating them a little, and you can see they are suitably downcast."

At this disarmingly frank admission, he smiled with a waiver of his head, side-to-side in the Hindu fashion.

With Rahul and his family over their dinner of saffron rice and dhal, I swore to visit him one day in Mumbai. His region, the graveyard of the Raj, was now the prime exporter of counterfeit pharmaceuticals, beside which African bush products were paltry indeed.

◯

I TOOK TO WANDERING on breaks down the sleet-ridden, snowy Cambridge streets, processing the HKS data overload, but also the mind-wounding subliminal gifts of the Six. At moments I thought them some Luciferean remedy, until I remembered the bruised eyes of the girl in Berlin, transformed in a single night to radiance. They seemed almost Rosicrucian alchemists, practicing before a mountain of Masonic manuscripts. Literature on visionary manifestations was not lacking at Harvard Medical School, where my appointment provided license to investigate. The phenomena about the Six were at first compelling, then irresistible. I began absorbing the works of James, Huxley, Klüver and La Barre on exceptional mental states.

Hagendas, with her plumage of Nordic hair, and Hammer slick as smoke, plucked me one night with their fond embrace from my private bailiwick of frozen Mass Ave. We watched, in the blameless quiet, as the moon came blindly out of the Charles. She was pink as a sea shell, discussing with happy absorption some arcane economic theory. Ice crystals were tickling frostily away, as Hammer attempted an air of sageness. Her low voice, even in her academic reveries, had a blue magnetism; the stars were afloat in her stream of perceptions. We often wondered how she trembled in bed.

Hagendas, with clouded breaths, had forgotten to remove her half-moon glasses. She had a fine, deliquescent charm, as though returning from tea sandwiches at the Pierre. At times it was a kind of sweet holiness, but one tempered by a pious evanescence, as if she already were initiated into some religious order with destinies at the World Bank. Hammer, next to her, had only a lax and faded coloring, fatigued even in these first weeks. We both observed her touchingly tremulous mouth.

We walked to stand by Johnson Gate, the oldest of the Yard, between Massachusetts and Harvard Halls, and through which the graduating class proceeds to and from Commencement under elms and oaks and great silk banners. The gate was imbued with rumors: adorned with Druidical mistletoe, a kiss under it would become a marriage, walking through it during term would lead to failure.

The snow fell fast; snowflakes were dissolving jewels in her hair. Hagendas, no matter the weather, had a consistent refinement of manner, as though our presence in Cambridge were some delicate secret affair of state, even as the whole silent inquisition unrolled.

Although that evening I thought her only a gifted student, for some seconds I divined her future as an elder analyst of financial enigmas and numbered accounts in Geneva, an overblown rose with a wicked air and a blush-proof secretary, replying in shocked tones to puzzled and thorny representatives from Interpol.

But now she was young, pure and curious, weaving a skein of bright thoughts before us in a kind of trance, as we all walked beneath the architectural circumlocutions of the Yard. Through Gothic windows, the lights recalled ballrooms of candelabras among the Viennese.

◯

MEMORIES OF THE SIX would occupy me relentlessly. It sometimes seemed I had witnessed some fearful blasphemy, the carefree surface of an immoral life. I then recalled their gentleness and precision, their mixture of courage and compassion, the fleeing black wings, the arching of the girl to the Godhead.

Harvard Square in the wintry deadness would burn up the nights. Dilapidated taxis loomed in lines, piloted by aggressively underbred Algerians and Dominicans, their ears festooned with tiny piratical rings. The easily discontented and disenfranchised roamed with no directions, or sat staring at the snow in some mental sloth.

Harvard's gates seemed like broken monoliths, or cairns, the murals of Widener like Pharaonic frescoes, the glass displays of rare manuscripts like swarming scrolls, the bewilderment of boots and voices some mad tattoo. The evenings streamed down until darkness snapped shut. I knew it was a remnant from the Six, and not from me, but I felt as though I were running from something.

◯

ON MY RIGHT in Criminal Justice section was the Chief of Police from Singapore. Although the territory of choice for laundering wizards from Chinese tongs and formidable Chui-Chow and Shanghai gangs, the streets of Singapore under his control remained as physically spotless as the white gloves of the traffic police. The city itself was a masterpiece of economic licentiousness. One of the last refuges for hard cash, it was inviting of uncontrolled currencies in large denominations, shipments that appeared in suitcases, private planes, jets, and bulk transfers forklifted on pallets. The Singaporean

6000-dollar bill remained the banknote of preference among smugglers, instantly exchangeable at banks from Lichtenstein to the Cook Islands to Nauru.

Yet this deceptively meek Singaporean official, like a long-legged spider on the black river of underground commerce, commanded thousands of well-trained police bristling with electronics and street savvy. Possessing an equanimity that deluded the inquisitive from the tortuous secrets within, he walked invisibly through the Cambridge nights, sublime and indistinguishable from the ubiquitous core of accomplished Asian grad students. Yet he made the Boston papers one morning after somehow gaining the uninvited attentions of a group of young black Roxbury gang members who were out-of-bounds near Harvard. They selected him, the only person by the Charles on a winter's afternoon, to mug in broad daylight.

Seriously ruffled but returning to class, he resumed his studies with visible bruises. He refused to comment, except for muted epithets of *low faan*, reflecting the Chinese view of Western culture as barbaric. His aura of severe control, his instincts, his glower and flashing of command, were impertinent to the gangs. They roamed like rare, cruising sharks through schools of intently occupied students, who dismissed obvious thugs as completely irrelevant. But the opposites – the gang and commander – instantly sparked each other.

"Yo, homes! Wachu lookin' at? Hey, I'm talkin' to you!"

Semi-literate teenagers with rhinestone grills for front teeth, wearing baggies and reversed baseball caps, closed around him with insults. Their fists and kicks brought him down hard. Filching his wallet, they strolled away in the brute cold and grey drizzle, someone laughing ("Bitch!"). In Singapore, this loose assortment of street thieves would have been hanged by their thumbs in secret stone dungeons.

It was a type of karma, alone in a country where no one knew or feared him, to be humiliated by a pack of mere undisciplined Negro youths, all unaware of the decisive violence meted out to the more severe street gangs of Singapore by the Chief of Police and his merciless troops.

Across the Charles from the beating, a dominant organized crime syndicate – the Boston Chinatown tong – occasionally dispensed discipline or retribution, subcontracting deniable muggings by hiring black repeat offenders through straw men. HKS policy students speculated that the humiliation was not from a provocation. Hammer weighed in.

"It would only take a call from the Singapore tongs to Boston about the Chief at Harvard."

Boston tongs were an ocean away from their toothless relatives in rags, hurriedly spooning fish broth underneath the baleful stare of my classmate's regiment of fearsome prison guards with their meter-long black batons, starched blue uniforms, and Chinese machine pistols. We concluded the mugging was random, as any successful deception intended.

IT HAD BEEN ONLY WEEKS since the mystical events in Salzburg, Vienna and Berlin. Stirred by the memories, I still was discomfited, worried that the phenomena might lead to magical thinking, like a belief in talismanic omens or a form of lunacy that engaged one fully. Other researchers at Harvard likely would dismiss my early reports as a very dubious thing, a doleful dream about a fanatical religion. There was no time for metaphysics, except at the Divinity School.

Yet light streamed across the Charles from a sharp little moon setting in the dusk of late winter, as the grace note of an untimely thaw. The encounters with the Six and the return to Cambridge, this quick transiting of divergent worlds, was a witching time. Idle thoughts drifted in star clusters: hesitant, milky, tentative at first.

In Peabody Museum's reading room, distant from others, sat a pensive cocoon of a girl. With long, black stockings, and pale skin too fevered to touch, she was slender but with devious curves. Grave beyond her age, she gave an impression of studied carelessness. She became restless only at the sounds of Memorial Church bells in the Yard, as though lapped by insistent tongues of memory. She was in Peabody for a fortnight, and so very near, engrossed in an ethnopharmacological text; it appeared to be on the religious use of psychoactive plants among the Buginese and Maasars in Celebes and West Borneo. She often coiled and uncoiled her long legs, then walked slowly along by me, passing like a novitiate with the innocent eyes of the mind. I, only an admirer, remained sensitive from the exorcism in Berlin. Although we never spoke, we seemed to share one consciousness, like V-1 and V-2 at moments. An unravished bride of quietness, her presence exercised one infinitely.

Blasts of late snow railed across Peabody's massive brace of bronze rhinoceri at its steps. The wintry deadness indignantly pouted, the shrill winds hardly less dispiriting than the tomes we were at a loss to decipher. I trudged to the Charles, where students meandered in small solemn processions, as if lessons could be conferred by tutelary watery nymphs. The chinking of river ice became a metronome inside our shrinking skulls. Our valiant efforts at cracking economic theory had descended during these walks to hopeful hyperbole and arm-waving, often yielding to the pelting of heavy sleet. The campus began to assume a transparency, something of a Byzantine provenance, for my perceptions were awash with fatigue, and had not yet accommodated the unspeakable.

◯

IN RECALLING THE SIX, I sometimes would disappear into a long black cloak, like a medieval cleric. Hulk and Surf, observing these silent ecclesiastical ruminations, then would rush to gather me up. We walked arm-in-arm, for warmth and friendship, with Hulk always full of distractions, endless Harvardiana, student lore, and extreme psychic acuity.

"The first Bible in North America was pressed by Harvard," he announced, close to my thoughts, forcing me to rise from the Berlin night and breach the surface, "a translation into the Wampanoag language by John Eliot, apostle to the tribes. We had an Indian College then."

"The fire," Surf interjected, as we passed Harvard Hall.

"Only *Christian Warfare* survived the burning of all Harvard's books in 1784," he said.

"Protected from above?" I tried to attend to his kind insight, admitting my theological perspective.

"A student returned it, fortunately overdue." was his mundane response.

"The university seems permeated with celestial light," I observed carelessly, at some risk of revealing one's fragility.

Surf either missed this cosmic inclination, or agreed, for she hastened to command the exchange, carrying on about the Calvinists' eternal damnation yielding to the Unitarians.

"In 1636 Harvard's mission was to 'perpetuate a learned ministry,' by 1924 thirteen colleges had daily prayers for 'Godless Harvard'."

Hulk was rambling about the Div School as the first non-denominational in America, the origin of religious pluralism, when I first noticed Surf's warm, shy smile at him. I was brought to reality by her heart. No longer an equivocal glance, Surf's look had the eagerness of a lover separated; she hardly was a love-proof girl. The hapless Hulk, in his long, touching vigil beside her withering academic directness, now was an object of lustful tenderness.

Surf had fought off constant admirers, most rejected for their psychic impotency. She had an intellectual nymphomania for learning and contacts, somehow attracting those with a perverse taste for her apparent innocence. One was a lightly stooped assistant professor with fair hair, from the ranks of *le monde*. Although Surf appeared to have a simple splendor, she was toned and sharply defined, a vessel of grace but also savagery. She had thought him a thinking weed, like a dry kiss, and his slippery overtures the machinations of some prurient fiend. The admirer soon found consolation by frequenting a little cabaret dancer: bosomed, tawny from assignations in the Caribbean, and with peacock blue eyes.

Surf had read the Cambridge stud book and racing form, and preferred to breed for cortex. Her voice to Hulk was like the flutter of eyelashes against mind, with a patient fidelity.

"You are aware," he continued, nervous and voluble at Surf's disturbing scent and linking of arms, "our rare books extend to our Hellenic/Pre-Columbian studies library at Dumbarton Oaks in Washington, D.C.? Spies and Virgil, anyone?"

Surf threw me a look of tolerance at the hopeless Hulk, then taunted him relentlessly about the origins of Harvard's color "Crimson" as we strolled along toward HKS. At these near-misses I kept smiling, saying little, blending in.

⬡

SPRING MIDTERMS SWIRLED on the horizon like some approaching storm of political diabolism. As the increased pounding of information began to deafen our minds, instructors tried imposing principles of clarity, accuracy and precision, but by then we were battered into various gradations of wreckage. Our hasty notes mounted into reams of hysterical codas, and students began showing signs of panic.

We were relieved to discover that a policy project outside Cambridge, albeit one entwined with the rigors of statistics, was required. Each HKS student was free to explore any topic as principal investigator, on the premise that unexpected regions of knowledge may be teased out with educated guesses disguised as equations. Hulk chose the interface of CIA and Silicon Valley, the front companies such as In-Q-Tel subsidizing startups. Surf considered rogue fissile material diversion in former Soviet satellite states, Hagendas the monitoring of European Union banking by the NSA, Hammer the legal services for distressed black communities in the rural South.

In an effort to detect and monitor the abuse of novel drugs, I began canvassing destroyed Boston: the junkies' havens, alleys of prostitutes, gang-riddled neighborhoods. The area still had addicts who had survived a clandestine batch of synthetic morphine-like substances – fentanyl and the exotic 3-methylfentanyl – drugs that appeared in localized pandemics in Boston, New York, and Moscow. An incoherent relief from the torment of the streets, pushers distributed such fragments of false heaven in the city's bristling slums.

Heroin and crack dealers were quizzical at this rare white student, thinking me some desperate user. Sapped by chronic deceits, their mood chilled the very air. Suspended idly among the glitter of refuse, enflamed by incessant overstimulation, the crack dealers had a wild insolence. The imprecations of the street were all about them like distant mourners; they studied newcomers keenly.

Their clients were the hooked and exposed, the least distrustful, often the innocent lured by smokable pleasure. "Toss-ups" abounded, desolate young mothers trading quick sex for crack; their obscene whispers, cajoleries and curses became a disorienting monotony.

The heroin dealers, by contrast, had a reptilian lassitude, a kind of perverted languor. It was their unknown land I sought to map, the isle of opium eaters. The seductive sirens of injectable opiates would beckon these many wretched of the streets to founder, their songs too often twisting at last into wails en route to Boston City morgue. Armed only with mathematics, a few of us left the sanctuary of HKS to assess – and propose containing – these maladies in the underbelly of the streets.

Clipboard in hand, and with a satchel of ninety-item questionnaires, I approached at dawn a line of sleepy but agitated junkies shuffling around the entrances to Boston's largest methadone clinic. Disarming a few with an admission of the prison years, I struck up conversations about my Harvard project on the probability of a fentanyl epidemic. A terminal heroin addict, a former RN in Vietnam, befriended me. She now stood for hours in the frigid Boston mornings to sip gratefully her tiny red methadone cocktail or, like many others, sell or trade it for balloons of heroin. She knew everyone, and rapidly arranged impromptu encounters for a small gratuity.

"Five dollars! Fill out this questionnaire!" she yelled, rushing around, spreading the word.

There were no end of takers. The addicts of Boston crowded into an archipelago of cheap coffeehouses, where in plastic booths they could nurse a cup of coffee for hours. With no conversation, they dully awaited all day their next fix, the only sound some tinny Muzak and the tapping of feet in anticipation of the candy man.

Age was meaningless. Wild, young junkies with tracks like teeth marks, really just fresh-faced dropout boys, sat near adolescent prostitutes – still pretty – who shot into the veins of their ankles in cosmetic deception. Older addicts vanished into nearby urinals to worship the anesthetic bliss of charred spoons and bubbling golden elixir. All presented their tales of the heroin street life.

The fentanyl was packaged as heroin, a product of the infamous manufacturer George Marquardt, with 116 deaths from Boston to Washington, D.C. in a year's time. I narrowed the study only to those actual fentanyl users who had survived this batch, to determine if they preferred it to heroin and why. By these means, one could assess the future proliferation of fentanyl in society.

"Hell yeah, I shot it. Nothin' happened at first, so I kept pokin'. Than wham! I wuz out. Woke up in a cold shower. My buddy Danger walked me 'round to keep my heart pumpin'. Where can we get some?"

A young user: "White girls wuz turnin' tricks in Roxbury. You got any?"

Still another: "Man…Homies were dyin' with needles still in they ahms."

Then another: "Honkies in cop cars cruisin', speakers on top, saying 'Don't use Tango and Cash.'"

He meant that police patrolled infested inner-city neighborhoods warning of this heroin brand, actually diluted fentanyl. Paradoxically, they attracted even more users seeking the powerful drug. During these many interviews, I sometimes saw through grimy windows the northern snowstorms shedding their frozen tears; their sleet was like needles on pockmarked arms, their dark clouds troubled above the unsteady audacity of the pitiable, the intemperate, and the grotesque.

Survivors clustered four to a booth in these dingy Boston coffee shops, thinking only of the next injection; they never ordered food, saving their paltry sums, borrowed or stolen, for a new bag. Yet this abjuring of society produced a cult of intimacy among these users who, for a glimpse of a painless earth, worshipped together with their impure sacrament. They shared their money, their syringes, even their bodies if anyone cared for the act. No one ever did, unless a non-addict offered to pay, for the drug itself surpassed all desire, all hunger, all human feeling.

They had special knowledge of a shadowy and insubstantial world, with the dimensionless, blunting airs of limited sensation. They breathed out contagion like fanged thoughts, the ravens of ill omen. They were like the cocaine addicts Crimson had described: all the pleasures of the world for them had been reduced to a trivial powder. It was small solace to realize that no drug could ever be stronger than our will, lest it run rampant and unopposed across the planet. Addicts have forgotten for a while, and some never remember, the triumph of the human spirit.

◯

INVITED TO A CRASHPAD of a users' commune, I found people sleeping on couches or floors, the kitchen devoid of food, everything sacrificed for heroin each day. I sat on a sprung, stained armchair while the woman RN injected each person with many grams of adulterated unknown substances. They gasped with the first rush, then nodded off as rubber tubing was loosened about the vein, blood trickling from flesh too white from sunless seas.

The RN, flashing between angel of mercy and harbinger of death, redeemed herself by opening their airways, then leaned their comatose bodies upon the couch, where they splayed like garish dolls. At this, she injected herself until falling into a deep reverie, her legs akimbo, her wrinkled smock pulled up past her panties. Just before unconsciousness, she managed a smile and an invitation.

"Wanna hit?"

After brushing her hair from her face and ensuring she could breathe, I waited for a moment, sharing among these lost the peace of Morpheus. Slipping away on the train for a long, empty ride to Cambridge, I stared out dirty windows at rows of despairing housing tracts; they stretched down the cold streets to become a white wake on Boston Harbor, like late moonlight thrown back from a filthy mirror.

Departing at Harvard Square, acquiring a jacket and tie, I darted across the Yard past the President's house on Quincy Street to arrive at the Harvard Faculty Club, transformed into the evening speaker as a new Fellow of the Interfaculty Initiative on Drugs and Addictions. After dinner with several professors of law, medicine, public policy and four other Fellows, I then stood and stopped the conversation by describing the cult of the needle, and the dismal world from which I had just come. To keep from crying, I discussed in purely academic terms the malevolent entity that fed upon the spirit of the opium eaters, as they lay dying.

◯

FINE RAIN AND WHITE PEBBLES of hail peppered the windows before Hammer and me, even while a few blades of sun cast prisms. Life in libraries had left us grey and opalescent, like Jesuit martyrs; we felt mentally bludgeoned. A shower of snow was melting at the edge of a hypothetical spring. As the rain slowly stopped tapping and dropping outside our stagnant silence, I retreated to the Yard, but so altered by weariness from study or contact with the Six that Widener seemed some cenotaph, battered into ruins.

Hulk and Surf tracked me to the Woodberry Poetry Room, where one could listen to recordings of Harvard's Nobelist Seamus Heaney. Seizing their captive, they marched me across the Square for croissants at the patisserie Au Bon Pain. Surf was in her Cambridge uniform: long red muffler, matching cashmere watch cap, black coat to ankles, tall boots, fine gloves. Hearing of my heroin research, the poetess opened with Ginsberg.

"I saw the best minds of my generation destroyed by madness, starving hysterical naked, dragging themselves through the Negro streets at dawn looking for an angry fix."

The Parisian freshmen with their narcissistic lethargy still engaged in priapic conspiracies over their espressos, fervently seeking young flesh in the snow, all while recalling their favorite tumbledown Seraglios in Morocco. Cambridge women being too fleet for them, they resorted to the easy, insouciant optimism of unprincipled libertines, concealing their darker introspections and fruitless mental debauchery. Gripping their cups in the still frosty weather, they stared like wolves at lone does from Pennypacker or Wigglesworth. The bookstalls were deserted, the sky low and toneless.

We darted across static traffic on Mass Ave and into Widener, where Hulk led us through its subterranean secret, the Pusey tunnel ("Pew-see" Hulk insisted, blushing). As they moved onward, the semi-lit tunnel contracted into a birth canal, humid and dark with claustrophobia gravida. The changes were beginning. Vienna, Berlin, the tunnel walls were engraved with the writhing girl, horned moons, angel wings, perfumed cryptic notes, the junkies' eyes.

Born into the cool, musty serenity of Houghton Library's rare book collection, I said nothing of the persistence from the Six; my friends at Harvard would never know. I tried focusing on the buoyant Hulk and Surf, for here we had special permission to explore the written record of our species.

Hulk, joyous, lectured. "Houghton's Modern Books and Manuscripts section starts at 800 BCE to the present; the Early Books of papyri and illuminated manuscripts range from 3000 to 1600 BCE."

Surf was reveling in original notes of the 19th Century authors, some still with pressed ferns and roses or the stains of blotted teardrops. Her mood became febrile, tending to the licentious.

"Louisa May Alcott! Oh, God! Emily Dickinson! (one never could be certain of her preferences). Emerson! Melville! Holmes Junior and Senior! Oh, God, Henry and Will James! (panting now) Loooongfellow!"

She pranced to the 20th Century writers, moaning all the while. Hulk stood transfixed at her, clutching some yellowed Tauchnitz edition, like a furtive priest acquiring a French letter.

"T.S. Eliot, ahhh. Thomas Wolfe. Frost! (now in a higher octave) Oh, oh…more, Updike! eee…eee…cummings!"

A librarian briefly looked in upon us, lightly flushed. Surf settled into the working papers of Dickinson's correspondence, loose and unbound in green morocco and grey watered silk. Hulk fled from her orgiastic theater to peruse original manuscripts of Copernicus, John Keats and Dante Alighieri. I found a leather chair among the handwritten letters of Goethe, Cervantes, and Tennessee Williams. But it was Surf's reading a poem of Cambridge mathematician Charles Lutwidge Dodgson to his young neighbor – Alice Pleasance Liddell – that triggered the event.

"Alice!

A childish story take,

And with a gentle hand,

Lay it where Childhood's dreams are twined

In Memory's mystic band.

Like pilgrim's withered wreath of flowers,

Plucked in a far-off land."

Surrounded by fairy tale books in the airless perfection of Houghton, I noticed again a puzzling luminosity, recalling camellias in the rain. As if the fabric of the world were transparent and bathed in light, like a pool into which droplets of my thoughts made rings outward, forever.

I was awakened by Hulk, as he detached himself from Newton's *Philosophiae Naturalis Principia Mathematica*. Surf, with her confederate's eyes, was making occasional groaning sounds at him. It was evident he was disturbed by the playful near-witch and priestess Surf, and admitted in his painfully opaque, academic way of being pulled into the gravitational field of her sun.

"We are more Copernican than Ptolemaic, don't you think?"

I hastened to agree. Surf was behind him, unseen by Hulk. In a *coup de théâtre*, she began twirling with her arms overhead and fingertips touching, like a small child pretending she was a sunrise.

⬡

SURF ENTERED midterms with her characteristic air of piety, but a fretful brow, while munching valerian cachets in a fever of anxiety. Hammer followed, walking blank and numb, then Hagendas with her helmet of bright blond hair. The silence was shrieking, our reason foundering.

The clock high upon the wall was open-faced and faintly malign. We bent to our task, the relentless assessment of our minds. There was only ink and haste, ghostly recall, hopeful conjecture, and the rare minor certainty.

Surf, in her dwindling last hour, made her grand gesture, as if executed on a guillotine. Hulk with frowning eyebrows kept writing with gale force in a tall fluent hand. Hammer had his fingertips on his Blue Book like a blessing, then consulted the ceiling as though it contained the future of his immortal soul. Maintaining a cool thrift, a classical indifference, Hagendas stood first. She drifted away in a long, thin Empire-waisted dress, suggesting a forgotten sophistication. Speechless, we fled to our commiserations. Midterms were over, but not the frigid truth of our grades.

⬡

LOST IN A MAZE of sleep-deprived, heavily pressed scholars, who awaited midterm scores and lunched in grad student cubicles, I noticed a blue index card pinned to the wall. Upon it was scrawled a quote from Josiah Quincy, the 16th President of Harvard.

"*Resistance to Tyrants is Obedience to God.*"

A phone rang. Hammer with a breathless demand.

"Find a jacket and rush upstairs."

It was that holy of holies: a special meeting of the National Security Fellows, hosting an unnamed guest speaker. Such impromptu gatherings of the unannounced could involve special drop-ins from the NSA Director to the Mayor of Tehran.

"And who might that be?"

"Why…the Administrator of the DEA…he runs 10,000 agents worldwide."

Not wanting to miss this overlapping ecliptic of vastly divergent worlds, and somehow sacrificing the pleasures of quiz points on Laffler curves and marginal costs, I – after a long pause and a bout of petit mal – became fully awake.

"Be right over. Who else is there?"

"Oh, some Nat Sec Fellows. You know, that group of agile fighter-bomber pilots and assorted spooks with the complicated watches, crew-cuts and sharkskin suits. And one of the Neiman Fellows, a gorgeous woman journalist, and let me see…Oh, yes, the Director of Intelligence for DEA, with a security detail."

I reflected in silence as Hammer went on.

"And there's a reception and dinner before the talk, semi-formal, small tables, maybe 20 people altogether."

More silence.

"And as a drug policy fellow, you can barge right in. I can't. By the way, DEA vets the Nat Sec list."

I gathered my wits and wafted upstairs. Laurie the Neiman Fellow, newspaper editor and friend, was ravishing in a clinging red dress; drinks were being served all about by white-coated HKS staff in a small reception area. One carrier pilot, known as "T-2" for his aircraft, was attempting to transfix her with stories of tail hooks and afterburners, so we launched abaft T-2 and navigated toward our table with a few others. But there was the Administrator suddenly, medium height, brown suit, steady demeanor but decidedly unintimidating to the unaware. He clutched a mineral water with lime.

I could only introduce myself as a drug policy fellow, bringing Laurie forth in a diverting way, and mentioning some scholarly interest in Afghan heroin and fentanyl outbreaks in Russia. Oddly, he seemed already well-briefed on these very subjects and, it seemed – as I projected an uneasy confidence – on me.

There was the clink of platitudes and glasses, a few beseeching smiles and solicitudes. Fragmentary friendships were formed, and new affections among the attendees. Yet it had the quality of some insidious dance, made morbid by suspicion.

Another of the drug policy fellows, already nearby, quickly responded to my call that the speaker would pique his interest. A former Harvard mathematician, he had in an orgy of practicality reinvented himself into Harvard Law School, and thereafter to his job as Assistant Attorney General of Massachusetts for narcotics, before retiring more happily into teaching undergraduates policy analysis. After introducing him to the Administrator, we repaired to dinner, I to all appearances just another distracted researcher in a cheap, ill-fitted jacket of unclear but definitely foreign origin.

The Administrator mounted a small podium, congratulating us on having security staff at the HKS entrances where he had created some flurry by his unexpected arrival. The DEA Intel Chief, florid and heavyset with white hair, and seated to his right, began in his knowing Irish manner a cool appraisal of the audience. I had the unsettling feeling of his eyes resting on me a little too long to suggest a random glance. Perhaps it was some unconscious mutual recognition beneath our masks, or perhaps the klaxons had sounded as he ran the attendees through the DEA's massive NADDIS database on persons of interest.

I meditated on this prospect while slowly pouring more Perrier, then appearing to push potatoes around. Self-consciously sweeping my gaze from Laurie's dress to observing T-2, who was fascinated with the Administrator's speech and nervously tinkering with the limitless dials and buttons on his Breitling chronometer, I slid my eyes back to the dais. There was the Intel Chief again, gimlet eyed and undeterred; I intuited we made each other in some extrasensory way. We entered into one of those subliminal but indiscrete reveries of "I wonder if you know that I know that you know" so risky and so dear to theoretical colleagues in covert activities. Yet these practices were useless at Harvard where I, now vulnerable but also unimpeachable, focused less on those eluding scrutiny than on public service.

The Administrator, a sanguine former New York state trooper, was giving his canned speech on the DEA's accomplishments, provided routinely to legislative committees for funding, but therein managed to insert a notable dig by suggesting that the spread of drug abuse originated in part from early researchers and "Harvard liberals" during the years of Dr. Leary. At this, I considered that an intel product, a background check, indeed had been produced on the Administrator's dinner guests.

Later disengaging, with due respects, into the freedom of the Cambridge night, I arrived interiorized at my desk, stripping off the Harvard tie, then my jacket from the Moscow GUM department store adjacent to the Kremlin. As the Administrator and Intel Chief returned to Headquarters at Arlington, Virginia on the DEA's Falcon jet, I entertained the prospect that they had made a special visit to Harvard on the incorrect assumption that a mole was burrowing rather too far into the system.

While it was true my research had begun to include investigative practices of federal agencies, I would not hear of the Intel Chief again for years, until an event in which he appeared as an avenging angel, in a setting devoid of civility, with only a few at the table and with his unilateral retention of the knives.

In the silence of late hours, broken only by the pricking of snow on black windows, I recalled the smiling Chinese nun scrubbing the floor at Hoshin-ji. My head was getting too far from my heart, and I wondered if I could survive this lying down with lions.

⬡

DAWN WAS SILVERING FRESH, still leaves in the mists of morning, at the advent of a brightly etched day. I wandered with Hulk, who knew of the Administrator's reception, down a trail around nearby Walden Pond. Limed by the last of the hoarfrost, Walden's incisive cold was yielding to the royal sunlight of late semester. We discovered a wooden sign, with a quote of Henry David Thoreau.

"I went to the woods because I wished to live deliberately,
to front only the essential facts of life,
and see if I could not learn what it had to teach,
and not, when I came to die,
discover that I had not lived."

Hulk, always the opportunist, was a litany of esoterica about Thoreau ("Class of 1837").

"You know that before Thoreau's two-year retreat at Walden Pond and his authoring of *Civil Disobedience*, he declined to pay Harvard five dollars for his master's degree?"

I didn't. We paid with our lives.

"DEA's visit reminded me of Thoreau," he continued.

I couldn't make the connection, and the topic was uncomfortable.

"When he refused, Thoreau told the Registrar, 'Let every sheep keep its own skin.'"

◯

POINT QUIETLY TAKEN from Hulk's too sensitive assessment, we returned to the Yard. The changing weather was just at the edge of an Aegean spring. There were masses of shallow vernal blossoms from the gravid earth, and dangling rosebuds under a painted blue sky. The glories of the university were but architectural afterthoughts.

Even in this radiance, Hulk saw ghosts everywhere, some from the origins of the United States. For uncertain reasons, he always, to me at least, characterized Harvard as an ancient sanctum for renegade thinking.

"In 1768 the senior class voted to defy British law and boycott tea. You know the rest."

He looked at me askance, but gently, as if he somehow knew I kept secrets.

"Imagine 1770. Boston mobs roaming with torch lights and muzzleloaders, random beatings of Loyalists. The General Court of Massachusetts Bay Colony moving to Harvard Hall in the Yard. Students seeing the great Revolutionary speakers, then forming oratory organizations."

"Do secret societies still exist?" I tried affecting some naïveté.

"They merged into the Hasty Pudding Club. Now theatrical, Man and Woman of the Year parades down Mass Ave, Hollywood celebs mostly…speak of the devil!"

Twenty young men and women burst from Sever Hall, quick as kingfishers, sprinting across the Yard. Undergraduates slowly emerged, traipsing under the elms.

"Eager for the first row?"

"Hasty Pudding initiates must run anywhere in Harvard Yard for a week, hence the term 'running for office'."

Dancing toward us gaily was Surf in a flimsy blue dress, with her long sinuous curves. Their relationship was the immortal story – still nebulous, describing a large parabola. Hulk gave his melancholy smile at her arrival, finding momentum for a little nervous lecture, a form of Cambridge courtship.

"Students wrote theses on untaxed paper, then confronted British troops at Lexington. Washington's men were billeted here in the Yard; in the parlor of Wadsworth House he drew up his plans to oust the Redcoats of George III."

Given our midterm debacle, Surf suggested it might be easier to get a degree for courage in warfare.

"And why not?" she said, in perfect and fond mimicry of Hulk. "Harvard presented an honorary degree to Washington a month after the British evacuated Boston."

I rang in. "Then sued the new United States for Mass Hall's melted doorknobs, and won."

"By George, he's *got* it," Surf sang, the expert dialectician and grammarian, whirling about as if at a ball.

We walked together for a while, as I considered Surf's honorarium for courage. There were no examples of such valor now, no outcasts with belief systems that might overcome hostile governments. The Six would acquire no advanced degrees in the divinities, I thought privately, with the reflective gravity of one permitted to watch the birth of religion.

Surf, with her own background in Eastern Europe a topic of gossip, often sensed my unclear history, nudging me delicately to confide in her.

"Warren House has a trap door that leads through a secret passageway into a hidden room. Part of the Underground Railroad."

I could only smile. With their devastating brightness, their familiarity with my dark, interior absences, they always teased me into the light. Our little ragged procession explored Cambridge until the dying of day and the burnished dusk, our unperfected thoughts borne on the breath of evening.

◯

WE FELL INTO A FIRELIT TRIBE of almost naked, barefoot natives in war paint, butchering a slaughtered goat with obsidian knives, turning the dripping carcasses over mounds of embers. They were, of course, Harvard students.

Surf had an invitation to Dunster House on the Charles, with its clock tower and crimson dome a nod to the Big Tom at Christ Church, Oxford. Its tarnished, chipped gilt-edged mirrors reflected the annual goat roast, initiated by anthropologist Daniel Lieberman.

In the spectral Venetian clusters of Dunster's great room windows, one saw the possessed dancing before throbbing fires, their lusterless countenances in trances, their pink rubicund faces now lotus-eating gods. Atop the roasted bananas and plantains were skinned goats' heads, their bulging eyes staring.

Most were trifling with chanting invocations from the rain forests, but a few affected serious miens, scowling or ecstatic. It was worrisome, this drunken revel mixed with sacred communion. I watched them as they toyed with the infinite, as if they were small children unaware by a great wall of fire. While they exulted, I remembered the frightened girl in Berlin, and thought of the dark entities who starved the women at Ravensbrück, and then of the doormen at Birkenau's ovens.

Hulk, observing this growing concern, tried his charmingly dry diversions. "Dunster, like Eliot and Lowell Houses, was built by the firm of Charles Coolidge ("1881"), who designed Stanford."

Several natives of the older tribe had a bardic verbosity in the tone of Welsh tabernacle. Fat capons of men had faces streaked with white grease paint in ceremonial tattoos, and wore authentic Yanomamo headdresses. Circling about the smoking, charred flesh, they could have been plaster cherubim, or Anglican clergymen, or Archdeacons lost in the jungles of Manaus. As we left the flaming celebration, moving down into the coolness of winding paths, a primitive with a bloody knife in one hand gave a small genteel wave with the other.

The air was heavy, redolent with perfume, rendered corpses, and ancient liturgies. The Anglicans' flock was lost in a grim quagmire of spirit worlds, unwittingly tempting invisible beasts, laughing at the night.

⬡

SPRING WAS A RAIN of white roses, the campus Athenian in twilight. The last tufts of north wind caressed the hair of a graduate student, a woman of lovely insinuation, as she crossed the Yard. I hurried at a frantic pace in running shoes over Weeks Footbridge, late in meeting Hammer and

Hagendas outside Harvard Stadium. Surf's dispute over the origins of the university's colors had spread, for just as I arrived, Hammer was attempting to defuse the matter decisively.

(Stretching, lunges) "1858 regatta…future Pres Eliot, bought six crimson silk handkerchiefs…tied 'em to heads of our rowers. Crimson stuck."

Golden Hagendas, now in ultra marathoners tiny black compression shorts, her long sinews and marvelous haunches distressingly evident, lunged back.

"Hardly. *The Crimson* newspaper, first published in 1893, was called *The Magenta*, after Harvard's original color."

Their banter was much too close. Trying to steer the conversation, without being obvious, I looked to the Charles. On the river the crews were straining after dusk, still preparing for the Head of the Charles regatta, the American version of the royal regatta at Henley, where in both they would compete with Oxford and Cambridge. The lightweight double sculls and pairs were out, the varsity lightweight eights, the heavyweight eights with coxswains, the Radcliffe crews. Hagendas, our fairest, had been infected by Hulk.

"The first intercollegiate sports event was between the Harvard-Yale heavy eight rowing crews, 1852."

Hammer, undeterred but distracted by the inspiringly supple Hagendas – who was spread wide as a devout yogini – resorted to challenging innuendo on other sports.

"Curves!" he announced astutely, before recovering, "the curve ball, rather."

Hagendas, a Princeton alum, rose to the bait.

"Introduced to baseball by Princeton in a game against Harvard. President Eliot, who was down on athletics, said of Princeton's curve ball, 'Deception is not a value we wish to cultivate at Harvard.'"

At this, she tossed me a meaningful look, although HKS was thick with spies. We ran and walked and sprinted for hours through early evening, Hagendas always slightly ahead in the default position to our admiration, her blond locks dancing under the moonlight. It was a honeyed night, among the last of the spring term. Under a dark, velvety sky, plaintive small owls began calling, some hidden in stadium rafters that bowed like penitents in a watchful silence.

Hagendas, gasping for breath, heart pounding, perspiring, stopped and began a desultory mooning about. Her lips kept moving like a prayer; we discerned she actually was reciting axioms for our imminent exams, like some goddess of concentration. In the frail starshine, for spilled seconds, one could imagine her flagrant beauty clad only in morning, spread on a huge four-poster with satin baldaquin, but it was only a historic afterthought to our mutual exercise.

"*Balls,*" she finally countered, picking up the game. "*Fast* balls."

Hammer looked caught out. He waivered, hung up in the duplicity of her wording. Hagendas was ruthless, a lacrosse captain at Princeton, who knew her baseball to offset sportsmen's fear of her intellect. Her mental nooses caused men to ejaculate when they were hanged.

"Fast balls were intimidating (her hands on hips, breathing heavily, clear blue eyes locked on shrinking Hammer). Harvard engineered the catcher's mask, based on our fencer's masks, 1876. Patented the mask…sold it to Spaulding…introduced to major leagues."

One could see her pulse race. Her skin was lilac bronze, wet like midnight dew. She suddenly relaxed her body, as if she were melting spring. It was at this unlikely instant that I saw Hagendas change, like a spell was summoned, although it could only be my projection. Her eloquent physique seemed magnetized, her Sibyl's eyes flashing yet unmoved in the dignity of her silence. One wrong word now would entrain new forces, new dangers. There were no real hauntings so far in Cambridge, though her magnificent arms and legs were ribbons of milky light, like quartz mirrors or dead stars.

Sea birds were flaming here and there. We were buffeted by a stout wind; there was the smell of brackish water. Brooding inwardly on the persistence of the phenomena, I turned to stretch after our run. Nonplussed, they joined me in slow, long healing postures. Clearly, one was fatigued.

⬡

OUR ANEMIC FLOCKS soon awakened to the warm weather. In the Radcliffe dorm one could hear down the late halls the small incoherent cries of divine rhythms, as mesdames and mademoiselles recovered from their alienated first year. Others, as yet unrealized and still frozen iron stiff, strove toward onanism in mirrors. The Charles had fireworks at night, kaleidoscopes of long-tailed box kites by day.

Just before finals, we sometimes would walk on the nether shore of the Charles, where there were charming vine trellises and shining limes. The river was mildly choppy as we plodded industriously past marble balconies and silhouettes of the Houses, their gardens under a spring moon starred with white lilies.

Like some passing fancy, we decided on a very late moonlit walk in the Yard. Hagendas and Surf, Hammer and Hulk, all became elated by the last silver spangles of lunar rays, the stars prickling out of darkness. Surf felt her way along the monuments in the desolate Yard, a serious admirer of Helen Keller, blind, deaf and dumb since the age of two (Hulk, "Class of 1905").

We convened mysteriously, guided by unseen hands, near the marble dragon in front of Boylston Hall. Carved during the reign of, and for, the young Emperor Chia-ch'ing (Hulk, "1796-1820"), the phallic statue was a gift from the Harvard Shanghai Club. Ten feet tall, with stylized serpents in grey Chinese marble, it was bright as a piece of moonlight, bright as a steel blade.

With our half-formulated thoughts, we wandered with graceful aimlessness, idle as fire-flies. In the half-light, it was the perfect moment for a kiss. Poor moonstruck Hulk considered the utter whiteness of Surf, the burning vastness of her, but got his dates wrong. Heartbeat-by-heartbeat, we proceeded in silence. The stars were cool, the roses black.

Hagendas began to dance with Surf in a slow, proud pavan, their entwined hands held high under the light of the dying moon, their frail sopranos lifting in a broken Puccini duet. An achingly beautiful moment, I see it even now.

> "We are like the goddesses of the moon,
> Who come down every night
> On a bridge from Heaven."

I recognized a song of Cio-Cio San, but thought then it could only be a coincidence with Berlin. Hulk looked on with the attenuated wraith of his fond hope, already an ill-starred love. We joined them at last, Hammer and Hulk and I, and we all danced on the steps of Widener, then danced through the Yard with our dazed endearments, irresponsible as flowers.

The pulse of the world followed us that night, we the moon-keepers; the stars were a glowing branch across the sky. We sang in the scented pools of air in these precious moments, for soon we would disperse throughout the nations, one day to be elders recollecting the magic of the time when we, from our lonely childhoods, finally found each other.

BY SOME UNSPOKEN AFFIRMATION OF MINDS, we arrived at William James Hall, the tallest building on campus, the lair of psychologists.

"You know that Tim Leary was a professor of psychology here, left in '63 for the psychedelic revolution," Surf whispered. I could only pretend not to know. We considered the James quote engraved in marble above the elevators.

"The community stagnates without the impulse of the individual,

the impulse dies away without the sympathy of the community."

The Memorial Church bell sounded its foundering, plunging tone. It was dawn, our night of dreams was over.

◯

FOR FINALS INSPIRATION the technocrats among us sometimes studied alone at Harvard's Museum of Historical Scientific Instruments, with its 20,000 artifacts donated since 1672. It had the chemical instruments of Lavoisier, the physics devices of Rutherford and Oppenheimer, the early computers of Gates, the dipping needles of the Santa Maria, the lenses of Leeuwenhoek. There were astronomical devices: globes, star atlases, astrolabes. With permission, we could access the telescopes of the Loomis-Michael Observatory.

I found a niche by Franklin's astronomical quadrant, the one he used to measure the heights of celestial bodies. Alone and stressed before the exam, I felt it come on again – the effect from the Six – but each time it seemed less frightening, and more as though new neural systems were associating. Accommodating the perceptions, I relaxed for a moment into the pasts underlying the instrument, as the quadrant resolved into Franklin himself, naked in his garret, taking his daily air bath in Paris, following the storms, trapping useless electricity in Leyden jars, his quill scribbling insights that now run worlds. Franklin's loving tears dropped onto his wife's decades of correspondence, each signed in her fragile hand:

"Yor afekshunit wif."

The Six were a matrix of ancient and novel belief systems. At times when others would make merry, I would rifle my notebooks peevishly, hunting for tokens of the miracle – the encrypted records of the Six – as if I were some papal emissary from other worlds. There came to be a kind of sorrow at their absence, the lure of a lost tribe threatened with extinction. In the pallid cold light of evenings in Harvard Square, sullen crowds had featureless faces as I repeated to infinity the fragments of songs and incantations from the visionary memories. The hindering thoughts of illusionists' creations, of a fearful magic, often were brushed aside by day.

⬡

BLUE SUNLIGHT, in the last week before finals, descended into blackest nights. The throbbing of crickets outside Radcliffe dorm was offset by the irresistible momentum of soft groans within. Serial paroxysms were unhindered, for fear can be an aphrodisiac. Most of us, though, lay stark and rigid, sleepless until dawn, like Crusaders' effigies.

In desperation we moved our study groups, forever seeking the perfect setting for revelation. For a controllable solitude, we sometimes found solace at Harvard's Fogg Museum, with its facades copied from the canons of the Church of Madonna di San Biagio in Montepulciano, Italy. I noticed, but thought nothing of it then, that as Surf and Hagendas passed under the facades they crossed themselves like serious penitents. We spread out beyond the Jean-Auguste-Dominque-Ingres collection, and even Monet's *Gare Saint-Lazare*, leaving Hulk by some pre-Raphaelite work.

Hagendas ignored the rooms of Degas and Renoir, finding her zone by the Hutchinson collection of English silver. Doleful, Hammer left her to settle out of eyesight at the Winthrop Bequest of European paintings. Surf disappeared into the Wertheim Collection of 19th and 20th Century drawings. I spent the next many hours within view of Hagendas, and on breaks admired the priceless silver masterpieces. One flagon was elaborately engraved with Celtic symbols, and seemed identical to Crimson's, the one he had by the fire, on the night the earth moved.

Very late, Hammer and Hagendas slipped discretely from a corridor; she was adjusting her coiffure, flushed, a little nervous, like desire expressed in heartbeats. They moved in slow gyres, embers aloft in fugitive afterglow from some conflagration. Hammer was rosy, but had crestfallen tones. Hagendas walked onward with her patrician simplicity, perhaps from the scene of some imprudence, and my stirred imaginings.

◯

I DECIDED TO FLEE on the remaining night to Harvard Medical School, now a talisman for surviving finals. Passing the Charles, I saw students among monuments like altars and tombs, still stargazing, and among them the drifting of brown-taffeta nightingales.

Harvard Medical School had a three percent acceptance rate, smaller than the College. Although the school in 1782 was housed in diminutive Holden Chapel in the Yard, the buildings and pavilion now occupied 26 acres. They were not like the Georgia Revival design of the Houses, but had an everlasting, coldly formalistic imperial style in white granite, a 1901 gift from J. Pierpoint Morgan, Huntington and Sears.

The blueish street lamps of Longwood Avenue looked upon only this single student at 2 AM, hunched under a book bag and dark sky, joining a cluster of med students at Countway Library. Arrayed under elfish yellow lights, some were sprawled among coffee cups, knuckling their eyes, unshaven. Concentration being futile, I passed the night with volumes from the 1800s by Havelock Ellis on artificial paradises and effects of the mescal button, *Anhalonium lewinii*.

Staring blankly at wavering print, I looked up to see a flickering grayness, a resonance upon the surface of the sky. As a flint pallor appeared on the horizon, the shuttle to HKS oversaw half-tone patches of green and white clover along the Charles. Divinity students moved reluctantly among heather blooms toward finals, counterfeiting pious walks while muttering blasphemies in true calf-slaying fashion.

At 8:07 Harvard time, realities moved. We arrived as if from vast, unforgiving deserts of incomprehension, the class finally entering like a train of fly-tormented, shuffle-footed camels, marching through heat mirages of numbers, airless towns of statistics, the tepid water of economics, and outcrops of palms and oases like rare correct solutions. We had parched voices; the proctors seemed grave and bearded elders of the tribe, the overhead lighting but paper lanterns covered in indecipherable inscriptions. It was a scene like a battlefield, littered with the survivors of this first year. Among those so blessed were personages worthy of recording.

Hammer stared as though into a crypt. Hagendas maintained her cooled efficiency with growing futility. We heard our Bangladeshi students uttering Hindu prayers *ex tempore*; there were spontaneous flights of nervous laughter. Some were absolutely drowned from floods of rhetoric, others were trembling like the leaves of fall. Even Surf managed small shrieks of death divining poetry.

Hulk seemed snuffed out, wrestling with the ungraspable in desultory torment. A few students seemed to have a progressive atrophy that cruelly emphasized their stress; one was a cadaverous shell with long sensitive hands, head askew on shoulders in resignation. A São Paulo girl was in an agony of apprehension, attentively listening to an interior monologue. In the germinal silence, someone snapped a pencil in half.

Even the occasional cocksure figure, having arrived in Cambridge poisoned by chronic narcissism, now seemed a trifle funereal. The first year had been a killing business, leaving us not quite *compos mentis*. For hours, we fell into a labyrinth of devoted uncertainty. One could hear only the clicking of pens, a whimper, perhaps a curse, for our day of reckoning was at hand. Outside by the river the Boston Pops was preparing for the season. At nearby Tanglewood, spirited cellists and tympanists spread picnic quilts under the amazed sky. Small children frolicked by the Charles, squeaking like mice.

Suddenly, it was over. Hulk, who never uttered a pejorative thought aloud, slapped his forehead and mouthed an expletive. The post-final fragmentation of our tender neurologies led to striking and distracted gazes. One or two lept about in dazed and premature self-congratulation, before their legendary qualities succumbed to the reality check of grades. But almost all of us were humbled, permanently.

⬡

THE BRILLIANT EARLY SUMMER, with the light keen air of that last morning, found me terminally undone at Logan Airport. I dumped impenetrable notes in the trash, as speakers blared boarding announcements and crowds of students from MIT, Harvard, Boston University, Brandeis and Amherst fled to Copenhagen, Rome, Peking or internships in New York and D.C.

I was connecting on a KLM flight, through Amsterdam and Moscow, for a possible public health project that required a remote trek in the Himalayas. As the ponderous azure dream of the Atlantic moved below the wing with infinite slowness, the stewardesses offered comforts in soft Dutch. I wondered about my study of the Six, for only Magenta and Cobalt had not appeared, and were unlikely to do so in Nepal. One hardly could be found by federal agencies there, much less a small clandestine group, where there were only footpaths trod by Tibetan monks with prayer flags.

The ever-widening circles of a working paranoia became but phantoms, as grueling studies finally yielded to the musical tones of advisories in Dutch, and then to sleep. At times I awoke with a start, mistaking the sounds for some obstinate clanging, as if they were distant warning bells.

Chapter 7.

Mother Goddess of the World

I have journeyed to sacred places in utter joy,
like a swan landing on a lotus lake,
and my heart is filled to the brim
with the nectar of their sublime qualities.

- Ngawang Kunga Tendzi
The 3d Khamtrul Rinpoche (1680-1728)

Numismatics, pharmacology and archeology have been reformed.
I understand that biology and mathematics are also awaiting their next avatar.
A scattered dynasty of recluses has changed the face of the earth
– and their work continues.

- JLB, *Tlön, Uqbar, Orbis Tertius*

With one quick look, you and I perceive wine glasses on a table;
Funes perceived every grape that had been pressed into the wine
and all the stalks and tendrils of its vineyard. He knew the forms
of the clouds in the Southern sky on the morning of April 30, 1882,
and he could compare them in his memory with the veins in the
marble of a book he had seen only once, or with the feathers of spray
lifted by an oar on the Rio Negro on the eve of the battle of Quebracho.

- JLB, *Funes, His Memory*

…whose intellects disgorged in total recall for seven days and nights with brilliant eyes…

- Ginsberg, *Howl*

Suffer little children to come unto me, for such is the Kingdom of Heaven.

- Matthew 15:13-15

THE LITTLE GIRL wore a filthy flour sack with holes for arms. A dirty-faced, black-haired six-year-old Nepalese orphan with bare feet, weakened and anemic from intestinal worms, she sat listlessly with a rusty iron pipe, breaking small rocks into gravel to sell for money. Her eight-year-old sisters were lost long ago, as they scavenged through garbage piles on the putrid outskirts of Kathmandu.

If she had shoes and a clean sari and someone to comb and weave her hair, she might be chosen by monks and fed rice and dhal and permitted to splash goats' blood as blessings on the tires of the Royal Nepal 707 jets at Pokhara Airport. If she were careful, she could wake before dawn after the monsoon rains and wander near the airfield to collect psilocybin mushrooms for the holy men and trekkers, before the other children beat her with sticks and drove her away. Now, she wearily struck rocks, then scooped up the gravel in her small hands to place in a toy pail, and carried it up the hill from the river's edge a hundred times a day, all for a few rupees if she were fortunate not to be cheated. She hoped to buy shoes one day. She drank from the river, where upstream men and animals defecated. Sometimes, she tearfully would lift her flour sack for the emaciated, cruel Indian vendor to feel her and worse. Her milk teeth were rotten from the Chiclets he gave her not to cry too loudly.

She looked up past the shining snowfields of Everest, rising beyond thousand-year-old stone columns of copulating tantric deities, where Radha was locked in ecstasy with legs around Krishna. She saw the distant silver capsule with vapor trails across the sky. She did not know that among its inhabitants, like visitors from another world, I sat surrounded by smiling Nepali stewardesses in silken saris, and scarlet-robed Tibetan monks with garlands and sunglasses. The monks sipped Perrier with lime, no ice.

But from the sky, she was just another speck of drab color, lost in the avalanche of suffering across the roof of the world. She was insignificant in the delirium of dancing effigies of gods and street-side shrines, each with their own blood sacrifices in this rainy season, to ensure prosperity the little girl never saw. She was not even desirable for the dissipated Rana princes in their sordid playpens near the King's palace, as they reveled in dispossessed children from Himalayan tribes, and discovered that among the frightened and illiterate and vulnerable, ruthless poverty and chronic hunger were the oldest of aphrodisiacs.

Across the planet again, from Cambridge and just up from Delhi, I was semiconscious, packed in the last row of tourists, half-dreaming of Crimson and Indigo and Vermilion, and their potential value to psychiatry. My presence in Kathmandu was a personal concern, to interview local ophthalmologists who returned sight to thousands of Nepalese blinded from the altitude, using cheap intraocular implants from Ram Dass's Seva Foundation. I awakened, musing that Ram Dass was the former psychologist Richard Alpert of Harvard, the early LSD researcher given his Hindu name in India by his teacher, who told Ram Dass to dedicate his life to *seva*, or service to others. Perhaps my slides would attract students at the Kennedy School or Harvard's School of Public Health to action among the peoples of Nepal and Tibet.

The rushing fields and paddies of Himalayan villages rose quickly, as the monks in business class offered prayers in Tibetan. My reverie soon transmuted into this reality of golden pagodas and temples, where covered palanquins of unnamable gods were paraded through streets by mobs in religious frenzies. Shouted prayers from a thousand voices protected Kathmandu valley from summer monsoon floods and landslides, as forests of bamboo and banana trees spread lush and tall. Hidden gardens concealed priceless Thanka paintings, while the elders within – their leathery brown skin burned at 18,000 feet for a lifetime – drank sacred potions for longevity. Their elixirs swirled with ground gemstones; the cups were lined with pounded silver and made from stained and polished skulls of deceased relatives.

It was the start of the festival season in Nepal, where at my trekkers' lodge Himalayan mountaineering expedition crews of Sherpa guides coiled prayer flags into bamboo baskets. From Tham in Eastern Tibet, their ancestors had migrated in the 1500's to the high valleys of sacred Everest, or *Chomolungma*, "Mother Goddess of the World."

I sat in my lodge's small veranda, where across a low stone wall and down the mud streets even the youngest girls wore brilliant saris. Eating dhal smeared onto an issue of *Rising Nepal*, I saw oxen pulling carts loaded with pressed bricks of tea, while above a hawk in mid-air dismembered a snake in its talons. The edges of crowds of small, dark Nepalese worshipers carrying garish displays of the elephant god Ganesh, the remover of obstacles, flowed past Tibetan stupas in a cataclysmic scene recalling Rimbaud's "calculated disordering of the senses."

Nearby, wearing a tattered shooting jacket for country weekends – but otherwise dressed like a Sherpa with flowing red and purple scarves and well-used hiking boots – a strongly built Englishman gripped a fearsomely carved walking stick. Speaking fluent Tibetan with a cluster of smiling monks, he glanced my way, noting the rare Westerner. The barefoot monks in rough brown robes approached me, I assumed to ask for alms. Instead, they bowed, then produced a white silk *khata*, a traditional blessing cloth, and with reverence wrapped it about my neck. The khata was intended to seal the doors to Samsara, the world of everyday thought and experience. Touching their foreheads to mine with a Tibetan prayer, they walked into the mad noon of Kathmandu. The younger monks, perhaps ten years of age, followed in leaping dances, playing blasts of atonal musical notes on *kanglings* – ritual trumpets made of human femurs – to cut through thoughts and invoke spirits.

The indigenous Englishman soon sat at my rough hewn table with a profound gravity, saying nothing, but holding my gaze steadfastly. He affected long grey hair, his hands calloused but bearing a silver class ring engraved with the heraldic coat of Oxford, and its inscription *Dominus Illuminatio Mea* ("May God Enlighten Me" or "The Lord is My Light"). His wrist bore a mala of sandalwood beads on a red thread, and a battered vintage Rolex Submariner. After long moments, when most would have engaged in cordialities or chattering banter, he merely lifted his formidable eyebrows.

More than I, he was quite comfortable with the protracted silence, one that presaged an altogether different encounter. He possessed a monk's harmlessness but projected a sense of absolute command. At earth's extreme, among the churning atmospheres of religious ecstasies, I already was overwhelmed with the unexpected, but not prepared for his eventual small bow and low, earnest singing of measures of the same Latin plainsong chant that had transformed the Berlin night.

Having reached the hostel on foot with a backpack, jostled within milling crowds of Nepalese celebrants, then randomly ambling down narrow, fragrant or fetid alleyways, I knew that few organizations could have tracked me to this world's end. Magenta waited as I sorted through this glorious coincidence, watching my face transform into recognition, then gratitude for their subtle and expert crafts. I was encompassed yet again, with no warning.

He requested from one small but immensely strong Sherpa some *tsampa*, strong roasted barley tea with yak butter, and unpalatable to most Westerners. I was provided the same. Remarkably, without introduction or pleasantries, he spoke of Vermilion as if he and I and the others of the Six were all family, merely continuing a long conversation within one mind. There seemed to be no discontinuity, but a seamless trust. He spoke in their manner of transferring information so rapidly that it broke open one's head. As if completing my thoughts, he began with a precious insight into Vermilion's lifestyle.

"…and he's hardly indulgent, one might note. As counterpoint to the *haute monde* quarters in which you were vetted in Berlin, Vermilion occasionally clothes the women in ethnic rags and sleeps with them for weeks in destroyed villages in Serbocroatia. Destitute, they have worn sarongs and raised chickens, living in thatched huts on stilts in rural Cambodia or Sri Lanka. Disguised and undetected, they have become refugees in Moldova and Dagestan. All for the balanced cultivation of the compassionate heart and mind. All between massive psychedelic batches and his elegant countersurveillance methods… and the more elevated, sensual pursuits you observed. Of course, he becomes impossible to track. They drink of life, and each other. Remarkable, no?"

Even exhausted from the rigors of overnight linking flights across Central Asia to this impoverished celestial kingdom, I managed to recall Vermilion's practice of juxtaposing from day to day the extremes of moralities and possessions.

"He mentioned experiencing the breadth of the human condition."

"So that he remains humble and focused," Magenta replied, "even with his consorts, and not distracted by the trappings of global mobility, the odd castle bedroom, and unabated sexuality. His responsibility as one of the Six permits little frivolity, if we are to be safe in preparing the medicine."

"And Indigo? We met in Salzburg and Vienna."

"Indigo considers ritual preparation of sacraments, the spiritual practices necessary to function while exposed to millions of doses. He knows the fine forms of kneeling or standing and praying across the religions, and the intricacies of counterintrusion electronics for clandestine labs. And he still has my six quarto minor volumes of Pope's *Iliad* translation," he said.

He stirred the pungent yak butter in his cup of tsampa, its rich exudate from the highly bred long-haired *dzo*, the yak cow.

"Crimson?"

"We are thankful for his Washington Rules, his security measures which constantly evolve, and for the Ivy Mike deception of DEA decades ago. Many of those young operatives fled to Nepal, Goa, and Southeast Asia. Cobalt will discuss the new paradigms for monitoring governments."

I nodded, observing privately his competency in Tibetan, Nepali and Hindi after years in the regions, but did not ask if he were an Ivy expat.

"And your specialty?" I inquired, hoping to confirm, yet not admit, his colleagues' earlier disclosures.

"Between batches, I research the future of psychoactives, sometimes requiring Vermilion's special services to penetrate government or industrial labs."

"And what will be the next major drug?"

"Nothing soon from the expansion of the psychedelic pharmacopeia. The spectrum of non-lethal compounds still merely reflects the diverse properties and self-limiting nature of classical hallucinogens. Rather, we track Big Pharma's, shall we say…special initiatives."

At that I gulped most of the tsampa, consuming the last of the dhal in haste, and thoughtlessly discarded the *Rising Nepal* as a one-eyed mongrel wanly followed its arc into a rancid bin.

A small girl wandered with her grandmother by the lodge, both wearing identical blue saris and gold nose rings, as above us at the edge of sky rose Everest's vast fields of ice and light. Her little hands clasped the wrinkled old woman's enduring mahogany fingers.

"Special initiatives?"

"Drug design of compounds significantly influencing learning and memory. And libido. By major pharmaceutical firms eager for billions in revenue, with little concern for the consequences of unleashed cognitive enhancers and erotogenics."

I was stricken by such scientific futurology among this most ancient of cultures. My charter was to examine a highly insular illicit manufacturing group, but now I looked from within it, as it spied upon global corporations that posed the next major societal hazard.

Even between the reeking mud and the star-scaped heavens in this remote outpost, we progressively were in a wilderness of mirrors – a net of secret agents – all looking at each other. As unknown observers submitted data to dossiers and implacable analysts, perhaps I was included as well. Magenta, at the loss of contact from these sober reflections, artfully relieved me from the ever-returning cycle of frightful conjectures.

Leading the way, he guided me past the stacked sacks of barley and rice, past bricks of compressed tea leaves, egg noodles, roasted tsampa and chilies, past the wooly, nut-brown Sherpa guides, the sharpened ice axes and crampons and bundles of emergency flares, out into the road beyond a decaying monastery, or *gompa*. We passed the dilapidated Hotel Shanker, a former Rana palace, and walked through clusters of holy men reciting the precepts of the Buddhist Dhammapada, or the Hindu Vedic sutras of the Upanishads. Beyond the tattered blue and red prayer flags hung from bamboo poles and mounds of rocks, we finally entered a foot path, where we trod through lavish rhododendrons and towering cypresses, as horses grazed under hemlock and prodigious firs. The path began to appear as Tibetan texts describe awakening: the earth itself bejeweled. Magenta's walking stick and boots beat steadily; I began to breathe deeply of the crystalline air. The fear was gone.

⬡

WE CAME upon the great stupa at Bodhinath, in ancient times representing the mythical Mount Meru of Hindu theology, now with its majestic white hemisphere painted with the eyes of Buddha and overlooking the valley cascading below. Thousands of monks were chanting mantras, their left hands extended to spin each of the hundreds of cylindrical wooden prayer wheels encircling Bodhinath. Carved in Tibetan symbols for *Om mani padme hum*, the Jewel in the Lotus, the inscribed prayers were sent outward to all sentient beings. I fell in behind Magenta; we spun each wheel so our vows to end suffering would be taken by the winds.

The inevitable contact high from one of the Six seemed amplified by the devotional resonance of Bodhinath. Magenta's walking stick tapped unceasingly like some secret code. We circled the mesmerizing ancient clockwork, telegraphing peace throughout the ten directions and untold realms. We became trekkers on the sacred mountain Meru with its rubies and amethysts and harlots and sanctified streams holding up the skies. The spinning became a spiral of reveries until we soon nodded at the wailing wall of Jerusalem, prostrated ourselves before the golden crucifixes of Florence, and ceaselessly recited a thousand sutras in Dharamsala. We whirled with our arms out and faces upwards like dervishes, and cycled among unknown lovers in the holy orgies of the Epidaurians.

We possessed the insights of Ptolemy, Kepler and Tycho Brahe of the cosmic mechanisms, freed from superstition and awed by the illimitable divinity revealed by science. The clicking of his staff became that of an abacus, and we naked Egyptian youths beneath the seven daughters of Atlas as the Pleiades rotated and the Nile flooded; the abacus again in our hands as we trembled before hundred-gated Thebes in the time of Diocletian. The repeated clicking and circling now induced seizures of déjà vu, and the incarnation of Plato's teaching in the 12th book of St. Augustine's *Civitas Dei* that all things happened again and again. The clicking now was that of particle counters, and we theoretical physicists rent asunder by differential equations of Maxwell and Bohr and Planck and Schrödinger, then spinning quarks and rotating quasars and vibrating strings and turning 24th dimensions and the eternal whirling ghosts of dark matter.

Onward we spun as the sun bore upon our necks, the prayer wheels for a fleeting and dismal moment merely dusty and futile contrivances – some ignorant, insane trickery – then resuming forever the fine transmissions of holiness, each a flower of civilization and benign awareness. Every step we took spoke its own prayer of Hallelujah at existence, until our interlacing comprehensions finally burst, and manifold tsunamis of compassionate thought radiated outward and inward to engulf the song of the whippoorwill and the merciful rains.

Everything stopped. It passed as though it never were, leaving us utterly transformed and completely untouched. Reacquiring my body, there remained only a cooling perspiration and an indefinable thirst. Breathless at the psychic devastations and rebirths, I rested against a low exterior wall and broke contact with Magenta who, without looking back but raising a hand, passed left into the broad curvature of Bodhinath. The incandescent haze of Kathmandu valley below rippled to the vast range of Himalayan crests, their pellucid glacial cirques brilliant and sunlit. I was alone at last.

In the wake of the cognitive phenomena, I rushed to pray for the children of the world, for the sick, for the grace of normal consciousness. It seemed the laboratory of our distant island earth, clandestine against countless diamond constellations, spun on its axis sending heavenward not only the orisons of the monks of Bodhinath, but the unfathomable emanations of all things, the prayers of every living being. We were infinitesimal, illuminated beneath our ungraspable and almost everlasting solar explosion, itself a forgotten pinprick in the boundless canopy of light.

At this simple gesture of devotion, a troop of thirty very young Tibetan monks, all about eight years old, and every one lean and barefoot with a shaved head, passed happily before me, chanting in sing-song Tibetan the pilgrims' prayer on the way to Mount Kailash.

"*Ka zher, lam khyer…*" (Whatever arises, bring it to the path)

Twirling the prayer wheels, each bowed to me, smiling brightly, then vanished into the curvature. At this portentous vision I could only follow in grateful reverence, my fingertips lightly grazing the cool enameled carvings of each slowly creaking wheel.

MAGENTA FOUND ME lost among the milling worshippers of Bodhinath, and collected this subdued researcher somberly and without comment. We hiked in silence to the lodge, then rode away in his scraped and beaten but perfectly tuned Land Rover, apparently some long decommissioned official consular car. The Rover swayed through a long series of directionless, rutted cow paths, its malas and bells tinkling, toward our destination: the Eye Clinic of Kathmandu.

A single, squat two-room building of painted hand-pressed slabs of mud and straw, the clinic contained a rudimentary office and a barren operating room with an old steel gurney. From this unassuming structure, thousands of Nepalese had been gifted with sight by the simple insertion of a cheap intraocular lens. Its only physician appeared. Genial, wearing thick sunglasses and with well-kept jet-black hair streaked with grey, he seemed gratified to find an ally. I offered to seek used, donated ophthalmological equipment in Boston for the clinic, and then gave him every rupee I had. As we left, Magenta considered my profligacy favorably.

"To leave this region with a rupee may be immoral."

Beggars by the clinic door shuffled toward us wearing shreds of dhotis and reeking head cloths, their darkly veined and knarled hands shaking in prayer, their lined faces and sightless eyes crowding us with earnest entreaties. One had white corneas, blasted by the high-altitude sun, the very glaucoma that would yield to a half-hour transplant just a few meters away. Blind since childhood, he had five children. I insisted he have surgery, and would pay for the eight-dollar lens.

"No, master. If see, no beg. No work me."

He chose to remain blind to support his children by begging. Magenta quickly dispatched a stack of soiled rupees, the currency's elegant portraiture of the King lost in the squalid grasping of desperate hands.

AS WE PASSED among the dispossessed of the earth and the profound concentration of religions, Magenta and I – only with some difficulty – spoke not of ethics or poverty or service, but of cognitive evolution, of neurology, of a future uncomprehended or perhaps foretold by these ancient faiths.

"How do the Six," I asked, "monitor drug development affecting learning and memory, or sexuality?"

The small brass bells hanging in the Land Rover's cab rang with every jolt as we slowly edged through almost impassable clearings occupied by increasingly dense and wildly colorful caravanserai. We were surrounded by free ranging mules, cows with painted horns and flowers, goats, and shoeless Nepalese families trudging in quiet migration toward the great edifices of Pashupanipath, the Mecca of Nepal.

"Drugs enhancing cognition and libido may be considered the modern moral equivalent of the first fires among ancestral hominids," he replied, "so that we are concerned with the first uncontrollable wildfires, those consuming children, cities and nations through abuse."

"Is that prospect not fanciful?"

Magenta wheeled slowly through masses of dark, mustached Nepalese men in dhotis, wreathed in yellow crocuses, while the delirium of creeds and cults intensified.

"Little thought has been given by governments or Big Pharma to drugs that would obsess whole populations: substances that significantly increase intelligence, or sexuality. Governments are reactive, we invite prescience."

"What abuse scenarios do you project?"

"For military uses of novel cognitive agents, not for interrogation but for aerosols over communities to subdue populations, your own Dr. M_____ at Harvard has proposed international controls."

"Yes, I've spoken with Matt M_____ about the Iraqis' Agent 15, used against the Kurds, perhaps a form of the florid hallucinogen JB-____."

"But few individuals would voluntarily self-administer those. Everyone wants heightened intellect and desire."

"What of the military aspects?"

"The Polish writer Stanisław Lem described an aerosol of Theologine, a hypothetical substance promoting religiosity. Whole villages prayed, prostrated themselves, self-flagellated."

"Somewhat like Pashupanipath."

"Quite so, but magnified, and inducible. Soldiers recoiled from their weapons, like the subjects of the early LSD experiments at Edgewood Arsenal at Fort Detrick, Maryland."

"And of eroticism?"

"The other Lem scenario concerned a theoretical compound that stimulated ardor. Entire neighborhoods engaged in frantic sexuality, mass orgies, indescribable lasciviousness."

"That's highly improbable in reality."

"Not so. We now see the advent of agonists for the melanocortin receptors. They induce lordosis, presentation for copulation, in females across the mammalia from mice to horses, and in microgram range doses. Experimental drugs for female sexual dysfunction pose a threat."

"Threat?"

"Rampant abuse, offshore manufacture, internet sales, chronic overdoses, prostitution, child abuse, date rape, gang rape of the unwitting, the wholesale dissolution of morals. A pharmaceutical wildfire beyond cocaine or methamphetamine."

⬡

WE SUDDENLY WERE SWEPT from the future into the past. The chanting bodies pressed heavily against our windows; it was best to walk. Pashupanipath lay before us in dreamlike array, the colossal temple complex where thousands of Hindus, Tibetans, Muslims and Nepalese swarmed before its spires and idols, anointing themselves and praying, singing, dancing and dying in myriad dialects and religious invocations. Clustered on hillsides for millennia, Pashupanipath was divided by a river cutting deeply between plunging stone stairways.

Far below by the river the dead were swathed in fabrics and herbs, then stacked on burning ghats; the bodies transformed from the incarnate to the ethereal, their crackling flesh, hands and skulls visible in the flames. Bereaved families cried in agonies, wailing wives knelt as spirits were rendered to the skies. I was spellbound at this ritual of death.

"Burning the wives with the bodies was outlawed some years ago," Magenta placidly observed, as we watched the infernal blazes. "The Tibetans prefer a sky burial at 20,000 feet, dismemberment in a charnel house for vultures."

Mixed crowds of Tibetans and Nepalese, Buddhists, Muslims, Hindus and nameless cults of zealots congregated past vendors of religious silks and incense and images. Their frenzied devotions became quiescent as they entered ceremonial halls no less sanctified among the heathen as the light from clerestory windows falling upon the nave in St. Paul's. In one palatial structure from antiquity, entry was forbidden to women and Christians but permitted to Hindus and Sikhs purified through *Puja*, or sacred offerings. They all bore *tilaks*, a finger of white paint pointing upward on their brows to show God-realization. Cautiously, I glimpsed within a portion of a twenty-meter high golden bullock, with oil lamps swaying from the ceiling, and as bearded worshippers in turbans cleansed themselves ceremonially under the gargantuan effigy.

○

AS WE WALKED up a narrow stone stairway two thousand feet to the isolated hilltop temples, we encountered a sturdy Hindu woman in a brown sari, sitting with her eyes closed. She clutched a newborn baby in an unwashed cloth, holding her hand out in the timeless posture of impoverished mothers from Vientiane to Guadalajara. A prominent umbilical cord, blackened with infection, protruded from the baby's abdomen like a snake impaling the Christ child. Agitated, I insisted Magenta instruct her to take the infant immediately to a hospital. He spoke to her in rapid, deferential Hindi.

"She has no money for a physician, but needs 500 rupees, about 20 dollars American."

I gave her a pile of rupees borrowed from Magenta. To much bowing and gestures of *Namaste*, she adjusted her sari and knit bags, then descended the stairs holding her baby carelessly. Flushed and semiconscious, it was too infected to cry.

"Shouldn't we escort her?" I asked, as she disappeared.

"What you see is likely a professional Hindu begging ring, preying on tourists. The baby may not be hers; they are purchased and used only to beg. If she is the mother, and she treats it, then she can't use the baby to feed her other children, like the blind man who refused the gift of sight. We can only hope for the mother's love. If we try taking it, we'll be mobbed."

She was gone into the mass of thousands of worshipers painting white tilaks on their foreheads and purifying themselves with Puja as they recited sutras over candles and milk and coconut shells. I walked on, with a sorrow that time has never extinguished.

○

WE CLIMBED HIGHER, confronting a type of karmic barrier – threatening tribes of wrathful Macaque monkeys – each almost a meter in height, with distressingly human faces and hands, all cachinnating in a din of shrieks and fierce incisors. Some were hanging from tree branches; other howling bipeds rushed at us. They were organized robbers who preyed on intimidated visitors.

"Move slowly and avoid eye contact," Magenta advised.

At the end of the steep, trailing stairway arose the planet of hermits, the retreatants of Pashupanipath who occupied single, small granite temples, each with sutras cut in stone above an open entryway, and just large enough to contain one holy man. These miniature temples dotted the hilltop, leaning precariously, randomly facing different directions. Many of the secluded were silent, standing or sitting in yogic asanas, with long beards wrapped around their heads and dressed in rags or less. There were *Sadhus*, with full facial paint in yellow and white, their hands and feet withdrawn in postures to mimic Vishnu. Their eyes were distant, focused on the dance of Kali on a ground of skulls, or on the eternal embrace of Krishna and Radha. Among these strange recluses, worshippers appeared to bring melons and rice. Fakirs with waist-length braids chanted in clouds of hashish, or sat pointing to lines of Vedic texts with long, wrinkled fingers. They read aloud whenever awake, never stopping, only reciting forever the sutras and names of deities.

○

WE SAT ON A BOULDER carved with religious symbols. No other visitors were present, save a very dark, slender and barefoot woman in a crude purple and grey sari. Her shoulder was exposed, and she wore a silver nose ring. She swept the crude stone paths, engraved with prehistoric markings, with a broom made of twigs. Magenta bowed to her ritually, and learned she had swept here each day since girlhood as a devotional practice. The silence of this primordial scene – hardly changed in a thousand years – was broken only by the scrapping of her ritual cleansing and the distant adorations of the fakirs and *Sadhus*. As we watched, Magenta began to address the future.

"At Pashupanipath, the most ancient of cultures strive for revelation, religious ecstasy, heightened consciousness. At the Kumbh Mela in India, at the confluence of the Ganges, more than ten million aggregate, the largest of the earth's celebrations. Our reptilian brain, overlain with stardust, grasps at logic, altruism, oneness with Glory. Yet, we soon can influence neuronal growth permanently, controlling evolution of the cortex, programming the Connectome. Not simply a transient drug experience. Again, the Godhead is providing the moral equivalent of the first languages and mathematics."

"I assume you mean the advent of nerve growth factors, brain gene therapy, cognitive enhancement?"

"And combined with computerized neurological assessment and training," he said, "to manage the instant access to the cloud's data sphere and communication among billions online. Our brains can evolve over decades, not only through natural selection but en mass biochemically, to cognitively encompass all data from the senses and beyond."

The Nepalese woman passed closely, her grey hair like silver threads woven in long, loose plaits, her dark skin shining with prayer oils and trailing the scent of myrrh. Her head was down as she recited mantras. Her bare, thickly calloused feet were white with dust as she gripped her twigs, sliding her feet carefully, the edges of her sari shredded from wear. She was mindful of her profound responsibility for the history of the world.

The dedicated purity of her intent seemed little different than the practices of the biochemists Magenta described, who each day sought medicines to revivicate senescent neurons, as they slowly adjusted instruments and recited the divine names of nucleotides. The sweeping devotee also reflected the Six, who bore ignominy to transmit the prisms of mind. We all awaited in reverence, in our different ways, the new comprehension.

"We are among the very first to experiment with novel compounds, to warn of any problems. Canaries in the pharmaceutical coal mine." He grinned broadly.

"Tell me of the self-administrations," I urged.

"We found the human toxicities quite early for first-generation cognitive enhancers: Desmopressin for short-term memory, the Russian's Phenylpiracetam, Galactamine to inhibit breakdown of acetylcholine, and Selegiline to increase dopamine through MAO-B inhibition. And for elders, one of Albert's ergoloids: Hydergine, based on lysergic acid. Very helpful in forestalling dementia and preventing sundowning, or loss of acuity in the evenings."

I deterred him from excursions into pharmacology, preferring to explore the social outcomes of new substances. "All of those have been used for a decade or more."

"Yes, but our extended family, so to speak, explored their human limits even before animal studies were complete. For the past few days, I've been exposed to various rare ampakines from researchers in Göttingen and Tübingen, which reduce cognitive deficits significantly. They markedly increase learning. Last evening, from a single reading, I absorbed a lengthy passage of Virgil that still is retained in the drug's absence."

With that, as the woman swept in time with his pacing and dramatic emphases, he repeated for over an hour the whole of Virgil's mysterious eclogues, even the fourth, one of the long poetic pastorals. As his voice rose in the perfect cadence of sheppards' utterances on a vanished hillside in antiquity, Magenta continued flawlessly, hypnotically, as one of the first humans to acquire such a novel capacity. He was possessed of a certain humility and awe, as it should be, in this demonstration of a gift.

His recitation ceased. There remained only the murmuring of worshippers chanting sutras – the essence of all information that ever was or ever will be. We heard from the hermitages a single saddhu who in his devotional chants never ceased repeating the million names of God. He did so from natural memory, but at the cost of extreme dysfunction and social isolation. It seemed caution was needed.

"But can these compounds be abused?"

"We feel that intelligence and memory without heart may be insect-like," he said, "dehumanizing, threatening to our species. Such drugs would confer selective advantages to the users, even nations. Economics, banking, science would be reformed even while personalities would shift in unanticipated ways. The militaries pose a central concern. More efficient killing machines with passions yet unknown."

"Perhaps forgetting can be a blessing. And intelligence not a survival factor."

"Certainly not if intelligence leads to a doomsday nuclear exchange. Our fear is that of Milton in *Paradise Lost*: the world began with eating from the Tree of Knowledge, and history will end when we eat from it again."

We stood and stretched, doing yogic asanas until our beings once again became light. As we began to leave, Magenta approached the sweeping woman and bowed in *Namaste*. She smiled to reveal a silver tooth. With a long, brown finger she tenderly touched the precise center of his forehead.

FROM THE DEVOTIONAL CYCLONE of Pashupanipath, Magenta led me for kilometers along muddy paths to a series of caves outside Kathmandu, all carved into a cliff face before the Buddha's time. Here, in the legends of the villagers, was where the Hindu seer Padmasambhava, practicing tantric union with his consort Sakyadevi, was said to have attained full enlightenment. We meditated and left alms, then returned through ever more elaborate and ruined temple complexes, crumbling and overgrown with thick roots. The pillars were of deities in erotic poses.

"In contrast to Big Pharma's frightful toying with erotogenics," I asked, "how do Tibetans and Nepalese view passion?"

Magenta was climbing through vines laden with lavish clusters of red peppers, concealing carved images of *Yab Yum*, or tantric sexual embraces of female consorts with many-armed beings who trampled on skulls. He arrived at an opening, through which the way ahead finally was clear for us. The afternoon sun through the passages was framed in luscious honeysuckle and wreaths of maiden's blush, their broad white flowers with pink centers.

"They await the siren call of the mischievous *dakinis*, the female spirits. The Tibetans practice polyandry and polygamy in the villages, but most are promiscuous. They see sexual drive as a spiritual longing arising from separateness, from endless duality, and know it can become compulsive, grasping and incomplete. When fully realized through holy union and tantric practices, the separateness disappears, transforming into compassion."

"And world distribution of erotogenic agents would become compulsive?"

"The longing would drive users mad."

"Would Vermilion not utilize them?"

"Vermilion's practices release Eros naturally; substances are used very rarely. With erotogenics, we fear the summoning of monsters from the Id."

Resting upon his staff, Magenta pointed to the crest of the Karakorum Range of the Himalayas.

"Beyond those peaks are the most remote parts of the earth, the trackless jungles of Shekalungpa near Tsampo Gorge, and Skelar-La, the pass into the Valley of the White Crystal. There are barriers of leech fields, which can consume staked packhorses. The women beyond the barrier, some say, capture trekkers and through constant tantra achieve God consciousness."

Our day had been overwhelming, for we had walked down dusy paths with little water and no food; we were forced to stop and rest. The local villagers received us with guarded looks, though, presenting conditions not encountered by most Westerners. Rude huts and itinerant vendors dotted a hillside. The stench from piles of refuse and burning plastic gathered in the haze from smoking fires. An oily, foul river flowed, almost stagnant. Half-naked ghosts of children toiled in gravel pits. In the reeking squalor, some wandered like tiny derelicts.

"There is a Pharisaic want of charity in this community," Magenta remarked.

He beckoned me to a crude table beneath desiccated palm fronds supported by bamboo sticks. We asked for food from a half-blind street merchant in a shredded loincloth. He had only a bowl of sticky rice and a sliced papaya. At this humble offering, we – without warning – were changed forever.

⬡

WE SAW ACROSS THE ALLEY a small, very dark and ragged Nepalese girl with bare feet, wearing only a dirty flour sack with holes for arms, and carrying a toy pail of gravel. She was being verbally abused by a thin, evil-looking Hindu vendor. Her hair was matted with excrement; a trickle of blood trailed down her leg. As he shouted, she trembled visibly, her small, fearful voice barely heard. Magenta, with his powerful arms, tensed. The vendor struck the girl across the face, sending her sprawling almost naked, her pail spilling as she clutched in one hand a wad of Chiclets.

Magenta and I lept forward, but the vendor disappeared into his hut of tin sheets and cardboard. He left his wares attended by an adolescent son, who displayed a sardonic smile and a *kuari*, a curved machete-like knife for chopping wood and slaughtering animals. We first approached the girl, where Magenta comforted her in Nepali.

"Is that your father?"

"No, Baba, I was give away. He hurt me sometimes."

She lifted her flour sack over her face for our examination. She stood there with her grubby hands held high, clutching the soiled sack and shaking, revealing her nakedness. Our hearts shattered.

"How old are you? What's your name?"

Dropping her sack, she spread uncertainly a few fingers. Her name was "You, girl."

I remained with her while Magenta, blanching with fury, stormed to the vendor's hut. After a violently heated exchange, the boy fled into the shelter. Returning, Magenta discovered from the girl that she was sold as a toddler into domestic servitude to a poor family, on most nights beaten and raped, then fled with her sisters. The vendor and his son molested her in exchange for scraps of tripe and spoiled candy. She was shivering, fearful of our intentions.

Magenta purchased a mango lassie from a vendor of fruits and ices and provided it to the girl. Her eyes widened with disbelief. She devoured the sweet drink in one pass, wiping a blemished arm across her swollen mouth. Spying a cart of used shoes, Magenta bought some pink plastic sandals that seemed to fit, while I located one Hello Kitty sock and one blue diamond argyle of a different size. We placed them on the girl's dirty feet and showed her how to wear the sandals. She smiled broadly with her few blackened milk teeth, then started to cry and shake terribly, lifting her flour sack again over her head to offer herself for the shoes. Her pudenda were bruised; her nipples were scratched and infected. She had cigarette burns.

"No, little one, you don't have to do that anymore," Magenta gently told her, as she stood with the sack above her head in her grimy fingers and covering the anguish of her face.

After some moments she released her flour sack and stared at the pink plastic sandals. A group of Nepalese elementary students approached, the boys in white uniforms and the girls in matching saris, with their chaperones. Some of the boys snickered loudly, ridiculing the girl in her sack. She darkened with shame. Her bowels released to flood diarrhea from the rich, strange mango lassie upon her Hello Kitty sock. She collapsed in her watery feces and sobbed helplessly. We gathered her up and stood her naked in a public fountain as Hindu wives, witnessing her bruises, shook their brooms at us in anger. As we went to clean her, she cried.

"Don't hurt me, Baba!"

Inconsolable, she clung to us in fright as we hiked to the Land Rover, then cowered in the back seat, while Magenta called upon every orphanage in Kathmandu unsuccessfully. We carried the girl to a one room open-air storefront beneath a handwritten sign scrawled with "A.M. Ramachandran Clinic" in English and Nepali, where a Hindu physician wearing a smudged white labcoat sat facing the crowds. He was blunt.

"These child, Sahib, have many healed fractures, facial and severe sexual trauma, and intestine…parasites. With nobody care, kind sir, she die soon."

Rummaging among donated boxes and waggling his head, he gave us antibiotics and medications for worms. A Seva volunteer quickly located a poor, elderly and lonely Tibetan couple whose children and grandchildren had fallen to their deaths in a bus accident near the remote high passes of Mustang.

We took our captive to their simple dwelling, with its pounded earthen floors, by a fresh stream and a banyan tree.

The white-haired elder and his wife, squatting by their cooking fire in tribal dress, stood and walked slowly to us, clearly intuiting the reason why two white Westerners had appeared with an abused and frightened young child. The grandmother brought barley soup, and coaxed the girl from the Land Rover. After several small bowls were consumed, she wet a ragged cloth in the stream and washed the girl, wrapping her in a lost granddaughter's thin worn sari.

Magenta provided rupees and the Seva volunteer's name, saying he would visit regularly. After some hours, as the grandmother sang by the fire a lullaby that once comforted her dead grandchildren, the girl, now with thumb in mouth, turned silently to hide in the priceless warmth of the old one's shabby robe. They embraced each other, rocking and whispering, the firelight reflected in the streaming of their tears.

We left the rustic shelter with its few pots, its herbs and cooking fire, and the bottomless eyes of our little lost soul, our mother goddess of the world. For some hours thereafter in the Land Rover, as tin-roofed slums transformed into the grounds surrounding the King's palace, we said absolutely nothing.

◯

THE WEEKS PASSED until my departure date, with conversation until dawn on the final night. As the sky lightened, Magenta was seated on a venerable Tabriz rug, holding a Tibetan bell in one hand and a vajra in the other, paired symbols of wisdom and heart. Behind him in this rude hut of an absent *Rinpoche*, or teacher, was a magnificent Thanka, a Tibetan scroll image; another wall displayed images of Buddhist paradises done in Shingham painting with plant pigments, crushed gems, and ashes of cremated bone. A mattress of straw occupied one corner, a small cooking fire the other. Nearing the end of my encounter with Magenta, we sought the delicious freshness of the early air, and did long, slow sun salutations. As we glimpsed the sunrise, he reached a conclusion on what must be done. It was a refrain to a very old hymn.

"We feel society would best be served, not so much by a pill for intellect or sexuality, but by one for compassion. A medicine for altruism. Perhaps we have one."

Above at first light, the wheel of stars turned in morning's ocean. We stood in contemplation, while before us Kathmandu valley was illuminated to the horizon. Our long drive to Pokhara Airport was subdued. I held the glances of the Nepalese children and elders, both so familiar and otherworldly, as we passed through copses of dark yews and alder, then thorn trees stretched across scorched meadows. Among the muddy trenches were the most fragrant of lilies, and white narcissi.

We entered again the elders' camp. The girl was still in their granddaughter's sari, but it was freshly washed and dried each day by the grandmother, who pounded it on stones in the stream. The girl wore her sandals with her Hello Kitty sock, and had been given the name Abeer, or Fragrance of Flowers. With a stick she proudly made an "A" in the dirt. I reached into my pack and produced from Berlin a little girl's feathered angel wings with a furry white halo, and showed her how to wear them. After she was exhausted from flying around the shelter, I asked Magenta to translate a few words for her.

"If you learn to read and write really well, you will be an angel one day."

The girl smiled shyly, and made another "A." The old couple put the wings and halo high on a shelf by the child's primer we had brought, one they barely could read, so wearing the angel wings would be a reward for her lessons.

At Pokhara Airport, Magenta waved farewell, then decided to join me. I noticed for the first time the forest of short specialized antennae protruding discreetly from his dented, thirty-year-old Rover. There had been no visible electronics in the cab, only malas and bells and incense burners and images of gurus. As the press of travelers surrounded us, and we were herded past Customs, I managed my last important questions.

"And the girl? Will you always see to her?"

"As long as we are able."

"What was the grandmother's song that first night? I know it's impossible, but the melody was haunting."

"They are illiterate and devout Tibetan Buddhists. But during her own childhood she was for a few weeks at a Himalayan mission school made of mud and sticks…before an avalanche destroyed it. Her song was her memory from Tibetan into crude Nepali. In English, it's close to this…"

Before he could finish, the insurmountable press of shouting Nepalese and Hindus and monks waving passports swept me onward to the tarmac. I boarded the Royal Nepal 707, watching for the ritual goat's blood on the nose wheel.

As we entered Indian airspace near Delhi, I declined the gratuity of Perrier and lime. I checked my email, decrypting a message that had been anonymized through thickets of privacy servers from Vanuatu to the Channel Islands. It read only:

"Jesus loves the little children,

all the children of the world.

Brown and yellow, black and white,

they are precious in His sight.

Jesus loves the little children of the world."

Chapter 8.

Von Neumann's Playground

Suddenly unable to bear walls, he wandered the campus at all hours through starlight and rain…
He took to the Bohemian life…talked of Greenwich Village and met Winter muses, unacademic,
cloistered by 42d and Broadway.

- Fitzgerald, *This Side of Paradise*

There was light coming out of his face.
It seemed to me that this was not a man in the ordinary sense,
that the face belonged to another, different species.
And then he smiled at me.

- Hiram Haydn, editor of *The American Scholar*
on encountering Einstein on a Princeton street (1935)

Der Herr Gott ist raffiniert aber Boschaft ist Er nicht.

(Subtle is the Lord, but malicious He is not.)

- Einstein (inscribed over the fireplace at Fine Hall,
Princeton's Mathematics Department)

If one can't be a great artist or a great soldier, the next best thing is to be a great criminal.

- Fitzgerald, ibid, describing *Arsene Lupine*, Act III

Qui custodiet ipsos custodes?

(Who shall guard the guardians?)

PRINCETON IN THE FALL, from the Tudor Gothic towers of the Graduate College to the hallowed sanctum of the Institute for Advanced Study, was indisputably a paradise for a diverse assortment of mathematical prodigies. They ranged from excitable teens just disgorged from Bronx Science and surviving their first term, to the tottering chalk-bound fathers of world-destroying nuclear devices, to highly-bred polymaths with secrecy clearances to decide the earth's future.

I was visiting Princeton's counterpart of HKS, the Woodrow Wilson School of Public Policy. Perusing the stacks at Firestone Library near the chapel-like Dulles Reading Room, I reminisced on entering Princeton at 17 with vague aspirations toward neuroscience, falling away undisciplined at 18 into the revolution of the time, and the long, tortuous road back to Harvard. From the comfort of Firestone in the bitter winter of my youth, we could glimpse future Nobelist John Nash hiding behind a tree. Caught between schizophrenic worlds of aliens and game theory insights, he hid for hours in the gentle snowfall, always whistling Bach's "Little" Fugue, and peeking at students while wearing his green tennis shoes. There were the couches at Firestone where, in his cogent times, Nash held forth with groups of enamored grad students amazed at his astral, steely intellect.

At a study carrel, poring over a volume of Suetonius, a young woman student seemed to observe my fond memories – the recollections she might one day have of her precious time here. The perfection of her waist-length auburn hair was sunlit with rays that filtered through leaded, stained glass windows inlaid with Princeton's standard and Latin inscriptions. The long mote-laden beams graced her like infinitesimal crystals of thought. She glanced at what appeared to be a dean, who had drawn alongside me in a courtly way, then returned to her readings on the emperors' dissolute retreats and savage licentiousness.

HE HAD A MILITARY DEPORTMENT, and an erect, finely muscular bearing, but wore an Ivy Club tie as an elder alum from the undergraduate dining societies. With a sport coat and jeans indistinguishable from any Princeton student, he had a tight crew-cut prematurely going to white. His eyes were aerial grey. He had little propensity for small talk, but projected the type of diplomatic ease that permeates embassies and high-level agencies, with the same solid awareness that – anywhere at anytime – nothing was ever as it seemed.

"It must be decades since you were here last," he finally remarked.

His knowing abruptness was unsettling. He was unlikely to be a former student who in his ripened years remembered my transient days. As he continued, the polished marble floors of Firestone began turning beneath me, for in a low voice he began to sing in perfect Tibetan the chant of the young, smiling monks encircling Bodhinath, "*Ka zher, lam khyer…*" To onlookers we appeared as colleagues in Buddhist and Asian Studies, one somewhat startled.

⬡

AT SEEING ME beginning to reel then recover, the student faltered at her Suetonius. Collecting her edition of *The Twelve Caesars*, she rose and passed by us – quite intent and without the slightest recognition. Stately and reserved, she wore a small scarf of silk chiffon in McLeod of Lewis tartan.

Seemingly a confirmed academic, but with a riveting syncopation, she floated toward the darkness of old Witherspoon Hall and its stonework remembrances, past Tudor spires and beds of hollyhock and forget-me-nots, toward the Graduate College pond and its weeping willows.

Spellbound, and wholly surprised by their fine tradecraft, I was led out of Firestone into the sunshine by Cobalt himself, one of the Six. We both knew the Princeton campus well, and said little as we considered the charms of the student, her sublime visage growing smaller along the promenades resplendent with dogwood trees. The lawns before her were beset with young men distracted by the theories of the late cyberneticist Warren McCulloch. Many wished for the resurrection of McColluch, with his prophet's stern and holy eyes burning above a long white beard and black leather jacket, as he motorcycled to and from Columbia or Greenwich Village to Princeton each day, arriving to the enchantment of grad students who were powerful with integrals but still awkward with the topology of the feminine.

Attempting to be cavalier at their masterful surveillance, I referred in an offhand manner to the student whose progress we followed.

"She would be worthy of Vermilion."

"You're becoming more observant," Cobalt coolly replied, neither confirming nor denying my admiring intuition about a young classicist with such presence. Although growing more comfortable with Cobalt, I privately braced myself for the inevitable contact high. It had not occurred yet, the proximity of others seemed to delay it.

⬡

WE FOLLOWED HER down Nassau Street, then turned left on Mercer to stand in veneration at Einstein's very modest 200-year-old white clapboard house with its unkempt lawn. We saw the open screened window into his upstairs study where he played violin among his stacks of notations on dimensions of mind, leaving only to amble in his old clothes and pork-pie hat to the Institute for Advanced Study, or to the lake to pilot his small sailboat. We admired the humility of the author of the transformative paper *Auf die Ausbreitung des Lichts*, On the Propagation of Light.

"Although Bohr thought Princeton 'the mathematical center of the universe,'" he remarked, 'Einstein considered it a 'quaint ceremonious village.'"

Nearby, around the corner on Library Place, was the former lair of the charming polymath Johnny von Neumann, the toast of the nascent military-industrial complex. Cobalt reminisced on von Neumann.

"He wore tailored suits, hosted week-long parties with canapés and drinks, and held forth in six languages on every topic in physics. Students considered him the 'Great Man,' but most privately thought he was an extraterrestrial who imitated a human perfectly."

"Who attended?"

"His government subsidies stocked von Neumann's playground with fast cars and a stream of doctoral candidates. He acquired fond collections of creative scholars, men and women who were not attracted to wealth or beauty, but to the power of thought."

ARRIVING AT THE MEDIEVAL, ecclesiastical setting of the Graduate College, we circulated among the last students who affected black academic gowns. As we took afternoon tea from the heavy silver service hosted by white-coated undergraduates, game theorists were locked in battle over Go boards, or played Kriegspiel in mock Prussian landscapes. Another duo was blindfolded, the opponents back to back and calling chess moves to the referee who oversaw the board.

Jousting conversations on mathematical arcana abounded, with friendly one-upmanship or cutting *ripostes*, for sniping on colleagues' relative abilities was habitual among those who were competitive thinkers, and who thereby culled the less than confident or plodding. Sipping tea from an eggshell china cup, but ignoring the cakes, all while engaging an intense cluster of number theorists, topologists and algebraic geometers, was our reader of Suetonius. I moved closer to her.

A rare classicist in this most esoteric of worlds, her presence among calculating wizards who spoke only variables was a prime example of improbability. She appeared to be a European undergraduate – hardly concerned with the men's halting advances – although fiercely attentive to the formulae espoused by even the most reticent of them. Extra dimensions of space, exoplanetary atmospherics – she followed precisely the most difficult concepts.

She sat and stroked with careless provocation the lush dark hair of an attractive young assistant professor in cosmology and theoretical physics, a thin and supple woman wearing round spectacles and a twinset, and who had small, pointed breasts. She attended with devotion both the cosmologist's growing tumescence and her discourse on the Unified Field Theory, then purred to her – not about the Caesars – but about supersymmetry and Langland's conjecture. Her mathematical knowledge was not that of some dazzled amateur, but of one with an agenda.

"You know of course," she murmured, her hand discretely on the cosmologist's lap and gazing into her eyes, "that André Weil here, when he was in prison in France during the Occupation, said that mathematical insights come from the mind of Vishnu, dispersing into different avatars, abstract structures, and that past the barriers of comprehension they somehow find each other and embrace, as if they were 'illicit liaisons.'"

The cosmologist became lightly heated, drinking her in but not moving, and trying to remain prim.

Our classicist persisted in her throaty *mysterioso* vein, "Weil wrote to his sister, 'Nothing gives more pleasure…to the *connoisseur*.'"

She was speaking in an indefinable European dialect – the emigré language from visiting faculty of many nations – known at Princeton as "Fine Hall English." Facing away now, I still could hear her mesmerizing overtures.

"And Frenkel at Berkeley, the Russian polymath, did a Noh play on a mathematician who found the *formula of love*, and hid it from the evil ones by tattooing it with bamboo on the body of her lover."

Recalling the earlier penetration at Princeton by V-2, I neglected to suggest to Cobalt that the girl was a perfect Vermilion operative. The multifarious societies of the Six now were so permuted as to defy characterization. In these delicate surroundings, it was best not to be too observant.

Cobalt, noticing me intent on the girl's tender crafts, proposed a diversion and some privacy by Princeton's Lake Carnegie. As we prepared to leave the Graduate College, she quickly glanced our way, then reddened, perceiving my sense of her. One's awareness of the Sapphic arts was forever heightened, after the sensuous liturgies of the exquisite Berlin night.

⬡

WE STROLLED past matching Whig and Clio Halls at the main campus, their Ionian columns and squat white marble Grecian domes concealing the Whig-Cliosophic Society, the debating forum. An old blue Whig-Cliosophic pass card remained my sole memoratum from Princeton days. We ambled underneath Holden's spires and towers, past my dormitory Patton Hall – with its greystone Gothic doorways and high battlements – and then along the placid slopes rolling down through prodigious oaks to the far playing fields.

On their cultivated lawns, the women's lacrosse teams struggled with civilized ferocity, their strong, fair legs urgent, their determined, clear countenances bright with vigor and capability and good fortune. I imagined Hagendas here in her undergrad days, the much-desired mistress of her flock. An elderly alumnus, in white ducks and a straw boater with orange headband, was seated on a shady bench and cherishing the sight. He turned in his wrinkled hands the pages of the *Daily Princetonian*. In our afternoon's mysterious idyll, the earth still remained firm, our exchanges simple, and the unexpected remote.

◯

AS WE RECLINED by the lakeside, the lightweight crews in the distance pulled in tandem on narrow wooden rowing sculls, sending rippling wavelets in slow, glassy sheets to the serenity of our moss-laden bank. A single heron spread its white finery, moving dreamlike through the transparent ocean above.

There had been no contact high, as with Crimson at a fireside reflected in fractal seas; with Indigo and an alpine sheppardess; in a secure manor with Vermilion; at a religious shrine with Magenta. After all, we were on the Princeton campus, very much among a conservative public, where the slightest errant behavior would summon security. Yet Cobalt began to whisper – in accelerating terms as he approached the light speed transmission of the Six – fragments of the past and future at the edges of one's grasp. During his soliloquy the campus itself began to loom and bend in gravity's curvature, and then dimple at the circumference as the visual field itself gradually started to unravel.

He described the initial detonation in 1967 in San Francisco when large populations first encountered LSD, the "million-hit drop" of Owsley and the "ten-million-hit drop" of Nick Sand and Tim Scully, their tablets of Orange Sunshine requiring synthesis of a kilogram. He spoke of illuminating youth globally, of dancing in the streets, the first large gatherings, impromptu love-ins and music celebrations, the transformation of art and music and science from their static flatlands, the dissolution and recreation of moralities and ethics, the refutation of war and materialism. He spoke of those first experienced, who learned to recognize each other by a word or gesture, an almost telepathic understanding.

He told of the legacies, the graduates of long-ago mystic nights, and how they infiltrated even federal intelligence agencies. He revealed the maturities of those youth transformed, their migration into law, medicine, politics, computer engineering, and spoke of how their devastating realizations by communal campfires still were remembered in private encounters. He alluded to the breeding of a secret society, to inherit without notice parts of our corrupted, glorious civilizations.

THE RIPPLES at the edge of vision became undone into trigonometric functions, sine waves crashing across the tranquil arbors and mirrored surfaces of the lake. Staccato rainbow lasers of secret information criss-crossed from Whig and Clio and the Mathematics Department at Fine Hall and the Institute of Advanced Study to NSA bunkers at Fort Meade, Georgia, Texas and Utah; to the applied physics labs of MIT and Caltech; to the campuses of Microsoft and Google. Their harvests of lonely, turned-on youth, now with PhDs in machine language, stripped everyone naked and drew them ever closer. In a world where governments still harbored the conceit they could keep secrets, our many watchers within every facility laughed.

The sky was churning heavenward, crystallizing in atomic lattices above us, as secure encoded communications laced the atmosphere from Cambridge to Princeton, to New Haven and Washington, D.C., to Austin and Madison and Los Alamos and Berkeley and Stanford. The great mind of optical fibers hustled revelations, and old children once more recalled the trumpeting heralds of evolution, and stood up to dance again by new fires.

Cobalt's image suddenly wavered like a broken transmission against the backdrop of the lake. A series of billowing immeasurable translucent domes instantly devoured all of life's fragility, a monstrous explosion shining with the face of Vishnu, the destroyer of worlds. Its blinding majestic evil pulsated with the images of newborns at mothers' breasts, then broiled, charred and vaporized at Hiroshima. The poisonous concentric domes seized the far horizons and ionospheres, throbbing like strobe lights with unearthly hues of red, white and blue, then gold and silver. The limitless power of this vile behemoth reached across the skies. Jeweled with the irresistible enticements of death, it was – incarnate – Satan's crown.

In the end, there was only a soundless purity, a gossamer feather lifting into nothingness. The weeping willows by the lake breathed quietly in their peaceful perfection; the lightest of rain had begun to fall intermittently, stopping as the warmth of the afternoon sun fell upon us.

Cobalt lay upon the verdant bank, contemplating two swans moving *à deux* across the lake. He made some reference to the Upanishads, but I could not recover so quickly. To fill the void as I reaggregated, he offered a little joke, recalling in a Boston drawl Harvard professor Kenneth Bainbridge's remark to

Oppenheimer, as both shielded their eyes from the Trinity blast and the bones of their hands were etched in light.

"Now we're all sons of bitches."

Cobalt smiled, then lay back and considered the Jacob's Ladder shining down, and the walking rain from the brightening cumulonimbi above us. Scarlet and gold tulips appeared like wood sprites, while a froth of bluebonnets spread luxuriously before my ancient eyes. The tranquility of the pale sky was disturbed only by the lazy flight of rooks and the cavorting of swallows. For a long time, we felt the cool earth beneath us, motionless, nurturing, silent.

⬡

RELAXING, he spoke to the clouds as I listened, his voice indistinguishable from my thoughts. He never again referred to the phenomena, as though nothing had happened. I could not forget so easily. He was unusually open, just for a moment, as was I. He preferred to speak simply – of anything – except that which we had beheld. He discussed the comparatively mundane for a while: the mechanics of spydom.

"My focus after synthesis is to monitor governments, those agencies and officials bearing upon our survival. I visit the Hill routinely under various pretexts, a convivial cipher for the most part, but sometimes with a *provocateuse*. We enter streams of embassy receptions or exclusive private dinners with political donors. I play pick-up games of softball at sandlots from Tyson's Corner to Arlington. We even can access green cards as defense contractor staff."

"Secrecy clearances?"

"We appear almost anywhere we wish. Interpol and UN meetings, DOJ official presentations; all the realms of D.C. players, from NSA conventions to DOD spectacles. The membrane between academia and government, corporate and intelligence, remains transparent to our methods."

"What methods exactly?"

"Vermilion disclosed the sensuous interface. And there are old academic relationships transcending duller government appointments. Friendship is porous. And we mustn't forget the graduates of the campfires. There are over one million people with Top Secret and Sensitive Compartmentalized Information – TS/SCI – clearances."

"The 'Twin Tickets'?"

"Precisely. One of every three hundred citizens is permitted information the rest aren't allowed. Most people don't understand or care, but we are an active domestic counterintelligence group. Not deleterious. Just checking."

"How far in are you?"

"Look, long ago one of our artists even designed the giant tulips and daises that adorn the subterranean tunnels of Crystal City, the green and blue card government contractor orgy across from the Pentagon. The building with nameless offices, and SCI card scanners on each door. We even have the floor plans, and total access."

"Only Crystal City?"

"No, no. Wherever we think there is data critical to our agenda. We run rampant through state and local, and socialize with the intel aggregators: Raytheon, L-3, SAIC – anywhere there are PhDs for whom reality is a fluid dynamic, not black or white but herringbone. I shouldn't go on…even with amusing anecdotes. It can be said that, after the warlocks at the intel agencies, we toy with DEA at conferences."

His image had reappeared and was steady, his voice echoing slightly, still finding a human chord, but warm. His reluctant disclosures seemed only a thin thread of a much grander conspiracy that was inaccessible to linear thinking. It was amorphous and inspired and based on the joyful, reverent convictions of those who were, physically at least, just like us.

"The initiates," he continued, "are now third and fourth generations. They are ultimately unstoppable, unrecordable by hostile analysts. They are lifelong sleeper agents. We watch the watchers."

Realizing his confidences, he pulled down the shade of consciousness, and said no more. I chose not to ask about secrets, for now.

◯

AS THE PSYCHIC AURORAE began to fade, we migrated northward like refugees from a war zone of cognition. The sculptured pediments of the Mathematics Department at Fine Hall soon manifested, announcing the algebraical labyrinths within. Drifting past the stained glass windows embedded with equations, we stood before the massive fireplace, carved with a fly contemplating a Moebius strip. Leaving Fine, we knelt and laid hands on the cornerstone like shamans; it contained a lead box with early Princeton mathematical papers, two pencils, one eraser and a piece of chalk, everything necessary to change the world's paradigms. We retired with fatigued delight to a small stone bench by a Picasso sculpture and reflecting pool. To students who passed, we must have appeared only as two scholars with open child-like faces, overwhelmed at some theory and analyzing the fabric of space-time.

Although the soundings of the carillon's bells still split the firmament, we reintegrated somewhat as last, watching with avuncular pleasure as masses of lanky undergrads walked before us. Already burdened with the duties conferred by privilege, some still had roses in their cheeks. They attended each other in oscillating groups like larks skyward; they were freewheeling and electrical in their thought and speech. Some gesticulated magisterially as they happily engaged in unrestrained expositions; others entertained similarly elated companions from the Princeton feeder schools of Groton, St. Paul's, Hotchkiss, Lawrenceville, and the Old South. As we listened, the phenomena ebbed and flowed. Their fingertips trailed light, as though they were magicians painting the sky.

We somehow managed to stand and ramble back to Nassau Hall, the nation's Capitol in 1783, captured from the British at the decisive Battle of Princeton by Washington's Revolutionary forces. We exited campus through Princeton's tall black iron gates, the barrier between town and gown that faced Nassau Street and the Nassau Inn. We took tea at a shop called the Alchemist and Barrister, aptly named for this voyage among the Six. Over a light repast of sliced fruits and cheeses, Cobalt considered enlightenment's inroads among the halls of power.

"There were numerous Damascene conversions, some remember, among youths who in adulthood became heads of state. Their doors may remain open to old passwords and shared hearts."

As he described a benign conspiracy of love and wonder, I was still reactive to the blossoming of imagery by the lake. The recurring memory was tempered only by that of the boathouse and playing fields, the highly bred lacrosse players like forest nymphs, and a fine, elderly man in a boater. Still restless, and torn between normalcy and the disturbing profundities of our afternoon, I suggested we find solace within the expansive grounds of the Institute for Advanced Study. It was a revered retreat, the monastic setting where Einstein and Oppenheimer and Gödel and von Neumann had been cloistered in a form of prayer, offering their glorias of physics and mathematics against the malevolence of mutually assured destruction. Both of us were refreshed from our cool drinks and ambrosia, and he agreed. We departed toward that holy ground.

⬡

COBALT WAS SINGULAR among the Six, darting among topics with a scientific glee; the range of his thought was exhilarating. Grand unified theories, the Randall-Sundrum model, hot Jupiter planets, interstellar probe-class instruments. He had access to old hidden spaces on campus, the Princeton Plasma Physics Stellarator, and the Tokamak fusion device. He moved across languages and technologies with ease.

"Our dear Tokamak," he said with a certain reverence, "old Soviet slang for *Toroidalnaya kamera s aksialnym magnitnym polem*, meaning 'toroidal chamber with an axial magnetic field.' Perhaps, for unlimited energy, we can capture a star."

His Russian was flawless, like Vermilion's. I wondered at the capacities and training of the Six, whose allegiances seemed less to any nation than to the planet. As I marveled at the elaborate physics, he embarked on a discussion of the Six and their superuser status at Mare Nostrum, the Barcelona supercomputer array in a pristine glass box in the nave of a 19th Century chapel.

Cobalt proved to be a mandarin-at-large, moving freely among the trading tables of the world's marketplaces in national security and intelligence. I discovered that he held, quite remarkably, Sophoclean secrets on governments' assessment of catastrophic extinction events. He could in his calm manner address near-earth asteroids and their collision paths. As we walked through the lawns of the Institute – hesitating now and then like a thoughtful cortège – he admitted such collateral intelligence was obtained by the Six, then launched into a litany of destruction for which I was wholly unprepared.

"Our prime directive is to anticipate and influence conscious evolution through chemistry and biotech. But through our access to national laboratories and agencies and embassies, we also learn of classified probabilities."

"Classified probabilities?"

"Outcomes inaccessible to the public. To prevent hysteria. Top-secret, secret or classified information. We hear of the likelihoods of coral reefs dying in acidic seas, watersheds evaporating in implacable hothouses, the specter of great terrestrial pandemics and die-offs of the species *Homo sapiens sapiens* from its own squalor and greed. We hear of the killings and mass rapes and starvation from disrupted food supplies, the rendering of man's remnants to mute creatures on footpaths to nowhere. We learn of the inversion of earth's magnetic fields, the ghastly descent of nuclear winter, the silent ice ages. We learn of epochal tornados sucking frightened life from its holes, pulverizing all human history. The time when we are all but dead leaves, moving across barren soils and into lifeless oceans."

I hardly could respond. "Certainly that's all…so extreme."

"The top-secret coteries of federal intelligence agencies, and the executive and legislative – all limited to less that fifty fully-briefed individuals – constantly assess the next hundred years. A few of the projected outcomes are very poor indeed."

"And futures are predicted to what dates?"

"With lessening confidence, through the long aftermath of nuclear exchanges or other catastrophes to the end of primates, to the eon where mutated survivors sketch crudely on subterranean walls the new religions, the chase of the remaining quadrupeds, the ancestral memories of beings with handheld communications devices and celestial halos."

At the latter, he smiled grimly. Across the fairway, two groundskeepers clipped tidy hedges while several young physicists, relaxing from hours of scribbling equations at Princeton's National Spherical Fusion Experiment, spread a quick supper on the tended lawns. They discussed atmospheric carbon, and the average global temperature increasing one degree centigrade.

"You speak of the end of civilization, of our species."

"Species evolve or become extinct, not static. In our very small way, we hope to illumine some of the future decision makers, by late adolescence or later."

⬡

NOT WANTING TO INDUCE ANXIETY in my vulnerable state, he distracted me from these horrors by speaking only of more pleasant memories. By then we had approached the bustling street of

Princeton's eating clubs, passing the houses where each undergraduate set was invited to dine together. The afternoon being challenging, I was grateful for the interlude.

The Quadrangle Club appeared, which attracted literary types, while adjacent was Cap and Gown, for the political and religious. The Ivy Club, like Harvard's Porcellian or Yale's Skull and Bones, was exclusive even of the meritocracy. Beyond these was the Cottage Club, the venue for adventurers, while the Tiger Club for athletes completed the row of large, old houses. Cobalt related anecdotes about the Triangle Club for dramatists and artists, which held an annual comedic musical review since the 20s. Traveling internationally in competition with the Yale Glee Club, and finally to Nassau in the Bahamas, its reluctant thespians returned to confront the severities of New Jersey winters and Princeton finals.

Cobalt, reflecting on the eating clubs, Princeton's substitute for banned fraternities, advised in his circuitous, formalistic way on the need for ferocious study by undergraduates.

"The frantic Reading Period even now quickly flushes out any leisurely dilettantes who, with a paucity of focus and effort, may mistake the university's privileges as some open license for indulgence."

"That's rather elevated. Can you rephrase it?"

"Don't miss class, *ever*."

○

COBALT'S OBSERVATION not being far from my own lack of rigor as a youth, I began to reminisce. It seemed almost yesterday when I, as a scholarship student at 17, and other classmen at then all-male Princeton, boarded buses on the occasional Saturday night for the rites of passage. We attended with growing trepidation, concealed by jackets, ties and cologne, the nervous mixers hosted by the flowers of society at the Seven Sisters: Bryn Mawr, Mt. Holyoke, Barnard, Radcliffe, Wellesley, Smith and Vassar.

While I dreamed of gilded days and nights, Cobalt still privately reflected on probabilities of catastrophes. After some time, he proposed that one likely scenario would be a drug epidemic to dwarf the great killers of alcohol and nicotine.

"Stravinsky composed an opera about the rebirth of the world after atomic cataclysm," he mused, "but it was aborted after the librettist, poet Dylan Thomas, died from alcohol poisoning at the Chelsea Hotel."

"You are concerned about a silent catastrophe?"

"We anticipate cataclysms that are not nuclear, but molecular. Magenta worries about erotogenic wildfires. Or abuse of learning and memory drugs, intelligence without the reins of compassion."

I seized on his consideration of drug epidemics to return to research on the Six. Cobalt knew of my progress among his peers, and their vetting of me. I tried a sensitive topic.

"May you speak of Ivy Mike?"

"Crimson's design. The first counterintelligence operation against DEA – or any federal agency – by a non-governmental organization. Criminal cocaine cartels later adopted the tactic, and walk-ins to agencies became suspect."

"Indigo mentioned only a remnant of Ivy Mike remains – monitoring trials and identifying actual informants and agents. Is there some version with senior officials?"

"Senior officials' identities are a matter of record. Their public appearances have a certain vulnerability. Every individual is human, no matter their vocation, and we begin with subtle overtures to that humanity. No official is overtly compromised; rather, we will develop a relationship over months or years, just to ask a single question."

"But where is the line in the sand, at that level?"

"It's an international sandbox. Who goes home with which toys is the game that is played. Would you, for example, disclose the location of a violent cocaine cartel leader, for a warning that would protect the psychedelic community?"

"Some would do that for nothing."

"Information is the trading post currency, as has been the timeless intelligence craft. But we prefer no direct contact with the friendly opposition, so neither law enforcement or underground sources are compromised. It's far less brutal just to invite leaks at convenient moments, and the pillows are so much softer."

I was mired in Cobalt's deft ambiguities, but thought it wise not to press. Although Princeton, like Harvard, was a type of intellectual and social reservation where the indigenous tribes openly shared data, my research now concerned those who acted very much off the reservation. I continued to corroborate his colleagues' accounts of themselves.

"Can you describe the others, their lifestyles?"

"Crimson lives very simply, as we all do, without personal possessions other than a few electronic devices and a suit. Indigo has only his great books and some 19th Century editions of ancient literature. Vermilion and his consorts only their clothes and disguises. Magenta essentially his trekking equipment and an old Land Rover.

"But they can't do syntheses and this vast range of counterintelligence as well."

"Just so. And it would be unwise to try, for we are quite delicate when we return. Rather, we remain isolated, introverted for the most part, within a very small circle. Operations are conducted primarily by trusted initiates at one or two degrees of separation. Some bathe in societies, with thousands of contacts, entering diverse worlds easily, filtering back the details we seek."

"But the Six are so remote from the real world of people and families and those simply working to survive."

"Not at all. We have found noble action is not elitist or affluent, but conferred by the democratic vision; our duty is to everyone. Ultimately, our effort is for the smallest of things, for the children."

"But we're behind the gates of Princeton," I returned crossly, "discussing embassies and governments and high-level intrusions into privileged realms."

"We each have our way of remaining grounded. Let me show you, if I may, how to remember what is most important."

○

HE GUIDED ME off campus to a bus stop on Nassau Street; we stood as a gaggle of students passed by, one holding forth on Boccaccio, another on Rabelais. The bus finally arrived, grinding to a noxious halt. We occupied ripped plastic seats, surrounded by slumped manual workers and bulky, exhausted maids. The bus slowly pulled out toward a depressed area of Trenton. As Princeton township and its well-kept suburb receded, old frame houses began to appear, some with torn screens and rotted wooden stairs. Their dormer windows were boarded and roofs patched; their miniscule yards were devoid of any life.

We arrived at a dreary red-brick state hospital with low buildings, wire fencing, and bleak, trash-strewn grounds. We were admitted perfunctorily by a tired nurse into a small visitor's enclosure adjacent to a secure ward. To prevent suicides by hanging, the doors had no handles. It was a playground, but not like von Neumann's for the gifted. It was for the most forsaken.

The enclosure was open to the sky, except for a rough net of chicken wire to discourage climbers. There were only a few hopeless, shriveled plants stacked upon unpainted wooden slats on cinder blocks, and an uneven patio of cracked cement.

Broken plastic children's toys were scattered about: dolls like tiny cadavers, their faces dirty and forlorn, their vacant eyes stuck open. Some had empty sockets. We sat on a peeling green park bench. The nurse with a ring of thick steel keys locked us in with a harsh, clanging finality.

An aged couple, white-haired and grieving, sat nearby as their granddaughter in her early twenties whirled in helpless circles, forever holding her hand to cover her face. Piteously hiding, she endlessly repeated, "Is it going to be all right?" Another visitor, a young man, hovered near his mother. She had unkempt hair and darting eyes, and made florid, writhing serpentine movements. She had oculogyric crises, the whites of her eyes locked upwards as she feigned masturbation with a deodorant bottle.

Cobalt whispered, "The young woman was isolated by her parents since childhood and made to sleep with them through her late teens. The older woman is a victim of tardive dyskinesia, a side effect of licit pharmaceuticals. Hospitals abound with them."

The harried, severe nurse soon ended visiting time; in the saddest of partings the visitors left. The girl still whirled, her hand concealing her face, meekly asking no one, "Is it going to be all right?" The older woman, her serpentine motions more exaggerated, reluctantly yielded the deodorant bottle. In a moment of lucidity at her predicament, she broke into inconsolable tears. With great difficulty, they each were coaxed into the chaos of blaring televisions and hypermanic or catatonic patients, swallowed alive by unending madness. Heavy steel doors closed upon them; we sat for some time in silence. Hearing the jingling of keys, Cobalt leaned to me.

"We have a special guest."

Another ward door creaked open, and a girl of about eight was ushered forth. She was shockingly white and thin, with knobby knees and short black hair, and wore a rumpled institutional blue shift and shower shoes. She seemed disconcerted in the sunlight, and had her hand in her mouth as if she were much younger than her years. The nurse pushed her forward. She staggered, taking a few steps with a bizarre, halting gait, as though some invisible object were before her. Upon seeing Cobalt, she made a cry like a frightened animal. I realized it was her gesture of surprise, and salutation. She staggered a few more steps, then looked away at a dead plant.

"May I introduce Eve," Cobalt murmured. "She had no name at six years old, when firemen found her by her father, who was dead from a self-inflicted gunshot wound. Mother also deceased, no relatives. She had crouched beside him for some weeks. One room apartment, rotten food containers stacked to the ceiling. He kept her in the room since birth; she was not allowed to leave. She was permitted to crawl only to the edge of the bed and back."

Cobalt approached her very carefully, then gently took her small, white hands. For the most poignant moments, they did some sort of shuffling dance together, the girl barely able to stand. She made a crooked semblance of a smile, except for the eyes. As they danced, Cobalt slowly sang to her, again and again in his soft tenor, as if it were a lullaby.

"I see skies of blue,
and clouds of white.
The bright blessed day,
the dark sacred night.
And I think to myself,
'What a wonderful world.'"

She looked up at him, her little hands lost in his, as though he were an angel. Her frail legs tried to follow. Forever confused and helpless, she brightened like a star just in these minutes of caring.

"I see trees of green
and red roses too
I see them bloom
for me and you
And I think to myself
'What a wonderful world.'"

They were swaying in their dance, the girl's face transfixed and utterly vulnerable, as if for a few seconds she imagined sunlit meadows, loving parents, a new dress, and walking with dignity among azaleas.

"I see friends shaking hands,

saying how do you do,

They're really saying

I love you."

When their dance and the song ended, she made her strange cry, put her hands in her mouth, tried to hop up and down, then looked away and froze. Cobalt found a ball, called her name, and rolled the ball to her. It bounced off her foot. She had no idea of the game, how to catch and return the ball. Cobalt carefully showed her, but she fell to her knees and seemed embarrassed. She could not play, or even speak, with other children. In her tragic loneliness she glimpsed them only rarely, but knew they grew year after year, and she did not.

I could look no longer, for the rush of feeling was too great. I attempted to walk it out in a section of the enclosure. As Cobalt continued singing and trying to play with her, the child looked at me with the eyes of a wild creature, yet painfully human. She knew she was locked in a horrific state; she knew other children laughed and played with each other, and that she could never be part of them. No foster parents would take her in.

Our eyes met, her gaze the eyes of the baby at Pashupanipath, the eyes of the blind beggars, the eyes of the cowering and abused girl in Nepal, the eyes of prisoners' children. I told her that she was loved, and that it would be all right.

As she and Cobalt crouched to examine the ball, I said I must go. He stood and turned from the girl, then took my hand.

"She is a reminder of why we risk our lives for medicines. Much of the world is like this precious one, locked in a cruel room. We wish to be, if you will, the firemen."

I turned to leave, and knocked on the door for the nurse. The girl tried to jump up and down, and made her cry of hello and farewell and suffering. Cobalt remained with her.

It was a somber bus ride back to Princeton. I watched the working-class houses pass, their streets with children who were beautiful and free. At the Wilson School, where I collected my notes, my phone rang. In the background, I could hear the ball bouncing, and Eve struggling to speak in her halting, fearful way. After wishing me a safe journey, Cobalt rushed to attend her. I heard only a few words, then singing.

"It's going to be all right, dear one, for there are skies of blue, and clouds of white...

I hear babies cry

I watch them grow

They'll learn much more

Than I'll ever know

And I think to myself

'What a wonderful world.'"

III

The Electric Supply

Keeping tabs on an entity that embraced the whole planet
was no trivial occupation.

- JLB, *The Congress*

When the sky is torn
When the seas pour forth…
Then a soul will know what it has been given
And what it left behind.

- Qur'an

I guess he felt he'd used up
'nuff of the electric supply.
I guess he knew that the
Angel of Death was nigh.

- Ginsberg, *Blue Gossip*

Chapter 9.

Crime's Own

We seek to train doers…we are not interested in producing
languid observers of the world.

- President Charles Wilson Eliot (A.B. 1853),
chemist from MIT who transformed Harvard

He has that gleam of radicalism so often found in men whose
environment would seem to foster only tradition and stability.

- President Eliot, on incoming President Lawrence Lowell

I won't philosophize, and I will be read.

- Byron, *Don Juan*, Canto X,
motto of The Magenta, Harvard Crimson's former name

Magenta is not now, and never has been, the right color of Harvard.

- *Crimson* newspaper, itself mocked by Advocate literary
journal as "Crime's Own," after all Departments voted
to avoid variations in colors worn by Harvard men at the races.

…but this is a snowscape in indigo, nubian, cobalt, ash Wednesday, gothic…

- Durrell, *The Black Book*

THE CHARLES IN THE FALL was like the echo of some tiny shell discovered by children who knew of the play of long tides, the last golden probes of sunlight, the twilit firmaments, the bondage of the kissed. I walked the embankment in reverent melancholy, as if one were the wind off the river, but thought of Abeer, the orphan girl in Nepal, and of crippled Eve, who had never heard the whisper of seashells.

The tenderness of the Six was omnipresent at Harvard, even on this sparkling afternoon. I tried spreading a blanket, then a small wicker-covered demijohn of juice and a basket of coarse brown bread and cheese. I watched the sun-drunk bodies, the flights of herring gulls. My thoughts remained a form of self-castigation though, little punishments at the sorrow of the world from this perspective of privilege.

I attempted small maneuvers to forget the Six, to concentrate, but pell-mell images of that which I had witnessed intruded. I fought off a white depression by intending to study at Harvard their ways, as other researchers in the Northwest Amazon had characterized indigenous ritual use of *Banisteriopsis caapi* – ayahusaca or yagé. The ballroom pandemonium of Cambridge receptions all too soon grew imminent, even as I arrived like some refugee from the latitudes of myth.

⬡

THESE WERE MIND-WARPING YEARS: the vaulting ambitions of Harvard's scholars, the Faustian bargain of the Six with their unearthly, heterodox science and experimentation, the poetic quantum of both groups. The sunlight began weakening into blue shadows; everywhere was like a world dream, the children of the earth, imploring.

I became more withdrawn over these first weeks of term, awakening early to study, when the Yard was like the Acropolis at dawn. Treasuries of wildflowers drank light morning rains, with their forgiving drifts of silver needles.

Even more sensitive now, I began to notice women in chartreuse taxis, thought of physicists being born, while lectures had the phrasing of newspaper demotic. Thin models drew my gaze in Harvard Square, for my reflections could not be extricated from the trio of Vermilion. I kept recalling V-1's fingertip trailing low down V-2's perfect abdomen, in their frank admission.

"We like to keep our appetite."

The trees dripped moisture from wet skies as the Houses became littered with the detritus of autumn, the ivy leaves finally withered and grey. These ruminations became a type of self-decortication. Mirrors troubled me. Grasping the Six had the futility of the infinitely complex.

⬡

ON ONE OCCASION I was maundering about as if in monastic rooms, deliberating on Vermilion *ex hypothesi* and having some internal dream colloquy, when I halted in holy wonder at the unfamiliar sunlight. It was then Hammer and Hagendas, with her teasing, foxy, classicist's voice and a shattering irreverence, awakened me. Caught wandering down Mass Ave while recalling Berlin, I was reciting some exorcism fragment from the Dark Ages.

"These are not the moors of Wuthering Heights, Heathcliffe," Hagendas observed.

Overhearing my last murmured Latin phrase, Hammer lightly quipped on President Eliot's demand that Henry Adams, an early reform-minded political journalist, teach a course on the 16th Century.

"But Mr. President, I know *nothing* about Medieval History."

"If you will point out anyone who knows *more*, Mr. Adams, I will appoint *him*."

They had me with their innocent wisdom. We looped through the Yard, the leaves filtering down, as Hammer engaged in fanciful mimicry of Hulk, and Hagendas crooned with joy. Pennypacker still seemed like a high donjon of some fortress, but their frenzy of piety over term projects, as they led me unerringly to HKS, brought one to the moment. As we passed a wedding at the Memorial Church, I began trailing Hammer and Hagendas somewhat dolorously, for the soprano was singing "Wenn die Frühlingslüfte."

⬡

THE LANGUID VIPERS and chess masters of Harvard Square proved no challenge, for we soon entered HKS, into its sea of matchless professionals. Spies, covert operatives and security experts – their presence unheralded and pervasive – riddled Harvard's Kennedy School. Hammer would discover that an innocuous student fiddling with a brown bag at lunch was a mid-career DOD analyst preparing a paper on "Destabilization of Despotic Regimes." In the interior quadrangle of HKS, where students clustered at wooden tables on warm days, Hagendas never looked up as a six-six Green Beret colonel in camos strode through the compound to the National Security Program. Hulk and Surf became oblivious to Secret Service agents routinely inspecting the building and their lockers in advance of a speech by the vice-president or the FBI or CIA Director.

Students were so concerned with constant exams and projects and speeches that they no longer noticed security teams from Lebanon, Israel, Russia and France accompanying US personnel, or entourages in limousines entering under HKS gates to discretely disgorge Presidents or Foreign Ministers. A trained observer might glimpse on HKS rooftops the barrels of SIG SSG 3000 sniper rifles, topped with Hensoldt scopes.

◯

PROFESSOR OF PUBLIC POLICY M___ considered an array of sixty HKS students, all suddenly poised in heightened alertness during an otherwise routine lecture on "authorizing environments of organizations." M___ had made such an impromptu, uncharacteristic personal reflection during his typically energetic, demanding presentation that his audience of future policy makers was startled. A prominent faculty member, himself surrounded by limitless faculty stars, M___'s cautionary statement may have been the singular phrase to survive in many students' memories.

"I have discovered through my years at Harvard that each and every person, from the lowliest freshman to the President of the University, thinks they don't deserve to be here."

The room quietened, for feelings of intellectual inadequacy were common. We were taught continually, or rather forced, to answer frequently unsolvable riddles during lectures, like insoluble Zen koans before a master. In these ongoing demonstrations of the Socratic method, students were asked question after question, each more incisive than the last. Problems were proposed to the entirety of the class and – failing that   to specific students, while everyone else offered prayers for invisibility.

Faculty, familiar with the syndrome, quickly encouraged the most reluctant students to "come in" to the public conversation at the unspoken risk of being considered irrelevant or unconscious. In the beginning, few were courageous enough to interact with the instructor, for fear of appearing incompetent. Lacking command of the information, we might provoke comment or laughter. Only very gradually did we become bold enough to try speaking, at first with a shaky confidence, before our august companions.

With little warning other than robins skirmishing impertinently, and grey-silver leaves ashiver, the sudden inclemencies of weather fell upon us. Cold whiplashes of wind yielded to brutal ice, while snow demons mounted the receptive white loins of earth.

Exposure to the Six – and to the Cambridge mind field – still gave rise to persistent phenomena: melting snows were mathematical cones, people spoke in literary cadences, the soothing ocean of light from the riverfront houses was infused by snatches of midnight chants. A benign madness had set in, a tingling cataclysm of nerves. Harvard, while retaining its genteel Edwardianisms, was a fairy land of breathing steeples; it seemed like an outpost of the stars.

⬡

SETTLING IN TO CONFRONT a tutorial by an unknown guest lecturer, our public policy class teemed with doggedly earnest scholars from the earth's far regions, offset by bright clusters of those blithe souls on an unimpeded Chapin-Choate-Princeton-Harvard-Oxford-Rhodes path. Having plodded over the truck-sized snowdrifts on Mass Ave on this formidable November morning, all were distinguished by various mufflers, mittens, earmuffs and rubberized high-top fleece-lined boots for heavy glacier trekking. It was during this lecture that our reluctance was freed, and we all found forever the courage to speak.

Before us appeared a dapper, smiling man. He had been described to me by an HKS faculty member – the smartest man I knew – as "the smartest man I know." MH was a former National Security Council member through several administrations, thus privileged to the secrets of the ages.

As thick grey clouds loomed over the frozen waste of the Charles, quiet began settling in over the room. To our surprise, MH's welcoming beam slowly darkened, until we all became utterly silent. In this somber setting, MH opened with a most serious question, grounding the class instantly.

"What are the limits on *torture*, if torture were required in the national interest to prevent mass causalities?"

Surf lifted her little Plantagenet chin and frowned at this impossible conundrum. On Hagendas's delicate neck, frail veins were pulsating. Hammer, with deep furrows in his brow, leaned over his desk. Hulk prepared to stand with a vague reply, then slumped at the moral perplexity.

MH as Socrates teased us out somewhat with questions, then stopped for a long dramatic moment. He carefully divulged, in his measured way, a highly classified history.

"In this special company, concerning torture, I will share with you a matter known by few outside of NSC and DOD, and impossible for any press to corroborate."

We fell into the uncertain rapture of those about to be anointed.

"During World War Two, in response to the success of German Intelligence in the run-up to the Normandy invasion – and at the risk of a million Allied lives – plans were developed by the Army to disinform the Axis Powers about the true site of Operation Overlord, the Allied invasion on D-Day. A misapprehension of thirty miles from Omaha Beach would change the course of the war, perhaps of civilization itself."

I noticed a carol of snow forming in a large parabola on an icy window overlooking the Charles, and thought of antidotes to war.

"There were many ruses, but knowledge of one of these plans was limited only to President Roosevelt, the Secretary of War, and to General Eisenhower, then Supreme Commander of Allied Forces in Europe. A top-secret call was made to the psychology staff of all Army divisions requesting a list of high-ranking officers with a career that could be publicly verified, and – a more difficult quality to assess – one who could tolerate prolonged torture without breaking."

I reflected on interrogation rooms, life sentences, of trembling in the grey afternoon, of the imbecile snow forever.

"After a short list of candidates was flown to a secret location in England, another requirement was added. The individual would resist interrogation until the point of death, but not die for an ideal. One man was chosen for this most critical of assignments, and bound to an oath of secrecy. He was told he would be parachuted behind German lines, to contact the French Resistance with a special message, and that the future of the free world depended on his success."

There was snow-rime in the dead flowerbeds before HKS; snow lines wavered along Memorial Drive in a wind of iron, crawling out of a northern winter. The sedge glittered with frost. In the calms, skirls of young snow were falling straight out of heaven.

"Air-lifted from Britain at night in a Lancaster bomber, he was briefed with Allied landing details. As the Lancaster flew low over France, he was dropped into isolated farmlands near Caen, which British Intelligence indicated had a heavy concentration of German sympathizers. Disguised as a farmer, he was seized quickly by German patrols and imprisoned. His asserted name and rank were determined to be fraudulent. Identified by fingerprints and military archives as a high-ranking American officer, he was tortured for weeks with specialized methods employed by the Gestapo. Alone, naked, starved, disoriented and confronted by skilled interrogators, he still refused to cooperate."

I recalled Indigo above Salzburg, and his disclosure of Ivy Mike, the spy-counterspy operation of the Six to infiltrate drug enforcement long ago. I thought of the diaspora of their young operatives, and how those captured still rotted in small steel enclosures.

"Before losing consciousness each session, he was told only a fool would give up his life, and his family, when he only had to say a few words to end it all."

Some of us groaned with relief, others said nothing, a microcosm of cowardice and bravery.

"As death neared, in the last moments, crying for his wife and children, then wildly praying to God, he finally broke, whispering the Allied landing coordinates. The Nazis let him live for further questioning. The invasion began within days. The Germans were waiting at the wrong place."

Hagendas, our paragon of a girl with eyes of blue lake, gripped her pen, rigid and tense, her fair English skin blanching.

"Managing to survive the war as a German prisoner, he was repatriated. The heavy concentration of Germans at the site he knew was noted, and he was discharged in disgrace from the military, stripped of his rank and command. Yet, he was the unknown hero of D-Day, the victim of a brilliant top-secret plan to disinform Hitler."

Surf could not resist. "What happened to him after the War?

"He lived out his life in silence and isolation, and without ever knowing the truth. He died as a very old man, down on his luck in some nondescript American town. Had he not acted dishonorably, a million lives would have been sacrificed in the European invasion. But this is only one example of how torture has been used in the national interest."

We entered into a profound silence, but for the ticking of sleet upon the windows.

"Now, what does this class consider to be the ethical limits on such ruthless use of humans today, to locate and penetrate, for example, terrorist organizations that cannot be approached without proof of willingness to die for jihad?"

National Security Council member MH then opened the floor to questions. At that moment, for the first time, we all as one broke through our hesitancies, fighting for position, arguing points. Bedlam ensued.

⬡

WE LEFT LECTURE that day in tight little groups, each one deciding when they would have broken under interrogation, or not. Hagendas and Surf led the way, intently carrying small backpacks, cutting across the lines of limousines and ignoring the occupants, unlikely to return for the evening speeches and question periods for diplomats. Hammer and Hulk and I managed to slip past Harvard security at one door, as they vetted the incoming students and faculty.

Unidentified assemblages of sharp-eyed men and women stood nearby wearing earpieces, their suits tailored to conceal holsters; they prohibited the public but not the weary HKS students from close proximity to the world's leaders. In a moment of frivolity I asked one apparent foreigner in faulty Russian if he was armed, unpermitted by the United States. He understood me, and responded with a fake Russian accent.

"Heckler and Koch MP55D6 silenced submachine gun with 7.62 NATO rounds."

⬡

WE GATHERED UNDER A MOON conflagration with high clouds, beneath a snow-glittering night sky. Focused on finding uncrowded reading rooms, we tried to cast aside thoughts of the Reich and deathheads and the Gestapo, but somehow arrived in the courtyards of Harvard's Busch-Reisinger Museum, the world's premier collection of German Expressionist art.

Hammer, peering in, recalled his great aunts at Treblinka, then observed the paintings.

"These acquisitions were purged from the major German museums and art dealers by the Nazis."

Pleading with a beefy, red-faced Irish guard, a fellow Southie from Charlestown, Surf managed our admission after hours.

Personal deceptions, no less sophisticated than any invasion of honor at Calais, soon riddled our emotional atmosphere. Hulk had followed the nonpareil Surf in his usual professorial way, but we soon discovered him looking at her with an incandescent admiration, as though she were some pelvic oracle. Flustered, he tried disavowing his expression as one of a trifling misadventure. But we all knew the truth of him, and of her.

Having trailed Surf through the great flocculence of snow before the Busch as if it were bedroom eiderdown, finally to settle at a broad reading table, Hulk proved to be the archetypical Platonist. He thought every movement of Surf's hands was some regal gesture, and the shifting of her hips next to him had a Botticellian elegance.

Surf that term still considered him with a gentle, charmed tolerance, but now and then with an unconscious contempt, preferring men with a marvelous prodigality. To Hulk's wondering about her heroine she once responded, to his dismay, with a polished indecency.

"Pythonice the courtesan, triple slave and triple harlot."

Yet between them there was a slow accretive growth of bonding, even though she openly described him as pusillanimous. At these fond insults he returned a metallic bluish gaze, and hardly ever blinked. She punctuated his efforts at frugality and chastity by great, tender yawns.

Hagendas detached from us to drift unescorted among the late medieval, Renaissance and Baroque sculpture, past the 18th Century porcelains, to admire the post-1945 Vienna Secessionist art. She reveled in art as a discipline of insubordination.

I watched her. With closed eyes, she moved her hands slowly in the air all over a painting, as if sensing the artist's presence. With her febrile slimness, Hagendas was a delirium to those who fantasized a love sandwich, a lithe *ménage à trois*, not realizing her innocence. This night she had arrived with Hammer through the dark winterscape, sheltered under Gothic arches from the powdery snowfall. I saw them approach from a moon white garden, where blue tits were scuffling in the snow. We studied until almost dawn, for we all were lovers, in these orgiastic rites of cognition.

◯

IN HARVARD SQUARE on an evening, when Hagendas passed the clutch of French pretenders, one became unsettled, breaking into a high girl's laughter. Another was drinking a Benedictine, yet another smoking a gold-tipped cigarette, the remainder chewing frozen croissants. They thought her some chaste seminarian, for they had arrived in Cambridge from the summer's almond-eyed whores in the Levant.

One of these *phalloi*, who was vaguely ornamental, seemed to have in her presence some paroxysm of the Id. From his expression I could see that he imagined her as a pneumatic Teuton, split invitingly across spilt blue silk, while he husbanded the white meat.

Another dirty little brute whispered *en Français* of her blanched nipples from the cold, yet another rakish type grinned at the withering flare of her hips, her high cheek bones, her graceful elongated figure. They were unprepared for fierce Hagendas, who with the audacity of purity, and her blue serene unshockable eyes, quickly subjected them to her beautiful mutilations.

The Parisian student foolish enough to actually approach her, a *lapin chaud* or "hot rabbit," was a little debased. He was a desultory student of everything. With his white vacuity of countenance, he suggested to her before his *amies* that he had serviced whole provinces of unsatisfied wives from the 15th *arrondissement* to the Côte d'Azur. He elaborated thusly, the vice of amateurs tentative in their arts. Hagendas, in perfect French from her childhood at Le Rosey, crisply retorted at length on the flaccid shortcomings, as it were, of bourgeois French males. At this, a vast paralysis seized her admirers. Scalded, they quit the field.

◯

OUR LITTLE STUDY GROUP was fond of Harvard's Museum of Natural History, the second most visited attraction after John Harvard's statue. We would lose ourselves in its three research collections: the Museum of Comparative Zoology, the Harvard Herbarium, and the Mineralogical and Geological Museum. In the courtyard twilight as Surf and Hulk entered to join us, a robin burst scarlet grey before them; I saw their rosy skin alight by the darkening bluish snow.

Surf found entrancing the seemingly limitless Blaschka glass models of plants, the thousands of perfect, hand-blown "glass flowers," each with a card of genus and species in Latin. Hammer hovered near the first *Triceratops* ever found, then advanced to the world's only mounted marine dinosaur, the *Kronosaurus*. Hagendas flung herself madly over a 1642-pound amethyst geode, channeling its spirits. It was among the glass flowers that I first noticed Hulk and Surf at the brink of some emotional precipice.

Surf obviously had experienced raffish circles; she sometimes pretended to be a gaunt mannequin, wheeling around an ardent bedroom. Hulk had only a charming diffidence; he was susceptible to the least politeness. When he brushed snow from her coat, he would inhale with discretion the fragrance of her body. He erred in thinking her cool as an ice-bound lake, so that she floated in his mirror, always unreachable.

Hulk spoke minutely, exactly, in his pedantic way, mesmerizing her with his artlessness, but also frustrating her. His bookish manner of exposition, as he wandered about her with the timeless inertia of a wrapped mummy, was intended to conceal what he felt were uncouth horns.

Surf tried tapping her nail upon a glass flower exhibit; to my concern it was *Turbina corymbosa*, the morning glory, the ancient *ololiúqui* used for divination by the Zapotecs in the highlands of Oaxaca. Peering in with her dense blue candid eyes, she invited him to come near, but Hulk was a myopic scholar.

He was a philosophical cutthroat though, and she at times on the basis of his intellect and companionship thought him a deist king. Yet she wanted to be owned by a lover, engulfed by him. To any of his beseeching looks, she stood fast unflinchingly, always aware of the walk of the sexually unawakened. One could see her winter spell, her whiteness turning under the moon, her infinite dispersion of starlight, her syncopated rhythms.

Hulk suffered in a benighted world, in a kind of deepwater trance of unrequited desire. She wanted to be broken and bridled, but Hulk was manifestly benign, with his archaic refinements. Unable to read her signals, he assumed any sense of command with her would be a terrible effrontery. They left the museum late, walking on under the frosty twinkling of the Pleiades, like great spectral creatures in the hush of falling snow.

HAMMER AND HAGENDAS by contrast frequently would study in our secret libraries and museum refuges until almost daybreak, occasionally dancing about if there were no other witnesses. Placed on a pedestal by most, Hagendas seemed to prefer dealing with an adventurer, a corsair, to be lost in the grip of savage, exultant kisses. I found her once with Hammer, a rolling storm outside, and passed their embrace with a fond complicity. She looked at me, flushing brightly, her eyes a troubled blue sea, the thunder beyond bellowing and insisting like shared desires.

I saw them once again, holding hands in the silent winter, listening to liquid music from a flute in Winthrop House. They stood there in some long communion, after a last magnetic pulse from the horizon, until they were bathed in pools of moon light, their faces turned silver and the snow dusted to a starscape.

⬡

MY MANNER, the esoteric path to Cambridge, and an aversion to personal disclosure provoked speculation by HKS students, who dubbed me "the Captain." My last name with its Norman origin was pronounced as that of the fictional Jean-Luc Picard, and in an earlier era that of the high-altitude balloon and deep-marine bathyscape explorers Jacques and Auguste.

Although a friendly gesture by students, I quickly found the prospect of such a role among these stars to be remote on merit-based grounds, so that I became a mere sweaty hand below the decks of the HKS freighter, one struggling to keep in sight others more skilled, as knowledge passed through us at the speed of light.

Professor M___, pacing the lectern on a snowbound morning before overwhelmed students in the run-up to midterms, suddenly uttered a provocation to our dense, worried group.

"Some students and faculty have a *secret agenda*."

We all alerted, this thought hanging for long moments before our confused or wary crowd. An HKS student, a single mother on her way to Yale Law, had an admirable habit of elaborating on faculty with her intuitions.

"You refer," she said, hands outlining in the air Professor M___'s observation, "to those covertly planning to use the HKS degree to influence third-world governments, or certain segments of our own, or to penetrate for personal reasons the world's political, economic and military establishments, or to use Harvard's imprimatur as a shield for directives from their country's intelligence agencies?"

"Precisely," he said, to light nervous laughter, but scrutinizing our reactions.

Buried in the fourth row center left, I continued to scribble notes furiously to stay abreast of M___. Many of us – as I – still had not learned to do the homework *before* the lecture, so that instruction was a reminder rather than a first exposure, and one could listen carefully while jotting just a few notes. I was an atavistic learner, always watching the horizon of my faster classmates as they receded into glorious comprehensions. Only paltry shadows of their competence occasionally reached me, so I slowly drowned in information. My hopeless notes were read only in desperation.

At M___'s intriguing proposition, those with actual secret agendas slowly withdrew, almost imperceptibly, into their winter clothing. Midcareer executives from the alphabet agencies assumed blank gazes fixed on notepads. Some students, those on friendly terms with their country's intelligence apparati, forgot to breathe. I was quite comfortable, even with multiple lives but no evil intent, until Hulk some distance away – before a hundred students facing each other in concentric rows – piped a heretofore unspoken consensus upon the still air, quite clearly.

"Well. We all know Captain Pickard is a *spy*."

The class howled as I flushed brightly and shrank. Recovering, I tried smiling with resignation at the outing and affected to look miserable, putting my head in my hands.

"What?" M___ offered encouragingly.

"We *all* know Pickard is a spy!"

Again laughter, then playful denial by the accosted to trivialize the event, until M___ graciously moved on to his days as a policy analyst at DEA Headquarters. Somehow the students had concluded that this ancient graduate student with a spotty heritage and an odd recent interest in strange tribal warriors in Afghanistan was a refuge from some intel agency. Demurring when asked about background only stimulated curiosity. Basic tradecraft described by the Six required that one limit the truth to a plausible, normal narrative among others, forsaking any memorable character and not attracting attention by the slightest evasiveness or braggadocio, but blending seamlessly and inconsequentially into any conversation. Thus newly inclined, I strove to be forgotten.

The playing field at HKS already was littered with actual spies, those seeking career advancement or a dignified convalescence from their multifarious deeds. Several students' fathers were CIA officials. Finally, though, it hardly mattered whence one arrived or ventured to, for we all became the improbable survivors of an education where every variety of ego and intelligence was demolished and refined until we were absolved of our backgrounds, washed as it were in the blood of crimson. Although individual agendas remained, our various pasts quickly dimmed, for we all were trained ruthlessly to confront the futures of nations.

⬡

FROM HULK'S COMMENT, I realized the undercurrents of public perception: that my intent walks about the Yard were viewed as a type of covertness. Magenta had advised avoiding a zealot's light, the fervor of a heretic, to not stalk about like a medieval *abbé*, eyes heavenward. Whatever moral or theological mysteries were confronted, it was time among my colleagues to stop mooning about, and to lighten up.

Hulk to the rescue, as we walked by the late 19th Century apartments of Harvard's former Gold Coast, where wealthy students resided *en prince* until all freshmen by 1915 were required to live in the Yard. He recited his doggerel.

> "I dwell 'neath the shades of Harvard
> in the state of the sacred cod,
> where the Lowells speak only to Cabots
> and the Cabots speak only to God."

I clucked a bit, albeit peckishly.

"No, really," he returned, "the Cabots arrived at Massachusetts Bay Colony on the Mayflower, then invested in slaves, rum, and opium. Hence, Cabot House for undergrads."

By then we were at the Lampoon on Mt. Auburn Street, where Harvard's comedians occupied a mock castle.

"Like some of our more *mysterious* colleagues, the Lampoon has five addresses." He gave me The Look.

"How curious, like Harvard students," I replied, not quite nonplussed.

"Notice the 16th Century Dutch and Flemish architecture has a face."

The castle had two round windows for eyes, a red lantern for a nose, and an entry of grinning mouth, with prominent incisors.

"What's inside the castle?

"The Lampoon study is the interior of a Dutch fisherman's cottage, with a circular humor library. It was funded by William Randolph Hearst – booted from Harvard for too many pranks."

"Pranks? Here?"

"Endlessly. Oh, good, the Egyptian Ibis is on the roof today. It's stolen routinely by staff of the rival *Crimson* newspaper."

He pointed to a large copper bird, resting imperturbably on the castle.

"What does the *Crimson* do with the Ibis?"

"After a 1946 theft, it appeared the same night with Orson Wells at the Opera House and as a prop for Blackstone the Magician. Once, the *Crimson* formally presented the Ibis to the Russian delegate to the United Nations, to be placed on the spire of Moscow University."

Hulk went on about creative thievery, the burglars forgiven by courts full of alumni.

"The Lampoon stole the Sacred Cod of Massachusetts in 1933, but insisted the cod-napping was real."

One could not help but be delighted. I began to smile, getting the spirit, as Hulk rolled on.

"The Lampoon also has parodied the *New York Times*, distributing copies to Boston subscribers, mostly Harvard students, before 7 AM. The headline read "Ancient Parthenon Topples as Quake Rocks Greece." Classes in Classics were cancelled that day, *in memoriam*."

We considered the Poonsters more favorably.

"Oh, and a cultivated pachyderm, with crown, has been received at the castle."

I stood mute, vacant. He prompted me by flapping motions, hands on ears, stamping his feet. I was dumfounded; Hulk rarely displayed his boyish charm.

"Even our favorite elephant has been to the Lampoon."

"Babar!" I suddenly was into the game.

"Right. Most French and American children have read 'Babar Comes to America,' where Babar squeezes into the Lampoon and occupies the Dutch fisherman's cottage."

Now encouraged to sporadic frivolity on winter days, we considered how outrageous one could be at Harvard, without meeting Hearst's fate.

⬡

I THOUGHT BACK to the very moment before I first entered the HKS entryway during orientation. A black hipster with a leather cowboy hat and pointy-toed boots seemed also to be seeking the Kennedy School name; we found it discretely arrayed in polished metal across a red brick Harvard edifice on JFK Street. Masses of cars urged forward over the Charles into Cambridge, as earnest undergrads unpacked their trunks in the four floors of the nearby spired and turreted Adams House. Venturing that the hipster might be a new HKS student, I offhandedly couched the question in street lingo.

To this square white boy who improbably spoke inner-city dialect, he responded with a grin and in Chaucerian English that he was, indeed, one of the chosen. A poet and survivor of the violent Cabrini Green housing projects in Chicago, he soon disappeared into the world beat of the HKS rhythm. Thereafter we passed each other on occasion, where he revealed his eternal search for the proper Cliffie of ethnic persuasion. As opposed to the black HKS students from second or third generation academic families, our hipster was the "real thing."

Soulful and goateed, incapable of enunciating the policy idioms but given to undercutting elevated discourse with your basic down-home reality check, said hipster – now known as "Hat" – was terminally irreverent. Cheerful at the rarified exchanges by which we armed ourselves each day, his refusal to adopt HKS policy speak provided a counterpoint to a certain scholarly overbreeding.

This tendency first bloomed in a seminar on drug policy, in the bowels of Crim Justice section. Greenboards were all around, subdued lighting matched students' pallors, and smooth oval conference tables were strewn with prostrate Yale alums who were now HKS grad students. All were inscribing on paper, with intent haste, mystical notations about comparative marginal benefits from marijuana legalization or incarceration.

Laurie the Neiman Fellow, no longer in her red dress donned for the DEA Administrator, but now wearing tight jeans and a bulky sweater, leaned against a wall next to a frosted window opening down onto the lights of ice-bound Harvard Square. Another star policymaker-to-be with good legs but serious demeanor – one of the Yale alumnae in the pipeline to Georgetown Law School – asked difficult questions about the economics of cannabis while filling the greenboard with mathematical nomenclature.

The presentation underway involved the heights of thinking on drug policy, but to Hat the concepts lived in some tenuous, abysmally detached *Weltanschauung* far from any pot smoker's reality. To all appearances definitely on the nod, my black acquaintance was moved to awaken and suddenly lift his leather cowboy hat, under which he had remained as quiet as Justice Clarence Thomas during oral arguments. He blithely launched a pronouncement upon the air in a slow, faux-Southern crack-fiend street corner voice, one that instantly humanized our desiccated seminar with its irrefutable accuracy.

"Ah think evvvvvry body, deep down inside, 'jis wants to smoke some goooooood reefer, take off dere clothes, 'n *dance neked* in de mooooon light.'"

Everyone froze. A pin dropping would have been like a iron crowbar against the steely surfaces of academic insularity. Each listener's mind, privately emerging from the shock, began parsing into mutually exclusive realms in which each truly wished they were high and dancing naked together right now, but quickly reaggregating into mutual consensus that his comment was irrelevant, and there was no precedent for stripping. Hat – who had experienced more marijuana use than Jimi Hendrix – became enveloped in an invisible cloak of nervous avoidance and suppressed titillation from which no similarly infectious meme could emanate further. Observing the white panic, he just leaned back and smiled broadly.

The lecturer, missing a beat or three somewhat unsteadily, regained her balance and folded the discussion quickly, while students fled to their own musings. I escorted Hat downstairs, remarking on the most outrageous flowering of the Id I had heard so bravely or recklessly uttered, since one of the Parisians in the Square had tried seducing Hagendas.

Sadly, a year later, he was tossed out of HKS for pestering women students, who were disinclined to disrobe either on moon phases or for multicultural experience, even to the hot sounds of Coltrane sax solos mixed with New England's presumptuous weed. Harvard's fairest yielded, it later was rumored, only on jasmine evenings to one who was stone cold straight, but with the mind of a true master, singing wild dreams of freedom and the possible.

○

HARDLY PASSIVE NOTE TAKERS, HKS students were required to speak out in class like Harvard Law students. Quickly analyzing masses of disparate information, we had to "stand and deliver" in a coherent and persuasive monologue, only to be torn apart by the faculty's incisive questioning. From our common fear of public speaking, through the relentless beat of lengthier presentations, we were trained to be comfortable and convincing, a fast study on any topic for boardroom or auditorium. Taking pleasure in these newfound powers of performance, students began to display their creative sides.

One black Oxonian provoked sprinkles of laughter, nudging huge red Las Vegas gambling dice onto a projector, magnifying them into a wall-sized set of tumbling crimson snake-eyes for his presentation on addiction and the gaming industry. On a different occasion I – released by the surprisingly free spirit at HKS – began to tease spectators at a mock conference on restructuring of the South African apartheid government.

Assuming the podium as the first speaker, faced with rows of very serious demeanors, then spreading my arms wide in the Transvaal tribal fashion of greeting, I announced slowly and loudly in Ki-swahili a welcoming in a *basso profundo* learned from chanting with the monks at Hoshin-ji.

"Jaaaaaaaaaaaaaaaaaaaaaaammmmbo!" (Welcome!)

This immediately prompted a surprised HKS student, who had worked in refugee camps in the Sudan, to stand up – her arms wide as well – and echo.

"Jambo!"

I went on.

"Jambo, rafiki!" (Wecome, friends!)

After long following lines in Ki-Swahili about the conference, I spread my arms wide again, and with a big smile repeated the same introduction in Afrikaans, then once more in English. Ice thus broken, the gathering went swimmingly, although it had taken days to memorize the Ki-Swahili and Afrikaans, and even the hand gestures and timing.

○

EMPOWERED WITH THE PLEASURE of public speaking but still timid, we would revert to dry recitation below visual aids that were devoid of humor, but when the event permitted we broke loose. I once appeared in a coat buttoned to my ankles, hiding in the last row of a lecture hall until the professor announced my speech: a proposal by a hypothetical firm providing policy analysis to Senate committees. Upon approaching the lectern to represent the fictional Blue Grass Beltway Analytical Services, I discarded the coat, revealing my working man's bib overalls labeled, promisingly, "Can't Bust 'Em."

I then recalled childhood Baptist sermons about truth, trust, and sharp country ways, while leaning against an honest-to-God hoe, chewing on a bit of straw and speaking in a slow Deep South accent, my first language. On this frigid Cambridge morning, slick students from New York City began to scurry to-and-fro, wondering how they would be graded on the curve. The Old Democratic South ultimately being convincing with its homespun integrity, I got the A.

◯

SOME TIME LATER, as we presented on containment of proliferating loose nuclear weapons in the Former Soviet Union, I adopted a long black coat, a Russian accent, and impersonated a scientist from a remote Siberian "atomic city" lost on the *taiga's* permafrost. My town was filled with post-*glasnost* scientists, no longer with special privileges, but worried about feeding their families while retaining fissile material. To provide a final example of nuclear devastation for the sober class, I snapped my fingers for my assistant "Dimtri" – actually a well-loved HKS student – to roll a film of our experiments near Tomsk-8.

Recognizing a clip from a popular science-fiction film showing a nuclear explosion passing across a city, the class went wild. Not anticipating it would be funny, I protested, prompting ever more glee.

"Nyet, nyet, verno!" (No, no, it's true!)

Fortunately, this deflation occurred near the end of the presentation, so with a wan and perplexed smile I managed to conserve some dignity with a quick little bow and a conciliatory *"Spaceebah!"* (Thank you!). Pushing back theatrical horn-rimmed glasses off my nose, I beat a hasty retreat, sulking offstage to the right through derisive hoots in Russian.

"Nasdarovye, Tovarich!" (To your health, Comrade!)

◯

LEVITY WAS SPORADIC, though. Being driven to achievement led us to trudge on in scholarly misery. We addressed ourselves eternally to sheaves of papers, gazed upwards in the night at the alphabetical stars, and pictured angels ascending into doctorates and tenure. HKS at times was like the concussion of the world.

The harsh truth sometimes stuck up jaggedly, as the smiles went away. Former Federal Judge Leon Higginbotham, in a democratic gesture, frequented lunch at HKS between his lectures, mingling with masses of students. A distinguished African-American jurist, Higginbotham typically was surrounded primarily by white law and policy students, together with the small retinue of young black academics considered "in high demand," and who in response to the need for competency and diversity would enter the World Bank or State or the UN or the private sector.

Higginbotham knew well of the street people not far from us, huddled in doorways along Mass Ave and Central Square in the severe Boston winter, or crouching in the city's howling jails. From exposure to the realities of the criminal justice system, I thought of the thousands of inner city blacks, Hispanics and poor whites Higginbotham had seen pass before his bench. His face sometimes was tired and lined, so close to the hard memories: the grim destinies of those countless youths and derelicts, most of whom hardly could spell.

In his visage, I saw an awareness transcending that of the students who accompanied him – many from privileged environments – and who smoothly transited to positions of influence without ever being hungry, or afraid, or considered disreputable, or without possessions and a place to sleep. His entourages were all on a golden path, far from drunken or drug-addicted parents, from the threats and shouting and blasting televisions, and no books.

Beyond the confident exchanges of our chosen, in the freezing doorways down Mass Ave, the black and old and grizzled peered out sightlessly, placating passersby with tragic slurring voices. The winds were like ravening mastiffs; the streets and alleys were a bestiary of the lost. Some of these refugees from life were impenetrable sad relics, while others had a skinny ferocity, strung out with sores in a noisome menagerie. All were amputated from the planet.

Higginbotham constantly felt the gravity of this other world just outside Harvard's gates, and knew that we – for the most part – did not. Recognizing this in him, I often wanted to say a few words, just enough to allude to the parallel reality, but usually managed only a simple overture.

"How are you today, Judge?"

He would nod, looking directly at me with that unspeakable sadness unnoticed by the inexperienced; I wondered if he might have sensed this atypical student had lived among the people of despair, and somehow survived.

⬡

FROM MY CONNING TOWER of the skull, I could see the arriving flights of deadlines at HKS. Our governmental projects were due soon, requiring contact with high-level officials at federal agencies. The congeries of loving emotions among us quickly would yield to endemic suspicions of each other's connections. CIA was the agency of choice for several classmates, for it constantly was present at the Kennedy School, perfectly soluble with the curriculum and students. From my unspoken perspective, I thought the agency was not unlike the ghosts of the Six, for all had the hubris to arrogate to themselves the power of deciding the world's futures.

The Six – like CIA and Harvard students – frequented *demimonde* haunts around the earth, although the agency could be wild as harpies, skillful with the *garrote*, recalling the stinking middens of our history. The Six consulted their breviaries more often than CIA, but like them still used a series of cut outs to protect what some observers might think a type of intoxicated anarchy.

⬡

I CREPT QUIETLY atop vertiginous spiraling stairways, high above the broad bronze HKS standard sunk into the floor below. It had a shield of horizontal stripes of the American flag, below open books embossed with *Veritas*. In a distant corner, the dim glow of a computer shone upon a Harvard security guard as he ran identifications. I discovered down a silent corridor the unlabeled plain wooden office door of a government employee on leave, the Director of Intelligence for CIA. In that each HKS student was required to have a senior official oversee a project, I quickly slipped my proposal for a

Policy Analysis Exercise (PAE), the equivalent of a master's thesis, beneath the Director's door. There was some possibility CIA might sponsor a PAE proposal that permitted studies in Russia and Central Asia during the reforms of *perestroika* and *glasnost*. Concerned with potential heroin and fentanyl epidemics that might devastate the naive Russian population, I entitled the CIA proposal "Synthetic Drug Epidemics in the Former Soviet Union."

For a different approach to the Agency, I checked with the alumni office, and was directed to HKS graduates who had been recruited by CIA. Calling a recent alumna and analyst who lived near Tyson's Corner, Virginia, I asked who might sponsor the PAE. After she referred me to a case officer at the Counternarcotics Center (CNC), created to prevent violent major cocaine and heroin traffickers from destabilizing governments, she also asked of my possibly applying to CIA.

"And what are you doing after graduation?"

I hesitated, entertaining visions of carloads of FBI agents interviewing friends, employers and landlords back through birth and beyond, and of being fluttered on polygraphs with unsettling questions. To her prospect, and with a rapid cost-benefit calculation, I could only weakly demur.

"My age and background make me an unlikely candidate."

I rang the CNC officer. The conversation was a reminder of the agency's almost self-defeating insularity. Opening with the alumna referral and the Harvard PAE, I rambled on about dangers from potent synthetic opioids and stimulants controlled by violent cartels. The officer preferred CIA's romance with expensive, well-funded orbital surveillance systems, reallocated from overflights of Soviet missile silos to narcotics agriculture.

"You know, we are only looking at major opium and coca crops visible by satellite," he opined.

Seeking to elevate consciousness on synthetic drugs, I offered other insights.

"But they can't see underground or indoor labs, and a single lab making the superpotent opioid 3-methylfentanyl can produce the equivalent of the world's annual heroin supply. And fit it into a briefcase."

He mused on the concept while I continued.

"And Congress may cut funding to the National Reconnaissance Office, right?"

"I can't talk about that," he continued, the prototypical end to every exchange of thought with a CIA employee.

We closed cordially. Some months later in an Amsterdam hotel room, overlooking CIA press releases, I discovered a speech by the Deputy Director of CNC, soliciting appropriations, and describing the future problems expected with new synthetic drugs. Chagrined at the hijacking of concept, I found consolation that evening with the Vermeer exhibits at the Rijksmuseum, followed by a spicy dinner of Indonesian *rijsttafel* near the Leidseplein.

Checking voicemail in Cambridge at 6 AM, there was a call from CIA, perhaps a response to the proposal to the Director of Intelligence. Groggy with the European time warp, I hit the delete button, inadvertently ending my dalliance with CIA for the moment. I sat up, fully awake, with mixed feelings at this crossroad. The path not taken may have been no less intriguing than the phenomenal psychedelic and erotic encounters, soon arising from the event horizon, across Holland's fields of flowers.

○

THE WIND WHIRLED in from a heavy Cambridge winter, as a frail ghost light came off the Charles, and the river locked up in a steel grip of ice. In the grey winterscapes, visibility was nil, our thoughts viscous. At clearing moments, when paths were untracked and the snowdrifts soothed themselves to sky, I felt sudden transports from memories of the Six, for they always remained a *Leitmotiv* to my quotidian studies. They each had found me somehow, except for the unavailable, unknown last of them.

My grasp of the Six still remained tenuous, for much more data was needed. They seemed elegant, mystical, connected with humanity and the unconscious, expert technocrats. On reflection they became winged seraphs or breathless messengers, or on the run from the hound of heaven. Opponents would view them merely as peddling the questionable nostrums of the day, but after Berlin and Kathmandu and Princeton, I knew they tread on holy ground.

But how they worked their magic, and their potions, became some terrible preoccupation. I had to wait for more contact, if it ever came at all, for nothing was promised. Only shadowy postulates were left of them, tenebrous floating visions, but since Berlin the sounds around me, the murmur of voices, even the winds off the Charles, were carved into nocturnes.

◯

HAMMER TOOK TO FLEEING to the special collections, often with Hagendas in tow. In his pursuit of her, I saw them everywhere, even in the Loeb Music Library, with its original scores from all the earth, and its impromptu performances of celebratory singing.

They frequented Harvard-Yenching Library, largest in the world for Asian Studies. There was Hagendas swanning about, affecting to be a slender, virginal adolescent lost in the Bodleian at Oxford, released for the afternoon by her headmistress at the Roedean or Lady Maragret Hall. Hammer, as yet undistracted, was cleansing his mental palate of relentless HKS statistics problems with a borrowed copy of Aristotle's *Poetics*, bound in calf.

It was a Monday. They had just come up from New York and Hagendas's parents' home in the canyons of the Upper East Sixties, with its original Audubons and winged bronzes. Meeting him at Central Park Scholar's Gate, Hagendas had insisted Hammer attend auctions at Sotheby's and Christie's, then visit the Whitney, entertaining him at the Russian Tea Room before the slow, dreary train back to Boston.

Beyond the cool, quiet rooms and tall parlor windows of Yenching Library, a light percussive hail began, offsetting the silence within. Hagendas reclined among the Chinese porcelains and silk shadowed lamps, her skin like snow dunes softened by winds.

She had a musical contempt for other suitors, but tormented Hammer in the presence of competitors by assuming a demonic meekness. She really thought most men were thoughtless swine or hazy brutes, their approaches a parody of love. Her quixotic temperament, though, gave others a decent equity to imagine themselves embraced in her private wickedness.

When Hammer first was stricken, he tried looking rather sinister around her, too cool a bird of prey. He displayed his litany of practiced, stylish moves, but when she combed her tresses with a silver-backed brush, her breasts lifting like spring plums, Hammer succumbed. He imagined her cadenza of flesh in the long winter moonlight. His voice sometimes became despondent at her elusiveness; we could hear this sadness even as he feigned the didactic.

I watched their obvious dance, so close to them each day, their intercourse like a rolling, majestic seascape by a great master. Hammer tried to probe her, failing that, to provoke her. His spirit became numb with the illusion of her dark star. Both had a brilliant sensuality and rhythm, a comprehension of each other. Hagendas at first would be sulky, profuse in her challenges, then ferocious, her eyes pale blue, almost plumbago.

Taunting him, she would find nooks with cushions, like belvederes in palace walls, and pretend pretty little seizures of the love act like a doll at her lover's every wish, only to meet his reproving glare. At other times she was a true bluestocking, and broke her spells with maidenly giggling.

○

LABORING UNDER THE UNCERTAINTY of CIA's response on the PAE, and with an imminent due date to find a government official as sponsor, I retreated to my cubicle, pondering stacks of research papers and wondering what authority to approach and how. Little time was left. Hammer rang.

"The Drug Policy Fellows are invited to a private seminar in fifteen minutes."

There were so many brown-bag lunches with mayors and junior Congressmen, I almost was too busy.

"Who is it?"

"The Assistant Secretary of State for International Narcotics Matters and Law Enforcement Affairs. The ASecState is the highest official you've met, even including the DEA Administrator."

I whisked from a chair my off-the-rack, ill-fitting Moscow GUM department store sports jacket, so worn the armholes were shredded, and pressed it into service as attire befitting the bedraggled and scholarly. I wore my one tie, a cheap dark blue silk version from the Harvard Coop with little crimson "H's" scattered discretely on the indigo field. The jacket and tie took more beating as I bounded upstairs and slid into the seminar room. Few faces acknowledged me.

Rather, our group of eight was rapt as the ASecState discussed the annual requirement for Blackhawk helicopters to combat the FARC rebels and suppress coca or poppy crops in Bolivia and Laos and Burma and 170 other countries for which he disbursed a billion each year for police training, paramilitaries, and air support.

The ASecState was sixty-ish, distinguished, excruciatingly bright, positive – the best of his kind. A career diplomat, a former Kennedy School alumnus and Ambassador to Bolivia with postings across the globe, he even spoke Quechua and other South American tribal languages. One policy-type shot me a glance suggesting this briefing was so sensitive I shouldn't be there. Sensing this attitude, the

ASecState began interspersing his talk with my early aside on the horrors of heroin and cocaine addiction, so that in his eyes I was welcome. By the end, he had won my enduring affection. I forgot about CIA.

Inside my operational cranium, I thought of Cobalt, constantly in perilous proximity to intelligence agencies. His every action was *sub rosa*, lest his colleagues become the authors of his professional misfortunes, and Cobalt trapped like some insect.

I wondered how Cobalt would manage the Kennedy School. He might be perfect as a mid-career student, or perhaps he would see a game of chance, where one's life was ventured. As the Fellows bantered afterwards, I thought of the freewheeling porosity between Harvard and the Hill and then – oddly – of a *croupier* at gaming tables in Monaco.

"Vingt-et-un rouge, impair et passe, Monsieur."

Whereas Cobalt might be duplicitous, my studies were straight forward and transparent. Useless to enforcement or intelligence agencies, they concerned only the public health aspects of opiates.

We dispersed, but being alight at so refreshing an official, I proposed hopefully, in an offhand manner, that he might consider sponsoring my research on Russian heroin and fentanyl problems in the wake of the economic reforms.

The ASecState was back and forth to Moscow routinely for meetings with the Russian Prosecutor General, attended occasionally by a subdued, effectively unknown FSB official from St. Petersburg named Putin. He also engaged with the MVD, the Russian equivalent of the FBI. We both understood the special allure of Moscow nights in January, when the Bolshoi was glittering, and the Kremlin spires with their hidden chambers still rose past defunct Stalin-era buildings, each topped by a Red Star.

He kindly accepted the proposal, and requested a short briefing paper on the ongoing fentanyl epidemic in Moscow. Suddenly I was transformed from alleged renegade anomaly into one blessed with the tacit approval of the State Department to conduct research in the interests of the United States.

The department chair and former Jesuit priest, Frank X, caught me leaving the seminar.

"You've got stars in your eyes," he said.

Infused with a thrilling, minor sort of terror, I tried to shake it off by plodding for hours through thin white snow as it lay under a sky of lead. Clouds fumed then dissipated, leaving the air dry and light, with patches of ice on balustraded terraces and ornate stone benches. As evening came, the sky seemed to go lilac, then started to bleed. The moon rose, and crawled over space hard and cold as a jewel. In my usual bemused dream, but stirred by contact with the Six, the pressures of Harvard, and now the project under State, I became prone to sudden fugues. Traveling down light-bewitched alleys, I fled into the brutal velvet of the Cambridge night.

⬡

OVER THE MONTH until Reading Period, I wrote and studied at Widener; through tall windows, black and white branches of yew trees were burdened with icicles. Snow lit up the ground. Memories of the Six, and of their parallel to Harvard students, often surfaced. Rather than dying piecemeal in life, as some shapeless, inelegant mediocrities, they both had chosen a world where frost-bound lovers go mad in the dark.

The weekdays became a kind of chrysalis, where I sometimes thought the ancient ways of the Six were medieval rubbish. At other moments they seemed a symphonic Bible, for we all wandered under ranges of staggering nebulae. My old consciousness then became but a weakened limb. V-1 and V-2 would appear as genteel spinsters in one's recollections, then nymphs lyrical with stars. I worried about my feeble private study of the Six, of their remote powder in sheath of hermetic symbols, and of false dawns breaking out.

When these concerns came, the evenings shut down, everything was paralyzed. As the nights became pricked with lamps, the Cambridge churchyards were a wilderness of falling tombstones. It was then I feared for the Six, even as I planned a HKS policy project to move about the earth studying heroin. This fear, this blending of their world with the demands of Harvard, soon distilled into icy metals of paranoia. The ruddy faces of the Square became, in fleeting moments, as rouged death masks.

Prismatic regiments of crystals, on the fronds of trees in the Yard, sometimes would reflect all that had been witnessed in the presence of the Six. I had arrived at Harvard, outside and looking in, but was now inside and looking out. With everything possible, nothing seemed real.

I wondered if and when and how they would be trapped by enforcement agencies: Crimson and Indigo, Vermilion and V-1, V-2, Magenta and Cobalt. For them, each and every day thereafter would follow like endless crucifixions. There was a glacier in my blood.

Possessed by these feelings, I labored about. Armorial bearings on university walls became tombs of masonry; rags of blown paper flew about the Square. Even the Druidical mistletoe above Johnson Gate looked on emptiness, forlorn in the whiteouts. There was no one to kiss.

◯

LONELY AND HARRIED with these many thoughts, I searched for friends in the Yenching collections, then the Fogg Museum, only to find Hulk standing with sadness before a Chinese vase and lighting joss sticks as though he were in prayer. Although somewhat a retiring violet, he harbored intense dreams of connubial felicities with Surf. I suggested he try for more intimacy, for whatever her response, he would at least know where he stood in her eyes.

He found her enthroned in a volume of Voltaire. She was tricked out for her amusement, in a subtle and modest fashion, with beads and licks of inky silk like an 19th Century palace courtesan. I waited, barely viewing them from another chamber. Hulk approached her with his precise little don's paces, and immediately forgot the rules. Surf addressed him in a husky and melodious voice.

"How may I *serve* thee, my lord?"

He quailed somewhat, with his china-blue eyes, while Surf's gaze had the grape-blue darkness of the sea. He imagined her naked as a sunrise, offering her pearly haunches, and lost his voice. They both wanted each other; I could tell from the awkwardness of their movements.

Lacking the linguistic skills of her previous lovers, he tried a furtive, wolfish look, what he thought a practiced womanizer might affect in proposing trysts, or secret assignations. At this, Surf became peevish and vexed, while Hulk's reserve was torn with wild pangs. A gracious tilting of her head announced he might try again. She cast eyes upon him.

Above them were gilded friezes and printed cherubs posturing in a ceiling of blue sky. To Hulk, she was sitting like an icon in a little chancel, or some shrine of Aphrodite.

While he thought of her as some delicate cathedral, and for him she later became that, Surf was hot, a true sensitive. Her crude admirers in Herzegovina villages, in her prior life of mysterious errands for unknown agencies, thought her an English hussy and besieged her with mash notes. But to Hulk's fumbling erotic maneuvers, she maintained the excellence of her teatime deportment.

The tension between them increased. The courtyard of the museum appeared as a million priapic blades of icy grass. I sensed her tastes were sybaritic, and that below her belly a leaping tropic flame drove her, but to Hulk she emanated the virginity of the rose.

She said nothing as he gathered himself, so that I wondered what she was dreaming about. I could see he was brooding, internally enumerating his sins, while thinking of her pale nipples like grapes, or diamond hard, polished with light. One could almost hear them trembling, like figs bursting.

In the first semester Hulk had thought of her as a small silver bowl of sweets, but now she was his shining darling, the last train at the world's end. From a distance I saw Hulk, in an act of fearful temerity, about to reach for her. I turned in silence, leaving them to their private glory.

At the end of term, all of these paths were interlacing: the intrigues of the Six, the diverse studies overseas, the hunters and the hunted, love at Harvard. I had become the man who knew too much.

○

CLASSES HAD EVOLVED into one large boardroom of eager participants, a free-for-all of controlled, analytical *repartee* and one-upmanship. Our confidence arose from daily exposure to wildly divergent perspectives of scholars from Vladivostok to Patagonia, from faculty and visiting physicians, physicists, bankers, and mathematicians, and from the several trained assassins in grad student clothing, temporarily supplanting their American, Chinese or Russian military uniforms.

Finals, the last barrier before we were released across the nations for our policy projects, began with an atmosphere of *brio*, our strengths *in potentia* no longer. The scene soon yielded to muttered heretical expletives.

Hagendas materialized indistinctly from a long night, like an abandoned rose garden at morning's light. She bore a little silver pen, and a current of loathing about standard deviation problems. One student, an early leader through his familiars at Exeter and Yale, was spoilt like a lord of creation no longer; he was shaken and unsteady before our blurring faces. We were covered in snowflakes, like a snowy island, our bodies blue and swollen, our clothing wet and smoking with a rank haze and pungent misery.

We had waded through huge icy drifts, past the university's tottering feudalisms, to collapse in a kind of splenetic apathy, as the dispirited, dull beasts that we were. With flamboyant gestures of her disengaged hand, Surf led a few choruses in humming the "Dead March" of *Saul*.

As the Blue Books circulated, the less-studied were on the fringes of outrage; the skilled had malignant euphorias. Beyond the Charles, long clouds rose into a ragged, fretful sky. We were all but a motionless sea of the watchful and impenitent. The thin snarl of a proctor, whom no one knew, instructed us to open our exams. His last word fell upon us like a headsman's axe.

"Begin."

At the first sighting of the problem sets, Hulk gave an involuntary start, then puffed and blew in his fussy way. He whispered to Surf, who was tense as a thread. Wide circles of sharp frosts, etched on a wall of windows above the Charles, were no less keen than our grief. Downcast expressions remained unhidden; mists of quaint oaths rose from the listless. One student, with not a trace of atomic insight on one exam section, sat frozen like a Trappist monk imagining some blameless purlieu.

Hammer peered at this most riveting document, and emitted a sigh, some sort of beastly grace note to the tragic silence. Hagendas, lifting her throat of silk, barely spoke, but raised her hand high and firm, our Gladiatrix in this Coliseum of mind.

"Morituri te salutamus."

Waves of premature speculation buffeted us, our futures dwindling each second. But over the hours, flights of fancy about the likelihood of survival replaced our resigned lethargy, until at last the class recaptured its vivacity. Bursts of swift lucidity soon followed, as we raised our ladders over castle walls of mathematical arcana. With our newfound seigecraft, we all somehow weathered the massed armies of incomprehension.

A lecture room voice, mordant and arrogant, hastened the shambling ones, including me. It all ended abruptly, followed by our nervous laughter. Suddenly, there were handclasps of parting, embraces of relief and fondness; our matrices of hesitant lovers were set adrift in their arks of desire. We sailed into the unborn morning, away from this ice storm of reason, and no one – not one – looked back.

THE LAST AFTERNOON was spent in alone in Pusey stacks, engrossed in the Harvard Map Collection with its 1569 Mercator Projection, and seeking city maps for an itinerary to Moscow-London-Central Asia and beyond. Rampant heroin traffic, which was undermining the New Russia with addiction and death, required months of research away from Cambridge. Deep in Pusey, envisioning encounters in Amsterdam, Basel, Zürich and Bangkok, I sketched the scenes of a modern Venetian argosy, a search for dark spirits and the lairs of dragons.

Tousled with lack of sleep but blessedly free of coursework, on an aircraft out of Logan to D.C., I reflected on the geometrical insanity of our second year, of our privileged white prison. Behind were the Yard's statues adorned in hoarfrost, the literary *bric-à-brac*, the moldering textbooks, our imminent degrees embossed with Harvard's crest, our equilibrium between life and heraldry.

Receding below, Boston's Back Bay was covered with a silver floccus; the seas shattered with forbidding lowlands and fingers of rock. Gone, for now, were the acres of beloved academic hysterias, the cabalistic rituals of probability and economics, the plotting of graphs upon the night. Before us in our projects abroad were the dead vocabularies of ancient cultures, and even greater ciphers.

At Dulles Airport, where customs officials usually said "Welcome back, Sir," passport control took a little too long this time. It was as if there were a "report but do not detain" flag in the system, either a courtesy to this traveling researcher or some implacable surveillance on a person of interest. Although Aeroflot to Moscow was replete with exotic agendas, a cold prickle of anxiety still ran through me.

The heavy signature of cloud above Dulles runway curled into *troikas* and sleighs and Slavic nights. The sea was lime-green, dark emerald. Below, the cold meniscus of the Atlantic was reaching out, then subsiding.

A tawny purple dusk extended until the twilight lingered no longer, for over the Atlantic we entered the edge of a partial eclipse, then a rare path of totality. Passengers rushed to stand in silence by the windows, as the cloud layers darkened to the horizons, like the passing of fate's somber hand.

The last of the sun was night-black. We flew toward the burning ring, so far away from the fear now. I thought only of the purity of the Russian winter landscapes, the opulence of the snows.

Chapter 10.

The Whisper of Stars

Alone, in a full coat
No hat and no snow boots
You are trying to be calm
A flaxen strand of your hair
Lights up your face…

Snow melts on your lashes
Sadness is in your eyes
It is as if your image
Your bravely erect figure
Were being etched forever
Upon my very heart.

- Pasternak, *Dr. Zhivago*, poem to Lara, at Varykino

We are in fear, thou, a man of learning, comest to us and hast seen
here of our best and worst, and whence thou goest hence thou wilt
tell of everything.

- Prince Basil III to the Monk Maxim, before imprisoning him
in a Moscow monastery

Back in the U.S.S.R., you don't know how lucky you are…

- McCartney/Lennon

A THIN GREY LINE in the frozen expanse of Russia, the road from Sheremetyvo Airport to Moscow was littered with Marlboro billboards. The radio of my private citizen's small car, in a ride negotiated by arm waving exchanges minutes earlier, played the Stones intermingled with Russian music. I could think only of our distant country.

There is no Cyrillic advertising from JFK to Manhattan. And when was the last time you heard a Russian song? They know us here far better than we know them, and we are so very much the lesser for that.

Fanatic chess players, voracious readers with books sold on card tables at street corners, a lust for the symphony and ballet, the Russians shared crowded communal tables in restaurants, making the couples *à deux* isolation of American dining out seem very poor indeed. Women danced on bars if in the mood, and there was pervasive respect for intellectuals and physicians making $60 a month. Full professors trustingly offered conveyance in rare personal automobiles for a few rubles, for people flagged each other down without incident in Moscow with its 15 million people and no taxicabs. This vibrant oil-rich white Nigeria with nukes and Czarists and narcotraficante oligarchs all mixed together, secure in the knowledge they were stronger than we who were weakened by television and technology and trash food and the lack of our own Stalingrad – the Russians victorious even during the sporadic cannibalism – and all within memory of many of the old ones with wrinkled eyes that saw too much, shuffling across Red Square.

Inching down Tverskoi Street in Moscow center, we passed a notorious club with "Night Train" emblazoned above its entrance, as crowds within Soviet-style markets examined fresh meats hung above tins of sweets stacked high enough to provide shelter from the milling streets for *babushkas* wrapped in shawls. Russian military officers strode with determined gaits in the cruel daylight toward the Kremlin wall and interrogation rooms of the Lubyanka. Beautiful Russian women attended posh shops here and there, as furtive Chechens drifted warily under the eyes of corrupt policemen shaking down the occasional vehicle. Teenage *cocottes* began to congregate along the sidewalks for their evening rides. Passing beneath the Stalinesque façades of decrepit buildings, we arrived among the chic entryways and multilingual staff of the Hotel Metropol, crossroads of the Bolshevik Revolution and habitat of Lenin as he secretly indulged in the pleasures of the Bolshoi *corps de ballet*.

Relieved of my unusual American passport at the Metropol desk, I was shown personally to a well-appointed, high-ceilinged room with filmy draperies and inviting percale sheets by a petite receptionist with finely-coifed black hair and tailored suit. She conversed in such excellent English; I inquired if she had learned in Britain.

"I've never been outside Russia," she purred confidingly, affecting a little *moue*.

She had been raised in the Soviet era of restricted travel, when presentable youth with language skills were recruited and trained by KGB as undercover Intourist guides who controlled itineraries during seldom visits by Western European and American visitors. It was a time when sultry chambermaids who were skilled KGB operatives succeeded in placing eavesdropping devices in the U.S. Embassy after seducing a Marine guard in heavily wired and dreamlike honey traps. A KGB compromise known as *provokatsya*, it was a tactic prohibited to U.S. intelligence agencies by our Puritan heritage. But this receptionist was only a talented girl chosen for her superior bearing, selected to welcome affluent international clientele to the new Russia, where the heavy blizzard of rubles and dollars blinded even the most avaricious. Across Tverskoi in Red Square, Lenin's waxy visage remained entombed in the red granite Mausoleum as the grand economic experiment of Communism marched into oblivion, its dirge only the mournful clicking heels of three stern goose-stepping guards, worried if their meager Army paychecks would arrive.

Thus immured in cultural shock, for few Americans then had appeared at this leading edge of *glasnost*, I confronted a menu in Cyrillic while Russian news and CNN Europe filtered through a haze of jet lag. Halfway across the planet, the movement finally had stopped. Yet it was only a few hours before I was due at the special entrance to the American Embassy for debriefing prior to meeting – at some indeterminate location in Moscow through even more locked doors and assorted examples of weaponry – a crafty Russian officer who coordinated 5000 armed secret agents across 11 time zones from St. Petersburg to Vladivostok. He was Major General Alexander Sergeev, the head of the MVD Drug Department of all Russia.

AFTER FILTERING through complementary *Pravda* and *Izvestia* newspapers and the English language *Moscow Times*, I unpacked my encrypted laptop and contacted the Moscow correspondent for the *Toronto Star*, who first reported fentanyl deaths in Russia. She advised me that the Metropol's resident *kahgebeyshnick* – the KGB man behind the lobby walls – listened to new arrivals' calls. To meet with the correspondent but still shaky, I descended to the atrium and inspected this new world.

A splendid brace of delicate swans, perfectly manicured Russian girls in the hotel's small bar, both brightened invitingly at my passage; they would entertain together in artful nocturnal arrays for 500 USD. It was simple to recognize nearby the groups of *biznismeni*, usually single brash figures gripping their mobiles – accompanied by dim bodyguards in long black leather coats – all looking surly, bored and malevolent.

Chancing upon an Oxford chemist in the atrium, and meeting with the *Toronto Star* correspondent, I secured four tickets for our evening at the Bolshoi ballet performance of Tchaikovsky's *La Bayadère*. My translator for the event soon appeared, an elegant and disturbingly comely woman with natural ice blond hair in a *chignon*, and who possessed blue, almost seraphic eyes. She spoke perfect English and Arabic and Russian. Poised and clearly practiced in the diplomatic and perhaps the sensual arts, she was the daughter of a leading mathematician at the Lebedev Institute, one of Moscow's think tanks. Although it would not have been surprising if her background were in clandestine intelligence, she had such a refined manner, with her laugher as gentle as soft bells, that such impressions were for the time allayed.

I experienced the Bolshoi that evening graced by one intimate with the ballerinas and dancers of Muscovite artistic society, as the *entreé* of our *pas de deux* moved into the final coda, the dance together. Thereafter, at the pace of lovers, we walked toward the Metropol as our breaths froze – sparking, silent, falling – the "whisper of stars" to Russians. It was as though old and distant civilizations comprehended a kiss. Beneath the Kremlin's spires the Red Star of past glories bathed her pale white skin, as we entered the long and forbidding night of the profound Russian winter.

IN THE BLEAKNESS of a grey and snowbound morning, chauffeured BMWs now crowded the lanes of Tverskoi, replacing the black Chaika limousines and Volga sedans of former Communist Party *apparatchiki*. The little Zhigulis of the few fortunate proletarians edged past the hotel entrance as the block-long ramparts of the Kremlin stood timeless, mute and unassailable. My driver Vladimir emerged in a dark green Mercedes, as heavily-bound *militizia* – the domestic police – waved him forward. At the mandatory visit to the U.S. Embassy, two impressive English-speaking Russian guards greeted me, wearing thick black uniforms, astrakhan wool collars and mink caps garlanded in ice crystals. Issuing a special pass, they permitted entry into the high walled grounds, unseen by the dreary, stalwart line of Russian nationals seeking visas.

A foreign service office provided an escort down a series of corridors to the Legal Attache Tom Robertson's office. Robertson, who knew in advance of my arrival, listened thoughtfully as I described the Russian drug market, the study at Harvard, and the ASecState's instructions on querying MVD Major General Sergeev about the fentanyl overdoses. Telephoning the MVD – the Russian Interior Ministry and equivalent of the FBI – he requested in flawless Russian an official interview with the General.

"What's Sergeev like?" I quizzed Robertson.

"He's a proud Russian," he replied in a careful non-description, "very strong. He loves his country."

The following day Vladimir and I gathered the fetching mathematician's daughter. She now appeared with her hair in a ballerina bun, wearing a clinging black suit by Fendi that swathed an hourglass figure and revealed her practice of serious physical disciplines. For the MVD, I thought it best to bring my usual student translator Dmitri, a gaunt, lumbering six-four twenty-two-year-old university student encumbered by a large backpack.

The Mercedes floated through the morning-after desolation of the Stary Arbat – the old market and its clusters of haunted opiate users. We passed hospitals and emergency rooms where I would conduct interviews of physicians overcome by Moscow's venomous tide of narcotics. Not yet school age boys played stickball, laughing beneath the spires of St. Basil's Cathedral, while beyond the windows of a small orphanage little girls in brown uniforms and pinafores sat attentively. I turned to watch, in their bright faces, Russia's future.

We fell into an introspective silence as our Mercedes approached with caution the fortress-like entrance to the *Ministerstvo Vnutrennikh Def*, the MVD of all Russia. Suddenly captive between four walls of impenetrable iron gates, we were held there for an interminable period of contemplative penitence. Our private reflections on the quality of our sins against the state were stimulated by the open muzzle of a 108-millimeter cannon attached to a 5-ton Russian tank at the entrance, and pointing directly through the Mercedes's windows at our heads.

Suitably unnerved, Vladimir gripped the steering wheel as our lady in Fendi remained unperturbed, cool and aloof in the back seat. Dmitri and I walked with a certain tremulousness toward the MVD building, for its hallways and their rough, wooden floors were populated by ghosts of the legions who had never returned, summarily executed in the Lubyanka or shipped to the nameless penal colonies flung across the Gulag archipelago like evil trails from Lucifer's wand.

○

AS WE ENTERED the MVD, several officials in non-descript grey suits quickly stepped forward, introduced themselves in Russian with smiles and handshakes, and led me around the metal detectors, while poor Dmitri was detained with an unceremonious and meticulous frisking by crowds of grim security staff. Properly intimidated, Dmitri managed to keep a reverent, murmured translation going as we were whisked to the top floor and into the private chambers of Major General Sergeev.

Sergeev stood at a small interview table, closely accompanied by two taciturn high-level MVD officials who affixed us with their steady, unerring gaze. After brief cordialities, he began to hold forth in a loud monolog as if he were on the dais before an auditorium. With permission I produced a recorder as Sergeev continued in a twenty-minute tribute to drug control efforts in Mother Russia; it was the obligatory *pokazukha*, a canned speech for the edification of foreign officials. I waited for this initial exposition to wind down, so we could begin our more thoughtful chess game of delicate, mutual questioning. He finally issued a proclamation on Russian resistance to addiction.

"We are stronger than Americans!" he cried.

"In many ways," I conceded dourly, knowing well the greater probability of Russians surviving a mass die off from catastrophic events.

The tales of Stalingrad, the voracious Stalinist pogroms, and the 20 million Russian deaths in the World Wars, was in somber contrast with the leisurely domestic peace of an untested American population. Such Russian strength came at unspeakable costs, as Gorbachev recalled when he first walked through a San Francisco supermarket. Seeing the abundance for all, he wept.

Sergeev, indeed the proud Russian, discouraged policy research into MVD efficiency.

"And we don't let academics examine our police matters."

Off balance, I glanced for a moment through the narrow, fortified window at the rooftops of Moscow and the white snarl of Soviet housing projects. The gold onion dome of the reconstructed Church of the Redeemer punctuated the winter sky. Thickly swaddled children gaily ice-skated at Sokolniki Park, unaware of the adolescent junkies who lay hidden nearby. Down-and-out in blasted tenements, and huddled near their smoky fires in steel drums, they shared needles in the piercing shadows.

"We've had some success with careful thinking by researchers." I returned. "You must agree that ideas can be generated outside law enforcement circles. Why not help each other on a public health issue?"

We had reached a standoff. Having exhausted our reserves of official points and counterpoints, I decided to break the cant and expose a few nerves.

"Can you tell me of the fentanyl outbreak in Moscow and the many Russian deaths?"

Sergeev darkened, moving toward me from behind his desk, and quickly ended the inquiry.

"We have that problem under control."

I knew the sources of this microgram-range killer were clandestine laboratories in Azerbaijan. The initial manufacturers, controlled by the Moscow-Kazan *mafiya*, were identified as the young student winners of the Russian Chemistry Olympiad. They were imprisoned for eight years. As destitute organic chemists became abundant, the formula was acquired by narcotics syndicates, while the growing ranks of cadavers at Botkin Hospital from overdoses slept undisturbed on steel trays.

Lightly feigning ignorance on such matters as just another researcher far from home, then using an old interrogation trick to assess Segeev's credibility, I asked him a question to which I knew the answer.

"Look, we think there is a growing population of Russian heroin addicts. And yes, we have many more of them in America, but discern the same problem is in its early stages here. Can you tell me the primary source countries?"

Sergeev looked at me for a long moment, then lied with absolute confidence.

"Ninety percent of our heroin comes from Vladivostok, up from Burma."

At best, this was a test by Sergeev. The bulk of Russian heroin was transported from Afghanistan through the former Russian satellite states Uzbekistan and Tajikistan, courtesy of old routes established by ancient smuggling families and reprobate Russian troops projecting Soviet power into Central Asia. Controlling the primary traffickers at the Uzbek/Afghan border was the former Communist Afghan warlord General Dostum.

Sergeev was practicing *vranyo* – disinformation accepted with knowing resignation by both parties – even as we both knew that covert and corrupt Red army officials harvested much of the billion or so in currencies transiting Russia. We did our little *pirouette* of feigned mutual deception but the point wasn't pressed, for we understood the need for operational fictions.

The other MVD officials present – Leonid Tancorov and Colonel Vladimir Ibragimov – said nothing for hours, remaining highly attentive as Dmitri quickly translated back and forth in exhaustingly detailed exchanges. At the conclusion of Sergeev's interview, I murmured to Dmitri in an aside.

"How do you say *quid pro quo* in Russian?"

Colonel Ibragimov, who had been utterly silent since our arrival, smoothly responded in impeccable Oxonian tones reminiscent of punting on the Thames or dining at high table at Jesus College.

"You simply say, '*quid pro quo.*'"

For hours, Ibragimov had feigned his inability to comprehend English. As the courtly Ibragimov and I emerged from Sergeev's office, the specters of those who lived their last days in these very rooms fled before the charms of my escort. Ibragimov, admitting he had been educated in England, vouchsafed a kind and intriguing farewell.

"I would love to talk with you at length, but Sergeev won't let me."

I promised that one day we would meet again, this time in freedom.

◯

SADLY WITHOUT THE MATHEMATICIAN'S DAUGHTER – with her softly musical laughter, piquant insights on Russian society, and her disarming and failed attempts at understated sensuality – Dmitri and I circulated among the insular circles, fiefdoms and turf wars of the new Russian drug control leadership. After interviewing prominent researchers, hospital directors, and high police officials, we arrived one grey afternoon at a copse of dying trees in the courtyard of a pedestrian one-story building on the periphery of Moscow.

We were to meet Vladimir Sorokin, the primary chemist for the Russian National Forensic Laboratory, who was responsible for analyzing samples of heroin from the street corners of Ekaterinburg to Omsk to the casinos of Moscow. Lost among tattered green buildings, Sorokin's lab was identified by its single sleepy guard leaning against a doorway and wearing rumpled olive military fatigues. He straightened up in a concerned manner, alarmed to see unrecognized visitors, especially one with a serious air bearing down on him in a black bespoke suit, accompanied by an attentive personal assistant advising in a low hush in English as our driver looked on.

We were welcomed cordially by Dr. Sorokin, with whom I had many exchanges earlier through the courtesy of Muscovite engineers at a nearby petroleum company, for the national laboratory had neither email nor fax. Sorokin and the facility occupied a single, modest room occupied by a few tables piled high with baggies of seized powders. In a corner resided an inoperable, antique gas chromatograph that alluded to the scientific but now was merely decorative.

We spoke of our fears that methamphetamine soon would make its appearance in Russia. He confided that no large clandestine labs of MDMA had been seized. After some friendly bantering and a round of toasts while sharing 100 milliliter glass lab beakers filled with hot *krepky* – strong, steaming black tea sweetened with jam – it seemed appropriate to query Sorokin about how Russia expected to monitor and stem the advance of limitless narcotics from Afghanistan, and synthetic opioids such as fentanyl from Azerbaijan. Vladimir was more taken with the evolving international MDMA club scene, perhaps stimulated by the volumes he proudly displayed on a shelf: Sasha and Ann Shulgin's *PIHKAL* (Phenethylamines I Have Known and Loved).

"I've read it all, in English!" he exclaimed with admiration.

It became painfully apparent that Russia rapidly was devolving into an emerging narcostate – one with thousands of nuclear weapons – controlled by increasingly strong crime syndicates. It was dispiriting to observe that, although his lab was the front line of defense, Sorokin could not analyze street samples of heroin or any other opiate, for he had no reference samples for his gas chromatograph. His machine effectively was blind. While we sipped hot tea from lab beakers, I proposed one solution.

"Why don't you, or someone at Moscow State, synthesize what you need? It's only a few grams of various substances, and Russia has hundreds of the world's most skilled organic chemists."

"Ah, yes, there are many who would do so," Sorokin explained with a despondent air, "but the Minister of Drugs, Eduard Babayan, must approve such syntheses, and he won't authorize it."

In essence, Russia could not identify the wave of opiates from which teenagers from Tomsk to Petropavlovsk naively derived their bliss, only to find their malaise, and not infrequently their deaths. And Russia could not do so because the permits for all drug possession throughout its 11 time zones, from the pharmaceutical giants to simple corner pharmacies, were signed by a single individual – Babayan – who did not trust university professors or the technical institutes or even his own national forensic personnel to prepare small quantities of reference samples of controlled substances. It was obvious we must intervene with Babayan – during my next trip to Russia in the fall – and resolve this absurdity.

Yet this hurried foray deep into Russia's drug leadership began to seem almost too easy for one of my ambiguous background. There was an unsettling feeling that my history – even overlain lately with Harvard's aegis and lightly with that of State – might have been detected within this old kingdom of covert operatives. Anticipating my return with the snows of November, Dr. Sorokin, sensing my hesitant mood, encouraged contact with Babayan but advised against further penetration of the Russian establishment through interviews at the FSB – the new counterintelligence arm of the former KGB – about their foci on drug trafficking.

"Don't go over there," he cautioned, "they think everyone's a *spy*."

Chapter 11.

Gigi

I wept, because my eyes had seen that secret, hypothetical object
which no man has ever truly looked upon, the inconceivable universe.
I had a sense of infinite veneration, infinite pity.

- JLB, *The Aleph*

Whenever you can, be the grey man.
Be the man no one remembers.

- Alex Berenson, *The Faithful Spy*

"What sort of government have you bequeathed to us, Sir?"

"A republic, Ma'am, if you can keep it."

- B. Franklin, to a woman on the street at the Second Drafting

THE SCEPTERED ISLE on a fogbound morning hath many jewels, among them the august sitting room of the Elgin marbles in the British Museum. A few hours of exploration in London led me here, perhaps drawn by the memory of Vermilion's heroines in Berlin, for the moonlit spectacle of their transformative ardors still endured. Abiding before the statues, one could contemplate the silken white figures of the Graces on the Parthenon's friezes and pediments and square metopes. For an imaginative hour – at last alone with them – I was in their embrace, they in mine. Our ecstatic reveries were unchanging, their kiss forever held.

At the periphery, like chickadees from branch to flowery branch, a small group of Scottish schoolchildren migrated, having moved agape through the Sarcophagi, armored knights, and ornate catafalques to arrive in this quiet, spacious room. They were all of nine years old, the girls like fragile budding roses pale from the northern light, the thin gangling boys no less, accompanied by a stout, florid matron with an Aberdeen brogue and sturdy shoes. She hobbled with a twisted mahogany cane that had a scarlet cairngorm set into the handle.

The children became silent, rapt at what seemed to be a polished museum official who described in charming and fanciful terms the glories of the marbles and their mysterious histories in Constantinople with Lord Elgin. At the performance's end, the flock of nascent scholars – all with fond glances at the official – were herded reluctantly toward the Rosetta Stone. It was as if some spell had been broken.

He studied the marbles, hands clasped behind him, his nails perfectly manicured. He wore a proper Saville Row double breasted suit, shoes from Loeb, and a red tie beset with the almost invisible standards of Christ Church College, Oxford. He affected thick black horn-rimmed glasses, and had very short, dark hair scrupulously trimmed by discrete London barbers. He emanated the authority of some erudite bureaucrat on a break from entertaining defected scientists at Whitehall.

Passing the marbles with the reflective pace of an athlete, he alighted at a respectable distance on the leather surface of the modernist bench upon which I sat alone, clasping copies of *The Guardian* and *International Herald Tribune*. My reveries thus broken, I was disinclined to converse. I returned to the alabaster elegance of a caryatid, a young priestess of Artemis supporting an entablature, and to the symmetrical etching of her ribs and lifted breasts, so undraped by her eternal, motionless robes.

"It does seem rather an *adoration*, in spectral lunar whiteness," he announced, uninvited.

He had the same Winchester public school accent so entertaining to Aberdeen youth. Yet his observation was alarmingly synchronous with my private – and most vivid – retrospectives.

"*Phoebe silvarumque Diana*," he continued, "the invocation to the moon."

I recalled V-1 and V-2 before the open French window in the heated night, arm-in-arm with their lithe neophyte, each dressed only in shining white rays of the horned orb, all urging its luminous seed to spill upon them.

"Phoebus and Diana, Queen of the Woods," he explained, "the opening line of *Carmen Saeculare*."

I looked at this classic historian and polite intruder, as he breached conventional social barriers. He seemed harmless enough.

"Pretty far from the tragic flophouse in San Francisco's Tenderloin," he said in pure Berkeleyese, "but not the nubile Berlin nights."

My heart leapt. It was Crimson. His hair was dyed, his eyes of autumn now the ice-blue of fjords, his bearing and speech flawless but pure theater. I admitted again the excellent crafts of the Six, their ability to find me across the earth. It was apparent they had access to the digital footprint of any individual, or retained teams of refined pavement artists with global mobility.

⬡

HE EXTENDED HIS HAND in greeting. In my shock, and the temporal dissonance of Greenwich Time, I seemed instantly to acquire his almost unearthly frequency. The shattering kaleidoscope of our first encounter on Limantour Beach was replaced by an ever more profound and immediate intertwining of our consciousness. It seemed now that a superhuman altruistic world gently caressed the very species from which it evolved.

As the moments intensified, we stood like somnambulists, moving through the dream of ancients. At the veil's parting, the physical collections of the museum's antiquities became infused with light and life, and the dead rose to dance. There was a rumble of cannon and whiff of grapeshot by Nelson's memorata, then blazing timbers, horses and shredded sails of the armada fell into the sea. Hieratic paintings and Greek crosses and gold inscriptions became weighty with meanings, all roadmaps to our cataclysmic realizations to come.

Overwhelmed, I staggered then sought balance, for the psychic effects heightened with each encounter of the Six. Distortions of physiognomies soon made stone Crusaders laugh like Mephistopheles, their robes alight with swirling languages and ecclesiastical scripts in rainbows of words. Sarcophagi disgorged fully formed Egyptian kings, and the reformer Amenhotep IV gazed sternly upon the adder and the asp, while the priestess whores of Babylon were anointed with oils and worshiped with gold.

The occult breathings thickened with harems' perfumes, as the eight full breasts of Diana Multimammia beckoned, filled with the sweet milk of apostolical labors. Scheherazade, naked but for wisps of Episcopal silks, trailed St. Elmo's fire from her arms, as Orpheus's lyre coaxed a fecund Eurydice back from Hades.

The phenomena both feigned and promised infinity, like the interminable number of hexagonal galleries in Borges's *Library of Babel*. Our elaborate brigantine of perception – at first issuing forth with following seas and a fair wind to fill its studding sail, topgallants, royals and flying jib – soon foundered in the roiling oceans of dissolving science and ethics and history and morals. We found a sacristan's bench and somehow, breathlessly, managed an exchange.

"But we can't *live* like this!" I cried, in the museum's hush.

○

THE CONCATENATIONS OF PHENOMENA continued to ensphere us. Polytheistic fancies abounded, as medieval Psalter leaves rapidly turned themselves. St. Augustine's palaces and his caverns of memory appeared, amid the cosmic miscellany and carousels of mind in the City of God.

"Yes, illuminations must be fleeting," Crimson returned, "they only guide us after reintegration."

The erotic component now incarcerated strongly, the lurid air softening and musky, the ripe bellies of nuns and queens and concubines and fertility effigies all swollen with the fruits of desire. A lush and inviting model of Catherine de Medici wickedly parted her robe. I thought of Vermilion's description of the Histrioni, or Abysmali, who believed their insatiable wantonness ensured their double in Heaven was sanctified. Crimson, in an unsettling feat of telepathy, sensed and externalized my memory.

"Ah…among them were the Nebuchadnezzars of Nitria, who refuted Christian dogma but loved God. They grazed on grasses like oxen, their hair wild like eagles."

"But one must have codes of behavior, social conventions," I opined hollowly in this vulnerable state, "or walk naked in the streets."

Crimson agreed, holding on to the varieties of religious spectra as if they were firm ground, while all about us the heavens raced.

"As they devoured wild plants," he said, "the Abysmali took their women openly, in daylight, and randomly. They mounted like herds of stallions and mares forever in heat. And before the eyes of others, precipitating waves of copulation with multiple partners."

"All of the Abysmali were without such restraint?"

"No. Others self-mutilated. Some of the ascetics lived in sewers. Their double in Heaven was pious when they were cruel, or did good deeds as they sinned."

I grew uncomfortable at the subject, and watched as the phantasms shifted from the erotic. The transfixing screams of lascivious couplings became holy liturgies of compassion within temples of virtue.

"Could psychedelic exposures in large populations alter civilization?"

"We certainly hope so. The effects are temporary, insightful, but available to – or chosen by – only a very few, not across entire societies. Use is self-limiting. Not some permanent state of frightful possession like the Abysmali. Many failed world-views, or errors of perception, have consumed religious groups before us."

"Errors of perception?"

"A trifling example would be in Isaiah. There are parts adopted by Händel for the *Messiah* oratorio, but the prophecies that open the work, seeming to celebrate Christ, were written in honor of Cyrus the Persian."

"But a failed world-view?"

"After the early work of Cosmas, the *Topographia Christiana*, it was thought for a thousand years the earth was foursquare like a tabernacle. Our modern illusions are held no less dearly."

The glories of civilization around us crumbled into the detritus of primitive culture, cruel emblems of the knife and fist. The museum now was a necropolis of our baser selves. As Crimson spoke in this setting, I noted the classicist and historical leanings of the Six. It seemed a contrast with their synthetic antidote for hatred, a substance some considered a gift from the future, or interdimensional worlds. I returned to the present, to Crimson's observations.

"And what modern illusions are held?"

"The spiritual descendants of the Abysmali, one might call them, are burying doomsday devices across the planet in fear and avarice. They are machine-gunning the last elephants, and rejoicing in carbon emissions, all sanctified by their avaricious rationales. They graze on flesh, convinced they are the chosen."

I looked up as the ceiling and walls vanished. There were malignant specters in the sky, and *autos-de-fé* burned on devastated hillsides like the dark, flickering campfires of post-apocalyptic tribes. Growing fearful at the wheel of alternative futures, I grasped at Crimson as an interview subject.

"But the Six, what are their religious preferences?"

"I am Judeo-Christian, Indigo is Vedanta, Vermilion Hedonist, Magenta Buddhist. Cobalt awaits the next visitation."

"And what are we now, at this moment?"

"We are as Sophocles described in *Antigone*, neither dwellers among men, nor ghosts."

⬡

SURROUNDED BY THE GREAT RELICS of divinity and bloodletting and passion, all still abundantly procreating, we tread with care across the museum's polished floors inlaid with tombstones and epitaphs. The surfaces still patterned in mandalas beneath us. We passed the Mesopotamian artifacts of Ur and Nineveh, then a magnificent gilded clock which seemed imbued with an astral magnetism that tugged at our spirits. Suddenly, as if through a transparent barrier no evil could pass, we entered a dimension of ineffable peace, and instantly were grounded into absolute clarity. It was by the very smallest of things.

Next to the exit, attended by her nanny, was a little girl playing with her set of stuffed animals, having a tea party. She was inviting Bunny to play with Gigi the Giraffe, who had a broken leg. She told Gigi that Dad would fix her leg one day so she could walk. They all prayed together for Gigi the Giraffe's leg. One of her guests was a little stuffed angel, with a halo and white wings, and who bowed her head in prayer.

Enchanted as we, the knights of the realms, the kings of kings, and the lions of lions, all again stood motionless in immemorial silence. Forever guarding the transcendent, they now protected the most gentle of beings.

We stepped lightly onto the flagstones of the British Museum entryway, and into the blessed daylight. Beneath the polled plane trees, finely cultivated rows of nasturtiums, fuchsias, geraniums and snapdragons burst from the earth before us. They were luxuriant, celestial, like lavish fairies created to please the children. At this delightful reminder of a benevolent deity, Crimson recalled the Sufi poet Rumi.

"We come spinning out of nothingness, like stars."

I was still recovering. Confronting a mountainous wave of consciousness, even repeatedly, has a fearsome aspect beside which the most expiatory baptism is but a flickering candle. One never grows cavalier at dying, and being born.

Returning from the mystic spheres, we began to get our bearings. We traveled along a road of ever lessening signs and omens, to encounter the drab rise of the mundane. Passing an 11th Century church, I noticed the cheap white plastic letters askew in a dusty frame. They proclaimed that to the evening's Rosary had been added a *De Profundis*.

⬡

WE WALKED ACROSS LONDON from the West End into Hyde Park, to rest upon a bench overlooking the Serpentine and the lakeside willows. Crimson said little, apparently touched by the little girl's tea party. Still fragile, he made a rare admission.

"*God*, I miss my children."

"Can you not call them?"

"Only with difficulty, to avoid tracking."

The severity of the covert life required the Six to be isolated during their operations, at such dreadful cost. They seemed to suffer most, not from fear or stress, but from the wounding of their hearts.

After long reflection, he led me into Claridge's, a grand dowager of a hotel, where there was a formal and delicate two-hour service of afternoon tea. We were seated on cream damask chairs, while an elegant lady in her eighties entertained well-behaved schoolgirls of seven or eight, all goslings in blue silk. Young women from Liverpool or Krakow discretely prepared tea services of trimmed cucumber sandwiches and cakes. A white piano was addressed with refined passion by a deferential pianist who displayed perfect teeth and slick black hair and patent leather slippers. The setting was of another age. Victorian and lovely in its simple perfections, it was the antithesis of the Goth tribal rebellion in San Francisco that Crimson often haunted. He rationalized both circumstances as tradecraft.

"A surveillance team would find this impossible."

The tea was served by a Slovenian 20-year-old with her fine hair in curled braids, possessing erect, disciplined movements and cultivated Eastern European manners. Under Crimson's knowing gaze and manner, and a few words I could not overhear, she palpably relaxed.

The pianist began playing the same Chopin Nocturne, Opus 9, Number 2, transposed from memory by V-1 on the harpsichord in Berlin. I tensed, then yielded to their demonstration of exquisite planning and foresight.

"That's quite a coincidence."

"We thought you might like it," he admitted.

"Is there no data the Six doesn't share?"

"For that answer, I must recall the Oxford Arabist T.E. Lawrence, who descended from the Bodleian Library in 1919 to rally the Howetat tribes on camels and fight against the Turks."

"That's a reach. How does Lawrence relate to the Six?"

"He was advised by Egyptologist Flinders Petrie, who deciphered the Merneptah stele, the first Egyptian historical mention of Israel. Petrie fondly tutored Lawrence that archeological research 'lies on the noting of the smallest details.' We adopted that advice. And part of our Washington Rules is to examine microscopically each other, and those around us. There are no secrets within our finite society."

We partook of cucumber sandwiches, arrayed on three tiers of a silver service, and found relief with the hot tea. I noticed it was chamomile, his favorite, and that Crimson had not asked. I said nothing, and tried a different tack.

"What do you do for pleasure?"

"My delight is family now, for time grows ever more precious. In earlier days, other than sailing, I hiked mountains, light technical climbing, nothing serious. The Eiger Nordwand. Bernese Oberland. Aconcagua. I failed K-2 by the Magic Line." He smiled. "That was too risky."

I laughed, for daily he faced an invisible guillotine, never knowing at whose gesture it may fall. Yet, he had grown more comfortable with me. I tried a bold inquiry, presumptuous of their trust, but with the remotest chance of disclosure.

"Where is Vermilion now?

"You might imagine him sunbathing on Tahiti Plage at St. Tropez, attending V-1 and V-2 in their glories. But they don't indulge, except as an operational necessity. Only for the seduction of information sources. I believe they are in some compartment on the Schweizerische Bundesbahn, the Swiss Railway, eliciting secrets from the Zürich Kantonpolizei. Or on the Blue Train south out of Paris. I don't know why, yet. They either target people, or experience diverse circumstances."

At this deft parry, he considered the smoky London rooftops through a gabled window, lifting his eyes to the distant Thames House. Within its digital confines, the analysts at MI-5 were kept late with a surfeit of terrorist sightings. The remote, arcane, cult-like agenda of the Six could not have concerned them.

"A few of their senior analysts might recall rumors of us, likely dismissed as fantasy, or in their more inspired moments may sense the reality. But we are a minor or non-existent issue to those who do not perceive a silent revolution of individual epiphanies."

I had no notes, and asked a question posed earlier to Vermilion, itself a fleeting but persistent augury from Indigo's ominous chronometer.

"Do you worry? That it all might end?"

"Professionally, each moment. That is my specialty. But not because of their ilk" – he indicated the Thames House – "for we are of no consequence to them. Terroristic violence is so much more newsworthy than the evolution of consciousness, sadly and thankfully. The first epidemics from neopharmacology may shift priorities."

"You mean learning and memory drugs, and erotogenics, as Magenta monitors?"

"Those, and drugs that shift personality, undermining authority, conferring selective advantages, instilling obeisance, or civil disobedience."

"But with the Six and the sacrament, a single error, a missed connection, a compromised individual, and it all becomes a nightmare?"

He considered our Slovenian miss, who was serving small sugared cookies to the quintet of merry and diminutive English girls – all proper in taffeta, curls and ribbons before their elderly empress. Heads barely above the keyboard, they had charmed the pianist, who acceded to playing some measures of Beethoven's 9th, the Ode to Joy. In tiny voices they attempted the chorale, several full octaves above the score. One was so amusing, after hushing the others, singing fragments of German in her high, wavering little girl's voice. In the most touching chorus, they all pounced on the refrain.

"We can never rest in the illusion we are safe," he said quietly, in brittle contrast to the innocence before us. "Almost all arrests are the result of informants, rarely from accidents. Nothing occurs from analysis or investigation alone. Exposure, we feel, is inversely proportional to meticulous care, but can never approach zero."

"But you ultimately are a target not only to 50 international DEA offices, and the UN programs and Interpol, but to every police agency in the world, across 170 countries. The global information grid for national security and law enforcement is being deployed."

"A working paranoia is a rational necessity" he replied, looking with benevolence upon the blossoms of English society as he whispered his words, "but there is no dignity in being afraid. We do not cower as criminals, for our intention is to end suffering in our small way, no less than any devoted priest or physician. We have the calm of feeling unchallenged on moral grounds, and persevere with a certain balanced tranquility, never in haste or self-defeating anxiety."

The cluster of silken little girls, all with garlands of small rosebuds in their hair, were circling the *grand dame* on tiptoes. Each had her arms raised over their heads and her fingertips interlaced, as if they were the spirits of spring over the wintry earth.

Crimson looked at them like a lost parent, almost grieving, then gathered himself. They were moving like pixies in a forest's magic circle, to the pianist doing lightly the Triumphal March from Aida. We left reluctantly, as worshippers from an entrancing sermon. Crimson, unsurprisingly, descended by means of the hotel kitchen elevator, then out the private exit in the direction of the Thames waterfront.

Oddly, there was no bill. The Slovenian miss only nodded slightly at me. I moved toward the entrance, confident we were not overheard, but became self-conscious at leaving to the piano's slow, matching cadence of Edelweiss.

◯

THE NATIONAL GALLERY was a few minutes' walk: its quiet hallways would permit reflection. Passing slowly down the galleries of 18th Century paintings, I stopped before a particularly fine 1784 rendition by Johann Nilson of Aloysia Lange, before she sang as Donna Anna in the first performance of Mozart's *Don Giovanni*. I retrieved the Overture for my headphones, and thought of Vermilion and his consorts, then of Mozart's platonic triad with Lange, the sister of his wife Constantine. At that moment, I may have detected one of their surveillance team.

She had a wasp waist, and was dressed in tight black satin pants. She wore a faux python cape from Harrods, posing as a student from the Royal School of Art, and affecting to read, of all things, the *Financial Times*. Perhaps the clarity of her skin gave her away, as if from cloudy days on the Isle of Skye. Or her flawless crimson nails. With an unconscious rhythmic allure – one could only feel from some imaginative *vita sexualis* – she moved across the hallway toward a distant gallery of portraits. The pale orange paper of the *Times* slowly rose, as a Geisha folds a fan with refined hesitancy, to conceal the perfect lipstick of her now hidden smile.

◯

UNCERTAIN AT THIS SOFT EMBRACE of the Six, I neglected to approach her. Rather, I wandered across Piccadilly to Charring Cross, then to my modest academic lodgings. A residence for Oxbridgians in town, it was a courtesy to an exchange visitor from the Harvard Club of Boston. The room was simple and inexpensive, without amenities, but endowed with sturdy Edwardian furniture, hand-knitted lace and a counterpane. I collapsed in wonder at the day, and awaited the night.

Crimson retrieved me without notice at a late hour, dressed in black Armani over an iridescent blue collarless shirt, with an invitation to a waiting cab. We traveled into the East End depths, to a pounding venue of electronica and the impassible body density of Euro youth, many on club drugs. He flashed a red passport at a surly guard. It was Dutch, perhaps diplomatic, bearing the imprimatur *Europese Unie Koninkrijk der Nederlanden*. The guard waved it away, grasped his hand heartily, and led us into the lasered magic of a celebratory midnight mass.

Crimson, more internalized than among the tribes of San Francisco, danced as if it were the last night of the world, the end of history. He still attended gently those in the ambient rooms, or the distressed, summoning memories of eternal love until they opened their immortal, luminous faces. Exhausted, we left for the silent, refreshing darkness, alone together. Upon farewell, he departed for the London terminus of Eurostar at St. Pancras Station. Unseen, I followed from some distance, reverently. He paid a working girl to use her phone. I saw him come undone – like a desperate father at 4 AM in another hemisphere – singing "Happy Birthday" to a beloved child.

Chapter 12.

A Tattoo for Thomas Hardy

Noon strikes on England, on Oxford town…
Good and godly kings hath built her, long ago
with her towers and tombs and statues all a row
With her fair and floral air
and the love that lingers there
And the street where the great men go.

- James Elroy Flecker, *The Dying Patriot*

Oxford, where the real and the unreal jostle in the streets
…where the river mists…and the gargoyles of Magdalen College
climb down at night and fight with those from Wykeham,
or fish under the bridges, or simply change their expressions overnight;
Oxford, where windows open into other worlds.

- Oscar Baedecker, *The Coasts of Bohemia*

What is it that breathes fire into the equations, and makes a universe
for them to describe?

- Stephen Hawking, Lucasian Professor of Mathematics, Cambridge

I AROSE EARLY, and went up to Oxford by a lively train filled with well-dressed families converging on Commemoration Day weekend, the end of the academic year. Crowds of giddy undergraduates and their dates and relatives packed High Street and Broad Street, but I soon found a small tea shop that had a tentative solitude and fresh scones, clotted cream and marmalade.

It was near Carfax, the thousand year-old intersection of four ancient Roman roads. I sipped a chamomile, for which I had asked. Around me the paths teemed with the living, but after the spectacle in the British Museum this haunted crossroad upon a reflection was a portal into millennia past. At a glance, one became conscious of the wraiths of Persian satraps and traders lost among ancestral tribes of Picts and Celts, or the ruined legions of Romans at the edge of empire with tattered heralds bearing the emperor's standard of SPQR. Ghostly heads lolled from public gibbets as rude tribes looked upon their grisly, festive punishments: the burning of witches, the executions of thieves and nobles, the rendering of scholars and saints on the wheel, the quartering of the possessed.

But on this bright day, the intersection transformed from the smell of death, for its modern inhabitants were of sublime heritages. Many here retained the courage of returning New World survivors, some the inspiration of Oxford writers gathered by James I to renew the scrolls and Vulgate and write the Biblical scriptures, and a few the genius of Faraday and Maxwell in the electrification – the illumination – of the world.

⬡

A STUDENT with woven flaxen tresses, still mounted on her bicycle, stood before me. She had a kindling glance, daringly soft, barely suppressing a sparkling vivacity. Her pale cheeks reflected the tint of roses. Long legs in black Danskins descended to highly polished black pumps with small, silver buckles. It was not her thin round glasses, but rather the sliver of Blackwatch tartan microskirt that gave me pause. Awakening me from a reverie, her greeting was in throaty Dutch.

"Huja morgen!"

I brightened, delighted. Changing her accents and languages, now in native Glaswegian from the banks of the river Clyde, she murmured an invitation before pedaling into the crowds with an obvious gymnast's pert control.

"The Sheldonian, if you please, *Herr Professor.*"

I could approach the medieval miracle of the octagonal Sheldonian Theatre on Commemoration Day weekend only indirectly, as great waves of pedal music tumbled about the choirs of thirty colleges comprising Oxford. The black-gowned students and scarlet-robed doctorates and masses of morning suits and fascinators overwhelmed the proctors and bowler-hatted bulldogs, the red-faced security staff. They stood in abject and unctuous rectitude, for enforcement of university regulations outside the colleges was futile.

The bells of Magdalen, Christ Church, Jesus, Balliol, Corpus Christi, and All Souls colleges competed in joy, their glory likely overheard even at the Wessex border. The Great Tom within Christ Church tolled relentlessly, as it did for five hundred years every evening at ten past nine, 101 times before the closing of the gate. All the colleges' pinnacles, decorated with Gothic ornaments and rising above indented battlements, forever pointed heavenward. Bach's Triple Fugue danced upon the air. The lush quadrangles – filled with graduates – had traceries of stonework that over-looked the promise of England's future, even as they tred on the illustrious bones of its past.

I walked underneath these many medieval window vaults and tall belfries, thinking of old Oxonian spirits who still roamed among the living crowds: Chaucer, Spenser, the Elizabethan spy Christopher Marlowe. Without warning, Crimson took my arm.

◯

HE GUIDED ME on a walk to an homage at 2 Polsted Road, the spacious red brick home of T.E. Lawrence as a youth, then visited briefly the Ashmolean Museum by Jesus College where Lawrence cataloged the relics of his excavations at Carchemish. Returning, we merged with the excited crowds, proceeding through revelers and choral singing, to admire the bells, organs and evangelicals at St. Alden's Church opposite Christ Church College and the Cathedral. Within one edifice, a baritone sang in German the favorite lieder of Lawrence: Wolf's "Verschwiegene Liebe." The streets were infused with elaborate liturgies, even the distant sound of a choir singing St. Anne's Fugue.

"Oh God Our Strength in Ages Past…"

Passing All Souls, we saw students and faculty dining at the last High Table, some in gowns and formal dress; others were entertaining in the common room over glasses of port. Crimson and I entered the Christ Church gate and quadrangle, flowing past the porter to whom Crimson nodded as though he were a visiting Fellow entertaining a guest. From a silver tray, Crimson took a glass of sherry that he never drank and soon discarded, then chatted with a merrily attended don. We somehow found an empty alcove with the most unlikely and austere silence. It had mezzotint portraits, with comfortable leather chairs and ottomans and antimacassars from another century. Beneath chintz window curtains on a refectory table were copies of *Der Spiegel*, *Le Monde*, *El País*, *Die Welt*, and Sweden's *Aftonbladet*.

Through the leaded windows we saw rows of pollarded willows, and grey stonework escutcheons emblazoned with heraldic crests. Hedge sparrows flitted to the music of a duo playfully engaged in Bach's Prelude for Cello Suite No. 1 in G-Major, with viola in counterpoint.

Crimson – ever the autodidact historian – reminisced at length on Lawrence's exploits in the extreme deserts, seeking rare water holes, only to find them poisoned with putrid camel carcasses by the Turks. Declining the array of drinks from a passing waiter, Crimson – to my enduring amusement – produced a small metal World War I canteen, noisily unscrewed the chained metal cap, and offered me a swig of water. He then withdrew from a worn leather pouch rations of sesame paste, almonds, olives, pistachios, dried apricots and dates, and arranged the feast carefully, in the manner of a Bedu herdsman. We ate communally, with two fingers of our right hands, and shared the canteen.

"You've gone *native*, friend," I observed.

"In memory of Lawrence," he explained.

Our meager lunch was common to the fighting near Damascus in 1919. Crimson long had admired Lawrence's seamless manner of disappearing into the suffering and courage of desert tribes, only to create nations. Like Lawrence, he changed his dress, speech, and lifestyles to elude detection and capture.

We ate thoughtfully, with Crimson casting his spell, as if food and water had been but a hopeless mirage. The quadrangle beyond our Spartan ceremony was alive with scholars in their gowns, all conversing intensely and clustering under a four-centered Tudor arch. Above Crimson in his reverential abstinence were paintings by Gainsborough, David and Hogarth, together with a laudable 1907 portrait by Sargent.

The revelers soon alighted from the turf to the cobbled street, as the shadowy spirits of Gibbon, Shelley, Raleigh and Harvey looked upon them. The future and the past intermingled easily here, so I put forth an unexpected question.

"Magenta mentioned epidemics from erotogenics and memory drugs, suggesting a future envisioned by Stanisław Lem. What epidemic do *you* fear?"

Crimson, nursed in the supernatural since his first realizations, described yet another Lem future.

"There may be a problem with anxiolytics – compounds reducing fear or distress. One Lem future involved a world where each citizen took a kind of vitamin, a world where everyone was perfect, men and women without blemish, cities of synthetic diamond, sweet air, rich seas, lavish sex and brilliance without end."

"The Holy Grail pill?"

"Not so. Without the medication, people awoke to reality. They were covered in rags, eating gruel from filthy bowls in dim caverns. The medicine was for melancholy."

"So you worry also about drugs that become ritualized and legitimized by governments for social control?"

"There may be a world in which the few awakened – those bravely disavowing drug use – secretly seek a normal mind for a night or so, then tell the others of what they have seen."

"And how are we to be protected from these strange futures, when even the normal mind is forgotten? Whom shall we trust, then?"

"I remember Lawrence, near death from thirst, who was wandering across the dry, shimmering furnace close to Rhum, where he found an ancient water hole on a rocky peak. The remote spring was only centimeters wide, with sparse green grasses, and a mere trickle of the holy substance. The rocks beside it bore Nabaethean inscriptions from migrations a thousand years earlier. In attendance was a blind beggar, crazed from the sun and dying, crouched in a corner. He kept repeating only one thing to Lawrence, in an Arabic dialect."

"What was that?"

"He said, 'The love is from God, and of God, and towards God.'"

⬡

OUR DEVOTIONAL REPAST slowly consumed, Crimson proposed an instructive afternoon trip through the Gloucestershire countryside before the evening's celebrations at Oxford. An unsmiling driver appeared, who said not a word the entirety of our journey. We passed in portentous silence by fields of hedgerows and stone walls, and along the parks of great houses, our curious transit softened only by the wafting herds of flying globes of thistledown. At some turnout, we embarked by foot onto a short trail rising to a shady escarpment, beyond which could be seen a contruction site with the skeletal outline of a vast silver saucer. Its stark modernity hovered over the farmlands and tilled soils that still yielded up the bodies of soldiers and spies who held in their mouths for millennia the coins of Hadrian.

Crimson seemed for a moment like an intelligence agent who had gone dark, and now was returning to the people. He pointed at the extraterrestrial device in the far meadows.

"This will be the Government Communication Headquarters Oakley complex at Cheltenham. GCHQ will have pods of Cray supercomputers at X Division linked to the Benhall center by fiber-optics. It will conduct surveillance for the Five Eyes: Britain, Canada, Australia, New Zealand and the United States. A futuristic Bletchley Park of code breakers and data miners, the silver torus will enclose a million square feet of space on 200 acres. The UK is acquiring talented personnel through public code-breaking competitions: the National Cypher Challenge and monitored online games."

"A competition to identify those with special capacities for disambiguating codes?"

"The last game required decrypting a secret message from Admiral Nelson to the Sea Lords, encrypted in two hundred year-old writings by Christopher Marlowe. The Five Eyes governments are filtering certain talents from the population – historically the province of universities – identifying special capacities useful for surveillance of populations. Cobalt no doubt will know early on the abilities sought. It's rather a type of capture – the harnessing of capabilities, if you will – to collect advanced mental breeds before they organize themselves outside government control."

He described the aggressive search for a narrow intellectual ability, the rendering of lonely youth at keyboards to saucers where their abilities would replicate, their visions constrained, their genes matched and inbred with gifted others. We sat for a while, considering this nexus of human thought, the saucer toward which the earth's conversations soon would flow.

"By the way, I have tried Magenta's experimental ampakines for memory," he remarked.

"To what end?"

"One GCHQ advertisement for linguists sought fluency in…"

At this he took a breath and – overcome by mirth as we stood and moved along the trail to our waiting driver – whimsically sang a litany of languages in a rapid, perfect melody from Gilbert and Sullivan.

"Albanian, Amharic, any other African languages, Arabic, Azeri, Balulchi, Basque, Bengali, Bulgarian, Chechen, Chinese, Dari, Georgian, Greek, Gujerati, Hindu, Indonesian, Japanese, Kashmiri, Kazakh, Korean, Kurdish-Sorani, Macedonian, Malay, Mirpuri, Nepali, Papiamento, Pashto, Paois/Creoles, Persian, Polish, Potohari, Punjabi, Romanian, Serbo-Croat, Shan, Somali, Tamil, Turkish, Ukrainian, Urdu, Uzbek, and Vietnamese."

He took another breath, and did the refrain with a grin.

"All the cryptolinguists
neatly in the torus,
and all their secrets
now arrayed before us."

"And accessible," I could only respond, "to the Six?"

"Perhaps through a few systems administrators, particularly the women. We may adopt Thomas More's advice to Henry VIII, 'You may tear down the laws to chase the Devil all over England, but when he turns 'round on you, where will you hide, then?'"

As we approached, the driver sat motionless, not looking at anything, really. I wondered at his employer. The plates, I later discovered, led only to a modestly functional elderly spinster in a bed sit in Devonshire.

OXFORD, that ecclesiastical romance in stone, lifted to the sky its varied spires as it embraced the leisurely Thames. Overlying the young turfs in the quadrangles of Oriel, Brasenose, and Corpus Christi colleges were crinkled battlements that protected the mullioned architecture of the facades. The halls, gables, chapels and gardens – the ensembles of this unrivaled panorama – reflected the setting sun behind us, their transomed windows burning like tongues of fire.

We neared the octagonal cupola of the Sheldonian Theatre, its ancient lantern revealing the blood-red robes of those holding doctoral degrees. From above the domes, in a glorious spectrum of audition, one could hear an Oxford choir rendering Henry Purcell's "Thou Knowest Lord The Secrets Of Our Hearts," while in another direction a soprano sang the Te Deum from Beethoven's C-Minor Mass. As the evening progressed, lamps began flickering in the rippled glass of Tudor windows as tardy students – too soon facing the morning's anxious dons – began to labor late in their lucubrations.

The scarlet gowns of the doctorates adorned earnest savants whose academic path never strayed from the Dragon School to Le Rosey to Eton, Harrow, Winchester, or Rugby, then forward to reading philosophy, politics, and economics at Balliol. One charming youth reading Greek history – whose confidence sprang forth like that of his accomplished peers – was happy in asserting to his fellow classicists the long view.

"Science is just a passing *fad*."

Yet, outside the blessed gardens of these gifted – past the privileged and down a dark alleyway like some tortuous defile – a troubling scene occurred. It was noticed first only by Crimson. On the plinth of a spiraling column blackened by time, a young and very pregnant working class woman sat, obviously lost and clutching the hands of two distressed and grimy children. She was being violently berated by a skinhead youth. She had the tawny russet hue of an impoverished field hand, and he the ghastly white that distinguished heroin's slaves.

Just beyond them the crowds were apotheosizing Newton, never even glancing at the pair, but the destitute family attracted Crimson's heightened sensitivities. The fellow had the startled, frightened look of one nearing the scaffold, about to join the sky. Like Hardy's *Jude the Obscure*, they forever were banished to infernal regions outside these august walls.

The fearful little girls, their bleak future assured, gripped their mother's hands. In the distance – as it passed Ruskin College – a massed row of marching pipers in Culloden tartan began a dead slow military tattoo. Caught in confusion and bewildered by their evil poverty in the midst of plenty, the mother and children sat forlorn and dazed in the alleyway. The skinhead's brow had a sinister furrow that only trouble traces. The pregnant young woman was reduced to making servile and humble gestures, enfeebled by her tragic circumstance.

The addict – a harsh cretin with a deathly pallor, and scared of everything – quickly left to satisfy his need. Crimson approached these remnants of a family and pressed 500 Euro notes into her hand, directing her to the rail station. He kneeled for a long while and spoke to the little girls, who in their miserable agitation and disarray had hidden in their mother's plain and unwashed skirts. With great tenderness, and singing a soft little song, he finally coaxed a smile from each one.

Encouraging the destitute family onward, he returned without the need to explain his actions. On his far circumambulations of the earth, he in his terrible loneliness seemed always to watch over the children.

〇

THE EVENING LINGERED. We shared a contemplative state in the quadrangle of Christ Church until only the waning shouts of celebrants were heard. He then took both my hands in his, and looked upon me with sadness.

"I must go, friend," he said with reluctance. "May your work inspire many."

I quickly asked, "Is there something you wish for others to remember?"

"Remember the price that was paid," he said.

I encouraged him to tarry, perhaps meeting again and parting nearer midnight. He gently demurred, albeit with uncertainty, as though he were preoccupied.

"*In'shallah*," he said at last.

In the manner of the Bedouin, like a desert phantom he blended with the night, leaving only the silence of the stars.

〇

HE NEVER RETURNED. It had been only a possibility, for the Six avoided a specific time and place to appear. I remained in a drawing room at Christ Church into the late evening, listening to plainsong from the time of Pope Gregory I drifting in from a remote choir, and reading the library's leather-bound volumes of Gibbon. There were chapters Crimson recommended on Julian the Apostate's conversion to paganism, and another on Constantine's conversion to Christianity. Within these readings, I reflected on the Six as conducting a type of priest craft, and in earlier times at risk of beheading for sorcery.

"For you, sir," a sanguine porter in green jacket said, bowing slightly.

At this I felt a profound absence, the sharp pang of a certain longing, as if I would never see Crimson again. He left only a note on foolscap. In the careful lettering of a monk scribe artfully illuminating manuscripts, there were four Latin words:

Vale, et me ama
(Farewell, and grant me your love)

Chapter 13.

A Ribbon for Detsky Mir

And the trees themselves white as specters,
Come out on the road, jostling and thronging
Just as they were waiving their farewells
To the white night which had witnessed
So very many things.

- Pasternak, *White Night*
poem of Zhivago

It is necessary, as politely as possible, to keep track of
the always too inquisitive foreigner lest he see things
as they are – which would be the greatest of inconveniences.

- The Marquis de Custine in Russia, 1839

A THIN, ELDERLY *BABUSHKA*, layered in old clothes, slowly swept snow from the steps of Babayan's building with a simple broom made of bound twigs. She was a grandmother in her eighties, grateful for the few rubles for her task. To her lined face and grey-blue eyes that had witnessed as a girl the horrors inflicted upon Russia by the Nazis, I could only offer a small bow and tentative good morning.

"Dobre outra!"

She gave a solemn nod as I entered the building where few dared venture. Babayan's secretary approached, leading me down dusty corridors into a modest sanctum. Within sat the man who controlled all pharmaceuticals in Russia – a genial, elderly Crimean with a knowing smile and wildly errant black eyebrows. For his idle hours, hand-bound volumes of Turgenev and Gogol rested comfortably next to a samovar. On the wall behind him, in an oval frame, remained an old, full-sized tinted photograph of Vladimir Illyich Lenin. A hallmark of tenacious party *nomenklatura* in these times of economic reform, Babayan had not forgotten to remove it, begrudging democratic forays into his absolute rule.

Yet Babayan hardly was a Leninist bureaucrat on the periphery of Kremlin power, or some elderly survivor of Young Pioneer meetings, with their recitations of Marx and Engels. For decades, he had represented the former Soviet Union and now the New Russia as the most enduring of the few members of the International Narcotics Control Board (INCB), thereby having veto rights over international trade of the world's metric tonnages of licit opiates. At Babayan's pleasure flowed the morphine of the earth.

His manner, to my delight, was guileless, so that we progressed into an intimate conversation about heroin trafficking from Afghanistan. Babayan – not so entrenched in institutional suspicion as General Sergeev at the MVD – revealed intragency details of intelligence successes.

"Why, just last week, we stopped thousands of kilos of acetic anhydride bound from Moscow to Mazar-i-Sharif," he divulged, "but we were unable to identify the true end user."

Acetic anhydride was an essential reagent for the conversion of crude morphine from opium to heroin, and Mazar was the lair of Afghan warlord General Dostum, where nothing could move absent cash tributes. While ruminating on this prospect, I found Babayan – like the forensic chemist Sorokin – more eager to discuss the influx of MDMA from Amsterdam into Moscow's exotic, on-the-edge rave scene and alternative culture; it now surpassed even the avalanche of cocaine into the glaring neon glamour of *mafiya*-controlled casinos such as *Melitizya* (Snowstorm).

DURING THE PREVIOUS EVENING in smoky student coffeehouses, I had met with a lively entourage of editors and writers from *Ptoch*, the Russian equivalent of *Rolling Stone*. Young and vibrant with gentle miens, they were suffused with the light of converts. They nursed a pot of tea for hours, assuring me the new generation of Russians had minds that no bureaucracy could contain. Vita, a lovely 20-year-old, described the evolution of raves in Moscow, and how all their hearts flew against oppression. Another young man, Volodya, told of their approach to Babayan in an effort to open research and moderate the laws.

"We tried to tell him of the changes, that entheogens would promote freedom after Communist rule, but he wouldn't listen."

As the café closed and I walked from their embrace, Vita smiled trustingly and lifted her voice, offering her farewell upon the evening air.

"Don't forget us!"

"I'll not forget you," I assured them.

Stepping slowly backward to hold their bright faces a little longer, I turned with regret, hands in pockets against the bitter cold, and leaned into the oblivion of Moscow's streets. I walked for hours in the brilliant tranquil night, through parks like country snowscapes. In their memory, I decided to confront Babayan on MDMA regulation.

BABAYAN NOW WAS COMPLETING his little *pokazuhka*, his obligatory speech for foreign officials, culminating with his views of club drugs. I suggested that entheogens had certain distinguishing characteristics.

"We feel the properties of this drug are less problematic than heroin or cocaine," I proposed, "and may have significant therapeutic aspects, so that society might best be served by more liberal control of MDMA."

Mention of psychiatric applications brought only a quizzical look. After listening politely but missing the point entirely, he became lightly agitated, then denied permitting even research. Sadly for my young Russian compatriots, Babayan lacked tolerance for any form of entheogen use.

I tried countering with an obvious problem that could not fail to attract even the most conservative decision makers, the need for analytical samples in the Russian drug lab so its chromatograph would not be blind to the toxic stream of opiates such as heroin and the lethal street drugs fentanyl and 3-methyfentanyl.

"Why don't you license a group of trusted organic chemists, as we do in America, to prepare small quantities of controlled substances for reference samples?"

In the protracted silence, we could hear sleet tapping upon the faded windowsills, pearling into icy sheets.

Babayan suddenly gripped the worn, wooden arms of his chair, then leaned forward, raised his black Crimean eyebrows and looked steadfastly at me.

"They might *sell* them, or *use* them, or *assist criminal groups* in manufacture," he said simply, with an apologetic air.

As Dr. Sorokin at the Russian drug lab had predicted, Babayan did not trust even reputable scientists, creating a bureaucratic impasse that left Russia vulnerable to violent narcotics syndicates. Yet Babayan himself was ethically sound, without sophism or compromise. He could not be bribed or threatened.

With this moral unassailability he continued to protect his beloved Russia, but he could extend his personal integrity to few others. Unwilling to permit even highly ethical, well-regarded chemists to conduct syntheses or research on drug topics, he was in this aspect a demagogue. Perhaps overwhelmed by his glimpse of Needle Park during an INCB meeting in Zürich, his fear was rational, for the wolves of addiction and their many malevolent breeds now paced at his country's doorstep.

Failing even on this front, I described to Babayan the American epidemic of methamphetamine, which had yet to appear in Russia. On more familiar ground, Babayan in an offhand manner remarked that twenty metric tons of ephedrine, the precursor for methamphetamine, was in a local plant – *Moscowpreparati* – for which he alone signed the permit.

"It is only lightly guarded," he observed with satisfaction, "because Russia has no methamphetamine problem."

I begged for an invitation to this remarkable sight. Babayan made a quick and cordial phone call to the president of *Moscowpreparati* to ask that I be given a personal tour of the security for Russia's largest reservoir of ephedrine. Putting his hand over the phone, he whispered a pretext for my arrival.

"You will appear as my personal emissary to check on security at *Moscowpreparati*."

⬡

MY DRIVER VLADIMIR proceeded on long loops through Moscow as befitted any tourist, or those who harbored the conceit of being pursued. In an ironic detour, we emerged at Feliks Dzerzhinsky Square – no longer with its statue of the Soviet secret police chief – then passed by the Lubyanka, the former KGB headquarters. Its barred windows were like sallow and merciless eyes, whose gaze no furtive movement or even thought could escape.

Across Dzerzhinsky Square from the Lubyanka, holiday crowds packed *Detsky Mir* (Children's World), a former state-sponsored emporium filled with stuffed hippopotami and dolls. A puppet theater from one of the 200 permanent Russian children's circuses performed in the street, provoking delighted shrieks from a cluster of otherwise wistful eight-year-old girls. Each had an identical blue ribbon in her hair. They were the daughters of dead addicts and alcoholics, from an orphanage in the First of May District on the outskirts of Moscow. Pinned to their dresses were plastic cards with no names, reading only "Children's Home No. 23."

We passed in silence through Pushkin Square, with its book tables strewn with the writings of Pasternak and Chekov, the poems of Anna Akhmatova, and old copies of *Literaturnaya Gazeta*. Moscow State students bent over chessboards and the Sicilian Defense. As we waited in light traffic across from Pushkin Gallery, one could see abstracts by Chagall and Kandinsky adorning the walls, admired by perplexed and prosperous new *chinoviki* (bureaucrats) posing in uncertain worldliness. Along the sidewalks, the pervasive and unwelcome Russian *vors* (outlaws) were collecting on every block their monthly protection fees from licit and illicit businesses – payments known as *krisha* ("the roof").

We moved through the extremes of Moscow: the blue dome of the Church of St. Nicholas gracing the sky above worshipful families; the young Russian soldiers and junkies interred at Vag Ankov Cemetery. Their peeling photographs were on tombstones, their cracked faces slowly disintegrating in the daylight, all alone. Thin blond girls from Murmansk, a thousand miles north at the Bering Sea, now stood pale and hungry in Moscow. They fended off poor *chuchniks* (Central Asian workers) as they entertained negotiating the price of the evening with multiple Chechen thugs, and fleetingly locked their eyes to mine.

At the massive *Moscowpreparati* plant, I entered a far more polished office than Babayan's. The president was a portly and unusually well-dressed woman. She seemed nervously deferential to this unknown American – in long black coat with Mercedes and driver – who questioned her about security for a king's ransom in ephedrine even while representing the official whose signature permitted her elegant couture. She appeared to profit from *blat* (favors), likely delivered under the table, or *nalevo* (on the left). We grazed warily on plates of *zakusi*, an assortment of cabbage salad, sliced fish, salami, beets, caviar and eggs.

We examined the simple locks and heavy tonnages of ephedrine precursor, and discussed the absence of security personnel in this land where street-level speed was only a bad dream portrayed in Western films. Weeks later, the first large-scale, *mafiya*-controlled methamphetamine laboratory in Russia was seized by General Sergeev's MVD agents; it was the harbinger of an everlasting plague of addictive stimulants, violence and psychosis, proliferating among simple villages and cities from Minsk to Nizhny Novgorod.

○

A TIMELY INTERVIEW of the leading organic chemists of Russia was at hand, to solicit their advice in somehow circumventing Babayan's intransigence. My driver waited as I, without Dmitri as translator, bounded the four flights of stairs within the chemistry building of the venerable *Moskovsky Gosundarstvenny Universitet* (MGU), beloved to Russian students and known as Moscow State to

Westerners. A fine ancient pile with dark filigreed spires, its hallways were tagged with inevitable bits of undergraduate graffiti, including one in English.

LSD for Democracy

Welcomed graciously after prior correspondence from Cambridge, I found it touching that these most well-trained of Russian scientists toiled in such difficult conditions. Science during *perestroika* had devalued from the era of isolated, heavily funded Russian atomic cities and the cultivation of the honored technical elite. No longer privileged thinkers who were gathered in special nameless towns, these true scientists labored among antique open-flamed Bunsen burners, wooden fume hoods, and a few elderly desktop computers. All appeared busy and earnest in their white lab coats, but I felt it was a mild form of *pokazuhka*, a small performance for the foreign guest, and I ached for them.

It was impossible not to reflect on the surfeit of technology in American labs, but I remained impressed with the impeccable science under such conditions. Recalling the humble cottage laboratory of my friend Sasha Shulgin – who created hundreds of analogues of entheogens – I indulged in tea with the eminent Dr. L. He spoke of academic economics during *perestroika*.

"PhDs who have cars are *de facto* taxicab drivers in order to live," he explained, "and department chairs earn 300-600 dollars a month."

Science was of little consequence to the new regime, for the oligarchs' venal harvesting of Russia's land, minerals and oil concerned the material and immediate. Progressive avarice threatened the light of learning. Constantly seeking small contracts from foreign firms to do research, the entire Russian scientific community was hostage to any plan subsidizing a living wage for its most gifted minds.

The graduate students so transparently engaged before me feared the imminent and mysterious *raspredeleniye* ("the distribution"), the annual transfer of those with new degrees throughout Russia, so that PhDs suddenly might find themselves thousands of miles from Moscow center in remote Siberian villages. They could be assigned as *vospitalelnitsi* (teachers, literally "up bringers") in the grimy industrial blot of Ulan-Ude near Lake Baikal, sadly unredeemed even by the presence of a single *umnitza* ("smart little one").

As I watched these fine organic chemists courageously adjusting instruments from the era of Madame Curie, I reflected that this impoverished excellence might be harnessed to synthesize legal analogs of Sasha's entheogens – or any promising medicine – even conducting human testing in a less restrictive research environment, as fetal stem cell research in Guangzhou had surpassed U.S. academics constrained by politically-based prohibitions.

Sitting on a wooden lab stool, while grad students attended reactions in round-bottom flasks, I glanced through the Tudor leaded windows at the spires of Moscow State. They receded into the onion domes near Markovsky Square, then became dismal rows of massive, anonymous *mafiya*-ridden Soviet cinderblock apartments in suburban Moscow. As magnetic stirrers whirred, and faculty apprised this unusual American in their midst, it seemed that only a pittance in funding might transform this earnest research group, if not the labored futility of the rare entheogen chemistry done in America.

"Funds might be found," I proposed with a certain hesitation, "small monthly stipends from American organizations such as MAPS – who espouse medicalization of psychedelics – to subsidize, for perhaps 2000 dollars a month, a team of four PhDs in medicinal chemistry to work full-time in drug development. Once organized, the teams might consider analogues of other medicines that are so costly due to Big Pharma."

Dr. L's welcoming demeanor quickly became serious; he asked if it might be so. We spoke of donors who were frustrated with the lack of new structures.

"It would seem a more promising use of donors' funds," he reasonably observed, "than limiting medicalization efforts solely to physicians' research on MDMA, LSD and DMT."

Sensing his comprehension, I took the concept a bit further.

"Young PhDs abroad in medicinal chemistry now are being neglected, but they could advance mind-brain research, creating novel compounds that improve cognition, perhaps even self-realization."

He considered the boldness of advances in neurochemistry against the faded light of Soviet chemistry allied to metallurgy, weapons research and rocketry. We spoke not of synthesizing controlled substances or defeating Babayan, but of the promise of transformative, new medicines.

The Moscow State chemists readily agreed. We vowed to remain in close contact as the concept was aired among U.S. groups. The former Soviet Union, once rigidly controlled but as yet unencumbered by thickets of laws, possessed freedoms unlikely to be seen again in America.

◯

STATESIDE AT HARVARD, to my surprise and the delight of student staff at the Kennedy School, faxes in Russian had appeared bearing the elaborately configured MVD letterhead and signed by General Sergeev. He formally requested 20 milligrams each of 10 compounds invented by Sasha Shulgin: DOB or STP ("Serenity, Tranquility, Peace") – the 72-hour wrenching phenethyamine later synthesized and distributed by underground chemist Owsley in the Haight-Ashbury in the Sixties; 2-CB, the modern variant treasured by experimentalists as a short-term empathogen, and 5-methoxy-DMT, a compound that provoked an ego death experience within 15 minutes in psychonauts courageous or foolish enough to self-administer it. Yet there was no mention of heroin or fentanyl samples. All were controlled substances.

At the bottom of the MVD list was an even more worrisome request. It seemed to confirm that my presence in Russia was accompanied by a secret agenda among the law enforcement community, for Sergeev's ending was provocative.

"We also request 20 milligrams of LSD."

This quantity would be sufficient to light up – as young voyagers might say – the entirety of the MVD building complex. Although compliance was an unlikely prospect, I regarded Sergeev's request with the utmost concern, agreeing to canvass licensed university chemists. The ASecState had remarked that samples easily could be transported by State Department couriers, but as the new envoy to Bosnia he became unavailable. Without government permission, I hardly could obtain a sample of the necessary purity – or possess or transport to Russia even this miniscule quantity of LSD, weighing less than a match head – without the risk of dire legal consequences.

It seemed rather a test of what I would do, or of Dr. Sorokin's passion for Sasha's compounds. The problem in Russia – and for that matter, the U.S. – was not the rare psychedelic or empathogen, but had long been the endemic presence of heroin and cocaine.

As I pondered these more subtle aspects, a mentor at HKS suggested a quick solution to Russia's impasse.

"Why don't you approach DEA directly?

Drifting through HKS hallways in a blank daze, I stumbled past students and faculty on their own far peregrinations of mind, then weighed the potential complications of such contact. My monk's simplicity was devolving into a byzantine labyrinth of encounters with CIA, the Pentagon, Customs, the State Department, the UN, the MVD, Congressmen, and heavily connected Cantabrigians and officials of every stripe. Each moment now was a universe away from ecstatic conversations around mountain campfires as we reached for the infinite. My head was gaining distance, but I had not yet misplaced my heart.

I knew that Sasha wisely had a formally circumscribed interaction with DEA to protect his research, and that my inestimable classmate and doctoral candidate Rick Doblin, the founder of MAPS, regularly interacted with DEA on regulatory matters involving medicalization. Privately, I wondered what Cobalt would do in these very circumstances. Recalling at last the privileges of earnest scholarship and the absolution of a new identity, I somewhat nervously called the agency from the Kennedy School. Locating a senior official, I assumed the mantle of academic researcher, and in this untroubled manner explained the problem with Babayan and Dr. Sorokin: the blind analytical equipment, the rise of post-Soviet violent narcotics cartels. The official, cordial and near retirement, refused.

"We don't want to be in the position of providing samples to every nation's forensic labs."

"But this is not Laos or Colombia. Russia is an emerging narco-state with nuclear capability," I opined. "Undetected, violent major heroin and cocaine traffickers could influence portions of the atomic arsenal."

The official duly acknowledged these special aspects, and we parted amicably. Some weeks later, on a call from HKS to Dr. Sorokin in Moscow, I found him elated.

"I will be traveling to Washington, D.C. in August, to visit DEA and pick up the samples."

Wincing at the prospect of General Sergeev's odd list of Sasha's phenethylamines, I cautioned Sorokin.

"Remember this is about the heroin and fentanyl standards."

Russia's forensic lab finally became sighted to opiates. It then began to discern in its ancient chromatograph's display – a precious white ribbon of paper now despoiled with undulating lines of black ink – the frightful image of a massive beast come round at last to feed upon the children. But its nemesis, the formidable Russian bear, was no longer blind.

I thought of the blue ribbons in the hair of the orphan girls at Detsky Mir, flowing bright and free above their wan faces and forlorn glances at real families so close they could almost touch them. To the little ones, with a long prayer for their great happiness, I folded my hands and bowed.

Chapter 14

An Exaltation of Thought

In spite of everything, I believe people are good at heart.

- Anne Frank, 14, before she was murdered at
Bergen-Belsen death camp, 1945

It's a boy.

- Edward Teller, father of the H-bomb,
in code to colleagues at Los Alamos
that the hydrogen bomb detonation
had been a success (telegram, 1953)

Women and girls dressed in long gowns traversed the street from house to house.
They were leisurely and perfumed. A trembling seized him and his eyes grew dim.
The yellow gas flames arose before his troubled vision against the vapoury sky,
burning as if before an altar. Before the doors and in the lighted halls groups
were gathered as if for some rite. He was in another world; he had awakened
from a slumber of centuries.

- Joyce, *A Portrait of the Artist as a Young Man*

THERE WERE FLOWERS in the Bloemenmarkt on a morning in Amsterdam; the 18th Century cafés rang with laughter, and entire families perched on single bicycles down cobbled streets. Narrow four-story wooden sea captains' houses leaned precariously left or right, looming over crooked lanes and rings of canals. Indonesians from Dutch Java prepared *rijsttafel*. The glories of Vermeer, Rembrandt and Van Gogh hung in the Rijksmuseum.

In this tallest of nations, six-foot white Dutch blond women strode through crowds or pedaled bicycles to the Universität, as precisely timed trams arrived and departed. As a courtesy to foreigners, many of the the 18 million people of Holland switched immediately to delightfully accented English.

Amsterdam was a gateway to experimental moralities. Coffee shops – from hip modernist venues to dark *boites* with Hindu gods – offered menus of cannabis, while *Psilocybe* fungi were retailed over counters like expensive perfumes by arty sales girls. Sporadic Somalis lurked with opiates, even as polite *politie* lit marijuana cigarettes for visitors, and the neon borders of Red Light District windows glowed upon startling displays of international attractions.

It was summer, Queens Day had passed. Dam Square was thronged with youth gathered at this crossroads to Europe and Asia, for America seemed to the Dutch a violent police state of overwrought consequence. With a fondness for Holland and a scientific meeting in Venlo, I arrived from Schiphol Airport to lodge in a small, cheap hotel down the Spuystraat and near the Café Luxembourg. Packed with locals sharing long tables and hot chocolate, the café had expansive windows opening upon an Amsterdam awash with leafy green parks and the quiet garden terraces of gabled houses. Under arched bridges with walkways, tour boats passed slowly like elongated glass swans on the canals, as the Amstel flowed to the sea.

One could have spent hours before finding an elderly person who recalled the jagged Nazi *Siegrunen* on arm bands during the *Einsatzgruppen* mass murders of the Shoah, or Holocaust. The truly civilized charms of Amsterdam stopped at the haunted doorway of the Anne Frank House, with its crying ghosts of the girls' death march to the chambers of Bergen-Belson.

I was in the evening symphony audience at the *Concertgebouw*, where the genocides were half-remembered only by a sprinkling of survivors with their wisps of white hair, and the Bavarian Orchestra now visited to play Beethoven's C Minor Mass with oboe and flute. At the intermission, I saw a sparkling, shapely woman in a tightly rolled blond chignon and black silk jacquard, speaking fluent German with an angular, well-toned man who had an academic air. At the bell, we returned for Mahler's Symphony Number Four, and then a pale, ethereal soprano singing *Die Liebchen*, on the heavenly life. At the third encore, I noticed them again quite nearby, more clearly now, the academic in a tailored, slightly worn herringbone jacket, and bearing a ragged, well-annotated paperback copy of Xenophon. He wore half-moon reading glasses as a distraction. His wrist, firm as a fencer's, bore yet another Breguet.

<hr/>

INDIGO, with the woman and without introduction, simply followed me and entered my cab. We passed along the Herengracht under a procession of antique amber lamps. In native Dutch, he instructed the driver to stop at a refined Amsterdam residence, where he kissed the woman's hand in a courtly, Platonic bow. With a soft fondness and proud bearing, she folded the silky fringes of her shawl and disappeared through elegant black wrought iron gates. Starlings flickered in droves from her rooftop, while above the great yellow moon hung heavily.

We left our cab near the Prinsengracht and the houseboats, and walked to a modest *pension* that projected a tolerant dignity. On Indigo's little headmaster's desk were stacked light and edifying readings: the classicist's vacation of Flaubert, Dumas, Balzac, Zola. A well-bred man, he had a zest and jollity I had not seen in him in Salzburg or Vienna.

His room was of utter simplicity. There was a kettle, and tea things, and packets of joss. His movements were reflected in a single cheval mirror. His private life – during his eternal transits of the earth – seemed that of beauty and introspection. On a rough library table with scratched leather inlay, and revealing the gravitas in him, there lay the antiquarian treasure of *De Revolutionibus Orbium Coelestium*.

His mood seemed flighty that evening, from long ruminative silences to an excited grandiloquence worthy of Bulwer-Lytton. He affected fabulous rhetorical flourishes, then long calms, sitting at the table with one hand splayed to his brow. He was an ever-growing question mark.

Indigo was fresh from a clandestine synthesis, not yet settled in a world where others assemble nuclear weapons. From some remote, silent retreat he was now forced into an espionage game, a planet of secret encounters that branded one with the iron of the covert. He was a hidden curate in a vast, mystic church.

There was no Sacher Torte on blue damask as in our first encounter, no child sheppardess in a distant alpine valley, no contact high in the Austrian Alps – only the waxing moon under which the Six always seemed to manifest. But Indigo and I had suffered among the peaks of experiences, so I began where we left off in Vienna – not abruptly – but following their own practice of a group mind conversing with itself.

"Tell me a story about the moment of creation in the laboratory, other than in allegorical terms."

As he visibly consulted his memory I watched his preoccupied face. In Vienna, he had alluded to the seconds of chemical transformation from crude reactants to their sacrament, but he was prudent about specifics.

"Perhaps a night in a far and quiet mountain retreat?" he began, almost confident of my vetting. "At the instant of psychoactivation – the linking of diethylamine to lysergic acid when 10 million doses flower in minutes – I was on my knees in a moon suit, praying. I pray standing as well, in the Judeo-Christian traditions, during this moment."

I leaned toward him, receptive to a rare disclosure; he continued, describing this Herculean task in an eerily resonant voice, as though recalling the fathomless.

"One hand was on a spherical glass reactor, feeling and blessing a portal into alternative dimensions. The isolated mountain chateau itself was deeply snowbound, buried beneath an ocean of ice, together with the laboratory and me. On the hard snowpack high above, there suddenly were dogs barking wildly; I could hear the crash of snowshoes, and shovels digging down for an hour almost to the top of the chateau doorway. All the while teams of men kept shouting."

"What were they shouting?"

"*Politie! Aufmachen!* Police, open up!"

"Where were you?"

"The chateau was up a trail. No roads, no neighbors within 10 kilometers or so. Beyond Gstaad, or Zug, or was it Cortina d'Ampezzo? Only the very tips of a forest of tall firs were visible, if one walked on the densely packed snow. Their apices were like tiny Christmas trees, scattered above 20-meter drifts. The chateau was inaccessible until spring. Food stocks and indoor cords of seasoned oak firewood were sufficient until the melt. Silenced diesel generators hummed slightly; there were long, narrow air vents, and others for the chimney smoke to escape upwards."

An ambulance klaxon burst onto the Prinsengracht. We waited as it lessened toward the Leidseplein theater district. Indigo began carefully preparing peppermint tea, then offered Austrian honey from the froths of blueberries far above the Mönchberg. He had a fine set of delicate, translucent china cups – Victorian or earlier, from the Raj – nestled in an old wicker case with a bamboo handle.

"You have my attention."

"Yes, well. I repeated the prayer reverently, then with a certain calm haste extracted my body from the moon suit, and sealed the facility door. Donning old slippers and a frowsy eiderdown robe, I entered the chateau living areas, passed an oak blaze, then in the atrium forced the door open a few centimeters against a wall of solid ice. Up a narrow white slit of 10 meters I could see part of an officer's face looking down at me. His beard had heavy stalactites of ice, his head a cowl of thick fur. A bandana covered his brow – a bright Red Cross on a field of white. I could only shout up to him: 'Are you in some difficulty?'

"'There's been an avalanche,' he returned, 'several killed. We are evacuating the area.'

"I declined, assuring him most gratefully I had adequate food, and that the chateau was on a ridge below which the tonnages of avalanche passed. I offered my assistance for their search, until they reluctantly went away. I could hear the dogs howling as their sleds passed into the next valley, diminishing until there was only the sound of resins crackling in the hearth. In the night's stillness, all was drowned in loneliness again. With a renewed ascetic piety, I performed the canticles of the Sacred Heart, and continued in indefatigable synthesis, for the fear had come and gone like a thief. There were visions during that first exposure, like St. Francis when he received the stigmata on Mount Vernia in the Apennines. They lasted until the morning, when the religious transports and I finally were spent."

"Did you dismantle the laboratory?"

"I remained until June, then decommissioned the site and practiced equanimity, repainted the chateau, gardened a little. There was a feeling of boundlessness, I remember, the beatitudes of peace being lord paramount. I seeded little showers of buttercups, and bowed out. Beyond, the sky was safe, the earth sodden. The heather was rosy that year."

He offered more tea, his gentle recollections belied by his wiry, disciplined physical strength from calisthenics in countless nights alone. His teapot had a hand-woven cozy, and was fired with the blue trumpets of morning glories, *Ipomoea violacea*, with its psychoactive amides.

"Where are the others now?"

"Do you miss them, as I do? I am aware of your encounter with four of us, Crimson thrice. I can speak of them in a small way."

"Please."

"Vermilion has completed three batches in sequence with no break, and is lost with V-1 and V-2 somewhere in South East Asia, their last contacts a series of jungle and forest meditation retreats in the Burma, Laos, Cambodia region. We might imagine him in a palm hut by a freshwater stream near Kuala Lumpur, when he elects to return to rural society. The three of them are bound like the rings of Saturn; their mirror is unclouded."

"Our night in Berlin was electrifying."

"I should think it was. They do such conversions as a practice. You'll see him again, most certainly, but I know not where or when. His batches – together with others each winter for the great summer distributions – are rather like a psychological H-bomb. We all must recover somehow. He heals with V-1 and V-2, in a holy trinity of romantics."

"Crimson?"

"Crimson, like our arterial blood. Near Oxford, in some thatched cottage, bicycling to Bodley or the Ashmolean reading rooms under an academic gown, darting here now and then, or with his dear family in London, Cannes, or San Francisco. He thinks of fundamental security as always, but a tidal sadness flows from him sometimes, the yearning for his children."

"He develops security further?"

"Something's on his mind these days, a fragment in a mosaic that won't fit. He confers with Cobalt more often."

"Magenta?"

"He has a lovely girl, whom you've not encountered. She's at the 16th Century training monastery Eihei-ji, practicing Zen forms, sometimes attending the baths. He's back in Northern India packing mules with Sherpas for the most remote lab site in his beloved Himalayas, one unlikely ever to be detected. He pops out for conferences on novel drugs, debriefs Vermilion's operatives, shows up in Bhutan, Lhasa, his various divine havens. He once reached me to speak of seeing the first violets, and hearing the unbearable throbbing of apple blossoms. Other than his voice, there was only the stamping of horses."

"Cobalt?"

"That's challenging. He is most elusive, unpredictable even among us. Travels in random, tight, rapid circles back through Princeton, D.C., ranges to Kyoto, Stanford, Silicon Valley, Taos. Usually near universities: the Sorbonne, Cambridge, Groningen, Bologna medical school. He's worried about NSA terrorism data mining, and its mission creep to enforcement agencies, where everyone not conforming becomes a second-class citizen."

"Where is he now?"

"His last call was broken, transient. I could hear his voice intermittently, and by a stream the singsong chanting of nightingales."

He stood with a certain stern quality.

"But enough," he said. "Let's walk, if not in the Austrian Alps, then in the mountainous, stony, moral crevasses of the Amsterdam night."

◯

I HAD GOTTEN TOO CLOSE, in his vulnerable state. We ambled onto the streets wet with summer fog from the North Sea. With a stronger pace we ranged more widely and aimlessly across the Eastern Canal ring, through artists' squats with huddled groups and sporadic music, and back past the shuttered Albert Cuyp Market.

His soul this night seemed riven. He moved with a breathless and exalted devotion, discussing the enigmas of nirvana, and conciliating the goodwill of passersby who at this hour hardly were the genuinely virtuous. The occasional skeptical mind may have considered him some overzealous ecclesiastic, having not been humbled by the truth of him, or having never known the mundane as luminous.

His giddiness in the free, cool night was merely a public affectation, for when there were no witnesses he returned to concrete details, pointing to addresses where the marches to Auschwitz and Bergen-Belsen began in 1945, and the offices of the Nazi raiding parties who conducted the *razzias*, or roundups of Jews. A siren in the night sounded shrill, like the shouting of seized children.

Indigo showed me the small apartment in Rivierenbuurt where Anne lived, as she overlooked the little square of Merwedeplein, then the flower business in the house on Prinsengracht where she hid for two years, with all Jews barred from parks, libraries and restaurants.

Indigo knew the very building housing special units of the *Schalkhaaders*, the Dutch police yielding to Nazi civil law. We passed the homes of *Reichskommissar* Arthur Seyss-Inquart, the fanatical anti-Semite who presided over the Anschluss in Austria in 1939 and who filled the cattle cars. Indigo stood for a long while by the houses of the Dutch resistance leaders who were hanged, each and every one.

We arrived at a small iron bridge over the Kloveniersburgwal canal, where in one direction we could see up and down café-cluttered tiny streets, and in the other timeworn gateways into flowered courtyards. He wondered if he was becoming a bore, a fervent. I told him of my uncles, among the first Americans to free the death camps. As the night wind tugged at us, I described how as a boy they told me of seeing 14-year-old girls, who – when the Wehrmacht were finished with them – were left hanging on meat hooks. I spoke of how my uncles in their old age still cried for them. He walked me to my hotel, and apologized. I knew not why.

◯

THE MORNING IN AMSTERDAM soothed our fierce hearts. The blood no longer ran, the dark wraiths slinking in disgrace to the shadows. The pale shell of moon effaced the blue sky, and the world was created afresh.

We stood in the Rijksmuseum, before Rembrandt's *The Night Watch*, his tribute to the civil guard, then moved to the brooding mystery of *De Staalmeesters*. A young artist quickly approached, oddly asking Indigo if he might do a fast sketch of him. As others of the Six, he disclaimed all random portraiture or photographs, to cultivate his personal obscurity.

The sublime aspirations of the Six had the disquieting aspect of imprisonment, so that their security practices were held in an unconquerable grip. Yet Indigo by his very presence sometimes seemed to emanate the radiance of enlightened teachers, beaming in waves like the silent Mumbai gurus whom followers adorned with garlands. He fought to suppress these phenomena, for then he was helpless to hide, to blend seamlessly.

On several occasions, among experienced youth, I saw complete strangers approach him, women art students in the Rijksmuseum, and men on a spiritual path. Without saying a word, they reached out to hold him. He simply embraced them momentarily, parting with a direct gaze and a blessing.

There were two instances of women walking up and stating in the frankest terms they wanted to sleep with him. He kissed their cheek or hand, declining with gentle modesty, saying only "In another time, in another world," then walking on with his heart white as a star. I asked how often this happened.

"More here than other places. San Francisco, Santa Fe. We all are linked subconsciously. We recognize each other in ways that can't be spoken."

○

HE SEEMED TO OCCUPY a highly evolved cognitive niche, a coalitional psychology excluding outsiders. It was as if he were a magical criminal in the bright openness of multidimensional mind, where the armed opposition merely were flat actors slithering across a trapezoid. I felt it coming on.

The Rijksmuseum assumed the nakedness of a theorem, the purity of space, and began to fill with archetypical imagery. We were reinfected once more by a dream. At first, there were conflicting, meaningless eruptions of the unconscious, blue tangerines and molting angels, a damaged moon.

We sat before a delicate Vermeer. Indigo's languages dispersed to the million voices above Salzburg, as he told of the Mithraists, the sun worshippers and Persian mystery religion that succumbed as the chief competitor to Christianity. He described their starry messengers, how belief systems imposed by blood inevitably disintegrated with time. As the stream of dead governments passed, he pointed to the satrapies of Darius with its tributes of gold and silver and 300 white horses and 500 boy eunuchs.

Across the visual field were images of ancients: the Minotaur and mazes, the face of Helen at the pyre of Troy. Our recursive thinking, alight with ethereal plasm, was an infinite set of thoughts within thoughts. We were satyr-monks erect with blind instinct, then hunted wretches fleeing ideological bloodletting, as the treasury of social distinctions was looted and the order of punishments revealed.

Indigo throughout maintained a patrician calm, his words now in Babylonian and Aramaic. It was as if the sunshine spoke. In a heartbeat, we were separated from this hushed, paradisiacal land, disgorged painlessly like some new parturition, bewitched into utter calm.

The experience this time was brief, as though now one could access at will the ungraspable. We retired with a reverent delicacy to the small cafeteria, where several art students inexplicably turned to look on. He began to sing softly – "Edelweiss" in German and Dutch – in a low, melodious voice, recalling our dazzling trek. We shared yoghurt, with mountains of fresh blueberries.

⬡

I WONDERED what saved them from becoming madmen or ecstatics, for the psychological pressures were constant. We took trams to Haarlem toward the sea, then crossed over the Saarne, walking alongside the banks of the Noordzeekanaal, and finally down the Keizergracht to an old, smoke-darkened brown café off Ree Straat. The sky was cloudless, hard as amethyst.

Indigo grew quiet with his musing, as though in order to speak at all he had to retrieve himself from inner meditation. We sat on rush-bottomed chairs, he with a silent dignity. His occasional surfacings were in a baritone voice that had the cultivated accents of his many mysterious heritages and languages, yet I needed more content for the ethnography of international psychedelic chemists, and tried to prompt him. He eluded me for a while with a string of commonplaces.

"What clandestine sites are preferred?" I suddenly inquired, at some risk, "I know of the mountains and deserts."

He rose to the moment, as though awakening from communion.

"The seashore has been attempted, but humidity was a problem with reactions that require elimination of water molecules."

"But what continents?"

"Magenta, of course, the remote Himalayas. I, Europe only. Vermilion, arid jungle estates. Crimson, Friesland north through Scandinavia and the Baltics. These vary, an identifiable *modus operandi* not being permitted. No one works in the States anymore."

"Why not?"

"Look around you. The United States is so much less civilized, less free."

"But Crimson and Cobalt often are in America."

"Crimson for his family. Distributions occur in America. Cobalt to monitor the friendly opposition, for threat assessment. He has some specific concern, recently."

A sense of foreboding crept over us. Stately and urbane, he managed to give me a martyred look. A nearby Amsterdammer was reading *Die Welt*, strangely attentive to our every murmur.

He stood, grim and sedate, paid in Euros, and with the tenacious pragmatism inherited from some saintly forebear, invited me into the sunlight.

People in public sometimes seemed to know him. Perhaps it was the recognizance he disclosed in the Rijksmuseum, the global community of friends, of seekers, of the truly human. Priests and shopkeepers gave fondest greetings, the Universität was a wave of smiles. As evening twilight approached, the sky became cloud veiled; we sauntered toward the Leidseplein, our still brimming thoughts a moving ocean of shifting perspectives.

"And the coffee shops? Are they society's future?"

"We see marijuana use, for ourselves, as an indulgence. The severity of our lives, the responsibility, does not permit it. We must be clear at all times, focused on our sacramental role. For safety, and to honor those who experiment."

"But for society?"

"Cannabis has a historical role in leading users to the forgotten mind: heightened aesthetics, the introspection available at any moment, music, philosophy, environment. We recommend only rare use, if any at all. The essential teaching is that normal mind is the ultimate glory."

"MDMA?"

"Our concern is the lethality. Useful emotionally for therapeutics. If it were a textbook, it would be a primer. Future medicinal chemists must resolve the toxicity from the entactogenic components."

We returned to his simple dwelling through cloaks of inky shadows, and the lights of a pearly nightfall. Our late evening in this violet, primal city promised to be unimaginable.

◯

INDIGO HAD NEVER MENTIONED the profane. In this he seemed less ardent than Vermilion, or even Magenta, perhaps thinking of the sensual world as frivolous. It was some time during our intercourse that he – feigning a demonic immaturity – proposed in a cavalier tone that we marvel at the sex district. I was unsteadied by this, for I knew he never wenched.

"It's an emotional maelstrom," he coolly continued, "a Thermopylae of the Psyche. To enter it, you may need a streak of coarseness."

"Why?"

"To not shudder at the terrible, glowing fresco of this world. Care to come?"

I tried assuming a Calvinist air, but could only hasten to agree. The Rijksmuseum and Concertgebouw were closed; no venue of the senses was left to us. As the tormented hour approached, we sat quietly, absorbed in our own anticipations. We walked along the Oudezijds Voorburgwal, finally arriving in the district at the Oude Kerk, with its 14th Century bell resounding in the night like judgment. It was a surrealist scene.

Crowds of couples and waves of single men – all pressed tightly together – funneled into alleys so narrow only one could pass. Nordic blonds in blue satin G-strings and heels danced provocatively or sat in lascivious restlessness behind large windows bordered in thin red neon. There were black-haired Greeks with whips, Swedes, Norwegians, Dutch, Somali, Ugandans, Portuguese, Serbs, the women of all nations having arrived in this Dutch port, long a refuge for tall ships and able seamen.

Shy customers – from high-school students through the elderly – knocked on black doors by the windows, then asked for the rates. As they disappeared inside, the door was locked with a snap, and red velvet curtains were drawn. Windows with only velvet drapes thus were occupied. After a half-hour, the customers stumbled onto the street, chagrined or transfigured, and fled into the night.

The curtain would open. The woman, again in her most alluring costume, would dance with sultry looks, seizing upon one of the thousands of wan, lonely, evil, or excited faces passing before her each shift. To some customers they were seraphs, to others salacious portals, to all they were the endless spectrum of one's tastes for girl flesh.

Men and not a few women – indecent in their haste and abandoning any reserve – pursued frail Circassian ash-blonds in diaphanous attire but with a large clientele, or became morose at weary black beasts in forsaken alleys. Indigo commented like Vermilion in Berlin on this primordial trade; his speech, compared to the spectacle of lust, was quaint.

"Cheops's daughter," he remarked – gazing at an Egyptian woman with mischievous Levantine eyes, wearing only a fine rose leather corset and sharp heels – "built the second of the three small pyramids that extend before the Great Pyramid at Giza. She prostituted herself for gold, and for each block of stone."

Indigo himself had no proclivity for wantonness. Through the spiritual rigors of his many transformative nights, he had become exiled in a universe of extinct vices. The folly before us he described, at first with an amiable irony, only by quoting Durrell.

"Through fornication the human shadow drinks."

Among the windows, the sex shops, the all-night falafel stands, the purse snatchers, and the cannabis smokers crushed into the Bulldog café, Indigo moved with serenity like a parish churchwarden – one whose mind was faster than light. Whatever scene displayed within the windows, he had perfect aplomb, for he was self-possessed, unruffled, even though he knew fully the extent of frantic human suffering.

The white women after each client were flushed and marked with deep pink blotches, the insatiable constantly flung at them. They gazed at us openly, fresh from the last debauch. Among such infinite lust, there was a maddening intoxication of the senses.

Indigo's lifestyle – in another – would have permitted the most extreme appetites to run free in the flesh, but he harbored the purest virtue. In an earlier time, he would conceal a miter, or pectoral cross. He refused to trade his perennial peace for some ephemeral carnal satisfaction, even though he had the simplicity and ease of the terminally experienced. I asked of his historical perspective.

"In Berlin, Vermilion mentioned the Adamites."

"The Adamites," he said, "among the earliest Christians, thought marriage sinful, women and men as common property. The first conventicles were held in caves, the religious service included mass sexual orgies. It was a form of unchastened raptures."

A few black harpies, priapic with cocaine and atavistic fervor, ravaged among the window workers for the indiscriminate and hooked. Quadroons and octoroons, devolved from the Boer occupations, ranged uncertainly among the palette of skins. It was a carnival of the last days: *carne vale*, the farewell to flesh, before all our lives were blown out like candles.

The regular Amsterdammers, with a nervous density, clustered among groups of foreign visitors. Now all freed from the age of piety to roam in sinful palaces, many here had compulsive thoughts, and were at the mercy of passing sentiments. The air reeked of fugitive perfumes; one might hear the sounds of steaming and furtive acts.

One magnificent woman, with the flare of child-bearing hips, intoned to the public the endearments of lovers. She had a small-boned litheness, and a sad poise, but her eyes revealed a sapphire-like brilliance. She sank back luxuriously in invitation, her legs parted in silken lavender repose. At the knock on the door, her white wrists flashed as she pulled the velvet curtain, the secrets shared therein a defense against the importuning of the world. She was the last dancer in a gutted ballroom.

INDIGO – undistracted by the many offerings – considered the penalties even for sanctity, describing the virgins who kept burning the sacred fires of Vesta, goddess of the hearth.

"The head Vestal priestess, accused of loss of virginity, was buried alive by brutal Domitian."

"And you? Do you never indulge?"

"I love only one. Thus, I am immune. She is…like drinking starlight."

Indigo had never spoken before of family, or lovers, though he clearly admired women. He seemed punished by the mere thought of any infidelities, his conscience rebuking the most vivid casual pleasures. Yet he was intimately familiar with the retailing of the expensive and affectionate.

"The highest rank visit only 5-star hotels. Others work elegant brothels such as the Yab-Yum, with fine Asian art, Champagne, and formally attired staff. All minister to those who, one might say, seek expiation from their desires."

"How would Vermilion, and V-1 and V-2, consider the district?"

"They would confront the entity within each person, on a mythic or religious level, as an exercise. They would choose someone to change, one by one. As in Berlin."

An imperious young hussy, a Nordic beauty with a regal impudence, retrieved her latest customer, then plunged under a tantalizing cloud of red velvet. A group stood agog, each still waiting in turn, some too fearful even to approach the door. A tout appeared.

"Have it off with her, then?"

Most visitors were penurious menial workers, here for the visual feast. They responded with hopeless denials. For those with only the minimal Euros, some window workers yielded with an air of involuntary boredom, wooden and methodical, their bodies the purest automatism.

One girl, a severe and stunning Goth in a black leather corset, looked up from a subterranean dungeon of bondage implements. A heroine of the night, with hard, white breasts, she challenged onlookers fearlessly by stretching across her livid teats chain links of steel like metal snakes. Behind her were saddles and stirrups and crops and chrome spreaders with ankle bindings. Her viewers, soon kindled under the spur, abandoned common sense for passion. Like delirious children among realms of sweets, men and a few bold women revived their fantasies and dismembered their ethics.

Indigo only quipped with Stendhal, "You must boldly face a little anatomy if you want to discover an unknown principle."

⬡

IT GREW LATER. There were big holes in the sky; moonlight blew about. Cruising couples retired, leaving only desperate predators prowling the windows, together with the drunken and the wired. A few intoxicated louts shrieked at the windows, pointing with rude gestures. They were small and mean, loud over trifles, part of an undistinguished herd. Indigo, by contrast, seemed respectful of the sex workers.

"The women could be – as we may be – passionate servants of that which is sacred, but considered profane. Handling the great rivers of human feeling – that which no one else will confront – we all are as outcasts."

I thought perhaps he overlooked, all about us, the ashen misery. "Do you come here sometimes?"

"No, it's too painful. But we now attend, and I think of how we might please them, these who please the lost."

Indigo, with a fearless detachment, located among the diversity of female powers the most ill-starred. He was drawn particularly to those furious with resentment and pain, like animals in traps. They had the coldness of victims, martyred to a stake of ice. Some were glaring at passersby, unable to sustain the fiction. We walked on in desolation, from the pitiable salaciousness of their trade. They were beyond Indigo's ministrations, this night.

◯

WE WANDERED to the ends of lamplit mazes and their draped windows, where the discrete lapping of nearby canals was audible on the blood. We saw a Copenhagen girl, fragile but like a boy, shod in Athenian sandals. She had lacquered nails and pliant limbs, offering to Indigo the most obscene night. He responded with gratitude and a chivalrous dissent. Another window worker gave ferocious glances of the *macabre* kind, whispering curses as a stimulant. All about, there was trading of underprivileged hearts for the bodies of nymphs.

One spectacular woman had a symmetrical renown. She was well-fleshed, well-haunched, with tantalizing roundels and an evolved undercarriage. For us, her expression had a lingering petulance. Another was a contemporary Botticelli, a Venus Anadyomene. She was aurcoled like an angel, concealing her pagan roots. Indigo, observing the almost sacred excitement of those before her window, redeemed her, and them.

"Postulants discharging their obligation to a god."

A row of spectacular and frolicking New Testament whores, arrayed in a writhing motif, laughed wildly at the parade before them: the passing drunkards, the unfocused eyes, the hangdog airs. One stern waif looked down at her admirers in cold reproof. She was querulous in manner, a child-like dominatrix. In a distant alley, a woman displayed an inflammable *hauteur* and delectable contours, yet was slim as the devil. Standing by her, a naked girl intently gilded her paramour's nipples.

"Sex is a fragile enterprise," Indigo remarked, "We see it not as an act, but a thought. Over mere wantonness, Love must reign."

We passed a woman who, with an onerous sadness, bid her clients a soft good night. The woman in the adjacent window had a simple insolence, with triumphant eyes. Another had a profound melancholia. Yet another threw jubilant glances, with a bristling flippancy. Two female customers described one window worker as having the longest tongue in Christendom. Indigo reflected on those unduly influenced by these diverse offerings.

"Much time in this world could alter the whole axis of one's human sensibility. Disenchanted, one might recoil into chastity or – like some inflexible moral puritan – break under certain exotic influences."

It seemed a kind of Stygian situation, offset by an insane gaiety, a theatrical and infernal happiness. Deflated satyrs, rendered immobile from overindulgence, stood at the ends of canal bridges like marble griffins. Their follies and deceits were measured out, hour by hour through the late night, by the relentless sour tang of the Oude Kerk bell.

Some customers returned only to the same woman. They were in the grip of an infatuation, thinking the district a mythical marriage feast. Others moved from window to window like malefic djinns among white slaves in their private Seraglio. Living from one mistress to another with a bloodthirsty jocularity, they circulated among the brothels of the world: from the civilized, quick and pleasant whoring of Amsterdam to the sordid, intolerable extremes of Cairo, Bombay and Bangkok.

The window workers – almost relieved by the blissful amnesia that excessive suffering brings – managed the thrusting profligacy with an amused irony. They knew they conducted a thrilling bazaar, offering fleeting and spurious romanticism like the sacrament of some breakaway sect.

Many had an overt friendliness. They were social adepts among the awkward public, the youthful and the elderly. Yet there were secretive ones as well, while others had an enigmatic disdain, as though physical congress were an act of self-castigation. Some had a candid intelligence, a knowledgeable impertinence. Others had only the prehistoric smiles of hunter-gatherers, primitive agriculturalists and breeders of men. They were vacuous, sweet, and silent as fruit.

◯

WALKING JUST AHEAD OF ME, Indigo sought out the most rarely visited alleys, with their narrow, centuries-old cobblestone walkways, and each window opening upon the unchosen. Some were aged, some obese, others refugees washed up from rude Indian Ocean islands. A few stank like the crazed, or were painted like ghouls, or sat undressed with scraps of pitiful costumes. All had sad eyes, waiting in the darkness, forever. They were used by the cruelest, poorest customers, destitute Moroccans or Afghans who in their home villages would stone them.

As in the Salzburg night, Indigo moved among these possessed, and the dispossessed. He first bowed – startling a few who had seen everything – then tapped lightly on the door. To each one he gave their fee, but refused entry, offering his cheek instead for just a kiss, or bringing their hands almost to his lips as though to ladies at a ball. He somehow instantly read them all, their pain, their thoughts, their buried feelings.

To one conscious of her unattractiveness he would say, "How lovely you look this evening."

To another, angry and confused, he murmured "Be at peace."

To the worst, he made a blessing, "Your life has been compassionate."

He moved like a humble Tibetan lama among a line of wild high-valley penitents. One young, frantic and derisive addict thought him only skittish, or fearful of being *impuissant*. Remarkably, he produced a small nosegay of flowers for her. As she clutched the bouquet, he tenderly pressed his hand upon her heart. He held her eyes for a long while, looking into her, like a baptism to another life. She reeled, the voice of her body rising. Breaking, she thanked him profusely in Croatian, then turned in tears as she held the flowers pressed to her breasts.

All responded to the first delicate warmth they encountered from the street, their hard eyes softening at lost memories of gentleness. It was like a religious meeting in an alleyway. With reluctance they let him pass, each moving to the edge of their window for a last glimpse.

⬡

THE DWINDLING CUSTOMERS – trying to forget the transfer of souls this night – imbibed stiff whiskies at the Bulldog, then left with disjointed lurches toward shabby squares. Everyone awaited time's vengeance, under fading sobs of moonlight.

He spoke to a few window-workers who were leaving their shifts, about to pedal away on their bicycles, as if they were tired schoolgirls. One was a sensuous tropical beauty without shame; others plundered themselves to provide licensed pleasures. They explained their evenings. "I have children." "My husband bartends nearby." "I work two year, then go village in Serbia." All were members of the Prostitutes Guild, with weekly medical checks. Fatigue tolled heavily on everyone, for we all had been swept away.

The hours wearied. There were sneaking cats and overturned dustbins, the smell of blocked drains. We heard the curdled crying of fat pigeons, the corpulence of ragged bells from the Oude Kerk. We bowed out from this incoherent and echoing world. Migrant customers dissipated to their dingy lodgings, their dignities expired.

He tried to cure my distress. "Imagine them all as serene peasant girls, with wreathes of blue flowers in their hair," he reflected, "under a white moon at sunset."

⬡

INDIGO WANTED to shake off the night. We entered the Leidseplein clubs, one known as the Melkweg (Milky Way), another called Chemistry, then settled on Trance Buddha, a small venue at the edge of the district. Indigo watched two women, alight with a fine flame under their skin, who were dancing closely in some adoration of each other. He came to them and said a few words. They embraced him like a lost lover, all swaying together in the web of dreamlike lasers. Parting from me, he left with both, and never thereafter explained how they recognized each other, or what they did that night, or by what magic all were recognized or summoned.

⬡

THE EARLY MORNING was grey and unreal, but brightened as Indigo collected me. From Centraal Station, with its thousands of bicycles gathered in black ranks, we began to travel across Holland by train. We passed through the grand Bloembollenstreek flower-producing region with its drifts of tulips and lilies-of-the-valley, its dykes of padded earthen embankments, its lattices of canals and the picture-book windmills, its roads under straight ash trees above gorse bushes and pink and white oleander. We gazed at the rushing landscape, and talked and mused and slept, until the sun was in its last conflagration before sunset.

By evening we arrived at Leiden. Seated on rough wooden chairs at an outdoor café on the edge of the Rhine, we had platters of thick sliced tomatoes and gouda. The North Sea air was salty and wet; one could hear the husky calling of old ships. An Albinoni *adagio* played in the café, while beyond us upon the Rhine were patches of black and silver moonlight.

We walked for hours through the big Vondelpark, where at our thoughtful passage birds rose in flocks, flinging about like spray. Near the Museumquarter, Indigo talked of the river gods of youth, the solitary life of the clandestine, the mind-bending years of survival and resistance. There then was silence, but for the trees dripping moisture from the sea.

I thought it my last chance. I already had asked Vermilion and Crimson. Ever since Vienna, one sensed or imagined some hostile surveillance of the Six, lurking in corners like prophetic inklings. These were my first tastes of ash and fear, and annihilating doubt.

"What if everything goes down?"

Indigo's eyes filled with the light of tragedy. He knew well of the insistent portents, of the plots and counterplots, of the invisible hand that turns over the chessboard.

"Such are the vagaries of fate," he replied. "If one 'goes down,' as you say, the others can switch it off, worldwide. We then would examine microscopically the system, altering identities and locations and procedures across the earth. But our fear is that – in the absence of the sacrament – toxic alternatives will proliferate, with addiction and loss of lives. Opiates, stimulants, bizarre lethal hallucinogens will enter the void. Governments would be wise to permit a certain availability of classical psychedelics, lest chemical horrors abound. There is not yet any non-lethal alternative that can be distributed widely."

It was characteristic of the Six that Indigo's primary concern was not imprisonment, but the outcome for society.

⬡

WE ENDED OUR TOUR at Delft, a few miles from the coast, at the Vondelstraat Hotel. We stood beneath the spire of the Nieuwe Kerk, its wet, grey grass before us and lichens on the church's stone walls. The moon in the clear sky was itself like some captive with unseen bonds. A phosphorescent penumbra began spreading all about us. I thought how sweet the graveyard, with its scattering of bluebells.

He had a third-class ticket for the ferry from Hoek van Holand to Harwich, then up to Oxford. He said only that he would see me very soon. I had merely a student pass to travel by boat from

Amsterdam through Cologne to Basel. While interventions by the Six seemed unlikely, I dared not underestimate them.

He was reflective, this truly occult mind, as though possessed of some informed fire. Behind us, the lamps of Delft shone in the haze like jeweled gloom. The low moan of sea wind arose, for a moment like a sad, slow coronach of bagpipes. Before us, there was a strange insistence of light from the sea. Just as he boarded the crowded ferry, he turned to me.

"If we switch it off, the darkness will return."

Chapter 15.

Sunrise at Midnight

For on his untruths and winged cunning, a majesty lies.

- Pindar

Survival is an infinite capacity for suspicion.

- Le Carré, *Tinker, Tailor, Solider, Spy*

Strong man, you know how it's done
you've done it again and again
sucking the spirit back
to us from its lair of smoke.

- (on a fireman with dying child) Rosanna Warren,
"In Creve Coeur, Missouri"

THE NIGHT PASSAGE to Zürich, out of the Gare de l'Est in Paris, harbored many obscure intrigues. It was a TGV bullet train, slowly passing the distant Latin Quarter under leaden clouds, then the Pont St. Louis and the floodlit Notre Dame. The observation and dining car windows finally showed only the blur of the rain-washed French countryside, as the train strung out in bluish light across the landscape, into the flying night.

A few days after the interception by Indigo in Amsterdam, there was no longer time for a leisurely boat down the Rhine for my meeting in Basel with other researchers. A cheap train from Centraal Station in Amsterdam quickly resolved the matter; some dwindling funds were spent in Paris on a night transfer ticket to Zürich and copies of the *Neue Zürcher Zeitung* and the *International Herald Tribune*. I had vague ambitions to hike in Kernwald's gloomy forest after the meeting.

The first-class quarters out of Paris were occupied only by several swarthy Corsicans, over from Calvi through Nice, and a sprinkling of French and Swiss arrived on the Blue Train from the Côte d'Azur. I took late tea, perusing the *NZZ*, when I noticed behind the Corsicans a devoted reader, his head concealed by a copy of Proust. Almost alarmed, I looked again, but acquiesced to my fate. The Breguet shone like the augury in Vienna, its face ticking the moments to glory or disgrace. It seemed impossible the Six could detect my last-minute change of plans. Indigo must have come down immediately from Oxford to Waterloo Station – taking the Eurostar to Paris – then boarded at Gare de l'Est. Perhaps it simply was coincidence. He said nothing, intent on the Proust. I listened to Brahms piano waltzes, pondering synchronicity and the darkling forests, until sleep came.

⬡

SWITZERLAND APPEARED like Yule-tide cake, the rainy vistas finally clearing at altitude. The bullet train slowed, then stopped with a sigh, awakening me to discover that Indigo's seat was empty. Engaging my driver, I passed along the cold waters edge of the *Zürichsee*. We failed to find a cheap room near the Zürich Savoy, then arrived at a crumbling hostel on the far side of the Zürichberg past the Dolder Grand Hotel.

It was a type of shabby Victorian doss-house. The desk clerk was thin as an insect, with an aquiline nose and tinted glasses. I relinquished my passport to a certain disposition of his eyebrows. With a whir of the lift the night porter ushered me to a nameless furnished room with a sprung bed, shaded night lamp, and an old green baize card table. I was sleepless, and it was a starry dawn.

At the bells of morning mass, I meandered instead this day to the Café Brioche. The night had been uneasy, but the early light and air had a terrestrial sweetness. The *Zürichsee* was like a looking-glass, under a washed-out, late moon.

The café rang with the dialects of Zürichdeutsch. I drank tea, worried about my extravagant transit and overdrafts, and thought of Indigo's lifestyle. Even burdened with the terrible cruelty of his isolation, he had a persistently amiable and equable demeanor. He was not quixotic, nor did he possess any exalted fanaticism. He did seem to reveal aspects of the Six more than the others – details I could add to my research ethnography on clandestine chemists – but I had learned never to force a confidence.

Lines of Zürchers were buying fresh hot loaves of Dinkelbrot, while beyond the window several uniformed officials from the Stadtpolizei Zürich gathered to look quizzically at the café. Suddenly fatigued, I left.

⬡

HE FOUND ME at a gallery in the Niederdorf – I no longer asked how. We walked with a studied casualness up the steep Zürichberg slope past the old villas, then down to Krähbühlstrasse, taking the tram to the terminal at Hauptbahnhof. As we exited, a tidy Spaniard turned the pages of *El Mundo*, then glanced at us, perhaps too long. We considered the trains to München, and wandered the subterranean shopping arcade. In the end, he resolved – almost as an act of faith – that there were no followers.

We came upon several furtive and distracted young women, who occupied empty storefronts. They shuffled restlessly, sniffling and checking their watches, looking down ancient streets like hungry dogs. Their eyes were clouded, ashamed, with a strange inner light that had no warmth. One seemed *déclassé*, but from a good family, fine-boned with a slender and gracile body.

"They are heroin addicts, circling back to Needle Park. 'Turning tricks,' as Americans say, and awaiting the next fix."

Seeking Indigo's perspective on addiction, I described the poppy fields of Central Asia, the kilos of opium at the farm gates, and of interviewing the final users in Boston.

"Can we visit the Park?"

"Indeed, we must. Let's begin, though, at the top."

⬡

WITH THAT, he led me along the exquisite shops of the Bahnhofstrasse, where we crossed the broad Paradeplatz – Zürich's grand financial complex – with Credit Suisse on one side, opposed by the Union Bank of Switzerland on the other.

"Much of the cartels' profit from the poisonous drug trade passes through banks near the Bahnhofstrasse: Colombian cocaine, Afghan morphine, Ugandan corruption, Nigerian deceits, Indian Quaaludes. Nazi lootings of gold and paintings are still stored in vaults below the Talstrasse."

"Is corruption really so public?"

"Nothing indiscrete. The real money movers, the primary fiduciaries, are small and private, more invisible even than the many *banques privées* of Monaco. The old mansions here have banks of only three rooms and five employees."

As we entered the quiet side streets between the Bahnhofstrasse and the Sihl River, the grandeur and generosity of Zürich seemed scattered about us like gems. Indigo was less enamored.

"The engineers of sin."

"What do you mean?"

"The private banks in these centuries-old townhouses are forbidden to solicit deposits for tax avoidance. Word of mouth only – for sensitive clients. Some have stolen Cézannes, Caravaggios, and platinum from the *Sicherheitsdienst*, the Nazi Security Organization. They are less regulated, with grandfathered numbered accounts, and elaborate offshore instruments."

We stopped on the Bärengasse, before a grey mausoleum identified only by a small brass plate. A lanky figure emerged. His bloodless face had eyes the color of arctic ice. Pretending to engage in some glacial calculation, he studiously avoided our gaze.

"Pig in clover," Indigo remarked.

We watched him pass, as did another observer in a dark green Barbour coat, woolen scarf, and a flat low cap more suitable for the hedgerows. He looked at us, as strange children do on the same playground. He walked toward the Sihl River in the direction of the railyard near the Zeughausstrasse, 100 meters from the Stadtpolizei. Perhaps I was becoming too sensitive.

"Let's follow the trail," Indigo proposed in a sorrowful tone, "down to the end users."

○

WE TRAVELED along the *Zürichsee* in the crisp morning light, the icy brilliance of the lake water broken only by massed spear-points of reeds. There were dreary plaster brick housing blocks south along the Sihl, and the crowded workers' slums of the Aussersihl and the Industrie-Quartier, where there were more Paks and Portuguese than Swiss. Indigo examined our hypothetical tail all through the one-way streets of Wiedikon and back over to the *Zürichsee*.

Needle Park itself was far too public for him. He led me to a derelict squat nearby, with its cracked pavements and scavenging feral cats; a door opened upon deranged structures with fallen masonry and shattered, candlelit rooms drifting with layers of incense. It was a chaotic oblivion, like an abandoned battlefield still edged with menace.

He changed form before my eyes. Indigo began to assume the light manner of a raffish Oxford don, but it was to conceal his distress at the prospect of encountering disease, like a surgeon at Dresden affecting cheerfulness before attending ghastly rows of burned men with no faces.

○

A SLIM, SMOLDERING GIRL came forth, standing the way tarts stand in doorways. Indigo approached her alone, almost out of earshot, rhapsodizing in some cryptic language with allusive mysteries about substances that would fan her blood to fire. In a beguiling and negligent Zürichdeutsch, she made a desultory response. From the interior I could hear fits of febrile weeping, and the sounds of women rutting in heat, as if with the endless pain there were unlimited pleasures. She admitted us, thinking we were users, or buyers.

Indigo, in the manner of a *paterfamilias*, offered pleasantries and Euros among the brethren. Out of sight, he faked snorting heroin, then crashed on a rotted timber. We feigned a heavy nod, as though dazed, then grinned lasciviously to deflect suspicion. We looked upon a gruesome scene.

○

IT APPEARED TO BE a vile clinic devoted to twilight sleep, echoing on and off with sobbing and hysterical orgasms. In payment for heroin or cocaine or methamphetamine – the monarchs of all vices – there was in the shadows constant and open whoring. Others sat with the red eyes of sheep, their spirits eviscerated.

One tattooed junkie, in his parasitic professional manner, heated spoons of heroin and cocaine mixtures over a candle. Describing it as dragon's blood, he offered the potion like a lord of the dark hosts. To our inexpressible dismay – for we could not caution them – a girl's flash of virtue evaporated very quickly before our eyes. Her veins tied off with rubber tubing, she was injected, laying back loose-legged against a wall, eyes glazed, sky-blue panties still new and fragrant, careless of the precipice. It moved through her, her body swooning. As she lay helpless, a perverse lout began pawing her unquickened flesh.

Some seemed mere children in their embryonic selves, drifting unresponsively around the alleys of society. A few were barbarian whelps, others overconfident delinquents. All assumed they were vastly augmented by latter-day laudanum, but their delicious vertigos were the cruel illusion of a cosmic malevolence. These blithe spirits lay dreaming, unaware they now were clad in the elegant livery of death.

One could only conclude that through chronic use their nervous systems had been butchered; they lay stranded here among the remains of their vanished neurologies. To them, no civilization existed beyond the candle and spoon; their universe was a giant maggotry.

I looked at the users more carefully. They had the pale hopelessness of wasted children, like the fruit of mirthless marriages, those that never had presents under a tree. These were the sacrificed, the first born of Moloch worshippers, poisoned by craving.

A lofty demoiselle of sixteen, cold as a Christmas rose, begged for another hit. In the low light, she waited for her masters' wishes. With an already dingy voice, her speech was broken, slurred. There was the idiot barking of savage dogs, perhaps from another world.

⬡

INDIGO SUGGESTED that we part the psychic veil, and look at the dark matter rather than the atoms. At this, he passed his hand over the scene – as if trailing a transparent curtain or rippling the surface of clear water – beyond which nothing and everything was changed. The young people were clutched in the folds of some high serpent. The girls were panting and breathless within the heavy reptile curl. The boys were wild and sweating, struggling, picked at by old carrion birds.

The walls moved with images of ghastly Aztec carvings. I felt like Orpheus looking back into Hell. Convent devils raged around us like clanging torments in this common, barren world. The snake of Aesculapius, god of medicine, coiled around the cross in a horrific caduceus. These debauched teenage acolytes of opiates and stimulants had dark-ringed eyes and fevered grimaces. Some were whining peevishly for needles; others in corners bent like squaws or kneeled before those unencumbered, in a room strewn with used prophylactics.

"They find the overdoses in crevasses on the Bernese Oberland," Indigo whispered, "thrown over and disguised as hiking mishaps."

One French girl, black-haired and pale-skinned in a leather jacket, had her blue jeans down her long legs to her ankles, offering herself for a dose. She would turn heads on the Bahnhofstrasse, with her wide grey eyes and white pallor. Removing her pointed silk brassiere of theoretical black, she looked as if she were temporarily absent from her family villa near Nidwalden, and now a roaming specter at the peak of the Jungfrau. Her right arm was stained in velvet, like blood drying.

"They come from Zug, Lucerne, Geneva, the rich into Kloten Airport and down the Zürichberg," Indigo said.

She was pathetic in the throes of craving, baffled, her new worldliness concealing an eye not yet embittered. Tearful and stammering, she still had starts of revulsion. In her scanty attire, with a listless and grim resolve, she invited the junkies, the ghostly horsemen, to ride her. We saw in the girl the next pestilences of this world, the drugged future Saturnalias, like the women and men copulating on graves in Milan during the plagues, as everyone grasped at dwindling life with the sibilance of machines. Evil was at the helm.

"And these are the oldest drugs," Indigo said, "Imagine the abuse of the next generation of erotogenics."

The deepest images were the most frightening. As we witnessed the mythic core, I almost bolted in horror. We saw the Christ child in a manger, infused with holy light, while surrounding Him were giant spiders feeding at His glory. Above Him stood the compassionate Mary, in her robe of stars, until her beatific countenance was drawn back to reveal horrible fangs. We saw who addiction truly was. I no longer could bear to look upon it. Indigo passed his hand across the panorama, trailing the images like strobes, and said from the Vulgate the last words of Christ on the Cross.

"Consummatum est." (It is finished)

The glissade of dimensions coalesced. There now were simply young people partying with spoons and pills and needles, a few aged junkies sharing their bags of powders. Some were dressing to flee into the cold Zürich air, spreading their secret infection.

As one sluggish fetus looked on with his dimmed swivel eyes, Indigo suddenly seized the French girl, pulling her forcibly behind a wall, as others had. Trembling, she exposed her young, sharp, uptilted breasts. She asked whether we each wanted her alone, or both together.

"Amour des quatres pattes? A tous la quatre vents?" (Love on all fours? At every opening?)

Indigo asked her if she would trade the drug for a loving husband and children who thought the sun rose in her eyes. She wavered at the unexpected truth.

He told the lost girl to cover herself, then offered her a pale mother of pearl rosary. She said it glowed like a string of moonlight and silver. Pressing it into her hand, he evoked a memory from her Catholic schoolgirl youth.

"Extirpandum Turcam." (Throw out the Devil)

He reminded her how to count the rosary, then they slowly repeated at least ten times the full *Ave Maria*. I heard them together, his voice first, her quavering refrain following, Indigo like a father guiding his children home.

"Ave Maria, gratia plena, dominus tecum, benedicta tu…"

She dressed, stumbling after us into the daylight, then joined us in a cab on the long ride to Kloten Airport. It was like Perseus's rescue of Andromeda. Indigo, in the manner of a seminarian with potent and sensuous beliefs, hovered protectively, bringing her back to a visionary, polite world.

We helped her board her flight to Geneva. Indigo retrieved her name and number; he said two women would visit her one day soon. Their names would be those of the Muses.

INDIGO ACCOMPANIED ME that same day from Kloten to Basel, where he seemed more relaxed. Each afternoon he trekked alone up the mountain, past streamlets and sunny bowers, as cowbells followed one another. He disappeared into a series of old summer houses that were completely brambled by roses and honeysuckle. Each morning, Indigo returned to collect me at the small hotel he recommended, once a haunt of Einstein's, away from the patent office in Bern.

I had anticipated some worldly, now modernist hideaway, but found a prim *châtelaine*, polished parquet floors and elderly Frauen in twinsets. There was silver plate from Utrecht and Paris, and an old creaking library with leaning landings crammed with quarto books bound in morocco and vellum. 18th Century clocks were in asynchrony beneath obliterated frescoes. Marquetry desks occupied window bays, upon which were clusters of white roses.

My room had a pallid reading light, and an old Portuguese writing desk with ivory handles. An etching of lions rampant hung on one whitewashed wall. There was a small crucifix of Christ on a cross of silver.

An ancient public telephone was used by guests, with subdued utterances and the greatest circumspection. Obscure and eccentric functionaries quietly padded by a 200 year-old Neufchâtel wall clock, with enameled dials and cameos, in three cases. A rubicund-faced charwoman was omnipresent. In the daylight, the ghosts of old spies from the Reich fled to hide under window planters filled with peonies. A favorite of Indigo, it long had been a crossroads for the highly experienced, and the covert.

○

I TOOK TO WANDERING the back streets of Basel, until I twice noticed the same girl peering into dusty shop windows. As I slid into the faded sepia anonymity of a bookstore, she entered and began perusing shopworn volumes of Petrarch. She was high-bred, with almost sepulchral skin, dressed in tightly fitted *crêpe de chine* and carrying a small Chanel handbag. Possessed of hot, shy eyes, she displayed a delectable – even sybaritic – fitness. Temporarily besotted, I soon recovered.

The pantheress from the Hotel Sacher in Vienna had rematerialized. She no longer wore the slit cheongsam embroidered with seed pearls and finches and lilacs, but retained the complexion of the young sheppardess. The girl could only be a diplomatic *agente provocateuse* of the Six, on some vital tryst or stealthy rendevous. I hardly was worthy of her time.

Her eyes were light, like morning. She moved about inscrutably, with an aristocratic subtlety, as though she were from the thoroughbred line of V-1 and V-2, with their obvious and electrical intelligences. As I watched, she looked over my shoulder at the window, then flushed vividly. Her eyes flashed the stars of infinite embrace, as if some flame were leaping from her belly to her heart. Crossing the street was Indigo. She turned away quickly, ignoring us, and assumed a wonderful remoteness. She purchased a copy of Strauss's *Die Frau Ohne Schatten (The Woman without a Shadow)*, and a volume of Yeats. With a Parisienne *chic*, she strutted away past a row of stiff alders.

I noticed her receding pumps were fashionable but sensible, the tradecraft of a pavement artist. She clearly was a monitor, but too sophisticated for Interpol. For an operative of the Six, she was almost careless, as if permitting one to see her. With some regret, I let it all go.

Indigo led me from the bookstore, and stared fixedly at the girl's figure as she turned the corner. At her passage he became silent, almost troubled.

"Who is she?" I asked.

"She has a hundred names, in many countries."

"What does she do?"

"She swims in all the oceans, as they say," he replied, "and she watches the watchers."

○

MARCHING BEFORE GILDED FRIEZES, the clockwork princes in a shop window of Basel struck the hours. We moved about the ramparts of crumbling centurion walls, and beneath the sable roofs, spires and sliding planes of the city's secret histories. Beyond vaulted passageways and massive iron-clamped doors, the besieged could keep up a raking fire. High above us, upon the mosaic of alpine fields, glaciers of white flowers melted away into the trees.

As we explored, Indigo happily engaged in a highly varied exposition on local manuscripts, ranging from More's *Utopia*, printed in Basel in 1518, to Kepler's *Mysterium Cosmographicum*. As we approached the University of Basel, he looked across the street. His face quenched, almost startled.

He changed tone in a subtle way, but without missing a beat, like a recording from which the humanity had been drained. He drew the fires as suddenly as he had stoked them. He circled among topics I knew to be patently apocryphal, then repeated himself with some absurd *idée fixe*, then descended into completely opaque phrases. To observers unfamiliar with his gifts, he appeared merely a casual tour guide, distracted at moments. Something was wrong.

We saw the girl. She no longer had the Yeats. She stood beneath an elaborate entry gate into the university near the Petersplatz, holding a fine pink Kyoto parasol, surrounded by a group of admiring students. One attractive woman *arriviste* held a pampered saluki on leash. Two of the men, some Hohenzollern or Hohenstaufen pretenders to extinct thrones, attempted to flummox international visitors. The girl easily multitasked between them, gushing on the surface but quite detached in reality, convincing one young man she was awed by his professed lineage. She smiled prettily, while discretely opening and closing the rigid folds of the dainty paper parasol, like a cherry blossom fluttering.

At this gesture, Indigo became frosty, consumed with the exigencies of business, hiding himself against the shadowed walls and quoting his beloved Le Carré.

"Jesus had twelve, old son, and one of them was a double."

I knew he was hunted as a criminal, the most vitiated class, but had never witnessed his response to the presence of danger.

He approached a park bench with a view of the street, initiating conversation with an ancient Basel resident in a rumpled tailored suit. I sat on the other side of the elder. He possessed a pronouced Parkinsonian tremor and senile demeanor, but welcomed us most warmly.

The girl folded her parasol and tapped the cobbled street. Down the line of sight of her parasol was a café in withering shade, off Petersgraben, on a back street redolent of bratwurst and *Schnapps*. The single table was occupied by a bottle of Rémy Martin cointreau – not a Basel drink at this hour – placed before a deplorable figure without a trace of discernable divinity.

Keeping up a respectful, effortless conversation with the elder, Indigo had a complete unaffectedness of delivery, as though the straggling discussion fascinated him entirely. They did halting, pleasant little exchanges on the best bakeries for Dinkelbrot, and the quickest hiking trails over the Vosges Mountains or through the Black Forest for those who fled the Reich and the Nazi collaborators on this very street in 1945. I was puzzled, but managed some lighthearted words. Prismatic dust hung in the mid-morning sunbeams; the world seemed void of any malice.

Not sipping the Rémy, but with a wary, belligerent expression, the observer carefully turned the pages of an out-of-town newspaper, the *Frankfurter Allgemeine Zeitung*. In the pastoral, civilized air of Basel he had a Philistine deportment, like some foreign and ruthless constabulary, perhaps a misplaced employee of the *Rauschgiftdezermat*, the German DEA. He was awkward, with a certain *gaucherie*, and boxy – even angular – like a distortion or mistransmission in the rainbow.

There had been a series of unheeded portents from Vienna to London to Zürich, auguries and premonitory signs of grave events. We saw him quite clearly.

○

A FLOCK of Japanese mothers with prams, with the children in bunny and frog costumes, were pointing out the museum-quality antique pink parasol. The girl, not remotely nonplussed in the midst of her spy craft and unwanted suitors, unfolded the parasol, twirling it slowly before the prams. She first moved with the meticulous, elegant posturing of a rigorously trained Geisha, and offered them a 17th Century haiku. The children looked on, open-mouthed.

Engulfed in the happy throng, she changed form, entering into an impromptu street theater. She told them a story in Japanese, acting out the alligators roaring and snakes hissing, rushing them as they screamed in delight. They clapped their tiny palms together uncertainly, small fingers spread.

A glint in a fourth-story window revealed the outline of a camera. The observer, looking over his *Zeitung*, forgot to smile. One could not easily estimate the size of the surveillance team, if it were that.

The girl danced onward with her entourage of suitors, and her cloud-soft laughter, to mothers and little ones waving farewell. Indigo took the sun lazily for a while, fully attentive to our pathetic companion. He stood reluctantly, then gently took the elder's shaking, palsied hand, and sang to him in Schweizerdeutsch a long nursery rhyme from the old man's childhood. Brightening with joy, the elder flailed his arm with attempted applause, until Indigo held them both steadily. He sang it for him again, more slowly and poignantly, then bowed. We departed at a leisurely pace toward my hostel. He never referred to the obvious sighting again, as if it were my imagination, merely a string of misinterpretations.

○

WE MET AT NOON for a hike to the Belchen peak above Basel. Indigo, ever the trekker, produced a hefty daypack with sleeping bags. We began walking from a trailhead up the slopes, at first with a kind of strenuous numbness. Witnesses began to fall away, until there were only goldfinches piping on thistle heads. I hoped he would tell me more.

"The girl at Needle Park. How did you know to provide a rosary?"

"Something in her light. And her Catholic background was apparent to me."

"And if it weren't?"

"Then another approach. Rosaries and saints and pilgrimages were condemned by Protestants since the Lutheran Reformation and the Augsburg Confession."

"So it wasn't specific to her religious tradition?"

"Yes and no. We had to evoke her earliest belief system, one beneath her psychic infection. We all once trusted the infinite, with the faith of children. It is a matter of remembering."

"Then addiction not always has an obvious neural component?"

"The medievalists can't be discarded entirely. Among those so foredoomed, phenomena occur that are recognizable by clinicians, but sometimes more accurately by modern demonologists."

A faint breeze passed through scarlet hibiscus, hanging in bushes along the way. The terrain began changing; marigolds flooded the uncultivated fields until they became sunken gardens. The sky was blue as a jay's eye.

After some hours, Basel spread far below us, its sublime histories and terror now remote. The last of tall fuchsia hedges gave way to wild copses of gnarly black oaks, then maple and birch. Among the grasses were sedge and ragweed, while thickets of blackberries grew along the remaining hedgerows.

Tiring, we stopped at a springhead – too high for the belled cows – and drank cold water from our cupped hands. We splashed our faces, exhilarated. Shoals of butterflies floated above a world of saffron and lion-gold.

He spread on a cloth some Emmental and Sbrinz cheeses, a loaf of Dinkelbrot, and apples. Within the pack was a large folder of detailed maps, and light reading – Fielding and Balzac. There was a difficult De Quincey – the *Suspiria de Profundis* – in a leather-bound 18th Century variorum edition, lightly foxed. Handwritten notes, inscribed with the fineness of quills, were in the margins. With hunger as the spice, we dined lavishly on light fare, while considering over distant Basel the sudden lowering of clouds.

⬡

WE HEARD only the hum of insects, and the incessant resonance of the life-giving brook. A murder of crows, perhaps fifty or so, roiled below us in slow helices. Indigo observed them in contemplation, remarking on their use for prophecy in primitive cultures. On a rough outcrop underneath them was a dead crow, its head curled under one wing.

"A funeral," he said.

"Do creatures honor their own?"

"Crows do, elephants, many other sentient beings."

One landed, inspecting the carcass, then flew off. The murder of crows scattered, then three more arrived, hopping to the body. With their beaks they placed twigs and grass by and on the deceased, as though they were nesting. Twenty landed, then forty. For a long while, they stood in silence.

"Vale et atque," Indigo said, "Hail and Farewell."

The crows blasted upwards as one, cawing bravely, circling ever higher. They dispersed to the winds, to the far rains, and into the thunderous sun. The dead crow lay under her twigs, flying with them always.

"They are altruistic?"

"It was altruism, not violence or force, which associated our higher cortex. Our intent is to awaken that memory."

"But how would the crows bode, as an omen, among the descendents of the Franks and Celts?"

"We disperse on pagan signs as well, in honor of forgotten truths, and warnings."

"At the whim of the wild?"

"At the majesty."

◯

AS TWILIGHT APPROACHED, there was some urgency to climb even higher. We packed our things, and hiked through a wall of three-meter gorse until it opened upon boulders and steep ravines. An imperceptible watershed led up to chasms, and labyrinths of defiles. Near the peak, the clouds began moving in alarming haste across a running moon.

The deep blue rotunda of the day shattered with a fierce freak storm. The sky began tearing, ripping wide into blackness; a vast disorder of flying shapes was whirling like some tide of dread. We huddled on this porch of the unknown as the moon, far above the vapory swiftness, opened its mystic door. It was not unlike the convulsive birth of the mistral, the iron north wind descending into France.

We hid in a grotto, waiting out the storm. There was no rain, only the demented dancing of Furies on ridge tops. In the loneliness of these highest ranges, where he had passed so many winters, Indigo seemed truly at home. I knew not how much longer we would be together, and encouraged his disclosures by pretending I had just thought of a question.

"What human had the largest exposure to LSD?"

Vermilion in Berlin had revealed Indigo's long night of the soul, but my polite little deception was futile.

"Vermilion is fond of that tale. We have no secrets from each other, an operational necessity."

I reddened, and remained silent. He continued with a fantastical drama.

"The event occurred before we adopted fully protective moon suits with face shields and air pumps. I had risen from praying – then stood by a custom glass reactor that contained ten million just activated doses. The elixir swirled under argon, beneath deep red illumination. The music was von Bingen, Gregorian, some Amazonian chants…"

The shrill wind of the mistral rose and fell. He looked out at the trailing clouds, as if he were recollecting some unspeakable magic.

"Standing several rungs up a ladder, and engaging a complex range of fine glassware, I began a purification method, decanting the ten million doses from a 12-liter flask into a large pear-shaped separatory funnel. It was attached to a stainless steel rack, high upon a ten-foot wall of delicate, specialized glass – a pilot plant, one might say."

"What happened?"

"My gloved hand, wet with solvent, slipped."

"And then?"

"The flask shattered. Ten million doses of the most potent psychoactive substance known – dissolved in a solvent that quickly penetrates skin – drenched me from head to foot."

"Oh, my."

"I thought I was dead. No human could survive such an exposure to any drug. I fell from the ladder onto my back, in a large pool of solvent and LSD. Screaming in fear, I staggered to the shower, shaking so I hardly could strip, awaiting the inevitable seizures, unconsciousness, and death."

"And then?"

"I was crying, shouting prayers to be protected, to live, to be spared, then I was on my knees naked and wailing before the blinding whiteness. I prayed in the timeless void, for it was the moment of birth and death."

He stopped as the mistral in its agonies disturbed the interface between this world and the next. The grotto was dark but for the cataclysmic shifting light.

"Please continue, if you can."

"The batch was irretrievable, of course, although no one cared. I couldn't call an ambulance, for the scene appeared like some other planet's holy wilderness of technology. I awaited the next life, grieving for my loved one. For a moment, demons shrieked and stellar hosts sang of forever peace."

"Go on."

"I somehow stood, praying, 'Please God…' I hung on the showerhead with the water over my face, carried by the river of life to the eternal mother ocean, the hiss of waves on beaches of worlds without end."

"And?"

"And trembling, I carefully bathed, ritually cleansing, then managed to dress in an old blue work shirt and jeans. I somehow moved about the rooms – which were billowing wildly in the currents of mind – and refreshed the votives, lit incense, and thanked God for my life that was passing."

"Yes?"

"I crawled to a veranda, on this summer night. I was in Northern Italy. The villa had an oceanic view, as we prefer for sites. Against the wall, resigned to fate, I sat with legs crossed, hands in prayer, gazing now and then at the spectacle before me."

"What did you see, or experience?"

"I saw the constant creation of the most perfect world imaginable by the mind of God, the luminous air of delicious gases like the perfume of lovers and goddesses, the rich earths made of gems, the fecund ground of being. I saw the union of all dualities, the crystallized souls of heaven, the galaxies of consciousness, and all life as mythic and sublime."

"How long did this last?"

"Oh, it never went away. Even now I can see it – if I wish."

"You mean the effects were permanent?"

"No. I mean the greatest gift is the natural mind, that which cannot be created or destroyed by any drug. That which we have always."

"How can you have seen what you described, if not for the overdose?"

"I saw the world as it truly is. God – or the ultimate consciousness – would not be so cruel as to make such glory dependent on a substance. Put another way, nothing happened that night."

"Nothing happened?"

"I was exposed to ten million doses in seconds – the only human to witness, or survive, such an exposure. Beyond the initial changes, there was no effect whatsoever. After the first few moments on the veranda, and the whirlwind of the unknown, the night became crystal clear. I could hear night birds stirring, and feel little freshets of cool wind. All was perfect, beautiful. The moon went bronze to white as it rose, its rays dispersing through the thick forests. No patterning; the world was vast and still."

"The exposure was so extreme that it had no effect?"

"By contrast, a milligram, 1000 micrograms, ten or twenty doses, would have been overwhelming. I would have writhed in rebirths for many hours. I was saved that night by Grace alone."

"Then the ultimate vision was our own mundane, magical world?"

"Yes, that's it. Perhaps the event was a reminder that we all already have that which we seek. Ultimate intelligence, ultimate beauty, universal peace, the final comprehension. Ultimate love."

"What did you do?"

"With humility and gratitude, I reflected on this great teaching, of enlightenment as the moment one recalls the divinity of normal mind, knowing it for the first time. And I looked at the forest in the moonlight, not moving through the night as the earth turned to day. After a final prayer, I rested for a few hours. Over the next weeks, I decontaminated the site with care, discarding every trace of the incident. There were esoteric acts of lustration, ceremonial purifications, with quite some use of smudge sticks, and candles, incense, chants and prayers. I ran kilometers each night, restoring physical energy, then with our formal traditions prepared the next batch."

At this he became quiet. We sat in meditation until the wind receded, the tranquil evening drifting upon us like a black silk gown at the commencement of understanding.

⬡

AS NIGHT FELL, the sky cleared to the horizons. We hurried to scale the mountain, gazing at the hundred peaks of the Alps as cascades of stars touched the earth. We made a small camp, then collected arm loads of downed wood shattered from the lightning strikes. We built a ceremonial fire, its flames burning with the heavy scent of juniper. All about us, the pale moonrise revealed a wilderness of jeweled crags. The valleys beneath were soft as eiderdown.

By the fireside, Indigo withdrew three sleeping bags, spreading their luxury over the stony ground.

"Three?"

"A friend."

Down the mountain trail all the way to Basel, nothing moved in the lunar landscape. The scene was motionless, like a luminous tomb. I expected some apparition to appear.

"And those lights at the edge of the city?"

"The pharmaceutical industry of Basel never sleeps, since the hermetic arts of the Middle Ages. We hope only that their medicines prove to be benevolent. They have been, and could be again in some small aspect, the factories of God."

LATE by the winking firelight – at this altitude under a startling white, piercing moon – he told old country tales of the Swiss. Fragrant smoke from the resins drifted like plumes of burnt offerings into the firmament's limitless black vault. He produced the De Quincey, and read from it, describing Paracelsus, the 16th Century physician and alchemist of Basel.

"Aureolus Philippus Theophrastus Bombastus von Hohenheim, or Paracelsus," he said. "In legend possessing a secret word that could transform matter, or recreate a rose from its own ashes."

"Heroic myths," I returned.

"You know the story? De Quincey reported it first, Borges illuminated it further."

"Not entirely."

"Paracelsus was approached by an acolyte, who wished to be taught the secret of alchemy. Rather like today's young medicinal chemist. Paracelsus explained that in alchemy it was not gold that was sought."

"Did Paracelsus reveal to him the knowledge?"

"The student first demanded some proof of the miraculous. He cast a rose into the fire, and challenged Paracelsus to restore it anew."

"What occurred?"

"Paracelsus did nothing. There could be no creation, for lack of faith, and the thought of gold. The student left, thinking him a charlatan. Paracelsus sat alone, letting the ashes flow through his hands, then said the word. The rose appeared."

"A children's tale. Impossible, of course."

"The modern parable would be the aspiring chemist, forced to be clandestine, who thinks psychedelics appear just from a recipe. A formula to be followed."

"But a synthesis can't be achieved by some invocation," I retorted. "We would be reduced to medieval, magical thinking."

"The rigorous precepts for synthesis must be followed, yes. But the requisite spirit is elusive, its absence creates insurmountable outcomes. Inexplicable failed reactions, poor yields if any, manifold threats, soul-draining fear and confusion. The tortures of insanity and greed. We have seen it many times."

"The spirit?"

"That which is ineffable, the purest intent, a flawless, diamond morality. Consider a similar spiritual error: the thought that making medicine is mechanistic entirely. Any physician has witnessed the miraculous, that not attributable solely to the molecular."

"And what else blocks the synthesis?"

"Any thought other than sustained reverence for the clarity of mind and heart. Any thought of power, control, riches, possessions, indulgences. Any thought other than the care of souls, the elevation of every being, the end of suffering by any and all means."

"Only then did the rose manifest for Paracelsus?

"Only then did he witness the ultimate nature of mind as pure and all-knowing."

"Can you show me the rose?"

○

HE NEITHER AGREED NOR REFUSED. Perhaps I was unworthy of the revelation. We sat by the firelight in silence, as iridescent packets of mist began gathering in the hollows below.

"Some old Navaho," he finally said, "have referred to the peyote spirit as 'Har yol lasch kla'a ash nee.'"

"Meaning?"

"The sunrise at midnight."

He began singing the prayers of a Navaho roadman. I felt it was a nocturnal benediction, the last time I would ever see him. Whether this night it was precipitated by tales of the substance, or the memory of Japanese childrens' laughter, or the sweet moon craft of our final evening, the varieties of religious experience displayed before us.

Indigo pointed at the heavens, his fingers pressing the invisible film of reality until it stretched and rang with bells. As he touched the field of vision, concentric ripples radiated outward, like drops of thought from within, falling into the transparent ocean of mind. He touched it again until there was no mistake, until we saw the external and internal as irrefutably interdependent, the bells ringing like soft choirs.

The present unfolded into the past. We saw our history of pain: the naked mothers with flesh hanging from their arms at Nagasaki, the cannibalism of children at Stalingrad, Nazi lampshades from tattooed human skin, the civil wars, the massacres by Cortez, beheadings, quarterings, rackings, immolations, the drowning of witches, the self-devouring of hominids back through time and the first stone knives, then through carnivorous reptiles and protozoans feeding upon themselves.

Before us, the visual field reversed to caring, moving to futurity, where we saw aggregation of unicellular organisms, the descent of mammals tending live young, the heliotrapies of sun worshippers, the traditions of Judaism, the advent of Christ and Mohammed, the end of human sacrifices, the settling of the New World, primitive physicians among the wounded, priests and nuns salving the hungry, the signing of truces and cessation of world wars, the bans on nuclear, chemical and biological weapons.

The field reversed again, and the future of pain unraveled: the catastrophic nuclear events, the poisoned seas, mutated plants and animals, world-wide infectious diseases and weaponized anthrax and smallpox and virulent cancers, the unbreathable air. We witnessed the corrupted machine-like corporatocracies dominating fragmented human tribes like vermin, until every word, every thought, every movement was tracked, filed, analyzed and predicted by anonymous overlords. We saw the end of the human species, the last woman suckling the last child at her necrotic breast.

The future field reversed into caring, and we saw healing medicines eliminating war, the genetic and pharmacological enhancement of cognition and altruism, the next human species brilliant and loving and tender and honoring the memory of the Old Ones.

"*Das Weltbewusstsein*," he said, "the consciousness of the world."

The universe suddenly became completely still, clear as plate glass. All creation was motionless, until a broad trail of sparks leapt from the blaze, like thoughts of sunlight firing into the night blue sky. We saw layers of distant black dust, illuminated from beyond. They were birds – clouds of crows – moving slowly as in a dream, across the face of the moon.

FAR BEYOND THE CIRCLE of firelight, from the nymph-begotten mists, a dark figure manifested before my astonished eyes. It swayed as if suspended above the ground, dancing to some celestial rhythm. The glaring moon shone upon her small, firm bare breasts, with their tips of light. She had no shadow. We went to her in silence, like lost ships drifting finally homeward, across the silver sea.

Her winged consciousness emitted streams from the sun. The girl floated with a lithe grace, softer than promises. She had thick, lustrous auburn hair, and the sinuous fluidity of immortals. Her breasts were high, she was slender and translucent, naked to the waist. Her countenance was wreathed in stars.

Indigo took her hand, and she smiled at me. She had left her pink Japanese parasol, and all of her possessions. She wore loose walking shorts, and light hiking boots, moving delicately like a fawn. A camouflage shirt was tied about her hips. Indigo had only the daypack. He left a sleeping bag for me, and a share of the food. The liquid moon was electric, the earth a white wake stretching out into nothingness. The sky and all the mountains were wild with divinity.

They turned to trek to the borders of other countries, to other identities, with only the hand of night to protect them. Indigo bowed to me, and gave a last blessing.

> "May you always be
> for those you love.
> May you forever see
> the moonlight dappled oceans
> and the long fires of freedom."

I returned the bow, feeling the precious last moment of them.

"And how shall I describe your lovely companion, the woman with so many names?'

"Rose," he said.

IV

Masters of War

Some people show evil as a great race horse shows breeding.

- Hemingway, *A Movable Feast*

"Why are you laughing?"

"Because I can see how easy it was for you to
get your troops in here. What I don't understand
is how you plan to get them out."

- Afghan Chieftain to British Commander,
who was dictating terms in First Anglo-Afghan War

Chapter 16.

Christian Warfare

…who passed through universities with radiant eyes
Hallucinating…Blake-light tragedy among
the scholars of war.

- Ginsberg, *Howl*

I felt fear's echo…and the unhinged, uncontrollable joy
which had been its opposite face, joy which had broken out
in those days like Northern Light across the black skies.

- John Knowles, *A Separate Peace*

In a bizarre profession anything that belongs to
every day routine gains great value.
He was always prepared to account for his actions,
even the most innocent, and he was strictly on time.

- Graham Greene, *The Human Factor*

THE GARDENS OF CAMBRIDGE in the last long march of summer days were resplendent with rare fireflies. Sails loitered on the Charles in rippled shadows; Eliot, Lowell and Winthrop Houses were a brilliantly colored frieze. Drum beats, clapping and dancing flutes sounded; the airless hot nights were harsh and clear. Crows melted into louvered belfries. After the encounters with Crimson and Indigo, the Charles brown water now had a magic surface. Silent ghostly craft spread wide the river, as the moon poured its molten light into the receptive, hallowed opalescence.

It was a new mind – not from some unwitting drug exposure – but from the presence of an advanced culture, as if one were a young girl taught by Amazons as her gifts kindled in youth. Normal consciousness seemed but a horrible dispersion of chaotic thoughts and feelings. At a glance now, colors were priceless, then reduced to ephemeral hues with a melancholy magnificence. To my delight, in lectures the skirmishes of words seemed great battles. At this diminution of archaic thought forces, worldly formulae began to ennoble the walls.

I often sought the pale rose of dawn, the morning still young upon the river. The Charles was cast in a bronze Pharaonic light, as the present was withered by memories. For one conscripted in a painstaking search for truth, the Six had a painful magnetism. Through unrelenting study at Harvard Medical School, down the dusty stacks, I sought some rational exegesis for them, lest they enlarge to gods or magi.

In Cambridge, one only could be skeptical of such prophesies as accompanied Indigo. Yet it was apparent that the souls of the Six truly were harrowed, for who could ever rescue them from their journey to the inevitable scaffold? Fresh from abroad, I at first maintained a perpetual silence, feigning ignorance of such psychic operatives and their mysterious portents, saying nothing but the commonplace. As the term at Harvard progressed, I could forget them only as our pitiable, disordered human world again drew my most devoted mercies. The evenings began to grow around my fellow students and researchers rather than the Six, and I rallied somewhat. The signs then augured well.

⬡

I THOUGHT I SAW V-1, by the flowering hibiscus and gilded torcieres of Lowell House. The last of the brazen sun had gone, the peach and almond blossoms yielding to the night's underwater mood. She was standing beneath rusty velvets and scrolled arms, enchanting an agreeable, orotund and sleek visiting professor of applied physics who spoke in grandiose tones. He drank dry, ochrous sherry, like the dons at Oxford.

I remembered from Berlin her tsunami of pleasure, the night wild with joy. Those unaware of such unassailable religious practices might think them the vilest debauchery, as if Vermilion's stellar triad procured slave girls – *Zeitfrauen* – as temporary concubines.

In the pallid candlelight, I could see the enthralling shimmer of her blond hair, her ravishing figure in a tight black tulip, her endless legs down to a set of red stilettos. But it was only golden Hagendas, oddly prying into research at the Large Hadron Collider under Geneva, and fishing for contacts with a researcher from CERN.

⬡

WITH THE FIRST DRY FROSTS, and the silent arrival of robins, the change of weather crept in. The ivy was mottled and grey; leaves rained down as we wound along before obstinate winds. As students huddled in study carrels deep within the Kennedy School, the sky through high windows became filled with winter tones. I plodded homeward in the dark afternoon through swatches of sodden mounds. The phone rang.

It was a collect call – one of hundreds from my prison confidante Akbar Bey – a Turkoman from Afghanistan. He was incarcerated at the maximum-security USP Florence in Colorado, serving a 14-year sentence for heroin importation. Akbar asked for help in contacting his associate General Abdul Rashid Dostum, the warlord then in control of all of Northern Afghanistan. After the destruction of Kabul in the years of tribal strife after the Russian pullout, I began connecting Akbar Bey weekly through Cambridge to Dostum on his satellite phone in the far deserts, or at his compounds in Tashkent, Uzbekistan and Mazar-i-Sharif, Afghanistan, occasionally greeting Dostum and listening to their long conversations in Dari. Their hypnotic exchanges recalled the old burnished faces of Central Asia, the crushing poverty and beauty of the royal city of Mazar, and Kabul itself – an *anus mundi* whose outskirts were littered with the whitening bones of its exiles.

Through a study window a foul grey rain fell on leafless oaks in a steady drizzle. I drifted to an economics text, their conversation in the background until they ended and I could disconnect them. After a hundred calls, I began panicking over tight deadlines for term papers and indecipherable problem sets.

Akbar – having served ten years – desperately wanted Dostum to plead with CIA or State to return him to his two wives and ten children at his home in the Wazir Akbar Khan district of Kabul. His house and family somehow had survived the shells and rockets lobbed into Kabul as Afghan mobs captured Communist President Naijbullah, hanging him in the public square after cutting off his testicles.

The rain gusted into a downpour, swirling in dark sheets, the rain like the dance of black Mevlevi dervishes as they slowly turned under crested palms in the last of the scarecrow principalities of the East.

Congress recently had given CIA sixty million dollars to reacquire hundreds of errant Stinger missiles from divisive warlords. Provided by CIA to kill Russian helicopters, thirty of these shoulder-fired heat-seeking weapons were retained by Dostum after the Soviets withdrew. Hidden across Northern Afghanistan, they were somewhere in the caverns of the Hindu Kush, or buried beneath shifting sand dunes, or in villages where sightless beggars roamed, or down dirt alleys past the captivating lilt and high ringing tones of the street story teller, or along the routes of the shuffling march of the last spice and opium caravans.

Dostum and Akbar agreed that I should approach U.S. officials and offer to trade four Stinger missiles as an inducement for Akbar's prosecutor to reduce his sentence. The prospect arose of negotiations in mud huts with floors of tamped soil, covered with carpets from Shiraz and Baluchistan, with rising wisps of incense traded from the Hejmz.

Akbar and I always left these calls to Dostum with a gravid depression about his endless prison term, a sense of enormous bereavement for his scattered wives and small children, all so vulnerable to the cruelties of the Taliban. I began a plan to help him.

⬡

AT THE KENNEDY SCHOOL, Hagendas and Hammer immediately recognized my proclivity – upon first returning from inexplicable tours – to have the forbidden heaven-occupied gaze.

"Aha! Our nursling of the moors," Hagendas noted, mistress of piquant repartee.

At this, one's internal spiritual majesty could only disperse like clouds in the storm. Hagendas always had an impish, teasing serenity. Hammer, no less than she, chimed in.

"You've got that look again. Like the last of a line of saintly forebears. I've got it! The Nazim of Hyderabad, right?"

Hagendas often seemed like a naiad to his Neptune; her eyes had the blue darkness of far ocean and starry sky. She was in fine voice that day, standing by a John Singleton Copley painting and looking into the HKS courtyard, while ignoring the beflagged diplomatic cars lined below. I thought then she had a kind of *Jungvolk* beauty, for her skin was like nacreous marble, but perhaps I had been caught too long in dreams.

Sabers of rain began slashing the drooping grey mists over the Charles. Storms from the edge of Boston Harbor brightened with magnesium flashes and claws of lightning, as sea winds rustled the foliage and the gutters clotted with leaves.

Surf appeared, our intellectual enigma with her affectionate fury. Buffeted by a fresh north wind, she had a wet *New York Times* over her head. As she stood by the reborn Hulk, her querulous spinster's voice – sometimes summoned to dismiss the various other pretenders to her throne – today seemed obedient, even pliant. She now treated him with an almost lachrymose tenderness, while he in turn drank the whole of her, with his hot sky glances.

◯

AS WE DISPERSED to faculty and projects, I did a cold call on former CIA Operations Officer Ken Knaus, who was still in his HKS office writing about his extraction of the Dalai Lama from Tibet. Driven by the friendship with Akbar Bey, I felt such an overture was permissible, even by a superannuated graduate student of uncertain lineage.

Knaus inevitably would run a CIA name check, so I preempted the subject by first mentioning Ron Rewald, another acquaintance in the same prison yard as Akbar Bey. Rewald had been a renegade CIA asset with the Domestic Monitor Program who had 70 more years on his sentence to complete for allegedly conducting a financial fraud on retired CIA officers. Knaus instantly recognized the Rewald affair.

"Oh, you mean that thing in Hawai'i."

"Yes, that thing in Hawai'i."

I quickly explained my own difficulties with errant lab equipment, "before coming to my senses and entering Harvard."

Knaus nodded somberly, but with a detectable air of guardedness, for this CIA operation officer had forgotten more secrets than most remember. He concluded that his new visitor, presumed at first to be an innocent HKS matriculant, had perhaps a roguish background that, as in Heisenberg's uncertainly principle, might shift perspective the closer it was observed.

Knaus, having seen every species of fauna, projected a sophisticated, almost indiscernible wariness tempered with the polish cultivated by the clandestine services. We kept it simple. I presented the issue of Afghanistan, and Dostum's offer of the Stingers for Akbar Bey. Knaus preferred known waters.

"I'll check with Langley."

◯

I QUICKLY FADED into the Kennedy School walls, invisible to all but my lively foursome. The new Hulk, previously docile to Surf's every calculation, now longed in anguish to take her completely, wildly. He wanted Surf posed in a barbaric spread in some hidden, warm conservatory as the attended her with neoreligious fervor.

Over the weeks, the winter settled in early upon Cambridge like an alabaster veil, leaving an untouched white expanse across the Charles embankment. As snow lit up our faces, we gathered on the river's slippery walkways and icy tracts, for we were rushing toward midterms, with its niggling and hair-splitting now substituting for our perennial certitude.

It was frightfully cold. Hulk seemed out of character, for Surf this week preferred frolicking in statistics solutions rather than in his arms. This cut him to the heart, putting him in a gnomic mood; he began uttering terse aphorisms.

"Love's labor lost." (Hulk then goes on with Bardic pain)

At these particularly felicitous passages, Surf accused him of childish cupidities. She lifted her powdered eyebrows, then linked her arms closely in his and argued stat problems as a long, heated exercise in academic lust, while they wandered down the Charles snow-bound paths.

◯

I WALKED ALONE one afternoon through the Square, with a quicksilver glaze still on the river, and Cambridge like some white land of magical realism. The students from Paris still were encamped at Au Bon Pain, and displayed their immense lethargic narcissism. Slow to piety, but not yet so dissolute they were in danger of being recalled to virtue, they all looked about to die from *ennui*. One aspiring but clumsy physics major displayed a tattoo of Erwin Schrödinger, describing the blemish as a *pointilliste* picture. They were discussing the pleasures of various succulent waifs they had rented near the Bois de Bologne. Even more to my unwarranted concern, evoking a hint of paranoia, they referred to the TGV train out of Paris from the Gare de L'Est. Perhaps I was growing too touchy.

A sheppard's pipe played in the winter's dusk, as the Square's denizens retreated in a limbo of oblivion. Everyone seemed to have a hopeless lack of initiative, as though the Square were a frozen, indolent serpentarium. Only when Hagendas passed would observers hasten to uncoil and show some sort of recurring moral scruples, slithering hopefully before a Madonna.

It was then I saw the surveillance. A man was standing rooted by the trees in a public garden. Alerted by my recognition, he began a prowling walk, like the predator he was. Sufficiently unprofessional to throw a sheet-metal glare, he had a smile of ill-concealed impatience in a thin, foxy face, like a tear in a sheet of paper. I began walking back and forth under a sky of palpitating fear, halting in doorways, a leaden weight about my heart. Finally convinced it was all an error of judgment, I left for the Kennedy School, assuming he must be here for someone else.

⬡

SLUGGING WITH DETERMINATION through formidable snow drifts, only to fail a horrendous economics quiz, I returned to Radcliffe dorm then spiraled into depression. The vulnerability of Akbar's two wives and ten children weighed on me; there were thousands of casualities in the constant rocket bombings of Kabul. I had promised Akbar to bring a bicycle to his young son, but the mechanics of getting the bicycle to Afghanistan through barriers of Uzbek and Afghan customs officials – then returning to Harvard for graduation while studying nights in cramped seats in Russian Ilyushin aircraft – were not yet solved.

Through the bitter winds of a New England winter, we arrived at HKS in the early mornings with thick textbooks in our frozen hands and our clothes steaming from melted snow, then pressed into study carrels like racehorses with blinders at the post gate. Unable to focus, I broke to visit Ken Knaus, still entertaining the hope that CIA would take the Stinger offer.

"Your name came back from Langley," he mused with a laconic air, watching me.

Long pause.

"What about the missiles?" I countered, men of the world that we were.

"We have Dostum well in hand," Knaus said, in a manner to deflect further inquiry.

"But you don't have the missiles," I ruefully observed.

Parting company affably, I encountered Knaus now and then on the cobbled alleys of Cambridge near the Brattle Theatre, courteously asking after his manuscript, but never again the still deadly and missing Stingers. There had to be another way.

⬡

HARVARD AT MIDTERMS, under sky keen with frosts, was a snowbound parish. The nights had a rosy moon upon the deeps of bluish ice banks. We bemoaned the reality check of these exams, for they inevitably cosseted our universal self-esteem. Entire regions of knowledge were still opaque to us, for even rigorous memorization failed to obviate our basic lack of comprehension. Our many students who were terminally maladroit about learning under pressure tended to develop cringing sorts of smiles, and were considered *outré* by others. The class thus suffered from these divisive factions of the skilled, and the frightened. I vacillated between these worlds as well, too often the latter.

At the midterm exam, Hulk strolled in with a conscious assurance, observed the desperate *mise-en-scène*, and began petulantly writing. Hammer, with an elaborate colored pen from the Harvard Coop in his mouth, looked like an old sheik smoking a long-shanked nargelih. But Surf summed it up for all of us, shouting out a quote of Mirabeau.

"Oh, *God*, give me *mediocrity*."

◯

ROBERT BLACKWILL'S CLASS was a *tour de force* of inner-circle Republican thinking. On hiatus at HKS after serving with Bush *père* as his National Security Advisor, Blackwill was in his early sixties, tall with a prominent forehead, grey temples, blue eyes and a razor wit. While Blackwill was the gateway for HKS graduates to become White House aides or analysts, his lectures became for us the entertainment *du jour*.

Blackwill was strict, hammering us for only seconds of tardiness. At seven minutes after the hour Harvard time, we were seated aghast but attentive. Blackwill – who fiercely observed any stragglers entering the lecture room balancing coffee cups, books and defrosting clothing – would bellow his statement on promptness.

"Being late is personally and professionally offensive!"

Yet Blackwill was no inflexible autocrat. As he discussed the trappings of presidential powers or the infighting at Camp David or the Executive Office, he commonly acknowledged arriving and attractive women students in the guise of a master of ceremonies for erotic dancers.

"And heeeere's _____!"

Stripping unfocused liberal students in class debates of any modesty, he would refer to those suspected of less moral or intellectual rigor in terms of late D.C. evening junkets and honey traps.

"That kind of thinking is down at the *Boom-Boom Room*."

We all had a precarious self-regard, but no one was even faintly shocked, for we were more delighted than annoyed as Blackwill expatiated on his themes. As he launched into his reminiscences of the president, or described Republicans who would never accept the most trite favor from lobbyists, the Democrats among us sought admiring ways to taunt him lightly but relentlessly. One lecture hour was consumed by forcing Blackwill into lofty and unsustainable moral states, where even a ride across D.C. by a lobbyist would attract Republican inquisitors. We were fond of him.

Blackwill proposed that the class offer simple solutions to the great environmental and social problems: war, food shortages, hatred. No one spoke. I finally raised my hand, not yet too far from the monastery at Hoshin-ji.

"Compassion."

Blackwill ridiculed this offering, which had no variables in the Kennedy School equations. The class joined him nervously, but had no alternatives; others dared not rise to the moment. No one ever brought up the human heart again.

Blackwill was on to me from the beginning, for as he discussed Nelson Mandela's twenty-six years of seclusion in an island prison cell, he opined wistfully, looking directly at me and smiling until it might become obvious to onlookers.

"I wish I had him here."

He unlocked his glance and hurled questions to the rows of students. I privately mused.

And what would you ask him? About the fear and hopelessness of endless nights, the humiliation of families, the prayers to God?

Wisely mute, I scribbled onward, marking his subliminal gesture and making a note to think about secret agendas among faculty and visiting researchers.

Blackwill saved us when we were overwhelmed by mountainous data and hurtling deadlines. He revealed his method of jockeying briefing books on Air Force One, while thoroughly shattered by events in all directions: the sleepless spectra of blending time zones, Somali potentates on CIA payrolls, brinksmanship by regional strongmen, and secret biological weapons. His students all forever recall his essential Blackwillian mantra, so dear to us in confronting impossible demands.

"If you take care of the small things, the big things take care of themselves."

◯

HULK LONG HAD SUFFOCATED his ardor, but no more. While Surf for the first year had a cunning that was alien to him, she now publicly ruffled his locks. Quick to notice my withdrawals into all obliterating introspections on the unspoken Six, Hulk accused me in the Peabody Museum of some Islamic intensity.

"Man, if you got any darker, we'd mistake you for Abu 'abd Allah."

I bit. "Who's that?"

"Muhammad XII," he said, "the last Moorish king of Grenada."

I began to compare Hulk's progress as a suitor with that of Hammer's. They both were prone at first to queer mixtures of feelings about the formidable Surf and Hagendas. Descendants of Venus, both were callipygous girls, which many men found infinitely alluring.

No longer regarded by Surf as having a total lack of codpiece, Hulk would dance in the Yard with her, under moonlit snowfalls, with soft snowflakes resting delicately like astronomical manna upon their hot, upturned faces. Once I found Surf in the Harvard Arboretum, in some mesmeric state, with Hulk taking quick, deliberate steps to her, pressing her by the cinerarias in the hothouse.

His seductions were in allegiance to his new ruling daemon; they had an almost terrifying grandeur. He would sing to her in his wavering tenor – Magnificat in D – beneath the white moon at sunset, or on faintly luminous, snowy evenings. I would discover them alone on the Peabody steps, grinding against the great bronze brace of rhinoceri rampant, so intent that I was unable to wrest my gaze from them, my heartbeats mercifully inaudible. Inspired by Hulk's resounding success, I neglected to escape their orbit altogether.

Hammer, no less enthralled, had delights that were much more fugitive. Hagendas often spoke to him in the tones that might spring from a freshly rosined bow. At this purring, he imagined her beneath the damascened wings of bed curtains drawn back, with Hagendas willingly secured by blue velvet ropes. She teased him incessantly, as if she were his pantomime fairy.

I chanced upon them one night in New York, alone together in the Museum of Natural History. He was behind her, both standing with hips tightly together, with Hagendas arching and flush as Hammer whispered in her ear his bloodthirsty tales. The walls were covered with the stained hides of a hundred assegai, captured at Omdurman.

"Lord Kitchener's troops," I heard Hammer breathe in a low growl, "forty-seven dead in the British Army…"

His strong grip on her now, Hagendas straining and taut, facing away, rising against him.

"Ten thousand Sudanese attacking on horseback with spears…all slain in a single morning by the Maxim guns…"

The horror – together with Hammer's full-length grip – seemed to excite her. Hammer soon took to writing her long letters of provocation, to reach this part of her, to turn her on. As she sat on some heavy Second Empire furniture at the Graduate School of Design, under a series of Edward Lear watercolors, I saw her reading his urgings, trembling with a restless heat.

Yet over the semester Hammer's access seemed to reduce, as Hulk's prospered. Hammer tried fiercer airs with Hagendas, to little avail. The master sensualist no more, he began to resort to supplicating looks, infuriating her. Lacking sufficient audacity, he found their encounters sometimes devolved to morose fencing.

I thought I saw them make up at the Yenching Library – discussing a Kennedy School decision tree with weighted lines and arrows – but the decision tree outcomes were on whether to never leave each other. Later, they were sitting quietly under the lights from a pagoda-shaped shade, while their alternative futures to my eyes trailed like wraiths behind them. Hammer, now the victim of small timidities, was reading to her from some ancient text with marbled end-papers, perhaps passages from Horace's *Epistles*.

Although both Hammer and Hulk were blatantly infatuated, in the end it was the former that struggled the most. One began to hear new notes of entreaties in his voice. He prayed for a sensational reconciliation.

⬡

I TRIED LIGHTENING their moments, inviting them all to the Harvard Faculty Club, with its 18th Century dining rooms of dark oak and bays of leaded windows. By now they knew of my inclinations toward Afghanistan, whereupon Hulk commenced describing the secret pleasures of mules.

"No, really, Abu 'abd Allah." (he insisted on addressing me thusly, in a flowery high Arabic style, with an Islamic bow)

Menus all around. Distinguished faculty close by like learned prelates.

"They often engage in *bestiality*, if there are no *captives*."

Silence. A few looks. I assured him my travels in the region would be conducted with care.

Surf, brightly. "Or horses. Their *mares*."

Surf was not inaccurate, having done a case study on the warlord Hekmatyar.

Hammer. "Harvard Faculty Club had horsemeat until the late eighties."

Hagendas. "Why not now? Activists?"

A waitperson, overhearing. "*Madame*, the Chef – who was from the Dordogne, three-stars – said the quality of horse from New York was inferior, and refused to prepare it."

I began with cantaloupe, yogurt and nuts. Mineral water.

Hulk, our historian, persisted.

"Imagine. The Great War. Brits chasing Germans in Africa. Fifty thousand horses dead in six weeks from tsetse flies. Inedible from the fly larvae. Commonly a company slaughtered twenty a day: horse soup, horse cutlets, horse gravy, horse jerky, horse sausage, jellies, aspics, terrines, pounded pink tartare…"

"*Do* tell us of your itinerary in Afghanistan," Hagendas interjected sweetly.

○

SOME WEEKS LATER, after Knaus ran my name through Langley, the CIA Near East Division Chief appeared. Over canapés and drinks in a small wood-paneled conference room hosted by HKS's Institute of Policy Fellows, Frank A_____ gave a leisurely yet desultory tutorial on Afghan issues. In his early fifties, with well-coifed hair, he had the mild manner of an MBA. A_____ was distressed about CIA's downsizing in the aftermath of the dissolution of the Soviet Union, for no major enemies yet had replaced the Russians.

Recruited out of the University of Illinois for the Operations Directorate, A_____ was responsible for all CIA activity from Morocco to Bangladesh; he oversaw disbursement of billions in cash and weaponry for the mujahidin to repulse the Soviets, including distribution of Stinger missiles.

With CIA Director Woolsey, A_____ just had named Congressmen Charlie Wilson as a CIA Honored Colleague for underwriting the Stinger Program. During the ceremony, A_____ in an odd aside commented on CIA's formation from the OSS and its long reliance on Ivy League feeder schools.

"This moment is about elitism," A_____ had said, "and one thing about elites is that they only care about approbation of the members of their own elites."

A_____ now found himself among the elite at the Kennedy School, long a source of CIA officials and analysts. He was being shaken – unhappily – out of CIA with many in the wake of Operation Nightstalker, where CIA analyst Aldrich Ames sold microfilm to the Soviets and caused U.S. assets in Moscow to be executed summarily.

After Ames was detected by concealed cameras in the Counter Terrorism Center as he photographed classified documents, he was sentenced to life in prison. At Allenwood Penitentiary, he smoked incessantly, played chess and was harassed by illiterate crack fiends, all while A_____ and Woolsey were clearing their desks and lunching with headhunters for outsourced intelligence firms.

While not mentioning the minor issue of General Dostum and the Stingers, I posed a question to A_____.

"Will CIA continue its focus on the mujahidin and warlords of the Afghan region, given the dissolution of the Soviet Union?"

A_____ said that with the Soviet collapse and the dismantling of CIA's Near East Division, a now meaningless backwater such as Afghanistan hardly would be a player on the world stage. The muj were just warring factions in an ancient ritual.

"Nothing there but rugs and drugs," he said.

As he spoke, A_____ seemed deflated. CIA now had neither A_____, nor much of the Operations staff, nor the errant Stinger missiles "well in hand." CIA's Afghanistan Desk no longer was a career path for aspiring intelligence analysts from the Kennedy School, so that reports of religious students from the madrassas, armed only with the Qur'an to assault and convert remote villages, aroused little interest. As the lights went out in Langley, no one noticed the unread documents on the almost empty Afghan Desk. Only a few barely mentioned these students, in Pashto the "Taliban."

○

COMING OUT OF WIDENER, then through Porcellian Gate into the crowds down Mass Ave, I again saw the surveillance. Sensing me, he began watching the street confusion coldly, with his pale water-rat face. His artful brown eyes were yellowed and bloodshot. This small confidence between us seemed to have on his part an animal resentment, denuded of all humanity. One assumed he ran with his intelligences, bleating them to his masters. An indefinable smell of tension began permeating the day. I could see him – separate from others – with the isolation of a gargoyle hung over the unconscious players in the Square.

The usual priests, gypsies and brigands around Mass Ave laughed, talked, plotted, and played Kriegspiel. Little minxes with pale skin and ravenous, scarlet mouths trotted about among various meth dealers. As I observed him indirectly, I saw that his baleful ferret's eyes had a type of malevolent fixity. He studiously turned away from me, which lent him the peculiar warped physiognomy of conscious avoidance. One could only ignore him, for the present.

○

I WAITED WITH SURF and other tall young women, all long-suffering HKS students, as we huddled along a chilly side street before a 1789 saltbox house. Our seminar within was conducted by the eminent disaster specialist Jennifer Leaning, M.D. of Harvard's School of Public Health. We awaited her memories and advice about remote refugee camps and war zones, and of disease outbreaks and mass causalities in regions forgotten by God.

Introductions across a crowded table in the packed seminar revealed a Serbian newscaster with tales of mass burials and gang rapes, an African graphically discussing the Hutu-Tutsi genocide, and a careful Chinese statistician monitoring lethal pharmaceutical donations in the unregulated third world. I managed some comments on those no longer on the world's stage, but left behind.

"Forty thousand dead from the shelling of Kabul by warlords Dostum, Massoud and Hekmatyar…"

My words came haltingly, for nights often were spent with Dostum and Akbar Bey, when I could hear the desperate gravity in their voices and, in the background, the sounds of barefoot children, translators, the calls to prayer, sporadic gunfire. I spoke of the downing of Russian HIND attack helicopters, and the Soviet withdrawal due to CIA's shoulder-launched Stinger missiles and automatic weapons. These advanced and portable machineries for killing had been released uncontrolled into the wilds of the Shamali Plains and Hindu Kush. They now continued to dismember the children of Afghanistan, who were caught between tribal leaders grown careless with living things.

I just had come from the presentation by Frank A_____, the CIA chief who ran the mujahidin program and signed for the missiles. At Dr. Leaning's seminar we discussed the less trumpeted human outcomes of weaponizing the barely civilized: the tent cities, cholera, the maimed four year-olds. The sightless and the crazed still wandered across rubbles of mosques and schools. Once-fertile valleys now were burned and littered with carcasses of animals, mothers, and little girls.

Disaster Management Seminar soon became a litany of mechanized death, corruption, and human suffering. Sensitive from exposure to the Six, I privately envisioned even greater tragedies. Only a few years afterward, Dr. Leaning would be one of the first to enter Northern Afghanistan's Shirberghan prison, where Dostum held surviving witnesses of the mass executions of Taliban prisoners by suffocation. Transported for days in sealed cargo containers with no air holes or water, they screamed and cried to Allah until their last prayers became silence. As the trailer doors finally opened at Shirberghan, corpses spilled out like wet fish. Stacked in pits in the desert near Dasht-i-Leili, Dostum's tractors buried them in a desolate necropolis.

While Jennifer Leaning inspected Shirberghan and the graves, then broke the story to Amnesty International, the human rights violation was sanitized on the directives of Bush's NSC due to Dostum's seizure of Kabul. Obama at last ordered Dostum's investigation for war crimes, resurrecting briefly those many who – beneath the unmarked Afghan sands – embraced each other in grisly tableau.

As the close of these unnerving roundtables with Dr. Leaning – after each witness provided a glimpse of some horror of famine or war – I walked the uneven cobblestones of Cambridge for hours in a long black coat with muffler and gloves, darkly internalized. Snow was falling like insidious white soot. Ruddy-faced undergraduates brushed past, drinking hot chocolate from Au Bon Pain and brightly discussing Spinoza, their voices disturbing me, as silence is by music.

A group of Tibetan Buddhist lamas in dark red robes was entering the Divinity School, together with a full-bearded Greek Orthodox priest in a black robe. He bore a cross lettered in Greek with IE XRN (Jesus Christ Conquers). The steps were whitewashed from the storm. My tears began scalding the snow, leaving little hollow blue shadows like the empty, cold monstrosities we could become. I tried to remember what meant anything in this world, and remembered my simple monk's vow to follow a compassionate path.

It almost had been extinguished by constantly engaging with lecturers on guidance systems for smart bombs through windows of mud huts in Waziristan, or the surgical efficiency of drone overflights that frequently missed the weddings, or the computer screens with ambiguous ghosts that were subject to kill orders.

As the snow fell, I knew that rapturous technicians with pristine computers snacked on donuts in air-conditioned rooms, glancing at the low-resolution images which could have been mongrel dogs or sheep or ragged children, or an illiterate father silently shaking his pre-WW I Enfield rifle at the implacable sky. They sacrificed these beings, in the national interest and without further reflection, by merely pushing a button.

○

BLACKWILL was one of the faculty to whom I proposed General Dostum's Stinger offer to extract Akbar Bey from prison. I entered his well-appointed office at HKS, where the *accoutrement* included his chairs with talons of ball and claw, several of his recent books on nuclear disarmament, his award from the German Chancellor for assisting in the reunification of Deutschland, and Bush memorabilia placed in strategic settings. Above his desk was a wooden plaque containing the small things quote. It was the first object petitioners saw upon entering Blackwill's sanctum.

"I have no interest in heroin traffickers. My concerns are with military matters," he instructed me.

I suggested that Dostum and the Taliban might be of military consequence one day, but Afghanistan was only fractious warring tribes then, and nothing to Blackwill. He had spent the summer leading an HKS Executive Program in Cambridge, teaching visiting high-level Chinese military officials about democracy and coordination of U.S.-China nuclear forces. Appealing to his pride in his connections on the Hill, I concluded my argument.

"Is there *any* way to make this thing fly?"

"Not from where *you're* sitting," he coolly replied.

Aware my seat was next to his, I countered.

"Some say ideas of merit have wings, irrespective of their origins."

With no interest by Blackwill, I took leave and – as part of my impending journeys to Central Asia and D.C. – decided to try it alone. A few years later, Dostum took Kabul with tanks and hardened Northern Alliance troops, backed by CIA and American forward air control teams directing B-52 strikes. I wondered if Blackwill remembered the missed opportunity to engage Dostum and employ his opposition to a ragged band of religious students, known only to a few Afghan analysts as the Taliban. But by then Blackwill was Bush II's Ambassador to India and – with such big things to consider – he probably forgot about the small stuff.

◯

SUDDENLY, FINALS. We all were like darting swallows – during term flying high and free – then falling into a breathtaking declivity. The social rubric in Cambridge required a certain stressed pallor during this event, so that as the proctor blithely expounded on the structure of the exam, Surf projected an adamantine misery. Hulk, still in his Islamic mood, did a sing-song lamentation in Arabic, his hands opened and raised like a mourner. Hammer, confounded by Hagendas if not the press of our imminent degrees, brooded over his Blue Book like some baroque incubus. Harvard, having conferred certain skills, also had wrecked our ignorance of our profound limitations.

In the afternoon, I wandered the Yard and Square, pondering the Six. Crimson and Indigo had found me in London, Oxford, Amsterdam and Zürich, but if the trend continued, how would Magenta, Vermilion and Cobalt appear? My itinerary – set only that day – led to remote destinations where the runways had potholes from shellfire, the men had cut-off hands, the women cut-off noses.

There he was again, the surveillance with his quiet venom. He knew I had made him, but he remained with a careless malice. His presence was like some bloodless dream; his smile a reopened wound. Tomorrow he would be gone, for then I would be on the far side of the planet, where there were no unfounded fears.

It was a smuggler's moon that night, glittering in the young snow. I slept with a sense of repletion – having decided to watch over Akbar Bey's family during these ventures – and dreamed of the blue spires of the Hindu Kush, the lowland fields of yellow-green barley, the trees with pomegranates like gleaming suns.

Morning came. Voices in the Square seemed clipped with Arab quarter-tones, the Charles embankment like the dirt streets of Mazar-i-Sharif with its feathery palms. As the climbing sunrise touched the cupolas of Winthrop House, I thought of minarets calling the faithful, the desert air sweet as the breath of a girl.

Chapter 17.

Our Man in Mazar

When you're wounded and left
On Afghanistan's plains
And the women come out
To cut up your remains,
Just roll on your rifle
And blow out your brains
And go to your Gawd
Like a soldier.

- Kipling, "The Young British Soldier"

Even fairy tales had a crimson atmosphere. Sensuality of the
grossest kind and murder, abominable cruelty, treachery or
violent death, are never long absent from the thoughts of a
people of whom none in the world are more delightful
companions, or of simpler, gentler nature.

- Sir George Robertson, *On the Siege of Chitral*

They cut off a man's head with as much indifference as we cut a radish.

- Mohan Lal, son of secretary to Mountstuart Elphinstone,
British envoy to Afghanistan and Governor of Bombay

THE UNDULATING BROWN PLAINS of Afghanistan passed slowly beneath my aircraft, their vast abysmal reaches dotted by clusters of mud huts below the pristine magnificence of the Hindu Kush. Seemingly unchanged since the medieval era, this land with its everlasting purity was an expanse of sparse fields and stony walls. It appeared peaceful from the air.

Yet behind this pastoral image was the hair-trigger of rapacious strife, for its peoples were the descendants of massacres in the three Anglo-Afghan Wars, in a land where the first sound a newborn heard was gunfire celebrating its birth as its mother sang of ancient battle. Children were reminded of how many British their ancestors killed as they played with East Indian Company coins handed down as heirlooms from British corpses.

This journey was a duty to Akbar Bey, one promised so often as we sat together on a prayer rug in prison. Sipping sweet black tea from crudely fired handmade cups beneath the only tree – a wretched little birch with few leaves for shade – we watched as disoriented inner-city crack addicts stumbled in circles nearby. The first to be released, I vowed to bring a gift to his family in Central Asia. We swore solemnly to share a proper tea, with rice and almonds, free one day beneath the arching blue sky and crystalline white peaks of Afghanistan.

Down from Kathmandu through Delhi – transported in a doubtful Russian Ilyushin-6 overflight across Afghanistan – I aimed first for Tashkent, Uzbekistan to meet with Afghan contacts. Tough Uzbeks, Hindu families and ethnic Slavs filled the rows. Sheets draped unoccupied seats and white fog poured from air vents as hostesses in blond bouffants and trim black microskirts offered paper cups of Coca-Cola as if it were sacramental wine at communion.

As our aircraft turned toward Uzbekistan, I could see the Fergana Valley – a finger of Afghanistan 218 miles long and only 11 miles wide at its narrowest – where rough brigands and noble tribes on horseback rode, traded and fought between the mountains of Uzbekistan, Turkmenistan, Pakistan and China. The British surveyor Durand created these borders to point at China as a barrier against northward movement of hordes from the Indian subcontinent. Durand arbitrarily drew the lines based on geology and the politics of Empire, separating the region's tribes into separate nations and producing endless strife. It was a triumph of geographic artifice that failed to comprehend these deeply interwoven bloodlines.

The Karakorum Range rose along the Hindu Kush (Killer of Hindus) mountains down into the fabled Khyber Pass, while the vista of peaks to the east included the spectacle of Chomolungma – Everest. I thought of little Abeer in Nepal, wearing her thin, worn sari and reading her primer by firelight, lost in the vast range of mud and snow.

Researchers on Central Asia at the Kennedy School had briefed me on the regional strongmen; Dostum of course, the French-speaking poet Massoud, the rapacious Hekmatyar, the Uzbek Karimov and other potentates. As Turkmenistan appeared on the shimmering horizon, I thought of its mad President Niyazov, the last of the Stalinists, whose ruthlessness included – commonly at gunpoint – a bizarre personality cult. He had banned libraries, dogs, men's beards and even lipstick on newscasters. In the capital of Ashgabat, his stern visage gazed at the oppressed from a multistory golden statue of himself. It rotated through the days of each week and the months he had renamed, even during April, now the name of his mother.

The Cambridge researchers advised caution. One emphatically recalled the last warning of British commander Sir William McNaughton in the First Anglo-Afghan War.

"*This country is one mass of loose gunpowder.*"

"McNaughton himself," another historian quickly interjected, "arrived triumphantly on elephants with an entourage of camp followers, but fell into disgrace."

"By what means?" I politely inquired.

"In the end he was quartered by sabers, his hands waved on sticks to taunt his captive men. They paraded his torso through Kabul."

"Where was his head?"

"Traded in the bazaar," he replied with a reluctant air, "cradled in his horse's *nosebag*."

The placid, limitless fields, falling away beneath the frozen couloirs of the Hindu Kush, thus belied the turbulent background of this country. Even now, as the Taliban crept northward in Toyota jeeps affixed with heavy machine guns, this same mythical land was occupied by remnants of the mujahedin – the former anti-Soviet freedom fighters armed by CIA. The researchers produced anecdotal reports that hard-pressed troops unflinchingly devoured, or copulated without shame, their donated Tennessee and Egyptian mules.

The only other Westerner on the aircraft was a war correspondent linking from Tashkent to Frankfurt, a lean, crew-cut German national with a ripped bush jacket and battered sunglasses. He asked of my intent, then gave advice about action in rural areas. I had a few questions.

"Analysts tell me there are pockets of renegade Russian soldiers that traffic heroin across the Tajik-Uzbek borders – and women down into Northern Afghanistan. Your experience?"

"Perhaps a few established groups who pay tributes to the warlords for protection. But in the countryside, lone survivors discovered by the muj after the Russian pullout were treated quite poorly. Held in desperate rooms. Other things."

"What do you mean?"

"British Special Forces sporadically repatriated captive Russian soldiers that the muj had driven into madness. They were severely diminished, barely functional, often hospitalized."

"How? Why?"

"The muj spared their lives only if they prostituted themselves on demand to circles of Afghan troops grown savage on *naswar*, opiated snuff. Passed around naked, surviving only on scraps of offal. For years."

Although this was a land of frequent bright smiles and formidable courtesy, it also was a maelstrom of periodic butchery, unpredictable lust and common treachery. It was a land into which I – sapped by growing trepidation – ever so slowly descended.

THE RECEPTION DESK at the rude Soviet-era Hotel Uzbekistan in Tashkent looked upon a sea of plastic chairs populated by disoriented arrivals and questionable transients who were murmuring confidences or shouting excitedly in Dari, Uzbek, Russian, Pashto, Urdu, esoteric Indian dialects – and most rarely – English. A mammoth cement rabbit warren with tiny cells, frequently workable showers, iron-hard narrow bunks, and steely Russian matrons guarding each floor and one's room key, the hotel was the Central Asian rendezvous for those who envisioned hustling the East.

This waiting room was a crossroad replete with silent Pak covert operatives, engaging Tajik conmen, insolent Bangladeshi hustlers, harried translators, raffish British refrigerator salesmen in cheap suits and florid Germans purportedly buying gypsum. Close by an abundance of risky deal making, a fearless and inspired missionary or two assumed the safety of rickety elevators while eyeing a discrete brothel of multicultural ingenues. Reigning in hidden hallways, most were the flowers of Karachi and Bombay, now cut off from their roots; a few others were the daughters of stranded post-*perestroika* Muscovite engineers, up from their tidy *dachas* along the renowned Silk Road and the deserts of Samarkand.

Suddenly embraced by Akbar Bey's "brother" Zalmay – smiling, besuited and trying his few lines of rough English – I soon was discomfited on a street with no name, accompanied on all sides by imposing, surly Muslims and obdurate Turkomen. We marched down through mazes of doors into the unlit basement of a crumbling building of uncertain function, all in a grim, unsettling silence. Entombed twelve thousand miles from home with unfriendly strangers who could dispatch me easily, I fell into reveries of the humble monks and nuns at Hoshin-ji, murmuring their prayers for world peace.

Escorted into a small office by a brusque and well-muscled Thugee who wore a thick black mustache – together with an elderly, hunched English speaker of threadbare competence – I spent some hours after perfunctory greetings in a hazardous standoff as speechless, unsmiling servants brought the ritual tea. A heavyset Turk at last appeared. Dark bloodshot eyes, open collar, expensive shirt. He settled behind the desk for a while. The only sound was the clicking of palms from a hot, dusty courtyard. With his commanding presence, the Turk made an abrupt, gruff demand.

"Why are you here?"

Everything focused on this moment. I presented a letter of introduction in Dari from Akbar Bey. The head man, wary and cautious, glanced at it with a dour look, then placed it on his desk and fixed his guarded eyes most unwelcomingly on me. The dry heat lay on my nerves. It was my turn.

"I bear greetings from your brother Akbar Bey. We were in prison together for years, and each day I promised him that in freedom I would look after his family. He sends the blessings of Allah upon you, your wife and your children."

To this, my interrogator at once broached the central, indelicate issue.

"By now he must have cooperated with the *police*."

The room waivered. The dismal, hand-plastered walls seemed tightly confined, foreign and askew. A fly drifted lazily too near a sticky strip thick with disemboweled insect carcasses. The ancient translator slowly struggled to deliver this accusation in English while his master stared at my expression for any sign of duplicity. Affecting uncertainty with the translation I waited, collecting my thoughts until he was quite finished. I assured them both most carefully that Akbar Bey had maintained his integrity.

"No. He has said nothing to them. He is serving all of his time. I know. I was with him, every hour of every day. For many years.

The Turk tapped his fingers for an endless moment, elbows on desk, and stared at me. I remained still, clearly at their mercy. After an uneasy and protracted period he finally smiled.

"How do you find Tashkent?" he asked, grandly presenting an elaborate business card.

We broke into cautious civilities. As he summoned more tea and the tangible aura of danger ebbed slightly, we spoke of his offices in Dubai, Istanbul, Moscow, and Delhi, and of the multifarious nature of his dubious enterprises. I lightly proposed he develop English customers and, as with the prospect of honor among thieves, we quickly became friends of convenience. The door to Central Asia was open.

○

MY ONE PAIR of shoes, disintegrating from the Cambridge winter, forced Zalmay to outfit me at the cobbler – a wiry Hazara with a mallet, sitting in a tin-roofed shack before a wall of hand-made footwear on wooden pegs. Suitably upgraded we meandered through the bazaar, stopping before a strapping Russian youth tending an eight-foot pile of raw pistachios. Refusing payment for a kilo bag, he said "Free for our visitor from America." The courtesy in Tashkent soon proved unbounded.

After my vetting Dostum's associates produced a surprise welcoming gift: an ethereal six-foot-one white Russian 22 year-old with a blond pixie coif, vulpine hips and filmy strapless shift. She appeared at my door and offered her most imaginative comforts. I insisted we dine. The evening became a carousel of secret clubs with exquisite Chinese hostesses, actual tribal daughters freshly imported from the Fergana Valley and now bound in fine leather corsets. Sturdy young waiters presented bottles of purified water and local sodas as if they were Dom Pérignon, while deafening cycles of the Beach Boys blasted beneath mirrored rotating spheres as my companion chatted gaily in Russian.

In the late night, we arrived at dimly lit boîte – fashionable as any in Copenhagen. Slender in silk, she began a slow samba about the tiny dance floor to appreciative gazes. An irresistible growth of sexual excitement moved throughout the room like some great heart beating. The music was subdued, then became very quiet. To this unmarried goddess I was only a distant scholar, a patron of sorrow for a girl who inflamed lonely men's hearts. Yet I felt for her a kind of haunted pity. Pulling her warm body closer, I accidentally touched her breast. A certain shyness overcome, I began to understand the pert, fleshly opiate of her, she who was shaped like a swan and who loved so well, yet so little. By silent agreement, we left into the great cobweb of the Tashkent night. Down the club's alleyway was a green Mercedes filled with sour, dark Chechen bodyguards. The empty streets of sand had no taxis; she flagged a ride for us by a forlorn statue of Lenin draped in dried flowers. In our private last hours, there was only a comb of brilliant stars above the whorled dunes, and thin mystic clouds traveling fast and free across the wild full moon and musky night of Uzbekistan. By these means, the economic and social advantages of the region were made quite apparent.

◯

BY MIDDAY I AWAKENED in haste from a dreamless sleep, for it was time to meet my evening's benefactor, the great warlord himself. Under the protection of fellow Uzbek President Karimov, Dostum maintained two homes in Tashkent – one for family and one for business – but his stronghold was his fairyland fortress near Mazar-i-Sharif, deep into the last narrow section of Afghanistan not yet under Taliban control. It was across the Friendship Bridge on the Amu Darya river – the Oxus in ancient times – one of the four sacred rivers flowing into the Aral Sea. In a salt-rusted orange Soviet Moskvitch auto with cracked windows, Zalmay and I headed south.

When the Red Army left Afghanistan to the muj, General Boris Gromov, commander of the 40th Army, was the last Russian to stand on the bridge and look down the iron tracks into Afghanistan, long the graveyard of empires. Elated turbaned warriors with rocket-propelled grenades hurriedly assumed control of the customs guard houses and made the bridge the province of Dostum and Akbar Bey's associates. They soon extracted taxes on trucks, waived Dostum's staff jeeps around customs, and provided a lifeline of slow trains to the South, although sometimes they inadvertently overlooked clandestine shipments of chemical death to the North. Akbar Bey proudly had explained that Durand's artificial borders were porous to old families and ancient tribes, so it was clear why Zalmay and I had no difficulty with customs.

"They are cousins," he said.

As the daylight receded, vultures still hovered in the cloudless mauve of dusk. After nightfall, passing into the still intense heat of a wild and abandoned landscape of ravines and schist, one saw the moonlight making desert sands into white ice. Although Zalmay had concerns, we camped in the Fergana Valley, then circled for hundreds of kilometers along areas of recent fighting in Badakhshan and Kunduz. Unshod farmers with abundant white mustaches – each wearing their flowing shalwar kameez and turban – harvested small plots of eternal poppies, or broiled goats on spits at festive tribal weddings for child brides.

The Tajik border region was infested with smuggler's havens and pure cheap heroin, attended by flocks of village girls and crones addicted into whoredom. Countless barefoot, raggedy children flew makeshift kites on rooftops. Like a vision from a Persian mystic, a long camel train passed – saddled with dusty women swaying in flowing black robes. Only their obsidian eyes peered out. They were fixed resolutely on the next paradise, far above these timeless legions of camels with their bells tinkling and their splayed pads plodding so delicately over shifting rivulets of sand carved like tawny drifting snow.

Returning down makeshift roads through boiling clouds of silky dust and then along black thorny promontories, we entered Mazar-i-Sharif, its name the Arabic for Tomb of the Nobleman. Zalmay seemed relieved.

"Here Blue Mosque," he said simply, sweaty and devoted.

The burial ground of Hazrat Ali, son-in-law of the Prophet Mohamed, the mosque's dome and minarets swarmed with white doves.

"Wash sin away," Zalmay assured me.

"So many white birds," I observed.

"Black before come here."

Dostum's large brass plaque – set into the Blue Mosque masonry – announced his contributions. A confounding array of tribesmen crowded the streets, from Mongol Hazaras to blue-eyed Nuristanis and Turkic Uzbeks. Scattered about on tattered rugs, they drank green tea and ate sugar-dusted almonds as small boys in white whisked away the flies. Toothless old men pounded hubcaps into spoons. Skinned lambs with glazed eyes hung motionless from nails, while the *azan* – the call to prayer – rose upon the evening air and called the faithful to their knees.

Like Niyazov in Turkmenistan, Dostum's image was everywhere, from portraits in shops to postcards in humble homes. Yet he refused to impose the Sharia law of the Taliban; the people dressed as they wished, small girls in head cloths went off to school, the nights had Afghan music and Bollywood cinemas. Liquor, sweet hashish and opium were traded freely.

We entered an alley of *halwaladars* – money changers in robes and turbans and long beards, several sharing an abacus, another with a calculator, all by thick stacks of inflated Afghanis piled by wads of dollars, rubles, pounds, Kyrgyz, Turkmen and Kazakh banknotes, all the Shan States' currencies. Heroin labs proliferated close to the Afghan borders in this nexus of the poppy trade, with Mazar as a free zone, for backchannel business among the cartels – even from Taliban sources – flourished underneath the bloodshed of divided armies.

In the desert near Mazar – and soon threatened by the encroaching Taliban – Dostum's palace was an ever-growing, gaily-painted cement edifice in the kitsch style favored from Goa to the Levant. We quickly were surrounded by ten hardened troops with war-torn faces and by Dostum's high-level commander – the craggy General Alem Rasim. With his translator Zia, Rasim examined my passport for the scent of intel agencies.

"Tourist," he sniffed.

I profited from my ambiguous affiliations.

"We thought it best under the circumstances."

He was wary, no-nonsense, a bad enemy. After Zalmay hurriedly explained our presence, I spoke of the effort to free Akbar Bey and of the prison years, then proposed a risky alternative. After all, we knew who we were.

"We could offer to trade heroin for Akbar Bey – perhaps 800 kilograms – rather than men or weapons. It is possible?"

"It is possible."

I knew that no government agency would entertain such a prospect – a feigned seizure – but also that the heroin would be diverted from street users. Although the ruse was never implemented, his answer revealed their concern for Akbar Bey. We were released to the main residence.

Local chieftains came and went under dying palms, paying tributes to Dostum in a form of corrupt suzerainty; we sat by an indoor pool now haphazardly filtered and spoiled like a ruined desert watering hole. Plastic deer grazed on fake foliage.

Zalmay was sad that Dostum's playpen no longer had the pliable English stewardess who graced the poolside off duty from Dostum's defunct private airline Balkh Air. At airstrips already pockmarked from mortars, the Taliban had grounded air travel with random firing. The hosts of imported Russian courtesans were gone as well, but Dostum's expansive larder of Blue Label Johnny Walker for honored guests still occupied an elaborate sideboard. An obsequious crew of translators ebbed and flowed in accord with his suspicions, reminiscent of the eunuchs attending Shah Shuja – the first Afghan king.

An oil pipeline roustabout during Communist rule and his early teens, he was born Abdul Rashid. By his fifteenth birthday, tribal leaders gave him 600 warriors to command. Soon called *dost*, or friend, the name of a popular Uzbek song, he became General Dostum by self-appointment, largesse and consensus. Diminutive and comfortably plump with black hair, he was physically unimpressive, but Dostum had the gift of oratory before his men as he recalled Uzbek and Afghan history and united divisive tribes. His troops grew to more than twenty thousand men; his armaments included often operational Soviet tanks, some Antonov transports, helicopters and a fighter jet or two.

Dostum's more ruthless warriors – the feared *kilim jams* – left nothing behind in their rape and pillage. With troops reduced by causalities and deserters to six thousand, his leadership was ensured by a loyal cadre and public displays of command. Hapless victims sometimes were tied between two opposing tanks and eviscerated, or dragged alive through the desert until only bloody pulp remained.

We entered to introductions and ritual tea. This was not a time for secrets. He was aware I had survived difficult years along with Akbar Bey, that I was reinvented in Cambridge, and had some academic, unofficial contact with State. I provided a letter to Dostum from Akbar Bey. Translator hovering, he had only a few questions for me.

"How was your evening?"

He knew of the late night in Tashkent. Through a window were mirages, like inverted stacks of cool lakes. I expressed my gratitude.

"The other matter is too complicated." He demurred on the proposal to Rasim. In the far distance on the horizon's edge were plumes of dust from Toyota jeeps. Taliban country. He confirmed the serial numbers of four Stingers.

"How is Akbar Bey's family?" I finally asked.

"The Taliban seized their house on the Wazir Akbar Khan. Boys are servants. Wives I cannot say."

"What will happen to Afghanistan?"

"Without American aid, it is falling to the Taliban. I will make my first trip to America soon, to ask for military support."

I knew Dostum had little hope of an official invitation from the State Department, and could only offer sympathy for his lost cause, but promised to visit D.C. as well and help in some social way as a minor researcher. Dostum, with his rogue's eyes, otherwise was a practiced host and master of diplomatic hand-offs. For covert discussions of uncertain legality, one was escorted into other rooms, to other men seated on rugs with a desperate and religious formality.

After a long night of rice and tea and unforgettable faces, sleeping among warfighters and weapons, we left at dawn for the eleven-hour drive to Tashkent. Under the shade of a straggling date palm, beneath a yellow-eyed nanny goat, a little brown girl sat naked as the desert wind. She tugged at the goat's teats, delivering a stream of milk into her mouth.

◯

AFTER AN INTROSPECTIVE FLIGHT from the heart of opium production in Central Asia to Cambridge to prepare for Dostum's arrival, I discovered that Customs officials never searched my bags. So courteous I suspected there was a free pass from unseen monitors – at least temporarily – they again said only the most comforting words.

"Welcome home, Sir."

At Harvard, with few options left for Akbar Bey, I devised a briefing paper, naming it INFRARED. A play on the heat-sensing missiles and on Dostum as a former communist pawn, it was circulated to analysts and officials proposing that Akbar Bey be traded for loose Stingers as a method to cultivate the persistently influential Dostum in this unstable region. Policy professors commented upon it encouragingly although uneventfully, unaware that in a few semesters one would chair a 9/11 Commission and Dostum would be Interim Minister of Defense in the new Afghanistan.

While frantic with cramming for an HKS statistics exam, I sought advice from Charlie Wilson, the flamboyant, womanizing six-foot-seven Congressman so endearing to his electorate in the East Texas district of Lufkin. In the House Appropriations Committee he had funded CIA's Stinger Program and authorized a billion in weapons and guerilla tactical training to the muj. Rejecting the U.S. position of opposing the Soviets to the last Afghan, Wilson described the muj as fighting with "stick and stones" and felt such courage should be enhanced, creating – to the further delight of his constituency – the largest covert program since World War Two.

I waited in my study in Cambridge as Wilson's covey of Texas secretaries with their magnolia-laden voices passed the call along to Wilson in his D.C. office. A message from Harvard inquiring about swapping Stinger missiles for an Afghan national's freedom piqued his interest. He took the call, lively and disarming with his East Texas rural accent.

"Hell. Ah got a Stinger right behind ma desk!"

Wilson referred to the 7-foot green launch tube with pistol grips, a gift from Engineer Gaffar, the Afghan who used it to destroy the first Russian helicopter. Wilson transferred me to a CIA officer in the Islamabad embassy who, listening politely to the proposal, concluded the matter dismally but left it open-ended.

"Dostum won't get anywhere on the Stinger issue," he summarily decided.

Undeterred, I still envisioned some physical transfer of the missiles to the American consulate in Tashkent. Only a handful of Western military or agents officially remained in Afghanistan.

"Can you tell me about the early Stinger deployment?"

After some hesitation, he plunged in with details he obviously had delivered in briefings.

"The adversary was the Russian HIND D helicopter gunship. Twenty million dollars each. Armored belly and cockpit. Hundred rounds per minute cannons. Four napalm bombs. Hundred twenty-eight rockets."

"Against untrained desert tribes with their grandfather's Enfield rifles, or their *jezails?*"

He knew I referred to the antique muzzle-loading matchlocks with a one-ounce ball, surprisingly accurate from a camel.

"Right. But then we armed them with Chinese-made Dashika 12.7 millimeter AK-47s with anti-tank rocket-propelled grenades. Shipped a few through Karachi on dhows."

"And those were not effective?"

"The HIND could just hover outside their 100-meter kill radius."

"So, the Stinger."

"HINDs were no match for the Stinger. Thirty thousand a pop. Twenty-four pounds. Five-foot long missile with less recoil than a shotgun. Housed in a shoulder-mounted 'fire-and-forget' launch tube."

"How stable in a desert environment?"

"It can be dropped into ravines, submerged in snowpack in the Hindu Kush or streams in the Shamali Plains. Stingers can be left in deserts at 120 degrees, stored for more than ten years, and still retain ninety-percent lethality up to five miles."

"How were they distributed?"

"Handouts to the muj leaders. Afghans known as 'cosmonauts' began riding through mountain defiles with empty green launch tubes strapped to their mules. To be exchanged for another Stinger."

As he spoke I reflected on the Russian graves at Vag Ankov Cemetery in Moscow, with their peeling photographs of young soldiers. Arming an ancient warrior society ensured that the line of "Black Tulips" – the tin caskets of Soviet airmen, each with a small window for grieving families – would continue to flow over the Friendship bridge into Uzbekistan. I signed off, but he left me with a little prompt.

"On Dostum we'd like to hear anything he's up to. Stay in touch."

I listened to the dial tone with growing anxiety, for I was running out of contacts who might act. The bartering system of the Hill – based on favors – was perplexing. Projects were getting out of control. I was due at a meeting on chemical weapons in England, for the Iraqis had just dispersed a cloud of psychoactive gas over Kurd families. A drug policy conference in Mexico was imminent. Dostum was due soon in D.C. – CIA wouldn't play on the Stinger issue, but State might. The Taliban were encamped about Mazar for the final assault. The six chemists were intercepting me unpredictably with their teachings. Harvard's demands were increasing like an exponential curve into stratospheres of thought. Caught inescapably among these kaleidoscoping involvements, I seemed blocked at every turn. At moments, I almost panicked.

Chapter 18.

The Gnomes of Ypres

You would think nothing could live through it.
No wonder they take men out raving mad.

- Braxton Bigelow ('09) of
British Royal Engineers
on trench warfare

A huge, rolling low-lying greenish cloud of smoke began to roll down on them.
One man said there were about one thousand Zouanes of the Batallion d'Afrique
in the lines, and only sixty got back – either suffocated or shot as they
climbed out of the trenches to escape…in any event, there's the Devil's work
going on in Ypres.

- Harvey Cushing (MD, 1895)
Harvard Medical School Professor of Surgery
Alumni Bulletin, Spring, 1914

As parades tem ouvidos.

(Walls have ears)

THE MASTERS of modern biological and chemical warfare arrived one-by-one. Their black cars and chauffeurs passed the expansive lawns, grazing sheep, groomed thoroughbreds, rose gardens, arboretum, and stone chapel of Wilton Park, an 18th Century manor in Sussex. Each of these special guests was attended by formal staff, then led through chambers rife with paintings, carved balustrades and stained glass. Assisted to their small room and reading lamp, they prepared to confront the malignancy of unrestricted weapons harbored by rogue and state actors with the technical capacity to disorient, infect, or kill individual targets or large populations. Academics, strategists and futurologists gathered to consider chemical clouds inducing psychoses, plumes of weaponized anthrax and smallpox, and vapors that paralyze or maim a political opponent or entire villages in an agonizing welter of uncontrollable suffocation, lacrimation, urination, defecation and blistered death.

Around the estate of Wilton Park manor, with its vaulted ceilings of painted white cherubs, were paths where pairs of young village equestriennes, girls of twelve or so, cantered their Bay geldings. By the Tudor entryway, there were fragrant beds of peonies and buttercups, and red poppies that the fresh-faced local children, in the evenings, gathered for Remembrance Day.

Following at Harvard the progress of international controls on cognitive agents for warfare, I appeared invitation in hand to be welcomed by staff, and introduced among the British chemists and military attaches from Porton Down, the U.K. version of American chemwar groups at Fort Detrick and Edgewood Arsenal. A striking – soon to be unforgettable – maid from Edinburgh, with dancing eyes and skin like milk, dressed in formal black with a fulsome bodice, served *hors d'oeuvres* from a silver tray.

The star-studded *vernissage* included officials from NATO, Whitehall, the Pentagon, private analytical firms, and the Chinese and Russian military. Most were concerned with containment, but the occasional face darkened with unholy powers. Like some *bête noire* stealing secrets from the unsuspecting, these few individuals were the antithesis of those fearful of great evil. They affected a careless hubris, but a sensitive observer could see they were riddled with mistrustfulness from their long-practiced deceits. Although distracted by the conflicting ethics, I tried to engage everyone cordially and indiscriminately, even though the lovers of light would consider the dark ones as Hyperborean swine. From Indigo I had learned to look for hidden agendas.

⬡

THE RECEPTION ATMOSPHERE, desiccated at first, evolved into collegial exchanges and comradeship as each found his own. It became an armed truce of the earth's paladins in scientific lethalities, for all were delighted to find a virgin ear. I had mingled with some lighthearted cluster when – across the polished oak-paneled room – a very fit Englishman glanced my way. With some transfixing anecdote, he was managing to hold down in a corner a brace of the local vampires – each of his prey with a name card and the manor sherry. His hair was tinted and trimmed almost to the scalp, his coat custom tailored yet unremarkable. At the edge of his cuff I glimpsed sandalwood mala beads and a new Rolex Submariner. Unseen by others, he bowed to me in a *Namaste*. Reflexively, I bowed as well, then started. Magenta.

It was rather a trek from Pashupanipath. I relaxed as if an old friend had come round, but felt his visit was not for me. The vampires were disguised as unethical pharmacologists from Islamabad in expensive suits. Magenta disengaged them with a hearty farewell, a craft to deflect their suspicion. He approached me oddly, without surprise or salutation, but raising his voice quite audibly among others in the room, and inquiring of the poetry of Blake.

"Have you *read* that rebellious disciple of Swedenborg's myths?"

He brandished instead copies of North's *Plutarch* and Holinshed's *Chronicles*, but avoided the usual Wilton Park references about binary bombs of hallucinogens or nerve gases or genetically modified Q fever. By this contrivance, he smoothly detached his companions who had ulterior plans. Ever the devoted Hellenist, he slipped Pope's *Iliad* translation into my jacket, then guided me outside through the delicate rose garden toward the 200-year-old chapel.

⬡

WE WERE ALONE, but not by a tranquil Princeton lake or isolated within Nepalese religious frenzies. A contact high here would precipitate among closely-knit circles of PhDs in unspeakable arts – all vastly skilled specialists in biochemical doomsday devices – as everyone took port, cheeses and teas in the Wilton Park libraries. These were the heirs of the first chemical assault at Ypres, Belgium in the Great War, where British soldiers choked in the trenches from the green death of chlorine. Collected here with us were many who defended civilization, but also those whose plagues would ensure a billion infectious corpses. I hoped the rose garden proved not to be that of Persephone, taken by Hades.

As we passed onto the safety of the stone chapel's consecrated ground, an astral brilliance began to envelop us, a light before which all evil quailed. It was as though we were gently acquired by an advanced civilization, one that looked back upon its baser selves from that bright land inconceivable to those who would harm. Magenta remained wordless, producing only an antique Malacca bamboo cane with an ivory handle. As at Bodhinath, he began circumambulating the ancient pews and vestry, tapping the floor as he slowly walked, reciting prayers in Latin and Tibetan.

The chapel walls were inlaid with centuries-old remembrances of the notable, the loved, and the brave. To the cadence of his muted prayers and the clicking of his staff, I walked silently as well – even as the chapel's liturgical paintings and triptych's of St. Paul began to quiver, then float in the windless and holy sanctum.

◯

IT BEGAN SUDDENLY, not as the luminous benevolent aesthetics in Nepal, but as a devastating parade of religious conflicts: the slaughtering of beggars in the mosques of Wazil Khan in Lahore, the bloodbaths in the Peloponnese and Aegean recalled by Thucydides and Xenophon, the carnage of Belfast troubles and the marching season and the Catholic schoolgirls' bodies desecrated by William of Orange at the Battle of Boyne, the countless slayings of infants from the extremes of Kierkegaardian Calvinism unrestrained even by the harsh wisdom of Talmudic Judaism.

By this circumambulating invitation we were transported out of our ken, beyond the celestial mechanisms of Bodhinath, beyond the concentric worlds of Ptolemy's astronomical treatise the

Almagest, to where the very stars burned. Trapped in a beastly black hole, we crawled on our bellies, the tapping that of some banshee tempest of brimstone upon our flayed backs, to the places of perdition where medieval crosses were inverted and images of Christ replaced by mirrors.

Long lines of hollow-eyed and starved women and children with shattered limbs moved over radioactive earth – many cannibalized by vicious hordes, or decimated by weaponized pestilences – with the last of human altruism but a single shriveled rose secretly held against a malnourished, diseased breast.

Within these phantasmagoria of moral repugnance – each second a thousand years – we were caught in an infinite regression of unspeakable suffering, until we fleetingly glimpsed through a crack in the grisly, bloody sky the morning light of heaven.

By Grace, we entered a rapturous contemplation recalling both the Sorrowful and Glorious Mysteries. There was the odor of aromatic oils distilled from the relics of saints, and finally the scent of valerian. Through the narrow stone window of the chapel, I saw in the early evening a funeral swirling of rooks. The stars looked turbid.

I turned, absorbed into the benign currents now manifesting, drawn at last into a laughing vortex of loving prophecies; yet the disquieting prospects could not be forgotten, for we had been exposed to the chthonic, the underworld.

It all stopped. Magenta was folding a chausable, perusing the Sanctus of High Mass. As I listened he began chanting a psalm, then intoned a *Te Deum* while clouds of incense enfolded our somber reveries. I wondered if some of the conference participants might be the ultimate arbiters of human fate, and we the people the endangered species, too late confronting extinction. We stood shriven in the garden of banksia roses, survivors freshly imbued with exquisite sensitivity to opposing forces. Magenta never again referred to the religiosity of our walk through the valley of shadows.

Among the roses, after we descended, he still demonstrated his findings on experimental memory drugs. He did a rapshode – comforting me greatly – by reciting long portions of the Homeric epics acquired from a single reading. At last, both somewhat more steady then, we turned to enter the high seas of gentlemanly deception.

AT THE CONFERENCE, among the formidable range of stellar talents, he exhibited Oxonian social amenities developed since birth. He first amused one official, who privately was a poet on Miltonian lines, with his mordant wit. More settled, we then engaged the wider *demimonde* of saviors and killers.

The abundant young Scottish housemaid with scarlet hair and sea-green eyes, but with the symmetry of a Titian, had by some innocent Highland coquetry infatuated one of the Pakistani scientists. His aggressive jocularity and ready-made phrases hardly concealed his lewd thoughts, so that she blushed charmingly but oddly did not move away. His Islamabad associate looked on from a distance, his face that of a desert butcher. Magenta whispered to me as he produced a bright smile and a respectful bow for the onlooker.

"Their science is criminal in the eyes of God."

In the subdued lighting, Magenta's targets both had ashen faces that reflected a contained ferocity, as if their dim recollection of virtue long had been routed. Their syntheses in underground labs in bunkers were accomplished by voodoo ceremony; their skills were a form of witchery, conducted by robots for petty tyrants. No one truly sensitive to the beauty of chemistry and medicine could manufacture annihilating poisons, the dark art only of malevolent, crude technicians.

While the benevolent stars of Whitehall and the Potomac managed light badinage on defense against biological and chemical weapons, surrounded by varying degrees of jovial and harmless sycophancy, Magenta had targeted his men. Both Pakistanis regrouped, abandoning prudent diplomacy for frightful states of frigid politeness. Magenta leaned near with a comment from his beloved Virgil's *Aeneid*, but still holding a friendly gaze with them.

"*Pallia morte future.*" (He is pale with impending death)

The housemaid managed to extract herself from the Paks' obscene intent, then departed upstairs. Magenta after some stealthy reconnaissance quickly sought to engage them, leaving me to the Porton Down masters with a parting from Virgil.

"*Si fata sinant.*" (If fate permits)

He moved in on them with a Muslim greeting and respectable Urdu. They provided toothy smiles. He mesmerized them with elaborate inventions ranging from anecdotes about a princely golfing acquaintance in the Murree Hills above Islamabad, to a bawdy night in the souks with Muslim bureaucrats and compliant English women, and ending with a scandalous starlit exit by dhow. He spoke of everything but weaponry, as if they were the most honorable of companions. I failed to understand his tactic, and decided to rest before dinner.

○

I AWOKE TO CONSIDER my attic room, with its knotted Exeter carpet, Japanese lacquered cabinet, single carved Chippendale chair, and rusticated door. I opened the leaded window of a deep embrasure, looking upon the night. A silent, heavy mist had gathered above the medieval overhangs and eyries of the village church. The dull crescent of a new moon, yellow and shaded like the eye of an Arabian viper, shone above copses of black oaks that once had sheltered Cromwell's men.

Magenta had appeared for an elaborate *ruse de guerre*, not to be interviewed by me. His clandestine art had the perfection of a Bach motet; I could only look upon it, a beautiful lie in the name of enlightenment. The sense of dread from the chapel vortex finally having receded, I withdrew from these reveries, then moved more confidently, preparing to descend to the Great Room and the taxing social maelstrom of those who conjured or banished deathly elixirs. At the first stairway, down the long, narrow hall with its wooden floors and Tabriz runner, I saw one of their counter-surveillance team. It was the girl from the National Gallery in London, without her *Financial Times* and her python cape.

○

SHE NOW WAS CHERRY-LIPPED, and wore skin-tight black Balenciaga pants over her long, lean legs. Her Balmain bracelet was chased with silver heraldic fauna. She was standing in high pumps with ankle straps, straining with insensate passion against the Scottish maid. The hard edge of her right hip repeatedly lifted into lavish, parting thighs. The maid, pressed into the doorway and flushing deeply, was yielding in the amorous locket of their bodies. There was the hint of rape.

She grasped the maid's prominent white breasts and fervently kissed her florid neck, her strong and insistent rhythm rising into the maid's voluptuous and immobile tension. The most indelicate advances of her hands were not repulsed. Unbuttoned, the maid revealed an expensive black silk chemise, loosened upon her ivory tautness. Her cheeks were all aflame, her eyes dreaming heavenward.

I heard them in small gasps swear eternal secrecy with the most sober and sublime virtue. I stood at the far edge of the stairs, unobtrusive; they remained unnoticed by the indiscrete. The close operatives of the Six were inferentially promiscuous – perhaps a bisexual anomaly among women – but *lingua franca*, it seemed, among this tribe. Their mental fecundity and diplomatic adroitness required sexual liberties enjoyed in another age by the ruling class. The maid with a stormy petulance reached for her keys. Trembling visibly, she opened the door to a manor bedroom. I withdrew to the evening session, the yearning of my heart thereafter but a memory.

⬡

THE GATHERING BELOW was in full bloom, a wild mix of capabilities and connections. There was the director of the *Bundeskriminalamt*, with his elegant manner and without a secretary, and the most charming elderly blue-eyed Russian with tales of decommissioning nerve gas depots. Magenta elicited from him details of the Russian OMON forces introducing fentanyl aerosol into a Moscow theater – one that had been seized by Chechen terrorists wrapped in dynamite – and the deaths or paralysis of hundreds of families from the anesthetic. With a merry, crinkled face from the Novosibirsk winters, he spoke of BZ and hallucinogenic glycolates diverted from binary bomb storages, and smoked on the streets of St. Petersburg.

A high Whitehall official of some secret service, overhearing us, promptly interceded with an eccentric diversion on General Allenby in the Great War, aboard his flagship Eurylus from Jiddha to Port Sudan.

"I *say*, dear man, the first chemical weapon was *gunpowder*. Imagine, the Stokes machine guns strafing Turkish trains, the guns brought over on the Eurylus, its funnels smoking in the desert air near Akaba in 1919. The biological weapons there were the infectious carcasses of pregnant Arab women. Yes, mounted on *pikes* our boys found them. Or eviscerated like camels, all unburied and unburned, left as toxins by the Ottoman. *Bloody* wogs, eh?"

He awaited our reaction, bemused. Gleaming as if he dealt in multiple identities and covert operations, he swirled then sipped a small glass of tawny port, peeking over it at us while gripping his portfolio bound in fine Russian leather. I reflected on the upstairs bedroom, and the special warfare he knew not, conducted through desire.

"That is," he continued *sotto voce* – speaking directly to Magenta – "before Lawrence became the national deity and fled into anonymity, as an RAF mechanic under an *assumed* name. Right?"

We sensed some complication, some barrier. Undefined threats did ricochet subtlely around the room; the guest list had been vetted by hostile analysts from twenty countries. We sought those with less evident liaisons, for Magenta's concern lay elsewhere.

⬡

MOVING IN THIS TARGET-RICH ENVIRONMENT beneath the library's plasterwork ceiling of roses, orange blossoms, grapes, pears and pomegranites, Magenta attracted a group of German biochemists who were developing cognitive agents and memory drugs. He entertained them in English – provoking hilarity with irreverent asides in the High German of the Reich – then provided an animated retrospective on Joseph Justus Scaliger, the French prodigy known as the "Phoenix of Europe" and considered the most learned man of all time.

"He acquired all of Homer, completely, in 21 days. Then became facile in Chaldean, Persian, Arabic, Ethiopic, Phoenician, and especially Syriac."

"By what means?" one Heidelberg researcher inquired, hooked and running.

"By concentration alone. During the brutal St. Bartholomew's Day massacre of Protestants by Pope Gregory XIII, he was so intent on his Hebrew he heard nothing of the fighting – the wailing of women, the groaning of children."

"But his attention to threat was diminished, a cognitive giving and taking away, yes?"

At this, Magenta launched into his thesis, his concerns about reaching for the sky of intelligence and recall.

"We can expect such shifts in personality with memory drugs, or certain cognitive enhancers, with a loss in other faculties or emotions. Consider Newton. His later years were wasted on a world chronology based on Jason's fabled Argonauts and their travel to Colchis for golden fleece."

Magenta held direct eye contact with the biochemists – but discretely circled to keep the nearby Pakistani pharmacologists in the periphery of his vision – then digressed, multitasking seamlessly.

"Newton thought the timing of Jason's voyage real, and the *Argo* to have beams from the trees of Dodona which could foretell the future, and were guarded by a sleeping dragon from whose teeth, when sowed, sprang fifty armed men."

For a moment the listeners were silent, for they were descendants of Visigoths who once paled before the legends of Athena. They then laughed broadly, for they were now sons of Bohr and Heisenberg with no time for children's tales.

"But how does Newton's deficit," one asked, "suggest increased risk for our experimental subjects with memory drugs?"

"Newton's stunning delusion occurred after his evolutionary cognitive leap: the mathematics of gravitation and the calculus. Enhancement of learning may have deleterious outcomes. For mind, as you say, is both given and taken away."

While he spoke I realized that if Magenta were correct, he intended by his self-sacrifice to be one of the first human victims, and to warn us of dangers. As our group pondered the social costs from artificial prowess, a bell softly sounded, summoning us to the Great Room. The German biochemists followed amicably; we all were seated for the keynote event amid anticipatory murmurs in Cantonese and Hindi, and the quiet exchanges with Oxbridgian and Kentish drawls.

GRECIAN DIVINITIES were frescoed across the vaulted ceilings, like the psychic displays of dryads and naiads in Berlin during the seduction of V-2. My eyes drifted to Aphrodite and her son Eros, my thoughts to the feminine nuclei of carnality now in the heat of fusion above us, for their vivid passions were unimaginable to those beneath the stairs.

An esteemed panel discussed the gold standard of chemical terrorism: the Tokyo subway attacks with nerve gas released by a fringe religious group, Aum Shin Rikyo. Hearing details of 6000 casualties among commuters, the Paks made notes furiously. After the conclusion, as we took tea, Magenta privately made a rare admission.

"V-1 and V-2 were at Kyoto University with Shinki Mochizuki's grad students to resolve the implications of his new mathematical nomenclature. They were somewhat a sensation there, among the artistic and fashion underground. But on the weekends, they visited police officials in the prefecture investigating Aum Shin Rikyo."

"Why would they?"

"The Aum group was a horribly deviant, ultimately malicious, polytheistic ideology that incorrectly claimed Shinto and Buddhist origins. It was led by a charismatic, blind figurehead. To affect his personal mind control of his inner circle, he held cabalistic ceremonies, providing hallucinogenic amphetamines in wine. As they drank, he intoned, 'This is the blood of Christ'."

"I wasn't aware."

"Problem was, while the devilish Aum leader maintained clandestine labs for the nerve gas, he instructed others of his group to seek five kilograms of ergotamine – the precursor to LSD – from Russian sources. Naturally, we immediately discovered their intent on the ergotamine, but not early enough to stop the nerve gas attacks."

"You are concerned about malevolent entities manipulating others with psychedelics?"

"Very much so. They usually acquire only small quantities – lacking skills and devotion – and self-destruct through arrest, indulgence or addiction. Yet they are exceedingly dangerous, like the vampires here. Cobalt is concerned with a situation in the Midwest. Perhaps he'll disclose that to you."

In the last evening, as we partook of canapés in convivial groups, and sampled desserts of blancmange, pistachio and cinnamon, I spied the sumptuous housemaid. Remarkably, she had assumed the demure purity of a Catholic serving girl. The Pakistani pharmacologists with the countenances of serpents seemed to hypnotize her, or she them. Backed into an alcove unseen by others, she began to pose in an inviting manner against a *chinoiserie* cabinet from Beijing. She now wore the Balmain bracelet.

As she commanded their attentions, I realized their briefcases and files easily were searched by her mistress. As if they were about to devour their prey, both Paks glanced around suspiciously. At this, she quickly peered at her watch, then looked imploringly across the room at Magenta. He was standing with discretion nearby, partially hidden by a Florentine marble obelisk, and blocking the stairway. He seemed stricken, signaling me to turn away without somehow attracting notice. The night with its intricate profundities had become too subtle for me, and I did as he wished.

IN THE MORNING, Magenta and the girl were not to be found. The Wilton Park staff confirmed, strangely, that no participants had departed. The maid, according to the manor housekeeper curious of my persistent inquiry, was a temporary.

"The lass was here only for the *receptions*, sire," she said, her wizened face friendly, but green eyes alert. "Why do ye *ask?*"

Magenta's sudden absence was like a revelation nearly grasped; one flailed at the emptiness. So many questions almost had surfaced, phantoms that hardly could be articulated. In the last night, I walked the hallways alone and dissatisfied, for these alluring global conspirators still were unfathomed.

Returning upstairs to prepare for a scientific meeting in Mexico, I stood by the doorway where the covert hearts secretly had thrilled, and recalled their deeply intruding, electromagnetic touches. I ran my fingers down the fine white ash, and dreamed of their interlude, but felt then I was inconsequential to them. But upon entering my room, I saw that by the turned-down bed had appeared a crystal vase. It contained a grand bouquet of freshly cut lilies, and white narcissi.

They were wild, from the ditches of Kathmandu. A torn fragment of *Rising Nepal* had been discarded. On the down pillow, scented with Eau de Givenchy, was a pressed copy of the *Financial Times*.

Chapter 19.

Our Lady of the Shadows

I imagined a labyrinth of labyrinths, a maze of mazes,
a twisting, turning, ever-widening labyrinth that contained
both the past and future and somehow implied the stars…
Absorbed in these illusory imaginings, I forgot I was a pursued man;
I felt myself for an indefinite while, the abstract perceiver of the world.

- JLB, *The Garden of Forking Paths*

"Good intelligence work,"
Control had always preached,
"is gradual, and rests on a kind of gentleness."

- Le Carré, *Tinker Tailor, Soldier, Spy*

ACAPULCO on a monstrously hot afternoon spread before me, as listless seagulls floated in the austere air. The encounter with Magenta at Wilton Park had been – it seemed – merely coincidental. I had grown accustomed to a new country from day to day, and took pleasure in the shock from divergent peoples and mores. I was late for the annual meeting of the College on Problems of Drug Dependency, held each summer in grand hotels past their prime during the heated unoccupancies. The drug policy leadership of America now gathered in Acapulco, as heroin smugglers conducted their dismal mutilations in the gardens of walled haciendas and in raw alleys.

On the streets were shrines to cartel leaders and lieutenants – beside their mausoleums – with each kingpin a sordid deity to illiterate boys who spoke only low-life patois, and revered cheap pistols. Displaying photos of some sallow, grimacing parasite, each shrine was embroidered with painted gypsum crosses and vulgar displays before which the people were reminded of the glorious rewards of addiction.

Acapulco oceanside was lined with impenetrable condominiums that wealthy Mexicans constructed for occasional holidays, across from open-air cafés on simple concrete slabs with ice and scratchy music, or nightclub pleasure domes dizzying to the most prodigal *Norteamericanos*. The small middle class lived in the hills, one wall of their modest casitas open to the sea. It was the periodic dreary aspect of a Maria that collapsed one's perspective to the fine point of true suffering.

They sat at the feet of passersby in artless misery, all absurdly young, one hand extended with open palm, the other clutching a baby. The detritus of Acapulco, they were ignored by all but the *policia*, who forced them back to the coarse depravity of a slum. Acapulco – chaos from the foundations up – was the febrile celebration of the moneyed, schoolgirls in white kneeling with missals on the steps of churches, the diabolical machinations of random torture and slayings, the rural farmers with mule-drawn carts and goats, and the Marias with glazed eyes, frozen in supplication, forever awaiting the fathers who never returned.

⬡

I ARRIVED at the hotel, a fallen princess with larded colors, but with the spacious, open air common to equatorial verandas. It had cool fruit drinks, and light that transited one's bones. Finding shorts and a robe, then collecting a daypack, juice and a book, I padded down long halls toward the ceaseless low roar of the implacable Pacific.

Like a sleeping god in the late afternoon, the beach vastly stretched its white emptiness. The ocean pounded with the foaming edge of heavy weather. Tall palms with curved erect trunks, laden with coconuts under efflorescent sprays of leaves, leaned oceanward before the sensuous hills.

I plunged underneath the breakers, as cross-currents tore left and right, and tried to body surf to little avail. I grew tired fighting a serious riptide, but a boiling surge of conflicting undercurrents pulled me far to sea. With a frantic swim almost to exhaustion I managed to gain a sandy footing, then staggered from its sucking maw to the safety of the pristine sands. As I lay on a towel and slowly regained breath, the low sun against my fatigued muscles and tightening skin evaporated the wetness into fine crystals of sea salt. I mused on these waters, in their splendid deceit.

Refreshed from drinking cool mango juice in the shade of a palapa, I began to read Homeric poetry from Magenta's book. It was Pope's 1724 translation of the *Iliad*, bound in leather and valued by scholars, handled thoughtfully for centuries. I opened the quarto volume to lines on the splendor of Achilles.

> *Her aegis Athenee o'er his shoulders throws*
> *Around his brow a golden cloud she spread*
> *A stream of glory flamed above his head…*

The sea was quieting. A lone figure came into being on the horizon, a girl aimlessly walking, barefoot at the edge of warm wavelets. I returned to Homer's description of the shield of Achilles, fashioned by the god Hephaestus, he of the strong arms.

> *Two cities radiant on the shield appear*
> *The image one of peace, and one of war,*
> *Here sacred pomp and genial feast delight.*
> *And solemn dance and hymeneal rite;*
> *Along the street the new-made brides are led,*
> *With torches flaming, to the nuptial bed…*

The girl's image grew larger. I first discerned she was slender, then I saw she was naked, but for a thin blue cotton shawl. She stopped for a while to place her toes in the lapping waters. She came much closer.

Her brilliant white skin was offset by the azure seas, as rumbling breakers announced her most delicate advances. Her hair was loose and darkly golden, her shape heartbreaking like the finest hourglass at the death of a queen. Her small pert breasts – framed with each swing of her garment – were achingly smooth like honeyed tulips, their pistils awaiting the caress of wind and pollen. Her belly was oval as a pink cameo below which new worlds arise. As she approached, I could not speak, but only dream.

She offered me her hand, her eyes alight with setting sun. She led me along the sands as if I were some slain warrior awakening in Elysium. She said nothing, but began to sing fragments of songs known to the Six, each in a different language or dialect, from Dutch to Ukrainian to rustic lullabies of the Hebrides.

"small and white, clean and bright, you look happy to meet me…"

Her nails were crimson.

"I see skies of blue, and clouds of white…"

She undulated with disturbing grace, tenderly holding my fingertips in her electric hand.

"All the children of the world…"

On the beach before us was a squatting man in blue work shirt rolled above his sinewy forearms. Wearing a straw Stetson, he looked intently at the sea, not moving as we came. The girl made no effort to hide her nakedness. He wore a silver ring, with the inscription *Dominus Illuminatio Mea*.

She released my hand and walked on, dropping her shawl onto the sand. I sat beside Magenta. We listened to the ocean's thousand voices, the cycle of prayers forever uttered. The girl wandered in serenity beyond us, a willowy, tall figure dancing to the whispers of the evening tide. As she stood for an eternal moment to weave loose, thick braids in hair – arms overhead and facing a far storm front – we could see through the wide cleft above her long, lean thighs the rolling, tropic blue waters. The fingers of the sea rushed to grasp her ankles, rising higher, coaxing, clinging then falling, failing to gather its tribute to Poseidon.

"V-3," he said at last. "Knows you well. National Gallery. Wilton Park. Other…places."

"Was the Wilton Park gambit successful?"

"We have the Pakistani's innermost secrets."

"The maid. A useful seduction?"

"Oh, right. No, they've been quite close since their teens at public school, Wycombe Abbey. The lady disguised as a maid is actually a distant relative of the Thane of Cawdor. She's one of us. The Balmain bracelet was hers, almost gave her away."

"And V-3?"

"I can give you a little. Parentage descending from diverse heroines, a baronetcy remotely, but the most interesting of marriages. Bloodlines include a double agent Teuton woman at the Peenemünde launch site during the Blitz, one from Salon Kitty where chosen damsels of Berlin society extracted secrets from *Einstatz* generals for Allied command in a secret brothel."

"Her languages are flawless."

"Perhaps from her polyglot forebear Nedezhda, a Russian fighter pilot who led the all-woman Soviet air regiment that firebombed the Axis. The 'Night Witches' they were called."

V-3 approached, her posture proud and free, her eyes transfixing with their subliminal flash of sapphires. Magenta gathered her shawl and – upon our promises to meet at the conference – walked with her toward the pink stucco hotel. Their fingers lightly touched. They passed through licentious fragrances of azaleas and rhododendrons and frangipani all promiscuously coupling, and into the thickening foliage and beckoning mysteries of the early Acapulco evening.

⬡

SHE NOW WORE A TIARA of small orchids at the conference reception, and the most mere blue shift fitted quite closely, but maintained an inspiring primness. She had gained the attentions of the American Drug Czar, Director of the Office of National Drug Control Policy, with his retinue of aides and researchers. A polished bureaucrat in his early sixties, he was fully in command, even among those blithely expounding in pedantic farragoes or with the occasional obsequious smile imprinted on their faces. V-3 and the Director seemed beguiled of each other in a fleeting way, he offering the fire of his wit, she responding with delicious subtleties perfectly matched to his background. They exchanged business cards, as researchers and officials so often do.

V-3 moved through the room with the illusory randomness of the fully briefed: a little German here, Russian there, the bell-like tones of a Wycombe Abbey girl up to Cambridge. As encounters demanded, she devolved to demotic American English. A lovely, seemingly confiding lass – but with an uncharted intelligence – she was so practiced at deception that even the inherently suspicious gushed at her apparently casual attentions. Magenta and I observed her progress.

"She honed her skills," he finally remarked, "among private intelligence contractors, then through industrial espionage, and across the diplomatic circuits."

V-3 collected her tenth card among the insular government officials. It was at that moment I saw, standing by a poster of a research presentation, a heavyset man with a dull, sunburned face and a too-neatly clipped moustache. He was a caricature really, unsophisticated at tradecraft, with the dead eyes common to low-level law enforcement.

He was looking at V-3, then Magenta, then me. Perhaps he sensed, while not comprehending, the covert social gambit underway. He tried affecting a casual air, glancing away, but it was too late. Everyone had made each other, then pretended otherwise.

We dispersed gaily in three different directions: V-3 arm-in-arm with a woman neurologist toward the elevators, Magenta fading to the ocean promenade with a lively gaggle of academics, and I to my poster entitled "The Future Drug Study – Drug Design and Policy Implications." Several researchers from Harvard's McLean Hospital and Hopkins were reading it. Pinned to the cork board were cards from universities and industry, and one from the Chief Pharmacologist at DEA.

⬡

WE MET AGAIN after midnight, as the high, sweet, warm ocean air whipped the ripening tips of stiff palms against the pitch-black sky. We drove toward the after-hours clubs of Acapulco, V-3 silent behind us, gripping her snakeskin Celine clutch, and wearing the tightest possible white tube microskirt above mid-thigh. Her long smooth legs ended in Chloe party booties. She slightly parted her window, and lay back to invite the luscious breeze. As we passed along sea walls worn by time, then through a poorly lit, depressed area, V-3 gasped.

She turned to look back at a lonely Maria, who was stumbling badly with her baby, collecting her shreds of blanket with her free hand. Her fast-receding image was lost among the sordid tiendas with their barred, smashed windows, and the revelry of affluent Acapulco youth racing beside us in the night to some ever fleeing, mindless glamour.

⬡

THE CLUB was a fantasy of tactile sound so dense and primal one's genitals tingled. Its ten-meter walls of glass peaked as though it were a temple, and inclined outward like an extraterrestrial presence hovering over Acapulco bay. Piercing red and blue lasers cross-hatched the sultry air of desire. It swarmed with striking Colombianas flocked from Bogota, thin Panamanians like elegant, lewd flamingos, and several Norwegians prowling for southern exposure. Well-dressed Hispanic youth with perfect complexions danced under epileptic strobes and laughed in wide leather booths under tumultuous ultraviolet art. A frenzied figure costumed as the god Quetzalcoatl – with a head dress of fluorescent flowers and snakes and covered in glowing body paint – danced madly on an elevated platform. Beneath the deep visceral electronica, the lights of Acapulco Bay extended to the horizon's curvature, blending with clouds of nebulae turning into the purple sea.

V-3 left her Celine clutch with Magenta, giving a serious instruction in Moldovan slang that eluded me. It appeared to contain high-denomination pesos and heavy gold Aztecas. There was a medallion from Indigo of Our Lady of Guadalupe in her robe of stars, standing on Satan's horns.

She moved to the dance floor alone, her syncopation born of the Sapphic rites. Besieged with offers, she chose two tall, svelte, Venezuelan models, identical twins with dark eyes, oval faces and the sheen of perfect olive skin. There was some instant recognition; they swayed in tandem, foreheads together. V-3 began responding; their tentative bodies became more insistent, their movement progressively torrid, as the blood rose.

The atmosphere turned hot, their motions like slow liquid. The crushing sound seemed to become silent. Our vision narrowed to the shameless urgency of V-3 caught between her bedazzled and frantic suitors. For a moment the women were the Bacchae, dancing in delirium, before they suckled young wolves and gazelles at their breasts, and tore apart calves with their bare hands, shredding them with their fierce nails into hooves and skin, the flesh on trees.

I sipped my drink, while Magenta made some sign to her. She was moving up and down between them, now against one, then the other, hands everywhere, her lips parted in some pre-orgasmic state.

She led the Venezuelans to the darkened stairs and to the grasping and the kisses, the women on each side, she firmly between them. As the door closed, I glimpsed V-3 pressed like the Scottish maid against a velvet wall. The models' long shining straight black hair swept slowly back and forth across their white microskirts and tensing legs, like dark pendula metering out the unbearable seconds of ecstatic apostasies. We waited until they took her – or she them – out into the cries of the night, out into the fevers of the initiated. She seemed to quell her fear, and release her passion, only in the celestial heat of others awakened.

⬡

AT THE HOTEL SUITE, apparently unconcerned about V-3's return, Magenta prepared iced punches of mango juice in sparkling water, then lit candles and incense, and extinguished the lights one by one. In the tropic heat, we wore only loose sarongs about our hips. The white noise of phosphorescent breakers hissed below us, while the occult sea beyond shone with broken trails of light from Orion and Vega.

"She'll be back before dawn, for an early flight to Tokyo. But there is the monastery on arrival and the *ofuros*, the mountain hot springs. I go another direction."

It grew quite late, as I imagined V-3 sampling her companions in convulsive pleasures. In the sobering night, I began to worry about her safety. The sea air became quiescent; between the soft rollers one could hear only the sawing lament of crickets, and the night birds' restive sighs. Almost imperceptibly, the door unlatched.

V-3 walked barefoot in the candlelight across the cool tiles, her Chloe party booties in one hand. She placed them together against the wall, as a Zen nun entering meditation. She lightly perspired. Her eyes looked within, to intense feelings only just passed. Pulling her microskirt above her head in one arching motion, she folded it carefully, placed it by the shoes, and bowed to us in the formal Japanese manner.

Gloriously nude – in a chiaroscuro of veiled shadow and ivory skin and candlelight – she lifted a tall, iced mango juice and slowly drank it. As a bead of juice trickled down the blue vein in her elongated neck, we considered the fine delicacy of her perfect posture. She eased us with a gentle smile, and walked over to the balcony, leaning forward over its edge. A magnificent vision, she straightened her legs firmly, and raised her arms to the heavens. The perfumed night wind, like the breath of Aphrodite, caressed her precious form.

She leaned outward toward the nocturnal display of distant light squalls. Through her cleft, there were far mists and lightning at sea. A gale was stirring, its magnitude irresistible.

Without a word Magenta arose, and went to one of three bedrooms. Placing her fingertips on the balcony railing, V-3 stood high upon her toes, extending her legs strongly and stretching her back, opening her breasts and everting her hips until she trembled. She breathed of the life-giving ocean in deep, amorous inhalations. The candles were going out. I felt we were at the doorway to some new world.

She turned, illuminated only by starlight, her small ripe breasts and belly the tears of angelic hosts. She wandered randomly at first, as if deciding. She walked very slowly toward me, halting with wordless, direct gazes. She was tantalizing, her presence the offering of an oracular priestess.

She leaned near. I could feel her body's heat, smell her cosmic scent, her musk. She spoke to me in the most loving way, with her voice of many colors: the simultaneous tones of children and mothers and harlots and the sanctity of the marriage bed and its fervent commencement. She said the most unexpected of things: Joyce's quote of Shelley.

> "Art thou pale for weariness
> of climbing heaven
> and gazing on the earth
> wandering companionless…"

She knew well of my own loneliness. She walked to the bedroom door, looking over her shoulder, then stood before it and saw me as if for the last time, like an elusive gift of grace for which one has only to reach out. Ghostly specters of bliss and emptiness danced about her, like alternate futures into other dimensions.

I hesitated. The contact high flowered, transforming her darkened body into the sun. She opened herself as the goddess Eo from the nuptial bed, her hair the rosy dawn. She turned, then moved upon Magenta, impaling herself on him in a classic tantric asana, her hair cascading like radiant beams.

Humbled at the perceived invitation, I dared not interrupt this spectacular union, remembering only a fragment of Joyce.

"She yielded to him,

radiant, warm and lavish-limbed,

enfolded him like a shining cloud…"

Concentric rings of unearthly light radiated outward from her, each inscribed with sutras and prayers and commandments across the religions.

She turned to face me now, almost motionless, riding above him in sustained tension, arms sweeping overhead, fingers dropping her hair in a scintillating halo. She clasped her hands behind her head, elbows forward, breathless, hips ever more urgent. Her breasts stiffened, erect in their white elegance, her rose circles blooming.

One could hear in the far sea the booming of great manta rays, their flat bellies and tons of weight slapping the surface of the waters.

In the starlight, she now was of the moon. She had a startling silkiness, with skin of cream and hair of silver. Her passion was in many languages, her voices thickening. Between gasps of adorations, they moved into each other with quiet, attentive force, as priests to the mystery.

She became the Night Witch and savior of skies, the flaming ignitions at Peenemünde, the groaning at Salon Kitty, her husking cries piercing the luminous and grandiose silence. One foot was off the bed and clenched, rising and falling hypnotically. A lightning conductor between God and man, she began a quavering coloratura chant, now with a tremulous shyness, now ardent, now involuntary and wholly indecent.

Her body was timid then uncontrollable and wild, like a virgin in the throes of love. She was abundantly female, as the Thracian goddess Cotys, worshipped in orgiastic rites. She and Magenta began a low moaning invocation, an invitation to sup at their fount.

I alone suffered the parched soul of mutual desires, and thought of Aeschylus beholding the sacred orgies.

"…and the roar of a terrible bull-like note keeps time,

from some invisible throat;

while a drum beats with fearful sound.

Like the voice of a thunderclap

underground."

I was near the center of a sensual whirlpool, their naked figures in paroxysms, their paradise profaned by love. The far squalls at sea themselves were mounting, the powers of a distant gale seemed forbidding, as lightning rippled under violent, running clouds. The weather was hot, crazed, destroying and creating. Heavy coconuts began to loosen and plunge, filmy draperies writhed, the waves in all directions debauched.

I too was torn, shivering, alive only by the warmth from their distant burning sun. I watched as they kneeled lasciviously before each other in utter devotion, then before Eros enthroned in their flesh, then skyward. Their salacious rite had the slow rhythm of a Gnostic initiation. The rapturous sea of love and lust opened its theatric doors.

She was a changeling with endless forms: a slave, a concubine, a Parisian doll before her lord and master, then a tyrannous Amazon as he wept under the cruelty of her nails. Mounted on him, she at last lifted her eyes and – for unbearable moments – showed me the infinity within. She suddenly seized, her frantic abdomen and teats and every sinew etched in lines of magnetic force, her face now the Godhead, her eyes emerald, then aquamarine, then white as alabaster as she consulted the hands of Grace above, and the fiery river beneath.

They were in a delirium of the most exalted devotion. With such knowledge, they could be with no other. I bowed in reverence and withdrew to my room, to the cold isolation from what might have been. After a time, I heard her singing; it was the most exquisite lullaby, in an indefinable language, as if for a lost child in another world.

IN THE MORNING, only the sounds of ceaseless waves remained, and a great light off the far and calming waters. I knew that they had gone. I didn't bother to check the registry.

Yet in the spare, lightly furnished suite – with its thin white curtains drifting with the open air, and its long balcony with majestic views of the sunlit Pacific – had appeared a service cart. It had white linen, fresh juices and fruits, *pan dulce*, and a purple vase of white lilies.

Filled with so many thoughts of the night, but barren with loss, I showered for a long while then dressed. I poured a glass of papaya juice and considered at length the sea's restless tranquility. Against the vase of lilies was a small envelope.

The note within was in a child's awkward and fragile hand, in pencil on smudged, lined paper. There was a photograph of a little girl with a big smile, standing all alone, quite small against a giant banyan tree. She had white, straight teeth just emerging, and wore a blue sari. I noticed her argyle sock on one foot, and a Hello Kitty sock on the other. She clutched a primer, and her eyes laughed. She wore angel wings, and a furry white halo. The note was simple, more precious than diamond.

I am angel now.

Love, Abeer.

◯

MY HEART AWOKE. I thought of where he still might be. Rushing into the brilliant morning, I took a crowded jitney down the palmed avenida into the outskirts of Acapulco. I passed decaying pink churches, some with bells long silenced, others with formidable matrons in black kneeling on their steps. Doleful street vendors of glazed ices looked on, with their faded, curled pictures of Christ. One church, between dubious alleys and garish narcotrafficante shrines, stood vacant and hopeless in the tepid morning shade.

There was even a Maria, cross-legged on a dirty blanket in the squalid chaos, one armed extended and hand open, the other protecting an infant. She was surrounded by two snarling dogs, and the hectoring cries of heroin dealers and users. Some subjected her to pitiless ridicule; others ignored her with impervious coldness.

Desolate among these obscure quarrels, she remained torpid as the filthy tides which crept past the seawall to and from these destroyed blocks. She had the face of an abused Madonna. Her diffident hopes were faint, but not her mortal ache. For her, all life's pleasure had been annulled; she was possessed of the despair that lacerates. Close by, an elderly prostitute looked upon the scene, her countenance scarred like the face of misery by eternal ravines. She shuffled away past the open sewage and through the smoke of burning trash.

I moved on to the empty church, with its ghosts of parishioners that never came, where I saw peeling walls with sacred renditions of the living presence from which I had just turned away. Walking back, I saw Magenta for the last time.

He was crouched over the Maria, while in lucid intervals from the maltreatment and anguish she comforted her baby. She seemed to be crying.

At the edge of the tattered, soiled cloth swaddling her newborn, barely visible just for seconds, was the slightest edge of the Celine clutch. Magenta stood by her like a benevolent spirit above the blood of innocents, as if plucking them from the gutter. He was offering a Tibetan prayer. The phrases were unknown to her, but not their meaning.

Perhaps the hope of the Six could be described in the last words I heard Magenta say. It was a blessing in French to the Maria and her sleeping child, with chaste kisses on their foreheads, as if they were his own.

"Que Dieu garde, ma fille."
(God protect you, my child)

Chapter 20.

Beneath the Veil

The Afghans are so crooked that when they die, you don't bury them,
you just screw them into the ground.

- Howard Hart, CIA Station Chief in Kabul

"Covert action," Casey once said, "has only one rule: 'Don't get caught.
If you do, don't admit it.'"

- Robert Woodward, *VEIL: The Secret Wars of the CIA*

Pickle, pickle, pickle.

- B-52 radio call to bomb Afghanistan

IT WAS TIME to intercept Dostum on his first visit to America, fresh from his miserable last stand in the ferocity of hand-to-hand combat near Mazar. I paced back and forth beneath the flags of 170 nations in the State Department lobby as courteous uniformed security staff attended computers – those to which intelligence analysts issued advisories on visitors.

It first seemed to be merely another undistinguished, mid-fifties 7-story office building in Washington, D.C., but through the heavy glass doors embossed with the seal of the United States lay the policy center of the earth's current superpower. Upon entering these halls, one became absorbed – not into some fearsome and cold bureaucracy – but into a fraternity of talented career diplomats who surprisingly were quite welcoming. One suddenly was on the inside of the intelligence and policy apparatus of the New World Order – at least once across the barrier – although I had a vestigial consciousness of shattered children's bodies as collateral damage from Blackhawk cannons and Predator drones, and of crops and then families withering from poison rain.

All were regrettable and officially unintended but perhaps necessary outcomes, thankfully distant from the quiet scribbling of signatures on checks and treaties after many handshakes and phone calls in the paneled offices at State. Such distracting thoughts often were banished from the minds of diplomats as the doors closed at the end of the day, for all sins were forgiven before dinner for those who served the national security interests of the United States.

⬡

DOSTUM – short, portly and lethal – descended from his limousine at the State Department *porte-cochère* on the appointed hour, together with his eclectic entourage of God-intoxicated mullahs and

Uzbek and Hazara commanders, all accompanied by one boyish mass-murderer of note. The tide of Dostum's men, the flotsam of foreign and unsettling moralities, began offering their own documents, presenting dubious credentials from a country close to the edge of extinction, their passports invisibly stained with opium and blood.

Fatigued but wearing an expensive ill-fitted suit, this warlord whose photograph was in every home and shop in Northern Afghanistan attracted not the slightest notice from American passersby. To those unaware of his absolute command on the ground in last non-Taliban areas, he could be mistaken for the manager of a Soviet tractor pavilion in Kyrgyzstan.

Among Dostum's group was his confidante Akbar J, a saturnine, charming Afghan national now a resident U.S. citizen. To untutored Americans he seemed obsequious to Dostum, but wisely so to Afghans who recalled the General's penchant for dismemberment of those who became afoul of his trust. Attah Mohammed Noor – a grey-bearded mullah in robes – rushed forward to take both my hands with a fervent *As Salaam Alaikum*. Reciting earnest incantations in Dari, he intently nodded, wide-eyed, in elaborate Islamic religious greetings.

Another was the silent yet polite General Naji Mohammed Mohaqeq, leader of the Hazara tribes, the Asiatic population oppressed throughout Afghanistan. But the last was a cocky, thin, dark and otherwise unmemorable thirty-year-old, the smiling and terrible Malik Khan Pehlwan. He limply shook my hand, blithely offering cash subsidies to help him secure a *pied-à-terre* close by the Hill, for he was immersed in a fantasy of repeated visits to D.C. and its nocturnal pleasures.

Roberta Chew appeared from the Pakistan, Afghanistan and Bangladesh section of South Asian Affairs, to lead us through the maze of halls within the State Department. We entered into the office staff suites of Robin Raphel, the Assistant Secretary of State for South Asia, who oversaw primarily Pakistani and far lesser Afghan matters.

Afghanistan after the Soviet withdrawal was of little consequence, having reverted to collections of rude brigands and fractious tribes. Its ancient nobilities had fallen into dissolute piracy. Brandishing aging but still effective U.S. and Chinese weapons, they fought each other relentlessly among rusted Soviet tanks and downed aircraft and the fleeing families of Kabul.

Hopeful for at least a diplomatic if not warm reception, Dostum and his men found themselves crowded into a small, dreary antechamber. I stood at the doorway, continually checking for Raphel's approach, only to turn and suddenly encounter her close by, her arms akimbo, her blue eyes stern and clearly unfriendly at Dostum's presence.

Raphel had little tolerance for unruly, corrupted warlords from the region. Dostum in turn was quite aware Raphel recently had lost her beloved husband – the late Ambassador to Pakistan – in an unexplained mid-air explosion in an aircraft that also carried Pak General Zia, who had assisted with the Stinger program. She stared coldly at the group.

I quickly made the semblance of introductions. Dostum, in a profusion of obeisances, offered her a fine Badakhshan rug. It was accepted and handed to a staffer, while a few perfunctory statements were exchanged at this decidedly hostile standoff.

Dostum spied a weaving tacked on the wall in Raphel's staff offices depicting a *bushkashi* game, where the headless carcass of a goat was struck toward goals by frolicking teams of horsemen in a form of medieval polo. Off balance, he tried to lighten the moment.

"The Taliban can never take the North," he hopefully proposed, "because they do not play *bushkashi*."

Dead expressions all around. Complete silence. Dostum was hustled off to his limousine, already late for his public speech at the Carnegie Endowment for International Peace. There he would make the last plea for American aid by confronting over 200 high-level attendees – in essence every bureaucrat in D.C. with any equity left in preventing the surrender to the Taliban of the remains of the legitimate Afghan government. Dostum, together with Mohaqeq and the warlord Massoud, controlled the last small section of Northern Afghanistan.

⬡

WALKING with a brisk but friendly officiousness offset by my single black suit and inherently preoccupied air, I simply cruised past the security staff at the Carnegie Endowment. The room where Dostum already was holding forth in Dari was packed with invitation-only officialdom. He faced a stony constellation of Beltway Afghan players – all old hands in the Great Game – from clusters of CIA, State and DOD analysts to astute, seasoned and incredulous regional diplomats and embassy officials. They included not only a plethora of nameless spooks, but also members of the National Security Council and the British Foreign Office; the former ambassadors to Pakistan and Bangladesh, and the Ambassador from Turkey. Sultan Ghazi looked on as the representative of 90-year-old Zahir Shah, the King of Afghanistan exiled at the age of 20 to his Italian palazzo.

Dostum's translator was the respectable Akbar J, speaking in tones much too deferential for the Hill. A call went out for a substitute. The new medium – Malekia – was a studious young Afghan woman with thin gold-rimmed round glasses, long black hair and a ready smile, but she was the daughter of aides close to Burhanuddin Rabbani, Dostum's fiercely genteel political rival. As she began a different spin on Dostum's words, he lost his pace but managed to recover his delivery if not his confidence.

With his few thousands of troops cornered into a limited area around Mazar-i-Sharif by the Taliban, the General pled for American intervention to prevent the fall of the nation. Weary of decades of bloodbaths from contentious warlords, even U.S. officials beyond Raphel assumed the Taliban were earnest religious students who could ensure peace by binding divisive tribes together under the banner of Islam. Many regarded Dostum as merely an ex-Soviet pawn on his way out, a heroin trafficker and money launderer who had reduced sections of Kabul to rubble.

As Dostum finished, a frenzy of incisive questions began. Four CIA employees in the back row abruptly stood, rumpled and in shirtsleeves. One opened with a pointed question.

"What is the source of your *funds*?"

No longer facing wizened, turbaned tribal elders predisposed to allegiance to this illiterate strongman, but confronting the cream of D.C. analysts with decades of electronic dossiers at their fingertips, Dostum faltered.

"*Emeralds*," he announced, "a hoard of emeralds. And currencies seized during the fighting in Kabul."

Dostum blinked, as an almost subliminal sigh collectively passed among the listeners. Everyone knew Dostum's money came from tributes from heroin traffickers exporting through his fields of command, together with weapons, smuggled trucks and household goods to keep up appearances. During the ricocheting murmurs, I privately recalled that crystallized morphine sometimes had the luster of dark green jewels. Financial structures and promises tended to dissolve in war zones – the 30 or so Stinger missiles he secreted away from CIA might yield $400,000 each for his coffers from terrorists, or be a trading chip for U.S. concessions, but still could be bartered for Akbar Bey's release.

Robin Raphel walked by with a little exchange, then disappeared into the enigmatic blend of unspoken agendas. Onlookers watched as Dostum was being laughed out of Washington, seemingly just another pudgy Middle Eastern demigod and unhesitating killer who came as yet one more unlikely applicant for Pentagon approval. His warnings seemed absurd that day, as he vowed that the intensely religious Taliban would prove to be disastrous. Central Asia researchers later would agree that the rejection of Dostum at the Carnegie meeting led directly to the rise of al-Qaida in Afghanistan and the destruction of the World Trade Center. The best intel analysts in D.C. were wrong. Dostum – who could not even read – was right.

◯

AS THE CARNEGIE CONFERENCE dispersed with hushed conversations, the CIA group to Langley and State officials to C Street, Dostum and Akbar J retreated to a small adjacent reception room hosting a towering display of canapés. Perhaps there were ten people in the room. With a consoling levity I offered that his talk had been well-received as he, drink in hand, bleakly awaited approaches that never came. While chatting with the personable Sig Harrison, the leading Afghan scholar, I was approached by former DOD official Michael Pillsbury, then a senior Fellow at the mysterious Atlantic Council.

Pillsbury, who in his tailored brown suit looked like Eisenhower at 5' 9", was a well-born conservative with a PhD in Chinese history from Columbia and fluent in Mandarin. He had been the Pentagon's Deputy Undersecretary overseeing covert programs, and almost single-handedly pushed the Stinger program through Congress. Pillsbury was cleared for VEIL – the compartmentalized system for non-routine use of CIA overseas, and also the ultra-secret Planning and Coordination Group. Both involved only a handful of officials at CIA, DOD, NSA and the Office of the President. In a Kennedy School case study on the Stinger Program, Pillsbury later admitted the limitless insularity of the clandestine services.

"The charmers in the covert action business are a club within a club."

Regarded as a foreign policy Machiavelli, at first he had failed to obtain approval for the Stinger deployment from the National Security Council, which was mired over concerns that an errant American missile in jihadist hands might lock onto the heat signature of a fully-loaded 747 leaving an international airport. Undaunted, he had flown Senators to Pakistan to lobby General Zia to distribute the Stingers to the mujahidin. After Zia agreed, Pillsbury then helped bury CIA concerns about plausible deniability of U.S. involvement. An all-woman workforce in El Segundo and Pomona, California began assembling a stream of the shoulder-fired rockets – each clearly labeled "General Dynamics" – beneath a large factory sign with a succinct motto.

"If it flies, it dies."

Some analysts from State were peeking into the Carnegie reception room but not approaching. The ravishing Ena Susi – editor of *The Diplomat* – passed by, along with her decades of mental archives on the intrigues of embassies and agencies. Viewed as a man with a long and honorable history of covert actions, Pillsbury hovered nearby. I stood with Dostum and Akbar J, assuring them of the favorable undercurrents in the audience, but they could see there were no smiles or supportive handshakes. Pillsbury – inferring I had Dostum's ear and uncertain of my lineage – asked me to invite Dostum to lunch at the Pentagon the following day. Presenting my Harvard credentials to Pillsbury, I did so, securing an invitation as well.

◯

INVESTING IN A TOWNCAR and driver for the day, I collected Maiwandi, the personable Dari/Pashto translator from the Voice of America. A friendly and educated Afghan woman with a buoyant countenance, Maiwandi had attracted my notice at the Carnegie meeting by her name, for Maiwand was the site of the worst British defeat in Asian history – during the Second Anglo-Afghan War – where the legendary heroine Malalai rallied Afghans by waiving her veil as the standard, before being cut down by British marksmen.

I planned to employ CIA's concerns about lost Stingers, even those retained in caves by Dostum, to secure Akbar Bey's release. CIA's Stinger Recovery Program sought to reacquire the many hundreds of missiles, any one of which could destroy a commercial aircraft and all its passengers. The bargain of Akbar Bey's life for the Stingers would have to be made while dining with Pillsbury, who had first unleashed the firestorm of heat-seeking weapons.

Maiwandi and I approached the North Entrance to the Pentagon, where Pillsbury waved us through security. Encountering Dostum and his translator General Payanda after their DOD interview, we repaired to the Pentagon dining room, where diversely uniformed, multilingual military officials from Omsk to Krakow to Spitsbergen were lunching on unremarkable meals served efficiently on green tablecloths.

French Officers with tall visored *capets* mingled with Ghurkas from Nepal, or discussed Pentagon business with British commanders from Hong Kong to the Falklands. Decorated German officials from the new Bundeswehr sat among odd sorts from the Gebirgsjäger, or mountain division. Decommissioned intelligence personnel from OMON confronted Russian Spetsnaz Special Forces as Mossad operatives whispered to outsourced contractors.

Among these diverse warfighters, it was the sprinkling of pale, hardly noticeable desk-bound analysts whom I found of greatest interest. Alumni of the ultra-secret Israeli cryptology Unit 8200, they posed even greater threats to clandestine state or rogue actors. I began to think of Cobalt, who engaged such dense, covert intel groups as a lifestyle. The annual conference on surveillance for contractors and federal agencies – the Wiretapper's Ball – was occurring right across the river at Crystal City; I wondered if Cobalt was there, or here.

Pleasantries dispensed, Dostum immediately arrived at his point; he needed weapons and U.S. assistance, or Afghanistan would be lost within weeks to the Taliban. He made a last attempt.

"We ask that the United States open a consulate in Mazar-i-Sharif."

This unlikely scenario, to plant an American flag on Afghan soil in recognition of the tatters of the Afghan government, seemed at that moment only a desperate fiction. Pillsbury was forced to hedge by circumstance. He reasonably suggested a grass-roots petition by Afghans supporting a U.S. presence, but the fall of Afghanistan was imminent, a matter of weeks.

The plea of an obscure Uzbek tribal leader – about to be exiled – meant nothing. Dostum's power was fading, his poorly equipped troops effectively were defeated, his absolute knowledge on the ground in Afghanistan was merely that of one of "our sons of bitches," now so easily discarded as a hindrance and embarrassment to U.S. interests.

There was no desert. Pillsbury provided a desultory tour for Dostum, Payanda, Maiwandi and me – circumambulating the Army, Air Force, Coast Guard, and Marines facets of the Pentagon's outer rings, some with their memorabilia dating back past the Revolution. I could only recall the clicking of Magenta's staff at Bodhinath. We concluded at the interior entry to the Joint Chiefs and the networks media room with its lectern and Pentagon seal. Afterward, our failed little group finally stood on the steps of the Pentagon and awaited our driver.

"Why didn't you ask Pillsbury or Raphel or DOD," I hopefully inquired through Maiwandi, "about trading the Stingers for Akbar Bey?"

He looked up at me and made a final admission with a frank irony, having sanitized the realities of drug export in an inspired effort to secure American support.

"I needed to distance myself from heroin traffickers."

Dostum had sealed Akbar Bey's fate.

◯

DOSTUM RETREATED to New York to receive Afghan families. While his troops huddled in meager camps and ditches about Mazar in imminent danger of being massacred by the Taliban, Dostum and Payanda found succor in a lavish marble site on the 40th floor of the New York Four Seasons Hotel. With dwindling hope for Akbar Bey, but with concern about Taliban domination, I entered the cool, expensive confines of the Four Seasons shining lobby, walking past subdued fountains and millimeter-thin waterfalls, a setting designed to extract exorbitant sums from those who imagined themselves king for a day.

In the royal surroundings of his suite, Dostum sat defeated, chagrinned from his glacial reception at State, his failure at the Pentagon, and his public outing before CIA and DOD at the Carnegie meeting. At best, he might one day receive a trivial CIA pension and periodic monitoring typical of America's retirement plan for regional strongmen who had been part-time assets. I thought it timely to propose one last method of engaging federal agencies' attention.

Seated across from Dostum while General Payanda translated, we shared a last cup of tea in the traditional Afghan manner. Remembering Akbar Bey's desperate family in Kabul, and the gift of a bicycle for his small son, I ruefully pushed a small envelope with some modest cash savings for them across a side table worth more than all my possessions. Perhaps this human gesture made Dostum more receptive, for there was a feeling of an opportunity that might never rise again.

"But there is another way out," I proposed, "for Akbar Bey and for you. The Taliban control heroin traffic out of Kandahar, and finance terroristic activities. You don't have to kill the Taliban leadership; you can just have high-level officials detained at international borders. Not your people. Their people."

"Is this possible?"

"You would have to meet with many State officials, and be interviewed by concerned analysts."

"I can do that. How can we begin?"

"The ASecState will want to meet you," I opined, only an assumption then.

After a few iterations on the scenario, and Dostum's reassurance he was eager to retain an operational relationship with American decision-makers, I asked him not to forget to deliver this paltry cash hoard to Akbar Bey's family. With a farewell to the Generals in the Afghan manner – a hand across the heart – I walked across the brilliant marble floor of the suite, and bowed out at the door, closing it in the monastic way.

Passing through the lobby, beyond the waterfalls and out into the cacophonous, dirty freedom of New York streets, I felt the promise of what might be: a settled Afghanistan with new schools and medical clinics and children with both their legs. Spirits still high with the boldness of Dostum's efforts, I remembered dourly that midterms at Harvard were just ahead, and I was very much behind.

Driven to JFK by a turbaned Sikh, I glimpsed through the rear window a last view of New York's gleaming corridors and the very emblem of benign globalization of the world's affluence – one day to be shared with a rising Central Asia and Afghanistan. Many floors above Dostum's suite, the twin towers of the Word Trade Center rose majestically, proud and free on a cloudless spring afternoon. Monoliths imperturbable as the Pyramids, for a moment their heights seemed to vanish into the sky.

⬡

IN CAMBRIDGE, students were adrift from lectures as the bells of venerable Lowell and Winthrop Houses chimed. While making explanations to faculty for several missed lectures, I began collecting signatures faxed from Afghan families in New York, petitioning for a consulate in Mazar. The effort was short-lived, for few government personnel supported Dostum – the Taliban were considered stabilizing. Conversation with the intrepid Pillsbury in D.C. soon devolved into reveries on his favorite basset hound.

At the Kennedy School I faxed the ASecState – thanking him for his sponsorship in Moscow – but included a document summarizing Dostum's stunning proposal. On the cover page was a handwritten note:

Do you want to act on this?

Although the ASecState had a significant interest in Dostum, he was overseas – having just been appointed as envoy to the Bosnian accords. Dostum's prescient offer to dismantle the Taliban leadership became a mere slip of paper, unread and seemingly inconsequential, buried in the forgotten stacks at State. It was trivial before the unassailable power of America, an unreachable shore for a few men whose only weapons were faith, cunning and madness.

Disheartened, I received an anguished call from Akbar Bey, and patched him through to Dostum's satellite phone, just as the Taliban were beginning their final offensive on Mazar-i-Sharif. Taunting the fathers and husbands of Mazar from across the trenches, the Taliban were brandishing their knives, clutching their genitals, and howling all through the nights.

"Wash up your women."

In a complex bout of fidelity and treachery in the fury around Mazar, Dostum's nefarious commander Malik Khan – who at State had sought a D.C. hideaway for imagined assignations – pretended to Taliban leaders to arrange the surrender of Dostum's troops for a $2 million dollar bribe. The Taliban were invited into Mazar where Dostum's men had sworn to give up their arms. At the last minute, General Mohaqiq – another of the visitors at State – organized a Hazara uprising and joined with Dostum's warriors. Over 6000 Taliban were encircled and slaughtered. Akbar, frantic, translated on a call to Dostum.

"They are throwing them down wells and killing them with machine guns…"

In one of Malik Khan's favorite ploys, his troops suffocated the captured Taliban *en masse* in cargo containers. But during the weeks of calls to Dostum from Akbar Bey, the Taliban main force regrouped and finally seized Mazar, forcing Dostum to flee overland with a few hundred men to

Tashkent. He reappeared in Istanbul with his wives and fifty bodyguards. The Taliban now controlled all of Afghanistan.

As the United States – and major oil companies – began to court the preferred new regime, Dostum and his inconvenient warnings were forgotten. At a loss then on how to proceed, I placed the many recordings of the pleas of Dostum and Akbar Bey into a folder, closing the file with a sad, long bow. I turned toward the last term, to interests ranging from novel drugs to the extent of opium production in Thailand, and – for so long only a bright dream – to the Harvard commencement.

Akbar Bey's young son precariously rode his new bicycle through the devastation of Kabul, as his mother submitted to any Talib, and his father railed against prison bars. Dostum, now powerless in Turkey, was for several years marginalized as inconsequential.

Within a few years, CIA helicoptered Dostum to a mountaintop overlooking Mazar, paid him ten million dollars in cash to subsidize thousands of troops, provided him with forward air control teams to coordinate B-52 airstrikes on Taliban positions, and supported Dostum's men on horses and mules and tanks as they fought down the Shamali Plains to seize Kabul. The demon Dostum knew, far better than we, had destroyed parts of New York, the World Trade Towers, the Pentagon, and the American soul.

V

The Machinery of Night

The performance of it is furtive, even clandestine, and its adepts do not speak of it.

- JLB, "The Cult of the Phoenix"

…angel-headed hipsters burning
for the ancient heavenly connection
to the starry dynamo
in the machinery of night.

- Ginsberg, *Howl*

The nymphs of the rivers,
the moist, grieving Echo.

- Cervantes, *Quixote* XXVI

Chapter 21.

Lucifer in Starlight

Travelers from the great spaces
when you see a girl
twisting in sumptuous hands
the vast blackness of her hair
and when moreover
you see
near a dark baker's
a horse lying near death
by these signs you will know
that you have come among men.

- Jean Follain *Transparence of the World*
(trans. W.S. Merwin)

Monks, I owned three palaces,
one for summer, one for winter and one for rainy season.
During all four months of the rains I remained inside the monsoon palace,
never passing the door.
Everywhere I was accompanied by courtesans
who danced and played music, sang and
looked on my pleasure without end.

- Siddhartha Gautama

Mystics invoke a rose, a kiss, a bird that is all birds,
a sun that is all suns and yet all stars,
a goatskin filled with wine, a garden or the sexual act.
None of these metaphors will serve for that long night of celebration
that took us to the very edge of day.

- JLB, *The Congress*

THE AIRPORT OF BANGKOK – or *Kreung Thep*, the city of angels – is overrun with teams of watchers from the French *Deuxième* to District Eight of the Royal Thai Police Force. All *farangs* or foreigners are suspect either of political or erotic perversities tolerated in modern Siam. In an unyielding plain of mauve jungle concealing 11 million Thai, Bangkok is punctuated by the golden needles of ancient Buddhist shrines and isolated glass skyscrapers that extend to the horizons. The girls of North West hill tribe long houses – their first shoes fluorescent stiletto heels – are asleep in air conditioned warrens under the blank, hot sky.

The only car in the muggy, fatigued airport dawn is a white Mercedes, beside which a thin, nut-brown Thai man bows to me, hands together in a *wai*, or blessing. I return the *wai* – used by all Thai for every greeting and farewell – for this country is a vast temple of monks and nuns and neon and cobras and schoolgirl whores and elephants in the streets and vendors of roasted insects. Its gentle people have a delicacy beside which Westerners appear as pale, ugly, warlike giants with the erotic sensitivity of dead coral.

We pass food stalls, aged tribal women sweeping empty sex cafés, and refined girls from Udon Thani in blue silk whose presence defines feminine beauty. We see the smoky fires and lean-tos of H'mong squatters and upcountry refugees under the Chao Phraya bridge, and strung-out *yaa-baa* dealers on motorbikes before meth burnout crashes them into careless graves. Barefoot young monks in saffron robes glance at newspaper headlines announcing the death of a priest. We cross before the barriers and razor wire of the American Embassy on Wireless Road, with their horney Marines having the Thai girlfriend experience for 50 American dollars a week, even though some of their paramours are *Katoeys*, or ladyboys, that trekked the porous borders from Cambodia, Laos, and Burma to leave their manhood sliced in a bucket.

◯

WE ARE JAMMED in traffic on Ratchada strip – the Bangkok Las Vegas with its gaming parlors – then turn onto Kaoshan Road. Young students – boy and girls in their gap years with backpacks and idealism – consider Thai sticks and the Samutprakhan crocodile farm, the Pattaya Beach sex district, and spicy deep-fried tofu with papayas. We are far from my hotel, and I grow nettled. I have only a few days to find my way to remote Chiang Rai near the Golden Triangle, hoping to crash an official conference on the heroin trade, where the American president's wife might speak.

My driver reassures me with an earnest *wai*. Through a blast of humid heat and into the crisp, cool Mercedes – with a pardon in French and excellent Thai – abruptly enters an elegant, wiry man in tropical whites, small round purple shades, and fine Panama hat. It is the time of roses in Bangkok, the season of joy, and it is Vermilion.

"We have almost a week together," he said, "an absence surely unnoticed by your colleagues, given the exotic circumstances. Game?"

My alluring memory of the Berlin night is reawakened by the specter of living with Vermilion and his consorts quite intimately, lost in the South East Asian heat and the evenings of Persian lilac and whirling bedrooms and the silhouettes of goddesses.

◯

ON THE FAR OUTSKIRTS of Bangkok, through clumps of steaming bamboo, we enter a rutted dirt road into heavy jungle. Our driver waits as two *tuk-tuk* cyclists pedal us on shrouded rickshaws miles deeper into thickets of tropical foliage. We finally proceed by foot down a precarious, narrow trail until we hear the single striking tone of a bell, then the soft singing of children. We enter into an opening, where an elderly Thai nun bows and walks meditatively to a far circle of cloaked figures. Small brown children in rags are gathered, smiling or in awe of two black-robed nuns.

The nuns sit erect, cross-legged on woven palm mats in the Zen tradition, singing nursery rhymes and simple hymns in poignant musical Thai with the black-haired children. Their songs have a lightness of heart, like the hand of simple peace, placed gently upon the fevered brows of those seeking refuge from the venality of Bangkok's grim procurers. We are in a forest monastery of the Thai Vipassana monk Ajahn Chah, where the practice is meditation on *metta*, or loving kindness.

In this anodyne atmosphere, where cruelty is banished, we see the nuns walk in slow meditation by clicking palmettos, the children behind them now like ducklings, all with hands folded and chanting in Pali the ancient sutras. The boys and girls, mostly H'mong or Lao, bow and take their bowls to the old nun, who ladles out noodle soup and bamboo shoots. With long embraces to the little ones, the other two nuns depart. A small girl rushes to them and tries to kiss the edge of their robes. They walk to us, their black robes swaying, their eyes down. Chanting prayers in Pali, they carefully place each bare foot on the jungle trail. They bow to us, and lift their cowls.

They have just ended a three-month practice period without electricity or running water, but with arduous early rising and intensive meditation and wood cutting, water bringing, and care of child refugees orphaned from opium addiction, alcoholism, AIDS, sexual abuse and abandonment. The nuns' hair and eyebrows are dyed black. They wear brown contact lenses. Their faces, necks, arms and feet are darkened by mud. It is V-1 and V-2, somber, divine.

⬡

WE PAD DOWN the trail to confront two startled *tuk-tuk* drivers, whereupon our teetering cyclists bring us to the Mercedes. As we flow through the fractured prism of Bangkok, V-1 and V-2 stare in compassion and revulsion at the sleazy, even barbaric cafés. The air is scented with aromatic foods, sweetmeats and diesel fuel, while tattered palms crackle in the spring wind. We walk through crowds of Thai, Khmer, and Malaysians gathered around rows of rude food stalls. A street vendor – seeing the drawn, destitute and holy V-1 and V-2 – gains merits by offering bowls of spicy cashew nut salad, thin rice noodles, and dipping sauces. His leathery hands sprinkle fried peanuts, chipped ginger, pepper, bits of lime, and curries. He refuses payment, and bows with a *wai*.

As we trail V-1 and V-2 into the lavish high-rise of the Dusit Thani Hotel on the Chao Phraya river, the flint-eyed security staff in their stiff tailored suits – all wearing thick dark glasses and ear buds – bow to the simple nuns they assume are seeking alms.

In the four-bedroom suite overlooking the river, V-1 and V-2 silently disappear to fold their robes and bathe.

"We are here to ground ourselves, after completing a psychedelic synthesis," Vermilion confides, "and for a special operation. Of course, the usual allures of Bangkok – for us – provide only opportunities for teaching."

He is aware of my nights in Amsterdam with Indigo. "You mean the sex trade?"

"We think of it as Tibetans do – the desire for union with the Godhead, too frequently torturously misdirected. Just for you tonight, though, a visit to the notorious Pat Pong area."

"How does Pat Pong differ from the Oudezijds Voorburgwal, the Red Light district in Amsterdam?"

"The spirit is more *malevolent* here," he replies to my concern, "closer to the surface, with manifestations not seen in the West."

We share sparkling juices on the balconies, observing the patternless cloudscapes. The sky is darkening; there is an incoming tide of mystical evening light. Rooster-tailed long boats pass slowly down the river under the ornate towers of the Grand Palace. Below, among the scattered novelties, the raucous flesh trades begin to be plied, while the river itself sweats with the scent of stale jasmine.

V-1 and V-2 appear in simple kimonos, freshened, their eyes sorrowful, fathomless from days encompassing naked children with easily treatable diseases and injuries, and now crystal and silver decanters and mint-green percale sheets. We descend to a rough pier where a ferryman sees us across the black marble water with its inky reflections of magical golden temples. Flocks of doves like clouds of platinum and topaz weave above us. V-1 and V-2 contemplate the river's swirling passage, while the sunset breaks open like a rose.

○

WE DISEMBARK at a lush bamboo hut with Thai woodcuts and fabrics, the hotel's massage retreat. We exchange *wais* with four strong, aged Cambodian refugee women. They have tough faces from the forgotten genocides of Pol Pot, but the kind eyes of survivors. They mistake us for the usual indulgent, uxorious couples. Two gather V-1 and me into a room with soft mats, where they gesture we should undress. I hurry with discretion into a light, loose cotton robe, but V-1 simply drops all her clothing and stands calmly, with perfect posture, her every muscle defined, utterly naked.

The masseuses, unaccustomed to bold *farang* women, are almost flirtatious as they titter in rural dialect. V-1's masseuse is blind, acutely sensitive to the body electric. They begin to pull our arms and legs, extending past the tension in the Thai manner, until I almost cry out. V-1 merely breathes, effortlessly allowing herself to be manipulated to extremes that cause the body workers to murmur about animal spirits, then the transcendent. It is as though they were children, tugging on their tolerant mother's hem. Their conversation becomes respectful, their voices lowered, then reverent. To them I am just another American male: tense, unconscious, and barely learning to release, but V-1 – with her magnificent radiance and evolved humility – confuses and fascinates them, stirring them like an erotic prayer.

After an hour – aching with soreness – I am wrung out, but bow and offer them payment in Thai *baht*. One leaves, but V-1's magnetism retains the blind woman, for to her secrets must be passed. V-1 – an exotic two meters of shining, white skin – somehow holds her unseeing gaze, then begins to chant softly in heartfelt tones of Pali memories from the old woman's childhood, when as a village girl she was instructed by nuns. In gratitude for her earnest, simple massage, V-1 shows her a spectrum of emotions through the wordless dimension of touch.

In a bold gesture, V-1 places her hand upon the woman's inner thigh, gripping her there until she shivers. She then slowly cups her *mons* in a most primitive way, like the insistent Cambodian males who grope rural women on foot paths or buses, or the Khmer Rouge in Phnom Penh before the rapes and killings. The masseuse flinches – almost faints – then recovers with tremulous shyness. V-1 tenderly moves her palm around the woman's belly, in elliptical orbits of the sun for each decade of her long life, in homage to the old woman's now dry wellspring. She moves along her ribcage to hold her flap of a breast, unashamed. She rests her hand above the old one's heart.

Singing in haunting Pali and perfect Thai, she presses her hand there with the rhythm of the heartbeat. After a long while, no longer balancing between heaven and hell, her patient's blind eyes soften and fill with trust. V-1 extends her fingertips so very slowly and lightly upon the woman's neck, sensing the very blood of her pulse, reading her every memory. She then touches her cheek with the most sublime adoration, like the tentative young lover long ago who still lived in the old woman's dreams. The touch is a beatific encounter, the blessing of a beloved child by her mother, the unforgettable caress of an angel.

The old masseuse – abused in her youth and now a pious woman of good faith – is led through the range of human feeling from fear to passion to glory. Taught this gentle art as a gift from a priestess, she begins crying and bowing, fingers interlaced in prayer as if before one awakened, a saint or arhat. V-1 in turn bows deeply to her, kisses her eyes, then guides the old one to the other waiting women. Mumuring devotions, they take her and bow to V-1 as though she were the most revered of teachers.

○

V-1 AND V-2, now a splendid pair in matching *rouge et noir* microskirts and high Armani heels, each with a thin silver necklace and a two-carat diamond that could only be paste, stride unrecognized through the Dusit Thani lobby past lavish arbors of forsythia and peach blossoms, followed by whispers and every eye.

I sit next to the driver, in front of V-1 and V-2 as they hold hands. The Mercedes windows reveal crowds of Thai laughing and *sabai* (feeling good) and *snuuk* (having fun), while elephants sway on street corners and drunken half-cast Vietnamese roar incomprehensible blasphemies. The polymorphous desires of the city reflect in swollen café mirrors, as the night burns ever more brightly. We move along walls of lurid iconography that spring up under pale moonlight, toward some confrontation with incorrigible hearts and minds, in this city of love and obscenity.

As we walk in the district, I notice a louche Khmer or Karen fighter in a checkered head cloth, crouched over a *Bangkok Post* and pretending to read. He has an ear of ironmongery. With reptilian cunning his one eye follows not the women, but Vermilion and me. There is a moment of galloping fear – the feeling he is a watcher – but I dismiss his unlikely attentions.

We cross Sukumvit junction into Soi 4, past the brothel hotels. At the Nana entertainment plaza in the center of Pat Pong, outside the big clubs Hollywood 2 and the Carousel, mama-sans provide cold Singha beer – with crunchy grasshoppers and fat grubs fried on a cluster of bright braziers. Laotian teenagers, dressed in tight pink latex schoolgirl outfits or bikinis, are all dancing to Thai rock over tinny loudspeakers as they tempt promiscuous males with their few words of English.

"Hansome man, I want go with yooooooouuuuuuu."

In a small, crude, open air bar in the Nana courtyard, below a picture of His Beloved Majesty the King, adolescent Mekong girls drink Kloster beers with "butterflies," or sex tourists. Cajoling them with vulgarities, they cut quick deals in Chinese dialects with Chui Chow bosses from Swatow, Pacific Rim businessmen, Sri Lankan pilots, and the occasional British and Russian ex-pats who frequent the thousands of bars in the side streets, or Sois.

As V-1 and V-2 engage several world-weary sixteen year-old girls named Nit-Nit, Noi, Nat and Kat, one threatening Khmer Rouge insists on buying the white women. V-2 abruptly quells his insolence with a particularly vulgar, loud and frightening six-birch expletive in flawless Thai. He quickly departs down another Soi, saving face with echoes of mad laughter from the idolatry of his dark gods.

A mama-san seats us in a broad booth at the Carousel, where V-1 and V-2 – the only women customers among lecherous and perspiring multinationals – are attracted to the long stage above the bar. Twenty tall, thin, naked tribal girls of fifteen or so move like restless, vacant automatons. Swaying aimlessly, their narrow hips twitch on *yaa-baa*, their taut brown nipples and flat bellies glowing purple with ultraviolet light. In luminous red and green, their backs are painted with fluorescent opium poppies.

They wear only G-strings and ionospheric heels rising into knee-length black latex boots stitched with the letters "O.K." Their dusky eyes are resigned, all shuffling for hours to a deafening continuous loop of Elvis Presley singing "Battle Hymn of the Republic." Each will go all night, in the sordid purlieu of tumbledown rooms in an adjacent brothel hotel, for 500 *baht* – fifteen dollars.

V-1, seized with aversion, summons one of the youngest girls. She gives her 5000 *baht*, and keeps her in the booth protectively – both with eyes lowered, heads together and never moving. V-1 embraces her in a long consolation, sharing the knowledge of women's suffering, holding the girl like the lost child she is.

Some of the dancers have eyes made up with kohl, and stand in corners behind colored glass panels that transform them into harlequins. They stagger uncertainly on unfamiliar heels, each taken standing for 200 *baht* by leering and corpulent one-time buyers. Other customers affect nonchalance, waiting in line to forsake bourgeois sensibilities for frantic adulterous enterprises. Some – not impelled by caprice or passing enthusiasms – are prone to less casual backsliding, preferring to rut nightly in the narrow upstairs cribs among the whips and needles. One bends to sniff the musky, perfumed thigh of a thin young Lao dancer, who is trembling violently from *yaa-baa* and moaning audibly from a near overdose.

Pressing *baht* into her cold hands, he turns her to the wall, considering her extreme stimulation as a gift to his prurient intentions.

"My word…I must say…for God's sake…ready?"

She manages to toss an arch look, but yields with filmy eyes. A rural Bangladeshi awaiting his turn rambles on with demeaning Victorian cockney allusions to "Tuppeny Uprights."

V-1, having had enough, slips away with her girl-child, buying her from the mama-san. At the exit, she makes a sign to a shaved-head American youth of twenty who has followed us into the Carousel, and who seems to know her. He gives every girl there 500 *baht* – a night's wages – bowing to each one with a respectful *wai*. In the ensuing and incredulous disarray, we all leave in haste.

○

WHILE V-1 DISAPPEARS with the girl down Soi Cowboy into the lizard nests of Pat Pong, Vermilion and V-2 and I travel across Bangkok on modern freeways above blocks of desolate slums. Their tin-roofed or thatched lean-tos have open sewers, lined with shaggy, untended tangerine trees thick with flowers and overpowering scents. Strange primeval creatures – legless Thai and opium addicts – roam under a blood-red new moon hanging in the forbidden sky like a gash.

We enter a twenty-story plain cement building with no windows, moving past bullet-proof glass and in secure elevators to an upscale industrial brothel. Through one-way glass we see masses of girls in their early teens – wearing silk cocktail dresses and gowns – all chattering hysterically or sitting in furious ennui. Exploited in a degenerate age, each has a foot-high number pinned to her back. Many have innocent faces, a few like imps from the underbelly of Paris, but all are veterans of at least ten men a day. Others are simple, stocky and dull, working animals fresh from muddy rice paddies. All remember to flash mechanical, queer, *art nouveau* smiles at the glass, behind which customers in their moral asphyxia choose among them like carp in a tank.

There are citron or bronze girls – Thai, H'mong, Khmer, Lao, Burmese – their pitiful glamour an intolerable bondage. A few earth-blue Negresses from the slums of Kuala Lumpur engage in trite conversations, while several Sudanese exhibit lascivious purple gums and tongues. Watching the girls beyond the mirrors, clusters of grotesque tourists – diabolists, every one – laugh and assay their prey.

Their spiritual impotency and unquenched grey flesh soon will grasp the supple, tender frailty of anesthetized youth.

V-2 chooses a very slim girl, among the youngest, who has a graceful form and an untamed glance. A squat gargoyle in a green suit, possessing an ominous suavity and a miserly frown, makes the arrangement. His eyes have no expression, save the wicked flicker of a wild boar.

Vermilion and I move past a series of couches before one-way mirrors, through which chambers can be viewed. One port opens onto two delicate Burmese girls, bending before a ribald pair of florid, porcine Chinese men. Nametags on cheap hanging jackets identify the customers as low-level workers from a rendering plant, an *abattoir* in Qing Dao. They grip the sweating girls' long black hair like reins. The girls' simple village faces are turned to us – heads moving to and fro like slow pistons – their half-feral eyes darting at first, then staring glassily for the longest while, then closing. Their frozen grimaces finally loosen, lips pouting as if the house liquor of absinthe finally has released them.

Seated in a private corner, we see an empty, white room with washable, enameled walls and a drain in the floor, illuminated by a bare single light bulb in a wire cage. There is a long, inclined board with bindings and restraints. I am stunned to see V-2 standing poised within, chanting softly in Pali. We can hear every sound through a vent. Her clothes are folded formally in a corner; she wears only the diamond necklace.

⬡

THE DOOR OPENS. The chosen girl enters, entirely naked, and facing away from the unknown client. She is Lao, with a slender olive form. Eyes closed, she begins gyrating lasciviously, tossing and whirling her long black satin hair, allowing it to cascade upon her narrow brown waist. Her hips are frantic, copulating the air. She carries a blaring radio in one hand, a large soapy natural sponge in the other. Putting the radio down and holding her ankles to exhibit her charms, she then stands and bolts the door.

Eyes still closed, she pretends to masturbate, yipping and shrieking to raucous Thai pop, her every gesture animated to excite, satisfy and quickly rid her room of the typical client. Her senses are scattered on *yaa-baa*, her gaiety the edge of madness. She humps invisible spirits and gasps, then turns and opens her eyes to view for the first time the inevitably intoxicated, rough brute who has rented her for an hour's fellatio. She drops the sponge.

V-2 bows to her with a devotional *wai*, then makes a blessing – not just in perfect Laotian, but in the girl's village dialect. The girl merely stares, her puffy, sullen mouth open, astonished.

V-2 commands her to turn off the radio. She does as she is told, thinking it a game, and affecting to be a naughty schoolgirl in penance. Her form is smooth, cleanly surfaced like dark opal; her burning eyes uncertain, her legs restless.

V-2 tells her this is the end of her great pain, the beginning of a new world. She leads the confused girl gently by the hand and reclines her standing against the board, facing us. She brushes the girl's hair from her eyes, spreads her long thin legs tenderly until she stands still and soft, unfolded like a velvet rind. V-2 cups her mount as V-1 did with the old masseuse.

The girl, assuming some perverse erotic theater, makes fake groaning noises and begins shaking her hips. Without removing her fingers, V-2 orders her to stop, then presses her lips against the girl's ear, and begins intoning the Pali sutras for healing. The girl grows fearful. V-2 strokes her intimately until she relaxes. She again feigns excitement. V-2 stops, reminding her not to pretend. The girl – a victim of thousands of calloused hands – simply freezes, letting this extraterrestrial white woman do whatever she wishes, but feeling nothing. She is, at first, unaware V-2 thinks her a wounded child. I know not how to describe the events that follow.

⬡

INCLINED ON THE BOARD and exposed completely, the girl is caught in a metaphysical quandary, at the frightening edge of a psychological cliff. She cannot deceive V-2. Her small tight breasts rise and fall in gasps of anticipation; her legs dance under the *yaa-baa* and V-2's insistent fingers. She is incapable of orgasm, entering the most crude prostitution at 14, as a poor illiterate village girl overcome by Bangkok neon, lurid new clothes and fraudulent affection. All men and women, no less than she, are objects to manipulate. She has the coldness of an arctic crevasse, her secret love and lust long buried in the glacial ice of hurt and despair. There she is pure and safe, and no one can ever find her.

Attentive to the most subtle recoil, V-2 synchronizes her hands and voice with every nuance of the girl's being: of her withdrawal or submission, of her gaming and disgust and fear, of her insensitivity and responsiveness, of her hunger. Carefully exploring her psyche, the unconscious realms glimpsed only in mythic dreams, she reads all the shades of feeling in the girl's bruised heart. No one has ever noticed her before, or the little girl within, forever needy and afraid. No one has ever waited for her desires. Not one deserves to witness her ecstatic innocence.

V-2 follows the girl's fleeing spirit with her fingertips, curling so lightly when she timidly returns, stopping when she runs with fright. She coaxes her thoughtfully, taming her slightly when she comes round, like feeding a wild beast bits of hot flesh. Inclined against the board with eyes closed, the girl suddenly tenses her abdomen, her knees bending. She is rising to the surface. V-2 ceases chanting in Pali, and begins singing a long poem from ancient women seers, the first slow phrases whispered in a deep, thrilling contralto English the girl does not comprehend.

> "I can count the sands,
> and I can measure the oceans.
> I have ears for the silent,
> and know what the dumb man meaneth."

As the erotic rite continues before us, I can not turn away. I quietly ask Vermilion for an explanation.

"It is what the Pythoness at Delphi said, answering in hexameter – before the Lydians even asked the question – as they entered the inner shrine of the oracle."

"But the girl doesn't understand."

"It is a formality with V-2, before she summons repressed memories from her patient. It is like St. Paul entering Greece, and encountering a slave girl – a damsel soothsayer – and commanding the spirit to come out of her."

As V-2 softly speaks, Vermilion translates the rural Thai. She regresses the girl to nights by a smoky fire pit in a flimsy, muddy hut in the highlands, when her drunken mother left and men she didn't know raped her at four. She speaks of the trance the little girl entered each dreadful night to escape the constant abuse, when the only warmth was from malevolent men who used her then cast her aside, and how her small child's heart knew it was wrong, and how she fed herself by pretending desire, and how no one ever cared.

V-2 speaks of the loneliest girl in the world, the yearning that never could be satisfied, the filth and squalor that replaced the sunlight of a pure child's radiant heart, and how one day the little girl's spirit hid from everyone, from that moment and forever after.

During V-2's soliloquy, the girl suddenly begins to contort her face, baring her teeth in hatred, eyes clenched to not see the horror. When she realizes she is with a client, she assumes her usual leer, and feigns sex with her hips.

V-2 speaks of the first hundred men, the first thousand, the village rags becoming harlot's dresses, her first shaky heels, the river of alcohol and opium, the nerve-shredding *yaa-baa* to writhe convincingly under ugly, sordid men with yellow teeth. She speaks of the human animals tearing at her sacred youth, the incessant beatings, the insults and humiliation, the brutal desecration of a trusting child.

When V-2 senses the girl's heart is crying, she speaks of simply remembered and very young playmates lost long ago, how they followed the water buffalo with laughter, and gathered the sweet sugar cane, and the magical nights of fairies. She speaks of the gentle time before the invasion of raging insects with the faces of cruel men devoured the children of light, and all that was human and holy.

The girl's face twists, her hands now freezing claws. Her skin darkens to a blue pallor, as though the life force has fled. As V-2 moves her hand, she awakens from the dismal past, inclined and naked, and does some feeble thrusts she assumes provocative. She falls again into the subconscious.

V-2 evokes the girl's wretched memories: of the young man's love she lost, of being passed around by careless gangs, of standing in wretched corners on *yaa-baa* for the faceless lines, the endless kneeling for oral sex, the laughter and derision, the poison in her mouth, the women who spat at her, the stealing for opium, the nameless miscarriages down public toilets or left in trash, all the miscreant seeds of darkness.

The girl's demonic face roars up from the abyss. Only the whites of her eyes show, locked upward, looking at some ghastly evil. She grinds herself against V-2's hand like an unfeeling machine, tearing at her with sharp nails. Her countenance assumes an unspeakable image. Her lips stretch back horribly, sharp incisors bared like death's grimace. The edges of her mouth draw cruelly downward. Her horrific expression remains frozen, not for moments, but over an hour or more, so that I can not be mistaken even as I grow more afraid. Her face is that of Lucifer.

I have never witnessed such an event. It is as though Satan has entered physical space and seized a human puppet. It is not an illusion, not a contact high. This hardly is an act by the girl – her personification of evil as crude psychodrama – but a matter of historical, religious consequence. I recall nothing in the medical or psychiatric literature to describe it. I turn to Vermilion, quite shaken.

"Good *Lord*, man, do you see this? She looks like the Devil incarnate."

"All the pain," he replies, "the parasite upon her true self, has assumed a face. It is annoyed by us."

Vermilion never takes his eyes from them, speaking as though during Communion. We both are transfixed.

"The expression you see sometimes is found by coroners in homicide cases where the victim died a violent death, or was tortured. Don't be alarmed, although it is real. In ancient times – perhaps accurately – it was thought possession. Among pathologists it is known as *Risus sardonicus* – a sardonic grimace in a cadaver. We are among the first – the very few – to see it in the living. It has occurred in MDMA or LSD interventions, but it is very rare. We are witnessing, if you will, a display of the miraculous. You'll never forget it. These things feed upon us."

The terror of a little girl's heart has grown into the vilest demon. Chanting the healing Pali, and liturgies from the *Pneumatologia occulta et vera*, V-2 taunts the beast to come forth. At this, the girl has a seizure. She is foaming spittle; her long legs go rigid with convulsions until they almost seem to break. It suddenly leaves the girl like wings fleeing a corpse – dark wings that can extinguish the stars one by one.

Placing her hand on the girl's heated forehead, V-2 sings for a long while, then moves her hand down to the girl's racing heart, singing and slowing the rhythm until its pace calms. The girl suddenly becomes limp. Gradually, ever so gently with her prayers and songs, she replaces the girl's great emptiness with the light of heaven.

The girl's face yields its hideous form, the features of a withered witch transform into a generous virtue. Emerging from her chrysalis – from her simulacrum of death – she becomes fine-boned and child-like. Her twisted hands gentle, reaching out timidly to touch a holy woman, as the pure and downtrodden hope for the transfer of blessings.

V-2's intimate caresses – a new sensation the girl has never felt before, nor foreseen nor even thought to permit – now cause her to catch her breath. Her voice is low in failed efforts to speak. The wild heart-sickness is gone.

V-2, with the reserve which delineates true power, sings and touches her in perfect synchrony with the giving and receiving of the girl's first flowering. Images of light, hoarded in the river of the girl's heart, reflect currents of a new desire.

The girl begins to shudder, her face brilliant with the awe of a Madonna, her sounds rapturous praise, the urgency of her hips the most heated, overt atonement. They fly together over the planet's rich, warm waves, beyond crystalline peaks and translucent choirs, and through the maternities of angels.

The girl is screaming as electric pleasure discharges through her loins; her long brown body is convulsive with ecstatic union, her legs fanning open to invite the heavenly hosts, her tears everywhere like hot rain. She is purified in an instant, communing at last with the irresistible, transforming furnace of Grace.

She begins sobbing and repeating the only prayer she knows from her lost mother's arms, "Ami dhaba, ami dhaba." Her ruffled long black hair, shining and wet, trails from her like the weeping ruins of desire.

V-2 holds her in her arms on the floor for a long while, rocking as the girl softly sobs. She comforts her with lullabies in her village dialect. V-2 finds the sponge and some water, and washes the girl slowly, teaching her to sing a little until they smile and cry together. She shows her how to bow. In a small, compressed voice, the girl asks how she could live now. V-2 tells her of the forest monastery, where she can stay as long as she wishes, until she finds herself and the one who loves her. She then removes her necklace, places it around the girl's neck, and kisses her. The diamond is real, worth more than a thousand nights.

The girl goes unerringly, like a sleepwalker, to find her clothes. We buy the girl off the management for the week, but never to return. At dawn, we help her board a jitney to the forest monastery, and bow to her. From a window, she turns to look at us, until her image is no more.

⬡

WE RIDE in the Mercedes toward the Dusit Thani, the early morning light on the mist-bound Chao Phraya river, until we stop in a grid-lock of *tuk-tuks* and smoking trucks. V-2 notices across lanes of choked traffic a hagridden, elderly tribal woman with long white hair, sitting in a lotus position on an elevated mat in a squalid corner of discarded boxes. With hopeless gestures, she is begging from the unseeing traffic. Her head is wrapped in a H'mong scarf. She is singing to herself. One eye is gone, and a foot. Her other eye peers out sightlessly. Her face is a mass of leathery winkles, her mouth innocent of teeth as a baby.

V-2 looks through the back window of the Mercedes at a Fiat with Bangkok plates. I first notice the 20 year-old from the Carousel, who has shadowed us all night. She nods to him. He blocks the traffic lanes, leaving his car running, then dodges irate Thai to arrive before the old woman. He discretely hands her a 5000 *baht* note, then bows to her with a deep *wai*. He is clearly an honorable devotee, a protector who watches the periphery. Our car moves on as though nothing has happened. I never see the young man again.

○

AT THE DUSIT THANI SUITE, a breakfast cart with embroidered white linen and silver place settings for four awaits us. Vermilion leads me to the balcony over a looking-glass world, the river below clearing and stippled with gold and silver. The sky is not yet the fierce blue of sunrise, but a milky, cloudy opal. Geraniums sprawl in planters before thin rails guarding the open space down to the river, as all Bangkok spills outward in the plain of temple spires like ornaments beneath a veil.

I turn and see through the fine draperies V-1, entering the suite alone and distraught. Her rumpled, smudged clothes are evidence of a profound night. She has no necklace. I hear both women speaking in rapid, low Thai from the bedroom, then their showering together for the longest time. Their tales are broken only by each other's heaving sobs, as they recall the tears of things, until at last there is only the sound of the water.

Vermilion distracts me, drawing my attention to some blackbird-haunted myrtles. He lights incense. The images of the evening are not easily forgotten, and I admit my bewilderment.

"That was the longest night of my life."

"And perhaps the girl's."

The phenomenon is almost ungraspable, and not easily put to rest. I rave on about emotions assuming the form of the Beast. Vermilion explains that one must turn away from the spectacle of death, rebirth and transfiguration, to not frighten others, and to care for the world without the gleam of zealotry. With difficulty, I change the subject.

"We've never talked, really, about acid. I've only seen what you've learned, or have become. There are many questions, if I may dare."

"We can discuss clandestine labs more rationally with temporal distance from the last batch. It is now permeating society, even among the peoples of South East Asia. We are feeling the changes, the karmic feedback. One night this week, certainly, your questions…"

He is subdued, for the reverent humility of the night still infuses us all. His voice trails away, until there is only the muted hooting of old water craft. He has the patrician calm of one whose slightest error yields perpetual infamy.

He is interrupted with a kiss. V-2 wears only the simple kimono of the forest, draw strings untied, flowing free in the perfumed air. She turns to me, her small, high, upturned breasts exposed, her ivory belly with livid scratches from the girl. She has an extreme sophisticate's careless naïveté, but a nun's sobering equanimity. She regards me gravely.

"We will follow the devil back to the girl's village, over the border of Laos. It will be…rather a serious affair."

V-1 approaches us, topless in a sarong tied low and loose below the deep curve of her waist. She is lean and finely muscled, arctic white. Her eyes are azure, candid, with the light of dawn. She places her hand upon my heart. I see for a moment ancient torches in sconces, and priestesses of Athena, spectrally slim and fair with hair the color of apricots and gold leaf. She beseeches me like a holy woman, with words I so long to hear.

"Come with us."

Chapter 22.

The Cloud Maidens

My vessel sails along that blessed shore
The dense sacred forest fills the air
Over nameless flowers huge palms soar
Cardamom weeps, rubber trees perspire
The unfound isle, announced by fragrances
Like courtesans…

- Sergio Corrazzini, *Il Mio Cuore* (My Heart)
fr. *Dolcezze* (Sweetness), 1904

Do not give dalliance too much reign;
the strongest oaths are straw
to the fire in the blood.

- Prospero, SS, *The Tempest*

And still you hold our longing gaze
With languorous look and lavish limb;
Are you not weary of ardent ways
Lure of the fallen seraphim?
Tell no more of ancient days.

- fragment of villanelle of Stephen Daedalus
Joyce, *A Portrait of the Artist as a Young Man*

REMOTE VILLAGES far north of Chiang Mai pass before the cracked windows of our dented van, their half-naked children staring in rows before rude huts. Dark men in conical straw hats and loincloths are immersed to their knees in rice paddies behind massive water buffalo with great grey horns. Old wives, with blackened teeth stained from betel nut, mix roasted crushed seashells and tobacco to extract the stimulant. The culture is infected by *yaa-baa* and opium, the illiteracy and poverty a conduit to Pat Pong.

We enter a jungle clearing by the Ping River – our base camp for the operation – to find a rambling ex-pat writer's shack, lit dimly by lanterns and candles. It has rooms of grand, artistic proportions, and walls of bamboo under a peaked thatched roof. The interior has some fine pieces, many tribal *objets d'art*, several scarred sea-stained tables, a musty library, and drawings of native women and children. Red brocade curtains hang as entryways to several bedrooms. Rickety windows, with wooden louvers for monsoons, open to little arbors of oleanders and thick moss-bound branches of oak. The women find their sarongs, loosely tie them about their hips, and move in barefoot silence through the rooms and gardens; they are topless with demure smiles, as though they are Geisha.

⬡

VERMILION RETREATS to the library with an air of Jesuitical seriousness, his philosophy of introspection almost a monomania. He peruses a copy of Tacitus, *The Annals of Imperial Rome*, then settles upon the lyrical poetry of Pindar and Sappho.

In the early dusk, V-1 and V-2 find a springhead leading into the Ping, and bathe each other like dryads. In the profusion of vibrating life, under a canopy of vines and exotic *Cymbidia*, the steep banks are a forest of giant ferns, with brambles of plump, ebony blackberries. Small native children soon appear to watch them – curious, shy and black-haired. They have never seen white women near their village, or so close and casual. Sitting in enchantment, they listen as the women both sing to them in the children's rural diaect. They scramble away giggling when V-1 and V-2 splash a few, chasing them into the thickets with great howls, like the tigresses their grandmothers assure them prowl after nightfall.

Low clouds of river mist gather like the dim smoke of a thousand blue irises. The women return through copses of wild blossoming orange trees, drying themselves in the twilit air, then tie their sarongs low and carelessly and enter the library. Devotees of Goethe, they are pleased to find his writings in German, stacked with Greek literature on round wicker stands. They read throughout the evening, occasionally stretching or floating about, or dancing together in a sort of quadrille. Their walk, I observe discretely, has a maddening fluidity. In the late hours, they grow quite serious, as though our retreat is a conventicle, a secret religious meeting unsanctioned by law.

We prepare fried rice, vegetables and tofu, eating with hand-carved chopsticks – mindfully and without speaking – from wooden begging bowls. We each wash our bowl, then consider the promising variety of beds. Hours pass alone in my room, the red brocade still, its beads parted slightly before the beckoning hallway and the streaming moon. There is the cooing of mourning doves. Sleep eludes me.

In the writer's library, I discover a mildewed volume of Elizabeth Barrett Browning, and read it in the dim light from a green shaded lamp by a rough deal table. The sticky-winged night is restive and dank. I write lines from Browning's *Morning for Prometheus* – her translation of Aeschylus – and leave it folded on a night stand for the women's Hellenic passions. It is a recollection of the possessed girl.

> "And black Hades roars up
> through the chasm of the ground,
> and the fountains of pure running rivers
> mourn low
> in a pathos of woe."

◯

WE ARE ALL SOLICITOUS DOMESTICS in this impeccable household, each with a monastic practice of careful placement and cleansing and honor of each other. In the dense tropic, with its heavy mingled scents, the voluptuous late evening begins to have an intemperate, sensual fascination. The house is quiet now, but for the incessant lust of trilling crickets, and the scratching of palmettos.

I have not heard the women or Vermilion for some hours, except for bare footfalls among the bedrooms, the shifting of beads, and the rustle of silks in some subtle and delicate luxury. The moon is late and wan, like the looks they cast.

Fighting an inclination to join them, I think of Pallas Athena intervening to curb the excesses of Odysseus. Of their boundless filial devotion – the height of felicity – I reflect on Prudence, the most tractable of the cardinal virtues. My musings are severed by the sound of a whip on skin, descending yet again, and long low moans.

In silence I move quickly toward the hall, in wildness thinking to protect if not serve. The sounds are indistinguishable: either loving abandon, or concealed ferocity. Through the edge of a doorway, past the brocade curtain – in a ray of moonlight across a woven mat floor and thin mattress with tangled sheets – I see only the two hands of a woman, tied at the wrists. They are splayed, trembling, palms up, reaching for thick stalks of dark green bamboo poles inserted into the mahogany floor.

Pulled and pushed by an ardent lover, she extends her fingers, grasping the bamboo. As if gagged by an intruder, she does not cry out. Her tightly bound wrists keep moving, her wet fingers flexing, clenching, slipping. Both her hands again hold the bamboo in a frantic grip, hanging on for unbearable moments. Her hands are then completely rotated, twisting the rope. Now they are palms down, then fingers interlaced, a captive nymph ravished at will. She is struggling, being devoured.

I back away, overcome with imagined passions. Returning to the library, thoughts rampant, I consider a rhombus of blue moonlight while my heart races. The muffled sounds continue, with the creaking of bamboo. I assume Vermilion and the women have some mutual need for bondage and dominance play. An hour later, the half-heard ardors still flagrant, I stumble in the blackness toward the kitchen at the far end of the hallway. A candle dimly reveals the crude teak floors, while surrussus of humid air breathe among the shuttered rooms.

He wears only a sarong, his lean musculature bright with perspiration. Vermilion stands at a block cutting table with some long French cutlery, parting the luscious orange flesh of a huge ripe mango. He extracts the hard oval seed, then cross-hatches the mango's tissue until it bleeds its delicious juice. He looks up at me, slowly spreading the mango wide with both hands, his fingers dripping with its fragrant contents. He knows my feelings.

"They are toughening themselves for the rigors of Laos."

"I thought it was you."

He opens the mango until the flesh glistens, the wetness so seductive I feel an existential hunger.

"Care for a slice? Now…or later?"

◯

THE FIRST UP from a restless night, I pass the monsoon windows, its slats open to the steaming dawn. On the nightstand, in vermilion ink, is a reply from the sleepless women. It is a poem of Baccylides, on Achilles, Ajax and Telamon rallying before the walls of Troy. V-1 and V-2 are ready for Laos.

> "Excellence, flaming out to all
> Does not black out
> Nor even dim
> Under the night's folding drifts
> But alive with light
> irrepressibly wings the earth
> and trackless skies."

◯

WE LEAVE THE WRITER'S SHACK in the long grave shadows of morning, driving far beyond even Chiang Rai, into the no-man's land of the Golden Triangle. We pass mad, remote markets of Vietnamese from Cu Chi and Da Nang selling papaya *pok pok* with twelve chilies and balls of sticky rice. We slow on unmarked roads near the Thai border; Laos looms in the heat, Burma to the west.

An hour down an almost impassable jeep trail hacked from the jungle, we gather our daypacks, leave the van and hike along barely perceptible footpaths for 10 kilometers or so. We arrive at a promontory, protected by low bushes and tattered palms, above a river and tidal plain waving away into swampy littorals and a low horizon. Laos is only a few hundred meters north, with its random, aimless smugglers' trails to the riverbank, and its rotted canoes to nowhere.

V-1 and V-2 wear their robes and kimonos and sandals, their skin again muddied, hair dyed, contacts in. They depart with deep *wais*, wordlessly moving down a vague trail. Vermilion and I crouch against a rough palm. Through a small opening we can see the women walking in meditation, chanting as they approach a decrepit ferryman with a ramshackle raft of lashed bamboo. Bowing, they beg assistance to the dismal Laotian village near the opposite bank. With reluctance, he begins to push a long pole into murky water, moving across the shallows with grim foreboding, like Charon, son of Erebus.

Vermilion retrieves two powerful spotting scopes from the backpacks – Leupold Ultras mounted on tripods. He steadies them, then opens an illegal military radio from the Hamburg free port and activates a linked channel. I can hear V-1 and V-2 speaking in Thai and fluent Lao to the ferryman, then to a village headman. Vermilion translates. They are seeking alms for the night, and the village priest, if there is one. We find them in the scopes at 300 meters. Both women wear cheap Timex watches, perhaps as trading goods.

The headman, dressed in purple and red rags, is leftover from the Lao brigades of Chiang Kai-shek. He leads them to a crude shelter of teak remnants, flyblown with ragged rat holes. The village is sparse, appearing unpopulated but for the elderly and hordes of naked children. It has poverty-stricken bean rows and melons overrun with fibrous creepers, and nearby a lamentable black swamp with barbed reeds. A single file of village women soon emerges from a longhouse, carrying pots down to the river, gathering the timeless bounty in their caring hands.

An elder approaches, bent and hollow with age as if from a thousand springs. He has thin white whiskers, and wears a patched saffron robe that is frayed and trails in dirt. Holding a brown bamboo staff, he bows with one hand to V-1 and V-2. He tells them he has performed the prayers over village births and deaths since he was a young monk. Offering bowls of rice brought by his granddaughter, he sits on a woven mat on the pounded earth outside their shelter. He has heard of Ajahn Chah's forest retreats, and he knows the girl from Bangkok.

The old priest tells them that many girls are bought from their parents, or run away, or are taken early. With a fearful look toward the palm thickets, he tells them much more. V-1 and V-2 sing to him in Pali until darkness falls, his eyes and toothless mouth smiling at last. The unjudging jungle stretches away into Laos, under a dead moon.

VERMILION AWAKENS ME at first light, our bags and netting thick with insects. At our scopes we can see the village elder, who has remained by the shelter all night sitting in meditation and – it seems – praying. V-1 and V-2 emerge, attracting the children, all their faces brightening at the tales and songs through the early morning. They walk and sing along paths overgrown with *Cymbidia*, with V-1 and V-2 drifting like wisps of cirrus clouds.

A magnetic blue haze settles on the banks as the sun grows hot. Two scruffy mongrel dogs rise from sleep, look about and snarl, then cowardly walk away. Anxious women hurry the children to the long house, leaving V-1 and V-2 by the river with the elder.

The palmetto groves remain still, the air now stagnant and foul. The brackish water stands in pools; the black mud begins to swarm with small stinging flies and mosquitoes like the forerunner of unearthly spirits. There is a fusillade of Laotian curses, and the stammer of horses on rocks.

A train of mercenaries and smugglers appear, edging down tortuous bridal paths, horses' manes tossing, saddles creaking; perhaps there are twenty men, most walking, others on mules. The officers wear sweat-stained khakis, and carry blackened, oiled AR-15s and M-16s over their shoulders. The men are in tribal dress and wear hobnail boots. They all have lined faces and long narrow moustaches under a melee of colored head cloths. The strained animals, strapped with layers of ropes over heavy gunny sacks, are slipping and snorting – wild-eyed – on the muddy track.

In the blurring heat haze, as locusts swirl in the unreality of their advance, I whisper anxiously to Vermilion.

"What are they carrying?"

"Heroin. And *yaa-baa*, methamphetamine."

They circle near an old wooden lean-to with unframed windows under the shade of a palm grove, and stop at a reservoir of rank emerald water for the horses and mules. Small brown owls flee one way, a kingfisher another.

The train is at the whim of one despot, a great brown toad, a fearsome troglodyte with a taurine neck and high cheekbones. With a scowling face and leathery hands, he is glowering, inflamed.

"Who's he?"

"A lord of the United Wa. No, Red Wa. Wa Shan. Burmese Army."

Women scurry from the longhouse, bringing broiled fish on palm leaves, then rice beer. Several of the older girls, with reluctance and tears and whispers, bring steamed rice and approach the men. The riders give them a few coins, then take the girls forcibly behind a windbreak of bulrushes. It is not enough.

Several drunken mercenaries, bored with attending the mules, break into the longhouse, and withdraw a leggy, frightened girl of about seventeen in a long narrow white sarong to her ankles. She is barefoot, with waist-length black hair and a conical hat tied over her shoulders. She is crying for her mother, who is restrained by two of the Wa Shan. A third holds her father, wrinkled and thin in a headscarf and loin cloth, at the point of an M-16. Laughing, two men rip off her sarong, exposing her thin brown body, they push her to the ground in the joyless heat behind sharp reeds. A small naked girl of four looks on, thumb in mouth.

The heat is like a brimstone fire, with clouds of black flies. The remaining men, the rice beer consumed, eye the village women, who are squatting on their haunches by the river to wash the men's bowls. Some of the Wa Shan stagger to them, pulling their victims' sarongs over their heads, the women on their knees wailing. They take them roughly, the men's heads thrown back with evil grimaces. One woman has her hands in the sand. As her long black hair loosens, a white chrysanthemum falls into the water, swirling slowly downstream.

The young girl's mother breaks free, running to to the leader, and kisses his stirrup irons. He beats her about the face and hands with his crop until she falls to her knees. He turns violently in his saddle and sees by the riverside V-1 and V-2, hands in prayer, insubstantial as rainbows.

⬡

HE POINTS AT THEM with his crop and screams. With shouts and threats, two riders bring them at gunpoint. V-1 and V-2 raise their begging bowls to the men, eyes down, chanting in Pali. The leader wheels his horse, looking at them carefully. He pulls an AR-15 from his shoulders, and with the barrel opens V-2's robe, revealing her skin of snow, her pink nipples. He prods her harshly, the gun sight cutting her breast slightly, and sees the scratches on her belly. Excited, he shouts for his troops, offering the women to his commanders with the most vile instructions.

The elder rushes forward, his hands pressed together, bowing and crying in shrill, rapid Lao. Vermilion turns to me, his sinews tensed.

"He says the women are devotees of Ajahn Chah – priestesses – and that if they are harmed a thousand monks will pray to Buddha that he is reincarnated as a hungry ghost."

"Have they assaulted missionaries?"

"Five Christian women were raped by forty Wa troops a few miles upriver some years ago. They kept them in bamboo cages, passed them around for months."

"What if they find the radio?"

We can – through the active channel of the device taped to V-1's thigh – hear the older girls nearby, terrorized and blindly satisfying their oppressors. They are groaning like a litter of pigs, their bare feet pushing in the dirt.

Several other riders – former herdsmen now fighters rich with weapons – have arms and hands of great power. Swaggering through pools of refuse, raving on rice beer and *yaa-baa*, they head for V-1 and V-2.

From the radio link we can hear the seventeen-year-old girl mewing, suffering appallingly, her small marionette voice incoherent. Ape-like silhouettes move incessantly over her, grunting. Within meters, a water buffalo is standing in the pungent ooze of blackwater, flicking flies with its tail, its immense horns and dewlap twisting from side to side, dripping with black slime.

The palms are brown and shiny, splintering themselves in the hot wind, like shivering mirrors of heartless worlds. The smoky cooking fires are sulfurous, from the bottomless pit.

The leader, still mounted, has a pockmarked face that is impassive and hawk-featured, with a single squinting eye. He spews invectives, but knows his eternal fate is at the elder's disposal. He whirls his mount around, gripping one rein, then shakes his AR-15, and points upriver.

The elder prostrates himself. V-1 and V-2 raise their begging bowls to each rider, but the leader and his commanders ignore them, moving on to the bulrushes and reeds. We follow the elder and the women as they pass out of sight of the shrieking village, toward the ferry.

The ferryman, crouched by a stream, seems surprised to see them. The women place their heads to the elder's for a long while, then bow. As they cross over the river, we hear from the village sporadic gunfire.

BY LATE NIGHT we are in Chiang Rai, packed in a stuffy, squalid little room above the market. Since the event – after our many embraces and exchanges – V-1 and V-2 have been mute. They shower then meditate, facing the wall through the night even as Vermilion and I try to sleep, half-awake, pressed against the door.

By morning, they both have retrieved their modest belongings, then confound me by transforming themselves, donning matching tropical business suits, with white blouses and sensible black pumps. They have fine leather portfolios and briefing books. They are cold and refined, wordless, like pure ice.

Vermilion knows my visit to Thailand is for a Harvard study on the public health aspects of heroin in the new Russia, the opiate smuggled through sources in Central Asia and – as General Sergeev in Moscow insists – the Golden Triangle. Chiang Rai, a remote crossroads for traffickers but also a small center of commerce in Northern Thailand, is hosting a reception this very day for Thai officials. It is to be attended for an hour by the American president's wife and well-armed Diplomatic Security Service staff. I hope to interview among the Thai, Burmese and Lao present, and assume V-1 and V-2 intend to crash the meeting somehow under my Harvard aegis. Even after the grisly Laotian village, Vermilion and the women have timed our arrival with perfection.

Yet V-1 and V-2, appearing as admirable researchers with business cards, references and fluent Thai, easily pass security and soon are mingling with crowds of embassy officials. Immediately closed in by formidable enforcement types, I fumble with my Harvard officer's credentials until V-1 intercedes with her elegance and charm, taking my arm.

The room is a sweating mass of Cambodian and Lao spooks, State analysts, those under non-official cover, DEA special agents-in-charge and field office personnel, military rogues, and uncertain professionals from Burma. V-1 and V-2 disperse, waiving their Montblanc pens to illustrate policy arguments, or gossiping about the Hill. Surrounded by vibrant young policy staff, even a few alums from HKS and the Wilson School, they seem in the quick confidence of several other women, perhaps State or Congressional staffers. They have endless little subterfuges, their movements stage-managed together, faultless in their precision.

I am psychically whip-lashed from the vivid memory that only yesterday they faced gang-rape and death by savage mercenaries and smugglers that prey on remote Laotian and Burmese villages. Given the agenda of the Six, this meeting itself hardly is a trifling danger to V-1 and V-2. I notice their reconnaissance of participants, their clever daring. Today – like each day – they confront the specters of life imprisonment: their faces and wombs desiccating, alone and forgotten in eternal dishonor. I wonder by what great gift the Six and their operatives maintain their equanimity, and manage their instant and utter transformations.

After some hours, with *wais* to the many gracious Thai, we depart through a shell game of intersecting *tuk-tuks* to elude surveillance. We meet with Vermilion parked in a van down a foul alley at the periphery of Chiang Rai. I noticed their portfolios are gone, as are their cheap Timex watches. After nightfall – as the moon rides with us through shining clouds over dense rainforest and sea – our small plane approaches a crude strip near a fishing village a thousand kilometers from Chiang Rai. V-1 and V-2 – when not silent in long periods of reflective horror – sing and pray and cry gently throughout the journey, their feelings finally free, to our sorrow and joy.

⬡

PHUKET LIES DISTANT on the horizon. The curls of the Andaman Sea are white and delicate as a spider's web, unraveling in slow glissades. The lyric southern waters lap over reefs, their surfaces coiling and wrinkling with small waves, while beyond they become tranquil, curving away to the edge of the world. The sun-touched horizon, like sea-bathing on a summer morning, is a shower of golden arrows.

At a jungle enclosed hilltop estate, opening to broad views of the bay and the fugitive lamps of far Phuket, we occupy cabanas illuminated only by candlelight. Vermilion, V-1 and V-2 each have their own, I a fourth. The retreat of a Japanese *keiretsu* director, the villa beyond has wooden eaves daubed with the knobby mud houses of swallows. There are overgrown sunken gardens, and fragrant lemon trees. The small cabanas enter upon a long, narrow crystalline lap pool, its depths black with dark purple fired ceramic inlays. In the evening, paper lanterns reveal swift, foot-long green geckos adorning the encircling walls, awaiting tides of moths or the errant dragonfly. Sandalwood incense burns in carved jade bowls. A bamboo flute mourns from the simple village huts below, the low, full moon forgetful of all it has witnessed.

V-1 and V-2 are by the pool each night, their skin shockingly bone-white in the moonlight. As they purify in these final days of peace, they silently do ablutions over each other, becoming tumescent from the cool water. They prepare votives on small palm leaves, and set them adrift. There is a white chrysanthemum, swirling.

They are healing from the proximity of great evil, from the vision of the ravaged, bleeding girl. They sing so softly, holding lengthy, low conversations in Thai and German and indescribable dialects. They begin to swim endlessly these nights, shimmering above the blackness, then do slow yoga, like visions in alabaster taut and naked before us. They stretch for hours in tandem by the candles, or under the fading moon, and finally by starlight. They read without cease from the estate library. After a long while, they don't cry anymore.

They write in elegant hands, notes on medieval rites, and drink fresh juices from a silver flask, or feed each other single grapes picked thoughtfully from freckled, warm clusters on a rattan mat. They compose letters with affectionate superscriptions to Vipassana, Zen and Thai priests. Soon strewn about the shade of the pool – all around their long, woven palm *chaises longues* – are diverse volumes on Lao history, Burmese heroin traffic, Gibbon's more prurient essays on the rape of Rome, the 13th Century works of the Cistercian monk Caesar of Heisterbcaj, and the corpus of exorcisms in the *Dialogue of Miracles*.

Beyond the white-washed walls in the evening are glittering streams of fireflies. Through the rustic gate one can see tracts of moon-polished sea, and hear the surf as it crumples and hisses. Sometimes V-1 and V-2 walk slowly by the pool for hours, their sarongs carelessly falling away, even as their mirror images on the still surface of the water seem to brood with sadness.

⬡

ONE MORNING AT DAWN – and each dawn thereafter – they appear in their nun's simple robes, and walk a trail down to the village; they remain until late afternoon, when our dinner is brought by two rotund Thai women from the estate. Twins, they have flowered sarongs and smiling round faces, and lay out pounded silver bowls of steaming rice, spicy deep-fried tofu, vegetable curries, and platters of sliced papaya. There are *wais* all around, but more deeply from the Thai women to V-1 and V-2. In their absence, I have hours with Vermilion, alone.

"For the cooks," he observes, "encountering V-1 and V-2 is like running into their mother's lap. They haven't met white women with the gravity of their village priest."

"Laos constantly enters my mind," I return, pressing the topic.

"I urged them not to go, but they are adamantine. Yet we now have close-ups and audio of the Wa Shan leaders, the Devils' apprentices. Or rather, State does."

"But those were simple spotting scopes."

"Not the Timex watches, as they lifted their begging bowls."

"At the risk of their lives?"

"Once V-2 saw their adversary, straining under the Bangkok girl's countenance like a vicious animal under human skin, they could only act."

We consider the great cloud mansions floating above us, in the expanse of hot lilac sky.

"The conference also was productive; the Montblanc pens have fine resolution. Some Thai are corrupted by the Wa, a few Americans. Meanwhile we have identified the regional office personnel. Cobalt will sort it out."

Vermilion is more open now that time is unhurried; I take the opportunity.

"How do they change form so easily?"

"Much practice. Dedication. Between laboratory sites they have begged on the cobbled streets of Prague, by the Vltava River, by the castle – then slept in its turrets."

"But how do they remember who they are, if they so often are chameleons?"

"One never forgets. You'll always remember the Berlin displays, the Bangkok girl, Laos. Imagine the phenomena around the actual psychedelic batches. Our memories compel us."

"But the delicacies of their interactions at the conference, as if they were among old friends."

"We think of V-1 and V-2 as akin to the Syracusan soldiers during the Peloponnesian War – who posed as allies and obtained passwords by mere conversation with enemy troops – then defeated Demosthenes at Epipolis. As with V-1 and V-2 before the warlord in Laos – or the corrupt officials at the conference – it was a consummate hypocrisy, a prelude to grand larceny."

The women begin relaxing over the days, now with open nudity. V-1 appears wearing only a *rivière* of green jade from the estate. They massage each other before us in the twilight. Yet they keep perfect time for rising, their frequent walking meditations, their one evening meal, and even the discrete practice of the smallest of things – the placement of flowers, even the arrangement of chopsticks. At the core of their apparently indulgent leisure is a deeply rigorous monasticism.

⬡

AS IF SUMMONED, I awake one night to the low, bull-like tone of a Tibetan invocation. Moving by the pool I glimpse through flimsy netting Vermilion, sitting in lotus posture and chanting in meditation. V-1 also is naked, embracing him completely – her legs tightly around his erect posture. Her arms are about his neck, their foreheads are touching, one inhaling as the other exhales. They are in a Tantric asana, the Yab-Yum union. The moon has set; the sky is hoary with stars.

V-2 is beside them, embracing both, running her hands very slowly up and down the length of their spines, from the crown of their heads to their locked, vibrating hips. As they visualize the white heat moving slowly up and down through each chakra, all intone the Tibetan prayers, their barely moving bodies like generators of electric spirit. After an hour, V-1 dismounts and V-2 takes her place, both alternating throughout the night. The long rite continues before my eyes, their intensity grows even as I – with a studied fascination – watch them. The branches of a whithered plum tree are flowing in the air in synchronicity with their chants; its flowers begin to blossom in the last starlight.

Their erotic meditations are focused, sublime, primal. It is not as though hidden satyr and maenads unite, or some frenzied adoration of the Bacchantes. They seem to acquire energy – and not dissipate – by living a dream.

⬡

VISITORS COME FOR DINNER. A thin young Thai woman with fine silver spectacles manifests with a gentle *wai*. V-1 and V-2 speak only Thai with her.

"She is the physician for the local village," Vermilion discloses. "She sees everything, and they assist her on…special occasions."

A young woman medical student, almost as tall as V-1 and V-2, appears from the island of Koh Samui, where Europeans gather for the full moon festivals. She is Ukrainian, elegant, with a daughter of eight who to the delight of the Thai has white-blond hair and blue eyes. V-1 and V-2 speak Ukrainian, Russian and Polish with her, and English and French with the little one. They sing Russian folk songs to the girl, laugh and dance with her, and comb her hair. I feel some unutterable sadness within the mother and child.

"She will be a neurologist soon," Vermilion remarks of the visitor from Koh Samui. "You'll recall V-1 took her doctorate in neuroscience in Leipzig, where they met." Of the visitor he vouchsafes, "Her husband is imprisoned forever. At some distance, he was one of us."

The twin Thai cooks in sarongs bring sticky rice and papaya from the estate, and we eat as the women talk late, accompanied only by the distant stabs of lightning at sea, and the sharp crying of gulls. V-1 and V-2 bow and pray over the sleeping child, for they know that in the little girl's secret heart she dreams of her loving father.

○

ONE EVENING, V-1 and V-2 discover a hand-carved jade chess set, and lie by the pool in the candle light during the humid night, both struggling and feverish with profound strategies.

"I'll take the winner," I propose, with a rueful grin.

"Remember V-2 has her easily accomplished international rating of 2100," Vermilion whispers, "the level of a candidate master. Rarely enters tournaments now. It would be unfair."

They stalemate, laugh, then kiss each other. I think of retreating to my cabana for consolation. Such formidable women, always attending Vermilion and one another, seem like Hesperides's nymphs, guarding a garden where a magic apple grows.

Upon the night air, they sing to each other, and to us. V-1 takes V-2's hand, and in a high coloratura offers Puccini's lovely "Che Gelida Manina" (Your tiny hand is freezing). As the moon wanes, V-2 caresses the prostrate V-1 with her long fingertips, looking directly at us and singing in her mezzo-soprano Dvořák's Song to the Moon from Rusalka, as though we were in Berlin. They wait, eyes turned to me, until they see I recall not the eroticism, but the profound conversion of that night. At dawn – as always – they leave for their mysterious errand in the village.

◯

THEY BEGIN to openly pleasure each other, careless of my presence. Vermilion explains their flagrant indiscretions.

"They are well now, and this is their lifestyle. They have accepted you, and care not to hide."

Their sublime amorousness is so advanced, I can never hope to reach them, and am grateful only to witness their beautiful freedoms. On a late afternoon, they return from their day in the village. Like a waking dream, I see them in a cabana behind the netting. They are moving together, inverted and opposed, their delectable V-shaped backs flaring into hips urged by spread fingers. They begin to swoon, each with little spasms. My self-command returns momentarily, and I manage to look away, but soon am so presumptuous as to consider the whiteness of their long necks, as both reach delicately, like swans feeding. My most enchanting suppositions are confirmed.

On an evening, V-1 lies on her back atop a cool duvet in the warm, honey-colored candlelight. Her knees are bent as she strokes the other's hair, sighing luxuriously. They are arrayed beneath a painting, a nude in repose by Vuillard. Their bodies are translucent, as a soft scroll of tongue probes downward. The vast bed has wavy patterns of watered silk. Owls are drifting from the moon-bright tree tops, slowly and silently as flakes of ash.

As V-2 draws her nails down along the cream-laden hollow of V-1's hip, her abdomen tenses, then begins to flutter. V-1 turns her head to look at me, flushing, her dream eyes brightening, changing from gentian blue to smoldering ultraviolet to the phosphorescence of the sea. She holds her gaze, as quick lithe ribbons move across her belly as swiftly as cloud shadows. They gather, contracting like the heart of a storm, vital, clenching, trembling. She closes her eyes, then looks upward at the radiance, shaking with triumphant cries.

It is the Floating World of an international conspiracy, unbreachable by those who dare not dream of it. The women can affiliate with any coterie, infatuated by their pure perfection. When thus not embraced, or singing, swimming, or reading, they dance with child-like naïveté in the almost unbearable heat, finally languishing on Kurd rugs, or good Shirazis, or upon the cool terra-cotta or teak floors. They dance as the bright four stars of the Southern Cross glint like mica, and the sea below tames itself in tideless long calms and lines of silk froth.

Their sensual love has the solemnity informed by thought. It is broken only by their laughter, like wild things. They sing in the morning garden, or while cleansing in the dawn seas, and often lie brow to brow, their eyes wide open. The moral atmosphere in which we are immersed sometimes makes it too hot to breathe, until it seems a mythic Aegean wind, like the ocean's sigh, saves us.

They sit together for hours, completely naked, their long thin toned legs spread wide and langorously over the edges of a broad rattan swing. They slowly swing back and forth in a lazy splendor, silent and gazing at us, their magnificent sibyls' eyes emanating a candid and advanced intellegence. They are a feast of perennial desire. Bathed in the thick, sweet scent of magnolia blossoms, they share sun-warmed grapes and pomegranates from the garden, careless of the juices. Above them, palm fronds dance restlessly, nibbled by the sea-wind in the cloudless sky.

⬡

IN SUCH CLOSENESS, I often hear V-1 and V-2 in their cabanas, which seem casually interchangeable. In the hours after dusk, V-1 is reading Aristophanes' *Hymn of the Clouds* to V-2, practicing her Greek, then softly intoning with Eastern European accents the lines in English.

"Cloud maidens that float on forever…
dew sprinkled, fleet bodies and fair,
and through the murmurs of rivers,
nymph-haunted,
the songs of the sea waves resound."

They are among the few surviving Hellenists, fond of Homeric hymns, speaking of violet-crowned, glistening Athens, and Apollo the Sky archer, until the mother of morning, and the rose fingered dawn.

⬡

THEIR SPIRITS RETURNING, they grow playful and teasing. V-1 with impish glee dons a Tam O'Shanter looted from the estate, taking also a recorder with batteries. To the music of ambient and chill electronica, she becomes an ecdysiast on the floors of fine Kilims and Baluch rugs. V-2, not to be outdone, does a *chaine chinoise* around the pool, then performs an erotic dance to Debussy's *Afternoon of a Faun.* They stretch with Hellenic perfection until the moon rises, both then falling together upon the rugs in an unnerving and inviting torpor.

At the end of each long evening, they always walk slowly in meditation, each holding a white beeswax votive in blue glass while circumambulating the pool. The still water reflects their passage like fairies, as they sing in high *bel canto* a benediction in Latin.

◯

THE WOMEN AWAKEN ME late one night in silence, by V-2 placing her hand softly on my forehead. We move with clouds of fireflies to the coastline, as it reveals its undraped whiteness. The moonlight waits patiently. Muted unearthly drum music comes from the dark village. As we enter the sea naked, their images are green violet reflections upon a surface quiet as a moonstone mirror lake. The gentle waters lick and relick their slender cherished bodies as they stand and extend their arms to bless the sky. They wade in the blue night, as the fragile moon freckles the sea in glimmering points to the edge of darkness. They trail their hands in the deepening phosphorescent water, dragging wide golden-green fire that flickers like quicksilver. V-1 and V-2 come to me, the pulse of their ocean like warm silk. We become a silver moon riding our nest of stars, as the fireflies follow our every motion, above the rhythm and cries of the night.

◯

THE LAST WORDS I hear V-1 and V-2 speak are in the final evening, as they sit together on a bed in a cabana; the outlines of their bodies are dimly candlelit, dancing behind ghostly, transparent netting. Perhaps they sense I am awake, watching the vision of them.

"We must make an offering to Aesculapius, the god of medicine," V-1 murmurs.

"See to it," V-2 softly replies, "and don't forget."

I recognize the final words of Socrates, to Crito, and fall into a dream, thinking they are saying it to me.

○

IN THE EARLY MORNING, as in Berlin, they all are gone. The privilege of being with them is replaced by emptiness. I manage my lonely bags, thinking that Vermilion and the women are not simply Hedonists or Buddhists, but truly pagan, mythical, polytheistic. Recalling their disappearance in Berlin, I remember their first gift – the white wings and halo now worn by Abeer in Kathmandu. I hurry to open my valise. Therein is a small stuffed angel, her head bowed in prayer.

It is identical to the angel at the little girl's tea party in the British Museum, when with Crimson the worlds moved. Every image and event by the Six has been thought out with precision, planted in my memory by these most excellent teachers. Honored by such devotion, I rush to find them.

Collecting the *tuk-tuk* driver, awaiting me for the long sojourn on the muddy road to Phuket, I enter the outskirts of the village. There are sounds of eager cocks crowing, and the melancholy, drowsy tinkling of goat's bells. Small tangerine trees stand alongside rude huts in the cool light, as flights of brilliant butterflies begin drifting in the pearly sky. Through the shade of vines, early sun dapples over deep garnet roses and the velvet of wine-red cyclamen. At the edge of hearing, there are small children singing.

The song is in Thai, then Pali, but their voices transmute to English, and finally to the flat, broad vowels of the American Deep South. It is an impossibility in Thailand, unless I have stumbled upon Mennonite or Southern Baptist missionaries.

"My latest sun is sinking fast
My race is nearly run
My strongest trials now are past
My triumph has begun."

It is overwhelming, a poignant bluegrass hymn from old Christians, sung in red-dirt backwoods twang, as though they are settlers from the foothills of the Blue Ridge at the edge of the Shenandoah Valley.

"Oh come, angel band
Come and around me stand."

I look everywhere. Most villagers are still in their palm shelters. The beaches are white as tusks, the sky like blue glass over the dawn-calm sea.

"O bear me away
On your snow white wings
To my immortal home."

Within sprawling brambles goats bleat, as the new day thickens with flower scents. There are ranks of marigolds, flame red, then moon white. Slim cypress trees move in the slight breeze, as if they are painting the sky.

"O bear my longing heart to Him
Who bled and died for me."

There they are, where they have gone every morning. V-1 and V-2 stand in their robes with many village children, some naked, most in tatters like defeated angels, the children all singing words they do not understand. As they lift their voices of heartbreaking sweetness, everyone waves and smiles, then bows as one to me.

"Whose blood now cleanses from all sin
And gives me victory."

Fighting tears, I bow to them.

"Oh come, angel band

Come and around me stand

Oh bear me away

On your snow white wings

To my immortal home."

Chapter 23.

Forever the Heart

…with the fine quiet of the Scholar,
which is the nearest of all things
to heavenly peace.

- Fitzgerald, *Tender Is the Night*

Rise from the sod, ye fair columns and arches,
tell their bright deeds to the ages unborn.

- Oliver Wendell Holmes (class of 1861),
commemorating Harvard dead in Civil War

What we need now to discover in the social realm is
the moral equivalent of war: something heroic
that will speak to men as universally as war does.

- William James (MD, class of 1869),
The Varieties of Religious Experience

It was carried out in a tumultary random manner,
and resembled a Cambridge commencement.

- William Douglas, describing the 1745 capture of Louisburg

STAGGERING IN from the green vulgar fecundity of Bangkok – and disoriented by cultural, temporal and spiritual shock – I entered the cool, limitless ocean of words in Cambridge. The Charles was a rare slate blue, the Houses' roses twined on climbing trellises, the warm sea winds brushing by us to dying strains of music.

Upon my desk were whole jeremiads of unanswered messages. Commencement invitations, itineraries for a post-graduation research tour, little notes from returning student friends about their own international projects, and reminders of due dates by insistent faculty.

From the extremes of nights with Magenta and Vermilion, I still had limited coherence. One became prone to recursive thinking, infinite Mandelbrot sets of thoughts. Of the electric, sensual women, my reveries ran free; their tantric and religious practices swarmed into one's heated imagination. Their translucent forms stippled the landscape; the very winds became their voices, aeolian with their sublime intelligence, their low moans.

At first they had seemed a cult of pleasure, with marvelous healing powers, whispering the splendors of secret languages and nights. Yet, after the transcendent realities of Bangkok and Phuket, I no longer could debauch them in great shining coils of erotic images, sketched upon my lonely silence.

The methods of the Six were a tenebrous affair. Captured, they would be vilified in the press. Most observers would consider them purveyors of iniquities, but they had delicate graces, as though teachers of holy court etiquette. After my contact with the Six, every physical object would yield to one's insight, dispersing into components. Now I saw not simply the sun above, but all the old heliotries, then flaming oceans of hydrogen boiling on the nearest Type O star, our mere White Dwarf a stellar explosion burning for only another billion years.

If I did more than glance at a chair, I would see the chewing death of sawmills, working men rubbing stains into wood, the great forest ranges and mountain mists, their roots and branches touching each other like consciousness, their crowns of sky and rain. No object or person existed alone, but was connected to all things.

Upon recollection of events with the Six, one's soul would become a simple votive, alight with memory's flame. Whether their actions were the result of bravery or vainglory, they had an essential aspect of personal freedom that perhaps was among the last in our society: the intoxication of a rupture with authority. I tried forcing myself to forget them at Harvard, and dared not speak of the phenomena I had witnessed in the covert world. On the pretense of academic demands, I avoided friends for weeks.

◯

AT LAST I SOUGHT refuge from these dreams by walking with Hulk, who was fond of long, quiet day hikes, on our favorite trail around Fresh Pond Reservoir. Well-treed, the reservoir provided the water for North Cambridge. The locals called it "The Pines." We often made the journey to cool out from the pressures of the Kennedy School. It was an elegaic morning of no classes; we padded along almost soundlessly, for our path was free in mid-week even from the occasional jogger or cyclist. Far down the trail, he abruptly stopped.

"We've never seen *that* before," he said.

I came alongside. Without notice or explanation, a mysterious entity had appeared. In a raised clearing, thick with pine straw and a view of the Pond, was a red granite bench set firmly into the ground. Four feet long, two feet high, eighteen inches wide, it must have weighed eight hundred pounds or more. Upon it was a perfectly chiseled, enigmatic, haunting inscription.

> "She whispered, giving herself in rapture to the cold embrace of the grass
> as she lay folded in her cloak in the hollow by the pool.
> Here I will lie. (A feather fell upon her brow)
> I have found a greener laurel than the bay. My forehead will be cool always,
> there are wild birds' feathers – the owls, the nightjars. I shall dream wild dreams…"

Hulk mused for a while, affecting to search his memory.

"Ah, Virginia Woolf. *Orlando*."

The origin of the bench, as of these writings years later, has never been solved. The donor remains unknown. By decision of the Water Board, it has never been removed. We stood in reverence, until he spoke again.

"Only in Cambridge."

I thought of his favorite near-witch. It was the perfect place for a moonlight assignation.

"You should bring Surf here."

○

IN MY SENSITIVE STATE Harvard Square was a *son et lumière* of the human condition, a whole anthology of the senses: the effervescence of early summer rain, the hard smells of iron gates and granite medallions upon entering the Yard, the cacophony of plebeian delights, bright pre-teens skylarking, growling traffic and clicking bicycles, strawberry ice creams and sticky fingers, a girl whirling to fragments of a Donizetti aria, Dominicans in queued taxis dreaming of the Caribbean's blue skin.

There seemed to be no surveillance in Cambridge anymore – at least none that was apparent – an absence which became even more worrisome to my slowly flagging paranoia. Before finally giving up and thinking such feelings illusory, I focused on every corner, every look, every car, my mind still as a burning glass.

○

IT WAS OUR SEASON of joy in Cambridge, for Commencement was imminent. On a late afternoon – in a rush of happiness at encountering old friends after the far and unspeakable lands of months abroad – I found Hammer and Hagendas in a rotunda with rose arbors. My recollection is dim on the encounter, perhaps it was Winthrop or Leverett House. He was reading to her from some dry Edwards Thompsons fascicles, rather than trying to excite her as before in the Museum of Natural History in

New York. No longer did he try tales of bloody assegai and ten thousand Sudanese dead from Maxim guns at Omdurman. He had learned the virtues of counter-imagination.

Hagendas had been attracted and repelled by Hammer since their erotic entwining before the assegai. No longer did she occupy all his mornings, *au naturel* and uncocooned.

During her more distant moments, he thought of her as some dire wench, one with the insolence of beauty. I began to sense her furious manner with him. She had decided that he had a sadistic impulse, but I knew he was devotedly humanitarian, even though in his miscalculation he had said and written anything to thrill her.

Although his scholarship remained excellent, this misunderstanding had driven Hammer into an emotional decline. In his overreaching eagerness to retain her affections, his usual monolithic poise now had desultory bursts of mania. While he retained his animal tenacity for her, Hammer felt persecuted, as though he were being pilloried by some beautiful harridan.

He had underestimated Hagendas's gifts, for she was not simply swans' down, falling angels and silk, but a formidable mental presence with elaborate ethics. As she stood beneath the slender chipped traceries and tall shanked columns, I could see that she had refused to be his pole star, and that they were on a winding road to some hopefully tranquil inevitability.

Hammer made a comment with a certain ghastly jauntiness, one I could not overhear. At this, she bridled haughtily. Eyes blazing, she heeled abruptly and left. At that moment he became utterly demoralized; all disposition of grace fell from his heart.

○

I GATHERED HAMMER at once, so that we walked together in these last days. The undergraduates – some with garlands of leafy ivy – were like young saplings crowded into the bony ruins of the Yard. By the Charles we saw the last voluptuaries of the sunset with their delightful insouciance, at least those students who had survived thus far. Many still crouched fearfully in Widener, Houghton, Peabody, Lamont or the Yenching Libraries.

Hammer – having never lost at anything – now had entered the *via dolorosa* of his life. With a surprisingly amiable futility, he began an amorous meditation, aiming his disposition obliquely at some invisible avatar of Hagendas. Rather than ignoble emotions, his delivery was a phalanx of sentiments, his final gesture of renunciation.

We walked quite late, until the new moon rolled across the surface of the Charles. Hammer, now nothing but a failed parvenu, muttered pained endearments to her recurring memory. He saw her face resonate upon the river, as if thrown back from a mirror, then shimmering and gone as a white wake stretched away under the moonlight.

Soon to be a Kentucky lawyer among the poor and illiterate, he looked at the heavens, and recalled an old country song.

"Fields of diamonds in the sky
Like the night you passed me by
I could reach you if I try
Fields of diamonds in the sky"

We saw the breathing beauty of the lonely water's reflections, the Charles stealing by us, flowing past the last lamps as if before the light of torches. Near the bosom of this ancient river, his passion was no longer a delirium.

We ambled in silence for a long while, halting now and then as he wrestled with sorrow. He remembered a poem by his childhood friend, now an elderly man, who still grieved over his lost lover, so very long ago.

"Into the river
Swollen with falling stars
I drop her promises.
They sink like stars of stone."

He withdrew from his pockets some tokens of remembrance, and let them go, one by one, into the water: her silver pen, her last note, a bundle of poems with a blue ribbon, a small scrap of torn and scented white silk.

〇

HAMMER TOOK HIS RETREAT to prepare for Commencement, so that I wandered alone, until Surf and Hulk came forth. They pretended our encounter was random, but Surf was acute to the scene with Hagendas, the pathos of the day.

When we first entered Harvard, she seemed quite capable of any excess. No stranger to coquetry then, Surf recently had developed a certain prudence, the duty of a heroine to a chivalric lover.

Hulk, who once anguished for her, covertly appraising her advantages – erotic and otherwise – now had her affections with only his disarming smile. He often enjoined Surf to various academic treasons, to which she rushed with a sensual sweetness. In the ashen light of the late moonscape, they sought my prediction that Hammer and Hagendas would prevail together somehow. Less than assured, they meandered down the Charles walkway dreaming of Commencement, a strewing of roses in the sky before them, under the last of our starry dawns.

On my morning trek down Mass Ave, during a prolonged bout of devoted introspections, Surf and Hulk rather insistently gathered me up. She was breathless, skipping about on those long legs like a girl.

"The Unitarians are having a *service*…no, the *Santo Daime* of Brazil…no, the High Church of *Scotland*…"

Her religious lodestar was spinning, perceptions I understood all too well. Surf had an uncanny sense of how to get to me. We idled arm-in-arm, appearing at Quincy House, to the unexpected sounds of swirling bagpipe music.

Quincy's House Master, dressed in formal kilts, appeared on the steps before a substantial crowd of cheering, whistling students. Shouting like a town crier in Chaucerian English, he was reading from an illuminated parchment. The piper's skirls accompanied his every word.

The Master was doing the annual exorcism. A Harvard tradition for decades, it was intended to ward off any spirits brought back from our Amazonian explorers, our archeologists' digs at Sardis, our perusal of heretic medieval tomes at Houghton Library, our proximity to sacred amulets and talismans at Peabody and the Botanical Museum, our prayers to diverse entities during Reading Period, and the theological confusions at the Div School.

"We herewith *exorcise*, exile, expel, exterminate and *exsufflate* all evil spirits…"

"Exsufflate?" I whispered.

Surf. "Blow them out one's *nose.*"

"…whether banshees or bogles, warlocks or witches, from our walls and floors and ceilings…"

I thought of dark wings fleeing the girl in Bangkok. In the Berlin night, there were smudge sticks and open French windows to let out the evil spirit, for there is only one.

"…our books and briefcases, our feather beds and waterbeds, our plumbing and pinball machines…"

Of course it was a frivolous, happy day for all, so that with some relief I rose to it and avoided looking harrowed. Although one was witnessing a parody of the unspeakable, it was no time to preach on street corners.

Hulk, indefatigable and relentless, insisted we also sprinkle ourselves from the drinking fountains near John Harvard's statue in the Yard. Knowing of my allusion to the statue as a religious pilgrimage site like the Meccan shroud, he pranced around us with irreverence, chanting in crude Arabic and splashing us lightly, to the horror of gaggles of tourists.

"Meccan holy water! From the well at Zem Zem!"

At this, with little shrieks of transfiguration, we brightened and danced about. The trails of darkness finally were gone from the campus, and from me, dispelled by gentle laughter, and the simple alchemy of caring friendships.

○

IT WAS SOON to be our last dance together. It seemed only yesterday that they first had coaxed me out of a furtive cubicle. Their sallies of joyous wit, their waylaying with ruthless mental ambuscades, had rolled on until my resolution foundered, and I began to play with them as well. It was a kind of charity on their part.

They had let me see their opening gambits of flirtation: Hulk like some ingrown virgin, with his guileless banter, even as his flesh slowly came alive. I saw his remorseless desire burst into summer kisses, until she became his cherished mistress. Once at Peabody I had to walk away, having come upon them embraced and inflamed, the lithe weight of her against him, and her husky voice fracturing the quiet with her throaty demands of "*Engorge-moi*." Now she obviously was his *amour-propre*, and his French had improved.

We toured the ongoing festivities at the undergraduate Houses, while Hulk instructed us on their histories. At Adams House, we stood under the motto, *Alteri Seculo*.

"Cicero," he translated, "For a future generation."

At Cabot house was Surf's favorite, *Semper Cor*.

"Forever the heart," she sang, dropping a slow Elizabethan courtesy, it seemed to us both.

○

WE FOUND HAGENDAS in Radcliffe Quad. She was in disarray, and quite tearful; we thought it was a reverberation from the distress with Hammer. She was pacing to-and-fro beneath some Frederick Church pastorals, past the fretwork and filigree, aimlessly pushing aside disordered Hepplewhite furniture. The afternoon sky had developed a fierce undertow of late spring clouds, blue-black and threatening, until the roiling sky finally burst. The rain began streaming down grey window panes, as if with a melancholy it could no longer bear.

We watched grim Hagendas, the slow clicking of her heels a metronome inside our silence, as the rain thrust downward.

"A promising sophomore girl," she said, "distraught at finals, killed herself and her roommate at Lowell House this morning."

At the news, a great nervous upheaval had spread across the Yard. The driven achievements, the overwhelming pace, the panic from mounting incomprehension, for some, provided no way out.

"The exorcism wasn't soon enough," Surf muttered gravely, as though in private she took such matters seriously.

We watched the steady rain. Through patches of clouds escaped ragged gusts and fumes of light, like harmless young spirits heavenward.

○

SUNSHINE WAS POURING into the Yard in the run-up to Commencement. Ribbons and bunting lined the seating between Widener and Memorial Church, while from the trees great silk banners of crimson furled and unfurled, wafting lightly in the air.

We all were autodidacts now, capable of quick study on any topic. The dispirited days of mastering infernal logic, the flights of galling failures – all were gone. Our fortunes no longer foundered, and seemed immutably fixed.

We had been reduced to ashes and reborn. Only a very few egos managed to reincarnate their grand seigneurial ways, walking about with the lofty destiny of the Harvardian overclass, as though the sons of gods had come unto the daughters of men. For almost all of us – we who suffered for our inspirations – it was a time of profound thanksgiving.

Class Day – the day before Commencement – was celebrated by undergrads in a less formal way. Four elected students gave speeches, two that were serious, and two inducing waves of hilarity. Prominent guest speakers typically included rock stars and presidents; a hand puppet – Kermit the Frog – once delivered the Class Day speech. Since 1838, gardeners mowed the Yard grass short before Class Day so students could dance unhindered. The gardeners grumbled that a cow could have done the job, since by a clause unobserved since 1772, professors still had the right to graze their herd in the Yard.

Several of the Parisians loitered about, a few with caps and gowns. Previously they had been scarcely animated corpses – languid, devious, impervious to the feminine. They now looked rather meek, with several pushing prams and constantly enlightened by their boisterous wives.

○

IT WAS A GATHERING OF WIZARDS, with a blue sky to crown it. Our futures were woven around these vivid memories; the valedictory images of Harvard's standards in silk hanging from all the oaks and elms. Every tree was festooned with great medieval gonfalons and banners bearing the heraldic devices of the various Houses and the professional schools; they passed softly overhead, like the gentle hands of Providence above those so blessed.

Commencement was always held outside, rain or snow, on the steps of Memorial Church. Among the thousands of onlookers, alumni and alumnae from every class for eighty years aggregated in small tents, some with elderly sprightliness, others wearing boaters and name tags – the last hurrah before subsiding into honored senescence.

Hulk rushed up in a gleeful spirit, his black gown overlain with the crimson mantle of Harvard College, as he breathlessly recalled the Commencement of 1797.

"A live elephant in the Yard. Calves with two heads. Women costumed as mermaids. Men wrapped like mummies."

"No sporting events?"

"Harvard students invited Native Americans from Natick for an archery competition."

"Who won?"

"They did…Oh, *bulls-eye*."

He had spotted his Queen. Surf glided through the crowd, her black graduate gown with an *alma mater* mantle of silk in dark Oxford blue. Oddly, she had never disclosed to us her prior training, or that she had a first in Greats at All Souls. And there was Hagendas, with her mantle of Princeton orange. Seeing them, I thought how perfect they would have been as operatives for the Six.

We sat with our Kennedy School class beneath our flowing crimson banner with the HKS shield upon it: three open books embossed with Veritas, above horizontal red and white stripes of the American flag. The vertiginous uncertainty of our fate was gone; our ganglia were made of steel.

Hagendas sat beside me, to her left was Surf, then Hulk. Hammer – perhaps sulking – was at the front row, on the right, with some voluminous bag of presumed party favors. He had an exhausted air, a princely detachment. No longer was Hagendas spread like spilt honey beneath cherub-haunted ceilings. Today she was a pale rose, fetching with her downy nape, and the open petal of her mouth.

The massive gravitational field of the Yard was pulsating. Galleons of great furry gowns – those of faculty, recipients of *honoris causa*, and other well-furnished minds – began sailing through the crowds to assemble for the regal, almost ecclesiastical form of procession begun at Oxford in the 14th Century.

At 9 AM, Morning Exercises were ending in Tercentenary Theater, the North Yard bounded by Widener, Memorial Church, Massachusetts Hall and University Hall. The Senior Class had gathered in the Church for their ceremony, surely now among the chosen.

The Harvard Band, assembled on Widener's steps before a sea of visitors, raised its brass for sustained fanfares, heralding the arrival of the presidential procession.

For over three hundred years the first to appear were the Sheriffs of Middlesex and Suffolk counties, in flowing purple and red robes, carrying long wooden staves. The lead Sheriff – bearing a great silver miter – walked ponderously, swaying from side to side like a saint at the Dead Sea.

The tapping of the miter inverted my world dream, to forever nights with only the ticking of flashlights on prison cell doors, and the ratcheting of handcuffs. It was a Zen priest's staff resounding at leaving ceremonies, then the sticks and crutches of legless Afghan orphans, then the sound of falling syringes from junkies dying in their own piss.

I was awakened from these private terrors by ever more elaborate trumpet fanfares launching skyward, like charging valkyries announcing the education of kings. The University Marshall followed the Sheriffs, with everyone in elaborate gowns: the current and former presidents in attendance, the Fellows of Harvard College, and the Board of Overseers. One of the procession seemed to carry – in both hands, on purple velvet – some precious amulet.

"The Harvard Seal," Hagendas remarked, "the escutcheon of the University, handed down from President Quincy, who discovered a 1693 hand-drawn version."

Surf, *sotto voce*. "It was opposed by Calvinists, who thought its exclusion of 'Christo et Ecclesiae' was a sign of Unitarian infidelity."

The Governor of Massachusetts was next, with all candidates for honorary degrees and their faculties, moving forward as if they were sanctified, like a march of Carmelites.

Hulk, leaning into Surf. "Ben Franklin was the first honorary, in 1753. U.S. presidents. John Singer Sargent, Frost, Churchill, Mother Teresa, Mandela, Gates."

The presidential procession was walking alongside the alumni tents through ranks of senior speakers, senior class officers, and candidates for *summa cum laude*.

It was a kind of joyous idolatry. In the palpitant moist heat of early summer; these passages of reverend gentlemen and women fed the hot flames of memory. I thought of the ghastly rictus of the Bangkok girl as her countenance became the Madonna, of Surf tramping through autumn leaves along the rain-swept Yard, of the liturgical nymphomania of Berlin, of watching the moon cloud over with Hagendas by the Charles.

Presently the Harvard faculties came, in rank of seniority, with their robes of many colors and the silk-lined borders of their *almae matres*. These were the men and women who had raised us to consciousness, who baptized us into a shock of recognition. Little girls with ribbons were frolicking by the procession, with garland of roses in their hair, waving to them. As the faculty noticed and waved back, their humanity truly shone.

Hagendas and Surf were holding hands tightly, like lovers, something I had never seen in them before. Their expressions were identical, as if they were the *Hetairae* – high courtesans of ancient Greece – about to entertain *à deux*.

The faculty was followed by former members of the Governing Boards, past professors, former alumni association officers; some were serious, other smiling at the trails of glory. I thought of the note from V-1 and V-2 in Chiang Rai, that excellence does not fade, or even dim.

Hagendas spotted two key figures for our fiercely competitive, soon to be graduates; two that assessed the fineness of thought among these young stars.

"That's the president and orator of Phi Beta Kappa," she said, "and the Trustee of the Charity of Edward Hopkiss, which awards academic prizes to undergraduates."

This bright and elevated spectacle – under my new eyes – was underlain with the tragic world at large: the twisted warrens of baked mud huts and earthen floors, flies and beggars and lepers, feeble lanterns in benighted little brothels, the unsalved pestilences, the insanity, the unheeded shrieks in brutish, filthy rooms.

The Ministers of the Six Towns – the clergy of Old Cambridge churches – came next, with their magnetic sway from lifelong curating of the spirit, for the ecclesiastics oversaw births and deaths, the transubstantiations, the scattering of peonies on gravestones.

Last were consuls to Boston, state and federal judges, past-honorary degree recipients, public officials and other guests.

Two stunning women, very thin, lofty and elegant twins in heels – adorned by crimson gowns – strode into the procession. Their heads were above the crowds. Petulant dignitaries were yielding to their charms, as sanctimonious expressions became childlike at their presence. An unnerving sight, I could see only their backs as they mingled with a few, then seemed to depart through the alumni tents, holding hands.

The president settled on stage into an old three-legged Jacobean chair. Hagendas, her silk robe rustling, her voice like afternoon flowers, observed the moment.

"The chair was President Holyoke's in the mid-1700s. Used ever since just for this day."

One hour and forty-five minutes after the procession first had gathered, everyone at the almost 400th Harvard Commencement bowed their heads for the Invocation, followed by the Commencement Choir with portions of Beethoven's *Missa Solemnis*. Like the tranquil dispersal of the Six to the remote earth, it was the last rapture of this mystical throng as well.

I remembered for a moment how it came to be – so improbably on this June morning – that I stood beneath the elms and flowing silk standards in Harvard Yard. I began to sing to myself, in a whisper so low that no one else could hear.

"We shall gather at the river, the beautiful, beautiful river…"

A senior rose on the dais to deliver the traditional Latin oratory. He opened somberly and at length, declaiming theatrically in flawless, complex Latin. Within the soliloquy seemed a few phrases on *Deus* and *lux* I had not heard uttered since the transfigurative nights.

Suddenly a mad giggle arose. Ripples of laughter began spreading among the hundreds of trained classicists in attendance, then howls as fluent insiders first realized he had begun telling ancient Roman jokes. In the end – to our relief, general comprehension, cheers and applause – he resorted to every popularly known Latin phrase, then mutilated the verb tenses.

"Hic haec hoc, huius, huius, huius, huic, huic, huic." (the Latin declensions, pronouced fancifully: heek hike hoke, hug us, hug us, hug us, quick, quick, quick)

Undergraduates took full advantage of the opportunity.

An advanced degree candidate rose to deliver the final student speech. Hulk, across from Surf and with hand covering mouth, knew no limit.

"Oliver Wendell Holmes did it in 1828, Teddy Roosevelt in 1880."

The grad student speech was no string of homilies, but accomplished and inspired, full of oracular phrases. He ended with resounding Goethe.

"The moment one definitely commits oneself
then Providence moves too.
Whatever you can do, or think you can, begin it.
Boldness has magic, power and genius in it."

A deep roaring began like a summer storm, growing ever louder, now with wild shouts and whistles, as we hovered by future's gates.

The Dean of the College rose. He conferred his blessing on the new graduates, followed by each Dean of the graduate schools. Rowdiness and disorder began breaking out.

The Schools of Science and Engineering stood, while their Dean addressed them. The moment he stopped, hundreds flung their mortar boards in the air, together with slide rules and calculators. Each graduate school class came prepared to out do each other with public spectacles.

Harvard School of Public Health students were summoned to stand and be anointed. Upon conferral, they produced from under their gowns a thousand packs of cigarettes, and yard-long plastic cigars, and threw them into onlookers as smokers went wild.

Hulk. "I never inhaled."

Harvard Medical School was next, the end of twenty years of rigorous study, standing for their blessing as healers. Plastic children's stethoscopes soon sailed about, hanging up on trees with the flowing medical school standard. Matters were increasingly unruly; people were coming undone. Surf, growing excited at this apex of a lifelong dream, began panting.

"Oh, my beating heart."

Monopoly money and real dollar bills zoomed in makeshift airplanes over the graduates as Harvard Business School rose, some waving fistfuls and other igniting dollars, rubles and rupees with lighters.

I teased Surf. "This could be their last orgasm, unless they short the next bear market."

It was the Law School that gave me pause. Here they sat in judicial solemnity, awaiting their Dean's conferral. Among them were future Supreme Court justices, presidents, federal and appeals courts judges, prosecutors, defense attorneys, Wall Street barons, and honest street lawyers fighting for civil rights. Their gravity soon was broken – perhaps by the longest cheers – as six-foot, pink-and-blue plastic sharks emerged, complete with raised dorsal fins and sets of great white teeth. A prolonged feeding frenzy mounted into an aerial lunacy, with sharks leaping and plunging into the massed students, finally thrown aloft by hundreds of hands into the shouting mobs.

We at the Kennedy School were last. Upon the Dean's profound laying on of hands, Hammer was seen handing out odd round objects he somehow had secreted into the festivities. Once inflated – somewhat like ourselves this morning – they became globes of the earth with blue seas and continents and cities; we twirled them overhead on our fingertips to the increasing amusement of the crowds.

Like great balloons at a rock festival, they began rolling over the former undergraduates, bouncing high and fast, riccocheting like volleyballs or exploding to our environmental concerns, as through the Benediction the madness increased exponentially.

To exuberant fanfares, we marched out of the gates of Harvard Yard. Our actual diplomas were awarded later – one by one – at ceremonies in the undergraduate houses and the professional schools. The Kennedy School had reception tents in green and pink stripes, with families everywhere, and ecstatic faces off to Congressional committees or the White House or *Médicine Sans Frontière* or Tibet or Serbia.

Diplomas in hand, we returned to the Yard for the final speech, that year by the Secretary of State. A forceful speaker, she related the menace from Chinese cyberwar, to the unease of our many students from the Mainland. The dragon statue by Boylston Hall looked on, carved in honor of a dead emperor of the oldest civilization, and wholly unperturbed.

It was when the Secretary departed the academic procession with her security – for lunch with the president of Harvard – that Commencement gained an irresolvable aspect of unreality. I again saw the two atmospherically tall models in the bright crimson gowns of doctoral candidates, close in with the Secretary and another woman, her Chief of Staff. Under their red caps, they wore matching black wigs in a French curl, and small purple-tinted eyeglasses with gold rims. I began struggling for a better view, imagining V-1 and V-2, but the press of the crowd forced me back, dispelling what could only have been an illusion. Perhaps – for that unforgettable moment – I was overwrought.

Passing at last through the gate of admirations, we came unto this lighted world, this spectacle of humankind, armed only with our charter to care for nations. We had entered to grow in wisdom. We departed to better serve our country, and our kind.

○

I TOOK a slow train down to New York City the next day, for a promised farewell lunch with Surf and Hagendas at the Harvard Club. They wore fine navy blue suits from Bergdorf's, very proper, all business. Hopelessly improvident, I had only my Moscow jacket, and was harried from packing for a cheap round-the-world research tour with countless stops and unlikely connections.

"You could contact the local Harvard Clubs worldwide," Hagendas proposed, "each of 170 countries has one. The oldest private intel network, next to the Vatican."

I advised them I would blend with the people, in the open markets and sometimes on footpaths, rather than traveling under the University's aegis. Back rooms might be lit by guttering wicks, floating in oil. They understood.

High on the wall above Hagendas loomed a massive mounted bull elephant's head with great tusks. Surf, seeing my distress, still had Hulk's historical virus.

"Victim of priapic Theodore Roosevelt. Class of 1880."

Hagendas was off to Switzerland, to her long-sought Banque Mondiale. Hammer already had left for the Southern Poverty Law Center. Hulk was on a plane to Paris as a consultant for some outsourced intelligence aggregator. Surf – whom we could never pin down – would be nearby in her beloved Eastern Europe, with remote political groups and uncertain affiliations to ambiguous agency fronts.

Both were almost white witches; without my divulging the Six, we often had discussed until first light the care of this earth, the sharing of consciousness, the spirit. Seated next to a landscape by Turner, they drank only mineral water, toying with little salads somewhat sadly.

We knew that we might not be together again. At last we toasted each other, competing with quotes in light play and honor. I opened with a line from Horace, then winced at the thought that Hammer might have read it to her.

"Incendi per igni." (I got through flames)

Hagendas raised her glass to us, with her somber, brow-bright gaze, and easily trumped me with Diderot.

"The present moment, great God! Tis the ark of the Lord. Woe be to him that lays hand upon it."

Surf's eyes darkened, interiorized, as if deciding what to say. Never before at a loss for the perfect *bon mot*, this time she begged forgiveness, then appeared to collect herself. We took each other's hands in silence, then stood with a long embrace.

They both were clad in the same light summer perfume, disturbingly reminiscent of Eau De Givenchy. Startled at the crossfire of their magnetism, and caught within their moonlit midnight, I suddenly felt the milk whiteness of them. They both began throbbing like the morning star. We walked to the entrance, I somewhat unsteadily, to where my cab to Grand Central was waiting.

Coincidence may be of such rarity that the divine in life is illuminated: a word, an act, some synchronicity, a reminder of the impossible that pierces the fabric of cognition. The Six had penetrated Oxford and Princeton but not – it seemed – Harvard. It is true that the ravishing Surf and Hagendas were Hellenists, not uncommon in Cambridge, and that we had discussed my interests in benign medicines. Yet, it had been highly improbable that these sensuous, talented women befriended one so easily in the first weeks, always rescuing me from disorienting sojourns, receptive of confidences but not prying. It was if they always knew precisely what to do.

As my cab began edging into traffic, Surf tapped on the window. I rolled the glass down. She and Hagendas, their hair flowing lightly in the warm wind, were standing together in the formal manner, hands in prayer. They bowed as one. As reality inverted, Surf spoke first.

"Make an offering to Aesculapius," she said.

"And don't forget," said shining Hagendas.

There were no waves of farewell, no smiles. The cab pulled away as I looked back at them. They stood with a flawless, trained posture, hands still together, as if their nakedness for endless mornings had been covered only by humble robes. Their images grew smaller. Even now, I see their eyes.

Chapter 24.

Al-Iksir
(The Elixir)

"What on earth prompted you to take a hand in this?"
"I don't know, my code of morals."
"Your code of morals? What code?"
"Comprehension."

- Camus, *The Plague*

Identity is the frail suggestion of coherence with which we have clad ourselves.

- Nietzsche

It was the technique of a man who selected thought
as one might select pieces of a jigsaw puzzle.

- Christie on H. Poiret, *The Third Girl*

IN A DEEP BLUE SUMMER KIMONO, she floated through the 16th Century wooden temple above Kyoto, out into the mountain forests of Japan thick with sycamores and red fescue. As she came to the bridge over a pond, then gazed at her reflection, she loosened her hair. A chrysanthemum fell into the water. At my cottage eave, she spread wide a curtain of falling lilac, then quietly slid open a shoji panel. As black-masked buntings fluttered among limbs laden with plum blossoms, a shakuhachi flute slowly moaned, gentling the night. Disrobing, she folded her kimono in perfect reverence and silence, then came naked to my futon, her slim silhouette outlined against moonlight. She stood for a moment with a gentle smile, kneeled, and bowed.

○

BUT I AWOKE on the dawn commuter train from New York to Washington, D.C., hours from Dulles airport and still a world from Kyoto. It was the first leg on the cheapest round the world ticket available, discounted only to fill seats as long as one moved west and tolerated complications of absurd connections on flimsy, risky carriers from Osh to Ashgabat.

The train was buried under foreign intrigues. The conveyed were not ebullient families on outings, or even Wall Street workers or laborers, but a passage of grim men and women clutching the *Post* or intent on computer screens. It was a train of thought, politics, subterfuge and surveillance.

With a jolt, we stopped at Princeton Junction to await the "Dinky," the shuttle out of the University on a private spur with only one car for students and faculty. A concession by the railroad to the University since the 1920s, it was ridden by Fitzgerald to Scribner's in New York, Oppenheimer to the A-Bomb hearings, Einstein to mathematical conferences and sailing off Long Island. Now CIA recruits, NSA analysts, and Institute for Advanced Study theorists all traveled on the spur – thinkers and actors casting a world-wide web where our every vibration was monitored by the unseen and attended by hosts of moral hobgoblins.

A lean, erect figure with refined features entered, quick as a lion and concentrated with a certain age and the quality of a serious male. Wearing a cherished blazer, and bearing an octavo volume – *The Life of Petrarch* – he sat beside me. He had the same sea-grey eyes, crystallized with a look of elation. In an eloquent understatement, we ignored each other for several hours.

I listened to Part 4 of Edward Elgar's *The Kingdom*, while Cobalt read the Petrarch. He floridly annotated the margins, occasionally making subtle gestures with his fine Montblanc. The conspirators all about us continued projecting normalcy, some destined for Langley or Fort Meade, some so silent and hostile they were obvious, others with an apparently vapid chatter carefully designed to dissemble.

As we neared D.C., a sad yellow sun hung over the slums in a liquid haze like used gauze. At the distant howling of dogs, I thought of the palpitating misery through which we passed, the poor and weak in bitter proximity to the powerful. Irony became unreal in Cobalt's presence though, for the scene slightly shifted with the edge of a contact high I fought to repress.

Rasping announcements began cutting through our reveries; everyone's artificial privacies were punctuated by society's electric overlord. Cobalt was engaged in some educated, forthright exchange with another passenger on extrajudicial killing by third-world controlled drones. His charitable, friendly effusion continued even as I noticed through the windows the demolished archways and skeletons of buildings among blocks infected by idle scruples.

With his heroic sentiment and refined diplomatic practices, Cobalt soon elicited the confidence of his temporary companion. The latter's initial hesitancy finally overcome, they exchanged business cards. Cobalt, clearly an informed source of intel – the currency of the Hill – was fully backstopped with a legend unassailable even to law enforcement. Seeing the card, his new contact became infused with a kind of gallant hypomania; with friendly assurances of a private meeting, he departed at the next stop.

Cobalt finally turned to me, with a whisper.

"Shall we circle this planet together? It may be our last opportunity."

Accustomed now to the impromptu, unpredictable, too-transient approaches of the Six, I was grateful for any sustained access to Cobalt. My toilsome personal journey would be transfigured by his mere presence, but I wondered how he divined my trip on short notice, or how he possibly could match my convoluted itinerary. He brought two cool drinks.

I mumbled about interviewing deans of foreign medical schools, hoping to establish international standardized exams on the U.S. model, but privately also to find a slot for a belated med student to go to ground. He just looked at me. I suggested that my connections would be labored.

"But that would include Sint Maarten," I said, in a transparent effort to discourage him, "and Stanford, Kyoto, Paris, Bologna, Groningen, and St. Petersburg. And a perplexity of unheated student hostels. And gunfire pockmarked runways…"

Environmental threats were trivial to Cobalt; he thought nothing of time and space. With the visionary intelligences of the Six, he was quick to dispense with small talk; he had an immediacy I had not seen before in any of them, as though there was some hurry to conclude my tutelage. For our journey, he made a most unexpected offering.

"Around the world, we could separate the visual field into Heaven and Hell."

I could only nod, acquiescing to this challenge of a painful, ecstatic teaching. As he spoke, a most subtle deviation in the dreary landscape began, a shining of things, where the common became precious. I thought of Ginsberg describing the area: "Baltimore gleamed in supernatural ecstasy." At this tenuous warp of perspective, our unconscious linked; it began as the most tender of touches, then rushed into an irresistible embrace.

The train's light shimmered, the roar and darkness fluorescing as through a tunnel of ion plasma, until the outlines of Washington, D.C. appeared. Near the station, a driver stood with a placard on which was written on "Xe," the atomic abbreviation for the element Xenon. I stumbled toward the safety of Cobalt's town car.

As he raised the driver's partition, we glided away as if on an affluent magnetic cushion. There was a light rain, and shivering beads of water on the car's black hood, but through wind-swept trickles the windows began to assume the lightest tawdry pattern, where the trails of grime suddenly were predominant. The smooth sounds of the powerful motor shifted to wrong chords, dark and *macabre, à la diable*.

Like Indigo in Zürich, he passed his conjurer's hand over the window, kindling my sense of the possible; at his gesture, perception was altered by an angstrom of emotion, or a light year of thought.

"Hell," he said.

There were no flagrant changes at first, rather a subtle shadowing of prospect. Then the spectacle of D.C. – FBI Headquarters, Main Justice, the Lincoln Memorial, the Washington Monument, the domes of the Senate – all were a *déjà vu* of the final days of Athens and Rome. The black hand of the dissolute moved among them. Their indulgences infuriated barbarian hordes, as all tore at vanishing grace and civility. The Pentagon stank with killing.

The verisimilitude of analysts and advisors was merely bogus fortunetelling. With ageless moral dissonance, impotent old men plotted shamelessly, consolidating power. It grew more intense.

The autumn was red with blood, hawthorn trees with pink and red petals shriveled into claw and fang before my eyes. All was ungovernable. Decision makers had a cold aridity, their staff a phlegmatic passivity. The elevated had only the low cunning of provincial public prosecutors, aflame with zeal and ignorance.

The vision almost was unbearable. We passed a ditch clogged with dead leaves. A deformed plastic baby lay trapped in a sewer, her innocent eyes unseeing.

"Now Heaven."

The best of us, dedicated to serve, moved with piety and self-abnegation in the quiet marble halls of the Capitol rotunda. Everyone was humanitarian, our government blessed with equable laws, our leaders resolute, impervious to intrigues. Our great monuments had a refined modernity and the heritage of truth; everywhere compassionate integrity reigned. The Hill was the bright fountain of evolution, the future of our species, the very heart of the world.

Our driver turned into the blocks surrounding NSA at Fort Meade. Cobalt displayed a stack of contractor green cards, all with different identities, his passports into any intel community.

"Here – once more – lightly," he said.

Gnarled pines at the entryways had the smell of decadence. Mammoth computers echoed with hysterical condemnations and distant cannonades of doom. The plotting and overfed were riddled with schisms, their rigor that of deceitful accountants rather than of angels.

Technicians were cloaked men whose calculating machines had the symmetry of black altars. Idolaters of Turing were servants to demons, their fear of everything a pernicous delusion. Computer arrays became a concentric holocaust, as clouds of data unraveled. A starless night of failed cognition descended, under a blurred moon. I began to panic.

"Now the opposite."

Angels of silver filled the hallways; brilliant young analysts with PhDs and kind eyes jostled in an intellectual paradise. Dazzling machines served the very least of us: the newly born, the lost, the falling sparrow. The intel tribes were guardians against errant weapons, disease and cruelty, keeping watch over us all like our loving mothers.

The driver en route back to Dulles detoured into the slums of Washington without being asked, as though everything this day were staged.

"Darkness," Cobalt said.

Twisted sidewalks and derelict houses swarmed with hungry children and addict mothers. Screaming leeches pranced on street corners with angry boom boxes and the glory road in their pockets. In this vale of tears, old men and babies had the same eyes.

"Now the other way…"

Equatorial rhythms linked everyone in the bass line world beat of sunny cookouts; elders danced with gleeful babies before open fire hydrants, mothers blossomed and children ran in joy as cool brothers laughed on doorsteps, sharing fine Jamaican ganja and high-fives.

Cobalt lowered the driver's partition. "His plane, please," he said.

◯

WE APPROACHED the air terminal at Dulles, where limos with embassy plates crowded into private jetways, and stern men in dark suits hastened to secret agendas. Colbalt turned to me, his eyes fathomless.

"What's the difference between Heaven and Hell?"

I had no answer, unable to speak a single word. My thoughts had congealed. Lying inanimate, head against the window, I had been sublimed completely by his *orbis tertius*, his illusory world. Consigned to more instruction, I awaited some resurrection.

He would take different transports to my next destinations, his identities and seats thereby uncertain. As I departed, the town car license plates were waving scriptures, a black anemone of changing Arabic characters from some Persian Gulf emirate. I boarded a jet to the Dutch-French island of Sint Maarten. The phenomena subsided but reoccurred, the aircraft screaming in bloody fragments one moment, the Caribbean a heavenly tropic in another, until these perspectives folded together and I sailed through the white clouds and brilliant warm sun of a loving deity.

◯

AS WE LANDED on the French side of the island, Sint Maarten's crescents of incandescent beaches edged waters of blue glass. At the American University medical school, I attended lectures with students in shorts, then slept on a burlap hammock — tied to palm trees behind the dormitories — loaned by a friendly young future physician. All were bright, talkative, and encouraging, eager for their clerkships in New York; their fine new campus — designed to withstand the autumnal Force Five hurricanes — had heavy louvered windows, overhead fans, and open-air laboratories with ranks of microscopes. In the evenings over simple meals *à la Provence*, I questioned students in rough lean-tos of palm fronds by Friar's Beach. Topless Parisiennes strolled by the seaside, holding hands. Others were mysterious, alone, slender and barefoot, feeling the salt warmth on their legs.

My skin was still pale from winter entombment in libraries. Drinking in the late rays of the sun, I swam with long, deeply pulling strokes until exhausted. Only eight miles offshore, the volcanic cone of thinly-populated Saba Island rose from the sea like a low thunderstorm. With its own medical school of eight students, weekly mail boat, and only a footpath between huts, it was the perfect retreat for one who wished to disappear.

◯

LEAN AND TONED in a woven hat and loose cotton trousers, Cobalt appeared at the edge of the beach; he was walking and reading, just another purposeless tourist. Sitting nearby, he requested fresh juice, some Camembert and Brie, then perused a volume on Alexander of Aphrodisias. A twelve-meter sloop was anchored just offshore, its sails reefed, halyards knotted neatly. At twilight, an alluring *madame* emerged from the barely-lit cabin, descended gracefully to the sea, and swam beyond us to walk on beach. She had a fine even smile and perfect teeth, with only a scrap of folded floral print twisted about her hips. In the manner common to the Côte d'Azur, her uptilted nipples were free, designed for yearning.

The conversation with Cobalt never really ceased; in his presence only the light of the world shone into different scenes: loving, fearsome, piteous, glorious, poignant. Near him one could only brace for waves of silent information – a sudden change of aesthetic, a difference in the prosaic, the periodic and absolute shifts in perspective.

I noticed the plants first. As we talked, they now appeared as strange life forms from unchartered planetary systems thriving in this atmosphere of mixed gases. People at a distance – then the far lights and buildings themselves – all seemed to walk about with the hiss of waves. I could only relax with it. The swirling stars above Cobalt reflected his recondite beliefs, but the visual field overhead was not so farfetched while the recognizable splendors of Vega and Altair still burned steadily in the sky. The sand became soft like clouds, while his voice was everywhere, inside and out, as though one were dreaming in echos.

"This planet," he finally said, "has the most glorious sunsets. Yet it is so very delicate."

At his observation, the marine-blue Caribbean snapshot in which we were framed tore in two, and doomed hominids gnashed with rotted gums on vile trash by toxic seas.

Seconds later, it again was a peaceful, warm, early evening. Small girls sang "*Adieu, chérie*" to each other, filling their toy pails with the purity of powdery, sun-washed sand. I reeled from the distortion, knowing that with Cobalt's teachings the earth might part at any moment, together with the blessing of our illusion called reality.

⬡

THE NEARBY VILLAGE of Marigot had small cafés dense with Amsterdammers and Parisiennes; tanned, attractive multilingual youth and harried *au pairs* flourished on French cuisine in the sultry, humid nights. Stacks of staring grouper, wall-eyed bonito, barracuda, and mottled green lobsters were piled in heaps by glowing charcoal in quayside firepits. The scents of Havana tobaccos, costly perfumes from Grenoble, and wines from Bordeaux laced the aromas of enticing cooking odors. Nubile, small-breasted, absurdly thin models from Luxembourg fluttered and strained against each other like storks, all wearing tight white tee-shirts and jeans, their manicured toes in Alexander Wang sandals, their wisps of sun-white hair like some signal of evolution.

We passed along the narrow streets in the Sint Maarten night, as elegant, sensuous French women in tight leopard pants gave longing looks, dining *al fresco* with their unconscious paramours in small, lively restaurants by the tiny harbor. During the day, they trolled in the *boulangeries* and *pâtisseries* with only slight bikinis adorning their lithe figures, their unspoken hunger apparent to the sensitive and discerning admirer.

○

WHILE CONFRONTING the divergent phenomena arising from the presence of one of the Six, I often tried to elicit details of their methods, the routines of their wondrous and frightful private worlds.

"Can you speak of actual, secular practices in the clandestine labs, other than the psychic events?"

Surprisingly, he without hesitation offered a little *vignette*.

"Within the rotary evaporators appears a pellucid, golden foam, the pure product before crystallization. It breathes argon, rising and falling like the transparent breath of some wild thing being born, until it becomes rigid, filling a pear-shaped flask, reticulated, cellular like a sponge."

I was at a loss to record such poetic mechanics of synthesis, thinking them better suited for academic journals.

"But of your personal conduct, I mean, excluding religious practices?"

"We are physically vigorous, exercising strongly, hiking on moonlit paths, sometimes bathing in streams or waterfalls. Yoga always. In winter, we run the high icy roads at midnight, even though there are no observers near our remote settings. The world then is a planet of snow crystals at high altitude, the stars so very close. Vast silence, one discovers, is comforting."

"Do you go out, other than for running?"

"Rarely. Only for communication – from distant towns through anonymizers – or for food, firewood."

In the late night, small sailboats and catamarans drifted before light winds in the channels, mooring near empty beaches of still warm white sand. In the far distance, a few lissome couples and threesomes swam naked – or took each other in translucent waters of secluded coves – beneath the heavy, waxing, forbearing moon.

As they passed eroded seamarks, the bow waves and wakes of returning boats were breaking with phosphorescence; the estuaries were alive with egrets and snowy pelicans, the summer ocean scattering and sucking about our ankles as we waded near the shoreline.

"There is a magnificent, mystical piezofluorescence in the pure substance, the twinkling of stars like blue lights from dissociation of crystal lattices. A single gram flashes when shaken in darkness, like foxfire, or a kind of fairy dust."

Cobalt was musing; I didn't interrupt.

"In covert settings, solitude is the central aspect, apart from the religiosity. There is only you and it, for weeks, months. No human contact. Isolation is painful after the first days; we yearn so very much for others. One walks incessantly, often in the night, with humility, focus, and deep prayers. We practice relaxations, to keep the fear at bay."

A lovely French girl, sitting legs crossed by a palm shelter, observed us from the beach. She wore only a garland of cowslips in her hair, and below her belly a thread of thong. She was covered in moonlight; her lap was full of flowers. She waved to us very slowly in a wide arc with an artist's delicate fingers – as if she knew everything about us – then gave a salutation in the accent of the Midi. We returned the simple greeting, Cobalt with a few charming words in French. Mademoiselle was – as we were – inviting, amused, *enchanté*. I wondered if she recognized him in some special way, like Indigo being approached by strangers in the Rijksmuseum.

The powder-white sand was littered with small beds of kelp, a few shattered shells, and the bleached remains of small crabs. We meandered, aimless, with an occasional exchange. I tried an orthogonal question.

"When you come into D.C., what then?"

He paused. With Cobalt, such delay meant I had reached some barrier.

"Upon re-integrating from the isolation of batches – for we are so fragile afterwards – I am fond of church and temple cookouts."

I thought he was joking.

"Other than gentle, earnest people with a Judeo-Christian ethos, they are cluttered with analysts – like receptions throughout the Beltway. Collecting and vetting intel contacts is my hobby; we have audiovisual of the most diverse layers of government. A word here, a look there – all included in our intel mosaic – and occasionally a rich vein mined from the odd and florid egomaniac."

A tepid sea-breeze moved along the cove. As the disposition of winds and countercurrents began settling the night into a long calm, the sea softly licked the prows of small vessels, then became still as a floor of glass, sliding beneath dreams.

"In Delft, Indigo said that if there were an arrest, the worldwide system would go dark. What would happen, precisely?"

"The variety of small independent chemists would continue, with availability at a lower level. We would place the event under ruthless scrutiny, perhaps neutralizing – of course in a legal, nonviolent manner – the devilish perpetrator, the informant."

"By what means?"

"Our Master-at-Arms – Magenta – says there is a parry to every thrust. The prime quality of his character is daring."

I had encountered by happenstance one of the *bona fides* of their sect. Cobalt continued with an apostolic air, as if ministering.

"We would never physically harm anyone, but some young operative conceivably might ensure the informant's detention for a while, reducing his credibility and providing karmic closure."

With the Six there was always – beneath the light from them – some swift and cold river fanning throughout the world. Delicious, life-giving to their adherents, but forceful and final.

"There is an issue," he finally revealed. "An independent chemist in San Francisco passed away, an elder who did small batches of perhaps four hundred grams or a kilo every year or so. We felt it first as a disturbance in the aether, if you will, like concentric rings in a pool of shared consciousness. His stored laboratory – however dysfunctional – has disappeared. It may have fallen into the wrong hands, those of some charlatan or mountebank."

"You mean stolen?"

"We have tracked it to the Midwest, where small remnants of batches – impure but active by-products really – are being distributed by some unscrupulous opportunist. We sense the outcomes – like a distress in the continuum."

"Magenta may have mentioned it at Wilton Park? And what will you do?"

"We will study it closely, then locate the lab and the thief."

After some days, he drove me down sandy roads by great marshes, past the chaotic calypso markets and along the lucid Caribbean to the dusty, meager airport. Throughout his tutorial of me on our world's journey, he never alluded to the missing lab again. By his hesitancy, I intuited they had serious concerns.

The jet climbed at a fearsome angle in full thrust, its fuselage barely evading the jagged, barren volcanic peaks of Sint Maarten. It was filled with sun-browned, sated French and Dutch couples and American medical students fresh from final exams, but not Cobalt. He had returned for a day at Friar's Beach near Marigot, to practice his Midi dialect with the girl in her garland of cowslips, and finish at leisure the Alexander of Aphrodesias.

⬡

THE REDWOOD VALLEYS and oaken hills of San Francisco Bay were off the wingtip; a silken glove of Pacific air with moist fog crept inland. The heirs of the great transformations of the Sixties roamed the universities, art museums and cafés. In wartime, nuns and elders and students doused the federal building in blood, chanting and falling under night sticks and sharp hooves.

From the City to Stanford, we thrilled at billboards with complex mathematical formulae, the public challenges to recruit talented programmers and cryptographers whose solutions and persons would be harvested by Google, Apple or Oracle. On Highway 280, with great ranges of heavy redwoods to the sea on one side, Stanford and Silicon Valley on the other, we passed the rural, equine Woodside community, now bought up by dot-com billionaires. Down Sand Hill Road past the Hoover Tower we entered campus.

Throughout the archways of the Stanford quad, and from the physics tank to the medical school, Cobalt engaged in casual, sometimes electrical exchanges with students and faculty; there seemed to be no science or technology in which he was not delightfully facile. On a sunlit patio by Tressider Union, over yoghurt and fruit, Cobalt related stories of Silicon Valley.

"Many of the early programmers had psychedelic experiences, to which they attributed increases in creativity and less rigid thinking. Jobs certainly, Gates, the Microsoft group of eleven. It was – and is – something of a tradition among California intellectuals and coders."

"And now computers permeate civiliztion." I observed, as researchers and investors began their ritual gatherings at Tressider.

"One must not be overwhelmed by any social change. Consider an eminent futurist who said in the 80s that "Computers are the most important advance since psychedelics," then later regretted his opinion, thinking psychedelics were trivialized as the world came online and computation dominated information."

"A billion-dollar industry versus a few young experimentalists? Surely they are different realms."

"We see the issue in several ways. Psychedelics evolve slowly. They appear historically in eras: Delphi, the ceremonial cup of Eleusis, the rituals of rainforest tribes, the discovery of the subjective effects of LSD during the Manhattan Project. Altering mind is a more fundamental concept than altering external information."

"But in what directions will psychedelics and computers go?"

"Psychedelics do two things with regard to computation, excluding their effects on creative programming. First, they point the way to enhanced wetware, the pharmacological and genetic neural modifications that we anticipate will help us process the Net's total information access. And second, the revelations – emotional, religious, philosophical insights – ensure that ultimately we must turn away from the machines, so that we can see the skies, so that we can see each other."

"You are suggesting that the proliferation of machine languages – in the end – must yield to the more subtle complexities of consciousness based on living DNA?"

He easily trumped my convoluted effort at paraphrasing him.

"We feel that conscious control of cognitive evolution – a point which is imminent – is a singularity. It is very much like the point at which AI – artificial intelligence – becomes self-instructive and exceeds our capacities. Rather a horse race between machines and flesh, if you will, but humans must predominate lest we are enslaved. Look, the chief of neurology at Harvard Medical School, you may recall, declared past decades as the age of the atom, the current era as the age of the computer, the near future – and forever after – as the age of the neuron."

I had attended the lecture. "How did you know that?"

"Our early surveillance and vetting of you, in Boston."

Leaving Stanford we drove through the University's eight thousand acres of rolling fields and forests, with hills atoped by great radiotelecopes. From SLAC – the massive Linear Accelerator – we continued along the great estates down Mountain Home Road in Woodside, and spiraled up two thousand feet on a serpentine among the redwoods. Past La Honda, we swept through the genuine heart balm of broad, quiet, fold-away valleys to the sea.

◯

SUDDENLY, we were on the beach. A natural Godhead and long a refuge for Stanford students fatigued with intellect, the sea was buffeted and breathless, with stentorian booms of surf. Beyond the dunes, desolate sands ran wild in elation.

At first, by the deafening roaring of the waves, Cobalt almost shouted as he flowered rhapsodically. We retreated to a jutting promontory, where the trembling waters below blew and sprayed like a gale. I could never anticipate Cobalt, and never knew what he might say next. By his practiced erraticism, one always felt a cognitive – and frequently emotional – delight.

A decent quiet came in the waves, with piles of cloud about the sky. There were no enigmas to be resolved just now, so that we walked for a time in blissful peace. The sunset was near, the keen air colorless and thinning from the golden gleaming sky. We reached a vast escarpment, below which stretched the Pacific like some great blue mystical beast, an apotheosis in the new pantheon of nature.

"Let's look deeply for a moment," he proposed, now that we were alone.

The water began streaming with torrents of fortunes and misfortunes, the battered rivers of light thick with hieroglyphs like secret languages in flux, or the beginning of words. The tumultuous sunset was the eye of a leopard flashing with the moon of Islam, then the Cross of Rome. Our terracqueous orb was haunted by a sphinx.

"Now come back," he said.

Our picturesque digression resolved only into waves of folly, the sunset with an electrical warmth like the gush of dawn. There were no full displays here, but the very edge of things remained; the mountain behind us was a slow wave with a frequency measured in eons, the world itself a bag full of God.

◯

COBALT ON OUR TOUR of the earth always was a wellspring of stories. He moved among topics seemingly randomly – fleetingly, subject to subject – the listener discovering only periodically the interlacing, crystalline perfection of his thought. At the sunset a satellite was visible, inducing some deep reticence in him. He began alluding to rituals, primitive peoples and the meaning of blood. I could see no connection to the transit in near-earth orbit.

"The Bushmen of the Kalahari," he said, "burn fires and offer prayers to the space station overhead. The astronauts, in turn, see remote lights north of the Orange River and south of Lake Ngami in Botswana, and know some of the fires are for them. An interdependency of faith and magic."

"In the South African deserts?"

"The same event occurs among outback Aboriginals. A massive international surveillance apparatus, gliding beyond the sky, looking down. Earth's ancestors by rude fires looking up, the future and past in reverence to each other."

"But the Bushmen may survive us."

"Ah, you know that. Our science may lead to mass extinction, with their flutes and dance and incantations surviving. Each culture is the height of its own evolution, the tips of divergent lines. Exquisite that we care for each other, they in the dignity of their songs and prayers, and we in our humble awareness."

We now were by the limitless ocean, as Cobalt ranged through the spectrum of what will come, speaking of computerized and holographic human simulacra: three-dimensional heads or bodies from advanced AI, with human identities. They related in any person's voice, incorporating every detail of one's lifelong digital record, and would be indistinguishable from a deceased parent or child.

He mentioned such wildly alternative futures casually, almost like a giddy friend on an outing. Yet he had a saintly aspect of each word being some great gift – its utterance a compassionate act. He was never an excited or blustering fellow; his every action, however minor, was considered.

"You've heard of the AI outcome where thinking machines unified to solve the unsolvable? It came from an early initiate – a biochemist at Boston University."

I assured him I hadn't.

"It's fiction, of course," he said, "even the narrator is an illusion."

He smiled. I felt the tug of multiple identities, of other dimensions and selves. Cobalt always took the long view, whether into past or future, myth or reality. He had a pronounced tendency to the cosmic – although with affection and balance – like an astrophysicist delighted at the presumption of mathematics embracing all of space and time, describing both tigers and galaxies.

"Computer data warehouses expanded," he began, flinging an arm into the air. "All information went to the Cloud. Data grew boundlessly for ceaseless generations, a billion years of every record maintained forever. Physicists, concerned with the inevitable death of the sun, asked the global computer an insoluble problem: "Can entropy be reversed?" Artificial intelligence devoted much of the Cloud's processing power to this conundrum, whether the running down of the universe – entropy – could be changed. The computer ultimately announced its conclusion.

"What was that?"

"Insufficient data at this time."

"But how was the conundrum solved?"

"Five hundred million years passed. The solar powered global computer now occupied much of the earth's surface. The specters of war and pestilence long had been eliminated, but data continued to aggregate. The seas died. Stellar migrations absorbed the populations. The last human on earth asked the question, "Can entropy be reversed?" The global computer updated its investigation.

"I know, 'Insufficient data at this time.'"

The last rays of the sun enlarged to a purple glow beyond our beachhead, then receded into blackness.

"Yes. The universe was dying. The supercluster gravitational lens CL 0024 + 1624 disappeared. The last stars went out. The Higgs Field, the cosmic microwave background radiation – all gone to black, absolute zero. The last mind of man was only a drifting spirit; the computer occupied all extra-dimensional space. Merging with it, the final consciousness asked, 'Can entropy be reversed?' The last thought: 'Insufficient data at this time.'"

Stars crept in the moonless sky above us, as if strewn by the forgiving hand of Grace.

"The hyperspace computer existed only to contemplate the insoluble solution. Countless eons passed. Suddenly expanding to the limits of the universe, it then contracted to a diameter less than that of an electron. It had arrived at a solution.

"What was it?" I asked.

"'Let there be Light,' the universal computer said. And there was Light."

WE WALKED in silence, but for the cosmic surf. The black waters and the horizon were indistinguishable; we were bathed in the radiance of nebulae already dead since the Paleozoic. I moved very slowy. There was regret at leaving Cobalt's presence this night, but I was due across the Pacific tomorrow in Japan, and I knew that – for my further illumination – he would on his mysterious errands somehow intercept me. As though we could read each other's thoughts, we turned in perfect synchrony, then outstretched our arms and raised our faces to the radiance above – the still living skies.

⬡

NEAR KYOTO, at the edge of the formal grounds of the great training monastery Eihei-ji, was a simple cluster of monks' retreats made of bamboo walls, each with shoji screens, tatami mats and futons. Eighteen hours from Stanford, down a mountain trail bordered with apple saplings, I entered my room to find a sitting robe folded for my arrival. On the wall was a simple calligraphic scroll. Beyond my rough wooden door, rose finches danced in the purple thrift, while down a gradual incline cascaded terraces bounded by balsam, firm juniper, yews and spruce trees. Nearby were the *ofuros* – the hot baths in which one recovered from intensive meditation and work practice. Swallows streamed overhead. Beyond the hickory and gnarly black oaks that spread on the monastery grounds was a young, lone doe, grazing by a small brook. The wind was soft as a nun's summer robe.

In the late evening peace – after the last sonorous ringing of the great temple bell from Eihei-ji – I gathered a kimono and walked in meditation down a pine-strewn trail to attend the ofuro. The lightly steaming room was empty, opening above to a canopy of wisteria blossoms and stars. Folding the robe in the ritual manner, I sat on a wooden stool and scrubbed my body in the Japanese tradtion, rinsed with cold water over my head from a rough oak bucket, then entered the fine silken heat of the ofuro.

Incense burned within a chipped brown glazed ceramic bowl, thin smoke curling into the moist air. The bowl was *wabi*, or well-used, broken but carefully repaired for centuries – considered much more valuable than a new bowl. Through a parted shoji screen, I could see a cherry tree, its branches outlined against fields of constellations.

A single monk floated along along the path, alone in silence. He had a fine, almost stealthy figure, flexuous from much training and work practice. His *Ki* – his personal energy field – seemed to bend the light from the stars. He entered the ofuro and bowed in the blackness. He folded his robe, washed his taut body, then with a blessing in Japanese entered the hot bath. It was some time before he lifted his eyes of aerial grey. Cobalt.

Pensive, earnest, he was slow to speak. "A story for you," he said. "One of politics and power, of government."

I could only wait for his instruction on the methods of the Six.

"A Grand Caliph – perhaps it was Al-Walid bin Abdal-Malik – was in early times a harsh ruler, engaging in common sorcery. He became jealous of a woman who rejected him, and by his magic extinguished the fires for fifty miles in every direction. Villagers only could ignite a torch by placing it between her legs."

Outside the door were starlit rock gardens and sitting areas with apple trees; beyond those were pink and white dogwoods in full bloom.

"The Caliph heard of a humble Sufi, who was rumored to have certain powers. He summoned the Sufi, perhaps the Sudanese mystic Abdurrahman Al-Masudi."

The night air moved with the scent of apple blossoms.

"The Caliph said to the Sufi, 'My people say you have magic exceeding my own. Prove it.'

"The Sufi simply asked for a bowl of water. The Caliph's slaves brought it forth. The Sufi sprinkled the water with a few drops of Al-Iksir, an elixir of Hermes, then invoked the name of Allah the Merciful. He invited the Caliph to peer into the Al-Iksir.

"'*I see no magic,*' the Caliph roared.

"The Sufi seized the Caliph by the hair, and plunged his face into the bowl.

"He was in rags, drowning in a tumultuous sea. Massive waves crushed his helpless body against mighty rocks, tearing from him his life force. He was lost, descending into blackness, perishing, his body growing limp and cold. The great light above him receded into nothingness…"

Cobalt hesitated. We looked up to see a shooting star, a long fireball trailing across the Sea of Japan, leaving only the newly risen and buoyant moon. As the meteor extinguished, we heard almost silent footsteps, like a hesitant fawn.

◯

THE FLOOR of the ofuro was warm, wet like obsidian. She glided within, wearing only a thin silk kimono of finches and lilacs. Disrobing, she folded the kimono in the ancient way. The open air was cool, the heavens were dense with stars. She bowed to us, then gave me a veiled nod, as if in memory of the doorway to a vanished betrothal. It was V-3.

Her body was slender and filled with light, her small breasts flawless. She had a lustrous, luxuriant whiteness, like some porcelain figurine from Arita. Her nipples of cream roses now were red lilies in the heat. She seemed a refugee from a band of mist fairies in some obscure forest.

Cobalt, discontinuing his story, bathed her very slowly on the stool with a sponge, then with a wooden bucket of water in the traditional manner. They said not a word. She entered the ofuro now and then throughout the night, occasionally flexing her body and exercising openly before us, or doing long yogic asanas. From a pouch, she produced onagiri rice balls rolled in sesame seeds, and a flagon of hot tea with small cups. Holding the cups in both hands, we took the tea gratefully, as though drinking from her fountain.

Her presence was like drifting pollens of radiance, the ofuro a castle of enchantment. The marble hardness of her form reflected in the waters; she extended herself before us, now prone, now on her sides, now supine as though Venus were exposed, and Mars rotated above her.

V-3 wore only a chrysanthemum in her hair. Undraped, she laughed softly, sometimes telling us haiku by Basho or singing in Japanese. Through the night, she massaged our hands and heads like a servant girl. We attended her feet in devotion.

In the shadows V-3 sometimes was backlit, only the line of her waist and thighs visible against the illuminated cherry tree, her willowy silhouette moving in dark postures. She then would come from the shadows, under the moon.

Cobalt floated her in the ofuro, his hands lifting her back and legs, until the lapping waters covered her in transparent gleaming films, and made her many-breasted like Cybele.

She would sit by him, or between us, or on him, and then look at me gravely. I remembered her alabaster eyes when she came with Magenta, her furnace turning heavenward, and her wild teats outlined with electrical fires.

Now she was gentle with us, like Kannon, goddess of compassion. She had a gold-leafed halo in the cloud of steam, her white heart of light looming against the black sky, as if that night we were baptized in wisdom.

"And did you discover the difference between Heaven and Hell?" she asked, placing my hand directly above the strong beat of her heart. Her nipples were quick and turgid. I could only shake my head in regret.

She read poetry during her monastic retreat. I asked of her preferences.

"Dickinson? Plath?" I was sophomoric to her refined tastes.

"I read the Perfumer. The Persian mystic poet Farid al-din Abi Hamid Muhammad ben Ibrahim Attar."

Her Arabic was perfect, using vocal stops and quarter tones of head notes in the flowery high style heard in the ruling salons of Abu Dhabi and Doha.

"His most recent work?" I was out of my element.

"He was murdered at Nishapur by troops of Genghis Khan."

We laughed. She had a diamond cortex, fast as summer lightning; together with her compassion and grace, it was the most attractive of her attributes. Playful then, perhaps some nostalgic little coquetry during her ofuro visit, she began to drape herself around Cobalt with a vulpine slyness like Scheherazade, climbing on him in a loose Yab-Yum posture. I started to rise, thinking it some erotic practice being initiated, but she held it at a modest level. Cobalt somehow retained a imperturbable equanimity.

Indulging in the appetite of the Six for Hellenic myths, she told us of how naiads played with meriads at the mouths of streams. She loved lightly, like a quicksilver haze, on Cobalt's river.

He had a vigorous prowess and a blood temperament; I knew his passion could become a delirium. Perhaps it was the inflamed necessity of her ignited by a falling star, but as her darkly flaxen tresses swung in the chiming silence, the starry vaults seemed to shower down desire. Her actions were more Shelleyan than Byronic though, for her tender movements and light touching became those of a trusted sister. Seeing my admiration, she at last was moved to some disclosure on beauty and passion.

"In youth, we have the radiance of early morning, before old age tears us to rags."

"What will you do then?" I asked, crudely.

"We instruct the young ones, and become advanced analysts, hosting in diplomatic and academic circles."

"And of lovers?"

"We are sated only by each other. All else is teaching, and healing."

I thought of the Acapulco night, as the river of light flowed through her, and how she looked at me until the gods took her. Her eyes in the mist were steady, moonflower blue.

In the late hours, ever faithful to her custom, she walked in meditations with exquisite slowness, chanting in her diaphanous soprano a reverent blessing, her hands pressed together in prayer. As she gathered camellias from a vase, then a fan and a bamboo comb, she was a vision in the silky air, trailing a languid perfume. Lying on heated wooden slats, she soon fell asleep. Unflinchingly nude, she had the suppleness of a young girl, chaste as a vestal.

I watched her sleeping nakedness until she relaxed and opened like a flower, as though the night spirits had charmed some sorrow away.

"She is resting," Cobalt said, "after her many nights in the Ginza."

"Ginza?"

"Tokyo's entertainment district. A jungle of neon and electronics and hordes of men. She begged for months in formal nun's robes – a monastic practice in the Rinzai tradition – by softly intoning prayers, eyes down, taking small meditative steps with each breath, holding out her empty bowl."

"What did the men do?"

"A few provided for her, those taught by their parents. Others – venal executives – rushed past her, unaware V-3 had instant global mobility, access to any intellectual, economic, or erotic coterie, to all possessions, to sensuality of which they hardly dreamed. Yet they discarded her as some simple nun of no consequence. She was rather like the Byzantine general Belisarius asking for alms."

"Where does she go now?"

"After the monastic practice period, to D.C. There is an issue."

The candles fluttered and danced in the light air, while above stars were prickling in a heavenly carpet. Cobalt closed her elegant fan, with its handle and struts of paulownia wood, then kissed her, evoking a contented sigh. He led me into the scriptorium, with its outer door open to the garden, then slid shut the shoji screen to the ofuro. Within were implements of a fastidious and sagacious bibliophile.

"*Aiba* is here sometimes," he said, using the Japanese for Indigo.

There was a tea tray set for two on a scrubbed deal table. Adorned with flower offerings for ancestral teachers, a Butsudan shrine occupied an alcove, while the walls had seasonal scrolls and Shinto texts and artifacts. Voluminous ancient manuscripts from the animism to the Meji periods revealed spidery starlit Kanji characters inscribed by quill. A mortar and pestle left from 15 centuries of grinding medicine sat beneath ranks of dried plants. Paper panes filtered moonlight. We could hear only a water wheel turning by a small brook in the Zen garden.

I dared ask. "Have her often?"

"Never. If she considers any man, it is Magenta. I am anhedonic...like a Jacobean friar, but untonsured." He laughed.

A rattan hat from Miyako had been placed with care beneath a museum quality example of calligraphy. Moon rays began bleeding around the scriptorium screens. I saw a fine pink parasol with a bamboo handle, spread open like a rose, just like the one in Basel. This simple, ancient room was some control center for the Six.

We passed outside by a drowsy dovecote, then walked at length in the broad garden among the pulses of the last fireflies.

"I must be...in Paris soon," I whispered in the hush, "near the Sorbonne." I knew of nothing else to say. The moon was shining against banks of soft cirrus. We walked among clusters of red and white manju flowers, with the percussion of water on stone from the water wheel the only sound.

Cobalt's robe of midnight blue had a pattern of tiny, almost imperceptible stars, from thousands of stitchings, each done by hand with a prayer. He wore a light blue kimono beneath this robe of starlight. Considering his priest's *okesa*, I remembered the story he began before V-3 appeared.

"But what of the cruel Caliph, the sorcerer who drowned?"

Autumn whispered to us. The receding new moon floated like a silver feather at dawn; from the foaming wisteria blooms a few small blue petals were falling.

"He was helpless, turning, gasping, drowning, lost under the sea, the light of the world darkening, then gone. His cold flesh only that of death."

A band of silver paleness began to spread along the eastern horizon. A violet to pink dawn, with its mysteries of light and shade, etched the far branches of evergreen oaks. Cobalt continued.

"Some small brown village children found the body washed upon the shore. It was naked, bruised, covered in sores. They tested it with their feet, then ran shrieking to a shelter of strange woven plants. The women came timidly, addressing the carcass in an unknown tongue. They gathered him, barely alive, and brought him to warm fires. They slowly healed his wounds. For years afterward he could not speak, for he had forgotten everything, like a newborn. He managed to learn elements of the language, although crudely."

In the nether mist of the garden, little bands of swallows were beginning to skim to and fro among the young green nettles.

"After a decade, poor and alone, he became a carver of sea shells. He encountered a village maiden with bright eyes. She felt compassion for his plight, and over time a certain affection. They lived in a rude hut. Children came forth. As many years passed, there was a plentitude of grandchildren. The old ones were happy, for they loved each other. They had nothing, and everything."

We sat on a bench in the garden, gazing at the dark outline of a Tori gate in a field by a giant *Cryptomeria*.

"In his timeless wizened old age – in the days of drinking his fill from their love and radiating to all – he was hobbling by the sea with his gnarled wooden staff. He thought of their great love, and their children's children, and how he was the most blessed of all beings. His heart expanded to encompass all the worlds. Suddenly a great wave arose, and washed him to sea. He was turning, gasping, drowning, the light above receding into darkness. He was dying, then cold and dead. All his loving world was lost forever."

"How very sad," I returned.

The edge of sunrise was dispelling the heavy night dews. We had talked throughout the night, and remained in the garden's quiet.

"But there is more," he finally said.

"What could there be?" I awaited his answer.

"The Sufi raised the Caliph's head from the bowl of Al-Iksir.

'I see,' the Caliph said.

He gently directed the guards' swords away from the Sufi's throat. For the remainder of his long life, he was the most benevolent of rulers."

We stood in our robes before the fair dawn, under the pink nebulousity of the last of the *Cymbidia koran*. Paris lay a world away. With devotion, we bowed to the rising sun.

Chapter 25.

The Omega Interview

The plan is so vast that the contribution of each…is infinitesimal.
The hypothesis of a single inventor, some infinite Leibnitz working
in obscurity and self-effacement, has been unanimously discarded.
It is conjectural that this 'brave new world' is the work of a secret society
of astronomers, biologists, engineers, metaphysicians, poets, chemists,
algebraists, moralists, printers, geometers…"

- JLB, *Tlön, Uqbar, Orbis Tertius*

The way we look to a distant constellation,
that's dying in a corner of the sky.
These are the days of miracles and wonder,
and don't cry, baby,
don't cry, don't cry, don't cry.

- Paul Simon, "The Boy in the Bubble"

It's so beautiful…they should have sent a poet up here.
I had no idea. I had no idea.

- Carl Sagan, *Contact*

THE CAFÉ off the Rue Saint Jacques had thick smoke-blackened beams; through its 18th Century windows one could see the pinnacled towers of the Sorbonne. In the Left Bank near Notre-Dame and the Île de la Cité, it no longer sheltered *petit bourgeois* wearing the smart tricorns of *La Belle Époque*; the café now was enlivened by eclectic convocations of students, some in black capes or silk academic gowns, others fixated on the works of Sartre and Genet. Thin Frenchwomen – graduate students with purple shadowed eyes – stretched their long, lithe and *recherche* bodies, then crossed and recrossed their legs to display black tights and fashionable black heels. They read de Beauvoir or Gide, then moonlighted as *modèles artistes* in sixth floor garrets.

Down from interviews at the Lille Medical School in the Norman stronghold of Picardy, I was visiting the Parisian version of Harvard's Kennedy School – Sorbonne's *l'École Libre des Sciences Politique*. While few students in the Latin Quarter still spoke Latin, the student café was engaging and thankfully cheap, and much more tolerant than the Sorbonne faculty retreats at the Café Dôme, the café Deux Magots, or Fouquet's in the Champs-Élysées.

Crushed among vibrant young scholars at my table was a distinguished philosopher, somewhat gone in the tooth but not yet broken of nerve and still scribbling his writings. He was accorded a great mystique by the students. Subjected to their momentous fictions, his long Gaulic face affected a horror of ostentation and pomposity. Outside a heavy shower ceased, but no one moved, all retaining their chapeaux and literary caprices, and brandishing overwritten manuscripts.

I first saw Cobalt, as usual ignoring me, pretending to read a fragrant letter from a lover in Bayonne. At my approach, he admitted a circuitous arrival from his spare lodging at the Hôtel du Nord in Nîmes. His very proximity altered one's perception like some viscous magnetic field.

Encountering him from city to city across the earth was increasingly hallucinatory, but oddly comforting, for we continued the conversation even as the world breathed all about us. We saw in the café divergent systems within systems: the sultry academic women and voluble students of course, but also impoverished metaphysicians and ineffectual *Luftmenschen* sitting idly over drams of grenadine, while through a glazed window an old man fed a dog, and an Arab in headgear wandered perplexed under a Coptic cross, then into the aisle of an open nave. Above these specters a fragment of waxing moon cut open the sky.

As waves of languages and cultures broke against us, I sought the unchangeable, the less disconcerting. Cobalt simply accepted the everlasting density of sensations among which we passed: the living cyclone of earnest priests and ripe *filles de nuit*, the Basque sheepherders and charwomen and rowdy *pescadors*, the fish and perfume, the cigars, filth and flowers.

"We swim in the Eleatic aporiae," he assured me unintelligibly, ever a proponent of Greek history, but noting my incomprehension.

"The paradox of the unity of our beings," he tried to explain, "against the unrealities of the constant motion and changes you now are experiencing."

He sipped a *tisane*, some infusion of herbs, while I had a *tasse de chocolat*. The *garçon* left us a plate of *petits fours*. Through narrow kitchen windows the chefs' white toques bobbed as they sliced ham and cheese to prepare realms of *croques monsieurs* for tourists.

I still was lost among the blending cities and cultures and psychic phenomena. "But where does one find rest?"

"Landscapes do alter, for the flickering stellar explosion irradiates the biosphere," he replied to my growing confusion, glancing at an adjacent table, "but underneath the seas of emotion and thought, our essence is still." I understood him only sometimes, like a sleepy child overhearing adults conversing.

I struggled to encompass the range of his thought. But he had been at the café too long, or our itineraries had drawn attention, or my fatigue had given way to baseless concerns, for there was a distraction.

◯

AS COBALT LAUNCHED into a monologue on Merlin's universal mirror, he tapped his index finger on the wine-stained oaken table like the girl in Basel did with her parasol on the Petersplatz. Nearby sat an old hack – a porcine, slumbering *gendarme* with piratical eyes, who seemed quietly attentive to the minutiae of our exchanges. He had two companions: one a portly goateed *professeur* with the air of hosting some fatuous dinner party, the other a saintly little pedant, bespectacled, placid and smug.

They occasionally murmured *au bon Dieu*, or an *enfin*, but primarily attended a plate full of biscuits. The pedant had plump white hands, and plentiful teeth, and considered his untouched *sirop de cassis*.

When we became silent, the *gendarme* attempted conversation with his companions. He seemed unhinged and unpracticed, beleaguering the others with awful drivel. The pedant, so unlikely an associate, kept replying in haste, with a kind of duplicitous sophistry. Their conversation was an act to explain their presence.

Cobalt and I went silent, using our senses to embrace the room. The *gendarme* assumed an unfocused, relentless glare as suspicion's shadow darkened his face, while a guarded note entered his voice. We had made him. He knew he was blown. The *professeur* descended to entries in a thin, discursive diary while we – too careful perhaps – chose to view the Sorbonne more thoughtfully elsewhere. It could have been an error in judgment, but the Six were forever prey – even among the most civilized – and certainly after recognizing the self-consciousness of poor actors.

◯

WITHOUT THE PSYCHICALLY OPPRESSIVE WEIGHT of the unexplained *flics* in the café, Cobalt later banished my spiraling concerns by providing a brief reminder of his high gift. His very presence freed memories and archetypes, like fleeting subcortical eruptions in the river of thought. We transcended paranoia and the prospect of physical force by entering the mythic.

As the night rose in the Parisian gardens, he pointed to the visual field of trees and spires and gypsies and the *lux anciens* of the 15th *arrondissement* of Paris. As he spoke and summoned a dream, it began to shift, all appearing to coalesce into an orb of symbols. Turning with fabled beasts and sorcerers, jaguars and islands of water hyacinths, it had runic alphabets engraved on Moebius strips with infinite surfaces. There were troubling portents in the orb though, fortelling the days ahead: the extinction of satyrs who were also gods, a lion falling from the moon.

Such disparate phenomena remained a private privilege between us, unreportable to any but mystics. All became still, reaggregating as the City of Light. Afterward we chose to recall the orb as a glimpse of the apostolic symphony, best forgotten in the day's concerns with trams and air flights and the fighting in Bagdad. We spoke instead of exhibitions at the Musée d'Orsay; the crack in the world was simply a transient error of the visual cortex, or a secret handshake within an anonymous society.

⬡

WE WALKED ACROSS PARIS to the edge of the Jardins Luxembourg. Bluebells, blue as water, flooded in a sea of azure like the dark fields of immortality. The gardens were sensible now, everlasting and motionless, but still weeping.

Cobalt's emanations grew more intense with each city, as though he were driven to teach constantly, as if time were running out for us. There again was some hurry, some urgency I had not seen before in any of the Six.

I began having difficulty, nearly drowning in the ocean of projected imagery and drifting cities. It was clear why they had never been interviewed – even ignoring the security concerns – for the phenomena around them were not limned even by mythic traditions. Almost frightened by the rush of dimensions, I sought a foothold – some tethering to firm ground – by blurting out questions, any questions, about their methods.

"Do you burn votives during batches? The others spoke of esoteric practices."

"Indigo began certain rituals around the synthesis," Cobalt replied, "the spiritual hosts for mechanistic chemistry. He included a votive of the Virgin of Guadalupe, an apparition of the Virgin Mary witnessed by an Indian – Juan Diego – on the hill of Tepeyac northeast of Mexico City. In the year 1531, *Anno Domini.*

"Is that not fanciful, such a protectress?"

"We have moved entire lab sites because such votives extinguished themselves. We observe the auguries of ancients, like the crows in Basel, when Indigo changed countries and identities."

He knew of my private moment with Indigo on a Swiss mountain overlooking the Jura. There were no secrets among the Six. I was transparent to them.

We went on foot down the Boulevard St. Michel, then over the Seine at Pont Neuf to arrive at Ieoh Ming Pei's luminous glass Pyramide at the Louvre. We hailed a cab on the Champs-Élysées, with its the Elysian Fields bordered by rows of chestnut trees and gardens. We passed the Place de la Concorde, where ghosts still attended the Obelisk of Luxor, but the soil no longer was freshened by beheadings, or the rolling faces and entrails of Louis XVI and Marie Antoinette. We stopped at the Avenue Foch and walked into the enduring night of the Bois de Boulogne, where in this violet city the late fireflies still were sparking.

◯

THE SIX WERE COMFORTABLE in moving quickly among any nations, tribes, villages, or peoples; they easily adapted to rapidly altering dialects, languages, dress, mores and behaviors. Constantly altering perceptions seemed but a familiar Philosopher's Stone to them. Cobalt sensed my disorientation.

"Fear not the phenomena," he said, "for we see only humanity's pathos and glory for just a moment. Consider the imagery we term 'Heaven and Hell.' We can turn it on and off. If we separate the fields, the polar opposites merge back to normalcy. Look before us. Look at the Bois, where it is just another night for public indulgences. Such erotic trysts in the Bois are of medieval heritage."

Adolescent twins opening their matching black *faux couture* stood by turnouts as headlights exposed their tumescent charms. Negroes from Martinique danced shirtless. Parisian couples parked together and opened *coupe* doors for *échangistes* and *ménages à trois, à quatre.*

"Now view it as Hell."

Underage prostitutes, riddled with needle marks and diseases, blew pox-fouled kisses and made sucking mouths to ravaging lechers; frightened girls were in rags, shivering, slaves to demons. Negro *émigrés* shook like voodoo dolls with sightless eyes and syphilitic skins. Married couples fled their hateful partners, young wives gave themselves to loathsome derelicts as cuckolded husbands mounted the profligate in revenge. All forever were unsated and debased, crazed with limitless promiscuity.

"Now Heaven."

Lovely Parisienne maidens, glowing with ardor and silken skins and luminous eyes, invited the lonely for the kiss of angels. Supple island dancers inflamed onlookers with tropic musks. Couples body-worshipped each other, sharing in a Satyricon of Dionysian raptures, lifting their scented gowns and parting their robes. Muses captured sylphs. The sisterhood was flagrant and shameless, all free as young beasts, conducting their sacred orgies under a celestial pleasure dome. Some spread ripened before thrusts of light, their moans the joyful prayers of innocents.

"Now come together."

At last there was only Paris – long either Paradiso or Inferno – for those who dared assume a difference.

⬡

"HOW MANY PHENOMENA ARE THERE?"

"We know of several classic transformations," he said, "God-consciousness, where one's thoughts seem kinesthetic, turning traffic lights green or inducing the sunrise, or where all songs are one's own voice, until in the end thankfully only God again has the power and glory."

"And other phenomena?"

"There are rebirths, where one writhes in gestations – the contractions are like seizures, one feels wet with blood – until all the world is born anew. Death experiences, where one's heart seems to stop – one becomes merely loose atoms in space and impossibly thought to be alive – and the grateful dead pull the chariot of the sun. But between us, it would take a lifetime to experience all of the possible changes."

"Are there other states of consciousness?"

"There are worlds where everything seems planned, then everything meaningless. Where there is a God, then no God. Where there is love, then no love. Where one is utterly isolated, then united. Where everything is alien, then erotic. In each of these states, one continually transits between the extremes, until the lesson is learned."

"Is that all?"

"No, the forms are limitless, but categorical. ESP experiences, where all people are one soul, all thoughts one's own, all music and literature and art the expression of a single being. Alpha and Omega experiences, where one is the first or last person in the world to know some ultimate cosmic secret."

I was exhausted, but grateful for being taught. Cobalt meanwhile had become more direct, more explicit with each day. Our end drew near; I risked making the questions quite personal.

◯

"AND OF THE OTHERS, how can they bear it through the years, with the constant loneliness and visions and fear?"

"Vermilion has the dual mistresses of his passion: V-1 and V-2. He once said they were like sleeping with electricity."

"And how do you, as anhedonic, view their way?"

"They have chosen to form a triune self, the merger of three separate solitudes. They see in all directions."

"Did you know Vermilion when the women came?"

"In Berlin with you that first night, he described his rescue by them into trinities of lovers, into their three-cornered desires. His batches had been the catalyst of these stranger loves."

"But before then?"

"Vermilion alone had an audacious lucidity." Cobalt smiled. "As a young man, we considered him the thinking girl's crumpet."

I left the question at that. Cobalt would adopt an extraordinary remoteness when one probed too deeply. He was without issue in his maturity; through his physical austerities he had vouchsafed his heart to undistracted synthesis. Yet I sensed some taciturn battle was arising in him, a concern over uncertain events.

◯

AN ELDERLY FRENCHMAN, slightly crazed, approached. He had the plaintive faded voice of a cloistered soul, but the hot fervor of a heretic. Somehow he detected us.

He accused Cobalt and me of dealing with Biblical revelations, and thought we were spies concealed under costumes of academics. He had that edge – the magical thinking of schizophrenics who are unnervingly hypersensitive, and with uncomfortably correct insights. His manner was too sophisticated to be law enforcement, and he knew we were on to something.

Cobalt gave him Euros and a blessing, reciting a healing chant of Aesculapius. We decided to move more deeply into the Bois, pretending to be lost or predatory tourists. We walked down a gravel carriageway from the time of Louis XIV, then over to the Seine, where we found a wrought iron bench under the oaks.

⬡

THERE WAS LITTLE REASON not to venture every inquiry now. Cobalt forewarned me of the dwindling hours we had together, and of some impending retreat and gathering of the Six. He offered to answer on any topic, and said he would show me all he could. At this I grew more reckless. I asked one question – disguised as several questions – that might be posed by a searching youth to a gentle, experienced elder.

"What do the Six see, at the peak of the highest experience? What is your most ultimate teaching? The results of all your exposures, your practices, the limit of your knowledge?"

Down the Seine, the *Bateaux Mouche* slowly glided into blackness, the soft light from their windowpanes reminiscent of candlelit offerings floating down the Ganges. The floodlit spires and flying buttresses of Notre-Dame were brilliant in the night.

He knew the question was coming, as if it were inevitable, as though he had been asked many times. He didn't hesitate, or divert me with blithe commonalities, but took the question quite earnestly.

"This is the most serious of matters," he said, falling into silence.

We observed the Basilisque du Sacré-Coeur, with its bell tower and onion dome, gleaming white atop Montmartre.

"Some say," he began, "we among them, that there is a wall beyond which – without reverting to madness – the incarnate mind of man cannot penetrate. Upon the wall, some have reported in various ways, is written the teaching. It has been revealed to many of the living, and at the interface of life and death to everyone. It appears historically, like the advent of Christ over the planetary gods. The teaching is a truth that occupies all of the sublunary world, comprising even sub-atomic forces."

I cared not for these grand and ambiguous mystical pronouncements, choosing instead to press him with a harsh insistence, then with outright irreverence.

"My rationalist self," I opined, "requires a less arcane, more concrete absolute truth. Can you disclose it?"

Cobalt sighed at great length. He sat erect like the head training monk at Eihei-ji monastery, slowly folding his hands in the formal manner, then told me a story I would never forget.

⬡

"I CAN ONLY RESPOND by framing it in a modern allegory, delivered in parts during our remaining journey. We will enter into an Omega experience in these final days together, where you are the last person in the world to know a secret. Is the revealed secret true? How lonely and meaningless and frightening it would be if the teaching were false."

"Tell me."

"Only limited groups know the most special form, designed for scientists and engineers with security clearances. We'll go with one of those."

"Very well."

"Johnny von Neumann," he began, "at Princeton in the 40s, told it to Einstein. Von Neumann later learned a variant had been circulated among Bohr, Schrödinger, Pauli and Ulam just before the Nazis canceled their nuclear program. Whispered at Los Alamos after the Trinity blast, it resulted in mass resignations. The first theoretical machines of the cyberneticists – at Harvard's Aiken lab, Caltech, Princeton's IAS, MIT, RAND – all calculated the same conclusion. The teaching was derived again with DARPA, coterminous with the end of the Cold War. It is highly fungible, evanescent, forgotten each generation then rediscovered as history repeats. It appears in waves of illuminations, with mass amnesias thereafter. The last time among the intellectual elite was at NSA Fort Meade two years ago."

"Fort Meade?"

"Do you wish the most recent version? We ourselves independently confirm it during each synthesis, alone and quite distant from NSA."

I nodded. Cobalt played daily among the leaderships of federal agencies, a people's counterintelligence agent whose humanity conferred upon him a certain invisibility.

"Fort Meade is linked to NSAs Georgia, Texas, Utah, Denver, Hawai'i. There reportedly was a software glitch, or some physical malfunction, that induced a meltdown, a complete freeze of all computer networks. Source unknown. NSA went dark. Emergency and Top Secret task forces convened; intel aggregators, contract analysts, people arriving but no one leaving. Lockdown of all facilities around the world. Independent cryptographers brought in with military escorts. Some transforming event – unheralded in the intelligence community since the Manhattan Project – had occurred."

The bells of Notre-Dame struck nine. I grew agitated at the interruption, but my fixed departure from Orly to Rome was soon. I begged forgiveness, then bowed out. He rose, always the tolerant colleague, and so accomplished at effortless interceptions during my arduous transit of the planet.

"Don't worry, friend," he said, "we'll speak again. You have the synchrony of a heartbeat."

⬡

BOLOGNA'S MEDICAL SCHOOL – among the most ancient – retained among its *professori* at ceremonies the long bird-like beaked caps of 14th Century physicians. The faculty robes were a heritage from an age when posies were acquired by children as protection against the Black Death, and Vesalius had not yet secretly excavated cadavers to illustrate the circulatory system. Set within a sturdy, classical rotting city, the medical school was rotund and amiable; the plasterwork and domes and art and doorways were like sepulchrally cringing eyes and jowls. Lecture rooms smelled like the interiors of clocks.

A shrouded horse with crowns of black feathers led a cortege as it threaded through somber crowds of Bolognese. An occasional priest walked the cobbled streets making baffling allusions to the Pentateuch, while the descendants of half-extinct, obscured and ruined noble families offered the fondest of greetings over espressos and pastries. The city had a halting grandeur, like a dream confected.

There were amber women in the shadows and in the sunlight; here and there were the heirs of the last faces that saw the living Christ. Gilded images abounded of the Tree, considered even by the heathen as a kind of gallows on which a god was murdered.

⬡

I WAS ENTERTAINING two second-year medical students from Bologna, a bright young ex-pat with fluent Italian and the daughter of a Milanese neurologist – a slender girl with the oval face of the Madonna. Having caught up with me, Cobalt slipped into a seat at a nearby table. The students soon hurried through the *arcades* – the sheltered medieval walkways – and down narrow, crooked streets to the university where Dante and Petrarch were scholars.

Ritual circumambulation of the world with Cobalt had an astronomical psychic density, as though one were a charged particle in the field of a neutron star, soon torn into equations with ungraspable variables. The buildings' perspective changed, the light refracted from some unseen radiance.

Our conversation from Paris continued unbroken, as though we were on a stage, around us one scene passing to another. He had revealed certain personal traits of Vermilion; I drew his attention to Magenta.

"His foci for some years," he replied, "have been novel erotogenics and cognitive enhancers."

"And his results? Are the Six concerned? Or the government?"

At Princeton, Cobalt had admitted access to the intel community's enlightened sector and its troubling projected futures for the earth.

"The last decades before any catastrophic event may well be – if we consider only one class of pharmaceuticals – orgiastic, propelled by erotogenic abuse."

"Why, that would require uncontrolled manufacture, unlimited precursors."

"Magenta knows the structures of microgram-range, easily synthesized aphrodisiacs, hidden from the public and the records sealed or destroyed by researchers. They – as we – fear the release of a chemical vampire."

"But of compounds for learning and memory?"

"Magenta feels that neural enhancement – only if including altruism and excluding deleterious personality shifts – may help us to comprehend exponential data from the Net. Our cognition is evolving to the next human form. We think of the first men and women as *Homo sapiens sapiens* var. *neopharmacologia.* Or the genetically engineered and heritable equivalent: var. *neoneurologia.*"

His face was alight. When he spoke of the ascent of the next evolved hominids, his eyes seemed as those of *Australopithecus* by ancestral fires, dreaming of distant heirs, of children who could calculate the motions of stars.

⬡

COBALT, fond of science fictions, told of a line of twenty very pregnant tribal women on horseback, with long hair and coronets of roses, and all of whom had coupled with the same post-apocalyptic sorcerer with a mutant neocortex. The children were linked with one mind, and grew to predominate the species.

His later freewheeling conjectures on erotogenics were punctuated with audible references to satyriasis, the heat of rutting, the varieties of abusive penetralia. Cobalt suddenly began masking some anxiety with facetious comments not like him at all. To our left, hiding under a stairwell, was an unkempt, desolate man who clearly understood English. From the stiltedness of his gestures and the awkwardness of his exchange with a passerby, we could tell that he was there for us. We could not dismiss him entirely, or think our conversation with its erotic asides had been overheard only by some grinning mooncalf.

He scuttled away. We resolved to trail him for a while, the iron hand of duty insistent, but he fled down a narrow passage hung with hand-washed laundry. Olive girls – perhaps of three and six – peered at us from a peeling rococo balcony.

"Out vaunted security is subject to all manner of ingenious contrivances," Cobalt observed with a resigned placidity.

We let it go. There were ravens' nests on rooftops. Women with shining black hair caught the last splashes of sunlight. In the long shadows, strumpets stood before dwindling shafts of bleached haze. A small shop offered quince and white rose trifle; another, necklaces of onion and garlic. I wondered about the limits of paranoia, whether constant reaction to prophetic inklings was a self-defeating strategy.

◯

WE ENTERED A PARK. Just for seconds, we imposed the Heaven and Hell paradigm upon Bologna. It was a trysting place, with moist woods. Lovers said wounding things, then placatory things. They first had a reserved listlessness, as though uncaring, then bounding steps eager for embrace. One suitor had a deceitful face, narrow as a dog's; he yawned about dirty as an Anchorite, his words the work of some mad magpie. Another moment he drifted glowing through ferns and rust-red mosses like an enchanted novitiate to a goddess astride her favored sorrel mare.

The rapidity of changes and threats somehow had grown less frightening. I acquiesced to the revolving new cultures each day, and began noting the similarities of humanity rather than the differences. I remembered Cobalt's unfinished story from Paris.

"Tell me more of the events at NSA two years ago," I suggested.

Unsurprised at this, he drew me to a stone bench where – to the bells of evening mass across the city – one could see flocks of matriarchs in black laboring up the steps of several of Bologna's 130 churches.

"There was no dysfunction at all of NSA computers," he said, as though it only had been minutes since he last described the meltdown, when NSA went dark. "Rather, all of their information – every database – had been replaced by an unintelligible random set, a series of unrecognizable symbols."

"Superuser malware of some sort? An intrusion? Some zero-day event?"

"Hardly. The vast data appeared simultaneously at every secure, classified NSA machine and its foreign counterparts, both friendly and hostile. Across the Five Eyes – the U.S., U.K, Canada, New Zealand, Australia. Then in the security establishments of the nuclear powers: France, Russia, Pakistan, China, India, Israel. Then Germany, Switzerland. All disavowed cyberwarfare. All had no explanation."

As vesper bells quieted, we began walking along the sheltered arcades and down twisted streets from the Dark Ages. Cobalt intermittently returned to the Fort Meade event. At first I considered it some fanciful rumor, or one of Cobalt's delicious little fictions.

"The number mounted, filling all foreign security databases. It was the ultimate hack; they appeared completely random. Some thought the set could lead to unbreakable encryptions. For a solution, the world's supercomputer arrays were linked in the first peaceful sharing. To the public, not the slightest disclosure. Emergency Congressional sessions of intel committees convened, but none knew we were prostrate before the deluge of unknown information. It was the Library of Babel – endless, meaningless, indecipherable. The word's best minds were humbled as every terminal drowned."

"This *must* be a myth." I was delighted at his somber delivery, just not taken in yet. I looked for holes in his narrative.

"Is it? The NSA scientists disclosing it to us were afraid of being outed. They did so only upon our most careful intervention, when we – with their awareness – separately exposed three young systems administrators to the Light. We all were there, and V-1, V-2, V-3. Each analyst was independent, none knowing of the other contractors. But listen, then decide for yourself."

He had guided me to the Pinacoteca Gallery, wherein we admired Raphael's resplendent *Saint Cecilia*. In this liturgical environment, his story had the reverence of a sermon, as if it were the undisputed truth.

"De-encryption of the smallest fragment – one barely manageable by the supercomputer array – proved futile. After every effort to unravel the code, if there was one, the figures remained senseless. Digital paleographers applied every known algorithm, every nation yielded their own secret versions. Insularity was suspended. International teams of formerly hostile analysts became transparent to each other."

We went from painting to painting in a measured way, arms crossed, surrounded by portrayals of instantaneous conversions and transubstantiations.

"Someone noticed that within the googolplexes of bytes, a tiny meaningless image repeated. This was the first of six great breakthroughs, each more profound than the last by a thousand orders of magnitude."

"What was the second?"

"Ah, a truly glorious event. From that foothold, an indecipherable pair of cryptographs – characters if you will – was detected. Variations of the same cryptographs seemed to repeat once every attabyte.

"But in a database of such size, the number or repetitions would approach infinity."

"Yes, quite. Exactly. The same small data, in an inaccessible nomenclature, almost like the refrain of a song from some majestic choir."

○

TRAVELING IN THESE DAYS with Cobalt almost was too much to bear. His constant subliminal transfer of wordless information, common to the Six, was coupled not only with demonstrations of classic psychic phenomena and imagery – the implications of which could influence theology and psychiatry – but also with his allegories, anecdotes and fantastic allusions. His story from Stanford – of the universal computer occupying hyperspace – was obviously fictitious. His relating in Kyoto of the Caliph and the Sufi may have been an Islamic tale from the al-Mu'tasim. He presented the NSA material as factual however, a matter I found troubling. Without material proof, it was worthy only of credulousness, or simple faith.

Under these worrisome auspices, we left Bologna to arrive at Harvard's 16th Century Florentine Villa I Tatti, where for days we perused the 50,000 volume library and hundreds of Italian Renaissance paintings. Among the boxwood *parterres*, the columnate cypress plumes, the lattice pavilions, the walled gardens and regiments of olives, Cobalt began to refer to the NSA event only in reluctant and minor asides. He read late during those last splendid evenings in Northern Italy, intent on certain rare volumes of the Moggam and other writings of blind ibn-Sinas. Our companions were only the murmur of Villa I Tatti's fountains, and the stars of early morning skies.

○

ARRRIVING THE NEXT DAY in the north of Holland, I began interviewing the students and rector of Groningen's medical school. Cobalt became fond of long treks alone near the Dutch border with Germany; the striking two-meter blond women of Groningen received only his appreciative gaze.

Like Indigo, he was a heavy walker and incessant reader, sometimes absorbing a volume even as he passed in thoughtful silence – like a native pathfinder – among branches covered in lichens or over piles of damp oaken twigs. He always bought cheese and bread and fruit for these excursions, reading

Voltaire and Diderot during one, Herschel and Linnaeus on another, Juvenal's *Satires* on a third – the last – accompanied by me.

The stars' cold pulses still were beating on that walk before dawn. We saw in the lessening darkness an anonymous Vauxhall occupied by men attired like Londoners – grey men in matching grey hats. They were sitting frozen, at a dead end, near a meadow quilted with dry stone walls. Cows began lowing in the singularly inexpressive twilight. The Pleiades were extinguishing. Some Swedes from Gothenburg tramped past us, all quite hale, then several straggling medical students up from Zeeland and late for lectures.

An untethered goat meditated under a walnut tree draped in moss. There was a setting half-moon, drawn and frail yet tarnished. Cobalt, standing under a fragrant branch of Artemisia, became almost enraptured at the roseate horizon and its broad mirrors of light. He was discussing, not the possible surveillance, but some book: a vindication of the Kaballah.

The sun was rising like a Dutch Proteus, with all the appearances of being, as the silvery-bluish air retreated from lowland fields and every possibility unfolded.

"Here's a conundrum for you," he finally said. "Look at the men in the car, from the perspective of Hell."

In the distance, they exited the Vauxhall, grimaced at us, pointed, then began walking quickly our way. I felt quite nervous.

"Now Heaven."

The men stopped. Two women on foot met them. They all drove away, laughing.

"In the merged view, they were here either for us, or for me," Cobalt said. "Or they weren't. Which is it?"

I couldn't tell, nor could Cobalt. The Six were not prescient, but observed signs and omens, thereby calculating with a certain fearless detachment only the implacable mounting of odds.

A simple Nederlander girl from the countryside passed us with a quiescent glide. She had a bearing of untrained but instinctive refinement; her honest beauty and innocence made the very atmosphere ring. At her passage, I realized yet again the transcendency of normal, natural mind – that every moment was tempted by art, and life itself was an illumination. She disappeared into a field of sylvan antiquity, where her ancestors in the time of blood and William the Silent, Prince of Orange, had pollarded the willows for bows.

◯

THE MORNING TWILIGHT had vanished, but not Cobalt's midnight airs. He still had intently fixed, abstracted eyes. We hiked in the cool freshness, his conversation typically unpredictable, ranging from Schopenhauer to the Tao Te Ching. He stopped speaking but increased his pace, silent for a long period, almost inviting. I managed to stay abreast somehow, recalling his disclosures in Bologna.

"And what of the third great breakthrough at NSA…after a pattern of repeating characters was detected in the infinity of random numbers?"

He drew up near a slight prominence, where beyond the low mists lay Germany.

"The third great breakthrough at NSA was of religious significance. The set of repeating patterns was matched against the human genome database. The code specifically correlated with repetitions within the vast silent regions of unknown functionality. The same sequence of nucleoides – adenine, thymine, guanine, cytosine – not only was spliced into DNA across the mammalia, but both kingdoms, the orders, the classes, across all life.

"Meaning that?"

"The still undeciphered data matched sequences – and effectively was embedded – in eels, cows, hummingbirds, aardvarks, ostriches, toads, gerbils, seahorses, giraffes and blue whales. The carnivorous hyenas. Sharks, smallpox, bacteria. Sequoias, bluebonnets, mastodons, daffodils. The pattern was self-replicating as long as life exists."

Cobalt, always the historian of science and classicist like each of the Six, also was fond of taxonomy: the families, genus, species, forms and variants of living things.

"The German cryptolinguists were the first to observe the matching sequence – finding in it the genes of planktonic protozoans," he recalled. "They had canvassed the seas. One eminent elderly geneticist, an heir of the 19th Century biologist Ernst Haeckel, kept shouting madly on a call from Bayreuth, "*Die Radiolarien! Die Radiolarien!*" It was the first conclusive identification of the mystery code in the *Radiolaria*, specifically the unicellular marine microorganism *Dictyoceras virchowii*. Lovely siliceous skeletons, those species, like the rays of small sunbeams."

At my fleeting comprehension of Cobalt's disclosures, the very earth vibrated as though a great bell had been struck. I felt the impulse of new religions. The information was a frenzy accumulating, like the irresistible urgency of frantic coupling at the point of no return. A slate-colored storm, a lake of limitless low clouds, began swirling near the German border like the inconsolable cry of unhonored gods. I knew not the dreams approaching.

◯

THE WHITE NIGHTS of summer at 60 degrees latitude brought out ivory ballerinas in flimsy slip tops. Their hair up in buns, the Kirov *corps de ballet* with their long, bare, formidably toned legs flocked into the Mariinsky Theatre of St. Petersburg. For his love of Holland, Czar Peter I had named this city of monarchs in Dutch: Sankt Piter Burkh.

The Neva River flowed past dozens of islands, under St. Petersburg's 500 bridges, and into the Gulf of Finland and the Baltic Sea. With as many canals as Amsterdam or Venice – and palaces, public squares and avenues comparable to Paris – this vision of Peter the Great arose at the mouth of the Neva from swamplands drained by slave labor.

I was visiting St. Petersburg State Polytechnic University, the University of St. Petersburg, and the pediatric neurology hospitals. The physicians and students all wore tall white hats, patients brought their own medicines, and Russia staggered under endemic alcoholism and addiction.

Cobalt awaited me, unannounced, at an emergency room exit. We walked long and well by the river, until the shady streets led into the lowlands of the Gulf, where blue kingfishers hurried among sharp-edged bulrushes. At the firm surface of the sea-line a young girl played, her white blond hair gleaming like spun glass. Fingers of currents rinsed the occasional beach of pebbles.

Despite our idyllic afternoon, I could repress the question no longer.

"What was the fourth great breakthrough at NSA?"

He had been waiting for me.

"The fourth breakthrough – and remember that the projected social impact of each stage increased by many orders of magnitude – involved the physicists, close on the heels of the evolutionary biologists who found the mystery code correlated to certain obscure dark regions of all life's DNA."

The girl found a whispering sea shell, and held its mysteries close to her ear. The Gulf, with its boisterous swirling waters, was in counterpoint to the peaceful sands; under this high latitude's colorless atmosphere, the beach was fine as ground silver.

"The physicists?" The matter now seemed completely out of hand.

"Mathematical physicists – only those heavily vetted with Top Secret clearances – observed the mystery sequence to be an algorithm underlying Maxwell's equations for electricity and magnetism. Others at CERN said it integrated quantum and string theory, as if the sequence solved discrepancies and symmetries in the Standard Model, linking electromagnetism with gravitation, strong and weak atomic forces. It was an evolutionary insight that destroyed existing paradigms, like the Randall-Sundrum revelation, the discovery of the atom, special relativity or the calculus."

For scientists, Cobalt's story essentially would consume all foregoing knowledge and history. The sea of the mystery sequence would dissolve the sciences: medicine, anthropology, paleontology, all human understanding. The sequence would be the seed from which all human thought and endeavor arose. It resolved the issues of where brain ended and mind began, where matter ended and space began; the interface between physical and spiritual.

In the blackness of our first unutterable night in Russia, as we rested on the south bank of the Neva, we could see the Peter and Paul Fortress, a mausoleum for the remains of Czars who once had limitless power. I was entranced by Cobalt's tale, and how it might relate to the ultimate knowledge of the Six, but concluded it was some allegory. Although he propounded the story with the unassailable demeanor of a world authority on subatomic particles, I knew nothing had changed in the journals, not in the *Annalen der Physik*, not in *Helvetica Chimica Acta*, not anywhere. There were no reports across the scientific literature of any new cosmology, or de-encryption, or fundamental equation, and certainly no novel array of nucleotides with a message from beyond. Distressed, I finally confronted him on the issue of his veracity.

"Of course, secrecy agreements are permeable," he said, "especially with such cataclysmic information. But listen, for the scientific outcome remarkably was like – as the old masters in Zen described – a form of *satori,* or enlightenment, where everything changes yet nothing is altered. The moon still rises, the swallow still exhalts skyward."

I listened. He would stop one line of thought and begin another, as though he had lost his way, only to weave them together again with the perfect structure of a Homeric epic. I struggled to prompt him back to the NSA matter, then realized his seemingly erratic delivery was that of a practiced, tolerant adult with a beloved and inattentive child.

I listened more trustingly, more closely. He spoke on apparently purposeless, unrelated topics, but I knew it was a finely arranged symphony, one I had yet to grasp. No matter how wild and free – even chaotic – it all would conclude on the same note, with an impeccable, startling coherence.

○

OUR PROGRESS through St. Petersburg was not without observers. We once saw in a sweaty peasant face the determined glower of combat, the hallmark of a sentinel figure. Stubby frame, hunched up. His smile was dangerously awry; he held a great willowy pitchfork in the malefic silence. He was unconventional, out of scale. Cranes flew drunkenly over the marshlands behind him. Yet, not everyone suspicious could be there for us. In the long shadows of evenings, I began to feel a coldness of fear in the proximity of the Six, as though my various lodgings were a tomblike niche beside some grand morality play.

Throughout the world, the Six and their progenitors somehow had found each other. They linked their special abilities as part of a secret society with a heritage extending from the discovery of the subjective effects of LSD in Basel in 1943 to Edgewood Arsenal in the 50s to CIA with MK-ULTRA. Ostensibly uncontrolled worldwide distribution actually was carefully – reverently – anticipated and planned.

At night, in my room in some student hostel, I took to making forlorn entries into a journal, reflecting on the Six: their ambiguous locations, the serenity of their retreats, their foreapprehending of destruction. Being with them, in their ascent to mystical plentitude, was as though one were in heavily freighted novel written by a Kabbalist. As I fell asleep over a fragment of the Petrarch that Cobalt had given me, a fine Dresden edition with commentary by Novalis, it floated from my hands like these rare beings and their international conspiracy soon also would retreat, drifting away like my own scant authority about them.

○

THE BRIGHT MORNING brought Cobalt, in a futurological mood, to a café near St. Petersburg State; it was filled with pale medical students stricken by the demanding oral examinations common to Russia. Although unfailingly courteous, Cobalt wasted no time on trivia.

"Magenta anticipates heighted addictions with future drugs," he said. "He thinks there will be irresistible compounds. We term them as 'from the astrolabe.'"

"From an advancement in pharmacology?"

I was barely awake. We began to sip fruit juices and mineral water, while med students forced themselves into hyper-alert, scattered caffeinism syndromes.

"No, no. The matter of the ancient Persian polymath Luft ali Azur, the dervish of Shiraz, as recalled by Borges."

Cobalt thought nothing of opening the morning conversation with the most difficult concepts, rather like vigorous calisthenics at dawn. I looked at him blankly.

"He discovered an astrolabe," he continued, "the first instrument to position celestial bodies. But thereafter he could think of nothing else."

"How does the dervish's monomania – about the astrolabe – relate to irresistible compounds?"

We were the only customers without coffee, for it was the practice of the Six to avoid even subtle addictions.

"We worry over some future chemical structures dominating all human thought, far more than cocaine, heroin and methamphetamine exclude the world from their addicts today. Until everyone seeks the compound. Until all personal activity focuses on the substance."

"But how was it that such persistent thought failed to overcome Persian civilization? What protected the desert tribes from compulsive thinking about the astrolabe?"

"Luft ali Azur threw it into the sea, so that men would not forget the universe. We believe there will be substances that will addict whole populations, entrancing the multitudes. But no sea then will contain that which fascinates."

◯

COBALT OFFERED NO REMEDY, but visibly censored himself. His usual serenity was replaced with some preternaturally vivid awareness; his thoughts seemed spectral, with a kind of melancholic compassion. At these times when there were no phenomena, but only the cold truths of the Six, I rushed to collect data. Something for Harvard, formal and real, not speculative. I tried another subject.

"Look, a matter troubles me. Are there any problems in the system?"

I remembered Indigo at Wilton Park, when he mentioned Cobalt conferring with Crimson on some security issue. He met the question unflinchingly.

"Among federal agencies, DEA soon will announce a new Special Enforcement Program titled 'Flashback.' The 800 percent increase in MDMA availability precipitated it; LSD was included even though use is stable and relatively rare."

"And the response of the Six?"

"We will study implementation of the program, selecting several of the 190 or so ongoing LSD investigations currently worldwide. We learn *ex ungue leonem*, from the claw of the lion, discerning the whole from a small part."

"But after you learn?"

It may be necessary to adopt the Greek approach."

"Greek?"

"The time when a father, with his small son, drove his horses and carriage into the forest near Athens, to a clearing in the woods where several Greek patriots had been hanged by the government. After their deaths, their families almost starved, their children were abused or lost. The father walked to the bodies, lifted the boy, and told him to kiss their feet. The boy did. They went away."

"And the lesson was?"

"The boy asked his father who they were, how he knew them. His father would say nothing. He simply shook his reins, driving the horses along. After a while, he said to his son, 'Always remember.'"

"Remember what?" I asked.

"'The taste of courage,' he said."

○

HE PREFERRED the early mornings or late evenings for the essence of things. The next day, as thrushes sang out and dawn drew bright the outlines of Peterhof – Peter the Great's summer residence – we saw the last of the primroses glimmering. As we walked among the palace's 150 fountains, Cobalt invited me to a bench where for a time we both reflected upon our immortal being. He spontaneously broke the silence.

"The astronomers made the fifth NSA breakthrough."

"Astronomers? How would they relate to a dataset?"

"They deduced that the sequence of repeating characters indicated no terrestrial origin."

I sat very quietly then, absorbed by what only could be a phantasm, but even a factual thread of which would be revolutionary.

"They went further, examining solar flare data, planetary ellipses, ion belt configurations from probes, deep-space infrared and X-ray maps, every influence on the electromagnetic spectrum. The mystery sequence had been generated by countless point sources within and without our galaxy, throughout time from the origin of the universe. Every civilization of every possible sufficiently advanced world was transmitting to each other. We were newborns overhearing an unknown song from all sentient beings with superior technologies."

I could say nothing to this, for I was lost in my own dissolving and reaggregating belief systems. Although I had long concluded the NSA tale inevitably would prove to be an elaborate fiction in which was couched some philosophical truism, Cobalt presented it with an absolute demeanor akin to that of the director of the Lowell Observatory. He answered – correctly and well – technical questions too extensive for these writings. He knew names, methods, formulae, nomenclatures, state of the art advances in every field. I could not fault him by any means within my grasp.

We walked in the receding mauve dawn of St. Petersburg; light blazed in us with some inviolable power, our understanding as stable as God would permit. Robins were calling in the passing twilight; there were catkins on big hazel bushes by the water. The bay was smooth at first under an early calm; only the old river craft grew plaintive as a turgid wind arose. There were no fictions to grasp, for now.

Some would think him a madman, others would consider him some cult figure, most certainly a criminal zealot. Yet Cobalt had the clarity, accuracy and precision of a pious ascetic. He could create worlds *ex nihilo*, like a scrivener on a blank slate. He had a profound nobility of aspect, his tone and gestures often that of one in a presbytery, saying his breviary.

At times he would burn bright, like a blue star, before my unprepared heart. It was one of these times, under the white silvery flowers of a godly moon, that we walked together over the bridges of the Neva. Almost in a whisper, he told me of the final great revelation at NSA.

○

"THE SIXTH and last breakthrough occurred when the cryptolinguists and exophilologists scanned the merest fragment of the database. They already had discovered that the unintelligible characters repeated infinitely, once every many googolplexes of entries. All de-encryption procedures failed. They assumed it was some intergalactic Rosetta Stone."

"But where was the key?"

"They thought the key to the cryptograms might be light years away. One day though, a philologist in Leiden found two symbols, a partial – perhaps still random – arrangement, with similarities to proto-human markings on the fire-blackened ceilings of Lascaux, made twenty millennia before Christ."

As we experienced the nations, Cobalt dispersed each day only small portions of his magical recollections. The morning awakened in St. Petersburg before he continued. It was a trance-like, pregnant summer. One could see the wheeling of larks, and hear goldfinches singing. The sky was a jewel overhead.

"Another symbol was found that mimicked the mythical markings on the obelisks and stone mirrors of the Axa Delta, the inlands of the Tsai Khaldun. Fantasy languages and fictional geographies were not excluded, having once resided in the mind of man."

On our early walk, he increased the pace somewhat, sensing I had focused my attention.

"Rudimentary dialects of forgotten villages were searched: the Rusha-Rungwa system of Tanzania, the Okavango-Huange of Botswana and Zimbabwe, the greater Limpopo of Mozambique."

By then we saw clusters of students with music scores and cellos and violas converging on morning classes at the Rimsky-Korsakov St. Petersburg State Conservatory, where the spirits of Prokofiev and Shostakovich still roamed in ancient wooden halls. A girl from Petropavlovsk seemed to recognize Cobalt, then told us that sometimes one could hear – in the chambers where Tchaikovsky once composed – the B-flat of the evening star, the high C of ecstasies, the A-natural of moonlight. Cobalt told her he sometimes heard the roses sing; we moved toward the summer palaces, to listen.

"Just when the code seemed to break," Cobalt said, "it mutated into more complex and elusive forms, as if it had detected our attention and was teaching us to expand our capacities."

The massive golden dome of the Tsar's Cathedral of Dalmatia appeared; the Russian Orthodox version of Bodhinath in Nepal, it called the faithful ever skyward.

"Some portion of the mystery code seemed to parallel extinct, exquisitely rare, or poorly curated Ural-Altaic languages. Other fragments seemed strange monosyllabic adjectives from spatial, wordless thought – insensible, wavering, sinuous numbers of alien mathematics – the inconceivable arcana of the universe. It was like some dialectical game, hopeless to our best minds."

He arrived at a low ridge beside the Neva, where one could see the Admiralty tower and spire of the old Naval headquarters dominating the Baltic horizon. Interiorized, Cobalt began skipping flat stones across the surface of the waters, where they promptly sank.

"Please continue."

"A few characters seemed almost nouns in the *Ursprache* of Babylonian Aramaic, or lost dialects of Arabic written right to left. Some were similar to the elegant quill of the Persian ascetic al-Gazzali, in his *Tahafut al-Falasifah*, *The Destruction of Philosophy*. One clue matched an early wax cylinder recording of the babbling in Syriac of a crazed Bedu captive staked under the desert sun near Damascus by the Turks in 1918."

We explored the city until near dusk, then the outskirts with its white wooden churches and blue-starred onion domes. At nightfall, under the early untroubled stars, blackbirds and thrushes nested within wild current bushes in the marshland. The husks of ruined dachas were forgotten in the stranded obsolescence, their lichened gables and falling rafters the last echos of the deaths and births they had harbored.

"Finally, indisputably instreamed within an infinitesimal fraction of the dataset – at only one cryptograph every attabyte – was what appeared to be a set of the earliest recorded known characters. Arguably, a few were utilized in Khalil's perfect work the Kitab al-Ayn, perhaps another seemed a letter from the 10th Century Anglo-Saxon, or the Icelandic sagas – one of the ballads of Maldon. Then – to some analysts – a truly recognizable character set appeared from vanished Indo-European languages. From chaos and emptiness, the suggestion of coherence was born."

He entered a deeply pensive state. I had learned not to press him. We returned to the city along the river bank, to arrive on a bridge overlooking the vast Heritage Museum. The leaded sky was a sepulcher for the gibbous moon; the clouded air was stagnant, then cleared with a fitful breeze.

"To dismiss the outcome," he announced without disclosing more, "would be to blaspheme against the human spirit."

I tried for factual proof of these events. "One hardly could obliterate all traces of such riveting documents."

He said nothing. Prompting him would be fraught with difficulties, yet only hours remained for our interactions. As we looked for the last time out over this land of bewitchment, the 18th Century palaces of Pavlovsk, Peterhof, and Tsarskoye Selo were all alight. The glories of Russia spread before us in the night, like a lost lover calling one home. With an indefinable sadness we turned to the western horizon. There lay uncertainty, loss and promise. There – tomorrow – lay the New World.

◯

THE TRAIN CAR was empty but for us. I feared this was my last encounter with the Six. We finally were northbound from D.C. to Cambridge and linking through Princeton – the end of our tour and his esoteric teachings. Cobalt, ever the Latinist, seemed intent on reading an old leatherbound copy of Pliny's *Epistulae X*.

He occasionally broke his concentration, entertaining me by raining dithyrambs from his eidetic memory. He then would assume again a stately peace, touching with inexplicable reverence the pages of the Pliny. As D.C. passed, he became fond of pithy, picturesque neologisms on government shortcomings, provoking my glee. Looking about, he suddenly became quite serious, returning to his disclosures in Russia.

"It was there," he said, pointing to the dull, receding face of the Pentagon. "It was a zero-day event, where all paradigms and algorithms changed, and there was no way back. We understand that the Joint Chiefs were the first to know, defense intelligence being supreme. The president and the National Security Council were there. All but eight were dismissed, only the highest level of Top Secret clearance remained."

"The Joint Chiefs were the first to know what?"

"The decryption of the first interstellar message, the key to great weapons, unbreakable cryptography, limitless power. The president opened a coded electronic briefcase, removed an envelope, and read the contents."

"What happened?"

One of those present said he was stricken, the look on his face grim, untrusting. The printout was passed among the select. One – among the more religious – knelt. Another sobbed. Others cursed at the likely deceit, the trickery, the falsity of dreams. Their power was gone into dust."

"What did it say?"

"It was the same message, a transmission repeated in all the languages of all the galaxies, from Alpha Andromedae to the planet circling the red dwarf GQ Lupi to the plutoid Makemake, from the beginning of time, the same message from all the dead worlds, all the exhausted stars."

The train lurched to a halt at Princeton junction; I accompanied Cobalt on the Dinky, the private rail to the university. He quickly disembarked, walking fast, his hand raised in invitation. I followed him out, then ran after him.

We had picked up some countersurveillance, one of the pleasing little opulences of the Six. At first she was an unknown, then became the girl from Firestone Library. I could tell from the way her hair swept out at the nape, and by her elegant bearing, and the fluidity of her walk. To the lonely, she would be like the promise of soft rain in a parched world. Sunlight fired from her. The ground seemed to issue tones under her feet. She moved across Princeton as if she had descended from the quiet streets of the Parthenon. But it was the last of my teachers whom I sought.

"Come now," I managed, out of breath, "what did it say?"

It had been described by Cobalt as the key to the hermetic mysteries, the difference between Heaven and Hell, existing *ab eternitate*.

"You asked initially about our ultimate vision, that which we also rediscover during each synthesis when we are exposed, destroyed and reborn. It is the same truth. It is always new and magnificent, yet the oldest of revelations. The culmination of all philosophy, all religion, all consciousness. Our very lives."

I could say nothing to this majestic claim.

"It may take some time to find it." He handed me the Pliny, bound in leather.

I opened the volume quickly. Under the title was the author – *Gaius Plinius Caecilius Secundus*. It was nothing but the writings of Pliny the Younger, in Latin, in the red and black print of a 16th Century edition. I was annoyed by this casual, ambiguous ending to his carefully delivered tale.

"I could see the *Bible* as the secret to the universe, or the Qur'an, or even the Mayan sacred text the *Popol Vuh*, the Book of the Dawn of Life. But *Pliny*?

He simply looked at me with sadness. I felt him begin to withdraw.

◯

THE PRINCETON CAMPUS was empty on this weekend evening, the sultry summer moon changing bronze to white as it rose, rolling across the pinnacles and towers of old Witherspoon Hall. This was it. They were going, fading back into their mysterious, inaccessible and anonymous international society.

Our minds began detaching, like the tendrils of a dream dissipating. Panicked, I asked my last question – one I had long harbored – on the pretext of pedagogical necessity.

"*Wait*. Wait. Who is the sixth man?"

He turned, then warmly took me by the shoulders.

"You don't know?"

I looked at him blankly. He threw his head back and laughed long and well, like a king receiving a bewildered and beloved prodigal brother in rags.

"You really *don't* know?"

I turned every shade of scarlet. In my perplexity, he released me. He said we could unravel these conundrums another way. Our minds linked. He looked up at the moonlit campus. I raised my eyes as well.

◯

TALL BOWED SKIES filled and emptied like great sails. Effusive honeysuckle vines spread across the battlements, while clumps of blackbirds exchanged secrets. The buildings were guarded by gryphons.

The bells of orison sounded under a high blast of moonlight. Every petal of the magnolias was a miniature reflection of the white-faced lunar orb. The earth became easy, then friable and molten, until we were surrounded by nymph-begotten groves. It was the strongest phenomenon yet, but peaceful and perfect, like the Islamic Night of Nights when heaven's portals open.

The sound of a lonely bagpipe skirled upon the air. Orphaned girls in blue ribbons and pinafores appeared from the shadows and danced happily, then ran to loving parents. I knew it was a prelude, and a finale. I stood helpless, under a vast range of great light.

The most fundamental elements manifested first. An endless series of long, formless alexandrines curved through Gothic entryways. Myths and religions blended: the tower mirrors of Tariq-ibn-Ziyad, then Ezekiel's angel with four faces to the North, East, South, West. Quicksilver reflections of the brilliant moon spelled everywhere the letters YHVH, the Hebraic Tetragrammaton, the ineffable name of God.

There were manifold, indecipherable lesser gods, yet all was utterly coherent. There were no meaningless transparent tigers or towers of blood, but the recorded revelations of prophets, sepulchers of fire and the cosmogonies of Gnostics. The moon's disc became blind with whiteness. All about was a sea of the heart that transformed one forever. I shall never forget it.

⬡

INDIGO APPEARED on the far peaks above Salzburg, singing "Edelweiss" to a young sheppardess with her row of simple geese. He was taking the hands of the destitute and hopeless, awakening the addicted girl with Ave Marias in Zürich, singing in Navaho by the fire on the Basel mountainside, offering a blessing with the luminous Rose under the alpine heavens.

The veil of St. Veronica lifted in the unanimous night, revealing scenes of irretrievable colors. There was Magenta, laughing with the young monks in Kathmandu, circumambulating Bodhinath, washing our little mother goddess of the world and finding a home for her, tending the Maria and her baby.

And yes, there was Crimson also, by the seaside fire that first night, with his tales of fear and courage, then caring for the illuminated youth with words of peace. Crimson, standing for a long while by the little girl with her broken giraffe, and singing to his distant child however he could reach her, then finally kneeling and comforting the fearful little ones in the Oxford alley.

And there were Vermilion and V-1 and V-2 as well, rescuing their acolyte in Berlin, singing with the naked children in the forest monastery, transforming the lost girl in Bangkok. I saw them comforting the blind roadside grandmother, splashing the children on the river Ping. There they were before me, walking in meditation and tears, leaving each morning to be surrounded by their band of small ragged angels in the poor village, and always singing.

They were all smiling now, waving their hands to me, saying goodbye forever with the gentleness born only of Grace. I knew it must be a tender illusion, but I could only bow to them. Everything had been a teaching – the secret formula of the Six was their unbreakable thread of compassionate acts. The last image was a white chrysanthemum, floating downstream in the air as if on an invisible river, all alone in the moonlight.

I at last was delivered of their shared consciousness, all the colors blending into me as I was born yet again into this lower realm. Under a Tudor arch stood Cobalt, trailing clouds of starlight.

"Farewell, friend," he said.

"Where do you go now?"

"I have a date with an angel."

He held a small posy of rosebuds. It was for little Eve, locked forever behind a steel door. He bowed, then turned and walked through the gates of Princeton and down Nassau Street. I would never see him again. He who circumambulated the globe now stood at a bus stop. I heard only his distant voice, as he sang of this earth.

"I see skies of blue
and clouds of white,
the bright precious day,
the dark sacred night,
and I think to myself,
'What a wonderful world.'"

Chapter 26.

The Smallest of Things

Nor is there any magic that can stain the whole truth for me,
or make me blind again.

- Euripides

Postscript to the Last Interview

FROM THAT NIGHT FORWARD, since the final contact with the Six, no such mystic phenomena have occurred. Their absence is an empty gate, opening only to the mundane. On the erotic anniversaries of Berlin or Phuket though, I sometimes notice the glance of women, some secret being shared, a kiss, an embrace. Everything looks the same, but infused with less light.

Even now, a few fragmented memories of the impossible persist. I may cross Harvard Yard to Widener Library, where through the branches of oaks and elms the sun is a boiling sea of fusion reactions and bright gods procreating. A nearby rose garden is an archive of ineffable mysteries beneath blue sky doors to worlds without end. I say nothing of this to anyone, recording the past only in private notes and furtive ink, the most fecund of liquids. My theological dread has vanished.

Passing the School of Divinity, I think of the larval selves therein, awaiting realization. In Widener and Firestone Library at Princeton, where sometimes I visit, there is a gravitational pull to books and scholarly lamps, for there one is supported by the twin staffs of Work and Solitude. I ride buses and subways in silence, holding fast to this dimension, until the day they may come for me again.

I notice certain small things: runic crosses bounded by circles, the flash of tartan, children everywhere, beggars, watchers at the edge, sometimes the crows. Nothing is beyond comprehension now, no human knowledge is alien to me. The most esoteric formulae seem simple, every language the same utterance, every history and future the same drama, every medicine the same potion.

The sacrament of the Six may be a model for all future psychoactive drugs of arguably benign consequence: those that are non-lethal, self-extinguishing. Those inducing aesthetic, learning, libido, altruism. Those which are unstoppable. Yet my afterthoughts can never be an *apologia* for the Six, for a researcher must take care not to become an *Illuminatus*, a convert to any world-view other than Veritas.

The memories wrought from these sorcerer's nights might lead others to cart about the world vials of hermetic powders, as if they were amphorae of the Damascene elixirs of St. Paul, but I must attend only to the old scriptures, to science and medicine, to thought. There is laughter and warmth, but I have lost some infinite thing.

There are times, when the moon is right, that I think back to the final night, to an event after the Six were no more. Then I smile. Sometimes, I cry.

⬡

COBALT HAD GONE. I sat by the Picasso sculpture and reflecting pool as the voices and colors faded to frail dreams. The moon was low, leaving the Princeton campus barren and grey. The only light was a cold fluorescence from the new Fine Hall mathematics library, the one that never closed, the last refuge for inspired cosmologists at 4 AM.

I entered, only to find two sleepless grad students waving chalk before a blackboard and arguing with one harried, rumpled doomsday theorist from the Institute for Advanced Study. Shuffling in an absent-minded way, I found an alcove. The night's events still were trailing, their profundities now checked by long open tables and the hush of pen and paper and mind.

Restless, I retrieved the Pliny, thumbing through passages in Latin. It was merely a copy of *Epistulae* Letters 96, printed in octavo major, with onionskins covering the woodcuts. At length I observed a false cover and spine, and began loosening them in frustration. An envelope fell onto the library's tattered Baluchi rug. I slit the seal. Within was a set of high-resolution photographs.

The headers stated "Ft. Meade Geospatial," another was "GCHQ On Her Majesty's Service." Another was from CERN in Geneva. Then Lockheed, General Dynamics, Raytheon. My first impression was of some harmless fiction by the Six. I took a closer look.

There were many pages in some sequence – clearly infinitesimal fragments of a massive dataset and presenting an insurmountable de-encryption challenge. The images were clouded, almost irretrievable, like dust on an infinitely fine lattice. It was indecipherable, with an almost invisible print so fine it was impossible to resolve the images with the library's magnifying glass. I prevailed upon the librarian for the bronze 1906 Zeiss microscope from a display case on the history of optics.

Under the high-powered objective lens of the Zeiss, the clouds now became barely viewable particles, each point with millions of columns and rows of repetitions of unintelligible symbols, a list of some kind. This had to be a sophisticated deception. The dogs of suspicion began tearing at me.

One blow-up showed that the density of information required characters to be formed of elemental atoms, symbols made of ten or twenty metal atoms against a carbon background, derived from a scanning-tunneling microscope at the edge of technology and beyond that publicly available. The data could only be processed by the first quantum computer, its very existence a magnificent secret.

I scanned the enlargement for days and nights, becoming ragged, devastated with fatigue. The librarians inquired as to my health. My right eye blurred, my left grew weak. I stopped only for water. Haunted, I intently walked the pre-dawn campus, pacing under the Tudor arches, then returning to roam Firestone and examine its collection of Babylonian seals and Egyptian papyri. Frustrated, I then returned to the list.

A physician from the Princeton health service appeared. White goatee, German accent. He had seen mathematicians undone from wrestling with alien formulae, and had watched John Nash fill backboards with arcana that even now remain undeciphered. He invited me for coffee. I assured him I was quite well. He checked my credentials, then offered eye drops.

Faculty peeked in, students aggregated in observant clumps, rumors spread of some solution of the Riemann hypothesis. Security visited more often. I was unshaven, with a coder's ashen pallor. I washed in the lavatories' sinks, wringing out my shirts and socks. On the fifth night, I found something.

The list began to be interspersed with recognizable symbols, but distorted as if parallel worlds had evolved but diverged. Some seemed as if they were inscribed by prehensile, non-human dactyls. The nomenclatures were not of this earth, perhaps from some mystic realm, or generated by exobiotic, intelligent organisms. When I saw the first proto-cuneiform, I began shaking uncontrollably. The list was the same phrase, repeated infininitely, in all the languages of all the galaxies. Maddening hours later, I recognized a dialect of Siberia, then saw the Russian. My heart went wild.

Almost hysterical and weeping, I began singing fragments of the songs of the Six. It was so childlike, maudlin, profound. It was the underpinning of coherent thought, words embedded in all primordial DNA, the whisper from countless advanced civilizations, from the Alpha to Omega, from the picosecond of creation to those who will hear the Trumpet.

⬡

It was the first message from the universe, the last message from the Six. At a barely perceptible resolution, forty atoms of silver were arrayed in perfect form. In English, they said only three words:

LOVE IS ALL

Final Report to the Human Subjects Committee

Harvard University

Faculty of Arts and Sciences

The prior enclosed writings constitute the undersigned's complete ethnography of the international drug trafficking organization described herein. Historical notes and recollections, in support of graduate studies and research appointments, are included as relevant to this record.

As the Committee will observe, the uncertain basis of the proximal psychic effects - and the subjects' inherent inaccessibility - likely preclude further investigation of this group.

However, it is suggested that this report - at the discretion of the Committee - be released to concerned researchers in the faculties of medicine, public health, law, government and divinity.

Accompanying this manuscript is a partial list of artifacts, examples of which are catalogued below. These items remain sealed, but may be available with prior permission to certain scholars in the reading rooms of the _____ Special Collections.

XA.487.SC: Two cancelled tickets to Mahler's Symphony No. 4 at the Concertgebouw, Amsterdam, purchased by research subject Indigo.

XA.487.SC: Police report on ergotamine acquisition by Aum Shin Rikyo (Japanese, with Eng. trans.).

XA.488.SC: List of Attendees, Conference on Chemical Arms and Disarmament, Wilton Park, Sussex, U.K. (original, scan available at _____).

XA.409.SC: Photograph of undersigned, by research subject V-3, at Wilton Park.

DOS/TS/1000.SCI: Fax from Kennedy School of Government to ASecState re Dostum (2 pp., original, scan available at _____).

XA.411.SC: Carnegie Meeting, Washington, D.C., List of Attendees (2 pp., original scan available at _____).

TS.11.SCI: Hand-drawn map to Laotian village, with foot paths delineated (pencil, on portion of *Bangkok Post*, irregular, appx. 7 x 12 cm.)

TS.12.SCI: Business card of research subject V-2, for Chiang Rai conference on South East Asian heroin trafficking, attended by principals and staff of EOP, DoS and DSS.

XB.617.SC: One fragment of *Rising Nepal* (Kathmandu), crushed, dimensions unavailable (29 gms.).

XB.618.SC: One copy of *Financial Times* (London), scented.

XB.619.SC. One dried sample of wild flowers, Genus *Narcissi*, white with short corona (34 gms.).

XC.809.SC: One music score (Berlin), Händel's Suite No. 4 in D minor (HWV437), with lip print in Laurent Rouge pur Couture.

XC.882.SC: One partly burned smudge stick (29 gms.), essentially sage, with red string binding.

TS.996.SC: Note on foolscap (5 x 9 cm.), India ink with broad quill, calligraphic, with parting in Latin.

TS.997.SC: Photocopy of register, bearing signature of Dr. Masoch of Geneva.

TS.999.SC: Handwritten excerpt of Baccylides, vermilion ink on ripped bond (appx.. 5 x 7 cm.), stained and scented.

TS.999.SC: Note in vermilion ink on blue linen (11 x 15 cm.), bearing portion of aria libretto by Puccini, scented.

TS.1000.SCI: Photocopy of *Epistulae X* Letters 96 of Pliny *Secundus*, 1665 private edition (original from Cawdor estate press, heavily distressed and unbound).

TS/SCI/(unregistered): Slip for deposit of thirty-six (36) alleged electron micrographs, Voyager probe transmissions and Cray outputs delivered to Director, Lowell Observatory.

PH.117:SC: Photograph of Nepalese girl (appx. age six) by banyan tree, and note on rag paper, double-spaced and blue-lined (5 x 9 cm.), in child's handwriting (pencil).

DIV/TS/SCI: Child's toy (appx. 5 x 9 cm.), stuffed angel with halo and wings, hands folded and head bowed in prayer.

Respectfully submitted,

———

Cambridge, Massachusetts

VI

The Christmas Tree

Now, at last, may there come to them
the white peace of the end.
In the knowledge they have achieved a deathless thing,
a lucent inspiration to the children of their race.

- TEL, *Seven Pillars of Wisdom*

Man is a stranger to his own research
He knows not whence he comes, nor whither goes
Tormented atoms in a bed of mud
But thinking atoms, whose far seeing eyes
Guided by thoughts, have measured the far stars.

- Voltaire

If I ventured in the slipstream,
Between the viaducts of your dream.
Would you find me?
Would you kiss my eyes?
Lay me down in silence.
It's easy to be born again.

- (apol) Van Morrison, *Astral Weeks*

Chapter 27.

Sasha's Balalaika

We waited, in the greatness of our sorrow
for he was like a father
of whom we were being bereaved
and we were about to pass
the rest of our lives as orphans.
Now, the hour of sunset was near…

- Plato, on the death of Socrates

Now cracks a noble heart.
Good night, sweet prince,
and flights of angels
sing thee to thy rest.

- *Hamlet*

Everyone must get to experience
a profound state like this.
I feel totally peaceful.
I have lived all of my life to get here,
and I feel I have come home.
I am complete.

- experimental journals of
Alexander Theodore Shulgin, PhD

ONE PASSED an old, dented orange Volkswagen, a Kharmann Ghia of better days, bearing the California license plate OSOMO – the Japanese for peace. From their artists' abode of rambling structures came Ann and Sasha Shulgin, elders and aristocrats of the spirit. Welcoming their many visitors with embraces, they guided them within, even while a small outbuilding contained the most productive, licensed psychedelic research laboratory on earth.

A painting of Sasha in his boyhood – dressed as the "Blue Boy" and holding his treasured viola – occupied an alcove. A piano crowded the rough living room, strewn with cushions and papers and books. Their hand-built residence on a mountaintop retained the most magnificent view of the entire Bay Area, with the hillside spilling down to a plain by the sea.

Bric-a-brac stuffed a tumbledown garage. Charming little patios of cracked cement had shaded umbrellas and wooden tables, while a narrow, flowered path led to the small, almost ramshackle but utterly refined laboratory where new worlds were dreamed.

I had retreated to Sasha and Ann's from Cambridge with a profound reserve, still saddened and baffled at the abrupt departure of the Six, but also with a new intellectual posture from my continuing interviews of users and manufacturers of addictive drugs.

In Sasha's study were all known references on entheogens, little gifts from friends and colleagues, and a plaque of appreciation from DEA for his scientific expertise on controlled substances. On a bookshelf was a jeweler's brass belt buckle of the Grateful Dead alembic – a skull split by a lightning bolt – labeled "No. 1" and signed by its creator: the legendary underground acid chemist Augustus Owsley Stanley III. Among Sasha's multiple computer terminals and thousands of books and files and memorabilia, one became lulled by the water music of pure thought and affection, and the companionable silence of games of destiny.

There was only one bedroom, for the other contained a massive, derelict Nuclear Magnetic Resonance machine for structural analysis of experimental substances. The small kitchen was in eternal disarray. Despite Ann's best ministrations, she often was overwhelmed by streams of convivial visitors. Old sage picked from a field rested on a faded chest of drawers. It was a peaceful place, a sanctuary. Here one could see clearly, so that to our no longer flawed vision all was sun-golden and leisurely, like a conservatory smothered in rose creepers.

⬡

A LEAN, six-foot-four mass of wizardly white hair and deeply welcoming bear hugs, Sasha loved word play and humor, science and music. The ultimate authority on psychedelic chemistry, he engaged all the world's primary researchers in the field, from the president of Aldrich laboratories – the chemists' chemists – to the pharmaceutical department of Sandoz in Basel, and those few with very long memories of how it all began.

Each month, a Friday Night Dinner or "FND" was held at a friend's house, with Sasha and Ann always present. They often hosted small dinners, or picnics on Easter and July 4th weekends at their home. Small children darted about fresh as roses, finding favor everywhere, like little birds among cherries and raspberries. The gatherings were melting townships, for airs of nervous preoccupations and sudden shynesses dissolved as ebullient Sasha sketched in the air his alchemies and divinations.

With their natural affability and the quality of their science, the compound was a magnet for artists, psychiatrists, neurologists, engineers, musicians, faculty from Berkeley, Stanford and UCSF, philosophers, a spectrum of seekers, underground figures, scientists of every specialty, dancing girls, Edgewood Arsenal alumni, Silicon Valley magnates, poets, forensic chemists, code warriors and writers. All were grateful something so fantastic existed. This blending of hermetic schools was synergistic; we were the moon people again those nights, the cloud-forged and blessed.

Their kindliness hardly reflected Sasha's 300 rigorous scientific papers, patents and books on the chemistry and pharmacology of entheogens he had invented. He was lively, with a theatrical note and rapid, soft, playful speech, his mane of white hair and beard in chaste silver points. Everyone confided in Ann, for she was receptive, understanding, with a slightly trailing and sophisticated trace of accent from her travels abroad. Exerting her social magic among so many, she sometimes would blush a damask rose. Ann was Earth Mother to a world tribe.

The pervading and disciplined science, with accomplished professionals all around, was not austere or forbidding. Those who were unaffiliated with academia, or not yet enfranchised into research, were welcomed by scholars who were experienced in personal transformations. Some people arrived as honorary attaches from unspeakable realms, and now were invited to rest here in the cool bosom of new consciousness. For others, appearing from the covert worlds and fearful of groups, it was like coming in from the cold. A special few returned from the far mountains and secret deserts, from their endless loneliness and practice of clandestine arts. To these, Sasha and Ann seemed angels of light.

Laughter was everywhere, serious asides here and there and – penetrating everything – the everlasting sunshine of simple compassion. Poignant, ghost-like presences sometimes were apparent: the deceased and luminous forebears of these arts, the remembered and loved, the imprisoned, and around the edges always the lost, or those too fearful to appear.

One entered into superlative esoteric states near Sasha and Ann, for one was in the company of like minds at last. With studied politeness, newcomers first stood in the violet shadows, while Sasha with his jilted Anglo-Saxon launched into abstractions and twinkled with kindly complicity, inevitably drawing out his fond listeners.

My experiences had been isolating, for events among the Six hardly could be discussed. Yet somehow my hosts knew. Over time, in the growing acceptance and friendship all around, the gatherings had a dream detachment – one's perception changed as if by evening river winds – so that in the brindled autumn and summer moonlight all was safe. We were home.

⬡

IN MY 20TH YEAR, visiting the stacks at Mallinckrodt laboratories at Harvard, I was reviewing articles in the *Journal of Organic Chemistry*. Through a Gothic window, as sunlight fell upon the page, I first became aware of Sasha's work. Although following forever after all of his papers, I – only after quite some years – braved writing him. Suddenly I was an invited, eager student in forensic chemistry at Berkeley, scribbling notes frantically as he lectured to packed classrooms. Ann often attended in devotion. Frequently her daughter Wendy would appear – fresh from Japan or Europe or the Levant, with her radiance and torrential golden hair.

By first announcing to his crowded classes that he would divulge some "dirty pictures," Sasha would introduce students to seemingly impenetrable molecular structures, precisely and rapidly drawn in chalk. It was not a reference to the licentious, of course, but his humor about the fearsome intricacies of organic chemistry so alarming to those with no background in the art. With his little joke, everyone relaxed. We were carried skyward, for everything became simple in his hands. Sasha rendered even the most arcane concepts elegant, even beautiful in a way.

After I completed my undergraduate degree in chemistry with Sasha's lectures, he wrote a recommendation to graduate school at Harvard. Learning of the acceptance, he gave me a great hug, as he often did with others.

"I'm so proud of you."

To young people fascinated with the advances in chemistry and pharmacology, and who showed persistence in their talents, Sasha always pointed out the path of advanced degrees, guiding them away from the uncertain and vulnerable covert life.

"Get that PhD!"

I sought refuge with them when I could. During my first dinners at their home, alone with them in the years before they wrote the seminal *PIHKAL* (Phenethylamines I have Known and Loved), Sasha brought out his voluminous handwritten notebooks. We sat outdoors, under a black sky, with its plates of brightness and a surprising moon. Sasha and Ann had eyes of unparalleled depth those evenings, the night flowing down to the white earth. Within his decades of records were drawings of molecular structures, calculations, elaborate syntheses he had created, and comments on subjective effects of hundreds of new psychoactive molecules. Exploring the journals with reverence, I teased him lightly.

"Where's the page that says 'Eureka'?"

Laughing, he pointed out the structures 2-CB and 2-CE, then described their teachings, eroticism and aesthetics. Of the mysterious Aleph-1, he fretted about mania, or ego-inflation.

Striding about the Berkeley campus or at conferences from Amsterdam to Heidelberg, Sasha was easily spotted, so tall he was, with his mane a wreath of white flowers. His personal vivacity was constant, for he possessed an innate joy. He would appear as suddenly as a star slides into the sky.

◯

HIS LABORATORY was out back. In the warm twilights, under a curtain of wisteria, the tiny cottage had a halo of starlight. Within, a God's eye and Huichol yarn paintings hung from a low roof, while an antique vacuum pump beat softly against the mountain silence. Old iron racks and lab benches held elaborate micro-glassware for reactions of hundreds of milligrams.

Sasha's lab was licensed by DEA and the State of California, so there was no fear of arrest. Doing thin-layer chromatograms to analyze new substances or monitor reactions-in-progress, Sasha's hands moved with refinement and accuracy as he described in muted tones the molecular mechanisms from which new medicines arose.

"But of the 5-MeO-DIPT," I once asked. "Although your journals describe its aphrodisiac qualities, other groups report it has no stimulant effect."

"The onset of effects must occur during love-making; it intensifies orgasm but does not induce longing."

After Sasha first tested a new substance upon himself to assess its psychoactivity – whether others might benefit from the experience – a circle of trusted friends, many with advanced degrees, then would try it together in a special session. Rules were set: not to leave during the experience, not to approach other's wives or husbands, not to forget to record one's recollections of the event. Through these courageous means, new probes to extend neuropharmacology were discovered.

My paltry skills were nothing beside his own. He once spoke of the major acid chemists of yore, all of whom he seemed to know.

"But why make the same thing repeatedly? Why not conceive new structures?"

I neglected to mention the Six, although if anyone were aware of them, Sasha would be. They clearly revered him, following his work carefully, even before they reviewed other newly-invented substances developed by Big Pharma, foreign researchers and maverick medicinal chemists across the nations.

We rarely spoke of the actual mechanisms of chemistry, but sometimes of the impact. Of his laborious bench syntheses of phenethylamine and tryptamine analogues – hundreds of them, one by one, each taking months or longer – I once suggested applying modern methods of pharmaceutical chemistry. These were rapid, costly, automated procedures.

"Why don't you oversee a team of foreign chemists, or use combinatorial techniques to generate thousands of novel structures, then assay them for psychoactivity with high-throughput screening?"

"Oh, but thinking of new molecules – then creating them – are the greatest delights. One would miss all the *fun*."

Sasha was born to the manor of chemistry, not simply educated. There will be no other like him.

SMALL OR LARGE, the gatherings could be long, for people were reluctant to leave. At the soft musical chime of a clock, and with the brilliant hilltop whiteness of the day receding, I wandered on the grounds one night to overlook a horizon of black ocean. Electric-lined clouds, mobilized in the lessening light, were suffused in glory. The far vivacity of discourse seemed on the very edge of comprehension, but in the titanic silence of the mountain falling away to the Bay, the rapid flow of ideas soon became quaint echoes. In those moments – for a beleaguered world – we all seemed to be, in some small way, the architects of fate.

Through personal revelation and distribution of new molecules, a few blithe or exuberant souls sought to overcome the cruelty of man. Other visitors, at first remote as ciphers in these gatherings, appeared to summon some desperate courage. Through Sasha and Ann's gateway, they hoped to enter the friendly society of academia, and the affectionate collusion among us.

In the westering moonlight, the nerve of feeling through us all grew ever stronger. Walking back among the crowd, I saw nearby Sasha's silver fingers raised high, and heard about him the silver waves of gentle banter. Those beguiled by his legend had found – to their delight – that he was playful and human, even as the sky stuck to him, and the birds sang through him. I thought of the Six, and of Sasha, and of the next experimental substances from their everlasting river of thought and skill.

Suddenly, there he was. Aggregating and introducing people rather than isolating them, moving about with invitations.

"And your wife and little one? You must bring them again. So burdened with studies?"

To the delight of her many suitors, Wendy's hair was caught in a golden mesh, while Sasha and Ann in their rustic setting were hosts in some wild villa, and even the dear planets themselves were aloft. The pulse of it all was not just from us, or projected from one's memory of the Six, but from a latticework of information, bravery and vision flowing in from hundreds or thousands of heirs, operatives and extended family over the earth. Such was the complexity of things.

⬡

SASHA, beyond his intellectual gifts and his pure love of the art, had fortunate circumstances and inclinations. He had no hunger for material objects; his simple needs were met. Their home, hand-made by his father, was the same cottage in which Sasha was born. The elevated acreage on the mountainside allowed friends to roam; their narrow quarter-mile driveway during gatherings was lined with cars. Named "Shulgin Road" on maps, the county had acceded to his gleeful request.

His small teaching salaries, his books, his scattering of patents, all somehow managed the electricity, heating and a few necessities. There were no luxuries other than excellence of thought and accomplishment, loving minds and floating hearts and lingering twilights in the amorous summers, and the chirping of visiting children running all about, blithe as larks.

At Sasha and Ann's little dining table, just off the impossible kitchen, we would converse late into the evening. It was like some humble, privileged family – we felt among the chosen. I would look at the countenances of those assembled, for in these moments we at last belonged, respected and welcomed and understood as those who had seen too much. The faces, it seemed sometimes, were those of poor children around their first Christmas tree.

⬡

THE ATMOSPHERE of intellect and friendship always was magnetically lit. On special holidays the book-filled shelves and gardens were interlaced with the shivers of tambourines and the spiritual thrills of Irish pipes.

One Halloween gathering had an amusement of women in full costume – all highly talented and serious – adorned as witches, wenches, angels, and harlots. Wendy's father, the inestimable Harvard psychiatrist John Perry, held court in a medieval gown. High clouds in that October night were wind-scarred, like our minds in their orgasms of flight.

Practicing as a lay monk at Hoshin-ji monastery – between the prison years and entering Harvard – I had no possessions other than a few clothes and a computer, so I wore my monk's formal sitting robe, kimono and tatami mat sandals. Fabulous creatures were all about: Wendy's fair maiden, assortments of ghouls and elves, even – to my delight – a Friar Tuck with rough robe and wooden staff. Blending in, I thought the robe would pass until a young woman with a wreath of rosebuds and in Elizabethan dress – perhaps a Zen student – whispered to me.

"That's no costume. It's real."

And so it was, but others were unaware each stitch had been hand-sewn with a prayer. I swore her to secrecy. Some of the white witches seemed real as well, but it was best then to say nothing. Sasha bounced up in his alchemist's cap, insisting I meet a distinguished couple observing the fun. It was the Director of the DEA Western Regional Laboratory and his wife.

We chatted, I an almost barefoot monastic, pretending my monk's robe was for Halloween. The Director, soon to be retired, certainly was amused, but polite. He had watched over Sasha for years, most fondly, a situation between government and private research unlikely ever to be seen again. We parted in a congenial manner.

⬡

SO MANY IMAGES remain, memories of them around the world. Buoyant exchanges in Amsterdam's cafés, the delight of neuroscientists at Harvard Medical School as Sasha lectured on entheogens with an aside about his freshman chemistry explosion in Harvard Yard. Sasha with Albert Hofmann and surrounded by scientists, students and youths with green Mohawks at 2 AM at European conferences on consciousness, picnics on Mt. Diablo with soft spring winds, Sasha looming with beatific mien after his presentations at American Chemical Society meetings, and always the magical nights, the unearthly flute music.

In Big Sur, at a small white frame house on a cliff over the Pacific, on a lawn with rare little Chinese apple and sour plum trees, the evening air the color of sunset, the mornings of bright showers shrouded in blue. Sasha discussing music as audible mathematics, cushions all about for a small circle of prominent figures: Czech psychiatrists, economists, a future Nobelist, professors of public policy and neuroscience from Harvard and Berkeley, a RAND thermonuclear war strategist, and Sasha always the prophesying oracle, settling under his hand our intellectual disarray and excitement.

In his talks and writings and among others, Sasha avoided any theological note in his references to the effects of newly-created molecules. Full of energy, there was a touch of bustle about him. He had a horror of pomposity, wearing the same simple coat he'd had for years, so that one saw only his heart and mind, bright always as the sun.

As his entheogen discoveries rippled outward, and old theologies yielded to the nakedness of thought, young people would approach Sasha and say they loved him. Yet he was uncomfortable with accolades.

Sasha was in his sixties then, hale and electrical, faster than anyone, the ultimate reservoir of knowledge on the psychedelic revolution. Yet, still the elder. In a sober moment, packed in an FND, I posed a question to other dear friends.

"What will happen when we lose him?"

"There will be a big hole in our lives," they said.

○

WE KNEW NOT of the crushing events that soon would surround us both. Years later, toward the end of his life, Sasha would lose his sight. No longer would he read music or play his viola in weekly quartets at the venerable Bohemian Club in San Francisco. It would all end in a kind of protracted foreboding, among those many with a preternatural fondness for this great man.

At Harvard one day I learned that DEA, in apparent retaliation for the publication of *PIHKAL*, or some misunderstanding about human use of unscheduled substances, had raided Sasha's house.

Appearing with lab teams, Sheriffs' deputies, federal agents, and the head of Special Testing at DEA Headquarters, they searched thoroughly, finding nothing.

One frustrated invader crushed under his boot heel Sasha's precious collection of botanicals, small flowering exemplars of *Lophophora williamsii*. The sacrament for the Native American Church peyote ceremonies, the Supreme Court had made it legal fifty years earlier. Although Sasha had a license for Schedule I substances, it was withdrawn after the incident, yet his continuing syntheses of new molecules was permitted. The research was all that was important.

In the last years, I would seek the company of Sasha and Ann, for after the Six my recent interviews of narcotics addicts and disreputable underground figures had become a most lamentable business. One individual in particular disturbed me greatly, one I might mention to Sasha for his advice.

The humble laboratory was alight within, like some great doorway to the morning after. Incense and music were drifting up the mountainside. A girl, thin as a reed and with eyes of drenched violets, passed out of the northern mists. Sasha and Ann's rustic door nearby was open to their table of friends; the scene was decorated in tints of heraldic light. In the finality of these evening skies, I saw the lowering of crows, but thought nothing of it, then.

He had concerns about my safety, even at Harvard, especially the research into manufacturers and distributors of addictive drugs: heroin, cocaine, methamphetamine. He thought such contact had a vulnerability, both from the treacheries of the subjects and from law enforcement. In this regard, Sasha was prescient.

Moonlight shown through him that night, like an ineffable spirit, as the music of a dulcimer led the path of dreams. I did not know these hours were to be among the last of my freedom. Sasha's lab hardly was the place to discuss dark deeds, but I felt compelled to reveal my latest interview subject. Aptly named Skinner, he lived in a converted missile silo in Kansas. He was a kind of preserved infant, but gargantuan, his face empty as a zero.

Upon my first description, Sasha became exceptionally quiet. Genius can be silence.

"And his behavior?" he finally asked.

"He tortures this simple, dependent young girl with drug overdoses, then in her confusion…indulges his prurience."

"And his manner? His voice?"

"A suave, undisciplined python. He keeps a bagful of odd stimulants and opiates – toxic as Hell. That poor girl…"

From Sasha's, I would travel to Kansas to interview this obvious demon. It was the last of my studies of abuse scenarios and addictive drug cults. Sasha was concerned about such encounters, so far from Cambridge and the moderation of established researchers.

"I wish you were back at Harvard," he said. His message was subtle, but clear.

"I will be, soon."

○

EVENING STORMS were rolling in from the Pacific – one could smell the wild sea and hear the troubling sky. As I left for the Midwest, Sasha and Ann's magical compound was high in the clouds, thinning away in whiteness. I worried about the meeting ahead, the strangeness of my new subject Skinner, his captive girl, the near-lethal drug mixtures he gave her, the coldness of his eyes.

Events happened quickly – frightening, cataclysmic events with no warning. I didn't know on the endless journey to Kansas that soon I would be incarcerated for life, or that these very words would be written from a remote and forgotten prison cell. Or that after a bleak decade – freezing and alone in a Special Housing Unit beneath a maximum-security federal prison – I sometimes would use my one monthly call to reach out to Sasha and Ann.

Even from this perspective of so many years entombed in cement and steel, I remember well the last night we spoke. I crouched beneath the narrow slit of a handcuff port in the 300-pound steel door of my cramped cell, and held the phone for the permitted fifteen minutes.

"I'm blind now," he confided, although Sasha's extended family throughout the world long had known.

"Galileo was blind the last ten years of his life," I reminded him.

Beloved by all that knew him, Sasha's life was truly blessed. Our last words together were not on chemistry, but on music.

"You could still play your balalaika."

His father was Russian, the fine triangular instrument a family heirloom. Sasha was ambulatory somewhat, due to the loving care of Ann and his Tibetan women caregivers, who daily massaged his legs and guided him to sit in his beloved laboratory with friends and colleagues who came to honor him.

"How many balalaika strings are there?" he asked.

"Six," I replied, uncertain (There are three).

"That's right," he said, for he never discouraged anyone by asserting his knowledge. Then he said his final words to me. It was the last time I would ever hear his voice.

"There are heavenly harmonics."

Chapter 28.

The Pool of Tears

I try to write all of this lightly
because my heart is full in drawing to an end.
But when I write of her,
my tears will have their way.

- Esther, Dickens *Bleak House*

And what about her, my Lord, what about her?
Is the kingdom of heaven only a step from her also
and will the passions of the earth
fall back and bow their heads
as she passes?

- W.S. Merwin, *The Miner's Small Children*
(describing a woman outside a prison wall each week
for seventeen years, unaware her husband long had
been executed.)

Woman who thunders am I, woman who sounds am I
Spider woman am I, hummingbird woman am I
Eagle woman am I, important eagle woman am I
Whirling woman of the whirlwind am I
Woman of a sacred enchanted place am I
Woman of the shooting stars am I.

- Oaxacan curandera Maria Sabina,
singing in Mazatec.

KANSAS. The sodden earth has frozen overnight and left the air crisp; the fall and all the world is caught and chained up in winter's grasp. Traveling overland to Skinner's bizarre setting, my vision darkens from some premonitory fear. Eight hours more of hard driving through the numbing irrelevance of endless, yawning grey landscapes. They arise from the roaring night, where the far lights of isolated villages seem distant, cold as the final stars. I do a propitiary prayer for survival.

But warmth and hope still reign, for within the years of interviewing the Six, and during the formidable study at Cambridge, my own parallel secret life has arisen like a flowering of the heart. I have fallen in love.

I withdraw from a briefcase a small bundle of letters to my lover, bound in blue ribbon and returned as a protective amulet for this journey. All were written in desperate rooms or hostels or manors or desert encampments, written under candlelight or moonlight, bare bulbs or oil wicks, lanterns or high-valley sunshine. Hours of anxious monotony lay before me, trapped in a silver Buick to nowhere. At turnouts and rest stops, I begin to read them.

"Dear Ms. _____,

Thank you for your research assistance in matters of public policy. Please provide contact information for forwarding of additional documents of interest. I look forward to further discussions, when our relative schedules permit.

Cordially,

_____ "

She has selected from awkward love letters even the dreadfully terse first note. Ah! A much later, more florid example.

"Dear _____,

It has been weeks since life was transformed by the votive joy of knowing you, of finding you at last. When we walked with the slow, delicate pace of lovers – as if one were walking a rainbow, with our arms entwined and our voices breathlessly congruent – I first realized we could never leave each other.

That night of changes still burns in me, with its bluish spring moon and the boom of celestial surf. Now forced apart by circumstance, I must write to record the blessed summoning of our spirits into one, for I remember forever the skies of old rose and the febrile ecstasy of your face.

Do you recall when we walked the natal coastline of the future, holding each other like a precious silver chalice or a rare book of mystic formulae? The fevered cities all began to disappear, and at the center of being only we were left.

Forgive me if I seem too unbearably prosy about all this, but tonight when we are alone together in different worlds there is no outlet for these feelings other than ink and light, the wordless lovers' code between our two hearts, our one heart.

I am stricken this evening by my interview with a most remarkable person in San Francisco, one of the experimental subjects, whose presence evoked cascades of realizations. Perhaps it is just my time in life that the veil is removed, but upon the last of the shimmering insights, I saw only you.

The nights and days since our embrace, as our love has flourished, have been both savage and lyrical, for your voice and body and touch have become like shivering mirrors. Every moment now we constantly throb up and down each other's spectrum.

It was the feeling of avidity that drew us near, our enduring eagerness on the first moonless dusk; the fading angle of sunlight was a stairway, showing us the way forward into the evening sky of our life together. When we whirled about on the edge of the newly rising moon – and then loved on the sand as the sky was covered in brilliants – I first felt the daffodil fragility of you, then knew the ferocious strength of your desire and the smell of the hot sea moon, until our dawn ritual of dance and prayer and fervent kisses.

Everything changed in an instant. The ochre sunsets became cloud-soft perfumed nights. The incipient flirtation of our minds launched us upon this sea of bewitchment, from which now we can never hope to return.

I have seen you revealed. When you bathed in the shallow water lagoon, your skin illuminated with silver light like some shy Psyche in the starlit air, I was terrified to feel at your mercy. Now I am but a humble supplicant before the majesty of you, surrounded by you always as though our one spirit were the ectoplasmic rose of the world.

I must quell these feelings, or wander in the streets quite mad. But no, love is the ultimate clarity, the rock of consciousness. It was the trembling of your ivy-soft fingers as I came to you, and you to me, that at once taught us the meaning of love craft. It is the ocean of you I remember most, when we joined our breath in the universal pattern, and I first saw your rapturous face and heard your wanton cries of delight. Now that you know the truth of me, and I of you, how can we ever be with another?

The edge of this page, the end of this letter, is like a heartless amnesia that can never be filled. I must stop for now. I know, I know.

Ever yours,

———"

San Francisco, after hours café in SOMA, and medical library at UCSF, and the UC Berkeley Genetics lunchroom

○

AFTER EACH LETTER, I kiss it, look out at the cold passing highway, and think of her. Big tandem tractor trailers the size of Jupiter blow past, leaving muddy streaks on the windshield. Grinding ten-wheeler Peterbilt diesel trucks winging to Omaha, Oklahoma City, Abilene, high plains drifters all the way down through the hard scrabble ravines of Texas and the black cypress swamps of Lousiana to Big Easy. They come up fast, flashing lights, but destiny is in no hurry. YIELD and STOP signs are proliferating, omens and cautions I had not seen so often before.

She is studying now, bent over her books, her hair falling by lamplight.

"Darling,

It is so cold. Autumn has fled from the air; there is the scent of approaching snow.

I am in Cambridge, at the crossroads of the world's knowledge, among the reasoning engines and dream calculations, with our paltry estimates of unknown futurities. The idle forebrain is no more, alas.

The last of the dashing flowers have gone; a snow moon has risen. I have put down the tomes and equations, for at the mere thought of you my heart must scribble the night with song.

A writer's greatest fear is madness, but one must push the border, breaking limits of the head and heart like a raider into new realms.

It is so late that I fear for morning lectures. A pallid light from the translucent dawn adorns the window in Radcliffe dorm. The chill is heavy, with a ringing frost. It is in this utter emptiness that I remember your lavender honey, as our new rhythm began.

I must be physical briefly, thinking of your magnificent carriage, like an unconscious patrician, when you would sing to me in quavering trails of songs in a seduction of almost carnal subtlety.

This pen must substitute to conjure these feelings between us, in the temporary sadness without you. Of course you know we have the same historic pedigree of thought and feeling, perfectly matched yet wildly divergent. In joy we have become each other's pillow consultant, strewing jewels of insight and laughter, but still our haunted eyes of hunger remain even as we climb together to the precipice, to the very edge of things.

I must share something. The night with the first research subject still troubles me in a way, although my private disclosures to you must be limited to the few words in these letters. Sometimes now the plants and trees seem almost paradisaical. I feel the portentous and profound silence of the rising moon. At other times there is a disposition to sing, as though one were on a terribly exciting Provençal summer. Yet are these not also manifestations of our affection?

Before the bitter frost, I would wander on the moonlit terraces in Harvard Yard, pouting at your absence, but a few times reveries of the experimental subjects would intrude. I venture to sketch this in because they are accompanied by an underworld of forebodings. The first subject, perhaps all of them, sometimes speaks in quaint Victorian English, even while possessing an infernal mystery and magic. But enough.

Students are serious now, further into term. Striking little stories abound of their prodigious youthful explorations of each other. I may write of them to turn you on. The dorm after Brain Break is like a research team investigating the Kama Sutra; their exuberant studies of such Indian mythology – under a velvet blue night sky – seem all engulfing.

My darling, these words are written in whispers, in a humble, late-night rapture. Some say it is difficult in America to do any serious thinking about passion, but during the

Austrian visit we can explore together through these writings the very limits. But why wait? We might try a little even now, before bed.

So often I breathe in the satin nakedness of your memory, as though you were the sun in her exaltation. At your first opening – my first opening – as our spirits began pouring into each other, our every movement and desire seemed to prosper with each breath.

Beneath your many layers of exemplary piety, I could feel the mouth of your thirsty womb suckling me. It was a kind of milking that laced my body with high tension wires and crackling currents until I was painfully rigid in an agony of impatience and satyriasis.

Distraught with wildness, we chose the probing scrolls of our tongues to free each other, our incessant warm lappings that forced us to kneel in loving obedience. When you seized so deeply, and seized yet again – so shameless before God – I felt the very blood-heat of your pulse beating. The taste of your fount was like my first drink on earth.

There is a lustful repletion in just knowing you read these words. Forgiveness, my love, I must now dispatch these writings, for there is a difficult and longish morning of work before lecture.

In honor that passes understanding,

———"

Cambridge, Yenching Library of Asian Studies, and Woodruff Poetry Room, and Widener Library stacks.

⬡

ILLUMINATED LIKE A MOON BASE, a truck stop looms in the smoking grey haze. EATS BEER BAIT. Taciturn drivers corralled into white Formica tables, ranks of toilets with coin locks, chili cheese fries in red plastic baskets, grey-haired waitresses who know every name, stuffed animals, chrome rims, strung-out truck stop dollies fellating obese drivers in steaming cabs, gallon jars of hot beef jerky, candy bar mountains, luminescent energy drinks, rivers of unrequested acrid coffee. Six hours of freeway limbo ahead. Unmarked car behind me, off to the right. White Ford LTD, no white walls, too many small antennae.

She is cooking, preferring home life to Americans sitting isolated in restaurants. Checking if her monthly bus pass has expired, arranging flowers, singing quietly.

"My Light,

The sun is rising upon our infinite bond, the ecstatic realization each morning that you are with child. We have surrendered ourselves at last – I am forever lost in your utter glory.

Without you in Salzburg I feel as Wordsworth described Newton, "voyaging through strange seas of thought, alone."

These must be heavily armored pages, written with a kind of tearless detachment, for the next experimental subject is quite phenomenal – like a desert Gnostic with global mobility. I can say only a little more, in caution, and because all else pales beside the miracle of you.

At my subject's invitation, I hiked in the false Austrian spring to alpine meadows, then looked upon dreamlike flights of doves, and dazzling, sumptuous brooks of crystal. A charming, very young sheppardess with a beatific face herded her flock of Imperial goslings, then danced for us, and gave us blueberries. Will our beloved child be so fair? How blessed we will be then, my love, for even now we live in a state of grace.

Salzburg proves the Greek poet's observation that "perils and absences sharpen desire." I did try to saunter along the Getreidegasse, but soon descended to looning about wan and bereft. Tonight is spent in this pension provided by my subject, as I try to record his world-view.

Your loving mind – I have found to my unfathomable delight – is so limitless I can fly gloriously without reaching any barriers. My pen thus freed, I can allude to changes that need not concern you, but which I must share in a small way.

While first with the subjects, it is as though one is skulking on the outskirts of reality, the edges of our planet's vast sanatorium. Then occurs a rigorous cleansing of cognition through a historical, religious panorama, before the condensing of one's wits back to – dare I say it – normalcy. One might think of the subjects as the *ne plus ultra* of non-linear theory. For you I cannot provide details, but must remain obscure, even opaque.

Some would consider their beliefs a cosmic absurdity, some severe, impossible magic. But near them one cannot but have a sense of immanence, under a manic sky. I now must go, for the darkness receives me, only to dream of you.

Morning in Vienna. At the Café Demel, contemplating an Anna Torte. The night was long, spent in your chiming, flashing heart. We appeared on a wide, mossy pathway, beneath thick sycamores and oaks, then in a meadow where our sensuality was violent and extreme as death and birth.

I awoke refreshed as if from your embrace, then in the slow morning light entered a hallway. A door was parted, opening to heaping bedclothes from a vigorous tryst. I thought only of our abandon, our strange posthumous feeling that sometimes occurs after loving, and your tousled sleepy awakening into bliss.

Just a few words today, my love,

_____ "

Salzburg, Pension Doktor Wirt
Vienna, near the Hotel König von Ungarn

ON THE ROAD. Rolling under speed limit, cruise control. Low slatternly hills to the horizon, wheat, corn, soybeans, hay ricks. Old barns with sad eyes looking upon the winds of memory. Lonely waterholes, emerald ponds. Repeat to infinity. Tornado whirlpools. Heavy, high clouds, roiling electrical atmospheres, armies of gods launching arrows, lightning like mad medicine men in the sky. Desolate red brick high schools, storm shelters, yellow buses with football teams. Patrol car on overpass, just sittin' by his lonesome.

She is rising before dawn, entering her future of compassion and research. Gentle, strong, committed. Her delicate hand of grace parts the simple worn curtains of our cheap little one-room place, where the radiance of the last knowing stars bathe her.

"*Liebchen*, my Beautiful Profligate,

Every moment I think of you swollen even more with our love, our dreaming child hearing your singing from on high, from beyond heaven's gates.

Today in Berlin, awaiting an aircraft, a phenomenon. I could feel the milky tightness of your breasts and hot belly. I was reading Lawrence's *Rainbow*, for all words now speak of you. The passage on the expectant heroine – listen.

'She lifted her throat in the breeze that came across the fields, and she felt it handling her like sisters fondling her, and she drank it in with the perfume of cowslips and apple blossoms.'

My aching night may stir your blood. Mysteriously intercepted for an interview, I was thunderstruck to encounter a subject who was attended by a sensational Sapphic duo. Rather than simply inducing in others a doe-like regard, they are truly accomplished, and caress each other with their minds to the point of inevitability. Can you imagine?

They appeared from entertaining *à trois*, to become like soft-footed Arab servants who gained in splendor throughout the night. In their presence an episodic vision occurred – perhaps I was mesmerized or exhausted – in which you manifested as a young girl alone on a moor. I yearned so, it seemed forever.

They came again in black cowls, their robes fashioned of moonlight. We retrieved a hapless girl from the cruel night, then in a breath-taking three-cornered passion they chanted a sort of litany as she rose to them, yielding completely with unintelligible cries. My notes are futile on the event. Perhaps we only dream when we are awake.

Under a theatrical moon, they were like a tapestry of medieval legends, then pre-Christian figures, then sacred relics of sensation. It was not profane, or even slightly lurid – although each writhed interminably in the anguish of delight – but some religious incantation, some rescue from the nether world. They were the Sisterhood of Eternal Love.

The spectacle brought memories of you in a scarlet leather corset, your model's thin body erect with the fury of heat, dancing over me like a veil of light, a will 'o the wisp, until we buried ourselves in redemption and delirium on some refectory table, and our minds slid northward into the pearl clouds of forgiving skies.

They left only a cryptic note and a little girl's angel wings. When I later passed the Reichstag, then the destroyed Kaiser-Wilhelm-Gedächtniskirche, I became restless, moody, alert. The shadows of the ruined Kirche were soundless as death, each moment fecundating into visions of future wars. Such thoughts must seem, for your gentle soul, only momentous fictions. For are we not now – with our every breath – the engineers of grace?

Always,

—————,"

Berlin, a spare student hostel near Tempelhof

◯

SIX HOURS NOW through the Land of Nowhere. Ancient, white clapboard town halls, vacant prairies, children and mothers and mayors long dust, nameless as the grey fields. Failed crops, dried creeks. Remnants of covered wagon trails, the great caravans to paradise, the broken-wheeled dreams. Dead wells, tin-roofed shacks, the faces of strong people who never left the land. Rock of Ages, every one. Children taught to say their prayers at night.

> "Now I lay me down to sleep,
> I pray the Lord my soul to keep.
> If I should die before I wake,
> I pray the Lord my soul to take."

She wonders where I am; her mind goes out to find me here. I feel her every gesture, her every move, every thought, for we are one river.

"*Radost Maya* (My Joy),

Moscow's frigid, pine-starred landscapes exhale clouds of ghosts; the grey winterset and vast snow meadows rest in silence.

Now in the tiny dacha of a medicinal chemist from MGU, near its rosy fire. Small children, all so very bright, are in bed each and every one. They have left two long-stemmed candles to write by, seeing me in a romantic melancholy, although I protested it was weariness from being sapped by economics texts. They knew.

Their dacha has the rustic simplicity of love, with little bits of found holly and mistletoe, laurel, moss, ferns, lichens. Chaplets of garlic hang over the fire, sweet meats and nuts are on the table. I crave your arms so. These short research trips are an eternity, unsalved by writing you each night.

The wind is solemn as it moves over snow-lit expanses. Yet in the great quietness of winter evenings there is an ecstasy, the joyful wounds of even knowing you, of feeling life growing within you.

In the pale hot candlelight I think of you in silks, like a sheath of silver drops, your ripening delicacy so pliantly feminine.

Ah, what of these brief but too burdensome travels? Are they not, in the end, temples of inconsequences?

You over there! Listen and dream, so we awaken together.

I saw an elderly *babushka* with a visage I can never forget – her eyes like the blue empyrean – sweeping snow in the bitter cold with a tattered broom of twigs. A just God must have ensured that she too – in her youth and in her children's eyes – knew some paradise of fire and light.

Will our child have eyes of blue like morning, or sea green or topaz?

You are creating each moment. Nature is reveling in the the inexhaustible wealth of you. All of wonder is flaming out behind you, beneath you, above you, before you.

The fire just burst at these thoughts. Each second is like the very heart of orgasm, the sweet lotus of insight.

Prosy again, damn the vagueness. I love you. 'Ya tibia lublu,' as lovers say here.

Until the morning, then,

——————,"

140 kilometers west of Moscow, north of the Mojaysk highway near Stepanova, at the family dacha of Professor L.

⬡

DIESEL MINNOWS LOTTERY. We take food stamps. The world is an automatic person ringing a cash register, distracted, mumbling 'Thank, you, thank you." Lines of grumpy drivers, hustlers, stone cold addicts, coffee fiends, boozehounds, kids eyeballing Mars bars, video game consoles, corn chips and bean dip, avalanches of icy Coca-Colas until we forget the delicious rain and sweet water streams and glades with springs. Let us pray. Sugar fat salt chocolate and the Lord be with you.

Tornado warning. The skies worry, soon to vacuum the Lice. Two squad cars end-to-end like gay boys, arms out flicking cigarettes, patches and badges, tinted windows, crackling radios. Nobody notices me, and why would they? Lots of murders on these plains. Lots of meth. Terminal users all sucked up, picking at sores, jittery, no teeth, looting pharmacies.

She walks in silence, feeling the weight of her, feeling the caldera of the unborn. She is thinking of life enfolding us, thinking of these letters being read, and how they will keep me safe.

"Mistress of Heaven,

Or would it excite you for me to be masterly again? I pray this caress releases warmth in your loins.

In a threadbare room at Harvard's funky retreat near Stratford-upon-Avon, jet-lagged among the kaleidoscope of nations. No, no – that's *miles* off. Rather, in a thatched-roofed cottage outside Oxford, scratching words to the mourning twining of clocks. It is Forever England, beloved.

Oxford is filled with Palladian galleries. Students and faculty quote noble poems over pints of Guinness in public houses, and Pindaric odes over sherry at All Souls.

The summer is high and warm, like a following wind, while Commemoration Day is a cumulus of thought. There is an intoxicating felicity among the students, a jollity of peers. I can see swallows and martins overhead by the light of the moon.

Along its rays I wander to Lawrence's house, musing on secret tribes of cognition, and how this study arose. Lawrence's dedication of his manuscript. How did it go?

"I loved you…
So I gathered these blessed ones into my hands
And wrote their names across the sky in stars,
That your eyes might be shining…"

But let's speak of our own secrets instead.

Outside the open window are apple blossoms with your scent and effervescence. I remember the night when your voice ran up inside me like fire, so that my blood also flamed, beating up in waves of desire, burning away in one consummation. It was then we became the doorway to each other.

Later in the night. Desperation. Alone. Do you hear the tears in my voice? I hear them so in your thoughts from afar.

Are not all attractions psychic? Among lovers, the physical following when it can? At this distance, the sublime pleasures of touch must wait, although it is not that which we seek, but the ineffable ecstasy.

Forgive this enigmatic portrait. It is only my etheric double, sailing in oceans of loneliness, looking for your verdant isle in the latitudes of heart.

Yours, Aye (as they say in Edinburgh)

——— ”

Oxford, in a cottage on Polstead Road, then a garret near the Old Parsonage

⬡

FIVE HOURS. "I'm just an Okie from Muskogee, don't get my kicks on LSD…" Twangy Merle and Conway Twitty rock the air waves, WWL 50,000 watts out of New Orleans right up the Mississippi, zig-zagging off the ionosphere to every little love shack out back, honey chile'. Highway to Heaven or Hell. Smashed armadillo guts and shredded armor too far north. Barn roofs painted JESUS SAVES, and He surely does. Three Kansas patrol cars flash past, red light racks in epilepsy and sirens silenced, rushing to crime scene shootout, mass causality, officer down or Mable's hot tart cherry slice, gratis for boys in blue, our finest. Gone now, specks on horizon, only the swish of wipers and – oddly – *Missa Solemnis* on the U Kansas FM out of Lawrence.

With the glorias I know she is moving like morning, kindness radiating. At a worn desk, her long fingers write notations in perfect script; she hesitates only to say a soft prayer for my return.

"Precious Light,

Have just scrambled down the mountains of the Schwarzwald near Basel. I draft this note in a quaint, even fastidious, little chamber; my writing table has drawers pulled by old ivory handles. It contrasts with the squat in Zürich, where bare bulbs hung in tenements and addicts' shooting galleries, and dawn chilled the night's unbridled paganism under a dazed-looking sky.

Here, there are sleepy ravens under the eaves, and gnarly carved window boxes, like some dusty villa buried in oleanders and poinsettias. Penurious artists abound, and the rates are low, thankfully.

I must tell you of a magnetic, startling couple – one an interview subject. We just were on the peaks of the _____, under the black, wind-washed skies of a tearing mistral.

In spectral moments, he sang to me in Navaho in a voice of thrilling deepness, like a shaman or roadman. His woman materialized, half-naked to the exultant stars. It has been only hours since they escaped into the violet night, into the graphic shadows down some *terrain vague* to the French border.

She was more than delectable; there was a faint chord of a different human species about her. I asked of their love; he said only the refrain to our song.

For him she was the galaxy, the way out, the beyond, at once sky and wild thing. He was mad with pride. They walked holding hands, the tide of pregnant peace descending over them like a silver robe. He said she had sunlight inside her.

Perhaps it was their white magnetism, their mind-thrill, or the instruments of Merlin or Faust.

Over Basel there is a fine late twilight; the horizon trembles with summer lightning. I pen this hastily, my love, as an expiatory device, for you are my journey back to sweet reason.

You taught me that nothing can withstand devotion. I must write tonight in ink rather than in tears, like the blue-black sky of infinite tenderness.

Te amo,

_____"

An artists' pension near the Teufelhof.

◯

WINDSHIELD WIPERS SLAPPIN' TIME, mile markers are little graves with numbers no names. Like small tombstones in the burying fields outside the state pen, one for each stack of prisoners' bodies, where everyone is free at last. Roadhouse strip joints with rough wooden chairs and floors, peanut shells, barbeque pork, Kansas City steaks and the best fried chicken this side of Natchez. Easy to hide here, as a son of the Old South, for the Midwest is Way Out West to country boys. I pretend I'm just passin' through, goin' home.

Big yellow school bus of Kansas kids, three girls of eight in back window with big smiles and a few teeth coming in, then three peace signs. Faces grow smaller, little hands wave bye-bye. I wave back, as if they were my own.

She is entering her day now, busing downtown, jostling crowds, feeling the soft emptiness of pink or blue baby booties. Pale, tired, coming home. Waiting.

"Lover,

It is vexatious hot. Your man is in a remote shelter of wattle smeared with clay, lost in a narrow finger of Uzbekistan into the Fergana Valley, encompassed within a few kilometers on all sides by the peaks of Tajikistan, China, Afghanistan, every one exalted with snow under an enamel sky.

The valley floor is a hysteria of dust; everything is steeped in sadness at your memory. Cheap Chinese recorders are playing tinny Arab songs in monotonous ululations of 'Aman, Aman' (Alas, Alas). The scent of incestuous musk spirals upon the night air, for in roadside tents the addict women entertain itinerant travlers, writhing on *naswar* (opiated snuff) and screaming in lascivious pulses as they feign sable orgasms.

There are wild horsemen here; they ride to the occasional blazing souk or choked bazaar. The dry heat is sulphurous, enervating.

While I am absent *en mission*, I carry your photograph in a pouch next to my heart as a talisman, but never show it when in some grubby café I am asked about family. The locals are mad about pink flesh.

A rare religious shrine – a simple mud dome, really – is atopped with the new moon crescent. In the wavering daylight, there are fictitious lakes suspended in the air like layers. Little rock doves hover in the desert fringe, until the great wind – the *khamseen* – whirls them skyward.

This is a queer, solitary life, penetrating into the heart of an alien culture. The children's lips are covered with ribbons of black flies, even as they stare (the elders carry a fly whisk for themselves). Ravaged paupers add to the putrescence of the humble village squares. There are about fifty mud huts; the few lamps are extinguished with a sheppard's crook.

Iron-black trees hang in the silence. Ravens hang across the moon. Even crude shelters – built of dried bundles of palm leaves and floors of straw – hang with every kind of *ex voto* to ward off evil spirits. The sulking bodies of the young hang about dust-tormented alleys. I hang about pensively, breathing the fresh, sweet air of your image, like a beloved mirage. I'm all hung up.

I hear a tumultuous clatter, for beyond the barely functional, rusted-out Toyotas a line of camels is growing ill-tempered. From these dingy lodgings one can hear the sound of their ragged bells.

The night is settling again into a shimmering haze of silence across the great silken mounds of dune. These are worlds of want and plenty.

At your memory everything changes. The sand becomes moist, pliant, cool. The morning skies have the marble whiteness of your skin, like some winged seraph. I am but a fledgling fallen from the nest, saved by the rainbow of your kiss. There is a jasmine afterglow, even as the dreams fade.

Restless on some clumsy, filthy divan. Through a doorless door the shapeless caravans are iridescent. The last Magellanic clouds brighten my private desert; in the clarity of the air one can see pinpricks of the sixth magnitude, actually globular clusters of a hundred million stars.

Dawn approaches again; the dry air is static with electricity. The desiccated wind frets and rises like the drowsy animals; everything is bathed in a ghost light of dimensionless obsolescence, as the dunes mirror the last starlight.

A water bearer has begun banging metal cups together; he bobs and rings them and says "Master…Master" to everyone as though he were sold into slavery as a boy. The dun mud floor is shining, reflecting the dense dew of morning.

Feathery dunes now are alight. Barbaric cafés hang with tattered Bokhara rugs. Somewhere there is a deep-throated flute, while to my inexpressible sorrow the eternal flies return and descend yet again into black ribbons on children's lips.

In'shallah,

————— "

Encampment somewhere in the Fergana Valley, Uzbekistan/Afghanistan/China/Tajikistan

○

FOUR HOURS to the missile base. Dull, smoking orange bus with barred windows, all somber men squeezed inside in neat, little immobile rows, eyes locked forward, no smiles. I know their iron misery, hear the silent chains. It hovers for miles, eases by me. Prisoners destined for cramped cells, then the screaming. Ten-twenty-thirty-forty-fifty-sixty-life plus a thousand years, handed out like traffic tickets. I look up, no one looks down. Finally one does – I raise my fist. He just stares, his hands cuffed tightly to waist chains, the waist chains to leg chains. Captives passing into The Machine. The air is sticky from a nearby feed lot and abattoir, with its narrow chute and black door, its blood and everlasting night from a bolt gun right through their incomprehension. Prison is only slower. I wonder if the herd knows.

She is making herbal tea and rice, then tutoring a ten-year-old girl. Her consciousness senses me. I see her always.

"Eagle woman,

Your faithful admirer is immured in the cities of debauch and casual venery in South East Asia, beneath a slur of blue sky hot as gun metal.

Before my fleeting study of opiates in Chiang Rai, the research subject from Berlin found me, together with his stunning diplomatic Geishas. They have proven to be Zen priestesses, skilled in the arts of transubstantiation in the medieval sense.

The women can project a hot lilac allure – or an icy serenity – issuing wicked invectives or transforming prayers in ten languages. They have a fathomless compassion for the abused, the aged, the very young, the lost. They appear to be advanced psychic physicians, casting spells with the blessing of Eros.

Casual observers in America or Europe, say, might first think them over-bred, or underestimate them as palace courtesans attending their liege lord, but the truth is unforgettable. One must regard them with a profound respect. I cannot write of the realizations they evoked, but must whisper them to you in person, practice them with you – I pray very soon.

Tonight we are students of love. May I excite your prurience? I thought so.

To prepare for the rigors of Laos, the women whipped each other – one tied at the wrists to bruise-dark bamboo staves, twisting under the lash, the whip rising and falling upon fair breasts and throats. In the midst of pain they descended slowly to ivory mounds with maidenhair ferns of white glass, just as I fall to your trimmed warmth, to the cries of your harsh triumph.

They live in a gossamer veil of passion and spiritual encounters, under a heated sky or in wet velvet darkness. They long have been stripped of the reticences of the sexually unawakened, for their daily practices include a profusion of erotica for heroines. In the presence of the initiated, they take each other openly.

Sometimes they wear only the merest of thin Chinese silk scarves, then walk in meditation about a lovely jungle demesne with candles and earnest brows and prayers in Latin and unknown tongues.

In the breathtaking dynamic of their triad, they love only each other. A tide of sadness flows from them though, when the moon is right. Master and mistresses interchangeably, they are three separate solitudes being born into one, like a band of forest nymphs writhing, becoming one angel.

True, the tropical heat has suspended the skepticism of your hardened rationalist, but in their fecund darkness I have learned from them.

Last night I heard the bass note of a chanted invocation, and found them all entwined in radiance, the women mounting him in turns in a lotus posture – constantly throughout the long night – each a palpitating victrix with her gleaming ruby core and her shining wet hair swinging in the intensity between hunger and abiding love. An electrical glow – an aura of speechless colors – generated from their incessant couplings, as each opened to the others, helpless, opening at last as a flower to the sun.

It was reminiscent of the night when I first heard your thunder gathering, then felt the epileptic bolt shoot up into our oneness, as the rays of the Almightly breathed through us, like the irresistible pulse of a massive fire. I know you can never forget.

This sea-stained stable on which I write is sheltered by a palm loggia beneath the delicate green pepper trees. It is early evening; there are soft footfalls to insatiable bliss and prayer. A ravenous air fills the dusk in this doll's house of mystics. If you were here, the women would want to kiss your globe, anoint you with oils. Shall I tell you of their frequent, casual encounters, conducted as though mere embraces by loving friends? They practice secret postures, erotic asanas, by which the initiated recognize themselves.

Close by I can hear a saturnalia in a creaking rattan chair, as a scholarly, naked white lily has surrendered her books. Fingers play about her sex, as though a precious viola is being tuned by a trio for a symphony. She is moon-drenched, the whites of her eyes heavenward reflect the silver night; she is arching with deepening breaths, convulsing in her spectrum of fantasies, birthing herself into the others.

You were born a sensualist, with no surcease, no rest, no apology for being a voluptuary. Life otherwise is but a stream of quietly flowing dead leaves.

By a flickering votive now. It is pitch dark, the moon-pearl black water is full of stars. I hurry to your arms, for they are the premonitions of my dawn. We will ignore the murmur of the telephone. In our tantric marriage and multifold embraces we will again share our yogic breaths in synchrony together, and extend forever the divine spasm. We will climb white stairways to the Hosts, engraving our voices and then our cries upon the dream cities of those awakened.

Deepest bow,
_____ "

Unidentified estate near village south of Phuket, Thailand

◯

LONG FETID CHICKEN HOUSES, packed alive in fear and greed like the imprisoned, where nothing can fly or walk or even move. Twenty thousand fryers in unbearable heat and stench, fed recycled, sterilized chicken excrement and entrails and ground feet, immobile from birth until death's harvesting. Beaks seared off tiny chicks, so when thousands go insane they don't peck each other to death and lower quarterly profits. Upside down feet caught in hangers, heads inverted in metal guides down blood alley as automatic knives go chop, chop, chop. Barrels of sightless heads ground into feed mush for beakless newborns.

SUPPORT YOUR LOCAL SHERIFF signs. Old billboards sprinkled with high caliber pistol fire. Radio says manhunt for three escapees.

She is reading now, soft light over her shoulder, perhaps Dickenson or Austin, for she loves forgotten manners from the Age of Innocence.

"Madame X,

I am late in joining you after Commencement, but must find consolation on this rose-trellised veranda. The old hurried morning is no more, there is only a deafening sunshine. Farewell until fall to this edifice of mentation, to the joyful foursome of student friends. Oh, the movers are here. Back soon.

Night has fallen, the summer stars are down. Our candles are bearded from hours of parting notes. The lightest of rains has begun, cool and gentle and blue.

You are a ripe peach now, so soon to burst into white-hearted light. I thought you might on that night when I reposed you back softly on the pillow after a few little *suçons*, love bites on your nape and thighs as our flight together departed. We sought then to divine our veiled future by coupling our minds; our bodies could only follow in the fateful rhythm. The bed was molten. Your belly began fluttering – quick as a swallow on her sky arching. You rippled when you came. Your breasts were wet, the night of blue silk, the stars on parade. You were like bathing in light.

My hand is shaking, teasing your dampness. I must stop.

Your enduring fantasist,

———"

PS: Oh, there is an admirable Gobelin tapestry at the Busch-Reisinger – you must see it. Fierce huntsmen, bloody stags, golden white maidens dreaming.

PPS: Sex. sex. sex. Forgive these terribly wordy priapisms – you know the real reason I love you is your dedication to science in service of others. And your eyes of future grace. So there. Veritas."

Cambridge, Radcliffe Quad and Museum of Economic Botany

◯

THREE HOURS. John Deere tractors lie fallow in frozen mud, Paramedics flying to smashed vehicles where the nursery rhymes suddenly stopped. Power lines and the last telephone poles dwindle toward far horizons like rows of wooden crosses; dried, muddy, aimless furrows are tank tracks across battle fields.

She is sewing now, pensive stitches, for she retains simple arts even in her unbounded science. The silence is too loud for her, like a sweltering Southern night before a gunshot.

"Dream-san,

Only a moment to write. Near Eihei-ji in Kyoto. Tomorrow Paris, another few days, your arms.

It was a chilled, black night; the sun rose like fire opal. I kneel before a monk's old writing desk in a meditation hut. The morning clouds trail so lightly with accents, misty with fine rain at the edges. The Japanese forests seem printed on dusty silk.

I must be dauntlessly candid. I fear for these subjects. Although there is no doubt at the bravura of their vision, they are so vulnerable to the brutish force of opposing agencies. I hope their philosophy will not prove to be tragic. They practice a high monogamy, even within the triad, so obviously in love with one another. They have a gentleness with children like the softest of winds, like the life-giving merciful rains.

I am half-stunned between love and sleep, wishing only for our nuptial bed and your warm pit of night, to rest my brow upon your self-perfected sphere of Dionysian force. Do you hear our angel singing?

No longer tourist hearts, we walk together through the concourse of maidens, where I am lost in you, wandering in the delicious unction of your hips, the nectar of your sweet ripeness.

These feelings must be distilled through the pale alembic of prose. But soon – the river will take us.

Konbanwa, Dream-san,

_____ ”

Eihei-Ji

⬡

PLENTY OF LAND, FOLKS. Barbed wire to the sky. Black buckshot mud dried hard as concrete. Bottomless when wet. Drivers numbed out, trashed back seats and popcorn, candy wrappers, 64-ounce soda cartons, pork rinds, lottery tickets. Truckers on CB spotting cops raiding RVs, dog teams hustling pot, coke, meth. Suspect one-way rentals, profiling LA thugs. Everything's under control, folks. Only two hours of clicking pavement now, as rolling hills replay like dime bags of street corner speed.

She descends into a slow bath, candle light and jasmine, Puccini in a darkened room. Breasts dripping with suds, belly slippery and warm and mysterious.

“*Ma Chou-chou* (well, maybe you're *not* a 'little cabbage'),

These winding tree-lined roads of Provence are blocked by village *fêtes*. I am reduced to eating stale *croissants* in an old cracked bistro, sustained only by vivid reveries of Madame. Elderly Frenchmen smoke *tabac* and gulp *anisette*, then contemplate the muddled roof tops beyond the river Rhône. Were you here, all would be transcendent, for then the harsh accents of the Midi would be lilting, seductive French. The wretched town clockwork with its annoying little robot would be a charming Jacquemart striking the bells of our vows.

From my interview in the Sorbonne, the subject hosted dinner at Closerie de Lilas and Dôme. I am now wagering against his intercepting me again, and am struggling to find a bed in the *auberges* of this village. The locals are by turn gay, bored or petulant. A tea kettle is snoring by a zinc bar. The countryside language is a queer, indecipherable argot. Clearly I am distressed – waiting – but my chimerical subject has sworn to collect me. Until then, I put down this pen so not to burden you.

Cheerio,

_____ ”

PS: *Mon Ange*, My Angel,

Stunning fortune! I so underestimate them; all are absurdly well-connected, socially advanced. Now in a well-loved, well lived-in, venerable chateau near Meurre, delivered with silent assiduity by a series of pensive cut-outs, including a woman in black with a scent of natural bruised sage and a complexion – no, a pallor – of white rose. Nameless, as are all the others. My perspective on these subjects hardly diminishes. I must remain for the night, during this round-the-world assessment of medical schools, to be instructed on their arts by my hovering guardian. There are almost unrecordable phenomena for the journals one day, although your absence may induce the madness. 'Work is hard, no work is harder' as the Greeks admit. I miss you unutterably.

A lyrical word on my companions of intrigue. Their *modus operandi* is compassion, refined by an astral theology. Their women are pierced by the horn of moon; each of their love-children will be like clear, flowing water. In their monkish cells, they examine fragments of reality with nude thought. At times their language is heroic, divine, as though common speech had the dull, empty cadence of a stagnant pond. Their love-making produces an amnesia in those invited to behold it, for it is like an uncontrollable wild fire, an explosion of light.

Is this too heavy, too esoteric, too tangential? Words fail me about them. I write in a long gallery with white panes of top light; a rustic door opens upon the sky-gold bracken and a few flowers on the gorse. There are flinty paths to hamlets with ancient churches and shuttered shops. In the field the Provençeaux sometime curry the cattle with leaves, then find some *boîte* where they eat *brioches* or puff cheroots and drink *vin du pays*. I am alone under a sharp, late moon.

In the old chateau there are Courbets and Bonnards – art everywhere – even in this tapering musicians' chamber where I compose the never-ending love letter that I pray you read so unerringly. We shall cast off this separation. Here's how.

As mere caprice – let us whisper magic together now, the weighty centuries of our hearts fanning into an anthology of sensations. Ah! Here is a cup of hot valerian infusion – a *tisane* they call it. Try a sip. Ummmmm.

Do you see the clear mistral sky tonight? The play of mists on the lowland fields like dream-memories, as they dance with the evanescent moonlight? I *knew* you could.

So there is no grey gloom, no morbid lassitude, no spiritless silence. Byzantium has not fallen. There are fresh spring shoots with their small-boned litheness, peaking from the furrows in the spectral air, for Life persists within us and without us. Do you see them? Good.

Then would it be intemperate of me to propose the vertiginous glories that might attend our affair? Let's run naked in starlight, your hot torrent of diamonds all over me, your moonlight-whited body under my black sky. *Viens, Cherie!* Running *au naturel* through the ivory, fleecy mist, yes. Along the lions-head fountains, the dilapidated urns, the crude stone *putti* peeing into the waters, yes. Delirious with love and freedom, running nude and wild until the Chargé d'Affaires revokes our visas. Yes.

Je t'aime,

———"

Lobby and bar of the Hôtel de Ville, Avignon
Village near Lutèce – no, somewhere in the southern Vauclose

⬡

ONLY TWO HOURS from Skinner's cement mausoleum, finally. Blew a turn-off, lost in a snake pit of freeway interchanges. ONE WAY HALT STOP DANGER signs for unsuspecting mammals. State Capitol coming up fast, thick with every known law enforcement agency, radio spectrum hot and furtive with mutterings of the Watchers.

She is drying herself, brushing her hair in meditation, padding without clothes across our one room where through the only window the high moon turns her ivory. She is dancing late, lifting her arms to the sacred night. She says a little prayer, always.

Ma Chérie, Ma Colleague,

They all have gone now. The last subject departed at dawn for a poignant dance with the most fragile, the most forgotten of us. The unspeakable final interview still holds me, infused with trails of the sacerdotal apparitions that occurred in their presence. I feel such illimitable loss, healed only by your blessed memory.

I write from a stone bench beneath the crenellated, smoky grey battlements of Princeton, awaiting the Dinky to slip up to Lowell Observatory in Cambridge to archive some – how do I say this – star maps. Perhaps some radio telescope data and encrypted deep space images that have been acquired. It may take some time to explain.

I have a new Pliny for you, heavily foxed but with the most brilliant Venetian leather bindings stamped and tooled in slipcases of centuries-old watered silk. A memento from the research, a mystery we could grow old with.

The campus tonight has a quiet greatness. There are no phenomena anymore, no predispositions to the ghostly infinities, no ethereal scents of invisible lemons and mandarins and honeysuckle and insensate musk, no secret trees and half-heard owls encoding whispers of what might be. The days of premonition have receded, like the subjects themselves, into moth-soft darkness. I am left to founder on the rock of your love. Clinging upon it, may I wander in the halls of memory?

John Nash's spirit lingers here, with his mathematician's early suspicion that future drugs will enhance intelligence. His labyrinth of nomenclatures in chalk are curated on old backboards (in new Fine Hall). I visit the little Japanese fountain at the Institute for Advanced Study, then muse about the IAS woods.

This is a land of Diophantine equations and Protestant respectability; our own wrestlers grapple with the slippery Riemann geometries and zeta-functions. Mathematicians engage in Joycean monologues, each teaching the listeners languages from theoretical dimensions.

Doves are swarming among the belfries now, while in Gothic doorways undergraduates secretly kiss. In this waning light the grounds recall the art of the Bolognese, their pale gardens, their Tiberian magnificence.

The research subjects. I worry about some sudden infamy they may incur, whether the women will bear violet-eyed children or be driven into a captive's decline. One of them always took the time to dance with little Eve, a very young crippled girl who is locked away forever. He danced with her when no one else – not one – ever really cared.

I shall not speak of them again to you, consigning them to the secret heart, to history. One could almost have become a habitué – no, a devotee – attracted to their magnetic blueness, their sense of tragic repose. At times they seemed dispossessed aristocrats from the sublime realms. The women had the countenances of Madonnas – broken only by a fugitive, stylish wickedness for their operational purposes – but which soon yielded to the sacred. They lived in shattered prisms and tumbledown rooms under enormous cavities of sky. At heart they had a generous innocence, with eyes set in their heads like jewels.

Not to take a high moral tone about all of this, but their world of secret meetings evoked some fragile recollection. I remember now. When we came together during our first realization, it was *you* that said to me: 'Love is all.'

Eternally yours,

——"

Princeton, bench by Witherspoon Hall, under a gibbous moon, then on the Dinky to Princeton Junction

◯

COFFEE SHOP of elderly farmers with lined faces and eyes of the precious land. Know every robin's nest for 20 miles. Ruined gas pump from 40s. Sporting goods, fishing tackle, heavy equipment rentals, funeral homes. Old settler lifts his calloused fingers off the wheel in greeting as he passes. Down home. Fresh eggs. Shotguns. Ammo. Crappie. Large-mouth bass. Catfish. Feed store with the smell of seed corn and oats and burlap and Red Man chewin' tobacco. Honest as the day one was born. Only the occasional psycho killer on the highways of the plains. Psycho killer, *qu'est-ce que c'est?*

To bed this night, she says a final prayer for baby and me, then for the world of sorrow, for it to become as light. She prays for guidance in helping others.

"Ma Fleur,

Our beloved child cometh, so very soon. Drifting in from heaven on wistful feet of beauty, just as your springtime arrived with the silence of a miracle.

I see you sometimes, dreaming naked in the night – your bigness moonlit – and through the white sleep I see the pale rose of your face, shining.

Moonlight always follows us, it seems, waiting patiently for us, like a poem. I have my secret compensation in your brief absences – in my mind live your eyes, your bright skin, your silken flanks, even the clothes that rustled and fell into a heap as we feasted on each other kiss by kiss.

Now I must awaken your recumbent figure from dreams. I feel from afar the throbbing throughout your splendid fullness, your authority as you drain me in the nights, the calm abiding of your understanding.

I see the receding facades of your images in late hours, for the surface of my mind is tumbled by the night of you, like the very wind.

Toujours,

——"

Grand Central Station, New York City, beneath the relentless ticking of the immortal clock

◯

ONE HOUR TO SHOWTIME at Skinner's underground asylum. Coming out of Topeka on Highway 24. Old raggedy-ass Pin-Oak motel. Tate's Bait Shop, minnows, craw-dads, lures. Brigg's Car Lot, Kick-Start motorcycle club bar.

She is dreaming, so I am dreaming.

"Darling,

I write this after our walk by the shore. The sky at dusk is a hot pearl – no – almost cherry, like some invention of an impossible, late summer. You are sleeping.

Your hand is on your fullness; our baby a small blossom and you the sun.

Last night we danced again, in the brilliant starlit air, the late moonlight like spindrift in your hair. The changing sea in the nether light was dark jade green, swirling into soft breakers like a regretful sigh.

Much later now. As you sleep, a gentle rain has begun falling, hissing like swans. It is youthful, refreshing, bringing in the smell of roses.

There is a cloistral calm, and I am fixed immutably on you. I must now share a secret. Please forgive me for this.

Sometimes I see behind your eyes some eternal tragedy – just a glimpse – as though your ancestors witnessed the starvations, or the death camps. I don't mean to unsettle you – it is the most fleeting of impressions. Surely I am deluded.

Once I said to you that life can change in an instant, then withdrew when you said I was frightening you. Of course I was mistaken – there is only joy always before us.

It is true, for now you walk glorified, a blaze from your heart, aching with beauty, each day happy in a shower of sunshine. You are dazzling from the womb, like a sacred vessel. Even as you sleep before me in this final night, you are polished by the light of heaven.

Farewell, Dream Lover,

_____ "

Undisclosed location

◯

PAYLESS SHOE STORE, Yamaha dealer. Topeka Boulevard over highway due south. SASNAK strip club, Kansas spelled backwards. Bored cashier warning 'skankiest girls in Kansas.' Inside dream sylphs beckon and sway to Schlitz bubbles. Pool tables, rack 'em. Cabaret Club about the same.

It is the crows that I notice first. There are thousands of them, all in a row for miles and miles, sitting on a power line to nowhere, staring like black-hooded harbingers of fate. Like black flies on children's lips.

She is restless, unconscious, groaning at black wings.

"My Love,

A God-fearing, very small town in Kansas. Hardworking, good people in Wamego. But how strange my destination – this decommissioned nuclear missile silo with a madman inside, like some huge cannon pointed toward millions of the unaware. It's just down from the funeral parlor.

I am mailing this home now with the other letters, tied in your blue ribbon for safekeeping. It is only minutes before a dismal interview at the silo. The subject gives one the uncomfortable impression of confronting an insect, one posing as human.

The exhausted landscapes trailed by me as I yearned for you. My heart has become an empty playground, waiting for children.

The wind has turned a point or two northward. It is a rogue wind, unpredictable. Rain and cloud swirl like smoke over the silo. The subject has a vicious face when he thinks I'm not looking. He keeps a damaged, dangerous girl – one he abuses in a magisterial fashion. A dirty sleet is prickling the car windows.

The subject – who is quite crazed but crafty and manipulative – has a kind of eloquent impersonality, as though educated in the cinema with only films of violence and treachery as his teachers. His lack of veracity worries me. The girl is forlorn with a mask of false laughter, and deserted by good sense.

A black hearse followed me the last many miles, like some ominous, long pursuit. The sliver of sky through the clouds is like a saber cut, as though one now enters the countries of sadness.

In some fearless way, I can only ask, 'Why am I here? With these unfortunates?' Polydrug abusers abound everywhere. The small funds offered may help with the baby, though.

The atmosphere has most worrisome implications; the lights in the clouds are changing too rapidly, like a secret storm.

Do you know of the Angel of Mons? In the Great War, after weeks of shelling and countless deaths in the trenches of Mons, Belgium, the British were in retreat, the sky shot through with blood and light. Many witnesses saw an angel in the sky, guiding the boys home. These clouds are like that – the Angel of Mons.

Know that all women were only shadows of you. Know that I go wrinkled before you, to prepare heaven. Know that you were always my sweet moon craft, the gift of the Risen Lord.

It is too late to discipline the heart. In loving triumph, I send you the secret formula for – the chemistry of tears.

Ever thine,

———"

P.S. An hour later, the world has stopped. The fear comes and goes, but I remain. A Dylan song is on the radio, Joan Baez singing. You remember, from the Old Days.

> May God's blessing keep you always,
> may your wishes all come true,
> may you always do for others,
> and let others do for you.
> May you build a ladder to the stars
> and climb on every rung,
> and may you stay
> Forever young.

If I don't make it back as soon as we hoped, all I have is a song by some roadside convenience store, reaching out to you and our little one, and to all our blessed children of light.

> May you grow up to be righteous,
> may you grow up to be true,
> may you always know the truth
> and see the light surrounding you.
> May you always be courageous,
> stand upright and be strong,
> and may you stay
> Forever young.
> Forever young, forever young,
> and may you stay
> Forever young.

I am slipping into sentimentality. But what of it? We all must drown in the pool of tears. I'll be home soon, my love. Kiss the baby for me.

Wamego, Kansas, parked behind a Quick-Stop

VII

Götterdämmerung

And lo! The Place
where thou hast need
to arm thy heart with strength.

- Dante, *Inferno*

'The banners of Hell's Monarch
do come forth toward us;
Therefore look' – so spake my guide –
'If thou discern him.'

- Ibid, Canto 34

Chapter 29.

Legion

Many devils were entered into him.

- Luke 8:30

His glassy essence, like an angry ape
Plays such tricks before high heaven
As makes the angels weep.

- Measure for Measure

Upon his head three faces…
At six eyes he wept, the tears
Down three chins distill'd with bloody foam.
At every mouth his teeth a sinner clamped.
'That upper Spirit,
Who hath the worst punishment," so spake my guide,
"Is Judas, he that hath his head within,
And plies the feet without."

- Dante, *Inferno*
(on the Devil, inverted and frozen)

Maid, arise.

- Luke 8:54

Apologia

MY MEMORIES must end here for the most sensitive readers, for all the future was but a nightmare. I include these final writings only for the few – with the utmost reluctance – but in fear of tarnishing those bright moments which have gone before. Thus, this volume might now be closed in a gentle way, or given to another, I hope with fondness.

Only at great risk of offending that remaining reader, one who unwittingly may venture into the malevolent – even lurid – do I continue. I beg forgiveness for the perceived excesses to come.

◯

PARKED BEHIND the rural store with engine running, I hesitated to meet with Skinner, for the interviews with this subject were not only bleak, but frightening. I remember now.

When he fucked her, it was like watching the caress of the mantis, for first he took her head. Devouring her mind at leisure, Skinner was savage, pumping this helpless girl – barely eighteen – as she jerked like a broken clockwork doll. In the throes of his unholy mixtures of tryptamines and meth overdoses, her long white coltish legs were embracing multifold deities in a series of near-death experiences. He preferred to think of her seizures as orgasms. It was easy to hate him.

Skinner, an Oklahoma con man, was mounting a lost young girl from the Kansas plains. "Dorothy," "Chantal," "Justine" – I never knew her last name, and remain uncertain of her first, for there were so many. We shall use the latter. He had a penchant for the underaged, both boys and girls, but a fatal indulgence for prodigal nymphs with lean, milky thighs. The last of them was this desultory teenage stripper, who first appeared in the final weeks before Skinner took my world away.

After a few days with him, she had no mind, no money, nowhere to go. Mute and crazed by then, Justine was a mere toy uncomprehending of her captivity. She was unaware that Skinner was the nadir of the psychedelic experience, forever barred from the illuminated family.

At the florid apex of her disorientations, some reported, he found it amusing to offer her temporarily vacant body to bellhops and girls. When his repeated drug injections failed, she would recoil as he reassumed his ghastly terrestrial form, but by then her spirit was gone.

He commanded her to walk about in hotel suites long and topless, and to wear only thin black stockings – stretched tight and split in great white ovals – to reveal sunless young flesh and livid scratches. Her scent was too musky from casual overuse and simple fear. Suddenly cut adrift from society by Skinner, and desperate on the dreary hinterlands for free food, cash and drugs, she would follow anything that moved.

To this poor child, who had never known real love, any attention was better than no attention, any controversy better than being ignored. Compelled to seek notoriety or even obloquy, she brightened at the rare praise. Forever she had sought the anonymous public eye, striving to replace her secret and utter desolation.

She became a dark cloud, wandering with a pervading melancholy, often forced to the ground or a wall or bed to service him. Around them arose a disturbing mixture of scents: love juice, blood, incense, the smell of illicit currencies, Skinner's unwashed breathings. I saw them the night her mind finally went.

◯

BUT HOW did they enter my life? This unfortunate girl in the last weeks of my freedom, and her master only a year and a few dinners earlier? It began with a young Asian man, close by in a Bay area hotel coffee shop, and thoughtless of his black leather jacket. As he drank a latte, I saw beneath the lapel a gold insignia of the DEA, its center labeled "US."

I was in San Francisco, attending the annual meeting of the American Academy of Forensic Science, with its thousands of coroners, county, state and federal chemists and lab techs. With official personnel all about, a name card with Harvard affiliation was pinned to my coat, even though DEA chemists present were required to file contact reports on any person of interest. Pondering the Asian agent, I was distracted by an elevator disgorging Skinner.

He wore a sleeveless white undershirt over an unruly belly – effectively a "wife-beater" as his fellow Okies would say. Although we were in a formal hotel lobby catering to affluent San Franciscans, and surrounded by forensic scientists, he had no sartorial sense, but an acute narcissism. Skinner's big erratic body was full of energy, his self-indulgent face already spewing malapropisms.

A mountain of ambiguous corpulence, and bald by his early twenties, he affected a thick, black Amish beard over the devastation of an acned youth. Hairy mats covered his back, neck and arms. Some thought Skinner odd – he was strange to both men and women – though it was not his appearance that was unsettling, but his demeanor. He gave one the uncomfortable impression of being some invertebrate. A dangerous specimen – one with secret poisons.

At his proximity, I felt a withering away inside myself, the feeling that occurs near a malevolent spirit. His ruling monomania proved to be raw cash: his solution for all sins, his bait for the many traps he set, the paper he preferred above intellect, kindness, and nobility. This singular drive was masked by a feigned friendliness. Even his name descended from forebears who long had rendered corpses.

He seemed vaguely familiar. Insisting we had met at some social event, he first tried on me his practiced allusions to great wealth, speaking like a poor man thinks a rich man talks. Although penurious myself, just a threadbare academic, I had encountered in Cambridge and abroad a few of the inordinately wealthy. A grifter was readily apparent.

"Ma family," he spoke in a rural drawl, "are all industrialists since the 1880s. We control most of the springs in America – little steel coils in every machine. We're worth hundreds of millions. I travel with staff, meeting with investors. I am one of the few working heirs."

I let him bloviate, watching this example of a plains con-man, one with pretensions to social emience.

"Ma mother has a staff of ten at her estate – butlers, cooks. She's the grand dame of Tulsa society. Big oil families, mostly."

Friends quietly ran a background check. He neglected to mention his sole income was from minor drug dealing and occasional handouts from his mother, a respectable and long-suffering woman who owned a small business, lived alone in a modest cottage, and otherwise sold chocolates.

An overfed outcast with a high school diploma and no life of the mind, he did have a ruthless cunning. Finding pleasure only in manipulating those who innately trusted others, Skinner was the kind of striving boor not uncommon in his socioeconomic stratum. He had encountered a few legitimate drug researchers at conferences he infiltrated, but most considered him a rogue personality, one riddled by excess. He would try to hurl himself into the delicate humilities of the psychedelic groups, but the experienced could see he was empty as the heart of the sun.

Skinner's *modus operandi* was to hypnotize drug-interested youth by referring to relatively unknown compounds, names he derived from glancing at Sasha's books and the publications of McKenna, Ott, and other distinguished researchers. Yet, he had no real chemical knowledge, a fact immediately obvious to the trained.

"What do you do?" he asked.

"A little research in Cambridge."

"On what?"

"Public policy only. Recently I studied fentanyl abuse in Russia. And the Kansas manufacturer – the infamous George Marquardt."

As he routinely did with his young neophytes, using buzz words he did not fully grasp, he began pretending he was a chemist – some ultimate drug authority. I neglected to reveal my degree in chemistry, or my reverence for the many who were much more advanced, but let him run wild to see how quickly he would stumble.

Skinner, I immediately observed, had no knowledge of how to draw molecular structures, or balance equations, or even the most rudimentary concept of atomic weights. He couldn't identify the formula of the simplest organic molecules, and would fail the first week's pop quiz for freshmen in Chem 1A. In short, at least to me, he was not a chemist, but a fraud.

I played with him as pre-med might. "Say, this fellow Avogadro, do you have his number?"

"Who's that?"

Perhaps he had no idea of how easily his level of competence was determined, but he was an overconfident schoolboy who thought 12th-grade chemistry was a whiz – one who avoided college with the arrogance of the untutored. Yet it was his claim of special expertise – or perhaps it was his silence-enobling voice – that troubled me most.

By handing out drugs and promises, he surrounded himself only with sycophants. Fearing being outed as technically incompetent, he avoided professionals. Skinner had the fraudster's heightened sensitivity to suspicions, so that between us there was a reciprocal distaste.

"You're from Oklahoma and Kansas, you say? Have you heard of the 300 fentanyl deaths from Marquardt's Wichita lab?"

He instantly claimed affiliation with Marquardt's associates, for he told others whatever they wanted to hear.

I was about to turn away. Seeing my disinterest, he quickly alluded to some long-stored stash of chemicals.

"Twenty kilograms of *ergotamine*."

It was the precursor to thirty million doses of LSD. Such quantities were known to – or influenced by – only the Six. If it were the stolen material of such concern to Magenta and Cobalt, in Skinner's hands it would devastate the community. Whether coached by federal agents or not, in an instant he had my enduring attention.

⬡

I BEGAN INTERVIEWING him once each month at costly restaurants where Skinner always paid in cash. His lifestyle – displays of money and arrogance – was that of an *arriviste* who had yet to arrive. He never noticed the aesthetics of life – the curve of white lilies nearby, the clouds racing, the crystalline dusks. He never read – certainly not the great works – or ever held the coats of his paramours. Perhaps he was a breech delivery, for he asked more from one's attention than he gave in return.

Affecting a certain craftiness, he was ingratiating with others, but each person was only the next mark in his lifelong confidence game. Overlarge, with blotching skin, he bragged about affluence and his carnal triumphs over loveless lives. In the silence of my misgivings, he was unaware that the temperature between us had fallen below zero.

At the end of dinner, he waived cash and paid with a cavalier obscenity, ignoring the realities of those who worked for a living. Skinner would toss his serviette on the table, then push back slowly as a sloth from a pile of rotten fruit.

"And where do you go now?" I would ask.

Ostentatiously searching his memory, he would allude to a night of extravagance.

"To my (he would emphasize an exorbitant sum) private suite at the (he would refer to some palatial hotel)."

At this disclosure he always smiled like a piano. Skinner displayed a terrifying cupidity – an inordinate desire for wealth – but in that far less effort was required, he was satisfied by the mere appearance of wealth.

Yet his was not even a generous spirit. There were no donations to the needy or deserving, no social sense or ever any kindnesses, no responsibility for the common good. Beneath Skinner's rented glitz remained a shoddiness, for he was frayed at the edges, the product of generations of hapless inbreeding.

Exhibiting some permanent manic phase of a bipolar illness, he practiced his chicaneries and artful subterfuges while living in costly hotels for weeks at a time. Burning through tens of thousands in cash from illicit and sporadic drug profits, he attracted unwanted attention even as he began to lose control.

He was, at best, a countryside confidence trickster, portraying himself as a spoilt rich boy or a globe-trotting *bon viveur*. Those not seduced by his illusions despised Skinner. I thought him bent as a hairpin.

SKINNER WAS GREGARIOUS, but only to advance his schemes. For his small coterie of easily-led youth, he proved to be a fast lane to the emergency room. The first rupture in his tale of being a world-beating financier was his disclosure of an incident at the Mandarin Oriental Hotel in San Francisco, a lavish high-rise overlooking the Bay. He divulged this event – in his usual dog rhetoric – during a dry recital of his accomplishments and connections.

"We had a little too much…called the hotel doc."

Friends later located a police report – Skinner had overdosed everyone in his penthouse. The door to the suite was ajar – a hotel employee heard continuous, wild shouting and physical violence. Police and paramedics found an 18-year-old girl in one bedroom, nude and on her knees, staring and unresponsive. An older couple was bloody from assaulting each other. Skinner was naked on the floor, twisting at the feet of police and yelling for oral sex. He was handcuffed to a gurney. All were removed through the lobby to ambulances, and to separate hospitals, then released a day later – after questioning.

Skinner represented the worse of the drug cults I had encountered. It was imperative to study him more closely.

⬡

ONE SOON DISCOVERED the truth of him. After a few months of dinners, he provided air fare to Nevada – ostensibly for interviews on his knowledge of novel substance use in the underground. Skinner avowed he conducted "pharmahuasca rituals," the quasi-religious use of an infusion of DMT-bearing Acacia bark mixed with Syrian Rue. It was a between-the-eyes, powerful psychedelic. I hardly could refuse, for such groups – for better or for worse – were proliferating. Skinner's was not in a supportive, secluded forest setting, or by the sea, but in the overwrought, brazen glamour of Las Vegas.

There were no religious practices at his expensive suites at the Bellagio, Paris and Venetian casinos and hotels, but only a bewilderment of transient young women and feckless boys. Among the street urchins he collected, those who survived nights with Skinner would become tomorrow's nuns. He heated his nymphs with a mixture of cash and claims of being a major industrialist, but most often with a pharmacopeia of free drugs. The hotels were Skinner's capitals of synthetic loves, where underage girls gazed over his faceless, pounding obesity at the pretty fireworks on the ceiling.

Skinner in Las Vegas was like a Greek voyager on Circe's Island, where the goddess changed men into pigs. Although the names varied with the sheets and the hours, his most recent conquest was to his undiscerning eye just another nubile, artless little vamp, a tumble with a doxy. I found them both *en suite*.

A vampire-snouted man, flushed with intoxicants, Skinner rose to offer a pale, dead handshake. He yelled for his latest – who was wandering in tearful disarray – as though she were an unresponsive servant in need of the whip.

"Justine…*git* in here!"

She was not a "stupid little tart" – as one of Skinner's prior wives had claimed – but somewhat tall for a girl. Dark-eyed, lean and fond of heels. He correctly thought her unsuspecting. Obedient. Easily caged.

His manner with her provoked an even greater awkwardness in me. Interviewing Skinner was like studying a live and reprehensible insect – I struggled not to reveal my feelings. Drawing closer to their private horrors, I could see she had swallowed whole the rigmarole of his story. From her delicate, limping walk and dazed expression, it was clear that he had overcome the last of her juvenile reserve.

He was unconscious that day of her final waves of tenderness, or the remains of her innate shyness. She in turn was unaware that his several previous marriages to mature women had become for them just emotional and intellectual babysitting.

With his dangerous overdoses of unwary girls, and a messianic fanaticism, he had learned to extract virgins' claws long before their time. He always would check young peoples' driver's licenses to assess his legal exposure, so that his predation was careful, a meticulous form of near-child molestation.

⬡

THEY WERE more than stoned in Las Vegas that day – they were crawling through a psychic wasteland. Enthralled on toxic levels of designer drug combinations, Skinner rocked his body back and forth for hours, the stereotypic schizophrenic. Gripped by his personal monotonies, he seemed thrust down into oblivion, even as he dreamed of omnipotence. My concern, though, was for the girl.

Justine had wounded eyes. As a teenager, her iniquitous catalog was limited at first. She was only a little stabled pleasure for him, defined by her poverty of affect, but in later years she proved to be quite a dangerous girl.

In the beginning, with Skinner over twice her age and weight, he displayed her on his bed like a pampered Borzoi, then more carelessly as his personal tethered ass. Before her devastation from

Skinner's calculated drug overexposures, she thought him a tedious mount, but one she could ride to glory.

Justine had turned just eighteen when he found her in a dissolute Kansas roadhouse outside Topeka, a place with raw wooden floors and rough clientele, sour half-drunk beers, and empty all day but for blaring heavy metal rock and one surly bartender.

A local girl of renown, resigned to a succession of rough hands, she was tired of warming the laps of drunken, itinerant farm workers and priapic college boys. She thought Skinner's sordid lifestyle paradisaical. Prior to being brutalized – then destroyed – by Skinner, she would slow kiss the occasional girl *à la française* to provoke him, as though she were in the Sapphic club. I could see she was a pretender.

Young and ardent as he began dissolving her will with noxious drugs, she swayed half-naked before the suite's expansive floor-length windows, arms raised high in worship of Mammon and mesmerized at the Brobdingnagian shiny objects of the Strip below. Her neurons already were a tepid soup of uncrystalized mysticism.

A drug ethnographer must not intrude into consensual adult sado-masochism, but Justine tugged at my sensibilities, for I knew what awaited her. She was of age – I often tried, but could not find her father. My first feeling for her was one of sadness, but over time – an infinite pathos.

⬡

IN REFLECTING on these events I must pause, in hope that the reader – while within these writings – will remember the apology. Recorded here – only with the greatest of personal difficulty – is a warning for those who may experiment without true friends to guide them home. In perhaps repellent scenes, we explore the progressive degradation of a bright young girl.

She long had been compliant to ogres, but never one with a malice so adroit. They both were exhibitionists, she with her body for the hollow affections of anonymous eyes and tips, he to be admired as puppet master. I remained nearby as strange people came and went, even as Skinner assessed his power over her, inviting witnesses into bedrooms or leaving doors ajar.

She was always free to leave, but chose not to, for craving had replaced her self-direction. Fighting impulses to severely discipline Skinner, I would not intervene – at least for now – but watched over her from the very edge of things, as perhaps her last protector.

Of course, they had an impoverished intellectual life, one of vexed resignation for Justine. With Skinner as ringmaster of his failed orgies, bedroom nights circled among the lavish Bellagio suites, then the Paris casino, then the Venetian. All were only dens of red crêpe or mirrored boudoirs that appealed to Skinner's luxurious bad taste. Too soon he would demand she entertain in the filthy cribs of his underground redoubt, a converted missile silo in Kansas. As he began stroking her into submission, both seated on a couch, her eyes would lock to mine across the room, frightened and wondering if he would order her to fellate anyone. Or perform for guests, blindfolded and cuffed.

First, though, he scattered her moralities. He forced her with his devilish liquids into abstruse Gnostic states, where for vanishing moments her thoughts catapulted, her theological distinctions blurred, and she felt herself to be the rose of all the earth.

Were it opiates rather than a melange of tryptamines and meth, she could have been a terminal morphinomane. She would give him a harlot's dry kiss, then – overwhelmed by the first drug rush – she would begin trembling, offering her naked breasts to his ghoulish white hands, even as she threw me a wild look of sadness.

At the peak of her unexpected, near-death overdoses, she would fall back in utter shock, then begin arching – pale and completely nude and legs open – like the last *femme fatale* among his countless dead. As he mouthed her, her tensing white abdomen and his thick lips were sticky as a fresh hymen.

He was pitiless when he finally took her loins, making her slave to his lust. He never lasted, thankfully, and would leave abruptly – he thought her only his receptacle. Dreams of haunting incoherence then possessed her, subconscious eruptions from the stimulants, until she was twilighting and half-awake, cut loose from her every mooring. One heard only her lonely moaning – for she still was unreleased – and saw her slow then rapid gyres as she humped the empty air. There was a secret poignancy to her, for she was fast becoming the wreck of the world.

After the worst scenes, when Skinner was gone, I would knock softly, enter, and wait to sense her feelings. Then in the quiet I would recite poems to her, or sing to her, for these words were her only connection to the world of light. Perhaps she heard some of them. This first time, while Skinner was away, I kneeled by her prostrate form. Her eyes were open but unseeing. I whispered to her.

"Justine."

Nothing.

"Love is an ever fixed mark…that looks on tempests and is never shaken."

⬡

WHEN SKINNER WAS GAMBLING, I walked her down the Strip for air and diversion, visiting other hotels, other scenes. At one tawdry, glittering casino, she stood dazzled – her retinas still patterning – trying to focus on the alluring trapeze artists. I attempted to lighten her night.

"You know what Hunter Thompson said about this place?"

"Tell me."

"The Circus-Circus is what the whole hep world would look like if the Nazis had won the war."

She gave me a little smile. I tried to kindle her self-regard by redeeming her posture – she often slumped from Skinner's abuse – for she was defeated but still protected the remnants of her spirit.

"If you stand up straight, it helps. Walk tall. Open a little. Imagine a string to the heavens from the top of your head. As if you're dancing with the sky."

With her gamine city appeal, she practiced it across the casino floor. I delayed escorting her back.

⬡

THESE DIFFICULT MEMORIES are not intended as a litany of mere sexual obsession, but as a record of mythic combat. Alone, I had not the skills of Vermilion and his consorts, those used in Berlin and Bangkok to evoke and banish the assumption of a physical form by – one must say it – evil.

They had completely different world-views. She had a hunger for the magic of love, but forever failed to find its frequency – it was so very far from Skinner's pestilences and pharmacological noise. He suspected that devoted threesomes existed – he imagined himself smothered in girls – but was unable to comprehend why they forever were forbidden to his kind.

Justine didn't know of his hidden bent for rapine and adolescents. I began demanding that she go. She always refused, sometimes withdrawing. At the thrill of the telephone I would answer, trying not to call the police, and remarking he was engaged. As yet undisciplined in the perverse – she was still being groomed – she insisted she was safe.

Upon his administration of the drugs – he always made her come on far too quickly – he would give her lurching looks and make vulgar gestures. At her perceptible coolness, he would display her in barbaric spread, forcing her legs apart or offering her to other compliant young addict women whom she had lured. However malicious his betrayal, she performed her arid duty, for she would do anything to avoid a plunge back into anonymity.

Many of the substances with which he abused her were not active orally. Skinner typically gave intravenous injections with his assortment of needles, but Justine feared the markings – at first – so that Skinner encouraged the rectal alternative.

Stretched out long and prone on the king-sized bed, she dug her nails into the headboard as though she were holding onto the very planet. Lubricating her, he often lied about the contents of his large syringes, even as she lifted her pallid whiteness, high and taut with anticipation and not a little fear. We later discovered it was not some light dose of MDMA for a few sensual hours as she thought, but an almost fatal quantity of drug combinations unexplored by any human. Pressing her down with one heavy hand, he began with the other an extremely slow injection.

The DMT and meth took her fast. Her mind shattered, her body completely unfolded. She was groaning deeply before the plunger was even half-way down the syringe. As untold doses of tryptamines and relentlessly horney meth ran up her legs to her cortex, repeated epileptiform seizures wiped her agenda clean. The whites of her eyes locked upward, her countenance became open and unlined, moonlike, her helpless body yielding to the slightest breeze. Anyone could have her then.

Skinner – excited now – forced it all into her. She gasped. Her thighs contracted involuntarily, then began to shake. I grew alarmed, but it was too late.

A lumbering man of fleshy waves and inversely proportionate testicles, Skinner could have been a monorchid or eunuch. While drugs distracted his young unfortunates from his insufficiency, he soon replaced the twenty-milliliter syringe with himself.

His awkward, impersonal thrusts – as she flailed about – to her became those of Apollo, the legions of Rome, the Lord of Hosts, the black ram over her white ewe, His Satanic Majesty. Flaming bright as he scorched her still-trusting heart, Skinner had obsessive thoughts while he copulated – poisonous thoughts – growling curses in her ear to defeat her last innocence.

As she contorted violently under the staggering dose, Justine's eyes began spiraling. Through the parted door, I could see in the low light that she wore only high, black Goth heels with ankle straps. Music was playing, some endless loop of driving electronica about visitations from the dark side. She began teetering between the great dichotomies: Eros and Thanatos, sex and purity, good and evil, for she now was the harlot of all time and space.

As a predator, he preferred to be this unnatural form of rapist. Others reported that Skinner's obsession – with those he rendered so vulnerable (I cannot put this delicately) – was ass play. As the DMT and meth effects intensified, she hung for hours on him, hooked and writhing. Manipulating her vacant body, his cruel ham-like hands slapped her buttocks into bruises, for Skinner was turned on by dominating those he had enfeebled psychically. He would be crazed with a cane. When at last her spirit surrendered, it was a travesty of everything human.

At moments of lucidity, when her eyes ceased to orbit, she began shrinking into postures of submission, crouching and pulling her arms and legs under her, but raising even higher for him. She looked like a child sleeping on its tummy, but having the worst of dreams.

She occasionally awakened, her wet hair across her face, then kept looking at the clock as if with a client, and praying it would end. When he was finished, he left to wash himself, as he did compulsively. The bitter fruits of her desecration were obvious: she was exhausted, downcast, lusterless, with a morbid spiritual lassitude.

She rolled over aghast, this forsaken child, then gazed at the rippling, breathing ceiling. She was dark and blank, like a fragile, much too young odalisque. At these times, she looked like a naked Arab girl of twelve – a desert *houri* – long trapped by some corpulent, rapacious Turk.

With a furtive but profound sympathy for her plight, I slipped in, kneeled beside her, and with gentleness brushed her hair from her eyes. She had heard of my wife and our baby, but the sacred heart – if she knew of it at all – was a distant world to her. I spoke in whispers.

"Justine, do you know what a man says to a woman he truly loves?"

"No," she admitted, in a tiny voice, ashamed.

"Lovely thou art as the sun,

White as the light of the moon

And the loveliest star

Is but a candle to thee."

○

I CHOSE to do my final interview of Skinner at the missile base, where he might be more cogent. During my last hour in Las Vegas, Skinner's office boys canvassed escort services, but fleets of women already were arriving on rumors of adolescent sex and rare drugs and easy cash. As I left the suite to fight through swarms of whores – all determined, steely 40-year-olds with rough desert skin – I saw Justine. Not yet recovered, she was naked but for six-inch fuck-me heels, climbing at Skinner's insistence upon the suite's grand piano.

Behind her the wall of glass had a vista overlooking the black Luxor pyramid. So confused and excited that her hips shuddered like a mare, she turned to extend wide her legs and lock her ankles over the edges of the polished Steinway. Adorned only by a thousand-dollar hairstyle of Rasta dreads in all the colors of the rainbow, she lay back on her elbows, and assumed a forced little smile. The hors d'oeuvre in place, Skinner opened the door.

After a flight from Las Vegas to LA that evening – as Justine groaned in the honeyed prison of her multiple consorts – I whirled in Alice's magic teacups with a curly-haired, precious little girl, a well-loved relative of five with eyes like the sky. Above us were the lasered castles of Disneyland, the happiest place on earth.

○

THE LAST VIOLETS were out. In the noontime distance, settled in a haze of prismatic dust, the missile base had seemed as empty as the catacombs. The sole above-ground objects were air vents for the rocket blast, sticking up like cremation chimneys with curling trails of white smoke and ash. Shriveled pussy willows stood in a muddy cow pond, surrounded by twenty-eight acres of pasture enclosed by chain-link fencing and military-grade razor wire. As a tattered peacock looked on, one undernourished pig and some unkempt turkeys wandered in a dying garden.

Beneath this Kansas pastoral was eighteen thousand square feet of decommissioned command center and launch facility for an Atlas-E intercontinental nuclear ballistic missile. Skinner, observing with surveillance cameras and tracking every movement, buzzed me in. As I looked back at the world for the last time, I saw in an uncaring twilight the advance of a thin, penetrating drizzle. The grey sky had dead clouds, like withered garlands.

Beyond the multi-ton steel doors, and down a hundred-yard blast tunnel into the missile bay, loomed Skinner. With his mud-eyed infant's gaze, and in a testy mood, he was undressed and incoherent. Skinner never gave anyone a warm embrace, but looked at them as if from some crevice. I noticed his smile in the half-light, the kind that for the oblivious might dig one's grave.

His enticements for guests – mostly excited and malleable country girls – were the usual drugs and his disturbed naïf Justine. The scene was absolutely virulent, with cheap scowling lurkers and the young and directionless. I could hear from above ground the distant crepitations of gunfire.

Skinner immediately rushed to the missile base offices to run some con by telephone. The base was a Faraday cage, where no electromagnetic signals could penetrate. Cell phones were useless. On one of his four landlines into the launch facility, he was in some full efflorescent paranoia, constantly attending the five closed-circuit video monitors with feed from post-mounted moveable cameras that surveyed the entirety of the base. For that moment, I was alone with Justine.

A kind of hebephrenia had arisen in her – no, a logorrhea – for she was perpetually talking nonsense in low ramblings. Gone astray in the forebrain, she was sick as an actress – one who was never offstage.

As imprisoned in this million tons of concrete and steel as in a medieval oubliette, she simply waited for him in her few minutes of peace, listening for the far crash of the blast doors, his strident voice like a loudspeaker calling for her, and then his ponderous breathing and meaty hands, and for the madness to begin.

⬡

SKINNER'S PROFESSION was by definition parasitic, so that he kept low company in his playground for derelict swingers. He never exercised, or washed his clothes or hung them, or made his bed. His sycophants did everything – sometimes. Only fits of a proprietary jealousy about Justine – when not so intoxicated he insisted she entertain guests – might overturn his world one day.

The missile base bedrooms were a dingy checkerboard of visitors: hanger-ons, day workers, addicts, farm girls, and refugees from raves. Sheets were unchanged, but heavy with cloying perfumes. Skinner affected a public piety among locals in Wamego – a kind of absurd modesty – although rumors sometimes were whispered on the steps of frowning churches. Gossip attended him, as though there were serious antecedents in his background.

The underground chambers were a constellation of mindless fevers, glib propositions and amateur bliss. Intoxicated with drug novelties, some kinetic personages stumbled about, others withdrew into their private stupefactions. Born to sin, Skinner chose among these almost-children, re-animating by feeding on their stark naïveté. Pathology, some say, begins at home.

Among the gathered youth, Skinner first hid as though he were a serpent in a bank of flowers, sinister and envenomed but a facsimile of joy to the unsuspecting. During their incapacities, Skinner romped among his pliable teenage lackeys. In the pre-dawn hours – grateful for inclusion into some underground scene – some curled up in trustful sleep, like innocent travelers in a bandit's lair.

He liked his admirers well enough as long as they remained in the background, and only he was the primal desecrator. As his dosed youth sat in reverence, he feigned a drunken dignity, making sloppy gestures with a Tibetan vajra and bell. Skinner had a slapstick holiness, for he considered religious implements toys, but hypnotized his anemic flocks by projecting a heavy liturgical air. After the Six, I knew it was a Luciferean trick.

$\bigcirc$

SKINNER LIVED in a complete hallucination, where he was lord of all, with dominion over every living thing. Justine was not a passionate servant, unless in the swirl of strange chemicals her blood was running. I always saw her heart, heavy as the pale shell of the moon.

He first had persuaded her with near-mortal stimulants and drug infusions, her legs opening like a scroll. Skinner though – the most crude of thieves – always failed to capture her inconceivably precious tiny scepter. She was never satisfied by him. He missed her mark so often that Justine was terminally aroused, quivering about on those long, thirsty legs, holding her head aloft in both hands lest it spill its oceanic consciousness.

When he slept, she would creep into the missile bay, so loaded she pleasured herself openly, and frequently. Often she failed to notice me crouched, thinking in the darkness, in the charged silence. Head thrown back over a ragged divan, legs askew and over the arms, her hands grew frantic as she reached for the lessening light. She would twist in silence, grimacing as though on a flaming pyre.

Justine first had thought of him as some ponderous alien, so that his puerile foreplay and grotesque penetrations were punctuated by her great yawns – until the plunge of the syringe. As the devastating rush took her, he would climb on her jerking body – it was white as death – with an air of grave preoccupation. He was dubious of his charms without the drugs.

Skinner had worn down her senses with these insurmountable injections, then reduced her further during the act – at his insistent mutterings – to fantasizing lines of muscular Nubians, drunken troops, rings of gardeners in sheds, constant private visits with the police. Unconscious in his profligacy, and uncaring of her mood, he hardly could know their relationship was her act of self-mutilation.

And so her perceptions cycled among these sordid impressions, until she pretended the grimy mattresses of the base were some gypsy brothel, where she was passed among a rabble of rogues. It was then she had the look of a wasted childhood.

After his abuse – until the next time – she would slink in disgrace with a certain ungainliness, almost halting. Her speech became fragmented, half-articulate. When no one else could, I heard – beneath his cumbersome gropings – the true voice of her body. It was always weeping, a sound like the softest of wailing, but wailing that never ended.

In the aftermaths of the worst scenes, in the blessed quiet of her rare solitudes – and careful that Skinner could not hear – I would approach and sing old country hymns to her, songs of the Good Lord and the Kansas plains. She liked that.

"His love made me free

He made me his own

And helped me cast off

Satan's Jeweled Crown."

⬡

ABOVE THE MISSILE BASE, one could walk within the electric fencing. I had to breathe untainted air, and left them alone one night – even while fearing for her. It was some empty, rural moon country, the sky asleep and unaware of the bitter story below. I tried not to think of her then, deep down inside, and what he was doing to her. When she stopped fighting and yielded, it was like the perishing of the stars.

I wondered how the Six would have intervened. V-3 could easily distract Skinner. Vermilion, V-1, and V-2 would seize the girl and transform her, likely with an exorcism. Magenta would control him through any extreme of force, as a mere exercise. Cobalt would debrief him – explain a few facts concerning Skinner's continued freedom and safety. Crimson would seize his phone records and documents, fluttering him with polygraphs, possibly arranging for his lengthy detention. Perhaps they were circling even now, for twenty kilograms of ergotamine from a deceased elder still was missing.

The cold smell of autumn was in the evening air. Skirls of fine rain hung over the missile base. I thought of her obsessive ablutions, how she tried to wash away the memories. Her brow – when not overheated and she relaxed into sleep – became uncrowded, like dark clouds unraveling.

In the moonlight, I walked about this grey mausoleum of razor wire. Designed for mass incineration of entire populations, the missile base would have been indistinguishable from the 400 murder camps from Buchenwald to Treblinka. Lair of the psychopath Skinner, who remotely controlled the military gates and blast doors, it was impenetrable and inescapable. What could a barefoot, penniless, psychically fragile girl do?

Justine came up. Alone, finally.

"A few friends could restrain him…have a little chat," I suggested, privately enraged.

"*Don't.* I'm OK."

"*Are* you, now?"

◯

SHE HAD YET TO ESCAPE from this underworld of forebodings. Drinking of the fresh night air, we descended into the missile bay. She turned to shower in the ornate lavatory in this early hour, when he would be unlikely to assault her. We could hear Skinner, in some far compartment, screaming insults to visitors. Nettled by his tone, she was blunt.

"He grabs my hair when we're alone, forces me to my knees, and makes me…do things."

The drumming of my heart could not save her.

Two Kansas State girls fled by us in a tearful huff, one shouting over her shoulder down the blast tunnel.

"That traitorous *shit*."

Older girls, or those actual students engaged with society, recognized his malevolence – and that he was a philanderer who offered counterfeit certificates for glory to the febrile and lost. His quick wits usurped the name of intelligence, though. A pied piper with infinite guile, he was capable of anything but honesty and altruism.

At the onset of his drugs – he invariably gave her a much higher dose than himself – his black eyebrows twisted as if in thought; then he became completely hysterical, pointing at his genitalia. When she failed to assume the position immediately, he was ashen with fury. He once lost his head in my presence, then came to when I seized his arm. Seeing my reproachful glare, he retreated to a corner in resentful isolation. His unchecked venality, though, deserved a lengthy horsewhipping.

In the missile bay or on random cushions, she began mounting him as acts of barren retaliation. As Skinner lashed about with his drunkard's unfocused eyes, a series of sinister, silent personages – Skinner's colleagues – sometimes would watch them for a while, then disappear.

Always sexually defeated by her, his revenge was to use her prone body as a pastime, upon his frequent demand, until she was limp with obeisance. One always heard his curses and her panting, then her whimpering like a mistreated animal, whimpering at last – as he continued – into a long, painful silence. He hardly noticed her.

The scene had an innate wrongness – a wicked, fairy-tale feel. The loops of dark electronica Skinner preferred would boom through the missile bay and tunnels, then stop, replaced only by an arrhythmic, awkward silence. Skinner would return and heave his gargantuan mass next to her, not moving until she straddled him with resignation and the same arrhythmia, her thin body rocking like a broken heart.

○

ALTHOUGH SKINNER considered Justine his *fille du jour*, I was not yet reconciled to the tragic nature of these things, and tried to quell the insanity. His earthy presence seemed to incarnate only a vast, lightless emptiness, but one that might swarm with abominations. One night I found her alone, then read to her from a ragged Bible I had retreived from Skinner's trash. Unaware of the scriptures, she found it comforting. In the candlelight, a page opened in Luke.

"Have you heard of the man from Gadara, who also lived in a tomb? The man they called 'Legion'?"

She had not.

"Within him, they say, were many devils."

Suddenly nervous, she glanced down the blast tunnel to see if Skinner overheard us.

"What happened to him?" she asked.

"Jesus drove his devils into a herd of swine, which then drowned themselves in a lake."

"But there is only one pig here," she said. "Where would the devils go?"

○

THE KIND READER must view these exploratory writings with tolerance, for in describing these last days I must shake off the bonds of narrative coherency – perhaps even propriety. One fears only a lapse into the prurient.

These were demon-haunted spaces. She began hiding from him in the airless darkness – so very like a prison – while to her befuddled mumblings, I nodded gravely, sympathetically. At times Justine had no mind – her slate was erased. To her eyes, I appeared only as another nameless form of pulsating colors, some multi-armed lesser deity.

At the approach of his footsteps, one could see queer mixtures of feelings run through her. On the edge of panicky flight, she began shaking.

"The bedroom, *bitch*."

Her little teats erected – turgid at his command, but involuntary and in lustless fear – like some terrified mannequin, like the well-trained rocking horse she was. Pale with apprehension of her night ahead, she seemed possessed. She fast was becoming an expressionless waxworks.

In the gathering hysteria, down the blast tunnel as she skirmished with Skinner, one could hear her pitiable and confused voice, his obscenities. A communicant who thought there was no absolution, she descended into the missile base bedroom as though into a crypt.

It was a common world they inhabited. Not even winter sunlight was in her eyes – but ice – for in her silence beneath his urgencies she finally realized he was inserting homunculi into her womb and brain. One could sense darkness closing upon her, enfolding her like great, taloned wings. The blackout curtains of their bedroom were a funereal crêpe; the single table had only clusters of dead white roses.

I saw by a bidet her lipstick marks on a porcelain tooth mug. Fatigue tolled heavily on her. The submarine master bedroom – scattered and disheveled like the work of some mad warlock – was the chamber where his dismemberments of her self-respect took place.

As he washed himself – for Skinner was as fastidious as a leper with his sexual organ – she would give a taut little parvenu's smile, then walk toward his hideous form with doglike trust, into her intolerable bondage.

The phenomena of the Six would reoccur during these most difficult scenes, overlying my vision like a memory. I saw her start to come apart, liquefying in multiple directions, her underprivileged heart fleeing out of a body borrowed from water spirits.

Each time – just before it began – one felt a foreshadowing of unreality, a warp in the dark matter, so that the air was pulsating with black trails. She would be skittish at first, hung over, unconnected, until some entity reached out of his psychic field and gripped her astral body. She was trivial to him, her hot tissue simply an aid for his – so very solitary – masturbation.

Pleading all the while in her doll's voice, she would slowly sink, then kneel again before him. With heartless gestures, he would adjust her face, listening to her practiced and vile adorations until she could speak no longer. He then would claw the length of her spine, as though drawing out her vital essence. There was only his roaring, his incomprehensible blasphemies – while through a nightmarish window one listened, or watched.

As Justine worshiped – quick to comply with his every command – he grew careless of witnesses to her debasement. A stoical immobility settled over his face, becoming a sneer. Finally – it took forever – his grossly overweight grey back would begin shivering, his matted hair raising like hackles, like the plumage of a nonentity. When at last she lifted her head, her exposition was blurred. I often could not understand her.

Afterward, she had a quiescent glide – a stealthy, vacant, unspeaking figure – belittled but thinking herself enthroned. Constantly intoxicated, Justine thought Skinner's sweat and acrid sperm were the world's ethereal plasm, and the base some castle argent. Locked into simple, repetitive behaviors by the enduring stimulants, she kept pretending her sullen mouth was greedy for him, always returning to nurse his flaccidity. She was so disoriented that she said Skinner made the rain fall.

○

ODD IMAGES of Justine remain. Standing by a mirror reciting her statement to police if ever arrested – "I am just a girl, an ornament." Over sleeping bodies, naked but for a white sheet worn like a robe, chanting fearsome invocations. Luring teenagers for Skinner with tales of drugs, money, lavish suites – her sex.

In the end – each time – he would command her to stand and bathe voluptuously by candlelight before others, as he basked like a viper in the warmth of their melancholy unison. It was only a parody of love. Justine's listless, dangerously awry smile escorted him everywhere, just as her eyes followed him with the look of a ravaged sheep.

○

IN A RARE MOMENT of silk – when she was somewhat cognizant – Justine and I stood above ground in the morning quiet, looking at a dawn of brutal carmine. We were at the end of a hundred-yard corrugated blast tunnel, just outside its foot-thick steel door. We exchanged quaint fictions, although such graceful ways seemed unfamiliar to her. I thought of Indigo with the lost French girl in Zürich, who traded herself for another dose.

"Justine, listen. I know what love is."

"Tell me."

"One who sees the sun rise in your eyes."

She looked at me like the wan orphan girls in Moscow, remembering their lost mothers. Like little Eve, when Cobalt sang to her. She fled into the tunnel, in tears.

⬡

THE DEAR READER must know that I cannot write of this with a steady coherence – there was none in these days. One can only recall disturbing, inchoate images as they flee from within. But I shall try.

An intense gloom gathered about them, for he harbored a white rage. She likely would remain barren – or without issue by choice – having never known the abidingness of love. Hence, she became ashenly miserable in her unlicensed shame. When he would take her the clouds fumed, the night uneasy, until she had a dangerous, glistening look in her eyes.

Slipping dimensions – being pillaged relentlessly – she forgot her childhood's dreams of lilacs and maidens, but awaited time's revenge. I imagined her growing more wrinkled each day, standing in the cold Kansas rain, remembering when she was victimized, when even the granite sky itself was entombed, and her every star trapped in ice. I sometimes saw her future as an elderly, childless charwoman – one whose unrelieved horror had given rise to a senile glee – so that to others she would sing unintelligibly of grave events long ago.

One underage but terminal meth addict reported that in the lavish bathroom of the missile base, with its mirror-like black-tiled chambers reflecting infinite regressions of her lean, pale body and degradation, he would cuff her to the shower heads, turn her helpless figure to see her image, and kick her ankles apart. As his polydrug mixtures of crazed stimulants rolled up her belly and blew off her cortical chakra, he ravaged her until she thought they were married in the shower. The hard, recycled grey water, with its miasmic stench, she thought was a trickling brook under her bridal bower.

When she was freshly taken from the shower but finally supine – another said – her unused, unquenched sex was livid, palpitating as if gasping for air. Arching her over pillows, her hands raised high and her wrists cuffed, he trimmed close the bleach-burned white hair of her Mons – in a crescent or star – as one who had been branded. Skinner, his sense of propriety vanished, would raise his licentious, sticky face, look up, and taunt those attending these black rites.

"Taste?"

She later would assume a vulpine slyness, spread in the yellow candlelight, with only a crooked, unfeeling smile for him. One could see that her eyes still cringed. Yet she insisted on remaining.

Yet, in the few times when she at last was away from Skinner, and coming down briefly between drug episodes, her feelings would coalesce into some ellipse of normalcy. In my shocked commiseration, I somehow managed to engage her. Finally alone together, I told her only simple things, words she might understand.

"In the springtime, some say, under a full moon, the roses sing."

Speechless then, she offered only a vacuous, gentle smile.

○

I MUST NOW DESCRIBE a scene for which prose is inadequate, so refractory does it seem to human logic.

Her uninhabited body – void of consciousness and conscience – still would struggle against him in his slime of plot and counterplot. He possessed her continually, furious and resentful that she could evoke desire, until at last she became the purest automaton.

Upon his intense drug injection one night – an extreme, perhaps deadly, overdose – she came on so fast she leapt from the bed in fright. He began searching every nook of the eighteen thousand square foot underground facility: the generator rooms, the sixteen-foot high ranks of storage batteries, the heavy machinery complex for the retractable atom bomb-proof roof, the command and control center, the electronic monitoring and surveillance rooms, the missile bay, the blast tunnel arrays, the safes, kitchens, saunas, offices, showers. She had disappeared.

I heard her screaming in the far blackness, She was in one of the launch control rooms – all alone and naked and wild – spread in heavy erotic contortions on the cement floor. Her thighs and hips contracted in lascivious gyres, her writhing body driven mad with stimulants. The queen of the night, she was frantic, breathless, fornicating with a group of invisible beings.

"Black mountain burning…leather wings…fangs…xoxxooooxxxonnoooxxoooaaaa," she shrieked to them, frenzied, making vile gestures with her hands, lashing her tongue.

"Justine. *Sister.* Do you know what true lovers say to each other sometimes?"

Her body still serpentine, she said in a guttural voice, "entrails…heads blown off…poison."

I took her cold, shaky hands and steadied them – in the way monks at Hoshin-ji were taught to hold the hands of the fearful and dying. After a while, she stopped convulsing. I spoke very slowly and clearly to her. "Listen, they say,

'How do I love thee?

Let me count the ways.

I love thee to the height and depth

and breadth my soul can fly,

when soaring, out of bounds,

to the ends of being and ideal grace.'"

She waivered, almost coming home.

"The angels will save me one day?"

"When one see the sun rise in your eyes, and can never turn away."

Skinner ran up in a jealous pique. I explained that Justine needed a drink of water, and had gotten lost. Bewildered and scared, she flinched at his unannounced touch. He led her into the darkened blast tunnel, faced her against the wall, and took her there. He never gave her water.

As his river of misfortune poured into her, her moans became low and abysmal. Giving up at last, she began drifting unresponsively – mindless, stricken, floating. In the red warning light of the launch panel, I could see only part of her. Her left hand was against the steel blast wall, her fingers splayed and trembling, her left leg danced in disjointed lurches. Then she was up on her toes, rocking steady now, facing inward, head down in the grim silence. But it was not over.

After some hours, I found them in the farthest chamber – a heavily fortified hole by the old liquid oxygen tanks. It was to be her ultimate sacrifice. Engaging in cosmic rape, and actually drooling over the lustrous flexibility of her body, Skinner was watching her arms and legs flail about aimlessly. A ragdoll in another world, there was no desire in her. She was gone.

He was moving her head however he wished to please himself. In the spell of a world-destroying tryptamine-crank mixture from a large syringe inserted far into her and not removed, her body was curling instinctively – like a restless fetus turning – for she was completely blind and superconscious and contracting in a thousand rebirths. Thinking of her writhings as those of some desirous slave only sent him into paroxysms.

As the hours passed, she began crying out – a noise like the musical calling of wolves. He loved to hear her groaning hysteria, for the sound of her spirit finally yielding was to him as satisfying as his enemies' throats being slit. To me, though, her sobs were the memories of some despairing infancy. They both had a mind-sickness.

They would never speak of his plutonic master to others, but I knew. As they entwined, I heard her shrill, incoherent cries worshipping Magoth with him, piercing me to the very quick of mind with their crudity. Such perverse elation was repellant, but in my long vigil of them that night I felt deeply for her, for in that moment he had stripped her of all human feeling.

When it was finished, she became restless and robotic, moving about the rooms of lethal machinery all alone. Her scattered senses thereafter consigned her to the corridors of the missile base, and – if the sun never rose in her eyes – to the corridors of society.

However long one lived, one would remember these nights of teenage slavery and hallucinatory palaces, with Skinner a fierce, sudden, black-winged harpy drinking at the waters of her annihilation.

LATE THE NEXT NIGHT at the missile base, I wandered sleepless through the launch bays, where one could hear in the distance Skinner snoring. With a marker I began scrawling in flowing Aramaic around a two-story cement pylon. Justine straggled up, shaken and aimless.

"What are you doing?"

"Oh, an ancient inscription. It's how we got the term 'the handwriting on the wall.'"

She was fond of incantations, being something of a confused witch, but uncertain of which race. Not wishing to toy with her, I said nothing more.

"What does it say?" she insisted.

"*Mene mene tekel parsin.*"

"What's that?" she asked.

"There are many translations, but only one for here. You'll not tell Skinner?"

"I promise."

"The Lord hath left this place," I said.

○

JUSTINE in the days of aftermath had a dissipated, shocking placidity, like the demolished submissive she had become. Even while Skinner raved around her with his boorish coarseness of expression, I still could see in Justine the last simple beauty of the very young, until sometimes I noticed her new, shameless glance.

Yet I alone knew part of her always was weeping. Though to Skinner her eyes were dry and bright, I could see her streams of anguish.

She would be eternally damaged by her recollections of these events. After the last, most repugnant scene, I pulled her aside and tried to immunize her.

"Justine. Listen."

"What?"

"Angels have no memory."

She came to me the final evening, when Skinner was done with her. Her mouth was puffy, riven, loose – so used as to be useless. Still trembling – even in my presence – she admitted to being an absolute captive, unable ever to free herself. The silence between us, as she waited for someone to save her, was impossible to repair.

In the harsh last morning, she wandered deranged and alone in the cow pasture above ground, always following the Argus-eyed tail of the missile base peacock. She thought it watched her every move, and spoke secrets to her. Having no food for days and nights, she was powered only by stars.

I approached her. She was half-nude, uncaring of her body, and wore only an open, filmy, torn shawl. Her abdomen still was clenching from his night inside her. She was shuddering – deep, uncontrollable heaving. It was as though Justine were sobbing, helplessly. Perhaps – among the remains of her pure spirit – she truly was.

"*Run*," I said.

"Where?"

"Why do you stay with him?" I asked.

This girl-child of the empty plains, where nothing ever changed, replied in the most sorrowful of tones.

"It's like being in a *movie*."

She suspected – but never knew – how the heart unfurls its splendor. In reverence, I bowed to her, wished her peace, then walked away. Never again – as a free man – would I see her. Along the path, I began crying for her, crying for all the lost and abused children, for all the motherless girls. Even now, so far from these memories, I am crying.

Chapter 30.

Kristallnacht

Six miles from earth,
loosened from this dream of life
I awoke to black flak and the nightmare fighters.
When I died they washed me out of the turret
with a hose.

- Randall Jarrell, *The Death of the Ball Turret Gunner*

The blood-dimmed tide is loosed,
and everywhere the ceremony of innocence
is drowned.
The best lack all conviction.

- Yeats, *The Second Coming*

In wartime, truth is so precious
she should always be accompanied by
a bodyguard of lies.

- Churchill, 1945

MY HEAD was on the steering wheel, motor running, still parked behind the convenience store. I had to drive to the base. Skinner was there.

A buried cathedral of the black arts awaited me down a long, unpaved access road – ten thousand tons of concrete slabs and rusted iron and Cold War delusions. Protected from incoming ICBMs armed with nuclear warheads, it was vulnerable only to corruption within. Although the base always had an eerie malevolence, a chilled hush, it seemed different that day.

Bells rang the hour in the distance, a feathery light snow was aloft in a slow wind. Thin streamers of grey smoke rose off to the horizon from concealed vents in the earth, disappearing like the ephemera we call our lives. The pallid shell of an evening moon gloated above it all, perhaps too candid for those who kept secrets. Scattered in a field were suspicious, silent crows, waiting as if for the reaper.

Driving in, I tried to suspend my moral judgments, tried to forget his deliberate savagery of the girl. As she lost all mastery of herself, her senses became permanently undone, her world gyrating forever. Perhaps she still wandered in the jangled dawns – half-dressed in a ragged coat, hair askew, mumbling, feeding the chickens. The troubled blue sea of her eyes had been foredoomed.

The base surveillance cameras turned to follow the car. An automatic electric gate of military razor wire parted, then sealed the exit. An empty guard house had dismal, shattered windows.

My friend Clyde had joined me, upon whom I had prevailed to help with matters. Eminently respectable, hard-working, he was from the best of loving families.

I knew not the perils ahead, just that everything seemed to be dying. Even the sky had a pearl-blue nescience.

THERE SKINNER WAS, braying like an ass in salutation. The first mere sight of him was like the ruins of an epoch. His legs seemed to give him away, though, for he approached in wide circles – almost with caution – in a kind of long penitential walk.

He feigned a quick embrace but it felt like the kiss of Judas. More furtive than usual, he eyed me with a grotesque squint, then became rather awkward, like an amateur actor in a difficult play. Skinner always had a shifting strangeness, but in the tension of those hours he seemed more nervous than ever, a jungle of impulses.

At his unsettling presence my angle of vision became disturbed, stripping the veil of familiarity between us. Within him I glimpsed the blur of the leopard. I couldn't hear or understand what he was saying, for the frequencies were all wrong. His voice of pretense kept reverberating like some great bruised gong.

Skinner was in clean clothes, oddly for him, and appeared not so intoxicated. His beard was unkempt, with his usual coarse plebeian growth. The girl was nowhere to be found. The utter quiet – the emptiness of the base – made illusory my memories of her sullen mouth, the dog collars and chains, the nights when the lights seemed to tremble.

Peevish this day for some reason, he soon caught himself, then faked a sort of a guilty solicitude. Living alone in some private cul-de-sac of the mind, Skinner possessed a dreadful sophistry in a way, always finding pleasure in deception. Unusually cocksure, his strands of motive forever were irretrievably knotted. As a distraction from the seriousness of our encounter, he tried some meager witticisms on me, but the missile base was a sinister place. It only accentuated his labyrinthine strategies.

Skinner had offered payment if I would return and assist him with some equipment, and to prepare for a licit pharmahuasca session for his sycophants using an infusion of Acacia bark and Syrian Rue. To such newcomers, he projected a type of excessive Puritan morality, for they had yet to hear the gruesome echoes of his excesses. Before their stoned eyes he would be reeking of God.

The girl was only a ghost now, forgotten. She had an insane frivolity after his abuse, as if reeling out of the brothel quarter after a long night. In her times of lucidity, when she realized he considered her only his private pelt, her tall skeltonic glances were like a sword thrust. I remembered her cries of sheer vexation as he forced himself into her, twisting like some vile saurian.

My minor social correspondence with Skinner had been increasingly acrimonious. After this, I intended never to see him again. His every action was like a running noose.

○

THE SCENES BEGAN unreeling in sections – sliced, choppy, interrupted. Words were spoken and not heard, everything was a little too fast, as if the irrevocable flow of existence were broken. It became dreamlike, but a harsh dream from which one could never awaken. Invisible events beat upon these very hours like fateful drums, for so many cold eyes were watching us.

I was unaware that the Attorney General of Kansas had been investigating Skinner for narcotics for years, or that his phone records were carefully analyzed each month to identify coconspirators nationally.

Or that for ten hours at the base Skinner had refused to take an unconscious opiate overdose victim to the nearby emergency room, instead repeatedly injecting him with drug mixtures until he died. Or that DEA and state agents also were investigating Skinner for his manslaughter. Or that the victim had been a DEA source of information.

Or that Skinner had a long defunct drug lab concealed on the premises, one he had stolen and was at a complete loss to operate.

Or that to unwitting young people he had been selling degraded by-products from the lab theft, first testing them on Justine and other girls, asserting he was a chemist and claiming the drops were "ergot wine" or "ALD-52."

To others Skinner still portrayed himself as some American industrialist, heir to this and that, but he was a minor drug dealer with no chemical skills and – with his only income from the toxic by-products – even his mythical fortunes were stagnating.

I didn't know that weeks earlier Skinner had left Justine alone at the base as he traveled to Mendocino, California to entertain his now pregnant teenage girlfriend – his earlier victim, hospitalized from her overdose by Skinner at the San Francisco hotel.

Or that Justine had sold rolls of MDMA to supplement the paltry sums Skinner permitted her, or that she was sleeping as well with her source when Skinner was away, or that DEA had discovered in her dealer's mail from Amsterdam a hundred doses, or that when DEA interviewed him Justine was in the next room on the phone to Skinner.

I was unaware that Skinner had been a lifelong federal informant since the age of nineteen, or that his step-father was a federal agent, or that he had evaded prosecution for his multiple bank frauds by testifying in two federal trials against his partners.

I didn't know that a few weeks earlier – while inviting me to Las Vegas and the missile base – he had in desperation solicited the Department of Justice to immunize him for the psychedelic laboratory he had stolen, offering to identify the chemist.

⬡

ONE OF THE BASE outbuildings contained about 20 large green military containers. In each were white sealed buckets that yielded only with difficulty to a special tool Skinner retained. I could not inspect them.

After viewing the containers, then registering at a local motel, I felt that things were not right. Skinner by phone reported that he was in Topeka. I saw a truck with someone just sitting in it, the same truck and individual twice but in a different location. As I made a slow pass, the occupant never moved, only staring straight ahead. Parking some miles from the base, I approached it on foot.

The multi-ton blast door was chained from the inside, something I'd never seen before. No one answered the base phone. Fearing some tragedy, I decided to look around, and left to buy the largest bolt cutters I could find.

One hardly suspected that a hundred DEA, state and local agents surrounded us, occupying observation posts and unmarked cars, all coordinated by the massive, High-Intensity Drug Trafficking Area (HIDTA) Investigative Support Center nearby, with its ranks of computers and radios and every federal agency represented therein.

The local Wamego police, the Pottawatomie County Sheriff's Department, Kansas Highway Patrol, Kansas Bureau of Investigation. DEA Headquarters officials, forensic chemists from DEA's Special

Testing Laboratory. Teams of federal agents from Kansas City, San Francisco, Washington, D.C. The command center personnel, the electronic monitoring technicians. Everyone was waiting.

I didn't know that Skinner was underground in the blast tunnel with agents, all on the surveillance system observing my every action. Or that he had convinced DEA I would set up the dismantled lab in a chamber at the base, one DEA wired with almost undetectable video devices. Secreted in the wall, they led to a trailer full of agents a mile away.

Returning with the bolt cutters, then approaching the missile base again on foot and severing the great chain, I pulled on the four-foot steel military handle of the blast door. Ordinarily it would open, but not that day. I spent hours forcing the unlatching mechanism, unaware that Skinner and agents were on the other side, holding the blast door closed in grim and frantic silence. Attempting to gain entry proved futile. I walked away, to a sunset of cruel saffron.

○

WE RETREATED to a nearby motel to rest. Sleep had been fretful – I still dreamed of being pursued across bleak, moonlit fields, running forever in the infinite night.

The last morning arrived. In the chalky, greasy dawn, a valedictory atmosphere seemed to permeate everything, a kind of remorseless apathy.

From the outbuilding, I looked at the chained entry to the base, and thought of the horrific scenes with the girl. I remembered from the chaos of those nights my feeble attempt to view the dark matter around them, seeing the flickering mythic core as congeries of eels breeding, electric eels with fine teeth and small yellow eyes. Although I had not the capacity to confront it, I sensed the half-birth of *Risus sardonicus* in her. As she struggled under the spilling of his demon seed, her face seized in a fiendish grimace, glistening with perspiration and the atonement of tears.

But the base was not a transient vision of evil, it was a reality. A machine designed to immolate civilizations, Skinner had chosen it as an altar upon which he sacrificed the very young. Recognizing at last this wretched incarnation, I knew then what my task must be.

The hundred buckets clearly were not the simple materials required for a pharmahuasca session, for I saw a bit of elaborate glass. I decided to destroy whatever strange laboratory equipment and chemicals Skinner had accumulated, everything one could find in the outbuilding. Before he harmed many others.

Over fatiguing and disorienting hours, we packed the buckets into a rental truck, together with many 20-liter containers of unknown liquids, working throughout the day and into the racing darkness.

Within the disarray in the outbuilding I found a votive object – my sitting robe and kimono from Hoshin-ji monastery. I never traveled without it, but in the distraction with the girl had left it behind. Skinner had ravaged my possessions, then – like some mad beast in a sacred space – he had crushed the robe into a filthy ball. At this dark portent, I grew afraid, for it was then I first realized my head had gotten too far from my heart.

Unfolding the robe with a prayer, I draped it about my shoulders. In the uncanny calm of that freezing Kansas night, I sat in meditation, breathing, centering, falling into consciousness. Time stopped. Destruction of the apparatus was a grave responsibility – one could not go back, or walk away. I said another prayer for our survival, for our safe return to our families.

A full moon transmuted the final scene. Staring at the pale monolith of the base, and across the echoing vistas, I thought I saw movement. Perhaps it was just a trick of the mists, the receding tide of Skinner's disenchantment, the fleeting lights of his apostasy.

I rang Skinner a last time, demanding to meet. He went on with an insufferable monotony, pretending he was at a Japanese restaurant, but he was surrounded by agents. While considering the spectrum of his disorders, I listened in tactful silence. Everything was recorded by the watchers.

We drove away and began to discard in dumpsters the sealed containers, whatever was in them. With sleet prickling upon the windshield and the grinding pavement in a grisly toccata, we slowly passed the funeral parlor. It was a paradoxical night – one felt the advent of an almost religious dilemma.

The groaning of the truck became the sound of his moaning over her, like the hum of an insect feeding. I still heard her doleful distant howling down the blast tunnels, her shrill cries as she was stretched into the fluidity of time.

No…it was a *siren*, growing louder.

◯

RED LIGHT RACKS were swirling on a patrol car, just behind me. A single patrol car, it seemed, a routine traffic stop. Hard to see at night. No, *many* of them, startling clusters of red lights, their hot flashes now everywhere, indistinguishable from the flood of adrenaline.

At the piercing sirens my neck hairs piloerected. Heat poured through me in a suffusion of super-human clarity. As the guillotine fell, I experienced the death of all the earth.

It was a set up by Skinner – for a massive clandestine laboratory. If incarcerated and utterly disempowered, one hardly could investigate or defend against these complexities. The suffering of family would be immeasurable.

It was a decision with only two possible outcomes. One was to outrun gunfire with a bead drawn on my back, for that was the way to the warmth of my child's arms, and by a hair's breadth of possible escape might be avoided the loss of all that was loved. The other was prison razor wire and death each dawn until burial out back or one's cadaver offered to whomever, if anyone cared or even remembered decades hence. Sheriff's cars were closing all around. I pulled the car to a halt, then bolted.

◯

I RAN into the night, into a rogue wind, into the cold blackness of an ice-bound forest. The stars were high, the moon too bright. Thorny brambles tore at my face, blinding me. Trained for distance, and crossing streams to throw off the dogs, I lost them in the first ten minutes. Looking back at the far conflagration of police cars, swarming federal agents and sweeping spotlights, I saw my dear friend, helpless.

The illuminated Kansas landscape was vast, barren and silent, suddenly shrieking as interminable trains split the night. Stumbling in the crying hours along iron rails and crossties, then beside rushing empty boxcars, I became only a breathless shadow running straight into nothingness. Isolated in the lunar fields were old white barns, radiating miles of icy furrows to nowhere. In the pre-dawn quietude, I finally found a ragged shed. Stopping to rest was my last mistake.

It began with a certain innocence, imperceptible as a fetal heartbeat. A soft flutter at edge of things gestated over minutes into the labored cacophony of a helicopter gunship circling overhead, with infrared detectors and armed pilots linked to a two hundred-fifty house manhunt.

This wild machinery stalked only me, frozen and huddled by some ancient tractor, a white-hot image on airborne surveillance screens. The heavy rotors tightened overhead, deafening now. My exhaustion terminal, the fear took hold. Everything looked dead, like the end of time.

As the first patrol car sped down the highway into the farm, I fled into freshly-tilled muddy fields, a viscous quagmire of a trap. Sheriffs were fishtailing fast behind me.

One pulled a gun and aimed it at my back, screaming.

And this is how the world came apart. Transparent panels were shifting in the heavens, there were great wheels in the sky. In the sun I saw her face, our baby's eyes, and reached for them. Forever after I heard the angels, singing...

Afterword

The few words that I have to add
to which I have written
are soon penned, and then I
and the unknown friend to whom I write,
will part forever.
Not without much dear remembrance on my part.
Not without some, I hope, on his or hers.

- Esther, in Dickens *Bleak House*

I imagine leaves must feel like this,
when they have fallen from the tree,
and until they die.

- T.E. Lawrence, at Clouds Hills, Dorset
a week before his death (1935)

And this prophecy Merlin must make,
for I live before his time.

- Lear

THE MOST PRECIOUS OF FLOWERS once bloomed, consumed by the fires of time and avarice. For the sensitive reader, may these writings reconstitute it yet again.

All the words were written in prison – in pencil, behind a heavy steel door. While surrounded by humans crowded in cages forever, it has become clear that long-term captivity of the non-violent is among the last evils of society before true civilization may appear.

Yet within these pages somehow arose embraces for a loved one, murmurs of blessings to a beloved child, notes of wonder to those who soon will inherit this planet. I pray the readings have been graceful to receptive hearts and minds, and nourishing as the gentle rain.

Even after decades, unsigned messages sometimes arrive in the prison mail. Postcards of rosy heather in the Alps, or bouquets of forget-me-nots in Provence. Some are of tiny, smiling children in Austria, Russia, the Himalayas, South East Asia. A few cards have an unfathomable scent like angels' breath, or are scribbled with lyrics of Beethoven's 9th. Others may show an old nun's hands in prayer, a froth of bluebells, an alpine valley covered in Edelweiss. One, perhaps from a geospatial satellite, was a photograph of this delicate island earth. By these subtleties I know some remember, and watch over me.

The beauty of the world is becoming frail, receding into unspeakable loss. In darkness, I think of her, of our sleeping child in the starlight. I think of the world-wide community of the loving and inspired, and with gratitude and joy for what may come. I think of the students at their texts and in lectures, of the artists, coders, musicians, the mavericks. The young researchers and physicians-to-be. The dreamers of the day. The future Merlin.

Sometimes when these words are read, even by one so very distant, I cannot help but feel it. I think of you.

When everything is taken away – all possessions, dignity, identity, touch, meaning, hope – all that remains is the love of one's family. If that goes, all is lost.

When the moon is right, and the late night is silent at last, I have a dream. It is always the same. I dream of her, our child, their warmth, their forgiveness. I hold them as if they are life itself. After a long time, I walk home together with them, stopping only to kiss the roses.

Epilogue

Very softly and so softly I could barely hear her
- I heard the girl whisper
'It had to live its whole life like that'?

- Donna Tartt, *The Goldfinch*
(on girl asking about Fabritius's
painting of a goldfinch
shackled to a perch)

Promise me, though
Promise me you'll never
put a living thing into it.

- Capote, *Breakfast at Tiffany's*
(Miss Holiday Golightly, on her gift of a birdcage)

The scratch of Jacob's quill is joined
by a not dissimilar noise from a rafter.
It is a rhythmic scrating, soon overlain
by a tiny sawing squeek.
A *he-rat*. the young man realizes
mounting his she-rat.

- David Mitchell, *The Thousand Autumns of Jacob van Zoet*

Scire volunt omnes, mecedem solvere nemo

(Everyone to know, no one to pay the price)

- Juvenal

SKINNER continued compromising unrelated MDMA and LSD distributors from Kansas to Poland – resulting in additional arrests and convictions.

Based on the incorrect and arguably fraudulent claims of low-level federal agents, senior DEA officials unwittingly cited – as a direct result of the seizure of the purported laboratory – a ninety-percent reduction in the availability of LSD in the United States. Unaware of the inaccuracy of the agents' data, a DEA Administrator – in seeking annual funding from a House judiciary and appropriations committee – described the seizure of "41.3 kilograms (90.86 pounds) of LSD."

The LSD investigation expanded from Kansas to Russia, the Caribbean and India. Multiple agencies participated under DOJ's Organized Crime Drug Enforcement Program (OCDETF), while two international OCDETF investigations lasted for years. An Attorney General, together with other highly reputable DOJ officials, unknowingly relied on agents' misstatements of quantity in press releases concerning OCDETF successes.

However, upon detailed cross-examination at trial, a government witness of integrity from DEA's Special Testing Laboratory undermined the agents' contentions and thereby the Administrator's statement to the House appropriations committee. The witness asserted that the LSD had been distributed in Europe rather than the United States, and admitted that less than one-percent of the quantity alleged actually was seized. Furthermore, the seized material was in an unusable form. These unfortunate events are an example of what one analyst has described as "continuing vitality of mythical numbers" generated by low-level agents.

Given these factors, and noting that there was no corresponding increase in LSD availability while the lab purportedly was operational, drug policy analysts indicated that the decrease in LSD availability after the Kansas seizure was a substitution effect from the eight-hundred percent increase in MDMA availability in the same time frame.

In perhaps the first example of its kind, the two costly, complex, multiagency and international OCDETF investigations led to no additional individuals sentenced to a prison term.

The federal trial lasted eleven weeks, one of the longest in Kansas history. Skinner testified for eleven days.

During trial, the defense discovered that DEA agents, to secure a warrant, permitted Skinner to arrange evidence at the missile base for several days without oversight. Government testimony confirmed that – months after the defendants' arrests – DEA determined that Skinner, even while working as the DEA's informant, had concealed in another location twice the amount of precursor that he had placed with the laboratory. No fingerprints other than those of Skinner and his employees were found on the sealed laboratory apparatus. Nevertheless, one defendant received a sentence of two life terms, the other a sentence of thirty years.

Years after trial, the defense investigation revealed that the jury foreman was an attorney and a law-school classmate of the prosecutor, matters undisclosed during jury selection. The defense also uncovered evidence that Skinner was a career informant, and – to avoid prosecution for bank fraud – was the principal government witness in two prior federal trials.

The defense later obtained a false document concerning Skinner – submitted at trial by a government agent to the Kansas district court and later to the appellate courts – with the document relied upon as authentic in their decisions. The defense further acquired records of DEA's blacklisting of Skinner – as wholly unreliable – to all DEA offices and other agencies. The federal agency blacklisting – which occurred during Skinner's actual eleven-day testimony – was not disclosed to the jury. Yet, within days after its blacklisting of Skinner, a government agent stated to an unsuspecting jury that "DOJ vouched for Mr. Skinner."

A few months after his testimony at trial, Skinner was arrested for drug trafficking at the Burning Man festival. Skinner and his most recent paramour both subsequently were arrested for the six-day interstate kidnapping and torture of her 18-year-old lover, with Skinner receiving consecutive sentences of life, sixty and thirty years, and the girl freed in exchange for her testimony against him.

Appeals in the Kansas case have continued for over 15 years, with 1000 motions filed in district and appellate courts in Kansas and California. In the appellate courts, the Kansas case and related FOIA proceedings have been reversed on four occasions based on allegations of government misconduct and withholding of documents.

By these records and decisions may be shed light on unconscionable government methods in this era of mass incarceration, during which our country stands alone – shamed among nations – in its extensive and prolonged incarceration of the non-violent. Litigation continues.

Acknowledgments

With the words going out like the cells of a brain
With the cities growing over us like the earth
We are saying thank you faster and faster
With nobody listening we are saying thank you
We are saying thank you and waving
Dark though it is.

- W.S. Merwin, *Thanks*

The research on fentanyl abuse in Moscow and Boston, and on international organizations and novel drugs, was facilitated by a grant through the Harpel fellows of the Interfaculty Initiative on Drugs and Addictions, and through an appointment in the Department of Neurobiology at Harvard Medical School, in accord with the Program on Mind, Brain and Behavior at Harvard.

Special gratitude is extended to staff at the Kennedy School Library, Tozzer Library and Economic Botany Library, and the Tina and Gordon Wasson Ethnomycological Collections at Harvard.

To the Human Subjects Committee, Faculty of Arts and Sciences at Harvard, for providing early guidance in research contact with underground chemists, leading to this ethnography of an international trafficking organization. To the faculty and fellows of the Interfaculty Initiative on Drugs and Addictions, to the staff of the Department of Neurobiology at Harvard Medical School, and to the faculty and students of the Kennedy School of Government. To the unnamed scholars who guided me along the way.

In my academic training and writing of this ethnography, I was inspired by the work of Albert Hofmann, Richard Evans Schultes, Wade Davis, Richard Alpert, Charles Grob, David Presti, Rick Strassman, Ralph Metzner, Stanislav Grof, Bob Knight, Marian Diamond, Franz Vollenweider, Michael Mithoefer, Torsten Passie, Roland Griffiths, Evgeny Krupitsky, Weston La Barre, Thomas Roberts, Alexander Sewell, Simon Brandt, Jason Wallach and other visionary researchers.

For correspondence, interviews and assistance in locating specific research materials, I am indebted to the curators, archivists and reference librarians at Harvard, particularly at the Harry Elkins Widener Library, Yenching Library, Houghton Library, Fogg Museum, Busch-Resinger Museum, Countway Library of Medicine at Harvard Medical School, and the Langdell Library at Harvard Law School.

At Princeton, to the staff of the Firestone Library, Dulles Reading Room and at the Department of

Mathematics at New Fine Hall. At Yale, the staff of the Beinecke Library. To the American Antiquarian Society, and to the scholars at Antiquarian Hall. At Oxford, to the staff of the Bodleian Library and the Ashmolean Museum, and in London the staff of the British Museum and the National Gallery.

In Vienna, to researchers at the United Nations Office of Drug Control and the Precursor Control Unit. To the staff of Wilton Park, Sussex, for their assistance during conferences on biological and chemical weapons and terrorism. To certain former and current unnamed researchers at Porton Down, U.K., Edgewood Arsenal and Fort Detrick, Maryland. To Enoch Callaway and Jack S. Ketchum. To Matt Meselson and Julian Perry Robinson of the Harvard-Sussex Program on Chemical and Biological Weapons Armament and Arms Limitations.

In Moscow, to the late Major General Alexander Sergeev and Colonel Vladimir Ibragimov of the MVD, forensic chemist Vladimir Sorokin, Eduard Babayan of the International Narcotics Control Board, and Tom Robertson at the American Embassy.

In Tashkent, Uzbekistan, I was assisted by many individuals, only a few of whom can be cited here, including Anna Goncharova and Dildora Muhammedjarnova, who brought me into the lives of Central Asia. Sakur, Zia, and Zalmay and his family welcomed me with the generosity and kindness of Afghans, and Zalmay guided me through the Fergana Valley and the streets of Mazar-i-Sharif, making possible interactions with factions of the Jumbesh-i-Melli.

In Tashkent, General Abdul Rashid Dostum and General Alem Rasim. In Washington, D.C., General Dostum, General Payanda and officials of the Carnegie Foundation for International Peace. At the Department of State I am grateful to Robert Gelbard, Robin Raphel, Donald Camp, and Roberta Chew, at the Pentagon to Michael Pillsbury and Spojmai Maiwandi.

To Akbar Bey (Akbar Bai) in Mazar-i-Sharif and Kabul.

My gratitude cannot be sufficiently expressed to the late Billy Rork and the staff of Rork Law Office in Topeka, Kansas, including Wendie Bryan Miller and Robin Alvarez, for their brave and enduring support through many difficult years.

To Mark Rumold of the Electronic Frontier Foundation, for his thoughtful and assiduous efforts.

In memory and honor of the late Alexander Theodore (Sasha) Shulgin, and to Anne Shulgin and Wendy Perry for their friendship over decades.

To Lester Grinspoon, Associate Professor of Psychiatry (Emeritus) at Harvard Medical School, to Julie Holland, Assistant Professor of Psychiatry at New York University, and to the late Michael Bauer of the University of New Mexico School of Medicine, for their friendship to one so very long imprisoned.

I am most indebted to poet and author Richard Shelton, Regents Professor of English (Emeritus) and Creative Writing at the University of Arizona, for his singularly penetrating review of the entire manuscript, his sensitive insights, and his personal example.

To volunteers Jan and Allyn Riding for their kind support and humanity in establishing writing and other classes for the incarcerated.

For their writings and arts, to Seth Ferranti, Don Lattin, Andy Roberts, Terence and Dennis McKenna, Daniel Pinchbeck, Martin Lee, Jesse Jarnow, Christian Rätsch, Peter Webster, Michael Horowitz and Cynthia Palmer. To Alex and Allyson Grey.

For friendship and moral support during this writing, I am thankful to:

Biographer Dennis McDougal, who suggested one might find freedom in the magic of pen and paper, and to documentarian Ira Abrams.

Mark Dowie and Wendie of Point Reyes, with whom I first became aware of the arts of running, writing and painting.

The late Dieter Hagenbach of Basel – friend, literary agent, and author of *Mystic Chemist*, the seminal biography of Albert Hofmann. Dieter most carefully edited this revision.

To Vanja Palmers at Puregg, Austria and Felsentor, Switzerland, for his kindnesses.

Many friends and colleagues helped me in the writing of this book, and several read part or all of the manuscript. My thanks go to:

Barth Beresford as general editor, for his early oversight of the entire work. His personal advice and assistance for many years are irreplaceable.

Danelle Morton, for her steadfast encouragement and editing, and for saving me from many lamentable blunders.

Richie Ryan, for line editing, fact checking, layout and other services which only he could have rendered, and who will – I hope – not spare his efforts on the present and future occasions through his indefatigable research and fine eye.

Ryan Place, explorer and researcher, for his detailed review of this work, his flawless provision of archival materials, and his most creative commentaries.

Caryn Graves, for her accuracy, reliability and insight in diverse matters.

To old friends in ways too various to specify, and who taught me of matters of the heart, I must be content in naming Bob and Jennifer Harris, Kenichi Sakai, John Omaha, Talitha Stills, Jim McLeod, J.A. Valliant, E.A. Zarlengo, L.T. Carriel, C.S. Dietrich, V. Twombly, M. Tate Schilling.

In memory of Bob Wallace of Microsoft, for his courage and vision.

For guidance on monastic practices and meditation, to the priests, staff and students at the monasteries of Hoshin-ji, Green Gulch and Tassajara, and especially to Blanche Hartman, Paul Haller, Michael Wegner, Vickie Austin, Jeffrey Schneider and the late Helen Dunham at the San Francisco Zen Center. To Mary Ishizaki. To the late Kobun Chino, Katrin and Maya, and to Chang-san for her gentle instruction.

To Lee Andrew Pinsky, without whose inspired efforts this volume would not have been possible, and to Sandy Meredith and young Aaron Morrison.

For good company through correspondence and their kind words of support, I am infinitely grateful to many friends, only a few of whom can be named: Henrik Dahl, C.J. Hinke, Bruce Van Dyke, Daniel Williams, Melissa and Bilbo, Michael and Natasha Townsand, Naiya Cominos, Chris Malone, Ben and Ruby Webb and baby Alec, Michael Golden, Chris Kilgus, Jamie Johnston, Ben Denio, John Chen, Martin Fleischer, Mats Fredriksson, Troy Brower, John Covington, Derek Hansen, Brandon Green, Bob and Kitty Shimek, Darren Murtha, Lauren Wickers, Peter Janney, Tara Anaise, Matty Shaw, Jack Nolan, Carrie Tyler, Mike Collard, and those special correspondents who must remain only in memory.

To Simon Tysko, Astrid Alben and Dudley Sutton, and with thanks to Artangel and to Resonance FM London for their recordings and spoken passages of *The Rose* from Oscar Wilde's former prison cell at Reading Gaol. To Greg Sams, and Neşe Devenot for their readings of *The Rose* at the University of Greenwich in London, and with appreciation to Ben Sessa, Julian Vayne, David Luke and Nikki Wyrd. To Rob Dickins, Rosalind Stone, and Dax DeFranco for their recordings of *The Rose* at Altered/Berlin.

I am especially indebted to the research subjects themselves, and with gratitude to V-1 and V-2 for permission to witness certain private liturgies in Berlin, Bangkok, Laos and Phuket. To Abeer of Kathmandu, and always to little Eve of Trenton, New Jersey.

For their careful guidance in sensitive practices, arts and dynamics, to Sister Moon, Diana the Huntress and a priestess of Athena.

For recalling the moonlight in Big Sur, to documentarian Lisa Stevens, and to author Jon Stephen Fink. To Peter Wilkinson and Jann Wenner. To Fire and Earth Erowid, and Jon Hanna. To filmmaker Cosmo Feilding Mellen. To Ganga White and Tracey Rich. To Sting.

With appreciation to Maria Kodama and the estate of Jorge Luis Borges, and to the Wylie Agency and Penguin Group USA. In honor of the poets, writers and musicians in the epigraphs, from whose canons these experimental writings evolve rhythms, pacing, syntactical elements and tones – perhaps interwoven with patterns and puzzles – for the pleasure of philologists and devoted readers.

To Amanda and Jamie.

To Carey and Claudia Turnbull for their compassion, courage, and vision.

To the staffs at Beckley Foundation, Heffter Foundation, Erowid and MAPS. To Rick Doblin.

To Tim Scully, for his enduring and intrepid support over the decades. To the late Augustus Owsley Stanley III, and with gratitude for the public presentations of Nick Sand.

To those who suffered and survived: Mark McCloud, Tim Tyler, and Amy Ralston.

To those who cannot be named. To those many who died in prison, including the late Roderick (Rudd) Walker. To those incarcerated for life. To those who remained standing. To Clyde Apperson.

To my father and mother, and to trauma surgeon Grigory Vorobee.

To my children, who were born in these days and now grow in the aftermath, so that within their secret hearts their father's love is not simply a whisper barely heard, and so that one day they will know the price that was paid. And in the white peace of the end – for teaching me of eternal love – to the one who wept.

Child of the pure unclouded brow

And dreaming eyes of wonder

Though time be fleet, and I and thou

Are but half a life asunder

Thy loving smile will surely hail

This love-gift of a fairy tale.

I have not seen thy sunny face

Nor hear thy silver laughter

No thought of me shall find a place

In thy young life's hereafter

Enough that now thou hath not failed

To listen to my fairy tale.

- (apol) Lewis Carroll, *Through the Looking Glass*

About the Author

William Leonard Pickard is a graduate of the Kennedy School of Government at Harvard, with degrees in chemistry and public policy. He was formerly a research associate in neurobiology at Harvard Medical School, a Fellow of the Interfaculty Initiative on Drugs and Addictions at Harvard, and Deputy Director of the Drug Policy Analysis Program at UCLA. His interests include Victorian-Edwardian literature, deincarceration technologies, the neuropolicy of cognitive enhancement, and the future of novel drugs. He encourages correspondence from the thoughtful reader.

www.theroseofparacelsus.com